SMITH'S LAW OF THEFT

SMITH'S LAW OF THEFT

NINTH EDITION

DAVID ORMEROD
Professor of Criminal Justice, Queen Mary, University of London
Barrister (Middle Temple)

DAVID HUW WILLIAMS
Barrister (Inner Temple)

OXFORD
UNIVERSITY PRESS

OXFORD
UNIVERSITY PRESS

Great Clarendon Street, Oxford ox2 6dp

Oxford University Press is a department of the University of Oxford.
It furthers the University's objective of excellence in research, scholarship,
and education by publishing worldwide in

Oxford New York

Auckland Cape Town Dar es Salaam Hong Kong Karachi
Kuala Lumpur Madrid Melbourne Mexico City Nairobi
New Delhi Shanghai Taipei Toronto

With offices in

Argentina Austria Brazil Chile Czech Republic France Greece
Guatemala Hungary Italy Japan Poland Portugal Singapore
South Korea Switzerland Thailand Turkey Ukraine Vietnam

Oxford is a registered trade mark of Oxford University Press
in the UK and in certain other countries

Published in the United States
by Oxford University Press Inc., New York

British Library Cataloguing in Publication Data

Data available

Library of Congress Cataloging-in-Publication Data
Smith, J. C. (John Cyril)
Smith's Law of theft—9th ed. / David Ormerod.
   p. cm.
Includes bibliographical references and index.
ISBN-13 : 978-0-19-929989-8 (pbk. : alk. paper) 1. Larceny—Great Britain.
I. Title: Law of theft. II. Ormerod, Daivd. III. Title
KD7992 . S6 2007
345 . 42'0262—dc22

2007034982

Typeset by Cepha Imaging Private Ltd, Bangalore, India
Printed in Great Britain
on acid-free paper by
Ashford Colour Press Limited, Gosport, Hampshire

ISBN 978–0–19–929989–8

1 3 5 7 9 10 8 6 4 2

PREFACE

The passing of ten years since the last edition of this work has necessitated a major review with large elements rewritten in full. The chapter on theft has been substantially revised taking into account, in particular, the House of Lords' decision in *Hinks* on theft and gifts. More significantly, there has been the enactment of the Fraud Act 2006. This represents the most radical change in this area of the law since 1968, replacing as it does all of the deception-based offences provided for by the 1968 and 1978 Theft Acts. Chapter 3 analyses in detail and, hopefully in a manner that emulates the lucid style of Sir John Smith in previous editions, the numerous issues arising from this beguilingly short and simple-looking legislation. That chapter draws upon the first named author's article in the *Criminal Law Review* ([2007] Crim LR 192). There is also a new chapter scrutinizing the common law offence of conspiracy to defraud and analysis of the future application of that offence. Chapter 13 on Handling includes a discussion of the principal money laundering offences, providing an opportunity for comparison between handling and money laundering regimes. Throughout the book, account has been taken of the voluminous statutory and case law developments since the last edition.

The book has a long-established popularity with a wide readership of students, academics, and practitioners. We have endeavoured to maintain its appeal by providing an accessible and useful companion for the practitioner without losing the depth of scholarly analysis for which Sir John Smith was renowned. In addition, new sections of a more practical nature have been added dealing with sentencing, jurisdiction, case management, material on the fraud protocol, and other procedural issues. To assist the reader, key materials including relevant legislation, the Fraud Protocol, and extracts from the Criminal Procedure Rules are appended.

Thanks are due to David Kirk for his valuable comments with regard to Chapter 3 (The Fraud Act) and to participants at numerous lectures on the Fraud Act presented in recent months. The assistance of Nigel Gravells, Graham Virgo, Michael Hirst, Rudi Fortson, and Andy Campbell for comments on various parts of drafts chapters is also gratefully acknowledged. Further thanks are due to Rebecca Young and Sattam Al-Mughery for reading through draft chapters. As representative student and practitioner readers respectively, they provided useful insights into the accessibility and clarity of the text. At OUP thanks are due to Jane Kavanagh, Marjorie Francois, Jodi Towler, and to Joy Ruskin-Tompkins for seeing the project through to completion. Any errors remaining are our responsibility.

This is a fast-developing area of law with further large-scale government reform ahead. We have tried to take account of all relevant changes in the law up to 30 April 2007.

David Ormerod and David Huw Williams

CONTENTS—SUMMARY

CONTENTS

5. Conspiracy to Defraud

Contents

13. Handling Stolen Goods and Related Offences

TABLE OF CASES

Australia

Canada

European Court

New Zealand

United States of America

TABLE OF STATUTES

TABLE OF SECONDARY LEGISLATION

FREQUENTLY CITED EDITIONS

'*Arlidge and Parry on Fraud*' refers to A Arlidge, J Parry, and I Gatt, *Arlidge and Parry on Fraud* (2nd edn, 1996), unless an alternative edition is specified.

'*CLGP*' refers to G Williams, *Criminal Law: The General Part* (1953).

'Griew' refers to EJ Griew, *The Theft Acts 1986 and 1978* (7th edn, 1995).

'*Russell on Crime*' indicates the 12th edn, 1964 unless otherwise specified.

'*Smith and Hogan, Criminal Law*' refers to DC Ormerod, *Smith and Hogan, Criminal Law* (11th edn, 2005), unless an alternative edition is specified.

'*TBCL*' refers to G Williams, *Textbook of Criminal Law* (2nd edn, 1983), unless an alternative edition is specified.

1

INTRODUCTION

The Theft Acts

Until 1968 the English law of stealing developed in a haphazard fashion over several **1.01** centuries. The common law began with a crude notion of stealing which covered only the most obvious and direct taking by one person of property which was in the possession of another. As the inadequacies of the law were exposed by the ingenuity of rogues, so the courts and, later, Parliament, extended the law to punish more sophisticated forms of dishonesty. The courts generally achieved their purpose by extending the ambit of the original crime of larceny by means of fictions and strained interpretations of the concepts which constitute the definition of that crime—particularly the concept of possession. Parliament's method was to create a new crime to supplement the old. As we shall see, history repeated itself with the judicial interpretations of the concept of deception leading to new legislation in the form of the Fraud Act 2006.

In one way or another before 1968 most varieties of dishonest appropriation of the **1.02** property of another were brought within the ambit of the criminal law and, with one or two exceptions, the gaps through which the dishonest might slip were narrow and did not present a serious problem. But this was at the price of tolerating an immensely and unnecessarily complicated structure, full of difficult distinctions of a purely technical character and bristling with traps for the judges, magistrates, prosecutors, and police who had to administer the law.

The Theft Act 1968, which was based largely on the Eighth Report of the Criminal Law **1.03** Revision Committee[1] (hereafter CLRC), swept all this away and gave us a completely fresh start. The definition of theft embraces all—or virtually all—of the kinds of dishonest conduct which came within the definitions of the old crimes of larceny (in all its various forms),

---

[1] Cmnd 2977, 'Theft and Related Offences'.

obtaining by false pretences, embezzlement, and fraudulent conversion. This was, in itself, an immense simplification, for the boundaries between these offences were difficult to draw precisely and, right up to the time of their repeal, were the subject of controversy.

1.04 It has, however, been decided that the simplification effected by the Act was greater than the CLRC intended. They did not think it practicable for the definition of theft to include the offence of obtaining by false pretences. The effect of the decision of the House of Lords in *Gomez*[2] was that it included that offence (then obtaining by deception, contrary to s 15) with the unimportant exception of obtaining land (and a few other minor instances).

1.05 Notwithstanding this simplification, many difficulties remain and some, at least, are unavoidable. Stealing consists in interference with other persons' rights in property, their rights of ownership, whether legal or equitable, their possession and control over chattels and things in action—intangible property. These rights are regulated by the civil law and, in an advanced society, their structure is inevitably complicated. This is something of which the reformer of the criminal law must take account in the legislation which he proposes, but which he cannot alter. The concepts of the civil law must be utilized in the definition of the crime. Moreover, while many borderlines are eliminated by the use of a broadly based definition of theft, there must always remain the borderline between interferences with another's property which are criminal and those which are not.[3]

1.06 Although generally well drafted, some offences under the Act proved in practice to be unworkable. One section of the 1968 Act, s 16 (notably a provision introduced while the Bill was passing through Parliament without scrutiny by the CLRC), proved to be so obscure and unsatisfactory that as early as 1972 it was referred to the CLRC for reconsideration. On the recommendation of the Committee, part of the section (s 16(1)(a)) was repealed and replaced by new offences in the Theft Act 1978. New methods of transferring funds created other difficulties, not foreseen by the CLRC, which were met by the Theft (Amendment) Act 1996 and have now been superseded by the Fraud Act 2006.

1.07 Unfortunately the interpretation of the Theft Acts has produced a mass of complex case-law. Whether this is due to inherent defects in the Acts or failures on the part of the courts to construe and apply them properly is debatable. The law of theft is still being considered by the Law Commission[4] who cite the opinion of Beldam LJ, a former chairman of the Commission, that it is 'in urgent need of simplification and modernisation, so that a jury of 12 ordinary citizens do not have to grapple with the antiquated "franglais" of choses in action and scarce public resources are not devoted to hours of semantic argument divorced from the true merits of the case'.[5] In fact the Acts do not use the expression

---

[2] [1993] 1 All ER 1, below, para 2.19.
[3] For a recent philosophical account of what rights might be protected by the Theft Act offences see A Simester and GR Sullivan, 'On the Nature and Rationale of Property Offences' in RA Duff and SP Green, *Defining Crimes: Essays on the Special Part of the Criminal Law* (2006).
[4] They began in 1994: Law Com No 228 (1994). For some proposals, see JC Smith (1996) 28 Bracton LJ 27.
[5] *Hallam* 1994, CA, No 92/4388. (The report in [1995] Crim LR 323 does not include this dictum.) Contrast the opinion of Lord Diplock, below, para 1.10. Lord Diplock was speaking before, and Beldam LJ after, the courts got seriously to work on the 1968 Act.

'chose in action' or any other franglais. If juries are being confused by the use of such terms, that is the fault of the judges. The law must utilize the concept of a thing in action because that is a variety of intangible property which is frequently the object of offences under the Acts. It is the duty of the judge to explain this and other legal concepts to the jury in terms which are intelligible to them.

Like many nineteenth-century statutes, the Larceny Acts of 1861 and 1916 created a mul-   **1.08**
titude of separate crimes to provide an aggravated punishment where a single circumstance of aggravation was present. Simple larceny was punishable with five years' imprisonment, but there were many types of stealing with greater or less penalties according to the nature of the property stolen, the place where it was stolen and the relationship between the thief and the owner. The fact that the subject of the larceny was a will, title deeds, or a mail-bag was a sufficient circumstance of aggravation to raise the maximum to life. Other single circumstances which allowed for an enhanced punishment were that the larceny was of cattle or goods in the process of manufacture, from the person, from a ship, by a clerk or servant, or by a tenant or lodger. On the other hand, lesser punishments were provided, for example, if the larceny was of ore from a mine or of a dog. Any court in sentencing a thief today will take account, in determining the sentence, of very many factors in addition to such single elements of aggravation or mitigation—indeed it is very unlikely that the factors enumerated will be the most important in the court's decision. Society's view as to what aggravates an offence changes from time to time.

In place of all these aggravated forms of larceny the 1968 Act provided a single offence of   **1.09**
theft with a single penalty.[6] As the definition comprehends within it offences which were formerly punishable with imprisonment for life and for fourteen years, it was thought right that the maximum penalty provided should be more than the five years available for simple larceny. Following the recommendation of the CLRC, s 7 of the Act provided a maximum of ten years. From 1 October 1992, this was reduced to seven years.[7] This is a more realistic maximum in the light of the practice of the courts, but it creates an anomaly in that fraud carries a maximum of ten. As with all the offences under the Act, these maxima should, in accordance with general principles,[8] be reserved for the worst type of the offence which comes before the court; and sentences in other cases should be proportionately lower.

The interpretation of the Thefts Act[9]

The Theft Acts represented an almost completely fresh start, and their words should be   **1.10**
interpreted in their natural meaning to produce sensible results,[10] without harking back unnecessarily to the concepts of the common law and the Larceny Acts.

> [The 1968 Act] is expressed in simple language as used and understood by ordinary literate men and women. It avoids so far as possible those terms of art which have acquired a special

---

[6] A step back was taken by the Criminal Justice Act 1991, providing a higher penalty for burglary when it is committed in a dwelling, below, para 8.66.

[7] Criminal Justice Act 1991, s 26(1).

[8] *Ambler* [1976] Crim LR 266.

[9] See R Brazier, 'The Theft Act: Three Principles of Interpretation' [1974] Crim LR 701.

[10] *Baxter* [1971] 2 All ER 359 at 362, per Sachs LJ.

meaning understood only by lawyers in which many of the penal enactments which it supersedes were couched.[11]

1.11 Historically, very little attention was paid to the actual words of the Larceny Act 1916. The courts constantly had recourse to the common law and assumed that the Act was intended to preserve it, even when the wording was somewhat difficult to reconcile with this view. The definition of larceny in the 1916 Act was a new statutory definition, but it did not purport to do more than codify the common law. There is therefore a fundamental difference between the Act of 1916 and the Theft Acts. The Theft Acts enact, for the most part, completely new law. Only in a limited number of cases is it necessary or desirable to resort to earlier case-law. When the 1968 bill was before the House of Lords, Lord Wilberforce introduced an amendment[12] to the effect that it should not be permissible 'to refer to any decisions of any Courts prior to the passing of this Act, other than decisions in general terms dealing with the interpretation of Statutes'. It is submitted that this amendment was wisely withdrawn. Such a rule might be workable in some statutes but only if they were drafted with such a rule of interpretation in mind, which the Theft Acts were not. In this field, moreover, it would simply not be possible to dispense with the previous case-law altogether. The Theft Acts assume the existence of the whole law of property, much of which is to be found only in decided cases; and any such Act must surely make a similar assumption. The Acts include expressions like 'thing in action', 'tenancy', 'proprietary right or interest', 'trust', and many other terms describing concepts of the civil law which it would be quite impracticable to spell out in an Act concerned with theft. The court can be informed as to the circumstances in which a person is 'under an obligation to make restoration' of property, its proceeds or its value,[13] only by reference to the law of contract and quasi-contract which is embodied in case-law.

1.12 No doubt Lord Wilberforce had in mind not the civil law, but the old cases on the criminal law of larceny and related offences with all their technicalities. Most of these cases are now irrelevant because the criminal concepts employed in the Act are new. Where the interpretation of the Act requires an answer to some question of civil law—for example, when the ownership in property passes—it is particularly undesirable that resort should be had[14] to those cases in which the concepts of the civil law were distorted in order to force a case within the confines of one of the old offences. Where, however, the Act incorporates the substance of the provisions of earlier statutes—as, for example, with the amended version of taking motor vehicles[15]—it is surely undesirable that the courts should have to go back to square one and reconsider points of construction previously settled, with perhaps different and not necessarily better results. Again, where terms with a well-settled meaning under the Larceny Acts have been used in a similar context in the Theft Act,

---

[11] *Treacy v DPP* [1971] AC 537 at 565, [1971] 1 All ER 110 at 124, per Lord Diplock.
[12] Parl Debates, Official Report, HL, vol 290, col 897.
[13] Section 5(4), below, para 2.250.
[14] As occurred in *Gilks* [1972] 3 All ER 280, below, para 2.264 where *Middleton* (1873) LR 2 CCR 38 was applied and extended. See [1972] Crim LR 586–90.
[15] Section 12, below, ch 10.

it would seem desirable—and certainly in accord with the intention of the framers of the Act—that those concepts should be given their well-settled meaning. Examples are the use of the word 'menaces' in blackmail[16] and 'receives' in handling stolen goods.[17]

The 'old' law is also relevant as an aid to construction insofar as its inadequacies illuminate **1.13** the mischief at which the 1968 Act is aimed and in that it may persuade the court that Parliament could not have intended to legalize conduct which it thinks ought to be criminal and which was criminal under the old law.[18] On the other hand, the courts should 'shun the temptation which sometimes presses on the mind of the judiciary, to suppose that because a particular course of conduct . . . was anti-social and undesirable, it can necessarily be fitted into some convenient criminal pigeon-hole'. And where an act was an offence under a provision repealed by the Theft Act, 'it does not follow that there is necessarily a convenient alternative criminal pigeon-hole provided which fits the facts under the provisions of the 1968 Act'.[19]

Lord Wilberforce's amendment would also have provided that the 1968 Act should be **1.14** interpreted 'according to the plain and natural meaning of the words used, read in the context of the Act as a whole, and given a fair, large and liberal construction'. It is submitted that the Acts should be interpreted according to the plain and natural meaning of the words used (if they have one) except where it appears that the word has a technical meaning which, in the context, it is intended to bear. Thus, if the word 'menaces' were given its plain and natural meaning, it might be held to be confined to threats of violence and the like. This would result in a drastic narrowing of the offence of blackmail and would plainly defeat the intention of Parliament. The word should be given the extended meaning which, in this context, it has long borne in the law.

No one could object to the words of the Acts being given a 'fair' construction but the **1.15** other expressions used in the amendment, 'large and liberal', are of much more doubtful import. They suggest that the Acts should be given an extensive meaning, so as to prohibit acts not clearly within their terms. It is submitted that the Act should not be so interpreted. There is much to be said for ignoring the rule (only applied spasmodically and inconsistently) that penal statutes should be strictly construed; but this is achieved by giving words their plain and natural meaning and adopting the 'fair' interpretation—'fair', that is, to both sides. It is not desirable that the courts should go to the other extreme and extend the meaning of penal provisions by a 'large and liberal' construction. The principle, *nulla poena sine lege*, is of as great importance today as ever it was. An important feature of the interpretation of the Act in practice has been the tendency of the courts to leave the meaning of words and phrases to be determined by the jury as 'a question of fact'. This has been criticized as an abdication of judicial responsibility leading to uncertainty and

---

[16] Section 21, below, ch 12.
[17] Section 22, below, ch 13.
[18] *Treacy v DPP* [1971] AC at 557–8, [1971] 1 All ER at 118, per Lord Hodson.
[19] *Charles* [1976] 1 All ER 659 at 666, per Bridge LJ.

inconsistency in the application of the law.[20] More recently, however, the courts have resumed their proper role as the interpreters of statutes.[21]

1.16 Where the words of the Act are ambiguous, reference may be made to the appropriate report of the CLRC in accordance with the general principles for the construction of statutes.[22] In numerous cases the courts have not hesitated to follow this course.[23] If only they had done so consistently, most of the difficulties which have arisen under the Acts would have been avoided. That they have not done so may be largely due to the fact that they were not invited by counsel to consider the Eighth Report. In *Gomez*,[24] however, the majority of the House of Lords declined to look at the Eighth Report, saying that to do so 'serves no useful purpose at the present time'. Their reason was that there was, in Lord Keith's opinion, a clear decision of the House on the point which had stood for twelve years; but the House in the earlier case did not have the advantage of reference to the Report; and not everyone agrees that it was a clear decision. Lord Lowry, dissenting, demonstrated pretty clearly that the decision of the majority defeated the intention of the Committee which Parliament had espoused by enacting provisions virtually identical with the Committee's draft bill.

1.17 In *Hinks*[25] the House of Lords were equally dismissive in rejecting the historical accounts which shed light on the intended interpretation of the Act. Counsel had cited, as evidence of the true intention of the draftsman, a passage from a note by Sir John Smith referring to a 'memorandum dated January 15, 1964 [by] the distinguished draftsman of the Theft Act (Mr JS Fiennes, as he then was) [who] wrote to members of the Larceny Sub-Committee of the Criminal Law Revision Committee'. This explained the clear intention of the provision. Lord Steyn noted that Sir John Smith 'returned to this point in "The Sad Fate of the Theft Act 1968", an essay in *The Search for Principle, Essays in Honour of Lord Goff of Chieveley,* ed. by W Swadling and G Jones, p 97, 100–101'. But his lordship dismissed the assistance it offered: 'While this anecdote is an interesting bit of legal history, it is not relevant to the question before the House.'

The law of stealing under the Larceny Acts

1.18 A very brief résumé of the position before the 1968 Act will assist the understanding of some of its provisions.[26] There existed the following crimes:

---

[20] See *Feely* [1973] QB 530, [1973] 1 All ER 341, below, para 2.292; *Hale* (1978) 68 Cr App R 415, below, para 7.17; *Dawson* [1976] Crim LR 692, below, para 7.12; *Reader* (1977) 66 Cr App R 33, below, para 13.98; DW Elliott, 'Law and Fact in Theft Act Cases' [1976] Crim LR 707. *Hayes* (1976) 64 Cr App R 82, an extreme case, seems, in effect, to have been overruled by *Mainwaring* (1981) 74 Cr App R 99, below, para 2.228.

[21] See DW Elliott, '*Brutus v Cozens,* Decline and Fall' [1989] Crim LR 323.

[22] *Black-Clawson International Ltd v Papierwerke Waldhof-Aschaffenburg AG* [1974] QB 660, [1974] 2 All ER 610, CA, [1975] AC 591, [1975] 1 All ER 810, HL. In exceptional circumstances the courts may now refer even to Hansard: *Pepper (Inspector of Taxes) v Hart* [1991] 1 All ER 42.

[23] See, for example, *Hall* [1968] 2 QB 788, [1968] 2 All ER 1009, CA; *Scott v Metropolitan Police Comr* [1975] AC 819, at 836–7, HL; *Ghosh* [1982] 2 All ER 689, CA; *Kassim* [1993] 3 All ER 713 at 718; *Kassim* [1992] 1 AC 9 at 16, HL; *Preddy* [1996] 3 All ER 481 at 486.

[24] [1993] 1 All ER 1 at 13. cf Lord Lowry at p 718.

[25] [2001] 2 AC 241.

[26] A full account is to be found in *Smith and Hogan, Criminal Law* (1st edn, 1965) and *Russell on Crime* (12th edn, 1964).

Simple larceny

Simple larceny was most commonly committed where D by a trespass took possession **1.19** of goods which were in the possession or custody of V without V's consent. It was from this notion that the common law began. The concept of 'taking' was expanded by the courts until, in the 1916 consolidation, it was defined to include:

obtaining the possession —
(a) by any trick;
(b) by intimidation;
(c) under a mistake on the part of the owner with knowledge on the part of the taker that possession has been so obtained;
(d) by finding, where at the time of the finding the finder believes that the owner can be discovered by taking reasonable steps.[27]

It was essential in all these forms of larceny that, as well as a taking there should be a 'carrying away' and the Act provided:

the expression 'carries away' includes any removal of anything from the place which it occupies, but in the case of a thing attached, only if it has been completely detached.[28]

At common law a possessor could not steal but legislation from 1857 onwards made it **1.20** larceny for a bailee to misappropriate the bailed goods and the 1916 Act provided:

. . . a person may be guilty of stealing any such thing notwithstanding that he has lawful possession thereof, if, being a bailee or part owner thereof, he fraudulently converts the same to his own use or the use of any person other than the owner.[29]

Here a physical 'taking and carrying away' was unnecessary. It was enough, for example, that D should have contracted to sell goods bailed to him, without laying hands on them at all. Though larceny was commonly (and, in general, accurately) described as an offence against possession, larceny by a bailee was plainly an offence by a possessor against ownership.

Larceny by a servant

Where a master (or, as we would now say, employer) entrusted his servant (employee) **1.21** with goods it was held at an early stage in the development of the common law that possession remained in the master and the servant merely had custody, so that a misappropriation of the goods by the servant amounted to a 'taking' out of the master's possession and, therefore, larceny. This was an aggravated form of larceny under s 17(1)(a) of the 1916 Act.

Embezzlement

The position was different where the servant received goods from a third party to transmit **1.22** to the possession of the master. Here the servant was held to acquire possession and therefore to be incapable of larceny at common law. He was, no doubt, a bailee; but, in 1799,

---

[27] Larceny Act 1916, s 1(2)(i).
[28] ibid, s 1(2)(ii).
[29] ibid, s 1(1), proviso.

before legislation dealt with bailees generally, Parliament created the offence of embezzlement to deal with the particular case here discussed. The distinction between embezzlement and larceny by a servant was a subtle one. If D received money for his master and put it straight into his pocket this was embezzlement; but if he put the money into his master's till and then took it out again this was larceny, since putting the money into the till reduced it into the possession of the master. Like larceny by a servant, embezzlement was punishable with fourteen years' imprisonment.[30]

Fraudulent conversion

1.23 By a series of statutes from 1812 onwards the offence known as fraudulent conversion was created and extended. By s 20 of the 1916 Act it was provided that anyone who had been entrusted or become entrusted[31] with property for various purposes or had received property for or on account of another should, if he converted the property, be guilty of a misdemeanour, punishable with seven years' imprisonment. On the face of it, the definition of this offence comprehended within it larceny by a bailee, larceny by a clerk or servant, and embezzlement. It also clearly applied to another category of persons—those who had been entrusted not merely with the possession but with the ownership of the property.

Obtaining by false pretences

1.24 Where D by a false statement induced V to transfer to him possession of the goods with intent to appropriate them, this was larceny by a trick at common law. Where D by a false pretence induced V to transfer to him *ownership* of the goods with intent to appropriate them, this was no offence at common law but was made a misdemeanour by statute in 1757; and, by s 32 of the 1916 Act, it was an offence punishable with five years' imprisonment. The distinction between larceny by a trick and obtaining by false pretences was a fine one and a fruitful source of difficulties. As an example, if D by false pretences induced V to let him have goods on hire purchase intending to appropriate them, this was larceny by a trick since the property did not pass; but if he induced him to let him have the same goods on credit-sale terms, this was obtaining by false pretences, since the property did pass.

1.25 As the Act has now been in force for almost forty years, a substantial body of very technical law has developed around the provisions with most of the key provisions having been before the House of Lords on at least one occasion. There is less need than ever to rely on the pre-1968 provisions for interpretative guidance, and the appellate court's approach to interpretation continues to be one favouring reference to the ordinary meaning of the statutory words rather than the draftsman's intended meaning—even where the concept is one of a technical legal nature. The result is that we are left with offences under the 1968 Act (and the sole survivor of the 1978 Act, s 3) which have a broader scope than intended. The reach of the Theft Acts in respect of dishonest conduct is nothing short of astonishing.

---

[30] Larceny Act 1916, s 17(1)(b).
[31] *Grubb* [1915] 2 KB 683.

The Fraud Act 2006

Common law approaches to fraud

It may seem surprising to many lawyers and certainly to the general public that there has **1.26** been no substantive offence of fraud in modern times in England and Wales. Conspiracy to defraud and fraudulent trading come closest, but neither is truly a general fraud offence.[32]

One consequence of the absence of any substantive general fraud offence in modern English **1.27** law is that there has been no attempt to provide a clear definition of what constitutes fraud.[33] The concept of fraud has evolved over the centuries rather than being a product of statutory design. It is notoriously difficult to define.[34] The classic attempt at definition in English law was that of the great Victorian jurist James Fitzjames Stephen:

Whenever the words 'fraud' or 'intent to defraud' or 'fraudulently' occur in the definition of a crime two elements at least are essential to the commission of the crime: namely, first, deceit or an intention to deceive or in some cases mere secrecy; and, secondly, either actual injury or possible injury or an intent to expose some person either to actual injury or to a risk of possible injury by means of that deceit or secrecy.[35]

Stephen's definition does not suggest that fraud is synonymous with 'deception'. As Buckley **1.28** J in *Re London and Globe Finance Corporation Ltd* [36] made clear:

To deceive is, I apprehend, to induce a man to believe that a thing is true which is false, and which the person practising the deceit knows or believes to be false. To defraud is to deprive by deceit: it is by deceit to induce a man to act to his injury. More tersely it may be put, that to deceive is by false-hood to induce a state of mind; to defraud is by deceit to induce a course of action.

Deception under the Theft Acts[37]

The Theft Act 1968 included a series of offences based on deception. In each it had to **1.29** be proved that D's conduct constituted a representation (whether by act or omission), that this representation caused the victim to form a false belief, that belief (caused by the representation) led the victim to behave in a certain way—transfer property, a valuable security, etc—and that as a result of the behaviour the defendant (or another) gained.

---

[32] Conspiracy because it requires conduct by two or more and fraudulent trading because it could only be committed by a corporate business.

[33] Astonishingly, the 2006 Act manages to introduce a general fraud offence, uses the term fraud as a label for the offences, and yet fails to provide any definition, instead producing three *descriptions* of proscribed conduct.

[34] See SP Green, *Lying, Cheating and Stealing: A Moral Theory of White Collar Crime* (2006).

[35] JFJ Stephen, *History of the Criminal Law* (1883) ii. 121.

[36] [1903] 1 Ch 728, 732–3.

[37] The offences were: Obtaining property: 1968, s 15; Obtaining a money transfer: 1968, s 15A; Obtaining a pecuniary advantage: 1968, s 16; Procuring the execution of a valuable security: 1968, s 20(2); Obtaining services: 1978, s 1; Securing the remission of a liability: 1978, s 2(1)(a); Inducing a creditor to wait for or to forgo payment: 1978, s 2(1)(b); Obtaining an exemption from or abatement of liability: 1978, s 2(1)(c). These offences were examined in full in earlier editions.

1.30 These offences caused problems for the courts from the outset. The requirement of an operative deception meant that the offences were restricted in application: if V knew that D's statement was false,[38] or if V would have acted in the same way even if he had known it,[39] or if V did not rely on the false statement but arrived at the same erroneous conclusion from his own observation or some other source,[40] or, of course, if V did not read or hear the false statement ATH made by D, no deception offence was committed. In addition, there were numerous more technical difficult issues surrounding the deception offences.[41] These involved such fundamental issues as: whether a representation could be made impliedly;[42] whether indifference as to the truth of a representation precluded a finding of an operative deception;[43] and whether there could be a deception of a machine.

1.31 The deception offences not only generated difficulty for the courts; some of the principal deception offences in the 1968 Act proved so unworkable as to require Parliamentary action. The Theft Act 1978[44] replaced the 'nightmare'[45] provisions of s 16(a) of the 1968 Act, which dealt with obtaining a 'pecuniary advantage'. Unfortunately, the 1978 Act itself created broad, overlapping and over-particularized offences to protect against deceptive conduct to secure services, and to avoid liabilities.[46] Similarly, following *Preddy*[47] the Theft (Amendment) Act 1996 introduced a further deception offence—obtaining a money transfer by deception—which was accepted as a less than ideal solution.[48]

1.32 Some greater good was to derive from *Preddy:* the case itself and the string of appeals in its wake, illustrated that the best that could be achieved by amendment would be a series of incremental repairs tackling individual lacunae as and when identified. As with the 1996 Act, there would be the problem that any amendment Parliament offered could never be retrospective, would create its own difficulties, and would be unlikely to have the flexibility to deal with every fraudster's future initiatives. It was realized that if English law was to offer adequate protection from fraud, a more structured and coherent package of offences was necessary to keep pace with technology, modern methods of property transfer and commercial transactions over the internet.[49]

1.33 Aside from the particular problems being identified by cases such as *Preddy*, there remained an underlying concern that 'deception' based offences were not working as effectively as

---

[38] *Ady* (1835) 7 C & P 140; *Mills* (1857) Dears & B 205; *Hensler* (1870) 11 Cox CC 570; *Light* (1915) 11 Cr App R 111.

[39] *Edwards* [1978] Crim LR 49, CA. See commentary at 50.

[40] *Roebuck* (1856) Dears & B 24. cf the similar principle which applies to misrepresentation in relation to the law of contract: *Attwood v Small* (1838) 6 Cl & Fin 232; *Smith v Chadwick* (1884) 9 App Cas 187, HL.

[41] For a detailed account see the previous editions of this work, ch 4.

[42] *Ray* [1974] AC 370.

[43] *Charles* [1977] AC 177; *Lambie* [1982] AC 449.

[44] See especially ATH Smith, 'Reforming Section 16 of the Theft Act' [1977] Crim LR 259.

[45] *Royle* (1971) 56 Cr App R 51, per Edmund Davies LJ.

[46] For a full examination of the 1978 Act see ch 4 of the previous edition.

[47] [1996] AC 815.

[48] See Law Com Report No 243, *Offences of Dishonesty: Money Transfers* (1996), and for criticism of the Act see JC Smith, *Current Law Statutes Annotated* (1996); C Osborn, 'Fraud Fudge' [1996] 93(41) Law Soc Gaz 24; the SFO was reported as seeing s 15A as a 'sticking plaster solution', *Financial Times*, 16 Oct 1996.

[49] See generally Law Com Report No 276 (2002).

they ought to. The courts had been forced to adopt broad interpretations to find operative deceptions. The concept was, arguably, being misconstrued. The Law Commission, Home Office (and the Attorney-General in debates on the Fraud Act in the House of Lords[50]) catalogued the problems with the old law: too many offences; with too much overlap; too much technicality;[51] over-particularized offences;[52] difficulty in selecting charges where it was unclear how D proposed to receive the property (money order/cash/cheque each involving different offences); obtaining by deception required an intention permanently to deprive. All of these led the prosecutor, quite naturally to place greater reliance on the 'safe option' of the all embracing conspiracy to defraud charge (at least where there was more than one offender).

The chosen solution to these problems was to repeal the deception offences and replace them with a general fraud offence in the Fraud Act 2006.[53]   **1.34**

Evolution of the 2006 Act

The immediate history of the Fraud Act 2006 can be traced to the reference to the Law Commission by the then Home Secretary Jack Straw: **1.35**

As part of their programme of work on dishonesty, to examine the law on fraud, and in particular to consider whether it: is readily comprehensible to juries; is adequate for effective prosecution; is fair to potential defendants; meets the need of developing technology including electronic means of transfer; and to make recommendations to improve the law in these respects with all due expedition. In making these recommendations to consider whether a general offence of fraud would improve the criminal law.

The response from the Law Commission began with Consultation Paper No 155 *Legislating*   **1.36** *the Criminal Code: Fraud and Deception* (1999),[54] and this was followed by Law Commission Report No 276, *Fraud* (2002).[55] In turn, the government responded with the Home Office Consultation Paper, *Fraud Law Reform* (2004)[56] which developed the Law Commission's proposals. However, calls for reform of the dishonesty offences, and in particular those based on deception have been circulating for many years.

The merits of a general fraud offence

The merits of general fraud offences have been debated for decades.[57] A general fraud   **1.37** offence was considered by the CLRC at the time the Theft Act 1968 was being drafted.[58]

---

50 See especially Hansard, HL, 22 June 2005, col 1652.
51 See also the comments in Hansard, HC, 12 June 2006, col 535 (Solicitor-General).
52 See Law Com Report No 276, paras 3.11–3.24.
53 Which came into force on 15 January 2007: Fraud Act 2006 (Commencement) Order 2006, SI 2006/3200. See also Fraud Act 2006, Sch 2, paras 2 and 3.
54 <http://www.lawcom.gov.uk/docs/cp155.pdf>
55 <http://www.lawcom.gov.uk/docs/lc276.pdf>. Described by Dominic Grieve MP as a 'model of its kind', Hansard, HC, 12 June 2006, col 546.
56 <http://www.homeoffice.gov.uk/documents/cons-fraud-law-reform/>
57 The merits were discussed in Law Commission Working Paper No 104 *Conspiracy to Defraud* (1987), and in CP 155, Parts 4 and 5. 'Any person who dishonestly causes another to suffer [financial] prejudice, or who dishonestly makes a gain for himself or another' (para 5.2) would commit the offence.
58 *Eighth Report* (1966) Cmnd 2977, paras 97–100.

The Committee recommended a very unusual form of fraud offence and included this in clause 12(3) of the CLRC Draft Bill of 1966: 'A person who dishonestly, with a view to gain for himself or another, by any deception induces a person to do or refrain from doing any act shall on conviction on indictment be liable to imprisonment for a term not exceeding two years.'

1.38 That form of fraud offence is very different from those under the 2006 Act because it requires as an express element of the offence, that the defendant deceived the victim. Once that proposal was rejected by Parliament, it seems that the general attitude, at least in the academic community, was against introducing such an offence. Several eminent commentators doubted whether a general fraud offence could ever be drafted which does not extend potential criminal liability too far.[59] There were however numerous strong supporters of such reform.[60]

Law Commission proposals

1.39 The Law Commission, in its CP 155, made recommendations to amend the deception offences, but declined to recommend any general fraud offence. This hesitant and unambitious approach was heavily criticized.[61] The Commission rejected a general fraud offence in which dishonesty, as currently understood, would be the principal element. Such an offence, it was said, would be 'undesirable in principle' and insufficiently certain to satisfy the European Convention on Human Rights (ECHR). A general offence resting almost exclusively on proof of deception was also rejected because it would extend the criminal law too far, and be too indeterminate. However, even in the Commission's tentative proposals to reform the deception offences in CP 155, there was a discernible shift away from focusing on the wrong of 'deceit' and towards criminalizing as fraud instances of imperilling economic interests and placing more emphasis on the *mens rea* of the offences than on any objectively discernible *actus reus*.

1.40 Unusually for the Law Commission, the Consultation Paper was revisited and a second round of proposals was circulated to a limited number of individuals, rather than as part of a full consultation process. These led to the final Report on Fraud No 276, which represented a complete volte-face from CP 155. The Report recommended enactment of a general fraud offence and the Draft Bill attached to it described three forms the offence should take. The proposals were endorsed by the Home Office in a further consultation in 2004, in which additional reforms were suggested. In addition to the deficiencies identified with the previous law, the government drew support for introducing broader, less technical offences from the fact that the volume of fraud being committed

---

[59] JC Smith, 'Fraud and The Criminal Law' in P Birks (ed.), *Criminal Justice and Human Rights—Pressing Problems in the Law*, i. 1 (1995) 49. Similar sentiments were expressed by another great theft scholar EJ Griew in *The Theft Acts* (7th edn, 1995) 141. See also the conclusions in Law Commission Working Paper No 56 *Criminal Law: Conspiracy to Defraud* (1974) paras 65, 81–2.

[60] See the excellent article by GR Sullivan, 'Fraud and Efficacy in the Criminal Law: A Proposal for a Wide Residual Offence' [1985] Crim LR 616; and also 'Framing an Acceptable General Offence of Fraud' (1989) 53 J Crim L 92.

[61] See DC Ormerod, 'A Bit of a Con' [1999] Crim LR 789.

in the UK continued to rise, with estimates that fraud cost the UK economy £16 billion in 2004.[62]

1.41 The Bill was, in general, very warmly received in the House of Lords in debates where current and former Law Lords approved of practically all of its terms (except the retention of the offence of conspiracy to defraud).[63] Similarly, in the Commons and in Standing Committee, the Bill was welcomed almost unchallenged. Indeed, it was rather surprising that it took eighteen months of Parliamentary time given the almost negligible changes which resulted from that process of scrutiny. The Act received Royal Assent on 8 November 2006.

1.42 The 2006 Act abolishes the eight heavily used[64] deception offences in the Theft Acts 1968 and 1978, including that inserted post-*Preddy* by the Theft (Amendment) Act 1996.[65] The principal replacement is the general fraud offence created by s 1. The offence of fraud can be committed in one of three ways as proscribed by ss 2–4. Each is based on dishonest conduct against property interests, and carries a maximum ten year sentence on indictment.

1.43 The offences are discussed in full in chapter 3. In short, liability arises by making false representations (s 2), failing to disclose information (s 3), or abusing a position of financial trust (s 4). Each form of the fraud offence is a conduct offence, complete on the accused's acts irrespective of any result caused, which represents a significant shift from the deception offences they replace. Obtaining services by deception is replaced by obtaining services dishonestly (s 11). Other provisions are discussed elsewhere in this edition.[66]

1.44 They are incredibly wide offences deliberately drafted to avoid technicality. Depite their scope and that intention, it is predicted that they will generate plenty of work for the courts, offering new intrepretative challenges. It is hoped that the courts keep a tighter rein on the new offences under the Fraud Act 2006 than they did with some of the offences under the 1968 Act, especially the offence of theft.

Conclusion

1.45 Over the last century English law has shifted its central focus in relation to acquisitive crimes from protecting the possession of tangible goods against transportation, to the protection of ownership of property (as broadly construed) against misuse. Those interests being protected and which form essential elements of the *actus reus*—property and ownership—have expanded. The constant concept has been that of *mens rea*—fraud or dishonesty. So it seems that it will be in the future. It may be that the *actus reus* of the offences will

---

[62] See HC Research Paper 06/31, p 3. See also press reports of 7 March 2007.
[63] See eg Hansard, HL, 22 June 2005, col 1661.
[64] There were 14,000 prosecutions in 2003: Hansard, HL, 22 June 2005, col 1652 (Attorney-General); for the anticipated impact on the efficiency of prosecutions see Home Office document <http://www.home office.gov.uk/documents/cons-fraud-law-reform/Fraud_Bill_RIA.pdf>
[65] See the 8th edition, para 4.64.
[66] See on ss 6 and 7, ch 9 below.

disappear almost to vanishing point as the interests the law seeks to protect become more diffuse, diverse, and indefinable.

The future

1.46 There seems little doubt that there will be an interesting period ahead with many possible areas for development, and many issues to be addressed.

1.47 How will the Fraud Act be prosecuted? Anecdotal evidence from prosecution policy makers is that the Act will be used in a restricted manner and that many of the most extreme possible uses of the legislation, identified below in chapter 3 and chapter 9, will never see the light of a court room. It is to be hoped that this is the case. However, that does not absolve the government of the blame for creating the widest and most ill-defined offences possible leaving to prosecutorial discretion the fair and efficient administration and application of the offences. Moreover, the prosecution agencies will not necessarily all adopt equally rigorous prosecution policies, nor will each necessarily apply the same rigour with internal consistency. The larger-scale frauds which come under scrutiny from the most senior lawyers are those to which most detailed attention is likely to be paid, and ironically it may be those to which the Act's provisions are applied most cautiously. No one relishes the prospect of a Jubilee Line type case failing because of the improper use of the new provisions. In addition, even if the prosecution agencies do all manage to achieve a sensible, measured, consistent approach to the new Act, that does not prevent inappropriate use by private prosecution and malcontents. These may be taken over and stopped by the CPS, but the damage has by then been done—arrests have been made and accusations levelled from which individuals and companies suffer.

1.48 What impact on the law of theft will the new Act have? The offence of theft is so wide, well established and so uncontroversial in practice that very few issues now arise on appeal. There may well remain a strong temptation for prosecutors to stick to what they know, even where the fraud offences would be potentially easier to prove. From the defence perspective, there is no doubt an argument to be made that the offence of theft and the element of appropriation no longer need to be as wide as they are since the conduct is likely to be within s 1 of the 2006 Act. It is highly unlikely however that the courts will recognize that the new fraud offences are of such breadth that it would be safe to reinterpret the offence of theft in a narrower fashion.

1.49 How will the courts intepret the Fraud Act? This will depend in large part on the way that the offences are prosecuted by the agencies. The courts could make the Act work well with some effort. It is hoped that in the early cases to be dealt with on appeal some of the fundamental principles will be established. Chief among those it is to be hoped is that the criminal law should not extend to those cases in which the defendant has a civil law right to be acting in the way that he has. The frontier of the criminal law ought, it is submitted, to be commensurate with that boundary. The likelihood is that the courts will adopt an approach treating the elements of the offences as 'ordinary English words' wherever possible. The legislation was designed to be non-technical and this will support what appears to be the Court of Appeal's current preferred approach to statutory intepretation in criminal law.

What will the government do next? This involves some very difficult crystal ball gazing. **1.50**
Will the government be prepared to allow the courts sufficient time to interpret the Act
and make it work? Disappointingly, that would seen unlikely. Modern governments are
not prepared to allow for legislative settling-in time. They must be seen to be relentless
in their action to combat crime (and of course the causes of crime). The likelihood is therefore that more legislation will follow. What is less clear is what form that legislation will
take. There is still scope for amendment of some of the Theft Act offences. There is also
a growing pressure to use the criminal law to protect other 'interests' from misuse—trade
secrets being a strong example. The law may need to be more forward-thinking by protecting 'rights' and 'interests' such as the 'use' and 'value' derived from 'having access'
to facilities. As these interests are harder to define the mental element of dishonesty
offences will become ever more important.

In addition, there is a very strong likelihood of more changes to the process of investigating **1.51**
and prosecuting theft and fraud, particularly serious fraud. The Attorney-General published the major Fraud Review in 2006.[67] The Review's recommendations include:

- A standardized method of measuring fraud on a consistent basis across the economy (p 40)
- Formulating a national strategy taking a holistic approach to dealing with fraud focusing on the
  causes of fraud as well as dealing with the effects (pp 47–8)
- Creating a 'National Fraud Strategic Authority' to devise a national strategy for dealing with fraud
  and to ensure that it is implemented (p 60)[68]
- Creating a new 'National Fraud Reporting Centre' to analyse reports on fraud and identify
  patterns and trends, to assist investigative agencies (p 92)
- Making fraud a 'policing priority' within the Naional Community Safety (Policing) Plan
- Creating a 'National Lead Force' based upon the City of London Police Fraud Squad (pp 136, 155)
- Increasing the maximum sentence for fraud to fourteen years, and extending other sentencing
  options available to the courts (chapters 8 and 10)
- Creating a 'Financial Court jurisdiction', with a specialist cadre of judges drawn from Crime,
  Commercial, and Chancery courts (pp 158–60)
- A plea bargain structure to be created with judicial oversight (chapter 11)

The government has more recently published its responses to consulation—*Fighting* **1.52**
Fraud Together [69] revealing that each of the proposals received very high levels of support
(all over 86% of respondents), with some recommendations being endorsed by 100%
of consultees (eg establishing the NFRC). With this level of support it seems inevitable that
these initiatives will be implemented.

---

[67] See the full 377 page report available from <http://www.attorneygeneral.gov.uk/attachements/Fraud
Review.pdf>
[68] See the concerns expressed by the Fraud Advisory Panel as to the accountability of such an organization
in 'Which Way Now: Evaluating the Government's Fraud Review' (2006) <www.fraudadvisorypanel.org>
[69] (2007), available from <www.attorneygeneral.gov.uk>

2

STEALING UNDER THE THEFT ACT

Section 1(1) of the Theft Act 1968 provides: **2.01**

A person is guilty of theft if he dishonestly appropriates property belonging to another with the intention of permanently depriving the other of it; and 'thief' and 'steal' shall be construed accordingly.

The offence is triable either way[1] It was originally punishable by a maximum ten years' imprisonment (s 7) but that was reduced to seven years by s 26 of the Criminal Justice Act 1991.[2] In 2005/6 there were 1,210,856 recorded thefts.[3]

Jurisdiction

Our courts will generally accept jurisdiction only over offences committed in England **2.02** and Wales.[4] A crime requiring proof of a result of some kind is usually regarded as committed here if conduct abroad causes that result in this country; but conduct in this country causing the prohibited result abroad is not. This rule caused serious difficulties which

---

[1] See Magistrates' Courts Act 1980, s 17 and Sch 1 para 28.

[2] Under the Penalties for Disorderly Behaviour (Amount of Penalty) (Amendment No 2) Order 2004, SI 2004/2468, made under the Criminal Justice and Police Act 2001, s 3(1), a fixed penalty (currently £80) may be awarded.

[3] See A Walker, C Kershaw, and S Nicholas, *Home Office Statistical Bulletin, Crime in England and Wales* 2005/2006 p 29, Recorded crime by offence 1996 to 2005/6 and percentage change between 2004/5 and 2005/6.

[4] See generally M Hirst, *Jurisdiction and the Ambit of the Criminal Law* (2001).

were the subject of a Law Commission Consultation Paper and Report[5] making recommendations which were enacted in the Criminal Justice Act 1993, brought into force only from 1 June 1999.

2.03 This Act applies to what it calls 'Group A' and 'Group B' offences. Group A offences include theft.[6] Group B offences are conspiracy, attempt, or incitement to commit a Group A offence, and conspiracy to defraud.

2.04 The 1993 Act, s 2, provides that a person may be guilty of a Group A offence if any relevant event occurs in England and Wales. The concept of a relevant event is crucial and is defined as 'any act or omission or other event (including any result of one or more acts or omissions) proof of which is required for conviction of the offence'.

2.05 So it is sufficient if any one element of the offence is committed or occurs in England and Wales. It is not sufficient that a merely preparatory act is done here; but if the act is more than merely preparatory to bringing about a result which is an element of a Group A offence, it will be an attempt triable here. It does not matter for the purposes of Group A or B offences (or conspiracy or attempt to commit them) whether a defendant was a British citizen at the time of the relevant event or whether he was in England and Wales at that time. It is also immaterial whether a Group A offence is an offence under the law of the foreign jurisdiction in which it takes place.

Conspiracy, attempt, and incitement to commit Group A offences triable here

2.06 The general principles of conspiracy, attempt, and incitement are stated in *Smith and Hogan, Criminal Law* (11th edn, 2005) chapter 12 and are not discussed in this book. These 'inchoate offences' are however, in general, confined to conspiracy, attempt, or incitement to commit an offence triable in England and Wales so it is necessary to note the extension of jurisdiction made by the 1993 Act for Theft Acts offences. Where a contemplated Group A offence—such as theft—includes an event in England and Wales, an agreement to commit it is a conspiracy under s 1 of the Criminal Law Act 1977, an attempt is an offence under s 1 of the Criminal Attempts Act 1981, and incitement is an offence at common law. It is immaterial that D joined the conspiracy or made the attempt outside England and Wales and that nothing was done here (s 3(2) and (3) of the 1993 Act); but the incitement must occur in England and Wales though the inciter need not be here. Section 3 does not apply where the charge is under s 1A of the Criminal Law Act 1977 (which allows for a prosecution where the conduct is an offence in the foreign state and an agreement to commit the offence in England would be an indictable conspiracy to commit those offences under s 1A of the Criminal Law Act 1977.[7]

---

[5] Law Com No 180 (1989).

[6] And many of the crimes with which this book is concerned—that is the offences under the Theft Act 1968 of theft (s 1), false accounting (s 17), false statements by company directors, etc (s 19), blackmail (s 21), handling stolen goods (s 22), and retaining credits from dishonest sources (s 24A). Other Group A offences are offences under ss 1, 2, 3, 4, and 5 of the Forgery and Counterfeiting Act 1981 and the common law offence of cheating the public revenue.

[7] See further, M Hirst, *Jurisdiction and the Ambit of the Criminal Law* (2001) 24–6.

Actus Reus of Theft

The *actus reus* consists simply in the *appropriation of property belonging to another*. The three **2.07** questions which require detailed consideration are: What is an appropriation? What is property? and, When does property belong to another?

Appropriation

By s 3(1) of the Act: **2.08**

Any assumption by a person of the rights of an owner amounts to an appropriation, and this includes, where he has come by the property (innocently or not) without stealing it, any later assumption of a right to it by keeping or dealing with it as owner.

This provision, said the CLRC,[8] is a 'partial definition . . . which is included partly to **2.09** indicate that this is the familiar concept of conversion . . .' 'Conversion' is the name of a tort concerning which there exists a substantial body of civil law.[9] It may be familiar to lawyers but it is certainly not familiar to laymen in its legal sense—essentially the usurpation of rights of property belonging to another. A similar concept already existed in the criminal law of larceny by a bailee and the offence of fraudulent conversion. The CLRC thought that 'appropriation' and 'conversion' had the same meaning but preferred 'appropriation' because it more aptly describes the whole range of acts it is intended to cover.

The above provisions now[10] have to be read in the light of three controversial decisions **2.10** of the House of Lords.

In *Morris*,[11] it was held that—

the assumption by a person of *any* of the rights of an owner in property amounts to an appropriation of the property.

In *Gomez*,[12] it was held that—

there may be an assumption of a right and, therefore, an appropriation of property belonging to another although the owner consents to or authorises the act in question.

---

[8] Cmnd 2977, para 34.
[9] See WVH Rogers, *Winfield and Jolowicz on Tort* (17th edn, 2006) 751 et seq.
[10] For early comment on this element of the offence see L Koffman, 'The Nature of Appropriation' [1982] Crim LR 331; D Stuart, 'Reform of the Law of Theft' (1967) 30 MLR 609.
[11] [1984] AC 320, [1983] 3 All ER 288. See LH Leigh, 'Some Remarks on Appropriation in the Law of Theft after *Morris*' (1985) 48 MLR 167.
[12] [1993] AC 442, HL, [1993] Crim LR 304 and commentary. On which see also M Davies, 'Consent after the House of Lords: Taking and Leading Astray the House of Lords' (1993) 13 LS 308; S Cooper and M Allen, 'Appropriation after *Gomez*' (1993) 57 J Crim Law 186.

In *Hinks*,[13] it was held that:

> it is immaterial whether the act was done with the owner's consent or authority. . . . [No differentia-tion is to be made] between cases of consent induced by fraud and consent given in any other circumstances. . . . An indefeasible gift of property can . . . amount to an appropriation.'[14]

2.11 It is questionable whether any one of these propositions is a correct interpretation of the Act but they have to be accepted as clear decisions of the highest tribunal. The effect is that the *actus reus* of theft is reduced to vanishing point. As Professor Smith commented, the decisions leave the law 'failing to perform a basic function or identifying with precision what constitutes the *actus reus* of theft.'[15] As interpreted by these cases, the definition of theft may now be more fully stated as follows:

> *Anyone doing anything whatever to property belonging to another, with or without the authority or consent of the owner, appropriates it; and, if he does so dishonestly and with intent, by that act or any subsequent act, permanently to deprive, he commits theft.*

Theft or fraud?

2.12 Astonishing though it may sound, despite the incredible breadth of the offence as currently interpreted, prosecutors may well be advised to prefer the offence of fraud in many cases since that is even wider and requires no proof of loss, gain, appropriation, or intention permanently to deprive. Where the defendant has obtained property (or sought to do so) by using a false representation, failing to disclose information which he is legally obliged to do or has abused a position of financial trust, section 1 of the Fraud Act 2006 offers a more straightforward charge and one carrying a higher maximum sentence. It is obvious that the combination of the interpretation of theft and the new offences of fraud provide English criminal law with some of the most wide-reaching dishonesty offences.

2.13 The elements of the concept of appropriation warrant close scrutiny, focusing initially on the impact of this trilogy of House of Lords cases.

Morris

2.14 An assumption of 'the rights of an owner', as the section puts it, seems prima facie to mean all the rights, not one, or some, of the rights of the owner in question. But in *Morris* Lord Roskill, having conceded that there was force in that view, nevertheless said, 'But the later words, "any assumption of a right" in subs (1) and the words in subs (2) "no later assump-tion by him of rights" seem to me to militate strongly against [that view]'. Remarkably, this citation from subsection (1) omits the subsequent and important words, 'to it'. Surely, if D assumes *a right to* the thing, he treats it as *his*, something in which he owns *all* the rights. As for the reference to subsection (2), it is hard to see how a reference to 'rights' can point to a conclusion that the assumption of 'a right' is sufficient.

---

[13] [2000] 4 All ER 833, [2001] Crim LR 162 and commentary. On which see also: ATH Smith, 'Theft or Sharp Practice: Who Cares Now' [2001] CLJ 21; J Beatson and A Simester, 'Stealing One's Own Property' (1999) 115 LQR 372; S Shute, 'Appropriation and the Law of Theft' [2002] Crim LR 445.

[14] Per Lord Steyn [2001] 2 AC 241, 253.

[15] ATH Smith, 'Theft or Sharp Practice Who Cares Now' [2001] CLJ 21, 22.

Though some may think Lord Roskill's conclusion was obviously wrong, it was an element **2.15** in the *ratio decidendi* of *Morris*, and in *Gomez*, where the House reconsidered *Morris*, Lord Keith said, without giving reasons, that it was obviously right; so, for better or worse, we must take it that the law is settled. Any assumption of *any of* the rights of an owner amounts to an appropriation. It is obvious that this extends the scope of the overall offence so that acts which might naturally be regarded as mere preparation or attempts would, because they involve the assumption of a single right, constitute the *actus reus* of the full offence.

Where V is the absolute owner of property the general principle is that only he has any **2.16** right to do anything to or with it. Anyone else who does anything to or with it is therefore exercising a right of the owner. If V has consented to or authorized the exercise of that right we would not, it is submitted, ordinarily describe that exercise as an 'assumption' or 'appropriation'; but, since it has been decided that consent and authority are immaterial, it is both. And, since the assumption of any one of the owner's rights in the property is an appropriation of the property itself, this amounts to theft if done dishonestly and with an intention permanently to deprive.

Morris also establishes that it is not necessary to prove an intention permanently to deprive **2.17** *by the act of appropriation;* it is sufficient that the appropriator has a present intention to deprive, either by that act or by some future act.

Applying *Morris*, D, who switches the labels on two articles lying on the shelves of a super- **2.18** market, with the intention of buying the more expensive article for the price of the less expensive one, steals the more expensive article.[16] Only the owner has the right to label the goods so D, by assuming that right of the owner, appropriates both articles. He has no intention to deprive the owner of the less expensive article, so he does not steal that.[17] The act of relabelling the more expensive article will not deprive the owner of it; but D intends to take it to the cash point, offer to buy it, and, when it has been sold to him, carry it off as his own. The theft, however, is complete as soon as the label switching is done. It is immaterial (so far as liability to conviction is concerned) that, for whatever reason, D thereupon desists. This does not look like theft because the article remains safely in the possession of its owner;[18] but, in law, the theft is complete. The article in D's hands was stolen goods. It ceased to be 'stolen' when it was replaced on the shelf[19] but that could not undo the theft that had been committed.

---

[16] [1984] AC 320, [1983] 3 All ER 288, HL, holding that *Anderton v Wish* (1980) 72 Cr App R 23, DC, followed (reluctantly) in *Oxford v Peers* (1980) 72 Cr App R 19, DC, was rightly decided. Lord Roskill at [1983] 3 All ER 293 thought it material that D had removed the goods from the shelves but, it appears, only as evidence that he intended to steal and was not merely a misguided practical joker. *Gomez* at p 9 makes it completely clear that the mere switching of the labels without more is an appropriation.

[17] Arguably he commits the general fraud offence contrary to s 1(2)(a) and s 2 of the Fraud Act 2006 in relation to *both* items as soon as he switches the labels. There is a false representation as to the more expensive item and by that representation D intends to cause loss to the shopkeeper. The cheaper item is now falsely represented to have a higher price. If D's intent is that X will pay that amount for it he intends to cause loss to X; if it is his intent that no one will, but if remains at its inflated price, he commits fraud against the shopkeeper because he intends the keeper to be exposed to the risk of loss on the sale of that item.

[18] It is of course a fraud offence under s 2 of the Fraud Act 2006.

[19] Theft Act 1968, s 24(3), below, para 13.22.

Gomez

2.19 The dishonest label switcher of course acted without the consent of the owner; but, following *Gomez*, even the shop assistant, performing his duty to label the goods, is appropriating them. Of course he has the authority of the owner to do this, but, so far as appropriation is concerned, that is immaterial. A customer taking goods from the shelf in the supermarket also has the consent of the owner but he is appropriating the goods[20] and, if he does so dishonestly intending permanently to remove the goods from the shop without paying, he commits theft then and there. Motorists are invited to fill their tanks at self-service petrol stations but when they do so, they appropriate the petrol. If a motorist, D, fills his tank intending to drive off without paying, he is guilty of theft when the petrol goes into his tank.[21] If the actions of the shopper and the motorist in these instances constitute a 'representation' of a willingness to pay they will also commit an offence of fraud under s 2 of the 2006 Act.

2.20 *Gomez* involved an issue that has troubled the courts for centuries. The common law recognized a form of stealing known as 'larceny by a trick' which was committed where D, dishonestly intending permanently to deprive V of property, used a trick or false pretence to induce V to transfer to D possession, but not ownership, of that property.[22] The issue had led to a conflict in two earlier unanimous pronouncements of the House of Lords interpreting the Theft Act. In *Lawrence v Metropolitan Police Comr*,[23] it was held that s 1 of the 1968 Act is not to be read as if it contained the words, 'without the consent of the owner' (words included in the definition of larceny in the Larceny Act 1916 and omitted from the 1968 Act), and that it followed that D was guilty of theft although he took the property with the consent of the owner. Eleven years later, in *Morris*,[24] the House was apparently unanimous in asserting that 'the concept of appropriation . . . involves not an act expressly or impliedly authorised by the owner but an act by way of adverse interference with or usurpation of the owner's rights'. Some judges attempted to reconcile these propositions (theft could be committed if D took with the owner's consent but not if he took with the owner's authority) but, generally, *Morris* rather than *Lawrence* was followed in the Court of Appeal, Criminal Division. In a case in the Civil Division, *Dobson v General Accident Fire and Life Assurance Corp plc*,[25] *Lawrence* was preferred.

2.21 In *Gomez*, the whole House acknowledged that the propositions are irreconcilable and, Lord Lowry dissenting, a majority held that *Lawrence* was right and *Morris* (in this

---

[20] *McPherson* [1973] Crim LR 191, approved in *Gomez* 11–12, as a case were goods were appropriated when taken from shelves and before being concealed in D's shopping bag. *Eddy v Niman* (1981) 73 Cr App R 237, DC, though not expressly overruled, must be regarded as wrongly decided.

[21] *McHugh (David)* (1976) 64 Cr App R 92.

[22] See for a historical review of the problem G Ferris, 'The Origins of Larceny by Trick and Constructive Possession' [1998] Crim LR 17.

[23] [1972] AC 626, [1971] 2 All ER 1253, HL. For an opinion as to the questions which the House ought to have been asked, see [1971] Crim LR 53, 54. For defence of *Lawrence* on pragmatic grounds see P Glazebrook, 'Thief or Swindler: Who Cares?' [1991] CLJ 389.

[24] [1984] AC 320, [1983] 3 All ER 288, HL.

[25] [1990] 1 QB 274, [1989] 3 All ER 927, CA (Civ Div). See further M Allen and S Cooper, 'Rethinking Appropriation' 56 J Crim L.

respect) wrong.[26] The majority gave scant consideration to the merits of the two views. The proposition in *Lawrence* was *ratio decidendi*, that in *Morris* was *obiter dictum*, and that was good enough for the majority. They thought[27] it would serve 'no useful purpose' to seek to construe the Act by reference to the CLRC Report. Lord Lowry, who did refer to the Report, demonstrated convincingly in his dissenting speech that it was the dictum in *Morris* which truly represented the intention of the CLRC and therefore that of Parliament which enacted the CLRC's proposals with no material change.[28]

The facts of Gomez

Gomez, the assistant manager of a shop, persuaded the manager to agree to sell goods to the   **2.22** value of £17,000 to his accomplice and to accept payment by two cheques. The cheques (as X and Gomez knew) were stolen and worthless. This was a straightforward case of what was then obtaining property by deception contrary to s 15 of the 1968 Act (and would now be an offence of general fraud contrary to s 1(2)(a) and (c), ss 2 and 4 of the Fraud Act 2006); but for some reason the defendants were charged with theft. The Court of Appeal, following *Morris*, quashed their convictions: the contract of sale, being induced by fraud, was voidable but not void, ownership in the goods passed to X and so there was no appropriation; X was entitled to take possession and did so with the consent and express authority of the owner.[29] The question certified for the House of Lords was:

> When theft is alleged and that which is alleged to be stolen passes to the defendant with the consent of the owner, but that has been obtained by a false representation has (a) an appropriation within the meaning of section 1 (1) of the Theft Act 1968 taken place, or (b) must such a passing of property necessarily involve an element of adverse interference with or usurpation of some right of the owner?

The House answered (a) in the affirmative and (b) in the negative.

Theft with or without deception

The questions for the House of Lords in *Gomez* were limited to cases involving deception.   **2.23** It was not necessary for the House to go beyond that; and there was powerful, though, it is submitted, mistaken, academic support for answering that question in the affirmative.[30] The House might have confined their ruling to such cases. They did not. No significance was attached to the fact that property was obtained by deception. The *ratio decidendi* is

---

[26] Note the cases in which the courts continue erroneously to search for an act 'adverse to' the rights of an owner—eg *Gallaso* [1993] Crim LR 459; *Ngan* [1998] Cr App R 331.

[27] [1993] 1 All ER 1 at 13.

[28] A small minority of academics welcomed this interpretation. For example, Simon Gardner, regarded the decision in *Gomez* as 'unimpeachable' in following the decision in *Lawrence*, and 'desirable from first principles . . . [since] the quality of the dishonest conduct is not necessarily altered by the victim's consent': S Gardner, 'Appropriation in Theft: The Last Word' (1993) 109 LQR 194. See also P Glazebrook, 'Revising the Theft Acts' [1993] CLJ 191 pointing out that D's moral blameworthiness is as great.

[29] For helpful consideration of when the ownership passed see R Heaton, 'Deceiving without Thieving' [2001] Crim LR 712. The House of Lords seems to assume that the appropriation occurred when X collected the goods, but as Heaton points out, at that point in time it is arguable that the goods already belonged to X by virtue of s 17 of the Sale of Goods Act 1979.

[30] See G Williams, 'Theft and Voidable Title' [1981] Crim LR 666, and see the reply by JC Smith at [1981] Crim LR 677. See also a letter by GV Hart [1982] Crim LR 391.

wider, namely that, whether there is a deception or not, it is no answer to a charge of theft that the act was done with the consent or authority of the owner.

2.24   This is consistent with *Lawrence v Metropolitan Police Comr*[31] which was followed by the majority. V, an Italian with very little English, asked D, a taxi-driver, to take him to a certain address and tendered £1, which was more than sufficient for the fare. D said it was not enough. V's wallet was still open and D took from it a further £6. Although V agreed that he had 'permitted' the taking of the money and although there was no finding that it was obtained by deception, D's conviction for stealing the excess was upheld. It was irrelevant that V consented to the taking. Such consent must have been to the passing of the entire interest in the money; but it was enough that 'the money in the wallet which [D] appropriated belonged to [V]'. There seems to have been ample evidence of obtaining by deception (contrary to s 15) but there was no finding to that effect and it was not an element in the decision.

2.25   If, as *Gomez* decides, a person who acquires ownership with consent may commit theft, *a fortiori*, one who takes only possession or custody with consent commits theft if he does so with the dishonest intention permanently to deprive the owner. A customer in a supermarket who removes goods from the shelves, dishonestly intending to deprive the owner of them, commits theft although the owner consents to, and indeed invites, the removal of the goods.[32] The customer practises no deception. In *Gomez*, Lord Browne-Wilkinson said:[33] 'For myself . . . I regard the word "appropriation" in isolation as being an objective description of the act done irrespective of the mental state of either the owner or the accused.'[34]

2.26   So it is irrelevant that D intended to deceive or that V was deceived. According to this opinion, both their mental states are irrelevant to the question whether there was an appropriation.[35]

Cases overruled by Gomez

2.27   *Fritschy*[36] was one of only two cases expressly overruled by *Gomez*. Fritschy was instructed by the owner of some krugerrands to collect them from bullion dealers in England and take them to Switzerland. He collected the property and took it to Switzerland, exactly as instructed, and there, as he intended from the beginning, disposed of it for his own benefit.[37] He committed no civil law wrong by taking the kruggerands to Switzerland. It was held, following *Morris*, that, as everything he did in England was authorized by the owner, he

---

[31] [1972] AC 626, [1971] 2 All ER 1253.

[32] Per Lord Keith at p 12.

[33] At p 39. But no meaning can sensibly be given to the word 'in isolation'. One has only to compare the phrase 'appropriates goods to the contract' in the Sale of Goods Act 1979 (see *Chitty on Contracts* (29th edn, 2004) ch 43) to see that its meaning depends entirely on the context in which it is used. When the word is read in either of these contexts it is submitted that it clearly imports a mental element.

[34] This was endorsed in *Hinks* see para 2.35 below.

[35] See S Shute and J Horder, 'Thieving and Deceiving—What's the Difference' (1993) 56 MLR 548; C Clarkson, 'Theft and Fair Labelling' (1993) 56 MLR 554.

[36] [1985] Crim LR 745.

[37] He would now be convicted of a Fraud Act offence as soon as he makes the false representation that he will transport the property as per his instructions (s 2) or when he abuses his position of financial responsibility (s 4) of the Fraud Act 2006. If the latter, this gives rise to a question of jurisdiction. See para 3.02 below.

committed no theft within the jurisdiction of the court.[38] According to the law in *Gomez*, he was guilty of theft at the latest when he got his hands on the property with intent to steal it.[39] Such a case would now be easier to prosecute as fraud under the 2006 Act.

The other case overruled was *Skipp*.[40] D, 'posing as a genuine haulage contractor', obtained **2.28** instructions to collect three loads from different places in London and deliver them to customers in Leicester. It was unsuccessfully argued that a single count for theft of the goods was bad for duplicity in that there were three separate appropriations. It was held that, though D may have had a dishonest intention permanently to deprive the owner at the time he received each load, he had done nothing inconsistent with the rights of the owner by loading the goods and probably not until he diverted the goods from their proper destination.[41] It is now clear that he committed three thefts.[42]

Other cases are impliedly overruled. In *Hircock*,[43] D obtained possession of a car under a **2.29** hire-purchase agreement by deception. Fourteen days later he dishonestly sold the car. It was held that he was guilty of an offence under s 15 of the 1968 Act (obtaining by deception) when he acquired the car and of theft contrary to s 1 when he sold it. The court distinguished between obtaining and appropriation and held that he did not commit theft when he obtained possession of the car, considering it significant that he acknowledged at that time that he was not the owner. It is now clear that he stole the car when he obtained possession and there was no separate or continuing theft when he sold it.[44] In *Dip Kaur v Chief Constable for Hampshire*,[45] a shop displayed two racks of shoes, one rack bearing a price label of £6.99 and the other of £4.99. D found in the £6.99 rack a pair of shoes, one of which was labelled £6.99 and the other £4.99. She took the shoes to the cashier, hoping that she would see the lower and not the higher price. This indeed occurred. D's conviction for theft was quashed on the ground that the cashier had authority to accept D's offer to buy at the lower price and the ownership passed to D. It now seems clear that D was guilty of theft as soon as she did anything with the shoes with the dishonest intent—probably when she picked them up, certainly not later than when she tendered them to the cashier.[46]

---

[38] Even if the theft was not committed until D disposed of the property in Switzerland such a case is triable here under Part I of the Criminal Justice Act 1993: the act of acquiring control of the property and taking it abroad being a 'relevant event': para 2.02 above.

[39] In *Gallasso*, the court thought *Fritschy* distinguishable probably because Fritschy 'took' the gold with a theftuous intent whereas Gallasso may have already taken the cheque when she formed her dishonest intention. It is submitted that this is an immaterial distinction.

[40] [1975] Crim LR 114.

[41] Again, this would be easier to prosecute as fraud: as soon as D makes the false representation that offence is complete, irrespective of what he obtains when and where.

[42] Whether the indictment should have been regarded as duplicitous is perhaps less clear. cf *DPP v McCabe* [1992] Crim LR 885, DC, where an information alleging theft of 76 library books from some or all of 32 different branch libraries over a period of two years was held not to be duplicitous. But in that case (i) the thefts were all from the same owner and (ii) it was impossible to particularize locations and dates.

[43] (1978) 67 Cr App R 278, [1979] Crim LR 184.

[44] cf *Atakpu* [1994] QB 69, [1993] 4 All ER 215.

[45] [1981] 2 All ER 430.

[46] D would, if dishonest, be guilty of fraud when she offered the cheaper item to the cashier falsely representing that was the true price for the pair.

Theft without taking

2.30 Most thefts (shoplifting, picking pockets, stealing of or from cars and in houses) involve a taking and, not unnaturally, Lord Keith spoke of taking with and without consent in discussing cases such as *Lawrence;* but 'taking' is not an element in the definition of theft. It was because the common law of larceny required a taking that Parliament had to create the offences of larceny by a bailee, embezzlement[47] and fraudulent conversion,[48] fraudulent conversion, and obtaining by false pretences. But all these (except obtaining by false pretences, ie deception) were abolished by the 1968 Act. The reintroduction of 'taking' would set the law back 200 years. The word 'appropriates' was used because it comprehended both taking and other assumptions of ownership. Section 3(1),[49] according to the CLRC, is a 'partial definition . . . which is included partly to indicate that this is the familiar concept of conversion'.[50]

2.31 It is submitted that the effect of the decision in *Gomez* is accurately described above, para 2.11, but if so, it was not immediately apparent to the Court of Appeal. On the very day that the Lords gave judgment in *Gomez* the Court of Appeal heard the appeal in *Gallasso*[51] which at face value appeared to reintroduce a requirement of 'taking' into the element of appropriation. D, a nurse responsible for the care of patients with mental disabilities, quite properly received cheques on behalf of one of them, J, who was incapable of managing his own affairs. Although there were already two trust accounts at a building society in existence in which J was named as the beneficiary, D opened a third trust account, a cashcard account at the same building society, and paid in a cheque belonging to J. The prosecution alleged that her purpose was to make it easier for her to make unauthorized withdrawals. The particular question for the court was whether the paying-in of the cheque,[52] if done dishonestly and with intent permanently to deprive, amounted to theft of the cheque. They held that it did not because there was no appropriation.

---

[47] A statutory offence involving the misappropriation by a servant of any property delivered to him on account of his employer.

[48] A statutory offence of conversion by a trustee or fiduciary of property entrusted to him.

[49] Above, para 2.08.

[50] *Eighth Report*, Cmnd 2977, para 34.

[51] (1992) 98 Cr App R 284, [1993] Crim LR 459. See commentary and criticism at [1993] Crim LR 307. Griew 2–91, thinks the case may 'defy rationalisation', ATH Smith, *Property Offences* (1994) 5–56, n 6, thinks it 'simply wrong' and *Archbold* (2007) 21–40 that it 'overlooks the essence of the decision in *Gomez*'. To the same effect, see *Arlidge and Parry on Fraud* 3–091, *Blackstones Criminal Practice* (2007) B4.26.

[52] Assuming that she had the dishonest intention alleged by the prosecution, D, when she paid in J's cheque, was exercising a right of the owner and, as consent and authority are irrelevant, she assumed that right and appropriated the cheque. When the cheque was honoured, J's property, a thing in action consisting in his right to sue the drawer of the cheque, ceased to exist. It was converted into another thing in action, namely J's right to sue the building society for the same amount of money. It was alleged that D intended to deprive J permanently of that thing, or part of it, by drawing on the account for her own purposes. If so, it is submitted that the theft was committed not later than when she paid in the cheque. If she had formed the dishonest intent when she took it from the envelope (which would be a dishonest taking), the theft began then and presumably continued until the cheque was paid in. In taking possession of the cheque and in paying it in D was exercising rights of the owner and it is immaterial that she was doing so with authority or consent.

The court was convinced by counsel's argument that, while *Gomez* makes clear that a **2.32** taking without consent may be an appropriation, 'there must still be a taking' and here there was no taking. Lloyd LJ, clearly with the law of larceny[53] in mind, said:

This is not to reintroduce the concept of carrying away into the definition of appropriation. It is to do no more than to give appropriation its ordinary meaning in section 1 and the same for the assumption of owner's rights in section 3 (1).

Sadly, only Lord Lowry in *Gomez* was prepared to give these words their ordinary meaning and the decision of the majority excludes it.

There is nothing in *Gomez* to support the argument that 'there must still be a taking'. On **2.33** the contrary, Lord Keith's opinion that mere label swapping with intent is theft is inconsistent with that view. As for authority, the cases in which convictions for theft have been upheld where there was a 'conversion' but no taking are legion. *Gallasso* is inconsistent with these decisions and must surely be regarded as decided wrongly and not a precedent binding on the Court of Appeal or lower courts. [54]

The Court of Appeal's apparent disbelief at the breadth of the offence of theft in the wake **2.34** of *Gomez* continues to manifest itself. In *Ashcroft*[55] D, a haulier, was alleged to have conspired to steal items from sealed containers in transit. The court regarded as 'some way removed from reality' D's argument that the theft occurred when D originally took possession of the goods in his lorries (in Scotland). The court commented that in this case 'there never was in any ordinary sense of the word an "appropriation" of the stolen goods until the conspirators removed them from the containers'.[56] True enough, but since *Gomez*, the word appropriation does not bear the 'ordinary' meaning that its drafters had intended.[57] There seem to be very small if any distinctions between this case and *Fritschy* (which was not cited). *Blackstone's Criminal Practice* points to the fact that in *Fritschy* the defendant removed all the goods whereas in *Ashcroft*, the intention was only ever to remove part of the goods, and until the goods it is intended to steal are ascertained there can be no appropriation of the property.[58] But is this a relevant distinction? Can it not be argued that D had appropriated the property in Scotland—he was assuming one of the rights of an owner over all of it, the element of consent he may have had is irrelevant.[59]

Hinks

Notwithstanding the apparently all-embracing nature of the decision in *Gomez*, it was **2.35** argued strenuously and cogently that there remained a number of qualifications to it: that

---

[53] Above, para 1.21.
[54] cf the erroneous comments of the Court of Appeal in *Ngan* [1998] 1 Cr App R 331 that the owner needs to be deprived in fact of the property.
[55] [2003] EWCA Crim 2365.
[56] Para 45.
[57] For an early discussion of the two senses of the word 'appropriation' see A Halpin, 'The Appropriate Appropriation' [1991] Crim LR 426; A Halpin, *Definitions in the Criminal Law* (2004), 166–81.
[58] (2007) B4.29.
[59] He might be argued to have a conditional intention to steal those parts he chose to be worth stealing once in England.

there could be no appropriation amounting to theft if D's act was lawful in civil law;[60] that there could be no appropriation unless the acts were dishonest and that there could be no appropriation where D acquired absolute indefeasible title. If D has a right to retain the property, or even to recover it from the alleged victim, it was argued that it could hardly be held to be theft for him to take and keep it. If it were theft, the civil law would be, by providing protection through the law relating to conversion, assisting D to enjoy, or to recover, the fruits of his crime! This argument underestimated the determination of some judges including, as it happened, a majority of a particular committee of the House of Lords in *Hinks*, to convict those deemed by a jury to be dishonest.

2.36 *Hinks* was the last in a trilogy of cases on similar facts: D received a substantial gift from V, a person of a vulnerable mental state, over whom D had acquired some influence. In each case V was of sufficient mental capacity in law to make a gift.[61] The gift might, in civil law, have been voidable because of the exercise of undue influence by D, but the juries were not asked to consider that question, so we must take it that it was not.[62]

2.37 In the first of these cases, *Mazo*,[63] a lady's maid was convicted of theft of large sums of money given to her by V. Quashing her conviction, the court, referring to *Gomez*, said that it was clear that an act could be theft notwithstanding the owner's consent *if* that consent was obtained by deception but no deception was proved in this case; and it was 'common ground that the receiver of a valid gift *inter vivos* should not be the subject of a conviction for theft'.

2.38 In the second case that of *Hopkins and Kendrick*[64] some doubt was cast on that premiss: 'It is not for these purposes necessary to consider whether or not that apparent gloss on *Gomez* is well-founded.'

The court considered 'bold and perhaps surprising' what was, it is submitted, a very sound submission from counsel 'if the donor's mind is such that the donor has the capacity to make a gift or to consent to the transfer of property, then there is no appropriation and no theft'. In *Hopkins*, in the court's judgment, the evidence of the lady's mental capacity was very different from that in *Mazo*; and the summing up could not have resulted in the jury being confused 'as to whether Mrs Clare was somebody who is just "not quite up to it", with reduced mental capacity, which was said of Lady S [in *Mazo*] or lacking the capacity to manage her own affairs'. An instruction to convict only if Mrs Clare lacked the capacity to manage her own affairs was, indeed, unnecessary if *Mazo* was wrong. If she lacked that capacity, the dispositions were invalid and the property continued to belong to her; and, if the appellants were aware of her incapacity, they intended a dishonest appropriation of her property. There was ample evidence to support the jury's verdict that they were dishonest.[65]

---

[60] G Williams, 'Theft, Consent and Illegality' [1977] Crim LR 127, *TBCL* 770–3. '. . . if the civil law sees no reason to permit the owner to complain of an interference with his property why should the criminal law do so?'—ATH Smith, *Property Offences* (1994) 5–49.

[61] See *Chitty on Contracts* (29th edn, 2004) vol i, part 2, ch 7.

[62] See the dissenting opinion of Lord Hobhouse in *Hinks* on this issue.

[63] [1996] Crim LR 435.

[64] [1997] Crim LR 359.

[65] All would probably now be guilty of the offence of fraud under s 4 of the 2006 Act.

In the third case, *Hinks,* H, a 38-year-old woman, was friendly with John Dolphin (J). She **2.39** described herself as J's main carer. There was evidence that J was extremely naive and gullible. It would have been easy to take advantage of him. But he understood the concept of ownership and was quite capable of making a gift. In a period of a few months he withdrew about £60,000 from his building society account. The money was deposited in H's account. J also gave H a television set. H was convicted of theft in four counts covering moneys and one count covering the television. The question left to the jury was 'Was [J] so mentally incapable that the defendant herself realised that ordinary and decent people would regard it as dishonest to accept a gift from him?' On appeal it was argued that, if the gift was valid, the acceptance of it could not be theft. The Court of Appeal confronted the problem directly and held that it was immaterial whether there was a valid gift: *Mazo* was based on a mistaken premiss. Rose LJ, dismissing the appeal, ruled:

in relation to theft, one of the ingredients for a jury to consider is not whether there has been a gift, valid or otherwise, but whether there has been an appropriation. A gift may be clear evidence of appropriation. But a jury should not, in our view, be asked to consider whether a gift has been validly made.

The only question was whether D, the donee of the gift, was dishonest—and the jury had found that she was.

The House of Lords in *Hinks,* having been referred to some of the voluminous academic **2.40** literature[66] supporting these qualifications to the *Gomez* decision, remained unpersuaded. It was held (Lords Hutton and Hobhouse dissenting), that there could be an appropriation where D was not acting contrary to the civil law and where he acquired absolute indefeasible title. The result is to create an offence turning almost exclusively on dishonesty. As Professor Smith commented, '[a]t its outer reaches theft becomes something akin to "thought crime"'.[67]

The conduct of the accused in all three of these cases was despicable. They were, as the jury **2.41** must have found, dishonestly taking an unfair advantage of a person with failing powers. It is submitted that the correct question in these cases, in the absence of proof of deception, duress, or undue influence, was whether the vulnerable individual was competent to make the disposition she did. If she was, it should be immaterial that her actions might be regarded by others as eccentric, imprudent, or irrational; and that the actions of the donee in relation to the gift were grasping and despicable. If a sane and wealthy woman, persuaded by reading the Bible that she should give her property to the poor, goes down the street and gives her Rolex watch to the first seller of *The Big Issue* she meets, he ought not to be guilty of theft, even if he tells his friends that she must be a 'complete nutter'.[68] Following *Hinks* he is at risk of conviction if the jury consider him to have been dishonest.[69]

---

[66] See for example, JC Smith [1993] Crim LR 304 and [1998] Crim LR 904; Griew 41–59; ATH Smith, 'Gifts and the Law of Theft' [1999] CLJ 10; J Beatson and A Simester, 'Stealing One's Own Property' [1999] LQR 372.

[67] 'Theft or Sharp Practice: Who Cares Now?' [2001] CLJ 21, 22.

[68] Arguably, it might be attempted theft under the Criminal Attempts Act 1981, s 1(1) and (3).

[69] 'The reasoning of the Court of Appeal [and the majority in the House] therefore depends upon the disturbing acceptance that a criminal conviction and the imposition of custodial sanctions may be based

2.42   The House of Lords decision has the effect of extending the offence of theft to produce an offence which offers maximum protection for the vulnerable,[70] but at an enormous cost to the certainty and coherence of the law of theft with its civil law foundations. The problems created by the decision are striking.[71]

The problems of Hinks: *(i) Theft and the civil law*[72]

2.43   *Hinks* opens up a general conflict with the civil law, and the problem of D's right to restitution in the goods is one obvious aspect of that major problem created by the decision. There are very strong arguments of principle for the criminal law respecting civil law doctrines, in particular in the area of theft where the criminal law is necessarily developed on the foundations of civil law concepts of property, ownership, etc. The vast majority of thefts do amount to civil wrongs but it does not necessarily follow that civil unlawfulness is a constituent of the offence. Section 1(1) of the 1968 Act does not include the word 'unlawfully' nor does it say 'misappropriate'. The mere removal of goods by a customer from the shelves of a supermarket and the filling of his tank by a motorist at a self-service petrol station do not amount to civil wrongs merely because the act is done with a secret dishonest intent. *Fritschy*[73] committed no civil offence by carrying out his employer's instructions to take the property to Switzerland but it is clear following *Gomez* that he committed theft by doing so. Not every theft must involve a civil law wrong, but it is submitted that the Act was intended to be construed such that there could be no theft where D acted within the civil law.

2.44   In *Hinks*, the majority of the House acknowledged, with surprising equanimity, that their decision does create a conflict between the civil and the criminal law. D who has V's consent to appropriate the property will commit no civil law wrong and, indeed, will be able to rely

---

upon conduct which involves no inherent illegality and may only be capable of being criticised on grounds of lack of morality. This approach itself raises fundamental questions. An essential function of the criminal law is to define the boundary between what conduct is criminal and what merely immoral. Both are the subject of the disapprobation of ordinary right-thinking citizens and the distinction is liable to be arbitrary or at least strongly influenced by considerations subjective to the individual members of the tribunal. To treat otherwise lawful conduct as criminal merely because it is open to such disapprobation would be contrary to principle and open to the objection that it fails to achieve the objective and transparent certainty required of the criminal law by the principles basic to human rights', per Lord Hobhouse of Woodborough dissenting at [59].

[70] It should be noted that the offence of theft was drafted with the purpose of protecting property rights, not protecting against exploitation per se; cf the interesting argument of AL Bogg and J Stanton-Ife, 'Protecting the Vulnerable: Legality, Harm and Theft' (2003) 23 LS 402 suggesting that the offence now better protects against exploitation of the vulnerable.

[71] See commentary at [2001] Crim LR 263; ATH Smith, 'Theft as Sharp Practice: Who Cares Now?' [2001] CLJ 21; and for a defence of the decision, S Shute, 'Appropriation and the Law of Theft' [2002] Crim LR 445. Shute suggests that dishonest conduct such as that in *Hinks*, although it might not constitute a civil law wrong, 'may nonetheless have a *tendency* to undermine property rights either directly by attacking the interests that they protect, or indirectly by weakening an established system of property rights and so threatening the public good that the system represents'. cf his view in the article in the *Modern Law Review* some years earlier: S Shute and J Horder, 'Thieving or Deceiving' (1993) 56 MLR 548.

[72] JC Smith, 'Civil Law Concepts in the Criminal Law' [1972B] CLJ 197; G Williams, 'Theft, Consent and Illegality' [1977] Crim LR 127 and 205; G Trietel, 'Contract and Crime' in C Tapper (ed), *Crime, Proof and Punishment: Essays in Memory of Sir Rupert Cross* (1981) 81.

[73] Above, para 2.27.

on the civil law to enforce the transfer of property, but will be exposed to prosecution for theft. Lord Steyn observed that:

Given the jury's conclusions, one is entitled to observe that the appellant's conduct *should* constitute theft, the only available charge. The tension between the civil and the criminal law is therefore not in my view a factor which justifies a departure from the law as stated in *Lawrence*'s case and *R v Gomez*. Moreover, these decisions of the House have a marked beneficial consequence. While in some contexts of the law of theft a judge cannot avoid explaining civil law concepts to a jury (eg in respect of s 2(1)(a)), the decisions of the House of Lords eliminate the need for such explanations in respect of appropriation. That is a great advantage in an overly complex corner of the law.

However, his Lordship also pointed out that: **2.45**

it would be wrong to assume on *a priori* grounds that the criminal law rather than the civil law is defective in creating this conflict. If we were constructing a new code of civil and criminal law, it would certainly be open to the legislator to prefer a principle of the criminal law to one of the civil law, but that is not the position. The Theft Acts assume the existence of the civil law of property rights and the criminal courts are, or should be, bound to take it as they find it.

The impact that the decision has in this respect can be illustrated by reference to examples **2.46** posed in the House of Lords in *Hinks* (and referred to in the speech of Lord Steyn):

(i) Suppose that V, becoming very excited on seeing D's painting of Salisbury Cathedral and, thinking he is about to get a bargain, offers D £100,000 for it. D realizes that V thinks the painting is by Constable but D knows that it was painted by his sister and is worth no more than £100. He accepts V's offer. D has made an enforceable contract and he is entitled to recover and to retain the money. Similarly, if a buyer knew that a picture was in fact by Constable and bought it for a very small sum from a seller, who, as the buyer was aware, did not know this, a jury might well regard D's conduct in these examples as dishonest—and, of course, V would not have consented, had he known the true facts. The effect of *Hinks* is that, if the jury is satisfied that these defendants were dishonest they are guilty of stealing the property—property to which they are absolutely entitled in civil law.

(ii) V makes a handsome gift to D because he believes that D has obtained a First in his degree. D has not and knows that V is acting under that misapprehension. V makes a gift. There is here a motivational mistake which, it is submitted, does not avoid the transaction.[74] Following *Hinks*, D is liable for theft if the jury find him dishonest.

(iii) 'A buys a roadside garage business from B, abutting on a public thoroughfare; unknown to A but known to B, it has already been decided to construct a bypass road which will divert substantially the whole of the traffic from passing A's garage. There is an enforceable contract and A is entitled to recover and retain the purchase price. The same would be true if B *knew* that A was unaware of the intended plan to construct a bypass road'.[75] B is liable for theft if he is dishonest.[76]

(iv) E, an employee of Z Co agrees to retire before the end of his contract of employment, receiving a sum of money by way of compensation from Z. Unknown to Z, E has committed serious breaches of contract which would have enabled Z to dismiss him without compensation. Assuming that E's failure to reveal his defaults does not affect the validity of the contract,

---

[74] G Williams, *Textbook of Criminal Law* (1st edn, 1978) 788.
[75] Compare Lord Atkin in *Bell v Lever Bros Ltd* [1932] AC 161 at 224, [1931] All ER Rep 1 at 30.
[76] B is of course guilty of fraud under s 2 if he makes a false representation and under s 3 if he has a duty to disclose the information to A.

so that E is entitled to sue for the promised compensation, E is liable to be arrested for the theft the moment he receives the money.[77] (E may be more easily prosecuted under the Fraud Act 2006, s 4.)

2.47   Lord Steyn remained unmoved by the impact that the decision would have in each of these examples:

> My Lords, at first glance these are rather telling examples. . . . On the facts set out in the examples a jury could possibly find that the acceptance of the transfer took place in the belief that the transferee had the right in law to deprive the other of it within the meaning of s 2(1)(a) of the 1968 Act. Moreover, in such cases a prosecution is hardly likely and, if mounted, is likely to founder on the basis that the jury will not be persuaded that there was dishonesty in the required sense. And one must retain a sense of perspective. At the extremity of the application of legal rules there are sometimes results which may seem strange. A matter of judgment is then involved.

The problems of Hinks: (ii) Theft where D acquires an absolute, indefeasible title

2.48   The effect of *Hinks* is to render any donee of a gift at risk of a theft conviction. In *Gomez* the property was in fact obtained by deception. The title which D obtained to it was, therefore, voidable. In *Morris* the article when taken from the supermarket shelves continued to belong to, and, indeed, probably to remain in the possession of, the shopkeeper. In *Lawrence*, there was no finding of any deception, but the dishonest taxi-driver certainly had no right to retain the fare which he knew exceeded that permitted by law. In all these cases any title D had to the property was defeasible. It was argued, before *Hinks,* that these were distinguishable from the case where D acquires an indefeasible right to the entire proprietary interest—ie, where there is no deception, duress, or other vitiating factor to render the transaction void or voidable, and its effect is to divest V wholly of his proprietary interest. *Hinks* rejects this.

2.49   If the gift in *Hinks* was valid in civil law—neither void nor voidable for fraud, duress, undue influence, or any other reason—the donee acquired an absolute, indefeasible title to the property. If it were seized from her by the police, she, not the donors or anyone else, would be entitled to recover it. She would have an action in conversion against the police—or the donor, if the police returned the property to her. It is as nonsensical as it sounds to suggest that although there is a theft there are never any stolen goods because the donor, *ex hypothesi*, never has any right to restitution:[78] the property belongs absolutely to D for ever.

2.50   The arguments in the last paragraph relating to gifts apply *a fortiori* to sale. Take a case like *Smith v Hughes*.[79] S contracted to sell some oats to H. Even on the assumption that S knew

---

[77] cf G Williams, 'Theft and Voidable Title' [1981] Crim LR 666 at 672.

[78] See s 24(3) of the Theft Act 1968, below 13.22. Assuming a valid gift, the goods were never out of lawful custody or possession and the donor never had a right to restitution. Hinks was ordered to pay £19,000 compensation to Dolphin. Compensation for what? For keeping a gift which she was legally entitled to keep? The jury's verdict did not decide that she did not have an *indefeasible* title to the property. Was the judge entitled to decide that her title was defeasible?—for misrepresentation, undue influence, or what? Could Hinks have an argument that the order was contrary to her right to peaceful enjoyment of her possessions under Article 1, protocol 1 of the ECHR? See R Clayton and H Tomlinson, *The Law of Human Rights* (2000) ch 18; C Weir and R Moules in J Simor and B Emmerson, (eds), *Human Rights Practice* (2000) ch 15.

[79] (1871) LR 6 QB 597.

(i) that the oats were new oats and (ii) that H was buying the oats only because he believed they were old, new oats being useless to him, it was held that S was entitled to recover the price. Suppose H had paid the price before discovering that the oats were new. S made no false pretence, but suppose he were now to be charged with theft. The question in the civil law was not 'what a man of scrupulous morality or nice honour would do under such circumstances'; and, in a criminal case, a jury might well consider such an unscrupulous and dishonourable seller to be 'dishonest' under the principle in *Ghosh*.[80] He obviously has an intention to deprive the buyer permanently of the money. But, logically if the law says he is entitled to recover the price, it cannot also say that he steals it. If this is theft then the law would be assisting him to commit the crime. To hold the conduct to be theft is, in effect, to alter the civil law. However, following the decision in *Hinks* this conduct is capable of amounting to theft.

Another example may be *Deller*.[81] D induced V to accept his car in part exchange for a **2.51** new one by representing that it was free from encumbrances. D had previously executed a document purporting to mortgage the car to a finance company. He probably believed that this was effective in which case the car was subject to an encumbrance. If so, he intended to tell a lie; but the document was probably void in law as an unregistered bill of sale. In that case the car was not subject to any encumbrance: 'quite accidentally and, strange as it may sound, dishonestly, the appellant had told the truth'. Clearly D could be guilty of attempting fraud by attempting to make a false representation (contrary to s 2 of the Fraud Act 2006) but would his dishonest obtaining of it also be theft? The orthodox answer is 'no', because the contract of part exchange was an enforceable contract. Whatever his intention, objectively he had done nothing wrong. If he is found to be dishonest, there is nothing preventing him being guilty of theft following *Hinks*.

The position is easier where D has no enforceable right to the property: the mere fact **2.52** that V has no civil remedy should not inhibit the court from finding that D has stolen V's property if the definition of theft is satisfied. For example, if D dishonestly and without authority offers to sell V's property to E,[82] D may not yet be guilty of any civil wrong against V but it would be strange to say that the civil law gave D a 'right' to do such an act; and it seems that, if the words of s 1 fit D's act, he may be convicted of theft. Even before *Gomez* such an unauthorized usurpation of the owner's rights in the thing was clearly 'an appropriation'.

The problems of Hinks: *(iii) Appropriation as a 'right' under civil law*

There are many cases where the civil law authorizes or *even requires* D to appropriate V's **2.53** property with the intention of permanently depriving V of it.[83] If, in such a case, D is aware of the law, it is submitted that he ought not to be considered to be acting dishonestly

---

[80] Below, para 2.270.

[81] (1952) 36 Cr App R 184, CCA.

[82] cf *Pitham and Hehl* (1976) 65 Cr App R 45, below, para 2.65. The position was the same under the Larceny Acts: *Rogers v Arnott* [1960] 2 QB 244, [1960] 2 All ER 417. Where goods are obtained by deception under a voidable contract of sale a receiver who knows the goods have been so obtained is guilty of handling, below, para 13.49; but, while the contract remains unrescinded, he is not guilty of conversion.

[83] eg a sale of uncollected goods under Sch 1 to the Torts (Interference with Goods) Act 1977.

and therefore he commits no offence, however evil his motive might be. Suppose, however, that D is unaware of the civil law which authorizes or requires him to act as he does and he proceeds in a furtive manner evincing a dishonest intention. He now falls literally within the terms of the Act unless 'dishonestly' is interpreted to include an objective element.[84]

2.54 In light of the decision in *Hinks*, could a future court find some means of avoiding the conviction of D for doing no more than the civil law expressly authorized or required him to do? An express authority or 'right' in the strict sense might be distinguished from a mere 'liberty' or 'power'. D has a liberty under the civil law to do an act if the performance of that act does not amount to a civil wrong. There is no reason why the criminal law should not curtail such liberties in appropriate cases,[85] and the Theft Act has done so in the case of a co-owner who dishonestly appropriates the joint property;[86] and where D has the power to pass a good title, he may nevertheless in some cases be properly convicted of theft when he does so. For instance, the mercantile agent who is in possession of goods with the consent of the owner passes a good title if he sells to a bona-fide purchaser, even though he does so dishonestly and in breach of the arrangement made with the owner.[87] This is clearly theft by the mercantile agent.

2.55 The distinction between power and right appears in s 48 of the Sale of Goods Act 1979 and it is instructive to consider the effect of the Theft Act upon the situations there envisaged. By subsections (1) and (2):

(1) Subject to the provisions of this section, a contract of sale is not rescinded by the mere exercise by an unpaid seller of his right of lien or retention or stoppage in transitu.

(2) Where an unpaid seller who has exercised his right of lien or retention or stoppage in transitu re-sells the goods, the buyer acquires a good title thereto as against the original buyer.

The unpaid seller who resells after the property has passed has clearly appropriated the property of another (the first buyer) and commits the *actus reus* of theft although in doing so he passes a good title to the second buyer. It is unlikely that he could be convicted in most cases, for it would be difficult to prove dishonesty where no part of the price had been paid. But a seller is unpaid[88] until he receives the *whole* price, and a seller would certainly be dishonest if, having received 90 per cent of the price, he were to resell the goods, intending not to repay. This subsection gives the seller a mere power, not a right. The resale is a wrongful one and the first buyer, if he were to tender the price, could sue in conversion. There seems to be no reason why this should not be a crime.

---

[84] At one time discerned by *Arlidge and Parry on Fraud* below, para 2.57.
[85] This passage in the seventh edition of this book is closely analysed by *Arlidge and Parry on Fraud* 1–063 to 1–069. They have particular difficulty with the distinction between a liberty and a right 'in the strict sense'. But the distinction between right *stricto sensu* and liberty has been recognized by jurists from Bentham onwards, though, admittedly, not in this context. See, eg, RWM Dias, *Jurisprudence* (2nd edn, 1964) 226.
[86] *Bonner*, below, para 2.201. There was a breach of contract in that case, but co-owners are not necessarily in a contractual relationship—they may have inherited the property—and this should make no difference to the liability for theft of the one who appropriates the other's proprietary interest.
[87] Factors Act 1889, s 2(1).
[88] Sale of Goods Act 1979, s 38.

A quite different situation is created by subsection (3):   **2.56**

Where the goods are of a perishable nature, or where the unpaid seller gives notice to the buyer of his intention to re-sell, and the buyer does not within a reasonable time pay or tender the price, the unpaid seller may re-sell the goods and recover from the original buyer damages for any loss occasioned by his breach of contract.

Though it is now established that the resale rescinds the contract and terminates the first buyer's property in the goods, the goods belong to the first buyer up to the moment of sale. It would be intolerable that the law should say, at one and the same time, that 'the unpaid seller may re-sell the goods' and that he is guilty of theft if he does this, not knowing that the law permits him to do so. He ought not to be guilty.[89] The position is the same under subsection (4):

Where the seller expressly reserves the right of re-sale in case the buyer should make default, and on the buyer making default, re-sells the goods, the original contract of sale is thereby rescinded, but without prejudice to any claim the seller may have for damages.

The problems of Hinks*: (iv) Appropriation which is not 'dishonest'*

Another argument[90] against convicting D of theft where the civil law authorizes or *even*   **2.57**
requires D to appropriate V's property with the intention of permanently depriving V of it is that the word 'dishonestly' has an objective as well as a subjective meaning. This is true, at least to the extent required by the first part of the *Ghosh* test,[91] to be applied by a jury for the meaning of 'dishonestly': was what was done dishonest according to the ordinary standards of reasonable and honest people? If not, D is not guilty. If a jury should think that shoplifting from supermarkets is not dishonest according to the ordinary standards of reasonable people like themselves, the particular shoplifting which has occurred is not a crime, whatever the state of mind of the shoplifter. A jury will, however, not usually be instructed to apply this test unless the defendant claims that he does not regard his conduct as dishonest. Moreover, 'what was done' refers to D's act *and* the state of mind with which he did it. A typical case is where D takes money from his employer's till but claims that this is not dishonest because he intended one day to pay it back. The first limb of the *Ghosh* test is really only a necessary first step to assessing the mind of the particular defendant.

Whether dishonesty qualifies the concept of appropriation generally is another matter.   **2.58**
There is a passage in the speech of Lord Browne-Wilkinson in *Gomez* which, at first sight, encourages the view that the appropriation must be objectively 'dishonest'. Lord Browne-Wilkinson said:[92] 'Parliament has used a composite phrase, "dishonest appropriation". Thus it is not every appropriation which falls within the section but only an act which answers the composite description.'

---

[89] *Ward Ltd v Bignall* [1967] 1 QB 534, [1967] 2 All ER 449, CA.
[90] *Arlidge and Parry on Fraud* (1st edn, 1985) 1.10.
[91] Below, para 2.295.
[92] [1993] 1 All ER 1 at 39. This is part of a longer passage cited by the court in *Hopkins and Kendrick*.

2.59   If that were right it would surely follow that only a *misappropriation*[93] would satisfy the Act. 'Appropriation' is neutral—it might be rightful (eg, by a bailiff) or wrongful. 'Dishonest appropriation' is certainly not neutral—if it describes the act, it must be, in some sense, a wrongful act. But in fact, the Theft Act nowhere uses the 'composite phrase, "dishonest appropriation"'. Lord Browne-Wilkinson seems to have been looking at an earlier analysis of the section by the Court of Appeal, not at the Act. The definition of theft in s 1 says 'dishonestly appropriates', which is not the same thing. 'Dishonestly' does not appear to qualify the objective meaning of 'appropriates' any more than 'maliciously wounds' qualifies 'wounds'. It is true that s 2 begins, 'A person's appropriation of property belonging to another is not to be regarded as dishonest . . .', but the sidenote to the section is 'Dishonestly', indicating that it is merely spelling out the meaning of the adverb, not qualifying the noun; and it then goes on to specify three beliefs, not objective facts, giving no support to the view that the word 'dishonestly' is meant to include anything other than a state of mind. Lord Browne-Wilkinson, in any event, failed to follow through his reading (or misreading) of the Act because he went on to hold that appropriation is entirely unqualified, except by the intent with which the act is done. He criticized *Morris* because it treated the word 'appropriation' as being tantamount to 'misappropriation'; but what could be wrong about treating the imagined 'composite phrase, "dishonest appropriation"', as tantamount to misappropriation? As the law stands, it seems that appropriation need not be 'dishonest' or misappropriation.

2.60   Following the decision in *Hinks*, it might be thought that there was little force remaining in this argument. Lord Hutton did offer a glimmer of hope by holding also that while the acquisition of an indefeasible title may amount to an appropriation, it will not amount to the *actus reus* of theft unless it is also a dishonest appropriation. He stated that: 'A direction based only on *Ghosh* is inadequate because it fails to make clear to the jury that if there was a valid gift there cannot be dishonesty . . .'[94] On that basis it does not matter how dishonest the jury may have considered D's conduct to be, or how clear D's belief that reasonable people would consider it dishonest, the appropriation is not, in Lord Hutton's opinion, 'dishonest' simply because it is a valid gift. 'Dishonest' must thus be an element in the *actus reus*. Lord Hutton concluded that:

> (1) It was necessary for the judge to make clear to the jury that if there was a valid gift the defendant could not be found to be dishonest no matter how much they thought her conduct morally reprehensible.

That conclusion did not differ in substance from that of Lord Hobhouse (dissenting), who simply held that the word 'appropriation' must be read in its context.

2.61   In *Wheatley v The Commissioner of Police of the British Virgin Islands*[95] W was a government official who had bestowed a lucrative contract on X and received payment from X for

---

[93] As the court stated in *R (A) v Snaresbrook Crown Court* [2001] All ER (D) 123 the act does not require a misappropriation.

[94] [47].

[95] [2006] UKPC 24.

doing so: straightforward corruption. The charges alleged theft contrary to laws[96] which reflect ss 1–6 of the Theft Act 1968 in all relevant respects. The magistrate acquitted W on the theft charges but the Court of Appeal of the British Virgin Islands entered convictions on the theft counts. Before the Privy Council, following the broad interpretation of the concept of appropriation in *Hinks*, it was conceded by W that there had been appropriations of government property—the price paid for the contract, even though that contract had been fulfilled by the completion of the required work for an appropriate price. Relying on the statements of Lord Hutton (above) it was submitted that there could be no dishonesty within the meaning of the Code where a contract had been made and services rendered for an appropriate price. The Board held that the convictions for theft were safe. There was no qualification to *Hinks* and no guarantee that the accused would be acquitted on the basis of a lack of dishonesty where the owner lost nothing. As Lord Bingham opined:

it is certainly true that in most cases of theft there will be an original owner of money or goods who will be poorer because of the defendant's conduct. But in one of the two cases in *Morris* the defendant was arrested before paying the reduced price for the goods, so that the supermarket suffered no loss, and in *R. (A) v Snaresbrook Crown Court* [2001] All E.R. (D.) 123, para. 25, it was accepted that the alleged theft was carried out for a purpose which could financially benefit the company. In providing that an appropriation may be dishonest even where there is a willingness to pay, [s 1(2)] shows that the prospect of loss is not determinative of dishonesty.[97]

The problems of Hinks: (v) Appropriation of property already owned

In the trilogy of cases *Mazo, Hopkins and Kedrick*, and *Hinks*, the property belonged to   **2.62**
the donor, V, until the instant when the dishonest act of receiving the gift was done. D's acquisition of the entire proprietary interest and the appropriation were simultaneous. In these circumstances, following *Lawrence*, it is established that D appropriates property belonging to another since the property still belongs to another immediately before he appropriates it. If, however, D acquires the entire interest first and then, after an interval, does the act alleged to be an appropriation, it would seem to be impossible for him to be guilty of theft. In *Hinks*, only Lord Hobhouse acknowledged the force of this argument, observing that D has not then appropriated property belonging to another—it is already his.[98] V, a poor person infatuated by a wealthy man, D, sends a valuable gift to D's house where it comes into his possession during his absence abroad. When he comes home, he treats it as his own—which it is. However dishonest a jury might think him to be, this ought not to be theft.

Appropriation by one already in possession

It has already been noticed that the most common method of appropriation is by taking   **2.63**
property from the possession of another. It is now time to take a closer look at other types of appropriation.

---

[96] Section 209(a) of the Criminal Code (Act No 1 of 1997) of the Laws of the British Virgin Islands.
[97] [11].
[98] See Lord Hobhouse at [2000] 4 All ER 855f–g.

2.64 It is very common for one person, D, to be in possession of property which belongs to another, V. Clearly V retains some of the rights of an owner which may be dishonestly assumed by D. The commonest examples are bailments, where V, the bailor, has entrusted D, the bailee, with possession for some limited purpose—he has loaned D a book, hired a car to him, let him have a television on hire purchase or pledged his watch to him as security for a loan. If, in any of these cases, D destroys the property or gives it away or sells it to another, he does something which only the owner, V, can lawfully do and he has assumed V's rights. He has appropriated and is, subject to *mens rea*, guilty of theft.

2.65 Even if D has only gone so far as to offer to sell the thing, he has assumed the right to dispose of the owner's entire interest and it is clear that there is an appropriation.[99] Even an invitation to E to make an offer to buy V's property might be regarded as an assumption of V's right. But a mere decision by D to sell V's property, even if it could be proved (he has declared his intention in a letter or by musing aloud), would not be enough. A decision to assume rights is not an assumption of them. Appropriation requires conduct of some kind even if it is no more than 'keeping' property already held.[100]

Exercise of one's own proprietary right is not an appropriation

2.66 Notwithstanding the decisions in *Gomez* and *Hinks* that appropriation may be committed by an authorized act, it is submitted that D, a bailee, does not commit an offence by any act which he has a right to do under the terms of the bailment. This is because the ownership in the thing is divided between bailor and bailee. The bailee has his own proprietary interest. In exercising the rights vested in him by the bailment, D is not assuming or appropriating any right 'belonging to another'. For example, D hires a car from V for a month. During the month he decides to take the car to a neighbouring town and sell it to a second-hand car dealer. He does not commit theft by driving the car to the dealer. As a bailee he has proprietary rights in the car which include, say, the right to drive the car anywhere in Great Britain. He is exercising his own rights, not assuming any right belonging to another. V has no right that he shall not drive the car to any place that the terms of the bailment permit.[101] Of course, D steals the car as soon as he offers to sell it, for he is now exercising a right which still belongs to V.

An agent, exercising his principal's rights, may steal

2.67 It is now clear that D may commit theft if, as V's authorized agent, he takes V's property into his possession or custody with intent to steal. But suppose that he does so without any such intention—eg that in *Fritschy*[102] D had obtained V's krugerrands from the depositary, as instructed by V, without any intention to steal but had conceived the theftuous intent

---

[99] *Pitham and Hehl* (1976) 65 Cr App R 45, CA. Though there is a complete theft at the instant the offer is made, it does not necessarily follow that the theft does not continue for some time thereafter. *Gregory* (1982) 77 Cr App R 41, [1982] Crim LR 229, CA, and below, para 2.103.

[100] cf the discussion of *Briggs* below, para 2.116.

[101] It was argued in *Rogers v Arnott* [1960] 2 QB 244, [1960] 2 All ER 417, DC. 'Once the defendant decided to keep the appointment to sell the tape recorder, and certainly once he had put it into the car, he committed an act of conversion' (Basil Wigoder); but the decision was that the offence of larceny was complete when the bailee of the tape recorder offered to sell it.

[102] Above, para 2.27.

before he left (again, as instructed) for Switzerland. Is it arguable that D, in taking the gold abroad, like the hirer of the car above (para 2.66) would have been exercising his own proprietary rights, not V's? It is submitted not. The agent (though he may be a bailee) is exercising the rights of the principal. His conduct is lawful in the civil law, not because he has a proprietary right but because he is authorized by the principal to do the act in question.[103] When he exercises a right belonging to the principal, even with the principal's consent, he appropriates it and if he has a theftuous intent, he steals the property.

Theft by possessors who are not bailees

A person may come into possession of the property of another in ways other than bailment **2.68** and may commit theft by the exercise of any proprietary right of the owner. Any possible doubts are dispelled by the provision of s 3(1) that appropriation includes 'where he has come by the property (innocently or not) without stealing it, any later assumption of a right to it by keeping or dealing with it as owner'.[104]

To the reader unfamiliar with the law of larceny, this provision probably seems quite **2.69** unnecessary—and indeed it is. It was a principle of larceny that, except in the case of a bailee, the intention to steal must exist at the moment of taking possession. The purpose of s 3(1) is to ensure that this principle was not applied to the new offence.

It is now entirely clear that the following acts amount to theft. **2.70**

  (i) D receives property which he knows to be stolen. He intends to restore it to the true owner or the police so he is not dishonest and commits no offence. Later he changes his mind and conceals the thing, dishonestly intending to deprive the owner permanently of it.

  (ii) D, a lorry-driver, receives a number of sacks of pig-meal into his employer's lorry for carriage from A to B. When he arrives, D discovers that ten sacks too many have been loaded. He keeps them for himself or sells them for his own benefit.

In these two examples, D did not assume *all* the rights of the owner when he first received the property; he intended to hold it for another. When he later assumed the entire rights of the owner he committed theft.

The same principle applies, however, where D intends innocently to assume the entire **2.71** ownership at the start. For example:

  (iii) D finds a banknote in the highway. There appears to be no reasonable means of ascertaining the owner and D decides to keep it for himself. This is no offence—D has 'come by the property . . . innocently'. Two days later, being still in possession of it, he discovers that V is the owner and then uses the note for his own purposes.

  (iv) In the dark V hands a banknote to D. Both believe it to be a £5 note. In fact it is a £20 note. Some time later, D discovers it is a £20 note and spends it. It is assumed that the property in the note does not pass in this situation. If this assumption is wrong, D will not escape liability, but it will then be necessary to rely on s 5(4).[105]

---

  [103] See generally, N Palmer, *Palmer on Bailment* (2nd edn, 1991) and E McKendrick in *Chitty on Contracts* (29th edn, 2004) ch 33.
  [104] Section 3(1).
  [105] cf *Ashwell* (1885) 16 QBD 190; below, para 2.250. See *Chitty on Contracts* (29th edn, 2004) para 33.002.

(v) D is handed his workmate's pay packet by mistake. When he has been in possession of it for some hours he discovers that it contains more than he is entitled to and appropriates the money.

In cases (iii), (iv), and (v), it has been suggested that, since D intended to assume *all* the rights of an owner when he first took the thing, there is no room for any 'later assumption of a right to it', ie that one cannot assume what one has already assumed. It is submitted, however, that the words 'later assumption' presuppose an earlier assumption; and that the later assumption envisaged may be an exercise of rights which have been assumed on 'coming by' the thing in question.[106]

Appropriation by acquiring ownership without possession

2.72 Ownership may pass under a contract of sale which is voidable because induced by deception, before possession is transferred. Under s 18, rule 1, of the Sale of Goods Act 1979, where there is an unconditional contract for the sale of specific goods in a deliverable state, the ownership, in the absence of a contrary intention, passes to the buyer when the contract is made and it is immaterial that the time of payment or delivery or both are postponed.[107] In *Dobson v General Accident Fire and Life Insurance Corpn plc*,[108] a civil action, the plaintiff claimed from his insurers the value of a watch and ring which a rogue had induced him to sell for a worthless cheque. The plaintiff's insurance policy covered loss by theft. It was not enough for him to prove that his property had been obtained by deception, contrary to s 15 of the Theft Act 1968 (as then in force). The insurers argued that the ownership in the goods passed when a contract was made over the telephone, two days before delivery; so that, when the rogue collected the goods, he was taking delivery of his own property. The response of Parker LJ to this argument was: 'the result would merely be that the making of the contract constituted the appropriation. It was by that act that the rogue assumed the rights of an owner and at that time the property did belong to the plaintiff'. The goods remain, for the time being, safely in the owner's possession; but they are already stolen.

2.73 As noted above (para 2.62) *Hinks* creates a further problem here. It is possible that D will have already obtained indefeasible title before the point at which D first appropriates the property which is being given to him. This is unlike the cases where D has obtained only voidable title to the property before he does the act which is alleged to constitute the appropriation. The circumstances in which a person may obtain ownership before obtaining possession are limited, but in some instances there will be a transfer of ownership before D has acquired physical possession.[109]

---

[106] The contrary view would be disastrous for, it should be noted, s 5(4), below, para 2.250, does no more than vest a fictitious property in the prosecutor and leaves open the necessity for an appropriation.

[107] See *Chitty on Contracts* (29th edn, 2004) ch 43.

[108] [1990] 1 QB 274, [1990] Crim LR 271, CA, Civ Div. Much of Parker LJ's judgment was cited with approval by Lord Keith in *Gomez*. This particular passage was not cited but is probably to be regarded as approved.

[109] This will be most likely where there is a specified article for sale, which has been clearly ascertained (s 16) and there has been an act of 'unconditional appropriation': for examples and discussion see R Heaton 'Deceiving without Thieving' [2001] Crim LR 712.

Appropriation by the mere assumption of the rights of an owner

When the common law of larceny required a taking and carrying away of the property **2.74**
alleged to have been stolen, the theft could occur only when and where that event took
place. But 'asportation', as it was known, is no longer necessary. It never was necessary in
the statutory extension of larceny—'conversion' by a bailee. Consequently it was held in
Rogers v Arnott that the bailee of a tape-recorder committed larceny when he offered to sell
it. That case has been doubted[110] and it has been argued[111] that the owner 'has no general
right that [others] shall not contract to sell [his property], or to purport to pass ownership
in it' and that there is therefore no assumption of the rights of the owner, no appropriation.
It is true that A, without the knowledge or consent of B, might lawfully *contract* to sell B's
car to C next week, a contract which he might be able to perform by buying the car from B
in the interval. But to purport to *sell,* or to purport to pass ownership, is a different matter.
Even here the purported sale will usually be ineffective and not amount to a civil wrong;
but it gives C a bona-fide, though invalid, claim to B's property, which it may not always be
easy to rebut. The right to sell is surely a right of the owner and, in normal circumstances,
of him alone.

The timing of appropriation

Under the 1968 Act it must be proved that D 'appropriated' the property and 'Any assump- **2.75**
tion by a person of the rights of an owner amounts to an appropriation . . .'. The question
arises: does D assume the rights of an owner, (i) as soon as he does acts in relation to the
property which only the owner may lawfully do or, (ii) only when those acts take effect
on the property? This problem arises most acutely in the case of thefts of credit balances
in banks.

In *Tomsett*,[112] the Court of Appeal acted on the assumption that the latter view was correct. **2.76**
The V Bank transferred US $7million to a New York bank to earn overnight interest. The
'money' should have been returned to England the next day. D, a telex operator employed
by the V Bank, sent a telex from London diverting the $7million plus interest to another
bank in New York for an account at its Geneva branch which his accomplice had opened
a month earlier. D covered up his dishonest conduct by making it appear that a second
telex had been sent giving the correct destination of the money but this was 'killed' before
it was transmitted. D's conviction for conspiracy to steal was quashed on the ground that
the theft took place either in Geneva or New York outside the jurisdiction of the court: the
alleged conspiracy was not, at that time,[113] an agreement to commit an offence 'triable in
England and Wales', as required by the Criminal Law Act 1977, s 1(1) and (4).

---

[110] ATH Smith, *Property Offences* (1994) 5–45, helpfully drawing attention to earlier conflicting cases
which have been overlooked.
[111] ibid, 5–49.
[112] [1985] Crim LR 369, CA.
[113] Even if *Tomsett* was rightly decided at the time, it seems clear that D could be convicted under Part I of
the Criminal Justice Act 1993. In order to establish the theft, proof would be required of D's act which was
therefore a 'relevant event' occurring in England. See para 2.02 above. He and his accomplices would be guilty
of conspiracy to steal.

2.77   However, in *Re Osman*,[114] an extradition case, a Divisional Court comprised of Lloyd LJ and French J, who were both members of the court in *Tomsett*, refused to follow that case. Prosecuting counsel in *Tomsett* had declined the court's invitation to argue that the theft was committed in England and, said Lloyd LJ, 'The law of England cannot be made or unmade by the willingness of counsel to argue a point . . . the present point was left undecided.' *Re Osman* was concerned with acts done in Hong Kong (the relevant law of theft was the same as in England) in relation to property in other countries; but the effect of the application of the *ratio decidendi* to *Tomsett* is that Tomsett would be guilty of stealing in England the property situated in New York when he, in England, assumed the rights of the owner by directing a disposition of the property which could be lawfully done only by the owner.

2.78   The property alleged to be stolen in both *Tomsett* and *Re Osman* was intangible property, a thing in action. In *Tomsett* it was the V Bank's credit balance with the New York bank, ie the debt owed by the New York bank to the V Bank. But the *ratio* of *Re Osman* is not confined to things in action. Suppose that V's Rolls-Royce is in Scotland. D has found the registration document and, purporting to be V, he in England produces the document and 'sells' the car to a bona-fide purchaser, E. Whether or not ownership in the car passes to E, this is surely an assumption by D of the rights of the owner, V, and theft is committed in England.[115] Of course, theft also requires an intention permanently to deprive the owner of his property. Whether such an intention can be discerned in circumstances such as these is considered below.[116]

2.79   Even in the light of *Re Osman* and of *Gomez*, the earlier decision in *Pitham*[117] is difficult to justify. D offered to sell V's property to Pitham. It was held that the mere offer to sell amounted to a completed theft so that when the goods were delivered to Pitham he received them 'otherwise than in the course of the stealing'[118] and was therefore guilty of handling the stolen goods. But in this case, unlike the example of the Rolls-Royce,[119] Pitham, the buyer, knew very well that D had no authority to sell V's property; and D knew that the buyer knew that. D did not purport to be the owner or to be acting with his authority. It was not really an offer to sell at all but a proposal for a joint theft of the goods. To demonstrate the absurdity of *Pitham*, Williams[120] puts the case of a butler who tells the maid that he has found the key to the Duke's safe and invites her to help herself to the silver. Williams says that it would be preposterous to hold that the butler has already stolen the silver.

---

[114] [1988] Crim LR 611. *Archbold* (44th edn, 1991) 21–9, doubted this proposition in *Osman*. In *Shuck* [1992] Crim LR 209 D was held liable for appropriations of property committed by his innocent agent in the Isle of Man—presumably because D directed them from England.
[115] See the discussion in the fifth and earlier editions of this book (5th edn, paras [25] and [26]), cf *Bloxham* (1943) 29 Cr App R 37, CCA.
[116] Para 2.332.
[117] (1976) 65 Cr App R 45.
[118] Below, para 13.72.
[119] Above, para 2.78. It is also unlike *Bloxham*, above, where D purported to sell his employer's refrigerator to a bona-fide purchaser and was held not guilty of an attempt to commit larceny because he had made no attempt (and presumably did not intend to make any attempt) to take the refrigerator and carry it away. Bloxham was not a bailee.
[120] *TBCL* 764.

It would indeed. The butler never purports to be, or to exercise any of the rights of, the owner or his agent. The maid does not acquire a claim of right to the property. To invite another to steal is not to assume or exercise any right of the owner. If it were otherwise, all those conspiring to steal specific property would already be guilty of theft.

In the case of credit balances, the question when the theft takes place is a more complex   **2.80**
matter. In *Kohn*, Lane LCJ said, 'The completion of the theft does not take place until the transaction has gone through to completion'—ie when the account is actually debited.[121] But in *Navvabi*[122] his Lordship himself treated that statement as *obiter*; and in *Re Osman*,[123] the Divisional Court, finding support in *Wille*[124] (which did not decide the point), held that the theft takes place when and where D issues the cheques, just as it occurs when and where D sends a telex dishonestly disposing of another's property. In *Ex p Levin*,[125] another extradition case, the court thought that the fact that a computer operator was physically in Russia was of far less significance than the fact that he was looking at and operating on magnetic discs in the USA: he had committed theft in the USA and could be extradited to that country.

Some confusion was caused by the case of *Ngan*[126] in which a large sum intended for V had   **2.81**
been mistakenly paid into D's bank account in England. By virtue of s 5(4) of the 1968 Act this property was to be regarded as belonging to V. D dishonestly drew blank cheques on the account and sent them to her sister in Scotland who presented them there for payment. The court, equating the presentation of the cheque with the sending of the telex in *Osman*, held that the theft took place in Scotland. The signing and issuing of the cheques were preparatory acts.[127]

The act of theft itself was the presentation of the cheque. Until then no right as against the Bank had been exercised . . . In [*Osman*] the Divisional Court held that appropriation occurs when a cheque is presented. We agree; but it does not follow that it cannot occur earlier . . . In one sense the very act of signing each cheque might be regarded as an assumption of a right. But it must be remembered that the right assumed is not to the cheque, but to the property or chose in action, that is, to the debt mistakenly due from the Bank. . . . [*Gomez*] has no application here, because until on each occasion a cheque was presented for payment there was no dealing with any of [the other's] rights to the balance mistakenly standing to the credit of the appellant. Her acts of signing the cheques and sending them to her sister were preparatory acts, and more needed to be done by or on behalf of the appellant before [the other] could be deprived of their property.[128]

There are problems with the views expressed in *Ngan*. It relies on *Osman* as authority for a   **2.82**
proposition for which it does not offer support. In *Osman*, the court had suggested, *obiter*, that the act of appropriation was complete on the drawing and issuing of the cheque by D.

---

[121] (1979) 69 Cr App R 395 at 407. To the same effect, see *Hilton* [1997] Crim LR 761 and commentary.
[122] Below para 2.177.
[123] Above, para 2.77.
[124] (1987) 86 Cr App R 296, CA.
[125] *Governor of Brixton Prison, ex p Levin* [1997] QB 65, [1997] 3 All ER 289, DC.
[126] [1998] 1 Cr App R 331.
[127] These problems are less likely arise since the bringing into force of Part I of the Criminal Justice Act 1993 and s 1A of Criminal Law Act 1977 but they are still significant and require resolution.
[128] Leggatt LJ, 335–6

Lloyd LJ concluded that 'a defendant "usurps" the customer's rights when he, without the customer's authority, dishonestly issues the cheque drawn on the customer's account'.[129] That approach was also supported by *Wille*.[130]

2.83 This view expressed in *Ngan*, that the theft occurs later—at the time of presentation—has eminent academic supporters. Professor Griew pointed out that the state of V's account may be much more difficult to ascertain when the cheque is issued than when it is presented to the bank.[131] The account might be overdrawn and any overdraft facility exhausted. This certainly shows that it is more difficult to *prove* a theft if it is committed when the cheque is issued but it does not establish that it *cannot be committed* at that time if it can be proved that the account was in credit or that the overdraft facility was not exhausted.

2.84 Take an analogous case. D has ostensible but not actual authority to sell V's goods which are lying in a warehouse. D dishonestly sells the goods to X, intending to keep the proceeds of sale for himself. Because D has ostensible authority, the ownership passes to X as soon as the contract is made. There is clearly an appropriation and D is guilty of theft. But now suppose that, when X goes to collect the goods, it appears that they have been removed from the warehouse by V and consumed or otherwise disposed of. It is difficult to determine whether the removal and disposition occurred before or after the sale by D to X. If it occurred after that sale, the removal and disposition cannot undo the theft which D has committed; but, if it occurred before that 'sale', the theft was never committed because there was nothing to sell and nothing to steal. This is precisely the same difficulty—a problem of proof—as arises when D issues the cheque to the payee and it is uncertain whether the account is in credit or not. The difficulty of proof is no argument for holding that there cannot be theft of goods where it is possible to prove that they were in the warehouse at the time of the sale; and, equally, it is no argument for holding that there can be no theft of the thing in action represented by the credit balance or overdraft facility where it can be proved to have existed at the time of the issue of the cheque. If it could not be proved that the goods were in the warehouse or the account in credit at the material time, D could be convicted of an attempt to steal. The case is exactly analogous to an attempt to steal from a pocket when it cannot be proved that there was anything in it.

2.85 Professor Griew concedes that 'A possible solution, not excluded by the cases [before the decision in *Ngan*], is to treat D's act as continuing (as an appropriation or potential appropriation) until the account is debited.' The continuing appropriation theory seems right. The effect of D's act may reasonably be held to continue, no less than the carrying away of tangible property which has already been taken. If there was nothing in the account (or nothing in the warehouse) when D purported to appropriate it, the offence would be committed when the account was credited (or when the warehouse was stocked).

---

[129] 295.

[130] *Wille* (1987) 86 Cr App R 296

[131] EJ Griew, 'Stealing and Obtaining Bank Credits' [1986] Crim LR 356 at 362; Griew 2–153, a passage cited in *R v Governor of Brixton Prison, ex p Levin* [1997] AC 741; but it does not appear that the court's attention was drawn to the argument in this section.

No appropriation by the sole owner

Although V consents to, and does, transfer his entire proprietary interest to D, D is guilty **2.86**
of theft if he receives that entire interest dishonestly and with intent permanently to deprive.
That is the effect of *Gomez* and of *Lawrence v Metropolitan Police Comr*.[132] But if D receives
the entire interest innocently he cannot thereafter be guilty of theft: there is no longer any
property 'belonging to another' for him to appropriate. It makes no difference that D is
dishonest. For example, where D, a motorist, fills his tank at a self-service petrol station,
intending to pay, and then dishonestly decides to drive off without paying, he commits
no theft.[133] The owner has consented to D's acquiring, and he has acquired, the entire
proprietary interest in the petrol. It no longer belongs to another. It is the same as where a
customer in a restaurant honestly consumes a meal and then dishonestly leaves without
paying. Clearly, he does not steal the food.[134] These acts are offences of making off without
payment under the Theft Act 1978, s 3.[135]

Since generally[136] D cannot steal from V after he has acquired V's entire proprietary **2.87**
interest, it is sometimes necessary to have recourse to the law of contract to determine
whether and, if so, when, the ownership in property has passed from V to D. Ownership
may pass under a contract for the sale of goods as soon as the contract is made and before
the price has been paid.[137] Whether or not it does so pass in any particular case is, however,
a question of intention; and it has been held that, in a sale in a supermarket, it is presumed
that the ownership in the goods is not intended to pass until the goods are paid for.[138]
In *Davies v Leighton*,[139] the presumption was held to be applicable, not only to the ordinary
case where the customer collects the goods and tenders them to the cashier, but also to the
case where the goods were weighed, bagged, priced, and handed by an assistant to a customer, D, who, instead of tendering them to the cashier, dishonestly removed them from
the store. It is possible that the contract of sale was made with the assistant but whether
it was so or not was immaterial. The ownership had not passed and D was guilty of theft.
In *Davies v Leighton* the court thought it might have been different if the assistant had been
in a managerial capacity. But, even if it had been intended that the ownership in the goods
should pass immediately to D, and therefore did pass to him, it is inconceivable that the
manager would have intended to give up the seller's lien, ie his right to retain possession
until the payment of the price. The customer would have only custody of the goods in his

---

[132] [1972] AC 626, above, para 2.23.
[133] *Greenberg* [1972] Crim LR 331 (Judge Friend); *Edwards v Ddin* [1976] 3 All ER 705, DC. It is
assumed that V, having parted with possession, has no lien. For the case where D dishonestly fills his tank, see
McHugh, para 2.19.
[134] *Corcoran v Whent* [1977] Crim LR 52, DC. D had arrived home before he formed the dishonest
intention; but it makes no difference to the result. The food was incapable of being stolen as soon as it was
consumed. cf *Buckmaster* (1887) 20 QBD 182, CCR (the welshing bookmaker), criticized in CS Kenny,
Outlines of Criminal Law (19th edn, 1965 by JWC Turner) 264–5, *Russell on Crime* 935–8, *Smith and Hogan,
Criminal Law* (1st edn, 1965) 352, n 15, and in the fifth edition of this book, para [41].
[135] Below, ch 6.
[136] For exceptions, see s 5(3) and (4) of the Act below, paras 2.219, 2.250.
[137] Sale of Goods Act 1979, s 18, r 1. See *Chitty on Contracts* (29th edn, 2004) ch 43. See also the discussion
in R Heaton, 'Deceiving without Thieving' [2001] Crim LR 712.
[138] *Martin v Puttick* [1968] 2 QB 82, [1967] 1 All ER 899, DC; *Lacis v Cashmarts* [1969] 2 QB 400, DC.
[139] (1978) 68 Cr App R 4, [1978] Crim LR 575, DC, and commentary.

hands, until he paid the price, possession continuing in the seller,[140] to whom the property would still therefore 'belong': s 5(1).

2.88 Similarly, it may be necessary to decide whether a contract has been rescinded so as to revest property in the seller. In *Walker*,[141] D sold to V an unsatisfactory video-recorder which was returned to him for repair. V then served on D a summons claiming the return of the price as the 'return of money paid for defective goods'. Two days later, D sold the recorder. He was convicted of theft of the recorder and obtaining the price by deception but his conviction was quashed. The service of the summons probably operated to rescind the contract. The effect would be to restore the parties to the position they were in before the contract was made. D would be the absolute owner, entitled to sell the recorder and to receive the price.[142] Even after *Hinks*, it is surely doubtful that he would nevertheless be a thief for doing so.

Appropriation by agent exceeding authority

2.89 Before *Gomez* it was held that where D has a limited authority to deal with V's property, he may appropriate it by dealing with it in excess of that authority. *A fortiori*, this is so after *Gomez*. Dealing with V's property is an appropriation whether authorized or not and the excess of authority is now important only as evidence of a dishonest intention permanently to deprive. The director of a company who has a general authority to deal in its export quotas (which, if assignable, is 'intangible property') commits theft if he dishonestly sells quotas at an undervalue.[143] In *Pilgram v Rice-Smith*,[144] goods were dishonestly underpriced by an assistant in a supermarket, acting in collusion with a customer, D, who then tendered the underpriced goods at the checkout. It is now clear that the underpricing of the goods by the assistant amounted to an appropriation. It was immaterial that the customer was going to behave as such, and not as owner, by offering to buy the goods at the checkout. In *Bhachu*,[145] a dishonest cashier in collusion with a customer undervalued the goods by ringing up a price below the authorized price. The court thought that the appropriation was committed by the customer when she put the goods in the wire basket provided and wheeled them out of the shop. It seems, however, that the cashier appropriated the goods when she sold them at an undervalue. If so, according to *Pitham*, the customer might have been convicted of handling as well as of theft.

---

[140] cf *Chissers* (1678) T Raym 275, 3 Salk 194.

[141] [1984] Crim LR 112, CA.

[142] cf Lord Roskill in *Morris*, 'it is on any view wrong to introduce into this branch of the criminal law questions whether particular contracts are void or voidable on the ground of mistake or fraud or whether any mistake is sufficiently fundamental to vitiate a contract': [1983] 3 All ER 288 at 294, [1983] Crim LR 813 and commentary. But, as Bingham LJ said in *Dobson v General Accident Fire and Life Insurance Corpn plc* [1989] 3 All ER 927 at 937: 'Whether, in the ordinary case . . . goods are to be regarded as belonging to another is a question to which the criminal law offers no answer and which can only be answered by reference to civil law principles.'

[143] *A-G of Hong Kong v Chan Nai-Keung* (1987) 86 Cr App R 174, [1988] Crim LR 125, PC.

[144] [1977] 2 All ER 658, DC.

[145] (1977) 65 Cr App R 261, CA.

Buyer not intending to pay

It appears that a buyer who receives the goods not intending to pay may now be guilty of **2.90** theft even though he practises no deception or does any other wrongful act. He appropriates the goods when he receives them and it is immaterial that the property passes to him with the owner's consent. He obviously intends permanently to deprive so the only question is whether he dishonestly appropriates. A jury which was satisfied that he never intended to pay would presumably answer the question in the affirmative. This is different from the *Smith v Hughes* example discussed in para 2.50 Because although there is a contract, the buyer has no indefeasible right to the goods: a court aware of his intention not to pay—a fundamental breach of contract—would not enforce any such right.[146] Since it is no bar to conviction for theft that D has an indefeasible right to the property, *a fortiori* where he has no such right. As discussed above, however, a decision not to pay after acquiring the ownership and possession of the property, however, cannot be theft because there is no longer any property belonging to another to appropriate.

Appropriation of property obtained by intimidation

Theft may be committed by intimidation falling short of force or threats of force and so not **2.91** amounting to robbery. In *Bruce*,[147] D generated such an 'atmosphere of menace' that V was frightened into parting with his money. A verdict of not guilty of robbery and guilty of theft was legitimate. Before *Gomez* it was thought that the outcome depended on whether the intimidation prevented the property passing from V to D. It seems that this is no longer material. There is no difference in this respect from the case in which property is obtained by deception. It is sufficient that the property belonged to V at the instant when D appropriated it and that he did so with a dishonest intention. If he knew that V parted with his property unwillingly and only because he was intimidated a jury would presumably find dishonesty proved.

Appropriation by a handler of stolen goods[148]

The wide definition of theft means that almost every person who would have been a receiver **2.92** of stolen goods under the Larceny Acts and almost everyone who is a 'handler' under the 1968 Act will be guilty of theft. Dishonest handling of stolen goods will normally amount to an appropriation of property belonging to another and will generally be done with the intention of permanently depriving the other of his property.

Appropriation by a purchaser in good faith of stolen goods

Section 3(2) creates an exception to the general rule that appropriation of the property of **2.93** another is theft. It provides:

Where property or a right or interest in property is or purports to be transferred for value to a person acting in good faith, no later assumption by him of rights which he believed himself to be acquiring shall, by reason of any defect in the transferor's title, amount to theft of the property.

---

[146] *Chitty on Contracts* (29th edn, 2004) vol i ch 14.
[147] (1975) 61 Cr App R 123, see the 6th edition of this work, para [45].
[148] See ATH Smith, 'Theft and or Handling' [1977] Crim LR 517. On the problem of proving theft or handling, see below, para 13.102.

2.94   The words, 'which he believed himself to be acquiring', relate to the moment when D received the property.[149] This subsection is designed to except from the law of theft the case where D purchases goods in good faith and for value and then later discovers that the seller had no title and that the goods still belong to a third party, V. V may simply have lost the goods or they may have been stolen from him. Having paid for the goods, D may well, in many cases, be innocent of any crime simply on the ground that he believes he has a right to keep them and is thus not dishonest. But suppose he is enough of a lawyer to appreciate that the goods are not his but V's: he is still not guilty—while he may have *mens rea*, the subsection makes it clear that there is no *actus reus*. The result is otherwise, however, if D has not given value, as where he received the property as a gift. If, for example, C purchases the property in good faith from the thief and gives it to D who later discovers the truth and decides to keep it, D is guilty. A purchaser for value who suspects that the goods may be stolen has been held[150] by a magistrates' court to be not 'acting in good faith' and so unable to rely on the subsection.

2.95   The protection afforded by s 3(2) is limited. D may with impunity keep the goods or give them away to an innocent donee. If, however, he sells the goods to an innocent buyer he will probably be guilty of fraud by the false representation that he is entitled to sell the goods.[151] Following *Gomez*, he may also be guilty of stealing the money. If he sells or gives the thing to one who knows it is the property of a third party, the recipient will be guilty of theft (and possibly of handling) and D, it seems, of abetting him. Section 3(2) does not seem wide enough to exempt him from liability for abetting theft or handling by another of the property.[152]

2.96   If D assumes rights over and above those which he believed himself to be acquiring, he may be guilty of theft. If C finds goods in such circumstances that he reasonably believes the owner cannot be discovered by taking reasonable steps, and sells the goods to D who knows these facts, D is aware that he is acquiring only the rights of a finder, not those of the owner. If, then, D subsequently discovers who the owner is, a later assumption of a right to keep the thing is the *actus reus* of theft.

2.97   It should be noted that there is no similar exemption for the handler of stolen goods which have been bought in good faith. Suppose D enters into a contract to buy a picture hanging in a gallery, delivery to be made at the end of the exhibition. Unknown to D, the picture has been stolen. Before the end of the exhibition, he discovers the truth, but dishonestly takes delivery of the picture. He is not guilty of theft (s 3(2)) but is apparently guilty of handling the picture by receiving it knowing it to be stolen, contrary to s 22.[153] Section 3(2)

---

[149] *Adams* [1993] Crim LR 72.

[150] *Broom v Crowther* (1984) 148 JP 592, DC, discussed by JR Spencer [1985] Crim LR 92 and 440 and by Williams [1985] Crim LR 432. D is not guilty of handling when he only 'suspects' and does not 'believe' that the goods are stolen: below, para 13.98.

[151] cf *Wheeler* (1990) 92 Cr App R 279, 282. It is arguable that there was no such representation where the sale took place in market overt, now abolished. If that were right in principle, it might apply to other situations in which a seller who has no title is able to give one.

[152] cf *Sockett* (1908) 1 Cr App R 101. This conclusion does not seem to be affected by the dicta of Lord Bridge in *Bloxham* (1982) 74 Cr App R 279, 283, which relate to liability for handling as a principal.

[153] Below, para 13.86.

would not exempt Ashwell.[154] He took the coin in good faith and for value (his promise to repay) and later (it is submitted) assumed rights of ownership which he believed himself to be acquiring when he received the coin; but his guilt would arise, not from any defect in the transferor's title, for there was none, but from a defect in his own title.

Multiple thefts of the same property?

If D, in a supermarket, dishonestly swaps labels, he assumes a right of the owner and steals **2.98** the article he dishonestly intends to buy for the lower price. If he then removes that article from the shelves he assumes another right; and when he buys the article he assumes yet a third right, ownership, which, until that moment, he, as a buyer, has acknowledged to belong to the seller. Has he committed three thefts of the same thing? If appropriation is the assumption of *a right* can there not be as many thefts of a thing as there are rights in or over it? The answer is to be found in s 3(1)[155] which provides that a later assumption of a right may be an appropriation when D has come by the property 'without stealing it'. This implies that where he has come by the property by stealing it, later assumptions of a right to it by keeping or dealing with it as owner do not amount to appropriations.[156] The draftsman was ensuring that a car thief does not steal the car afresh each morning when he gets into it.

In *Atakpu and Roberts*,[157] DD obtained cars on hire by deception in Germany and Belgium, **2.99** and drove them to England, dishonestly intending to sell them here. In the pre-*Gomez* case of *Hircock*,[158] where the facts were similar except that the whole transaction took place within the jurisdiction, a conviction for theft of a car was upheld: the fact that D had already obtained the car by deception contrary to s 15 did not preclude a charge of stealing it by the subsequent sale. But, after *Gomez*, it is clear that Hircock stole the car when he obtained it. In *Atakpu*, it was held, reluctantly following *Gomez*, that DD had stolen the cars when they obtained them abroad and could not steal them again by the projected sale in England. *Hircock* is impliedly overruled by *Gomez*. In *Atakpu*, convictions for conspiracy to steal the cars were quashed because the plan did not involve the commission of theft of the cars within the jurisdiction of the English court. The offences of obtaining and theft in Germany would still not be triable here under the Criminal Justice Act 1993, s 2, because no 'relevant event' occurred in England and Wales; but, assuming the act was an offence under German law, the agreement in England would be an indictable conspiracy to commit those offences under s 1A of the Criminal Law Act 1977: Criminal Justice Act 1993, s 5(1).[159]

---

[154] Below, para 2.251.

[155] Above, para 2.08.

[156] It is different where rights are assumed, abandoned, and resumed. Where D steals property but leaves it on the owner's premises because his van will not go, his later removal of it may amount to a second theft: *Starling* [1969] Crim LR 556, CA (larceny). cf *DPP v Spriggs* [1993] Crim LR 622.

[157] [1994] QB 69, [1993] 4 All ER 215, CA.

[158] (1978) 67 Cr App R 278, [1979] Crim LR 184 and commentary.

[159] See further, M Hirst, *Jurisdiction and the Ambit of the Criminal Law* (2001) 24–6. Presumably even at the time of the offence Atakpu and his accomplices could have been successfully prosecuted for conspiring to obtain by deception, and therefore to steal, *the price* which they intended to get from unsuspecting purchasers of the cars in England.

Is theft abroad 'theft'?

2.100 Professors Sullivan and Warbrick[160] argue that the court in *Atakpu* was misled by the phrase 'theft abroad is not triable in England'. They contend that so-called 'theft abroad' is not 'theft' under English law. DD had, therefore, come by the cars *without* stealing them[161] so their later assumption of a right to the cars in England would have amounted to an appropriation, a theft under English law for the first time. The cars, according to that view, were to be stolen in English law for the first time when appropriated in England. The court had relied on s 24(1) of the Theft Act 1968 which it is convenient to set out here and which provides that:

> The provisions of this Act relating to goods which have been stolen shall apply whether the stealing occurred in England or Wales or elsewhere, and whether it occurred before or after the commencement of this Act, provided that the stealing (if not an offence under this Act) amounted to an offence where and at the time when the goods were stolen . . .

2.101 Sullivan and Warbrick argue that this points to a conclusion opposite to that of the court— the subsection provides an extended definition of 'stolen goods' for the purposes only of the offence of handling and it acknowledges that stealing goods outside England and Wales is 'not an offence [sc. theft] under this Act'. It might, however, be argued to the contrary that the words in parentheses imply that some stealing outside England and Wales is an offence under the Act. In some jurisdictions, eg Canada, taking with intent *temporarily* to deprive is theft. It may well be that these words[162] are properly construed to cover cases such as the handling in England of goods stolen in Canada by Canadian law, whether or not there was an intent permanently to deprive. It is debatable whether such conduct should be an offence under English law.

2.102 The preceding paragraphs have implications for cases like *Shuck*.[163] D, a company director, acting within the scope of his authority, transferred the company's funds to a subsidiary in the Isle of Man, a place outside the jurisdiction of the English courts, with intent there to dispose of them dishonestly for his own benefit. It was held that he stole the property when it was disposed of by his innocent agent in the Isle of Man, presumably because D, directing operations in England, was assuming the rights of an owner here.[164] No doubt, pre-*Gomez*, it was assumed that the transfer of assets to the Isle of Man, being authorized, could not be theft. If so, we now know that that assumption was unfounded. It seems that D stole the property when he transferred it with theftuous intent. If so, even if theft abroad is theft by English law, he could not steal it again by the dispositions in the Isle of Man and he was wrongly convicted. Appropriation in the Isle of Man, directed from England, is unquestionably capable of being theft triable here under the Criminal Justice Act 1993—but not if the appropriator has already committed theft of the property in England.

---

[160] [1994] Crim LR 650, 659.

[161] See s 3(1) of the 1968 Act, above, para 2.08.

[162] The words in parentheses cannot be intended to apply to stealing in England and Wales *before* the commencement of the 1993 Act, because that could never be an offence under the Act.

[163] [1992] Crim LR 209, CA.

[164] See *Ex p Osman* (1990) 90 Cr App R 281, 289, above, para 2.77.

Appropriation as a continuing act[165]

An offence may be committed in an instant yet continue being committed for some time **2.103** thereafter. It is often important to know how long a particular theft continued. A person may be guilty of a theft by aiding and abetting it while it is being committed by another, but he cannot aid and abet the theft once it is over. A person may be guilty of robbery if he uses force while theft is being committed but not by using force when the theft is at an end.[166] A person may be guilty of the offence of handling stolen goods only if he does a proscribed act 'otherwise than in the course of the stealing'. Theft may certainly be committed in an instant, so that D could be convicted of the offence even if he was immediately arrested. It does not follow that the offence is over in an instant, though that seems to have been the opinion of the court in *Pitham*.[167] D stole V's property by inviting E to buy it. It was held that the theft was over and done with, so that, when E agreed to buy and received the property, he was receiving stolen goods 'otherwise than in the course of the stealing'. That is a very doubtful decision.

In *Atakpu*,[168] after a careful review of the pre-*Gomez* authorities, Ward J summarized the **2.104** law as follows:[169]

(1) theft can occur in an instant by a single appropriation but it can also involve a course of dealing with property lasting longer and involving several appropriations before the transaction is complete; (2) theft is a finite act—it has a beginning and it has an end; (3) at what point the transaction is complete is a matter for the jury to decide upon the facts of each case; (4) though there may be several appropriations in the course of a single theft or several appropriations of different goods each constituting a separate theft as in *R v Skipp*, no case suggests that there can be successive thefts of the same property . . .

The court thought that, on a strict construction, *Gomez* left 'little room for a continuous **2.105** course of action' but they would not wish that to be the law and preferred the view that appropriation continues so long as the thief can sensibly be regarded as in the act of stealing, 'or in more understandable words, so long as he is "on the job" ' as it was put in *Smith & Hogan*.[170] It was not necessary for the court to decide the matter because no jury could have reasonably concluded that the theft of the cars in Frankfurt or Brussels in that case was continuing when the cars were brought, days later, into England. It is thought that this is the better view and that to treat appropriation simply as an instantaneous act would be inconsistent with the provisions of the Act relating to robbery and handling which presuppose that there can be a course of stealing.

So if D enters a house and seizes a jewellery box with theftuous intent he is guilty of theft **2.106** as soon as he does so, but the theft continues while he is in the course of removing it from

---

[165] See G Williams [1978] Crim LR 69; V Tunkel [1978] Crim LR 313.
[166] cf *Bowden* [2002] EWCA Crim 1279 where the question was whether the theft was complete or whether it was ongoing at the time D used force to prevent what he thought was a crime (relying on s 3 of the Criminal Law Act 1967).
[167] Above, para 2.65.
[168] Above, para 2.99.
[169] [1994] 4 All ER 215 at 223.
[170] 7th edition, 513.

the premises: see *Hale*,[171] where the court held that, as a matter of common sense, D was in the course of committing theft for the purposes of s 8 and that it was for the jury to decide whether or not the act of appropriation was finished.

2.107 In *Meech*,[172] D, with V's authority, cashed V's cheque, dishonestly intending to deprive him of the money. He took it to a prearranged destination where E and F staged a fake robbery to account for its loss. The court assumed that if D had appropriated the money when he drew it from the bank (and, since *Gomez*, we know he did) the theft would have been over by the time of the rendezvous, so that E and F could not be abettors in such a theft. Whether it could be regarded as continuing probably depends on the distance in time, place, and circumstance between the initial appropriation and the division of the spoils, which does not appear in the report.

An act or omission as an essential element of appropriation

Mere state of mind insufficient

2.108 A mere decision in D's mind to assume the rights of an owner is not enough to amount to an appropriation.[173] In *Eddy v Niman*,[174] it was said that 'some overt act . . . inconsistent with the true owner's rights' is required; but that case must now be regarded as overruled by *Gomez*. What is now required is conduct which is, or would be, inconsistent with the owner's rights if he had not consented to or authorized it. It seems that a secret dishonest intention may now turn an authorized act into theft.

Omission may suffice

2.109 Appropriation can be performed by omission as well as by act. This seems to be implicit in the provision in s 3(1) that a person may appropriate by 'keeping . . . as owner' property which he has come by innocently. 'Keeping' would not seem necessarily to involve doing any act but to be satisfied by D's omission, with the appropriate intent, to divest himself of possession. If D's 7-year-old child brings home V's tricycle and D, knowing that the child has come by it unlawfully, does nothing about it,[175] intending that V shall be permanently deprived of the tricycle, it is submitted that this would be theft by D. This might be regarded as an assumption of ownership through the innocent agency of the child who, no doubt, would continue to act as owner. If D were to say to his wife, 'Let Richard keep it', this, it is thought, would probably be sufficient assumption of ownership. Even where D does nothing at all, as where sheep stray from V's land on to D's and he simply allows them

---

[171] (1978) 68 Cr App R 415, [1979] Crim LR 596. cf *Gregory* (1981) 74 Cr App R 154, [1982] Crim LR 229; *Lockley* [1995] Crim LR 656.

[172] [1974] QB 549. According to the report of *Anderson v Wish* in [1980] Crim LR 319, 320, Roskill LJ, approving the principle of 'continuing appropriation', said that a passage of his judgment in *Meech* reading 'the misappropriation only took place when the three men divided up the money at the scene of the robbery' should read 'the misappropriation took place *not later than* when the three men . . .'. But this passage (though cited in the immediately preceding case of *Oxford v Peers* (1980) 72 Cr App R 19 where the court doubted the decision in *Anderton v Wish*) was omitted from the report (presumably revised by the judge) in (1980) 72 Cr App R 23.

[173] *Eddy v Niman* (1981) 73 Cr App R 237, DC.

[174] (1981) 73 Cr App R 237 at 241.

[175] cf *Walters v Lunt* [1951] 2 All ER 645. cf *Police v Subritzky* [1990] 2 NZLR 717 (mother guilty of theft by not preventing 4-year-old child from wheeling pushchair home from toyshop).

to remain there,[176] treating them as part of his own flock, he ought to be guilty. In such circumstances it may, however, be difficult or impossible to prove any intention to 'keep' and the charge will then fail, not merely on the ground of lack of *mens rea*, but because there was no appropriation.

Suppose that D, having borrowed V's cycle for a week, resolves on the expiry of that period to keep it. It would clearly be an appropriation, at the expiry of the period, to refuse to return it on demand,[177] or to deny V access to it, or for D to claim it as his own. Such conduct shows that he is keeping it as owner. It would also constitute appropriation if D were to use the cycle after the expiry of the loan because this is an assumption of one of the owner's rights. But what if D, on the expiry of the loan, merely leaves the cycle where it is in his garage hoping that V will forget about it and intending to keep it? Literally the case falls within the section since D is 'keeping . . . it as owner' and there would appear to be no warrant for giving the words other than their plain meaning. Of course it would be very difficult to prove D's *mens rea* in the form of the intention permanently to deprive, but he satisfies the appropriation requirement of keeping as owner. As the court has recently underlined in *Gresham*[178] 'keeping' as owner in relation to a bank account may be difficult to prove in a case where [D] does no more than refrain from bringing the mistake to the attention of the bank'.[179] That is of course strictly a matter of evidence, but in practical terms, some positive act such as drawing a cheque on the account may be necessary. **2.110**

Theft by D's acts which induce V to transfer property?

In general terms, the concept of appropriation, being defined in terms of an 'assumption' of the rights of another would seem clearly to require conduct on D's part demonstrating such an assumption. What of cases in which D induces V to transfer property to him? Can there be an appropriation before the point in time at which D has physical contact, possession, or control of the property ie when V has initiated the transfer? The problem becomes most acute in cases involving alleged thefts of things in action, especially credit balances. **2.111**

In *Hilton*,[180] where D, who had direct control of a bank account belonging to a charity, gave instructions for the transfer of the charity's funds to settle his personal debts, it was held that he stole the thing in action (the charity's right to payment of that sum from its bank) belonging to the charity. There was clearly an act by D, and *Hilton* might be regarded as a straightforward case since D always had control of the bank account and instructed his agent (the bank) to act in relation to the property. It would make no difference whether D had authorized the payments to be made by a cheque drawn by D or by telegraphic or other transfers which he directed. D stole the credit balance, ie the charity's right as creditor to recover the debt owed to it by the bank. **2.112**

---

[176] cf *Thomas* (1953) 37 Cr App R 169.
[177] cf *Wakeman* (1912) 8 Cr App R 18.
[178] [2003] EWCA Crim 2070.
[179] Approving the statements in *Ngan* [1998] 1 Cr App R 331 at 336, *Gresham*, para 22.
[180] [1997] 2 Cr App R 445, [1997] Crim LR 761 and commentary.

2.113   Is the position different where D, by deception, induces, V, the owner and controller of the bank account, to transfer[181] funds from it because although V's credit balance, or part of it, has gone, D did not 'appropriate' it?[182] The prevailing view is that in such a case V exercises his own rights of ownership over his own bank balance, so as to destroy it in whole or in part.[183] Two categories of case may need to be distinguished. In the case of a transfer initiated by D causing V to draw a cheque in his favour, there seems to be no difficulty in saying that D has stolen V's credit balance, probably[184] at the time of presentation. In *Williams*[185] the defendant, a builder, defrauded numerous elderly householders by overcharging for work once he had gained their trust by completing work on initial jobs at reasonable prices. D was charged, inter alia, with stealing things in action by cashing the householders' cheques made payable to him/his company. The Court of Appeal held that the presentation of a cheque by or on behalf of the defendant, causing a diminution of the victim's credit balance in his bank account, amounted to an appropriation of the victim's property.[186] The convictions were upheld.[187] D stole V's credit balance or right to overdraw his account. By presenting the cheque D destroyed that thing, or part of it, and the exercise of the power to destroy is the clearest possible assumption of the rights of an owner with intent permanently to deprive, because it extinguishes those rights—all of them. However, D's presentation of the cheque did not *immediately* destroy V's thing in action. That occurred only after the cheque been processed by the bank. If that process was effected automatically without human intervention, concluding that D has caused the destruction and, therefore, has appropriated the thing is straightforward. If the process is effected by human hand, D can still be said to have caused the destruction of V's thing in action by the innocent agency of the bank clerks.

2.114   The position is less straightforward where D dishonestly and by deception procures V to 'transfer' funds by telegraphic transfer or CHAPS or similar order, as in *Preddy*.[188] Can D be said to have stolen the credit balance by destroying it when he has instructed/deceived V to make the transfer? In particular, can V be properly treated as an 'innocent agent' acting on D's behalf in the chain leading to the destruction of the bank balance? There is no reason in principle why the victim cannot be an innocent agent of the accused, but Sir John Smith advanced two reasons why V is not acting as D's innocent agent when he authorizes the telegraphic transfer which diminishes his bank balance. (i) The bank clerks who process the

---

[181] The so-called 'transfer' of property is not really a transfer at all, as *Preddy* makes clear, one thing in action is extinguished and another created. It might properly be regarded as a transfer of value.

[182] Reliance was placed on *Caresana* [1996] Crim LR 667, *Naviede* [1997] Crim LR 662. See also JC Smith, Archbold News, Issue 9, 14 Nov 1996.

[183] This was the view Sir John Smith preferred: see *Smith and Hogan, Criminal Law* (9th edn, 1999) 515, 1.

[184] See *Ngan* above where the court held there was no assumption of any right to the mistaken credit balance in D's account until the cheques were presented.

[185] [2001] 1 Cr App R 362.

[186] See R Heaton, 'Cheques and Balances' [2005] Crim LR 747, 750.

[187] D had dishonestly and by deception, procured V to draw in his favour and deliver to him a cheque, D acquired a thing in action—the right to sue on the cheque—but, following *Preddy* he would not have been guilty of obtaining that thing from V, contrary to s 15 of the Theft Act; the thing in action was never 'property belonging to another', as s 15 required.

[188] [1996] AC 815. On the CHAPS system see *Paget's Law of Banking* (13th edn, 2006) para 17.43 and R. Cranston, *Principles of Banking Law* (2nd edn, 2002) 280–2.

cheque, like the postman, are merely following their regular daily routine, not involving any exercise of judgment, their acts being automatic; whereas, V, when he authorizes the telegraphic transfer, is not doing a routine act but exercising his judgment;[189] (ii) the chain of causation is broken by the intervention of a 'fully voluntary' act. If V is fully aware of the nature of the act he is doing, that act breaks the chain of causation, even, it is submitted, if V was deceived into doing it. The person who authorizes the telegraphic transfer knows exactly what he is doing. His mistake is not as to the nature of the act. It is his, and only his, act.

The Court of Appeal in *Naviede*[190] confirmed that it was not satisfied that 'a misrepresenta- **2.115** tion which persuades the account holder to direct payment out of his account is an assumption of the rights of the account holder as owner such as to amount to an appropriation of his rights within section 3(1) of the 1968 Act.'[191] Subsequently, following Sir John Smith's commentary on that case (and on *Caresana*[192]) the Court of Appeal confirmed in *Briggs*[193] that there is no theft of V's credit balance in such a case.

In *Briggs*, D had, by deception, induced her elderly relatives to transfer to her proceeds of **2.116** their house sale. D had arranged for the sale of the victims' property to be handled by a firm of licensed conveyancers, but handled the purchase of the new house herself. D wrote instructing the conveyancers with a letter of authority signed by the victims, authorizing £49,950 from the proceeds of the sale to be sent to D's solicitors, and for the outstanding balance to be transferred to the victim's bank account. The conveyancers transferred proceeds as per those instructions. Title to the new property was transferred to and subsequently registered in the name of D. Counsel for the Crown argued that the credit balance was appropriated by D when she caused the licensed conveyancers to transfer the sale proceeds to her solicitors for her own purposes, ie to buy the new property and transfer it into her name, against the wishes of her elderly relatives.

The Court of Appeal quashed the conviction for theft of the credit balance representing **2.117** the proceeds of the sale (there was some confusion as to what D was alleged to have stolen—it was either the credit balance in the conveyancing company's account or the debt owed by the conveyancing company to the elderly victims). The court held that the word 'appropriation' connoted a physical act rather than a more remote action triggering the payment that gave rise to the charge.[194] The court relied heavily on Sir John Smith's commentary on *Caresena*:

It is true that D procures the whole course of events resulting in V's account being debited; but the telegraphic transfer is initiated by V and his voluntary intervening acts break the chain of causation.

---

[189] Relying on *Stringer and Banks* [1991] Crim LR 639 where, in holding that intervening acts were done by innocent agents, the court stated 'If they had exercised an independent judgment as to whether or not to pass the invoice for payment it might be different.'

[190] [1997] Crim LR 662.

[191] ibid.

[192] [1996] Crim LR 667, see also JC Smith's note in [1996] 9 Archbold News 4.

[193] [2004] EWCA Crim 3662, [2004] Crim LR 455.

[194] Despite the court's approving reference to the *Oxford English Dictionary* definition of appropriation involving a 'taking', it is submitted that a physical 'taking' or 'touching' is only a sufficient but not a necessary element of the offence, otherwise there would be no protection for intangible property.

It is the same as if V is induced by deception to take money out of his safe to pay to D. D does not at that moment 'appropriate' it—V is not acting as his agent. D commits theft only if and when the money is put into his hands.

2.118   Although following earlier authority and the views of Sir John Smith, *Briggs* is an unsatisfactory authority.[195] Neither *Gomez* nor *Hinks* was cited to the court. Although neither of those cases expressly precludes the approach taken in *Briggs* and *Naviede*, they do make it very much harder to draw any clear distinction between (i) D's direct acts towards V's property, with V's fraudulently obtained consent, and (ii) D's acts causing V to transfer his property (or extinguish his chose in action) with V's fraudulently obtained consent. Arguably they are distinguishable on the basis that V's act of transfer in (ii) breaks the chain of causation since V will not be acting in a free informed manner (having been deceived). However, if D used an innocent agent, E, to effect the transfer of V's property, or to extinguish it, there would be no difficulty in establishing a theft charge at the moment that E assumes any right in relation to V's property. Why are things different when D causes V to act towards his own property in a way that will lead to its being destroyed or transferred to D? Both the agent and V appear to have been deceived. The fact that V has the authority to act in this way by transferring the property and consenting is, according to *Gomez* and *Hinks*, irrelevant. D's setting in motion of the transaction could be regarded as the commencement of the continuing act of appropriation. It is therefore arguable that where D, by deceit of V, causes a transfer of property that act is itself an appropriation. This possibility flows from the shift in emphasis in interpreting the concept of appropriation generally.

2.119   It remains the case that theft requires proof of an 'act' by D towards the property that belongs to another, subject to what was said above about keeping and dealing. 'Appropriation' is quite different from 'obtaining' in this respect. Whereas appropriation requires an act by D, in s 15 the element of 'obtaining' was satisfied by passivity on D's part: the crucial element of criminal conduct for that offence was D's deception.

Attempted theft

2.120   An attempt, with *mens rea*, to assume the rights of an owner, is an attempt to steal.[196] The fact that any assumption of any of the rights of an owner is an appropriation and therefore the complete crime of theft means that there is often little, if any, room for an offence of attempt. D's first dishonest act will be the complete crime. Common sense might suggest that the act of swapping the price labels in a supermarket is merely an act preparatory to obtaining an article by deception; but it is the full offence of theft of the article.[197] One of the practical effects of *Gomez*[198] is to enlarge the offence of theft to include acts which were formerly (and sensibly) held to be preparatory acts. In the *Asil Nadir* case Tucker J asked:[199]

If for example, a Defendant has authority to arrange the disposition of goods in a warehouse, and he places certain goods near the door so that his accomplices can come and steal them, is the

---

[195] See the commentary by DC Ormerod at [2004] Crim LR 495 and R Heaton, 'Cheques and Balances' [2005] Crim LR 747.
[196] Criminal Attempts Act 1981, s 1(1).
[197] Above, para 2.19.
[198] Above, para 2.22.
[199] *R v Central Criminal Court, ex p Director of Serious Fraud Office* [1993] 2 All ER 399, 401.

Defendant's act an unauthorised act so as to amount to an appropriation and theft? Or is it merely a preparatory act?

Following *Morris*, the authority then prevailing, Tucker J opined that this was a preparatory **2.121** act. It now appears to be theft. Tucker J was posing an analogy to the allegations before him that D, a company director with authority to transfer the company's funds to a subsidiary abroad, did so with the intention of there disposing of them, not for the company's benefit but for his own private interests. He held that this was a merely preparatory act. After *Gomez*, it is theft.

A person may be guilty of an attempt although the facts are such that the commission of **2.122** the offence is impossible, as where D tries to steal from a pocket, wallet, car, or other place which is in fact empty. He attempts to steal a thing in action if he dishonestly draws a cheque on V's bank account which is overdrawn and has no overdraft facility. He may be guilty of attempting to steal from V property which is in fact his own if, because he is making a mistake of fact, he believes the property belongs to V. If his mistake is one of civil law, the matter is more doubtful. D's *mens rea* is the same—he intends to appropriate property belonging to another—but the case would probably be held to fall outside the terms of the Criminal Attempts Act 1981, s 2(1), which provides: 'A person may be guilty of attempting to commit an offence . . . even though the facts are such that the commission of the offence is impossible.'[200]

Theft only of specific property

Theft can be committed only in respect of some specific thing, tangible or intangible, **2.123** described in the indictment or information. It is not necessary for the prosecution to prove that D stole the whole of the property mentioned, but the sentence imposed should relate only to the property proved to have been stolen.[201] It follows from the need to specify the property stolen that merely to cause V to become indebted to X, however dishonestly, is not to steal from V.

In *Navvabi*[202] D, by the unauthorized use of his cheque book and cheque card, obtained **2.124** gaming chips in a casino, causing his bank to become indebted to the casino for the amount of the cheques. He was convicted of theft, apparently of money, on a direction that 'writing a cheque backing it with a cheque card is an appropriation of the assets of the bank'. That was wrong.[203] It was impossible to specify any property of the bank that had been appropriated. The appellant's counsel's concession that an appropriation took place when funds were transferred by the bank to the casino was doubted by the court and was surely also wrong. The 'appropriation' of funds to pay the debt was the act of the bank, not that of D, nor was it done as D's agent.

---

[200] See commentary on *Huskinson* [1988] Crim LR 620 at 622.

[201] *Parker* [1969] 2 QB 248, [1969] 2 All ER 15, CA; *Machent v Quinn* [1970] 2 All ER 255; cf *Levene v Pearcey* [1976] Crim LR 63.

[202] (1986) 83 Cr App R 271, [1987] Crim LR 57, CA. Probably D ought to have been charged with obtaining a pecuniary advantage by deception, contrary to s 16(2)(b) of the Theft Act 1968.

[203] This would now be an offence of fraud under s 2 of the Fraud Act 2006 at the time D offers the cheque without authority.

2.125   Difficult to reconcile with this principle is *Monaghan*.[204] D, a supermarket cashier, received the price of goods from a customer and put the notes and coins in the till without ringing up the purchase. She was then arrested, charged with and convicted of stealing that money. She admitted that she intended to steal. At the end of her shift, or perhaps when some earlier opportunity occurred, she would have taken from the till a sum equivalent to that unrecorded. Had that occurred, she would undoubtedly have been guilty of stealing the money so taken. Since *Gomez* it is no longer an objection that she had dealt with the money exactly as her duty required by putting it in the till; but how could it be said that she had appropriated, or, if she had carried out her plan, would have appropriated, *that* money? That money may well have gone into her employer's safe, while she stole money paid by some other, as yet unascertained, customer. It was impossible to prove the appropriation of any *specific* money. Even after *Gomez*, this seems to be a case of a merely preparatory act.

2.126   A case which presents even greater difficulty is *Thompson*.[205] D, a computer operator employed by a bank in Kuwait, opened accounts in his own name there. He programmed the computer to debit the accounts of wealthy customers of the bank and credit his own accounts with corresponding amounts. He then took off for England and the program operated while he was in the air. In England he opened other accounts and instructed the Kuwait bank to telex his credit balance to his English banks. The Kuwait bank obliged and D withdrew money from those accounts and spent it. He appealed against his conviction for obtaining money by deception contrary to s 15, arguing that he obtained the property in Kuwait, outside the jurisdiction of the court. But the court held that the transaction in Kuwait was a nullity. The programming of the computer was no different in substance from forging the accounts with a pen. It was held that 'the only realistic view of the undisputed facts' was that property was obtained by deception 'when the relevant sums of money were received by the appellant's banks in England'. But clearly no 'money' in the sense of banknotes was received. Nor was any other property belonging to the Kuwait bank obtained. The credit balances at the English banks (if not void) were things in action belonging to D; and they had never belonged to anyone else.[206] Far from receiving any property, the English banks were undertaking (or thought they were undertaking) the burden of a supposed debt owed by the Kuwait bank to D. No doubt this created a corresponding indebtedness of the Kuwait bank to the English bank. Presumably the loss would fall in the end on the Kuwait bank; but, as we have seen, to cause V to become indebted to X is not to steal from V. Property may have been obtained by deception when D drew on the English accounts; but this was not the offence with which he was charged.

Theft without loss

2.127   The popular conception of theft is that the thief makes a gain and his victim suffers a corresponding loss. This was indeed the situation at common law and under the Larceny Acts; but the extended definition of stealing in the Theft Act 1968 and, particularly, its

---

[204] [1979] Crim LR 673, CA, and commentary.
[205] (1984) 79 Cr App R 191, CA, criticised in [1984] Crim LR 427, 428, Griew 6.11, *Arlidge and Parry on Fraud* 3.07.
[206] *Preddy* confirms this view of the law.

application to things in action, means that there may now sometimes be theft without loss. In *Chan Man-sin v A-G of Hong Kong*,[207] it was held that a company accountant who drew a forged cheque on the company's account stole from the company the thing in action consisting in its credit balance or its contractual right to overdraw. Yet it was settled law[208] that the honouring of the forged cheque and the debiting of the company's account was a nullity and the company, on discovering the unauthorized debit, was entitled to have it reversed. It was nothing more than an error in the books of the bank. In law, the company was never a penny worse off. Yet it was held that there was both an appropriation—because D had assumed the rights of an owner over the credit balance—and an intention permanently to deprive—because he intended to treat the thing as his own to dispose of—regardless of the company's rights.[209]

Similarly, in *Wille*,[210] D, the director of a company issued cheques on the company's bank **2.128** account for his own benefit. He was the sole signatory to each cheque, and the bank had met these despite the fact that the bank mandate from the company required all cheques to bear two signatures. The bank was not therefore entitled to debit the amounts of the cheques to the company's account, and there was no loss to the company. Nevertheless, the Court of Appeal held D was rightly convicted of stealing the debts owed by the bank to the company.

The fact that no loss arises in fact does not preclude a finding of dishonesty.[211] Nor is **2.129** there a difficulty in finding an appropriation where the defendant has not obtained something. That was a crucial difference between the offence of theft and that under s 15 of obtaining by deception.[212] It is sufficient that D has caused V's property to be destroyed without himself obtaining it as most obviously in the case of a theft of a chose in action belonging to V being destroyed by D's act. If D dishonestly causes a bank to debit V's account, D does not appropriate V's money, he appropriates a thing in action belonging to V (V's right to payment of that sum from the bank) and may be guilty of theft of that property.[213]

Property

Stealing is the dishonest appropriation of property and, by s 4(1): '"Property" includes **2.130** money and all other property, real or personal, including things in action and other intangible property.'

---

[207] [1988] 1 All ER 1, [1988] Crim LR 319, PC. See also *Burke* [2000] Crim LR 413. *Wille* (1987) 86 Cr App R 296 is to the same effect. See also *Hilton* [1997] Crim LR 761.
[208] By *Tai Hing Cotton Mill Ltd v Liu Chong Hing Bank Ltd* [1986] AC 80, [1985] 2 All ER 947, PC.
[209] Theft Act 1968, s 6, below, para 2.316.
[210] (1987) 86 Cr App R 296.
[211] See s 1(2) below para 2.272 and *Wheatley v Commissioner of Police of the British Virgin Islands* [2006] 1 WLR 1683; [2006] UKPC 24.
[212] See the commentary by Professor Sir John Smith, QC at [1997] Crim LR 344 cited with approval by the Court of Appeal in *Williams* [2001] 1 Cr App R 362.
[213] *Chan Man-sin v A-G for Hong Kong* [1988] 1 All ER 1, PC, 662; *Ex p Osman* [1989] 3 All ER 701, DC; *Williams* [2001] 1 Cr App R 362.

2.131 It should be noted at once that this definition is highly qualified, so far as land and wild creatures are concerned, by subsections (2), (3), and (4) of s 4.[214] Under the Larceny Acts there could be no larceny of land or things in action or other intangible property (because they could not be taken and carried away as the law then required) nor wild creatures while at large as they had no owner. Each of these items requires separate consideration under the 1968 Act.

Land

2.132 Since appropriation can occur under the 1968 Act without any taking and carrying away the technical obstacle to land being the subject of theft has disappeared. Land was formerly a possible subject of fraudulent conversion[215] and, since fraudulent conversion is now swallowed by theft, it was essential that land should, in some circumstances at least, be stealable. It would have been possible to leave s 4(1) unqualified and a perfectly workable law would have resulted. The Committee, for reasons of policy, decided against this course.

2.133 Section 4(2) provides:

> A person cannot steal land, or things forming part of land and severed from it by him or by his directions, except in the following cases, that is to say—
>
> (a) when he is a trustee or personal representative, or is authorised by power of attorney, or as liquidator of a company, or otherwise, to sell or dispose of land belonging to another, and he appropriates the land or anything forming part of it by dealing with it in breach of the confidence reposed in him; or
>
> (b) when he is not in possession of the land and appropriates anything forming part of the land by severing it or causing it to be severed, or after it has been severed; or
>
> (c) when, being in possession of the land under a tenancy, he appropriates the whole or part of any fixture or structure let to be used with the land.
>
> For purposes of this subsection 'land' does not include incorporeal hereditaments; 'tenancy' means a tenancy for years or any less period and includes an agreement for such a tenancy, but a person who after the end of a tenancy remains in possession as statutory tenant or otherwise is to be treated as having possession under the tenancy, and 'let' shall be construed accordingly.

2.134 It is helpful to spell out the possible liability of the various categories of persons in detail.

Trustees, personal representatives, and others authorized to dispose of land belonging to another

2.135 Any of these persons may steal the land or anything forming part of it by dealing with it in breach of the confidence reposed in him. So if he sells or gives away the land or any fixture or structure forming part of it, he commits theft provided the land belongs to another.[216]

Other persons not in possession

2.136 Such a person may steal only by severing, or causing to be severed, or appropriating the thing after severance. A purported sale by such a person of the land would not be theft. An attempt to sever, as by starting to dig out a sapling, is an assumption which is not a

---

[214] Below, paras 2.135, 2.146, and 2.150.
[215] Above, para 1.23.
[216] See generally R Brazier, 'Criminal Trustees' (1975) 39 Conv 29.

sufficient appropriation, though no doubt an attempt to steal.[217] The general rule is that a person who is not in possession of land can steal fixtures, growing things, and even the substance of the land itself, if, in each case, he first severs it from the realty. The following acts are theft: D enters upon land in the possession of V and

   (i) demolishes a brick wall and carries away the bricks;
   (ii) removes a stone statue fixed in the land;
   (iii) digs sand from a sand pit and takes it away;
   (iv) cuts grass growing on the land[218] and at once loads it on to a cart to drive away;
   (v) takes away V's farm gate.[219]

It is not theft for D to appropriate land without severing it, as where he moves his boundary **2.137** fence so as to incorporate a strip of V's land into his own.[220]

Other persons in possession as tenants

If a tenant removes a fixture—for example a washbasin or fireplace—he may be guilty of **2.138** stealing it. Likewise if he removes any structure—for example a shed or greenhouse which is fixed to the land. If the structure is resting on its own weight and not a fixture then it is, of course, stealable under the general rule and there is no need to rely on s 4(2)(c). But the tenant will not be guilty if he digs soil or sand from the land and appropriates that. This exemption applies only to the person in possession of the land. If his wife or a member of the family were to dig and sell sand, it would seem that s 4(2)(b) would be applicable and theft would be committed. In such a case, there is some authority for suggesting that the husband could be convicted as an aider and abettor.[221] If the husband were the principal in the act it is possible that anyone assisting him might be held liable as an aider and abettor, even though he could not himself be convicted.[222]

Unlike s 4(2)(b), 4(2)(c) does not require that the thing be severed. It appears then that if **2.139** the tenant contracted to sell the unsevered fireplace in his house he would be guilty of theft, even where there was no intention to sever it, as where it is sold to the tenant's successor in the tenancy. If the tenant purports to sell the land he commits no offence and a purported sale of an ordinary house would be indistinguishable from a sale of the land. The house could hardly be held to be a 'structure let to be used with the land'. The phrase implies that the structure is of an ancillary nature.

Other persons in possession otherwise than as tenants

A person may be in possession of a land as a licensee.[223] Curiously, he is not within the terms **2.140** of s 4(2)(c) and so is incapable of stealing the land or anything forming part of it. He thus

---

[217] The rule formerly was that a person could not be convicted of stealing anything which he had severed from the realty (subject to specific statutory exceptions) unless he first abandoned and then retook possession.

[218] cf *Foley* (1889) 17 Cox CC 142.

[219] cf *Skujins* [1956] Crim LR 266.

[220] The arguments for and against making land the subject of theft are summarized in *Eighth Report*, Cmnd 2977 at 21–2.

[221] *Sockett* (1908) 1 Cr App R 101.

[222] cf *Bourne* (1952) 36 Cr App R 125; *Cogan and Leak* [1976] QB 217, [1975] 2 All ER 1059; *Millward* [1994] Crim LR 257; *Smith and Hogan, Criminal Law* ch 8, p 511.

[223] *Errington v Errington and Woods* [1952] 1 KB 290, [1952] 1 All ER 149; see J Furber (ed), *Hill and Redman's Law of Landlord and Tenant* ch1 para A.643.

commits no offence if he dishonestly appropriates fixtures or digs sand or ore from the land. This appears to be an oversight in the Act. He of course may be guilty of stealing structures not forming part of the land.

2.141   It may be important to determine whether a particular article forms part of the land. Generally appropriation will involve severance, so non-possessors will be caught by s 4(2)(b) while tenants are caught by s 4(2)(c). But if a licensee in possession appropriates a structure, it is vital to know whether it forms part of the land. This is a question of the land law and the answer depends on the degree of annexation and the object of annexation.[224] The chattel must be actually fixed to the land, not for its more convenient use as a chattel, but for the more convenient use of the land.[225]

2.142   Incorporeal hereditaments[226] are stealable. The most important of these are easements, profits, and rents. The main purpose of the provision would seem to be to cover the theft of a rent-charge.[227] Instances of theft of the other interests can only be extremely rare. For example, V has a right of way over O's land—an easement. D executes a deed purporting to relieve O's land of the burden of the easement. Or D, a tenant of V's land, purporting to be the freeholder, allows O, the adjoining landowner, to erect a building which will necessarily obstruct the flow of light to windows on V's land which have an easement of light. These acts seem to be appropriations of the easement which, if done with the necessary *mens rea* will amount to theft. The most obvious instances will be those where a trustee or personal representative disposes of an easement, profit, or rent for his own benefit. These cases are not covered by s 4(2)(a) but incorporeal hereditaments can be stolen by persons generally.

2.143   It will be noted that these examples relate to existing incorporeal hereditaments. Dishonestly to purport to create an easement in the land of another would not seem to amount to an offence unless it is done by one of the persons mentioned in s 4(2)(a). In the latter case, such an act would seem to amount to 'dealing with the land in breach of the confidence reposed in him'.

2.144   The fact that D's efforts to dispose of an interest in V's land in these cases would be ineffective to do so would not seem to affect the result in the criminal law. When a bailee of goods purports to sell the goods, he is unable (in general) to pass a good title; yet it cannot be doubted that his purporting to do so amounts to an appropriation of the goods. The same is now true of a person who has no proprietary or possessory interest of any sort in the goods. The position must be the same in the case of a purported disposal of an interest in land.[228] In addition it should be noted that the simpler and more appropriate course will be to charge him with an offence of fraud under s 1 of the 2006 Act.

---

[224]   See *Elitestone Ltd v Morris* [1997] 2 All ER 513, [1997] 1 WLR 687 HL.

[225]   Compare *Elitestone v Morris* [1997] 2 All ER 513—timber bungalow on concrete stand on land only removable by destroying part of land, held to be part of land; cf *Chelsea Yacht and Boat Club v Pope* [2001] 2 All ER 409—houseboat secured to riverbed pontoon and river walls by mooring ropes is not part of land.

[226]   See *Hillman and Redman* above, n 223, para A. 904.

[227]   No doubt this was the subject of fraudulent conversion under the old law, and called for a provision of this kind.

[228]   The problem of 'intention permanently to deprive' is the same as that discussed below, para 2.316. See also *Chan Wai Lam* [1981] Crim LR 497, below, para 2.337, n 1.

A rather strange anomaly resulting from the exception of incorporeal hereditaments **2.145** from the meaning of 'land' is that if D, not being one of the persons mentioned in s 4(2)(a), purports to dispose of the whole of V's interest in the land (for example, the fee simple) he will not commit theft (though he might be guilty of fraud); whereas if, as in the examples given, he purports to dispose of a comparatively small part of V's interest he will be guilty of theft.

Exception of things growing wild

Things growing wild on land undoubtedly fall within the definition of property in the Act **2.146** and, but for an exception, could be stolen by a person not in possession of land if he severed and appropriated them. Section 4(3), however, provides:

A person who picks mushrooms growing wild on any land, or who picks flowers, fruit or foliage from a plant growing wild on any land, does not (although not in possession of the land) steal what he picks, unless he does it for reward or for sale or other commercial purpose.

For purposes of this subsection 'mushroom' includes any fungus, and 'plant' includes any shrub or tree.

The effect is in general to exempt things growing wild from the law of theft. It will be theft **2.147** however if:

(i) (except in the case of a mushroom) D removes the whole plant. For example, he pulls out a primrose or a sapling by the roots. This is not picking from a plant and so is not within the exception.

(ii) D removes the plant or part of it by an act which cannot be described as 'picking'. For example, he saws off the top of a Christmas tree growing wild on V's land, or cuts the grass growing wild on V's land with a reaper or a scythe.

(iii) D picks mushrooms or wild flowers, fruit, or foliage, for a commercial purpose—for example, mushrooms for sale in his shop or holly to sell from door to door at Christmas.[229] The provision is no doubt intended to be used against depredation on a fairly large scale but it would seem to cover such cases as where D, a schoolboy, picks mushrooms intending to sell them to his mother or the neighbours. It is possible, however, that such a single isolated case might be held not to fall within the law as not being a 'commercial' purpose—for it will be noted that the wording of the subsection requires that sale, as well as other purposes, be 'commercial'. It might be argued that this requires that D, to some extent, must be making a business of dealing in the things in question.[230]

It is, of course, theft to pick a single *cultivated* flower, wherever it is growing.

Wild creatures

The distinction between wild creatures (*ferae naturae*) and tame creatures (*mansuetae* **2.148** *naturae*) is a matter of common law.[231] Some tame animals, like dogs and cats, could not be stolen at common law; but now, all tame animals may be stolen. Wild creatures could not,

---

[229] What then of the popularity of removal of articles for farmer's markets etc (popularized by eg Hugh Fearnley-Whittingstall's use of wild things for his River Cottage produce)? See generally M Welstead, 'Season of Mists and Mellow Fruitfulness' (1995) 150 NLJ 1499. On the potential for charges of theft when protestors destroy GM crops, see M Stallworthy, 'Damage to Crops' (2000) 150 NLJ 728.

[230] But cf G Williams, *Textbook of Criminal Law* (1st edn, 1978) 683, n 1.

[231] See East 2 PC 607; Russell 2, 903.

while at large, be stolen at common law or under the Larceny Acts because no one had any property in them until they were taken or killed. The owner of the land on which they happened to be had an exclusive right to take them which was protected by the criminal law relating to poaching but was not protected by the heavier guns of larceny. When the wild creature was killed or taken, the property in it vested in the owner of the land on which this was done,[232] but the thing was now in the possession of the taker who could not therefore steal it. If, however, he abandoned the thing on V's land, then possession of it vested in V and a subsequent removal of it by D was larceny. Difficult questions could arise whether D had abandoned the creature or not. If he put rabbits into bags or bundles and hid them in a ditch on V's land, he retained possession so that it was no larceny if he returned later and appropriated them;[233] whereas if he merely left the things lying on the surface of the land, this might well have constituted abandonment of the thing.[234]

2.149 Though this result was rightly criticized, it was the logical consequence of the rule of the civil law which provided that the thing was owned by no one until it was taken. Had no special provisions been made in the Theft Act for wild animals they could probably have been stolen by virtue of s 3(1): though there would have been no appropriation at the instant of taking (because the thing was no one's property) any subsequent assumption of ownership (as by carrying the thing away) would have been theft from the owner of the land on which it was taken.

2.150 For reasons of policy, it was decided that it was undesirable to turn poaching[235] generally into theft; and accordingly, s 4(4) provides:

Wild creatures, tamed or untamed, shall be regarded as property; but a person cannot steal a wild creature not tamed nor ordinarily kept in captivity, or the carcase of any such creature, unless either it has been reduced into possession by or on behalf of another person and possession of it has not since been lost or abandoned, or another person is in course of reducing it into possession.

2.151 The effect of s 4(4) is that wild creatures cannot be stolen, except in the following two cases:

(i) The creature is tamed or ordinarily kept in captivity. For example, V's tame jackdaw, the mink which he keeps in cages, the animals in Whipsnade Zoo. The eagle which escaped many years ago from London Zoo could be stolen while at large, because it was ordinarily kept in captivity. (This phrase seems clearly to refer to the specific animal and not to the species of animal.[236]) Animals like bees or pigeons which roam freely are sufficiently reduced into possession if they

---

[232] *Blades v Higgs* (1865) 11 HL Cas 621.

[233] *Townley* (1871) LR 1 CCR 315; *Petch* (1878) 14 Cox CC 116.

[234] cf *Foley* (1889) 17 Cox CC 142.

[235] On salmon poaching see W Howarth, 'Handling Stolen Goods and Handling Salmon' [197] Crim LR 460, considering the Salmon Act 1986.

[236] In *Nye v Niblett* [1918] 1 KB 23, it was held that the words of s 41 of the Malicious Damage Act 1861 (now repealed, see Criminal Damage Act 1971) '. . . being ordinarily kept . . . for any domestic purpose' referred to the species of animal; but Darling J thought the section also protected a particular animal which was kept for a domestic purpose though the class to which it belonged was not so ordinarily kept. In the present section, however, the interpretation actually adopted in *Nye v Niblett* is untenable. Even though the great majority of animals of a particular wild species are ordinarily kept in captivity, a particular wild animal of that species which is and always has been in fact at large can hardly be stolen.

have acquired a habit of returning to their home (*animus revertendi*).[237] Possession is not lost because they are flying at a distance. If bees swarm, the common law rule is that the owner retains his possession only so long as he can keep them in sight and follow them. Possession is lost even though they are in sight if they have swarmed on land where he cannot lawfully follow.[238] A person who then takes them, or destroys them, does not commit theft or criminal damage. Bees could not be said to be 'tamed' or 'ordinarily kept in captivity'.

(ii) The creature has been reduced into and remains in the possession of another person or is in the course of being so reduced.[239] For example, V, a poacher, takes or is in course of taking a rabbit on O's land. This is not an offence under the Act. D takes the rabbit from V. This is theft by D from both V and O.

Except in these two cases, wild creatures cannot be stolen; so it will not be theft to take **2.152** mussels from a mussel bed on an area of the foreshore which belongs to V and which V has tended in order to maintain and improve it.[240]

The effect is that the poacher who reduces game into possession, abandons it and later **2.153** resumes possession (so that he was guilty, under the old law, of larceny from the owner of land) no longer commits any offence of theft. The creature has not been reduced into possession by or on behalf of another person. The landowner may have acquired possession when the game was left on his land[241] but it can hardly be said that the reduction into possession was by him on his behalf. [242]

In *Cresswell v DPP*[243] the Divisional Court considered whether badgers which had been **2.154** enticed into traps set by officials from DEFRA had become 'property' for the purposes of the Criminal Damage Act 1971 (identically worded in this respect to the Theft Act). The defendants sought to argue that the badgers were property and that a defence to destroying the traps was available on the basis that they were protecting property—the badgers. Keene LJ, rejecting the argument, stated that 'merely to entice a wild animal, whether it be a badger or a game bird or a deer, to a particular spot from time to time by providing food there, even with the objective ultimately of killing it in due course, does not form part of the course normally of reducing it into possession. If the creature were thereby to become the property, say, of the landowner providing the food, it would mean that it could not then be lawfully shot by the adjoining landowner on or over whose land it passed'.[244] Walker J was more hesitant, declining to express a concluded view on what constitutes property. His lordship did express some more general views on the concept of wild animals:

In broad terms, (a) it is a question of law whether an animal is wild or domestic. . . . (b) Once a wild animal is killed or dies, absolute property in the dead animal vests in the owner of the land or, in a case where relevant shooting or sporting rights have been granted, in the owner of those rights.

---

237 Blackstone *Commentaries* ii. 392–3. On whether an animal is tamed if kept in captivity, see *Hamps v Derby* [1948] 2 KB 311 (pigeons), cf *Cory* (1864) 10 Cox CC 23 (pheasants).
238 *Kearry v Pattinson* [1939] 1 KB 471, [1939] 1 All ER 65, CA.
239 Section 4(4).
240 *Howlett and Howlett* [1968] Crim LR 222, CA.
241 *Hibbert v McKiernan* [1948] 2 KB 142, [1948] 1 All ER 860; above, para 2.148.
242 Clearly, this slight narrowing by the 1968 Act of the law of stealing is of no great significance.
243 [2006] EWHC 3379.
244 [11].

(c) While a wild animal is alive there is no absolute property in that animal. There may, however, be what is known as a qualified property in them in three circumstances. The first is described as a qualified property *per industriam*. Wild animals become the property of a person who takes or tames or reclaims them until they regain their natural liberty and have not the intention to return. Examples of that kind of property include animals such as deer, swans and doves. A second qualified property is described as *ratione impotentiae et loci*. The owner of land has a qualified property in the young of animals born on the land until they can fly or run away. A third type of qualified property is described as *ratione soli* and *ratione privilegii*. An owner of land who has retained the exclusive right to hunt, take and kill wild animals on his land has a qualified property in them for the time being while they are there but if he grants to another the right to hunt, take or kill them then the grantee has a qualified property. [245]

2.155 For the purposes of theft, if the creature, having been reduced into possession, escapes again (and it is not a creature ordinarily kept in captivity) it cannot be stolen since possession of it has been lost. A more difficult case is that where the possession of the carcase of the creature is lost. V buys a pheasant and loses it on the way home. D picks it up and reads V's name and address on the packaging but determines to keep it for himself. If possession of the pheasant has been lost then D is not guilty and we have a curious case of a particular kind of chattel where there can be no stealing by finding. It is clearly arguable, however, that even in this case, theft is committed. [246] If so then there is another rather anomalous distinction between the loss of a dead wild creature and the loss of a live one—for the Act clearly contemplates that it is possible to lose possession of a wild creature and, even if this is inapplicable to the carcase, it must apply at least to the living animal. This is one of very few instances where possession is important under the Act and, significantly, it presents problems.

Poaching

2.156 Poaching may amount to an offence under a variety of enactments[247]—the Night Poaching Act 1828, the Game Act 1831[248] as amended by the Game Laws (Amendment) Act 1960, and the Poaching Prevention Act 1862,[249] Deer are protected by the Deer Act 1991. In addition certain provisions relating to the poaching of deer and fish were dealt with in the Larceny Act 1861 and, in view of the decision to repeal the whole of that Act, these were reproduced in Schedule 1 to the 1968 Act (below, Appendix 1) in a simplified form and with revised maximum penalties. These provisions were put in the Schedule rather than in the body of the Act to avoid giving the impression that they are intended to be a permanent part of the law of theft.[250] The CLRC long ago suggested that there should be a review of

---

[245] [38].
[246] The old law of larceny by finding must have proceeded on the assumption that even the person who had lost goods retained possession of them—otherwise there would not have been that trespass which was an essential element of larceny at common law. 'It appears clear on the old authorities that every person who takes a thing upon a finding is civilly a trespasser, except in the one case of a person who finding a thing when it is really lost takes it "in charity to save for its owner"': F Pollock and RS Wright, *Possession in the Common Law* (1888) 171.
[247] See generally the Wildlife and Countryside Act 1981, ss 1, 9, and Sch 5.
[248] Section 24 protects against the destruction or taking of game eggs.
[249] Which protects, inter alia, game eggs.
[250] CLRC, *Eighth Report*, Cmnd 2977 (1966) para 53.

the whole law of poaching followed by comprehensive legislation which would replace Schedule 1.[251]

Criminal damage

The Criminal Damage Act 1971 defines 'property' in such a way as to exclude those wild **2.157** creatures and those growing things which cannot be stolen; so the provisions of the Theft Act cannot be circumvented by a charge of criminal damage.

Things in action

A thing in action is property which does not exist in a physical state but which may be **2.158** vindicated by a legal action.[252] Examples are a debt, shares in a company, a copyright or a trade mark. The Patents Act 1977, s 30, declares that a patent or an application for a patent is not a thing in action but is personal property so it is clearly 'other intangible property' and is capable of being stolen. An invention for which no patent has been granted or applied for is clearly another form of intangible property,[253] whether or not it is a thing in action. So is a company's export quota if it is transferable for value.[254]

Intent to deprive of a thing in action

It is only in exceptional cases that the thief of a chattel deprives, or intends to deprive, the **2.159** owner of his ownership. Usually he deprives him, and intends to deprive him, only of possession. The thief intends to deprive the owner of all the *benefits* of ownership but he knows very well that the chattel continues to belong to his victim and that there is nothing he can do about that. He knows he is handling stolen goods and that, if he is found out, the goods will be taken from him and restored to their owner. So the intent permanently to deprive in the law of larceny referred to an intention to deprive the owner permanently of *possession*, no more. We thus encounter a difficulty when theft is extended to things in action: by definition, they do not exist in possession. An intention to deprive permanently of possession is an impossibility. Things in action are owned but not possessed. So the questions arise (i) whether, in order to amount to an appropriation, there has to be an actual deprivation of ownership; and (ii) whether there has to be an intention to deprive of ownership. The first question is easily answered in the light of the case-law: any assumption of any of the rights of an owner amounts to an appropriation[255] and such an assumption may fall far short of a deprivation of ownership or possession. The second question also requires a negative answer in the light of s 6 of the 1968 Act, as construed by the courts.[256] D's intention 'to treat the thing as his own to dispose of regardless of the other's rights' is to be regarded as an intention permanently to deprive.

---

[251] ibid.

[252] See generally M Bridge, *Personal Property Law* (3rd edn, 2002).

[253] See Patents Act 1977, s 7(2)(b).

[254] *A-G of Hong Kong v Nai Keung* (1987) 86 Cr App R 174, PC. The strange notion to be found in *Williams and Crick* (1993) (No 91/3265/W3) that, following *Nai-Keung*, 'a transfer' of property could be a thing in action, received no encouragement in *Preddy* [1996] 3 All ER 481 at 489. The export quota was 'an asset capable of being traded on a market'—per Lord Goff.

[255] *Morris* [1984] AC 320, HL, above, paras 2.14–2.20.

[256] *Chan Man-sin v A-G of Hong Kong* [1988] 1 All ER 1, above, para 2.127; *Hilton* [1997] Crim LR 662.

Theft of bank balances[257]

2.160   A credit balance in a bank account and a contractual right to overdraw the account are things in action belonging to the customer. If D dishonestly draws a cheque on V's account and causes the credit balance to be reduced or eliminated, or the overdraft facility to be reduced or exhausted, he appropriates the thing in action. In *Kohn*,[258] which decided these points, D's convictions of theft on other counts were quashed because the account on which the cheques were drawn was already overdrawn beyond the agreed limit: there was nothing in the account to steal. It would seem that today,[259] whatever the position then, D might be convicted of an attempt—it is the same in principle as attempting to steal from an empty pocket. D would of course be liable for fraud under the 2006 Act by making a false representation.

2.161   It is important to realize that the item of property being stolen in such cases is the credit balance owned by V (ie his right to sue the bank for the debt they owe him). In some cases the Crown has circumvented problems of whether there was a thing in action (and indeed whether it belonged to another), by charging attempted theft of the cash from the bank. In *Hendricks*,[260] the Court of Appeal upheld a conviction for attempted theft of £41,000 where D had paid a stolen cheque into his account and then sought to withdraw £41,000 in cash from that account.

Theft of cheques

2.162   Before 1968 the courts seem to have had no difficulty in holding that a person could steal a cheque or obtain it by false pretences.[261] Since 1968 courts and commentators alike have tended to consider the question of obtaining cheques primarily as one of obtaining a thing in action, apparently losing sight of the fact that cheques were undoubtedly the subject of theft and obtaining by false pretences before there was any possibility of committing an offence by stealing or obtaining a thing in action as such.[262] An alternative approach was to treat the cheque as 'a piece of paper'. In *Preddy*. Lord Goff noted that it does belong to V but said that D would not be guilty because he had no intention permanently to deprive— he knew that the cheque form would, after presentation, be returned to V via his bank (or at least be available for V's collection).[263] Since the House was not required to decide whether D might be guilty of obtaining this item of property, it is submitted that this was

---

[257] See also the discussion above, para 2.111–2.119.
[258] (1979) 69 Cr App R 395, CA. cf *Forsyth* [1997] Crim LR.
[259] Criminal Attempts Act 1981, s 1.
[260] [2003] EWCA Crim 1040.
[261] *Pople* [1951] 1 KB 53, sub nom *Smith* [1950] 2 All ER 679. See also *Essex* (1857) 7 Cox CC 384, CCCR (conviction quashed on other grounds); *Hudson* [1943] KB 458, CCA; and *Arnold* [1997] 4 All ER 1, [1997] Crim LR 833. D was convicted of stealing a valuable security, a bill of exchange, signed by V, creating a thing in action which V could never own, but was nevertheless, property belonging to him.
[262] This trend seems to have begun with *Duru* [1973] 3 All ER 715 and continued through the decision of the House of Lord in *Preddy* [1996] AC 815, [1996] 3 All ER 481. The House at last rejected the erroneous notion that D obtains a thing in action from V when he induces him to draw a cheque in his favour; but it did not (and was not called on to) recognize that, though D does not obtain a thing in action from V, he obtains something more than a piece of paper from him. Lord Goff's statements are clearly *obiter* on the matter. See also *Chitty on Contracts* (29th edn, 2004) 34.003.
[263] This assumes they will all be retained for V. Modern practice is not to do so.

obiter (as well as wrong) but the Court of Appeal in *Graham*[264] treated it as ratio and in *Clark*[265] held that it was bound by that decision. So at present a cheque form cannot be stolen or obtained.

The arguments about whether there was theft of a 'thing in action' or a 'piece of paper' have **2.163** obscured the fact that the cheque form may be a 'valuable security' capable of being stolen. As acknowledged in the Larceny Act 1916,[266] this is something tangible (something that could be stolen from the person or from a house), not a mere piece of paper, any more than a key is just a piece of metal or a swipe card is a piece of plastic, or a theatre or railway ticket a piece of pasteboard. The physical thing—the cheque—has special properties.[267] It is not any piece of paper which will cause, say, a bank clerk to hand over £1,000; but a cheque will do that. Of course the cheque *is* (i) a piece of paper which (ii) *creates* a thing in action but it is also (certainly if given for value) (iii) a valuable security. The Theft Act 1968 does not specifically refer to valuable securities as property which may be stolen or obtained, any more than it refers to title deeds to land, or dogs, or other things which the Larceny Acts had to mention expressly because they could not be stolen at common law. There is no need to refer to any of these, because they are all 'property', as widely defined for the purposes of theft and obtaining by s 4(1) of the 1968 Act. Just as a dog or title deeds may be stolen, so may a valuable security; and that means, not the thing in action, nor a mere piece of paper, but the instrument, the physical thing with certain writing on it.[268]

It is important to note that not all cheques do create things in action. An action on the **2.164** cheque will lie only if it is given for valuable consideration—ie, any consideration sufficient to support a simple contract or an antecedent liability.[269] If D induces V to make him a gift of a cheque for £50, that cheque does not create any thing in action—but it is still a cheque and, it is submitted, a valuable security.[270] Unless V stops it, the cheque will enable D to deprive V of £50. When D gets his hands on it, he has a valuable, tangible thing in his possession. It is worth noting that, because a cheque need not be a thing in action, it is immaterial that the drawer's promise is voidable for fraud.[271] The cheque remains a valuable security because it is an effective key to the drawer's bank account. When D obtains the

---

[264] [1997] 1 Cr App R 302.

[265] [2001] Crim LR 572, [2001] EWCA Crim 884. The court did not refer to the decision in *Arnold* [1997] 4 All ER 1, 15, where the court had stated that 'there is a good reason for the application of s 6(1) if the intention of the transferee at the time of the appropriation is that the document should find its way back to the transferor only after all the benefit to the transferor has been lost or removed as a result of its use.'

[266] Inter alia, ss 13 (larceny in dwelling-houses), 14 (larceny from the person), and 32 (false pretences).

[267] 'A cheque is not a piece of paper and no more. . . . It is a piece of paper with certain special characteristics' *Kohn* (1979) 69 Cr App R 395 at 409, per Lord Lane CJ. See also *Chitty on Contracts* (29th edn, 2004) para 21.073.

[268] It is certain that the wide definition of property in the Theft Act 1968 was intended to include anything which could be stolen under the Larceny Acts or at common law.

[269] Bills of Exchange Act 1882, s 27(1). cf *Davis* (1988) 88 Cr App R 347, [1988] Crim LR 762, CA.

[270] In *Yates* (1827) 1 Moody 170 it was held that an unstamped order was not a valuable security because it would have been illegal for the drawer to pay out on it; but there is nothing illegal in honouring a cheque given without consideration. A document authorizing the payment of money, which such a cheque does, is a valuable security: Theft Act 1968, s 20(3).

[271] In *Danger* (1857) 7 Cox CC 303. Lord Campbell CJ said at p 309: 'We should not have given weight to the argument, that even in the prisoner's hands it was not a valuable security by reason of the fraud which would prevent him from enforcing it.'

document he has acquired a tangible thing which is of real value to him, and to V, who has parted with it. In *Kohn*[272] the Court of Appeal held that where D dishonestly drew a cheque on a company's account for his own purposes he was guilty of two thefts—(i) of the cheque and (ii) of the thing in action consisting in the company's bank account which the honouring of the cheque destroyed in whole or in part.[273]

2.165 When D has dishonestly obtained a cheque from V, he usually acquires a voidable right of action against V on the cheque. When he presents the cheque and it is honoured, any right of action he had against V terminates. If his account is overdrawn and the cheque merely reduces his indebtedness, the property is extinguished. If D's account is in credit he has converted his own property (his right of action against V) into another form. The indebtedness of D's bank to D has been increased by the amount of the cheque and D's thing in action is now his right to sue his own bank for the credit balance represented by the cheque. This new thing in action belongs, in law if not in equity, to D. But, V's own bank balance, a thing in action belonging to him, is debited with the amount of the cheque. D has not obtained anything from V[274] but it seems that, by his use of the cheque—the 'key' to V's bank balance—he has appropriated that balance, or V's right to overdraw, as the case may be. Since *Gomez*, it is no longer an objection that D's dealing with the cheque signed by V was authorized by V. It is not theft of the increased balance in D's account since that was never property belonging to another, but it is clearly theft of a different thing in action which does belong to V, namely V's credit balance (or right to overdraw if such a facility exists), at his bank.[275] On presenting the cheque,[276] D has assumed V's right to destroy that part of V's property.

2.166 An objection to a conviction of theft in a case like *Kohn* is that, almost inevitably, the cheque is a forgery and it is settled law that the honouring of a forged cheque, and the consequent debiting of the customer's account, is a nullity;[277] so that (i) in fact the thing is not 'appropriated', and (ii) there is (if the drawer of the cheque knows the law) no intention permanently to deprive. But the answer accepted by the Privy Council[278] is (i) that 'Any assumption by a person of [a right] of an owner amounts to an appropriation' and the

---

[272] (1979) 69 Cr App R 395.

[273] *Arlidge and Parry on Fraud* 3–010, criticize the case because 'the court appears to have treated the cheques as intangible property'; but it is submitted that Lane CJ distinguished clearly between the 'cheque counts' and the 'thing in action counts' (p 410). The relevance, for the former counts, of the paper ceasing 'to be a thing in action' was that the tangible thing, the paper, changed its character on being stamped, so that the thing appropriated was (like a melted-down key) not the thing returned to the owner. While both thefts are undoubtedly committed where Vs account is in credit, it would be wrong to punish D twice for what is, in substance, a single offence. If V's account is overdrawn, this in no way impairs the conviction for theft of the cheque. The real value of the valuable security is the factor which ought to be taken into account in sentencing, not the value of a mere piece of paper.

[274] This is the effect of *Preddy* [1986] AC 815, [1996] 3 All ER 481, HL.

[275] *Williams (Roy)* [2001] 1 Cr App R 362, [2001] Crim LR 253.

[276] *Ngan* [1998] 1 Cr App R 331.

[277] *Tai Hing Cotton Mill Ltd v Liu Chong Hing Bank* [1986] AC 80, [1985] 2 All ER 947, PC.

[278] *Chan Man-sin v A-G of Hong Kong*, above, para 2.127. The Board held that the assumption of 'a right' was enough, following *Morris;* but the drawer of the forged cheque assumes the right to destroy (in whole or part) the credit balance and that is surely an assumption of all the rights of the owner of the balance, or the part of it alleged to be stolen. cf *Wille* (1987) 86 Cr App R 296, CA.

drawing of a cheque on the account is undoubtedly a right of the owner of the account, and (ii) D's intention to 'treat the thing as his own to dispose of regardless of the other's rights' is a sufficient intention permanently to deprive.

In this type of case the theft is of a somewhat artificial nature because the victim of the theft, **2.167** the owner (account holder), never loses anything. The loss falls on the bank against which no theft is committed, unless the customer has 'held out' the rogue as having authority to draw the cheque. It also makes little sense to talk about an 'intention' permanently to deprive in the natural meaning of the phrase because 'the thief' is unlikely to have any knowledge of the effect of forgery, 'holding out', or any other considerations which, in law, determine whether there will be any actual deprivation of the owner of the cheque if he carries out his intention. The intention 'to treat the thing as his own to dispose of is, however, easily recognized.

The question whether D 'procuring' V to make such a transfer might amount to an appro- **2.168** priation was considered above, para 2.111. It is important here to consider whether in such a case there is *property* which is capable of being stolen. First, as we have noted in connection with cheques, the credit balance in V's account at the beginning of the transaction is undoubtedly property belonging to V. When the transfer takes place, that thing in action belonging to V, to the value of £X, has not gone *anywhere*, as *Preddy* decides, but it has, nevertheless, gone for ever—it is extinguished. If it is a loan transaction, as most of the pre-*Preddy* cases were, D may have had an intention to repay, but that would have been an intention to create a new thing in action. Where a loan of cash is obtained by deception, the intention of the borrower to repay may possibly negative dishonesty but it does not negative the intention permanently to deprive. The principle is the same whether we are concerned with cash or things in action. The difficulty lies if theft is charged—then it is necessary to find an appropriation. If D or his agent caused the diminution in that balance, it is submitted that D stole it. As argued above, if D was paid by a cheque which he presented and which was honoured, it seems clear that he did appropriate V's balance. Unless the processing of the cheque was fully automated, the actions of one or more persons would intervene, but these were in effect innocent agents.

The position is, on the present view of the Court of Appeal, the same where funds are **2.169** transferred by telegraphic transfer or CHAPS order. If the process is initiated by D as in *Hilton*[279] where D had direct control of a bank account belonging to a charity and he gave instructions for the transfer of the charity's funds in order to settle his personal debts, D steals the thing in action when the funds were transferred. The position is less clear where D does not have control of the bank account and does not personally initiate the process by which V's account is debited (as was the norm in the mortgage fraud situation). Where D, by deception, induces V to agree to lend him £X and V does so by instructing his bank to transfer the funds by telegraphic transfer or CHAPS order, D procures the whole course of events by his deception. However, it is questionable whether D can be guilty of theft: the voluntary intervening acts of V break the chain of causation. D may not even be aware of

---

[279] [1997] 2 Cr App R 445.

the process by which the transfer of funds is effected.[280] The Court of Appeal recently affirmed this view in *Briggs*[281] considered above 2.120.

2.170 The second property which D may have stolen in such cases is the credit balance acquired by D. This could not be property belonging to V before the deception because it did not exist. It does not follow that it did not become property belonging to V at the moment of its creation. This question was not in issue in *Preddy*. D is the primary owner of the thing in action but it does not follow that no one else has any proprietary interest in it. In *West Deutsche Landesbank Grozentrale v Islington London Borough Council*[282] Lord Browne-Wilkinson said, 'Although it is difficult to find clear authority for the proposition, when property has been obtained by fraud equity imposes a constructive trust on the fraudulent recipient: The property is recoverable and traceable in equity.' The thing in action is the proceeds of V's property.

2.171 In *Governor of Brixton Prison, ex p Levin*,[283] D, a dishonest computer operator, caused V's bank account in the United States to be debited and the account of D's accomplice, E, with a different US bank to be credited. The question was whether E's drawing on this credit would have amounted to theft if done in England. Beldam LJ said[284] that the property appropriated was not the thing in action consisting in V's bank balance but different property; yet V retained, until the balance was restored, an interest in the funds representing it. If so, in a case like *Preddy* D has, in the words of s 3(1) of the 1968 Act, 'come by the property (innocently or not [in this case, not!]) without stealing it' and therefore 'any later assumption of a right to it by keeping or dealing with it as owner' amounts to an appropriation of property belonging to V. It does not appear whether any argument on these lines as canvassed in *Preddy* but, if it is right, it is possible that a conviction for theft could have been substituted in some of these cases.

No theft by breach of copyright

2.172 It is thought that theft would not be committed by a mere breach of copyright. If D, in writing a book, were to copy out large sections of another book in which V owned the copyright, this would be a breach of copyright but it would not be theft. It is an assumption of a right of the owner and so might now be regarded as an appropriation, but there would seem to be no evidence of an intent to deprive V permanently of his property. D is not treating the thing as his own 'to dispose of'. It would be more analogous to making a merely temporary use of another's chattel.[285]

---

[280] cf *Caresana* [1996] Crim LR 667 and commentary and *Naviede* [1997] Crim LR 'We are not satisfied that a misrepresentation which persuades the account holder to direct payment out of his account is an assumption of the rights of the owner such as to amount to an appropriation of his rights within s 3 (1) of the 1968 Act'.

[281] [2004] EWCA Crim 3662, [2004] Crim LR 455.

[282] [1996] 2 All ER 961 at 996.

[283] [1994] 4 All ER 350, DC.

[284] p 364.

[285] If D is regarded as dishonest, and his conduct is regarded as making a false representation, he may be liable for fraud if he also intends to gain or to cause loss to V or to expose V to a risk of loss. See generally Ladie, Prescott, and Vitoria, *The Modern Law of Copyright and Design* (3rd edn, 2000) ch 40.34.

In the light of the broad notion of appropriation followed since *Gomez*, it may be that the **2.173**
theft is committed where and when D does some act which only the owner could properly
do; but that it continues to the time when and place where it affects the property.

Miscellaneous categories not regarded as property

Confidential information

Confidential information is not property. Thus, an undergraduate who unlawfully acquires **2.174**
and reads or makes a copy of an examination question paper may not be convicted of
stealing intangible property, namely confidential information belonging to the University.[286]
It follows that the wrongful acquisition and use of trade secrets is not theft.[287] While the
'theft' of information is a serious problem, particularly in the form of industrial espionage,
for which the civil law may not provide adequate remedies, it seems, as Griew observes,[288]
that the Theft Act is not the appropriate instrument to deal with this specialized kind
of mischief. The Law Commission has reviewed the possibility of introducing a specific
offence of the misuse of trade secrets,[289] and in view of the significance and prevalence of
the problem, legislation would seem desirable. The Law Commission's proposal was to
criminalize non-consensual use or disclosure of another's trade secrets.[290]

Services

Services do not constitute property, so it is not theft for D dishonestly to walk off without **2.175**
paying for his haircut. This is particularly important in relation to s 11 of the Fraud Act
2006, discussed below para 3.188.

Electricity

On the face of it all property is capable of appropriation but there were formerly doubts **2.176**
whether electricity was capable of appropriation. The dishonest use, wasting, or diverting
of electricity was a separate offence under the Larceny Acts and the position was preserved
by s 13 of the Theft Act. The CLRC observed that, 'This has to be a separate offence
because owing to its nature electricity is excluded from the definition of stealing in . . .
[s] 1(1) of the [Act].'[291] The Committee's view was endorsed in *Low v Blease*[292] where it was
held that, electricity not being property capable of appropriation, D could not be convicted

---

[286] *Oxford v Moss* [1979] Crim LR 119. But might he have been convicted of stealing the question paper
on the ground that the 'virtue' had gone out of it when he put it back? Below, paras 2.324–5 and commentary
at [1979] Crim LR 120.

[287] Griew 2–21, 2–83; Williams, *TBCL* 688–9, 722–3.

[288] Griew 2–25. See further R Hammond, 'Theft of Information' (1984) 100 LQR 252; JT Cross,
'Protecting Confidential Information under the Criminal Law of Theft and Fraud' (1991) OJLS 264; A
Coleman, *Intellectual Property Law* (1994); A Endeshaw, 'Theft of Information Revisited' (1997) J Bus Law
187. See also L Weinreib, 'Information and Property' (1988) 38 UTLJ 117, and the Canadian Supreme Court
in *Stewart* (1988) 50 DLR 1.

[289] See Law Com Consultation Paper No 150, *Legislating the Criminal Code: Misuses of Trade Secrets*
(1997), and the review by J Hull, 'Stealing Secrets: A Review of the Law Commission Consultation Paper'
[1998] Crim LR 246. For a recent review of the criminal law's general protection for intellectual property see
C Davies, 'Protection of Intellectual Property—A Myth?' [2004] J Crim Law 398.

[290] The suggestion to extend the scope of the Fraud Bill to include dishonesty towards trade secrets was
rejected by the government. See ch 3 below.

[291] Cmnd 2977, para 85.

[292] [1975] Crim LR 513, DC.

of burglary in entering premises and making a telephone call from them.[293] Heat is a thing of value, as anyone paying the bills well knows, but it seems that it would not be theft to assume the right to heat belonging to V, by diverting V's hot water so as to warm D's premises.[294] The heat is energy (as is electricity) but is not property

The necessity for specific property

2.177 We have noted that theft can be committed only of some specified property[295] but it is not necessary that the property be 'specific' in the sense in which that term is used in the Sale of Goods Act 1979.[296] It would be enough under the Theft Act that D had appropriated an unascertained part of an ascertained whole though such property would not be 'specific' for the purposes of the Sale of Goods Act. If D is charged with stealing five out of a consignment of ten tins and it emerges at the trial that he was guilty of stealing all ten, he may be convicted of stealing the five.[297] Conversely, if he is charged with stealing ten tins and it emerges that he stole only five of them, he may be convicted of stealing the five. It is not an objection that it is impossible to point to the five which have been stolen.

2.178 In *Tideswell*,[298] V's servant, E, weighed a quantity of ashes into trucks for D, but entered a less quantity in V's books and charged D for that less quantity. It was held that D was guilty of larceny of the balance of the ashes over those for which he had paid. D's contract with V was not to buy the whole bulk of the ashes at so much per ton, but only to buy such as he might want at that price. The court took the view that E had no authority to pass the property except in those ashes for which he charged; that the balance therefore remained V's property, and it was immaterial that it was not distinguishable from the bulk.[299] It is submitted that this is theft under the Theft Act. Indeed, it would be more accurate in such a case to charge D with theft of the whole; for it is difficult to see how property passes in any of the ashes since 'Where there is a contract for the sale of unascertained goods no property in the goods is transferred to the buyer unless and until the goods are ascertained.'[300] The goods appear never to have been ascertained in that case.[301] On the other hand, it may be said that, while there is an appropriation of the whole quantity (an *actus reus*), D has a claim of right in respect of the quantity for which he has paid or agreed to pay. Such reasoning

---

[293] See *P* (2000) 11 Aug, CA, No 0003586 Y5, where D entered his neighbour's property as a trespasser and made phone calls to premium rate sex chat lines.

[294] *Clinton v Cahill* [1998] NI 200. Nor is it theft of the hot water, unless all, or substantially all, of the heat is exhausted, so as to deprive the water of its 'virtue'.

[295] *Navvabi* (1986) 83 Cr App R 271, above, para 2.123.

[296] Section 62. See *Chitty on Contracts* (29th edn, 2004), 43.002.

[297] cf *Pilgram v Rice-Smith* [1977] 2 All ER 658, above, para 2.89; *Davis* [1988] Crim LR 762, CA, commentary at 765.

[298] [1905] 2 KB 273. See further *Chitty on Contracts* (29th edn, 2004) para 43.163.

[299] In *Lacis v Cashmarts* [1969] 2 QB 400 at 411 (discussed in [1972B] CLJ at 204–8), the Divisional Court thought it an unavoidable and apparently fatal difficulty on a larceny charge that it was impossible to distinguish the goods alleged to be stolen from other goods lawfully taken. The court thought there would be no difficulty under the Theft Act. It is thought that it is as much, or as little, a difficulty for theft as for larceny; and that it is not a real difficulty in either case. The court seems to have overlooked *Tideswell*. Difficulties do arise, of course, if there is a charge of handling and the stolen goods cannot be identified.

[300] Sale of Goods Act 1979, s 6.

[301] cf *Re Wait* [1927] 1 Ch 606.

was not, however, used in *Middleton*[302] where D was convicted of stealing the whole sum of money although he was entitled to a less sum.

A more intractable problem than that of *Tideswell* is presented by *Tomlin*.[303] D was the **2.179** manager of V's shoe shop. Between stocktaking in March 1953 and September 1953 goods to the value of £420 had gone from the shop without the proceeds of sale being accounted for. D's conviction for embezzlement of that sum was upheld. The court[304] rejected the argument that there could be no conviction for embezzling a general deficiency and that embezzlement of specific sums on specific dates must be proved. Clearly in cases of this kind it is virtually impossible to prove that D took the money for a particular pair of shoes and put it straight into his pocket; and it is submitted that the defence that there can be no theft of a general deficiency would fail under the Theft Act. D has not in fact appropriated 'a deficiency'; he has appropriated a sum of money, no doubt on a number of different occasions, but between specific dates. Thus far *Tomlin* should present no problems; but a further point which was not argued is not easily solved. On the evidence it is very difficult to see how the jury could have been satisfied beyond reasonable doubt that D took money and not shoes.[305] If D has appropriated shoes, it is difficult to see how he can properly be convicted on an indictment alleging that he stole money, even to the same value. If the jury are satisfied that he took the shoes or the money it may well be that, in practice, they will convict him of stealing the money if that is what he is charged with and they think it the more likely event; but strictly speaking, they ought not to do so unless satisfied beyond reasonable doubt; and, if the defence is raised, it would seem that the judge would be bound so to direct the jury.

There are other instances of dishonest profit making which may be morally indistin- **2.180** guishable from theft but which are not punishable under the Act because of absence of an appropriation of any specific thing. For example, an employer withholds part of his servant's wages as a contribution to a pension fund and dishonestly omits to make that contribution. However, the employer will probably now be guilty of fraud.

Finally, there is the example discussed *obiter* in *Tideswell*: **2.181**

Suppose the owner of a flock of sheep were to offer to sell, and a purchaser agreed to buy, the whole flock at so much a head, the owner leaving it to his bailiff to count the sheep and ascertain the exact number of the flock, and subsequently the purchaser was to fraudulently arrange with the bailiff that whereas there were in fact thirty sheep they should be counted as twenty-five and the purchaser should be charged with twenty-five only, there would be no larceny, because the property would have passed to the purchaser before the fraudulent agreement was entered into.[306]

---

[302] (1873) LR 2 CCR 38, above, para 2.82.

[303] [1954] 2 QB 274, [1954] 2 All ER 272.

[304] Following *Balls* (1871) LR 1 CCR 328. In substance, such an indictment alleges an indefinite number of offences but it is not bad for duplicity: *Archbold* (2007) 1–144; *Cain* [1983] Crim LR 802, CA. cf *DPP v McCabe* [1992] Crim LR 885, DC.

[305] Or that he took the money before he put it into the till (embezzlement) and not after (larceny). As both types of appropriation are now theft, this problem need not be pursued.

[306] Per Lord Alverstone CJ [1905] 2 KB 273 at 277; see to the same effect, Channell J, ibid at 279.

If the property in the whole flock had passed, then it might be argued that there was no appropriation of 'property belonging to another'. The answer is that the owner retained his lien on the whole flock for the unpaid part of the true price, and that the bailiff appropriated it by delivering the sheep. Whether the property would have passed before the appropriation is, however, less clear than the learned judges appear to have thought; for, under the Sale of Goods Act 1979, s 18, r 3, where 'the seller is bound to weigh, measure, test, or *do some other act or thing* with reference to the goods for the purpose of ascertaining the price, the property does not pass until such thing be done, and the buyer has notice thereof'. The easier solution is to charge fraud under s 1 of the 2006 Act.

2.182 If the bailiff agreed to deliver the whole flock of sheep before he counted them the agreement would be a sufficient act of appropriation of V's property.[307] When the bailiff accounted to the owner for the price of 25 sheep, he would be guilty of fraud under s 1 of the 2006 Act and he and the purchaser would be guilty of a conspiracy to commit that offence.

Property 'belonging to another'

2.183 The property alleged to have been stolen must 'belong to another'. 'Belonging to another' is, however, widely defined to include almost any legally recognized interest in property. By s 5(1) of the Act:

Property shall be regarded as belonging to any person having possession or control of it, or having in it any proprietary right or interest (not being an equitable interest arising only from an agreement to transfer or grant an interest).

No theft from self by sole owner

2.184 D may be guilty of stealing his own property if another person, V, has any proprietary interest in it; but if D owns the entire proprietary interest in the thing he cannot steal it; there is no property 'belonging to another' for him to appropriate. No one can steal from himself.

2.185 The onus is on the prosecution to prove that the property in question belonged to V. Frequently this is self-evident and not a live issue, but not always. In *Marshall*[308] D obtained part-used underground tickets and travelcards from members of the public passing through railway barriers and resold them to other potential customers, so depriving London Underground Ltd (LUL) of the revenue it would have gained from the potential customers. D was convicted of theft of the part-used tickets from LUL. The court assumed that those tickets, though in the possession of the passengers, continued to belong to LUL because there was a term to that effect on the reverse of each ticket. That issue was not contested, but the existence of the term is not conclusive. The term was operative only if it was proved that reasonable steps had been taken by LUL to bring that condition to the

---

[307] cf *Rogers v Arnott*, above, para 2.74.
[308] [1998] 2 Cr App R 282, discussed by JC Smith, 'Stealing Tickets' [1998] Crim LR 723. For consideration of the case and offences that may have been committed see also K Reid and J MacLeod, 'Ticket Touts or Theft of Tickets and Related Offences' (1999) 63(6) J Crim Law 593.

notice of the 'buyer', as the passenger probably thought himself to be.[309] If he had been given sufficient notice, he was not a buyer but a mere bailee of the ticket[310]—he was in possession of a ticket belonging to LUL. If sufficient notice was not given, the ticket belonged only to the passenger who had originally purchased it, LUL had no proprietary interest in it, and D could not properly be convicted of stealing from LUL.

Abandonment

If the property belongs to no one, it cannot be stolen. If property is abandoned there can **2.186** be no theft of it. Whether an owner has abandoned his property or not is a question of the intention evinced by him in disposing of his property. If he intends to exclude others from it, he does not abandon it, though it may be clear that he intends to make no further use of it himself. So it will be theft for D to appropriate diseased carcases which V has buried on his land.[311] A householder does not abandon goods which he puts in his dustbin. Prima facie, he intends the goods for the agency which collects the refuse, so that a refuse operative (aka dustman) may be guilty of theft if he appropriates the goods knowing that he is not entitled to do so.[312] A person who loses property does not necessarily abandon it because he abandons the search for it.[313] The test is whether V[314] has evinced an intention to relinquish his *entire* interest in the property, without conferring an interest on anyone else. Of course, if D mistakenly believes that V has abandoned his interest in the property, D's appropriation cannot be theft, he does not intend to appropriate property belonging to another, he has no intent permanently to deprive, and he is not dishonest.[315] This is another aspect of the law of theft in which the courts should take their lead from the civil law relating to property, and not assume that the criminal law's determination of the issue of abandonment itself settles the civil law position.[316]

Unknown owner of property

If the prosecution are unable to establish the identity of the owner, a charge of stealing **2.187** from a person unknown should lie.[317] It will be necessary to prove that the accused knew,

---

[309] A question posed by the law of contract, to be answered by the jury, as it would formerly have been in the civil law: *Parker v South Eastern Rly Co* (1877) 2 CPD 416, CA.

[310] He was a buyer of the right to travel on the railway, a thing in action.

[311] *Edwards* (1877) 13 Cox CC 384. On abandonment see AH Hudson (1984) 100 LQR 110; 'Abandonment' in N Palmer and E McKendrick, *Interests in Property* (1993). See also the interesting recent article reviewing the law in the light of the decision in *Rostron* [2003] EWCA Crim 2206 discussing the civil and criminal law approaches to abandonment: R Hickey, 'Stealing Abandoned Goods: Possessory Title in Proceedings for Theft' (2006) 26 LS 584.

[312] *Williams v Phillips* (1957) 41 Cr App R 5, DC. The availability of theft charges in such circumstances is important in dealing with those who rummage through the refuse of celebrities for information to sell to tabloid newspapers, and those who appropriate confidential industrial or financial information from refuse.

[313] cf *Hibbert v McKiernan* [1948] 2 KB 142, DC.

[314] Lord Goddard in *Hibbert* seems to suggest that D's intentions can affect this—plainly they cannot affect the title in the goods—see Hickey, above, at 592.

[315] *Small* [1987] Crim LR 777, CA, below, para 2.271; *Ellerman's Wilson Line Ltd v Webster* [1952] 1 Lloyd's Rep 179, DC.

[316] See Hickey above, for a detailed analysis of the issue.

[317] cf *Gregory* [1972] 2 All ER 861, below, para 13.100 (handling stolen goods belonging to a person unknown); *Pike v Morrison* [1981] Crim LR 492, DC (criminal damage—name of owner an immaterial averment).

or believed that by taking reasonable steps he could find out, who was the owner.[318] A mis-statement of the owner is not a material averment if the accused is not prejudiced thereby.[319]

Property of the deceased

2.188 In *Sullivan and Ballion*,[320] the defendants had appropriated the £50,000 they found on their friend who had died of natural causes in their company the night before. The deceased was a drug dealer and the money represented his takings. Dismissing the charge of theft of the money, the trial judge ruled that the property did not 'belong to another' when it was taken.[321] As pointed out in the commentary to the case, the property must have belonged to someone other than the thieves (who had no rights to it). Since there may be a conviction of theft of property of a person unknown, it follows that it is enough to show that the property must have belonged to someone and that the defendants knew it belonged to someone other than themselves. The money did not belong to those who had purchased drugs from the deceased (in this case a group known as 'The Firm') because, as the judge held, they had parted with their entire proprietary interest in the money; but the proprietary interest can hardly have vanished into thin air—it passed to the deceased or, if he was acting as an agent, his principal. At the time of the alleged theft, the money must have belonged either to D's principal, if any; or to those entitled under his (or their) will or intestacy; or, if they did not exist, to the Crown as *bona vacantia*.[322] There remains the difficulty in establishing the defendants' *mens rea*. If the defendants supposed, or may have supposed, that the property belonged to no one and could be taken by the first person to come across it, then they are not guilty. But if they knew it must belong to someone other than themselves, it is immaterial that they did not know who that person was.

Ownership, possession, and control

2.189 Since the law protects all interests in property, where two or more persons have different interests in the same property, any one of them may steal the property from the other or others by appropriating the other's interest in it. As was the case with larceny,[323] an owner in the strict sense can be guilty of stealing his own property from one who has mere possession or custody of it. For example, D pledges his watch with V as security for a loan but

---

[318] See s 2(1)(c), below, para 2.283.
[319] *Etim v Hatfield* [1975] Crim LR 234.
[320] [2002] Crim LR 758.
[321] Hale, *Pleas of the Crown* (1736) i. 514: 'If A dies intestate, and the goods of the intestate are stolen before administration committed, it is felony, and the goods shall be supposed to be bona episcopi de D. ordinary of the diocese, and if he made B his executor the goods shall be supposed bona B tho he hath not proved the will, and they need not show specifically their title as ordinary or executor because it is of their own possession, in which case a general indictment as well as a general action of trespass lies without naming themselves as executor or ordinary, and so for an administrator'. East, *Pleas of the Crown* (1803) ii. 652 and *Russell on Crime* (2nd edn, 1843) ii. 99 state the law in similar terms.
[322] A suggested direction for such cases is 'Before you can convict the defendants of theft, you must be sure (i) that the deceased died in possession of the money; (ii) that D took it for their own use; (iii) knowing that the money was not theirs to take; and that it must have belonged to someone other than themselves; (iv) intending to deprive whoever was entitled to the money permanently of it; and (v) that they did so dishonestly'. See commentary, n 320 above.
[323] cf *Rose v Matt* [1951] 1 KB 810, DC.

takes it back again without repaying V and without his consent. This is an appropriation by D of property which belongs to V for the purposes of the section. The position is precisely the same where D bids for a car at an auction, it is knocked down to him, and he then takes the car without paying the auctioneer, V, and without his (V's) consent.[324] The car became D's property on the fall of the hammer but V retained his seller's lien for the price and D has therefore appropriated V's property.

The owner may steal from his bailee at will. Though he has a right to terminate the bail- **2.190** ment at any time, he will be guilty of theft if he simply dishonestly appropriates the bailed chattel. It is only in exceptional cases that the problem will arise, because it will usually be clear that the bailor had a claim of right to recover possession. In *Turner (No 2)*,[325] however, D, who had delivered his car to V to be repaired, took it back, dishonestly intending not to pay for the repairs which V had carried out. In truth, V probably was not a mere bailee at will, having a lien on the car. But the judge directed the jury that they were not concerned with liens and so the Court of Appeal had to decide the appeal on the basis that there was no lien. An argument that V's possession as a bailee at will was insufficient was rejected. The court said there was no ground for qualifying the words 'possession or control' in any way.

It looks more than a little odd that, where D has a better right to possession than V, he can **2.191** nevertheless commit theft by the exercise (however dishonestly) of that 'right'. It might have been thought that a thing does not belong to a possessor, V, as against D who has an immediate right to take possession from him. Possibly *Turner (No 2)* may be explained by holding that a bailor has no right, even in the civil law, to take back the chattel bailed, without notice to the bailee at will.[326]

Suppose D's car is stolen by V, and D later finds the car standing outside V's house (or the **2.192** house of a bona-fide purchaser, V). D has, of course, a right to take it back. But suppose he does not know this, and thinks that a court order is necessary to enable him lawfully to resume possession. Believing that he has no right in law to do so (ie dishonestly), he takes the car. According to *Turner (No 2)*, he is guilty of theft. If he were convicted and the court asked to exercise its power to order the car to be restored to the person entitled to it,[327] the incongruous result would be that the car should be given to the convicted thief, who was and always had been the person entitled to it. Perhaps the decision in *Turner (No 2)* would not be pressed so far.[328]

---

[324] cf *Dennant v Skinner and Collom* [1948] 2 KB 164, Hallett J.

[325] [1971] 2 All ER 441, [1971] Crim LR 373, discussed in [1972B] CLJ at 215–17. Described by Williams as 'one of the most extraordinary cases under the the Theft Act': *TBCL* s. 33.8. It is hard to believe the decision represents the law. *Arlidge and Parry on Fraud*, para 1.14, regard the decision as 'absurd' because D did nothing dishonest (in the objective sense they attribute to the word, 'dishonestly'), however dishonest his state of mind.

[326] Insofar as *Turner* decided that V's possession need not be lawful, it is obviously right and was approved on this point in *Kelly* [1998] 3 All ER 741 at 750. It may be theft to take the stolen property from a thief; the law protects his possession. But the point in *Turner* is that D (in the absence of a lien) had every right to take his own property back. If the owner takes his property from a thief who is unlawfully detaining it, does he steal it if he mistakenly thinks it is someone else's property?

[327] See below, para 14.27.

[328] *Meredith* [1973] Crim LR 253 (Judge Da Cunha) seems inconsistent but right in principle (no theft of impounded car from police because police had no right to retain it).

2.193   Similar problems arise where D retains possession as well as ownership and V has the lower interest which is described as 'control' in the Act. D, an employer, entrusts his employee, V, with goods for use in the course of his employment. D continues both to own and to possess the goods; but, if he dishonestly deprives V of control, he may, to the same extent as the bailor at will, be guilty of theft. It was larceny at common law for a master who had entrusted money to his servant to retake it, intending to charge the hundred for an alleged theft. So if today an employer takes his own property from the custody of his employee, intending to claim against his insurers for its loss, he might be held to have stolen it. The more natural charge would be one of fraud or attempted fraud under the 2006 Act.

2.194   Where the property belongs to more than one person, as may easily occur under s 5(1), and D appropriates it for himself, it follows that he may be convicted of stealing it from any one, or all, of the persons to whom it belongs. V lets a lawnmower on hire to X who hands it over to his employee, Z, to mow the lawn. V remains the owner, X remains in possession as bailee and Z has control. If D now appropriates the lawnmower for himself, he commits theft from all three of them. If, in order to appropriate the lawnmower, he uses force on Z, he commits robbery from V, X, and Z.[329]

2.195   D may appropriate property which belongs to V in any of the senses described in s 5(1). It does not matter that V's interest is precarious or that it may be short-lived; wild birds reared by V may belong to V although they may 'betake themselves to the woods and fields' as soon as they are old enough to fly,[330] and flowers left on a grave remain the property of the leaver.[331] Nor does it matter that someone exists who has a better right to the property than V: a thief may steal from a thief.[332] This is a well-established principle. It does not matter that it is impossible for the victim (the original thief) to assert his title in a civil court: public policy which prevents the wrongdoer from enforcing a property right should have no application to criminal proceedings brought in the name of the Crown. The criminal law is concerned with keeping the Queen's peace, not vindicating individual property rights.

Equitable interests

2.196   The clear implication of s 5(1) is that equitable as well as legal interests are generally protected.[333] 'An equitable interest arising only from an agreement to transfer or grant an interest' is the only recognized exception. Where property is subject to a trust it 'belongs to' both the trustee (legal interest) and the beneficiary (equitable interest). A third party who appropriates it steals it from both of them; and the one may steal it from the other. The question whether V has an equitable interest in property alleged to have been stolen from him may involve difficult issues of civil law.

---

[329] See s 8 of the Act. At common law, it would have been robbery only from Z, and similarly under the Larceny Acts. cf *Harding* (1929) 21 Cr App R 166.

[330] cf *Shickle* (1868) LR 1 CCR 158.

[331] According to *Bustler v State* 184 SE 2d 24 (1944) (SC of Tennessee). cf *Edwards and Stacey* (1877) 13 Cox CC 384.

[332] cf *Clarke*, referred to at [1956] Crim LR 369–70; *Meech* [1974] QB 549, [1973] 3 All ER 939, CA.

[333] But cf *A-G's Reference (No 1 of 1985)* [1986] 2 All ER 219 at 226, below, para 2.246 suggesting that some equitable interests are not protected.

In *Clowes (No 2)*[334] the question was whether investors, who had subscribed money for **2.197** investment in gilts by a company controlled by D, had an equitable interest in certain assets of the company. In deciding that they did, the court found it necessary to consider various Chancery decisions and to rely on the principle, inter alia, that where a trustee mixes trust money with his own, the beneficiaries have a first charge on, and therefore an equitable interest in, the mixed fund. A person dishonestly withdrawing money from the fund may therefore be guilty of stealing it from the beneficiaries. Changes in the civil law may affect the reach of the law of theft. So a decision that the payer of money under a mistake of fact retains an equitable interest in the money so paid and is not, as was previously thought, a mere creditor, means that the dishonest appropriation of the money by the payee may be theft according to general principles, removing the necessity for reliance on the tortuous provisions of s 5(4).[335]

The parenthesis in s 5(1) excludes from the protection of the law 'an equitable interest **2.198** arising only from an agreement to transfer or grant an interest'. If D, the owner of land, enters into a specifically enforceable contract to sell it to V, an equitable interest in the land passes to V, and D is, in some respects, a trustee of the property for V. If D were to sell the land to a third party, it might have been held, but for the parenthesis, that this was theft of the land under s 4(2)(a).[336] If, after D has contracted to sell to V, a third party, E, enters on the land and appropriates something forming part of the land by severing it, this will be theft from D but, because of the parenthesis, it will not be theft from V. An equitable interest similarly passes to the buyer under a specifically enforceable agreement to buy shares.[337] The seller who dishonestly resells is protected. It does not follow that the buyer's contractual right is not a thing in action capable of being stolen.[338]

A contract for the sale of goods may be a sale or an agreement to sell. If it is a sale, the legal **2.199** interest passes to the buyer and a resale by the seller who remains in possession may thus constitute theft from the buyer.[339] If, however, it is an agreement to sell, the buyer usually acquires neither a legal, nor (since contracts for the sale of goods are generally not specifically enforceable) an equitable interest,[340] so the provision will not generally be required in such cases. It may be, however, that in the exceptional case where a contract for the sale of goods is specifically enforceable, an equitable interest does pass to the buyer before the legal ownership does so. Again, the parenthesis makes it clear that there can be no theft from the buyer. The reason for the parenthesis probably is that an action for breach of contract is a sufficient sanction against a person who, having contracted to sell to X, resells in breach of contract to Y. Such conduct is, perhaps, not generally thought to be more

---

[334] [1994] 2 All ER 316. On which see M Davies, 'After *R v Clowes (No 2)*: An Act of Theft Empowered a Jury Impoverished?' (1997) J Crim Law 99 commenting that with a trial based on complex legal issues the effect is to reduce the issues that fall to be determined by the jury, potentially displacing the importance of eg s 2(1)(a) of Theft Act 1968.

[335] Below, para 2.250.

[336] Above para 2.135.

[337] M Arden (ed), *Buckley on the Companies Acts* ch 21.

[338] See [1979] Crim LR 220 at 224–5.

[339] See above, para 2.181.

[340] *Re Wait* [1927] 1 Ch 606, CA.

reprehensible than other breaches of contract. It is probably incidental that an appropriation by a third party is not a theft from the buyer; but this is not serious since it is inevitably a theft from the seller.

Co-owners and partners

2.200 D and V are co-owners of a car, D sells the car without V's consent. Since V has a proprietary right in the car, it belongs to him under s 5(1). The position is precisely the same where a partner dishonestly appropriates the partnership property. Whether or not his conduct constitutes the tort of conversion, it is theft.[341]

Trustee and beneficiary

2.201 Conversion by a trustee was a special offence under s 21 of the Larceny Act 1916. Now it is ordinary theft.[342] The beneficiary, by definition, has a proprietary interest in the trust property and any dishonest appropriation of it by the trustee is theft. Section 5(2) provides:

> Where property is subject to a trust, the persons to whom it belongs shall be regarded as including any person having a right to enforce the trust, and an intention to defeat the trust shall be regarded accordingly as an intention to deprive of the property any person having that right.

2.202 Where the trust is a charitable one, its object is to effect some purpose beneficial to the public, rather than to benefit particular individuals. Such trusts are enforceable by the Attorney-General, and an appropriation of the trust property by a charitable trustee will, accordingly, be regarded as theft from that officer. When a donor puts money into a collecting box for charity, the property passes at that point. The dishonest appropriation of money which has been put into a collecting box for the benefit of a charity is theft from the Attorney-General, as well as from the person in possession of the box and money. Each has a proprietary interest in the money.[343]

2.203 Trusts for the purpose of erecting or maintaining monuments[344] or maintaining animals[345] have been held valid, though unenforceable for lack of a human beneficiary or a charitable intent. If the trustee of such a trust were to appropriate the funds for himself it would seem clear that he would commit theft from anyone who was entitled to the residue. It would be no defence that he believed the residuary legatee to be undiscoverable: s 2(1)(c). If the trustee were himself entitled to the residue, he could not commit theft, since he would be, in effect, the absolute and exclusive owner of the property.

2.204 In *Sanders*,[346] D, the executor of a will appropriated £100,000 of the legacy. He admitted doing so and admitted that he did so dishonestly. He argued that this was not theft since subsequently it had come to light that there was a second will naming him as the beneficiary. The Court of Appeal upheld his conviction. Once probate had been granted a trust was

---

[341] *Bonner* [1970] 2 All ER 97 n. The Torts (Interference with Goods) Act 1977, s 10, amends the law of conversion. cf *McHugh* (1988) 88 Cr App R 385 at 393.

[342] R Brazier, 'Criminal Trustees?' (1975) 39 Conv (NS) 29.

[343] *Dyke and Munro* [2002] Crim LR 153, [2002] 1 Cr App R 404. See also the offences under Part 3 of the Charities Act 2006.

[344] *Trimmer v Danby* (1856) 25 LJ Ch 424; *Re Hooper* [1932] 1 Ch 38.

[345] *Pettingall v Pettingall* (1842) 11 LJ Ch 176; *Re Dean* (1889) 41 Ch D 552.

[346] [2003] EWCA Crim 3079.

established and if D had discovered that he was the beneficiary under a second will he ought to have sought an amendment of probate. As the court noted, in some cases there would be a ground for arguing that D was not dishonest in such action.

Things in or on the land

A person in possession of land has sufficient possession or control of articles in or on the **2.205** land, even if he is unaware that they are there, at least if he intends to exclude trespassers from entering and taking any such thing.[347] It is not, then, essential that V's intent to possess should exist in respect of a specific thing: it may be enough for V's intent to exist in respect of all the goods situated about his premises. In *Woodman*[348] V sold all the scrap metal on certain disused business premises to X; X removed most of it but left some as being too inaccessible to be worth the expense of removal. D then entered the premises to take some of this scrap and was held to have been rightly convicted of theft from V. V continued to control the site and his conduct in erecting fences and posting notices showed that he intended to exclude others from it; that was enough to give him control of the scrap which V did not wish to remove.

This principle was exemplified in the recent case involving the theft of golf balls from lakes **2.206** and water features on courses with a view to the balls being resold (reportedly producing a £15,000–30,000 annual turnover). In *Rostron*,[349] the Court of Appeal confirmed that the issue was whether there was evidence that golf balls hit into a lake were property belonging to another—the club owning the course.[350] It remains necessary for the prosecution to prove that the golf ball retrievers were acting dishonestly in order to sustain a theft conviction, and that may be no easy task. Possibly a finder who was not trespassing—a visitor playing a round of golf or a person crossing the course under a public right of way—would have a better right than the club to the ball. If so (and it is a question of civil law turning on whether they had exercised control over the course to assert title to the property on it), it is submitted that he could not be guilty of theft. See also Hickey (above, n 311) considering whether it would matter if the balls were in the ground (in a water feature or embedded etc) or on the ground.

Proprietary interests and treasure trove

At common law any article of gold or silver hidden by its owner with a view to its subsequent **2.207** recovery was 'treasure trove'. In the absence of its original owner and his successors in title, treasure trove belonged to the Crown. The Crown did not have possession or control of the treasure if it was found on someone else's land, but it did have a proprietary interest in it. It was therefore capable of being stolen from the Crown by any person including the owner or possessor of the land in or on which it was found. In *Hancock*[351] D was charged

---

[347] *Woodman* [1974] QB 754, [1974] 2 All ER 955, CA.
[348] [1974] QB 754, [1974] 2 All ER 955, CA. See also *Hibbert v McKiernan* [1948] 2 KB 142, [1948] 1 All ER 860, DC (theft of golf balls 'lost' on club premises); *Williams v Phillips* (1957) 41 Cr App R 5, DC (theft of refuse from dustbins).
[349] [2003] All ER (D) 269 (Jul), [2003] EWCA Crim 2206.
[350] See L Toczek, 'Never Plead Guilty!' (2002) 146 SJ 455.
[351] (1989) 90 Cr App R 422, [1990] Crim LR 125.

with stealing from the Crown Celtic silver coins which he had found using a metal detector on another person's land. It was not established that the coins were treasure trove but it was argued that the Crown's right to have their doubtful status determined was itself a 'proprietary interest'. If a finder conceals his find from the Crown, the Crown has lost something of value—the chance that, on investigation, the find would prove to be treasure trove. It was held, however, that such a chance is not a proprietary interest. If A and B each claims to be the sole owner of certain property, and the dispute is eventually resolved in favour of A, it would be odd to hold that B had a proprietary interest in the property up to the moment when it was determined that he had never had any interest in it. Another way of looking at this is to treat the 'chance' not as a property right in the disputed treasure, but as a free-standing item of property derived from the existence of the treasure.

2.208 The Treasure Act 1996 abolished the law relating to 'treasure trove', replacing it by a wide concept of 'treasure' including, as well as any object which would previously have been treasure trove, other specified objects at least 300, or in some cases 200, years old.[352] As previously with treasure trove, when 'treasure' is found it vests in the Crown (or the Crown's franchisee). The finder of treasure who takes it for himself commits the *actus reus* of theft: he has appropriated property belonging to the Crown. To prove theft, it has to be shown that he knew the Crown was, or at least might be,[353] the owner—that is, that the property had the factual characteristics of treasure—for example, that a bracelet is at least 300 years old and is made of at least 10 per cent by weight of precious metal. But a defendant might know that the property had the factual characteristics of treasure and still be unaware of the Crown's proprietary interest because of his understandable ignorance of the law of treasure.[354] So proving theft may be very difficult. The court in *Hancock* was sceptical about the alternative of charging the finder with theft from the owner of the land.

2.209 The law has been clarified by *Waverley Borough Council v Fletcher*.[355] F, using a metal detector in a public park belonging to the council, found a medieval gold brooch. A coroner's inquest decided that it was not treasure trove and the coroner returned it to F. It was held that the council was entitled to a declaration that the brooch was its property. Auld LJ stated two principles of general importance in the law of theft:

1. Where an article is found in or attached to land, the owner or possessor of the land has a better title than the finder.

2. Where an article is found unattached on land, the owner or possessor of the land has a better title than the finder only if he exercised such manifest control over the land as to indicate an intention to control the land and anything that might be found on it.[356]

---

[352] See generally J Marston and L Ross, 'Treasure and Portable Antiquities in the 1990s still Chained to the Ghosts of the Past: The Treasure Act 1996' [1997] Conv 273, criticizing the Act for offering only piecemeal protection.

[353] 'Might be' because the finder may be aware that 'reasonable steps' might reveal that the find was of silver and that it had been concealed, not lost: Theft Act 1968, s 2(1)(c).

[354] Ignorance of the civil law may negative *mens rea*.

[355] [1996] QB 334, [1995] 4 All ER 756, CA.

[356] In *Bridges v Hawkesworth* (1851) 21 LJQB 75 the plaintiff, the finder of banknotes, apparently lost by someone on the floor of a shop, was held to have a better right to the money than the owner of the shop: 'The notes were never in the custody of the defendant nor within the protection of his house, before they were

In the *Waverley* case it was immaterial that the land was held by the council as a public
open space to be used for various sports and recreations. Digging in the land was an act of
trespass. A digger who dishonestly intended to keep anything he found for himself would
be guilty of attempted theft and of stealing from the council anything he found and kept
for himself.[357] The owner of the land in which articles are buried has a proprietary interest
in those articles because they are in his possession or control. The property may also, if it is
treasure trove, belong to the Crown. The proprietary interest of the owner of the land is
much easier to prove than that of the Crown. If the intent to steal from the landowner can
be proved, the way may be opened for proving theft from the Crown. Under the doctrine
of 'transferred malice',[358] the finder's intention dishonestly to deprive the landowner of the
property may be treated as an intention dishonestly to deprive the Crown. If the property
turns out to be treasure trove, the finder may be guilty of stealing it both from the landowner and from the Crown. **2.210**

The property of a corporation and its controlling officers

A corporation such as a limited company is a person distinct from its members. A member
can steal the property of the corporation. It is property 'belonging to another'. A director
of a limited company can steal the property of that company. The injury is suffered by the
shareholders or, if the company is insolvent, by its creditors; but the property does not
belong to them and the theft is not from them but from the company. Suppose, however,
that D and E are the sole directors and sole shareholders in the company ('a sole director
case'). The property still 'belongs to another'—the company—but, before *Gomez*, it was
difficult to see that there could be an appropriation under the principle in *Morris*: the only
persons who could speak for the company, D and E, had authorized and consented to the
Act in question. As the majority in *Gomez*[359] said, this argument is no longer open—the
consent or authority of the owner is no longer a bar to theft. They added (and here the
dissenting judge, Lord Lowry, agreed)[360] that even if *Morris* had been right on this issue, **2.211**

---

found, as they would have been if they had been intentionally deposited there.' In *Parker v British Airways
Board* [1982] QB 1004 a passenger who found a gold bracelet in a British Airways Executive lounge was held
to have a better right to it than British Airways. Even if the finder, being unaware of his rights, had taken the
bracelet with a dishonest intention, he could not, presumably, have been guilty of theft, since he was doing no
more than he was entitled to do; but he might then (theoretically) have been guilty of attempted theft. On the
other hand in *Hibbert v McKiernan* [1948] 2 KB 142 a trespasser on a golf course was held guilty of larceny
from the secretary and members of the golf club of balls lost by golfers. He was aware of the intent of the
club to exclude him as a 'pilferer' of lost balls, so the case is distinguishable. See also *Rostron* [2003] EWCA
Crim 2206 and Hickey, above, n 311.

[357] In *Rowe* (1859) 8 Cox CC 139 R was convicted of larceny from a Canal Company of iron found in the
bed of a canal when it was drained. The true owner of the iron was unknown but the Canal Company had a
sufficient property in it. *Rowe* was followed by Chitty J in *Elwes v Brigg Gas Co* (1886) 33 Ch D 562 where an
ancient boat, buried in land belonging to the plaintiff was discovered by his lessee, the defendant, excavating
the site for a gasholder. The boat was held to belong to the plaintiff. In *South Staffordshire Water Co v Sharman*
[1896] 2 QB 44 two gold rings were found in the mud in the Minster Pool in Lichfield by one of a number of
labourers employed to clean it out. It was held by Lord Russell of Killowen CJ that the owner of the pool had
a better right than the finder. And cf *Woodman* (1974) 59 Cr App R 200, CA, above, para 2.205.

[358] *Smith and Hogan, Criminal Law* 113.

[359] [1993] 1 All ER at p 40, per Lord Browne-Wilkinson.

[360] At pp 35–8.

the directors would still be guilty: the principle that the mind of the controlling officers is the mind of the company does not apply to offences committed against the company.

2.212   It was thought that there was nevertheless still some difficulty in saying that property belonging to another has been *dishonestly* appropriated.[361] Clearly the appropriator is not dishonest vis-à-vis the shareholder because he is the shareholder and therefore it is very artificial to say that he is dishonest with respect to the company which exists for the benefit of the shareholders. He may of course be dishonest vis-à-vis the company's creditors—but the property does not belong to them. They are not the victims of the alleged theft, though they will be the ones to suffer if the company becomes insolvent and the assets have been dispersed by the directors. It is clear, however, that the members of a partnership facing insolvency commit no offence under the Theft Acts if they dissipate the partnership's assets to the detriment of its creditors. They cannot steal from the partnership because they are the partnership; but their creditors are in no different situation from those of the company. It has been argued that the interests of the creditors of an insolvent or doubtfully solvent company are the interests of the company,[362] but it is not clear that this is an established principle or that it is the foundation of the cases holding that the sole director may steal the company's property.[363]

2.213   In *R v A (A) v Snaresbrook Crown Court*[364] the Divisional Court concluded that there are circumstances of theft from a company, including the facts of the instant case, where it was possible to identify dishonesty.

The human body and parts of it[365]

2.214   There could be no larceny of a corpse at common law[366] and it remains the law that there is no property in a corpse. However executors or administrators or others with the legal duty to inter a body have a right to custody and possession of it until it is properly buried. They do not 'own' the corpse in the strict sense of the word but, while they have custody or possession, it appears to belong to them for the purposes of the Act, so it is possible that a charge of theft would lie against one who took the corpse from them.

---

[361] DW Elliott, 'Directors' Thefts and Dishonesty' [1991] Crim LR 732.

[362] See correspondence [1991] Crim LR at 929.

[363] *A-G's Reference (No 2 of 1982)* [1984] QB 624, [1984] 2 All ER 216, CA, and *Philippou* (1989) 89 Cr App R 290, both approved in *Gomez. McHugh* (1988) 88 Cr App R 385 at 393 and *Roffel* [1985] VR 511 were disapproved. cf *Pearlberg and O'Brien* [1982] Crim LR 829; *Painter* [1983] Crim LR 819, CA, and commentaries; GR Sullivan [1983] Crim LR 512, [1984] Crim LR 505, J Dine [1984] Crim LR 387, Williams, *TBCL* 811.

[364] [2001] EWHC Admin 456.

[365] See ATH Smith, 'Stealing the Body and its Parts' [1976] Crim LR 622 and *Property Offences*, paras 3.03 to 3.06; P Skegg, 'Criminal Liability for the Unauthorized Use of Corpses for Medical Education and Research' (1992) 32 Med Sci Law 51; M Pawlowski, 'Dead Bodies as Property' (1996) 146 NLJ 1828; A Maclean, 'Resurrection of the Body Snatchers' (2000) 150 NLJ 174.

[366] *Handyside's Case* (1749) 2 East PC 652; *Sharpe* (1857) Dears & B 160. See ATH Smith 'Stealing the Body and its Parts' [1976] Crim LR 622; P Matthews, 'Whose Body' (1983) 36 CLP 193. For other offences which might be committed, see Williams, *TBCL* 679–80. *Doodeward v Spence* (1908) 6 CLR 406, 95R (NSW) 107.

In *Doodeward v Spence*,[367] a decision of the High Court of New South Wales where the **2.215** English authorities are examined, it was held that a proprietary interest could be acquired by one who expended work and skill on the corpse with a view to its preservation on scientific or other grounds. A skeleton which has been prepared for anatomical study, or a corpse which has been stuffed or embalmed, is the subject of property in the ordinary way. The snatching of the embalmed Jeremy Bentham from University College would no doubt be regarded as a serious theft. In *Dobson v North Tyneside Health Authority*,[368] where these principles were confirmed, a brain which had been removed at an autopsy was preserved in paraffin, in pursuance of an obligation to preserve material bearing on the cause of death for as long as the coroner thought fit. It was held that this (i) was not on a par with embalming and (ii) did not entitle the next of kin to the brain for burial purposes. Their civil action failed because they had neither ownership nor the right to possession of the brain. But if they had taken it from the Health Authority they could presumably have been guilty of theft.

These decisions were applied in the controversial case of *Kelly*[369] where parts of bodies **2.216** preserved as anatomical specimens and taken from the Royal College of Surgeons were held to have been stolen. The Royal College of Surgeons had control and possession of the body parts within s 5(1).

The Human Tissue Act 2004[370] now provides a framework for issues of donation, storage, **2.217** and use of body parts, organs, and tissue. The Act is a response to the concerns raised by events at Alder Hay and Bristol Royal Infirmary.[371]

Parts from a living body

Fluids taken from the living body are property. So a motorist has been convicted of stealing **2.218** a specimen of his own urine provided by him for analysis.[372] The same rule should clearly apply to a blood sample.[373] It is probable that parts of the living body may be stolen from the living person. Thus, a magistrates' court has held a man guilty of larceny when he cut some hair from a girl's head without her consent:[374] and this seems entirely reasonable. It would be extraordinary if a person did not own his own hair!

---

[367] (1908) 95 R (NSW) 107.

[368] [1996] 4 All ER 474, [1997] 1 WLR 596, CA.

[369] [1999] QB 621; [1998] 3 All ER 741. See also *A v Leeds Teaching Hospital* [2005] QB 506 on a pathologist's right to possession of organs removed at post mortem of a child.

[370] The Human Tissue Act 2004 provides safeguards and penalties in relation to improper retention of tissue and organs without consent. The Act sets up an overarching authority which will rationalize existing regulation and will introduce regulation of post mortems and the retention of tissue for purposes like education and research and provides for the Human Tissue Authority to issue Codes of practice giving practical guidance on the conduct of activities within its remit: Department of Health Guidelines <http://www.dh.gov.uk/PolicyAndGuidance/HealthAndSocialCareTopics/Tissue/fs/en>

[371] See Department of Health guidelines: *The Removal, Retention and Use of Human Organs and Tissue from Post-mortem Examination* (2001).

[372] *Welsh* [1974] RTR 478, CA.

[373] cf *Rothery* [1976] RTR 550, CA.

[374] (1960) The Times, 22 Dec. 'For centuries human hair has been bought and sold without controversy': M Bridge, *The Sale of Goods* (1998) 26–7. This is also now capable of being charged as actual bodily harm contrary to s 47 of the Offences Against the Person Act 1861: *DPP v Smith* [2006] EWHC 94.

Property vested in V where D has obligation to retain and deal with property

2.219 Section 5(3) povides:

> Where a person receives property from or on account of another, and is under an obligation to the other to retain and deal with that property or its proceeds in a particular way, the property or proceeds shall be regarded (as against him) as belonging to the other.

2.220 This covers a very wide range of cases. In *Arnold*[375] the Court of Appeal confirmed the breadth of the provision, emphasizing that 'no words of limitation in relation to the interest of the transferor's interest' should be introduced over and above those demanded by s 5(3). The obligation need only be one 'which clearly requires the recipient of the property to retain and deal with that property or its proceeds in a particular way for the benefit of the transferor [of the property]'.[376]

2.221 Every bailment seems to be included. So does every trust. So where D has received property from or on account of V in the circumstances described in this subsection it will almost always (if not always) be the case that V has a legal or an equitable interest in the property or proceeds. This case then is covered by s 5(1) and subsection (3) is unnecessary.

2.222 In *Klineberg and Marsden*[377] the court referred to the previous sentences in the previous edition commenting that this did not anticipate the unreported case of *Smith (Paul Adrian)*, 14 May 1997, 'in which, when cheques from investors were paid into Intercity's [Smith's] bank account, the person on whose account the money was received (GRE) did not have a legal or equitable interest in the credit balance but it was nevertheless to be regarded under s 5(3) as belonging to GRE'. Since Smith was under a contractual obligation to GRE to forward all the monies received, it was unnecessary to decide, and the court does not appear to have decided, whether GRE had an equitable interest. *Klineberg* seems, in this respect, straightforward. D had been provided with monies by his investors under a scheme to provide timeshares and the scheme provided that the monies would be 'safeguarded by trusteeship'.[378]

2.223 Even if it is the position that in many cases s 5(1) is sufficient to secure conviction, section 5(3) is useful because it enables the prosecution to make out its case without the need to resort to the technical question whether V retains an equitable interest. It extends the meaning of 'belonging to another' as widely as is practicable. If there is no legal obligation on D to retain and deal with the property in a particular way, it is his to do as he likes with, and it cannot be theft for him to do what he is entitled to do. But where there is such an obligation, it seems right that the property should be capable of being stolen by D.

2.224 The subsection may, however, go beyond this and apply to cases of mere breach of contract not covered by s 5(1). For example, D who buys a non-transferable ticket may become

---

[375] [1997] 4 All ER 1.
[376] p 9.
[377] [1999] Crim LR 419.
[378] See also *Adams* [2003] EWCA Crim 3620 where D was an insolvency practitioner who administered bank accounts into which monies were paid specifically for the purposes of paying creditors. D's dealings with the accounts were charged as thefts of the things in action—debts owed to the creditors. The Court of Appeal also acknowledged that the insolvent debtor retained an interest in the property by virtue of s 5(3).

the owner of the ticket, but be under a contractual obligation to 'retain and deal with it in a particular manner' in the sense of 'not dealing' with it.[379] In the case of a rail ticket, such as that in *Marshall*, his ownership of the ticket involved his contractual obligation not to assign it to another. But note that the property must be 'received'. Where D enters into a contract to deal with his own property in his own possession the subsection does not apply.[380]

D receives property from or on account of

It has been held that D 'receives property from' V within the meaning of the subsection **2.225** when V returns a proforma bill of exchange supplied by D, signed by V as acceptor and by V's bank as guarantor, although D is the owner of the paper throughout.[381] If D then dishonestly disposes of the bill, contrary to the terms on which V had returned it to him, he commits theft of a valuable security. If D had put the proforma before V for signature while retaining possession and control, s 5(3) could not have applied and D could have been guilty of theft only if the circumstances were such as to give V an equitable interest in the bill.

The requirement that the property is 'received from or on account of another' creates a **2.226** difficulty where the property is credited to D's account by a bank transfer.[382] *Preddy* decides that, since the credit is new item of property (a thing in action which belongs to D and has never belonged to anyone else), D could not be guilty of obtaining property *belonging to another* by deception. The property had only ever been D's. This is significant for the offence of theft, since it seems necessarily to follow that D has not 'received' the property from another or on account of another. The property of the other, V, was the thing in action—V's right to sue his bank—and that was extinguished when D's new item of property was created. It would seem then that, s 5(3) does not apply and D can be guilty of theft only if the person whose bank account has been debited retains an equitable interest in the new property owned by D.

Although in *Klineberg*,[383] the court did not distinguish between funds provided by cash, **2.227** cheque, or bank transfer, it is clear that the first two are property 'received' from another, the third is not. The point was similarly overlooked in *Kumar*[384] where Turner J had 'no difficulty in concluding that if money in whatever form and on whatever number of occasions, is credited to a person who is under an obligation to account and pay over to a named recipient on a given date, but it is not so paid, the inference may safely be drawn that the trustee and debtor, has been guilty of theft if in the period between the receipt of the money and the due date he does not pay in accordance with the terms of the trust' but did not distinguish between the methods of payment.

---

[379] cf JC Smith, 'Stealing Tickets' [1998] Crim LR 723 at 726. It is pointed out that this is not theft of the thing in action, but whether it is theft of the thing in possession (the ticket) is not considered.
[380] It may however create an equitable interest. cf commentary on *Arnold* [1997] Crim LR 833 at 834.
[381] *Arnold* [1997] 4 All ER 1, [1997] Crim LR 833, CA. cf *Danger* above.
[382] Though it is commonly called a bank transfer, in law it is not a 'transfer' of property at all.
[383] [1999] Crim LR 417.
[384] [2000] Crim LR 504

Obligation

2.228 It is settled that 'obligation' in s 5(3) and (4) means a legal, not a merely moral or social, obligation.[385] Where the relevant transaction is wholly in writing, it is for the judge to decide as a matter of law whether it does create the legal obligation alleged and to direct the jury accordingly.[386] Where the obligation is alleged to have been created wholly or partly by word of mouth, or by conduct, the judge should direct them that, if they find the necessary facts (which he must specify) proved, there *is* an obligation—not that it is 'open to them' to find—that there is an obligation.[387] Aside from the correct procedure for determining whether a legal obligation existed, the substance of that question will often involve complex issues of civil law.[388]

2.229 If D is under no legal obligation to retain and deal with property which has been delivered to him or its proceeds, he can lawfully do what he likes with it and it is incapable of being stolen. This is ordinarily the position where money is lent. Assuming that D, the borrower, received the money honestly, his subsequent decision to dispose of money loaned and never to repay it, however dishonest, cannot be theft. It is not always easy to determine whether D was under an obligation to retain and deal or at liberty to dispose of the property entirely as he wished.

2.230 The subsection applies only where the obligation exists in law and D has personal knowledge of its nature and extent.[389] The knowledge of his agents cannot be imputed to him. It is probably not enough that he is aware of the facts giving rise to that obligation, unless he also realizes that it is an obligation. If he does not do so, it would be difficult to prove dishonesty.

Obligation to V

2.231 It is plain that the obligation must be owed by D to his victim, V. It is not enough that D is under an obligation to a third party to deal with the property for the benefit of V. The case of *Floyd v DPP*[390] is difficult to square with this principle (at least on the law as it stood at that time). D collected money in weekly premiums from colleagues who had ordered goods from a Christmas hamper company—V Ltd. She failed to pay the money to V Ltd and her conviction for stealing it from V Ltd was upheld in reliance on s 5(3). The court said it was unnecessary to show that V Ltd had any legal or equitable interest in the money. The only remaining source of an obligation seems to be a contract; but D had made no contract with V Ltd that she would collect and hand over the money. There was probably a contract between D and her colleagues that she would 'retain and deal' with the money they gave

---

[385] *Gilks* [1972] 3 All ER 280 (s 5(4)); *Meech* [1974] QB 549, [1973] 3 All ER 939; *Wakeman v Farrar* [1974] Crim LR 136, DC. See also *Chitty on Contracts* (29th edn, 2004) para 40.30.
[386] *Clowes (No 2)* [1994] 2 All ER 316, holding that a brochure inviting the payment of money for investment in gilts was a contractual document creating a trust.
[387] *Dubar* [1995] 1 All ER 781, following *Mainwaring* (1981) 74 Cr App R 99, CA and disapproving dicta in *Hall* [1972] 2 All ER 1009 at 1012 and *Hayes* (1976) 64 Cr App R 82 at 85 and 87.
[388] See eg *Breaks and Huggan* [1998] Crim LR 349 (contractual obligations of insurance brokers placing insurance with Lloyds).
[389] *Wills* (1990) 92 Cr App R 297, CA.
[390] [2000] Crim LR 411, DC.

her for the benefit of V Ltd but V Ltd was not privy to that contract and acquired no rights at common law. The position is different now under the Contracts (Rights of Third Parties) Act 1999:[391] as the term in the contract between D and her colleagues requiring her to retain and deal with the money by paying it to V apparently 'purports to confer a benefit' on V, V will under s 1(1)(b) of the 1999 Act be able to enforce that term, 'in their own right'. The money will then be regarded as belonging to them under s 5(3).

Charity payments/collections

A common occasion for the application of s 5(3) is that where D receives property from C **2.232** for onward transmission to, or for the benefit of, E. The required obligation may be imposed on D either by D's relationship with C, or his relationship with E, or both. In *Lewis v Lethbridge*,[392] D obtained sponsorships in favour of a charity (E) and received £54 from the sponsors (C). He did not deliver the money to the charity and was convicted of theft. His conviction was quashed because the magistrates had made no finding of any rule of the charity requiring D to hand over the actual cash received, or to maintain a separate fund. It might have been different if he had been supplied with a collecting box. No consideration was given to the question whether any obligation was imposed by the sponsors. They might have been surprised to hear that they were giving money to D to do as he liked with. In *Wain*,[393] the Court of Appeal, disapproving *Lethbridge*, held that the approach was unduly narrow and that, on similar facts, D was under an obligation and accordingly guilty.

In *Lewis v Lethbridge*, the court concentrated exclusively on the relationship between D **2.233** and E. In *Huskinson*,[394] by contrast, the obligation could only arise out of the relationship between C and D. D applied for, and received from the Housing Services Department, C, housing benefit to enable him to pay his rent to his landlord, E. D gave some of the money to E but, as the court thought, dishonestly,[395] spent the remainder on himself. It was held that he was not guilty of theft. No obligation to pay the money to E could be found in the statutory provisions authorizing the payment of housing benefit. The housing benefit was, apparently, the tenant's money to do as he liked with.

Obligation to deal with property or its proceeds

The obligation is to deal with that property or its proceeds in a particular way. The words, **2.234** 'or its proceeds', make it clear that D need not be under an obligation to retain particular monies. It is sufficient that he is under an obligation to keep in existence a fund equivalent to that which he has received. If the arrangement permits D to do what he likes with the money, his only obligation being to account in due course for an equivalent sum, the subsection does not apply.

---

[391] Applying to contracts made on or after 11 May 2000.
[392] [1987] Crim LR 59, DC.
[393] [1995] 2 Cr App R 660.
[394] [1988] Crim LR 620 and commentary.
[395] His conduct was not 'dishonest' in the objective sense favoured by *Arlidge and Parry on Fraud*, above, para 2.57, since he was entitled to do what he liked with the money. Presumably he thought he was bound to give it to E and so had a dishonest mind.

2.235 Therefore the appropriation of an advance payment for work to be done by D will be theft only if the money was given with an obligation to use it for a specific purpose.[396] Suppose, for example, D agrees to paint V's house for £500 and simply asks for 'an advance payment of £100'. If he appropriates the £100 to his own use this will not be theft for V has no proprietary right or interest in it nor is D under any obligation to deal with that property in any particular way. The result should be different where D agrees to paint V's house and asks for £100 to buy the paint which he will use on the job. If he appropriates the £100, it is submitted that this now will be theft.[397] Similar situations arise where D employs V and requires him to deposit a sum of money as security for his honesty. If the terms of the arrangement are that D can do what he likes with the money then D cannot steal it[398] but if D has agreed to retain the money, as by depositing it at a bank,[399] then it is capable of being stolen.

2.236 Similarly where D is a debt collector who is required by the terms of his contract to hand over the money he collects, less a certain percentage, to the creditors: if he is under an obligation to keep in existence a separate fund, then the money he receives is capable of being stolen.[400] If, however, the arrangement with the creditors is such that D is merely their debtor to the extent of the debts collected, less commission, the money he receives from the debtors is his and he is under no obligation to deal with that money in a particular way. It is a question of the construction of the contract between the debt collector and the creditors.

2.237 A travel agent who receives money from clients to pay for travel arrangements is under an obligation to provide tickets, etc, but not necessarily under an obligation to retain and deal with the money in a particular way. In *Hall*,[401] the agent paid the money into his firm's general trading account—a fact which was not decisive since it did not affect any interest his clients might have in the money[402]—and applied it in the firm's business. The firm failed and the clients received neither tickets nor the return of their money. Not a penny remained. In the absence of evidence of a special arrangement imposing an obligation on the agent it was held that he was not guilty of stealing from the clients. If he was entitled to use the money for the general purposes of the firm's business, he committed no theft from the clients even if he was completely profligate in its expenditure or had spent it all at the races.[403]

2.238 In *Hall* the court accepted that cases could 'conceivably arise where by some special arrangement (preferably evidenced by documents), the client could impose on the travel agent an 'obligation' falling within s 5(3)'.[404]

---

[396] In this respect, the Act seems to reproduce the old law of fraudulent conversion. See [1961] Crim LR 741 at 797.

[397] cf *Jones* (1948) 33 Cr App R 11; *Bryce* (1955) 40 Cr App R 62; *Hughes* [1956] Crim LR 835.

[398] As in *Hotine* (1904) 68 JP 143.

[399] As in *Smith* [1924] 2 KB 194.

[400] *Lord* (1905) 69 JP 467.

[401] [1973] QB 126, [1972] 2 All ER 1009, [1972] Crim LR 453 and commentary.

[402] *Yule* [1964] 1 QB 5, [1963] 2 All ER 780.

[403] In the latter case it might have been theft from his partners.

[404] [1972] 2 All ER 1009 at 1011. For an example of such see the extradition case of *Re Kumar* [2000] Crim LR 504, DC, where there was such an obligation.

An insurance broker who receives premiums for a number of insurance companies on **2.239** terms that the premiums will vest and remain in them is guilty of theft if he dishonestly uses the money for his own purposes. It was so held in *Brewster*,[405] notwithstanding that it was known by the principals that brokers, as a matter of general practice, did use the premium monies for the purposes of their own businesses and ultimately accounted for equivalent amounts. If the contract had been varied to allow D to use the money in this way, he would not have been guilty. The decision was based on a finding that there was no evidence of such a variation but only an 'indulgence'—the companies were tolerating a breach of contract. If so, it seems that the agent using the monies without dishonest intent, was appropriating them and committing the *actus reus* of theft. There is a nice question as to the point at which D became dishonest. Presumably so long as he was confident of his ability to repay and intended to do so, a jury would be unlikely to find him dishonest. When he continued to use the money knowing that there was a risk that he might not be able to repay, a jury would probably find him to be dishonest; and they would certainly do so if he used the money knowing that he could not hope to repay it. There are also difficult questions of civil law as to the effect on the rights and duties of the parties of such an 'indulgence' or waiver of contractual rights.

In *Cullen*,[406] V gave his mistress, D, £20 to buy food for their consumption and to pay **2.240** certain debts. She spent the money on herself. The Court of Appeal held that this was a plain case of theft, rejecting D's argument that it was a domestic transaction not intended to create, and so not creating, legal relations.[407] The court does not seem to have answered a serious argument. If the civil courts would not regard it as even a breach of contract for a wife to spend the housekeeping money on a new hat, the criminal courts should not regard it as theft.

Relationship to civil law obligation?

It is submitted that a person cannot be under a legal obligation to 'retain and deal' unless **2.241** a failure to retain and deal would involve him in civil liability to some other person—the victim of the alleged theft. That obligation must have been in existence at the moment of the appropriation. Property is regarded as belonging to V where D 'receives property from [V] . . . and is under an obligation' to V. If D receives property from V with an obligation at the moment of receipt but the obligation is later terminated the property ceases to 'belong' to V from that moment. It is thereafter no longer possible for D to appropriate property 'belonging to V'. In determining whether there was an obligation at the relevant time, the court must have regard to all the material facts which are proved to have existed at that time.

A case which is difficult to reconcile with these principles is *Meech*, the facts of which have **2.242** been given above.[408] The court held that the proceeds of the cheque 'belonged to' V only through the operation of s 5(3). It had been argued that V was under no obligation to D

---

[405] (1979) 69 Cr App R 375, [1979] Crim LR 798. cf *Robertson* [1977] Crim LR 629 (Judge Rubin QC).
[406] (1974) Unreported (No 968/C/74). cf *Davidge v Bunnett* [1984] Crim LR 297.
[407] *Balfour v Balfour* [1919] 2 KB 571 was relied on.
[408] Para 2.107. See commentary [1973] Crim LR 772.

because D had obtained the cheque by forgery. The court held that D assumed an obligation when he received the cheque because he was ignorant of its dishonest origin; that the
cheque therefore belonged to V and that it did not cease to belong to him when D learned
the truth about its origin, even (apparently) if the effect was that D was no longer under any
obligation.

The fact that on the true facts if known [V] might not and indeed would not subsequently have been
permitted to enforce that obligation in a civil court does not prevent that obligation on [D] having
arisen. The argument confuses the creation of the obligation with the subsequent discharge of that
obligation either by performance or otherwise. That the obligation might become impossible
of performance by [D] or of enforcement by [V] on grounds of illegality or for reasons of public
policy is irrelevant. The opening words of s 5 (3) clearly look to the creation of, or the acceptance of,
the obligation by the bailee and not to the time of performance by him of the obligation so created
and accepted by him.[409]

2.243   It is submitted that if, in light of all the proved facts, V would have had no civil claim to the
cheque or its proceeds, s 5(3) was inapplicable. It is agreed that, where reliance is placed
on s 5(3), it must be proved that D knew of the facts which gave rise to the obligation (and
probably that there was an obligation, mistake of civil law being a defence here). But, while
this is necessary, it is not enough. There must also be an *actus reus* as well as *mens rea*. The
section says 'is under an obligation', not 'believes he is under an obligation'.

2.244   It is advisable to rely on s 5(3) where there is some doubt whether V has a proprietary interest within s 5(1). Where there is no such doubt, that subsection could add an unnecessary
complication. A bailor of property alleged to be stolen by his bailee has a proprietary right.
No question whether the bailee owes any 'obligation' arises. It would be no answer that the
bailor had himself stolen the property or obtained it by deception and might have difficulty
in suing for it. It was clear at common law, and is clear under the Theft Act, that property
may be stolen from a person who has himself stolen it from a third person. The law protects
the possession even of a thief against one who would dishonestly dispossess him. V will
usually have not merely possession of the property obtained, but also ownership, at least
until the third person takes steps to avoid the transaction under which the property was
obtained. Thus in *Meech*, V was probably the owner of the cheque which he had obtained
by a forged instrument from the hire-purchase company. If the cheque had been stolen
from him, there would have been no difficulty. The problem arose because there was no
evidence of dishonest appropriation until after D had paid the cheque into his bank. The
question was whether V could follow his interest into the proceeds. It is submitted that V
could have done so under the principle of *Taylor v Plumer;*[410] where an agent converts his
principal's property into another form (even wrongfully) the property in the changed form
continues to belong to the principal. Since the court held that the money withdrawn by
D was the proceeds of V's cheque,[411] the money belonged to V and it was unnecessary to
rely on s 5(3).

---

[409] [1974] QB 549 at 554, [1973] 3 All ER 939 at 942, CA.
[410] (1815) 3 M & S 562. See *Paget's Law of Banking* (13th edn, 2006) para 19.34.
[411] This conclusion may, however, be questionable on the facts since V's 'money' became mixed with D's
money in D's bank account. See *Re J Leslie Engineers Co Ltd* [1976] 2 All ER 85 at 89–91 (Oliver J).

Where reliance is placed on s 5(3) the property is regarded as belonging to another only 'as **2.245** against him', that is, the person owing the obligation. If, therefore, in *Meech* the property belonged to V only by virtue of s 5(3), E and F who dishonestly appropriated part of the proceeds of the cheque could not commit theft from V except as aiders and abettors of D. Only D had assumed an obligation to V. If the argument that D's theft was over and done with had been accepted, they could not have been guilty of theft at all but only of handling. If, however, V retained a proprietary interest in the proceeds then D and E were guilty of an independent theft.

A duty to account is not a duty to retain and deal

A duty to account, creating a relationship of debtor and creditor, is not an 'obligation . . . **2.246** to retain and deal' within the meaning of s 5(3). It has been held that an employee who makes and dishonestly retains a profit from his misuse of his employer's property or his position as employee is bound to account for the profit, but only as debtor and so cannot steal the profit. D, the salaried manager of a public house, in breach of contract, sold his own beer instead of that of his employer and retained the takings instead of paying them into his employer's account. On an Attorney-General's reference,[412] it was held that the trial judge had rightly ruled that D had no case to answer on a charge of stealing the secret profit he had made: (i) he was under no obligation to 'retain and deal with' the proceeds of sale within the meaning of s 5(3); (ii) he did not hold the secret profit on a constructive trust or, if he did, it was not such a trust as fell within the ambit of s 5(1) of the Theft Act 1968; and (iii) the employer had no proprietary interest in the secret profit. D was under an obligation in the civil law to account for the profit he had made, but this (subject to the doubt about the 'constructive trust') was merely a debt.[413]

The conclusion depends on civil law and, particularly, *Lister & Co v Stubbs*,[414] where the **2.247** Court of Appeal held that an agent, D, who receives a bribe in breach of his duty to his principal, V, must account to V for the amount of the bribe but is only a debtor and not a trustee. V has no proprietary interest in the money. In *A-G for Hong Kong v Reid*,[415] the Privy Council has now held that *Lister & Co v Stubbs* is wrongly decided. It is unlikely that the Court of Appeal, Criminal Division, will regard itself as bound by *Lister & Co v Stubbs*.[416] If *Reid* is followed, as is expected, it will substantially enlarge the criminal law.[417]

---

[412] See *A-G's Reference (No 1 of 1985)* [1986] 2 All ER 219, [1986] Crim LR 476 and commentary.

[413] The case would be more easily prosecuted under s 4 of the Fraud Act 2006. Statements on the case of *Re Holmes* [2005] 1 WLR 1857 support the finding of a constructive trust where the property is fraudulently obtained from another.

[414] (1890) 45 Ch D 1. See also *Cullum* (1873) LR 2 CCR 28; CLRC, *Eighth Report*, Cmnd 2977 (1966), para 38; Williams, *TBCL* 756; ATH Smith, 'Constructive Trusts in the Law of Theft' [1977] Crim LR 395; JC Smith (1956) 19 MLR 39, 46. It has been said that in none of the cases in which a fiduciary has been held liable to account for profits did the question arise whether the defendant was a trustee as opposed to being merely accountable: J Martin, *Hanbury and Martin, Modern Equity* (17th edn, 2005).

[415] [1994] 1 AC 324, [1994] 1 All ER 1, PC.

[416] This is the attitude taken by the court in the law of provocation where a similar situation has arisen: *Karimi* [2006] EWCA Crim 14. *Reid* had been followed, or discussed with approval, in numerous cases eg *Daraydan Holdings Ltd v Solland* [2004] EWHC 622 (Ch), [2005] Ch 119 (secret commissions); *Clark v Cutland* [2003] EWCA Civ 810, [2003] 4 All ER 733; *Smalley v Bracken Partners* [2003] EWCA Civ 1875, [2004] WTLR 599.

[417] See JC Smith (1994) 110 LQR 180.

2.248   It will be noted, however, that the court in the *Attorney-General's Reference* thought (i) that not all constructive trusts fell within the ambit of s 5(1); (ii) that the profit which was the subject of any trust was not identifiable; and (iii) that there would be serious difficulties about proving dishonesty on the part of the profiteering publican. As to (i), s 5(1) refers to 'any proprietary right or interest' and it is difficult to see why, or on what principle, some proprietary interests recognized by the civil law should be excluded. As to (ii), if D appropriates the whole, knowing that V is entitled to part, there seems to be no real difficulty in holding that D has appropriated the part belonging to V, though it is not identifiable as separate property.[418] And as to (iii), the alleged difficulties of proving dishonesty do not seem to have bothered the courts in the least in *Cooke*[419] where, in similar circumstances, it was held that employees might be convicted of conspiracy to defraud their employer. Conspiracy to defraud, no less than theft, requires proof of dishonesty. As the profiteering publican and his barman together rolled out the illicit barrels in the dead of night, there seems no reason why they should not similarly have been convicted of conspiracy to defraud They can also be convicted under s 4 of the Fraud Act 2006.

2.249   In *Lister & Co v Stubbs*, the secret profit took the form of a bribe to an agent who naturally did not account to his principal for it. Similarly where D, a turnstile operator, was improperly given £2 to admit to Wembley Stadium a person who had no ticket, it was held that D had not stolen the £2 from his employer, V.[420] No doubt, D was bound to account to V for the £2, but the relationship between them was that of debtor and creditor. In *Tarling v Government of Singapore*,[421] a majority of the House of Lords decided that evidence of an agreement by company directors to acquire and retain a secret profit for which they were accountable to the shareholders was not evidence of an agreement to defraud. Lord Wilberforce said that 'the making of a secret profit is no criminal offence, whatever other epithet may be appropriate'. That may require reconsideration in the light of the *Hong Kong* case. In any event, it is now caught by s 4 of the Fraud Act 2006.

An obligation to make restoration of property acquired by mistake

2.250   Suppose that D acquires possession of property by another's mistake and is liable (a question of civil law) to account to V for the value of the property so obtained. The ownership in the property may pass to D, or it may remain in V, depending on the character of the mistake. If the ownership remains in V, then, under the rules already discussed, D may steal the property: but if the ownership passes to D and V retains no proprietary right or interest, D can commit no offence under the provisions so far discussed. Such a case is, however, covered by s 5(4) which provides:

Where a person gets property by another's mistake, and is under an obligation to make restoration (in whole or in part) of the property or its proceeds or of the value thereof, then to the extent of that obligation the property or proceeds shall be regarded (as against him) as belonging to the person

---

[418] It may, however, be difficult to prove that D intended to appropriate property *belonging to another*; see 110 LQR 180 at 184 and *Arlidge and Parry on Fraud* 3–062.

[419] [1986] AC 909, [1986] 2 All ER 985, HL.

[420] *Powell v MacRae* [1977] Crim LR 571, DC.

[421] (1979) 70 Cr App R 77, [1978] Crim LR 490, HL; discussed [1979] Crim LR 220.

entitled to restoration, and an intention not to make restoration shall be regarded accordingly as an intention to deprive that person of the property or proceeds.

This provision is obviously apt to cover such a case as *Ashwell*.[422] V, in the dark, gave D a **2.251** sovereign in mistake for a shilling. When, some time later, D discovered that he had a sovereign and not a shilling, he at once decided to keep it for himself. Likewise with the case of *Middleton*.[423] V, a post office clerk, referred to the wrong letter of advice and handed to D, a depositor in the Post Office Savings Bank, a sum which ought to have gone to another depositor. D took it, knowing that it was a much larger sum than he was entitled to.

In neither of these cases, however, is s 5(4) strictly necessary. Mistake of identity vitiates **2.252** consent in the civil law.[424] In *Ashwell*, it was implicit in the decision (and rightly so) that no property in the sovereign passed to D (a sovereign is necessarily a different coin from a shilling—it was a mistake of identity)—so D today would be guilty of appropriating property belonging to another under s 1(1) and s 3(1) of the Act.[425] The basis of *Middleton*, too, was that no property in the money passed to D because of a mistake as to the identity either of the deposit or of the depositor. If, however, *Ashwell* and *Middleton* should have been wrongly decided (because the property did pass)—and both have been criticized[426]— s 5(4) makes it quite clear that, under the Act, persons who act as they did should nevertheless be convicted. Even if the property in the money did pass to D in each of those cases, it is clear that D would be under an obligation to make restoration, if not of the actual property or its proceeds, at least of its value; and therefore the property would be treated as belonging to V. The only slight distinction is this: Middleton received £8 16s. 10d. and was convicted of stealing that sum—rightly on the basis of mistake of identity. He was, however, entitled to 10s. and, if the property had passed, he would under the Act be guilty of stealing only £8 6s. 10d.—the amount which he was bound to restore.

The real object of s 5(4) (or at least of that part of it which deals with the value of the goods) **2.253** was to remove the mischief (as it was seen) of the decision in *Moynes v Coopper*.[427] D, a labourer, had received most of his week's wages in advance from his employer. It was the employer's intention to tell the wages clerk to deduct the amount of the advance when paying D at the end of the week. He forgot to do so. The clerk therefore gave D a packet containing the full amount of his wages. D did not discover this until he arrived home when he opened the envelope and, knowing he was not entitled to it, decided to keep the whole sum. The Divisional Court dismissed the prosecutor's appeal on the ground that D had no larcenous intent at the time of taking as required by the Larceny Act 1916. This is no longer a problem: see s 3(1). The Court of Quarter Sessions (chairman, Mr Thesiger, QC), however, had acquitted Moynes on the more fundamental grounds that (a) D received ownership in the money and (b) D took the money with the consent of the owner. These were

---

[422] (1885) 16 QBD 190.
[423] (1873) LR 2 CCR 38.
[424] *Chitty on Contracts* (29th edn, 2004) para 5.076.
[425] Above, paras 2.08–2.129.
[426] *Russell on Crime* (19th edn, 1966) 970–4, 979–82, 1553–74 but see the issue of unjust enrichment, below, para 2.262.
[427] [1956] 1 QB 439, [1956] 1 All ER 450, criticized in [1956] Crim LR 516.

valid grounds.[428] The wages clerk, no doubt, had a general authority to pay each workman the weekly wage due to him. You do not revoke your agent's authority by deciding to do so and then forgetting about it. When the clerk handed the wages packet to D it seems clear that he transferred to him both ownership and possession in the money. In that case, it was quite impossible for D to be guilty of larceny of the money and it was really irrelevant (as Mr Thesiger decided) whether D decided to keep the money for himself at the wages table, or later when he got home. No one else (or so it was then thought) had any legal interest in the money—D was merely under a quasi-contractual obligation to repay to his employer an equivalent sum. He was in fact merely a particular kind of debtor.

2.254 On such an analysis, there is a good deal to be said in favour of Moynes's acquittal; but few cases have attracted so much adverse criticism and it is hardly surprising that it was thought necessary to bring this case within the new law of theft; and s 5(4) (and particularly the words 'or the value thereof') does so. Though the money would still be D's, a notional property in it would be vested in V for the purposes of this Act; and D's intention not to repay would be regarded as an intention to deprive V of the money.

2.255 *Moynes v Coopper* was concerned with tangible property. Section 5(4) was applied to intangible property in *A-G's Reference (No 1 of 1983)*[429] where, through an error on the part of her employer, a policewoman's bank account was credited by means of a direct debit operation with £74 to which she was not entitled. There was some evidence that, when she discovered the error, she decided to say nothing about it and to keep the unexpected windfall. The judge withdrew the case from the jury. The Court of Appeal held that the thing in action— the debt of £74 due to D from her bank—belonged to her; but that she was under an obligation to make restoration (which the court thought is the same as 'make restitution'). For the purposes of the law of theft, the thing belonged notionally to the employer and D would be guilty of theft if it were proved (i) that she intended not to make restoration, (ii) that she had 'appropriated' the thing, and (iii) that she had acted dishonestly. [430]

2.256 The CLRC seems to have assumed that in cases like *Moynes v Coopper* the entire proprietary interest in the property passes to D and that, in the civil law, he is a mere debtor. Subsequently, however, it was held by Goulding J in *Chase Manhattan Bank NA v Israel-British Bank (London) Ltd* [431] that, where an action will lie to recover money paid under a mistake of fact, the payer retains an equitable proprietary interest. If that is so, there is no need to rely on s 5(4) to attribute a 'notional' proprietary interest to the payer. The property belongs to him within s 5(1). *Chase Manhattan* was considered by Lord Browne-Wilkinson in *Westdeutche v Islington London Borough Council*.[432] In his opinion, contrary to that of Goulding J, receipt of the moneys in ignorance of the mistake gave rise to no trust, but the fact that the

---

[428] This is implicitly recognized by the Act which, by s. 5(4), circumvents ground (a). Ground (b) has become irrelevant with the disappearance of trespass as a constituent of stealing.

[429] [1985] QB 182, [1984] 3 All ER 369, [1984] Crim LR 570, followed in *Stalham* [1993] Crim LR 310, CA, rejecting an argument that the case could not stand with *Davis*, below, para 2.261.

[430] See also *Ngan* [1998] Cr App R 331.

[431] [1981] Ch 105, [1979] 3 All ER 1025, Ch D.

[432] [1996] 2 All ER 961 at 966, HL. See also *Chitty on Contracts* (29th edn, 2004) para 29.074. *Westdeutche* has been followed in *Bank of America v Arnell* [1999] Lloyd's Rep 399; *Clark v Cutland* [2003] EWCA Civ 810, [2003] 4 All ER 733; *Sinclair Investment Holdings SA v Versailles Trade Finance Ltd* [2005] EWCA Civ 722;

payee learned of the mistake two days later 'may well' have provided a proper foundation for the decision.

In the meantime, *Chase Manhattan* had been applied by the Criminal Division of the **2.257** Court of Appeal in *Shadrokh-Cigari*.[433] A bank in the USA, by mistake, credited the account of a child at an English bank with £286,000 instead of the £286 actually due. D, the child's guardian, procured the child to sign authority for the issue of large banker's drafts which D paid into bank accounts of his own. When D was arrested only £21,000 remained in the child's account. His conviction of theft from the English bank was upheld. Although the things in action created by the drafts did not, and could not, belong to the bank (because the 'thing' was a right to sue the bank and the bank could not sue itself) the draft itself, the document or instrument, when first drawn by the bank's employee on the bank's paper, clearly belonged to the bank. When the bank delivered it under a mistake of fact, to D or the child, it parted with the legal ownership but retained an equitable interest by virtue of the principle in *Chase Manhattan*. It was not necessary to rely on s 5(4); but the court held that the subsection was an alternative route to the same conclusion. D got the drafts by the mistake of the bank and was under an obligation to make restoration of the proceeds or value. Since D knew of the mistake from the start, *Shadrokh-Cigari* does not seem to be affected by *Westdeutsche*.

Subsequent Court of Appeal decisions have applied *Shadrokh-Cigari* without hesitation. **2.258** In *Webster*,[434] the Court Martial Appeal Court upheld D's conviction for theft of a medal which he had sold on e-bay. The medal was sent in error to Captain X (it was an unsolicited duplicate), X gave it to D, his admin officer to deal with. There was some confusion as to what the procedure was for the issue and return of medals, but the court had no doubt that medals are akin to gifts from the sovereign, and that in this case there had been a fundamental error by the Ministry of Defence in supplying a duplicate. The Crown retained an interest in that medal, it was property belonging to another as against D.[435]

Mistake induced by deception

In *Gresham*,[436] D's mother had been in receipt of pension payments from her former **2.259** employer which were made by automatic transfers to her bank account. D failed to inform her employer (the Department of Education) and the bank of his mother's death. The payments continued to be credited for ten years after her death and D, having had the power of attorney to act for her when she was alive, continued to use this power to cash cheques drawn on her account. The cheques drawn by D reduced the credit balance in his

---

Campden Hill Ltd v Chakrani [2005] EWHC 911 (Ch). For a helpful discussion see G Virgo, *Principles of the Law of Restitution* (2nd edn, 2006) 608–12.

[433] [1988] Crim LR 465. See further G MacCormack, 'Mistaken Payments and Proprietary Claims' [1996] Conv 86.

[434] [2006] EWCA Crim 2894.

[435] Was this not obvious? Was there not also X's proprietary interest? He had not authorized the sale, and after *Gomez* that would not matter in any event. See also the comments of the Administrative Court in *Re Holmes* [2004] EWHC 2020 expressing the provisional view that the property which D had fraudulently transferred by automated process from a German to a Dutch bank was subject to a constructive trust. cf *Ngan* [1998] 1 Cr App R 331 in which s 5(4) was not discussed.

[436] [2003] EWCA Crim 2070.

mother's account. D was convicted of theft and obtaining a money transfer by deception (contrary to s 15A of the 1968 Act). The credit balance that D diminished by drawing cheques was not an item of property that belonged to the Dept of Education within the terms of s 5(1). The prosecution relied instead on the fact that the payments had been by mistake and that s 5(4) applied. The court upheld convictions for theft on this basis, rejecting as 'eccentric' an argument that s 5(4) has no application where D has induced V's mistake by deception.

Whether the overpayment must be identified

2.260 Section 5(4) does not create any offence. It merely vests a notional property[437] in V which D might then appropriate. Only identifiable property can be appropriated. Suppose that Moynes, on his way home, had given his pay packet to a beggar without opening it and before he knew that it contained the full amount of his wages. He would presumably remain obliged to repay the excess but his failure to do so would be a mere refusal to pay a debt and no offence. He could no longer be guilty of theft because there would be no identifiable property to appropriate. It would be the same if, being unaware of the mistake, he had spent the whole of the wages on beer which was consumed by himself and his workmates. But if he had bought a bicycle with the wages and then realized that he had been overpaid, he might appropriate, and therefore steal, the bicycle in which the employer now had a 'notional' (or, according to *Chase Manhattan*, a 'real', equitable) proprietary interest. There is, however, a sufficient identification of the property if it is an unascertained part of an identifiable whole.[438]

2.261 In *Davis*,[439] D was entitled to housing benefit from the local authority, V. By mistake, V's computer, every month during a certain period, sent D two cheques, each for the full amount due.[440] D, dishonestly, did not return either of the duplicates but endorsed them to shopkeepers for cash or to his landlord for his rent, etc. He was convicted of theft of money. The court quashed his convictions on those counts where there was no evidence that he had received cash in exchange for the cheques. Paying the rent by endorsement and delivery of the cheque may have been theft of the cheque but it was not theft of money. Where he received cash for the cheque, his conviction was upheld. The cash was the proceeds of property (a cheque) got by another's mistake and, by virtue of s 5(4), was to be regarded as belonging to V. No reference was made to the case or principle of *Chase Manhattan Bank*. D was entitled to one of each pair of cheques but it was not necessary to identify one of them as that sent by mistake. When an overpayment is made, the whole sum is got by mistake within the meaning of the section, but the payee is, of course, liable to

---

[437] All proprietary interests are 'notional' in the sense that they are legal concepts or notions existing only in the minds of men. What is meant by 'notional' in this context is that the proprietary interest does not exist in the civil law, that branch of the law which properly determines the existence and extent of such interests.

[438] Above, para 2.178.

[439] [1988] Crim LR 762.

[440] Does the malfunctioning of a machine constitute a 'mistake' within the meaning of the subsection? If the computer was wrongly programmed, the mistake was that of a human mind. But if the automatic chocolate machine, because of a mechanical fault, gives me ten bars when I have paid only for one, it seems plain that property in the nine does not pass, because the owner of the machine does not intend it to pass. It is no different from the case where the machine falls apart and spills its contents on the floor. I might be convicted of theft without recourse to s 5(4).

repay only the excess and may be convicted of stealing the excess if the other conditions of theft are satisfied. The court equated the case with that where an excessive number of coins is inserted in a pay packet. It is unnecessary to identify certain of the coins as having been included by mistake. It would be otherwise, however, if a cheque was properly sent and then, by a subsequent mistake, a second cheque was sent. Then, only the second cheque or its proceeds could be stolen.

Plainly, s 5(4), the decision in *Chase Manhattan*, and the developments in recent years in **2.262** the law of unjust enrichment extend the scope of stealing quite dramatically. In *Kleinwort Benson Ltd v Lincoln City Council*[441] a bare majority of the House of Lords held that money paid under a mistake of fact or law was recoverable on the ground that its receipt by the defendant would, prima facie, lead to his unjust enrichment. The majority also held that money paid under a void contract may be recovered even though the void contract is fully performed.

The scope of liability for theft includes for example, where V pays money to D under the **2.263** mistaken belief that the property of D has been lost through a peril insured against. D receives the money under the same belief.[442] Or V pays money to D under a contract for the sale of a fishery. In fact the fishery already belongs to V.[443] In both these cases, D discovers the truth and resolves not to make restoration. In legal analysis, D's situation is indistinguishable from that of Moynes: he has received money under a mistake and is under an obligation to make restoration of the value thereof. Plainly, then, the money (notionally under s 5(4) and actually under *Chase Manhattan*) belongs to V in both these cases and (if D's resolution not to repay can be regarded as dishonest) D is guilty of theft if he appropriates the money or the proceeds (eg the Rolls-Royce which he has bought with it). Only if the money cannot be traced into some property in his possession will he be exempt. Whether such cases are wisely brought within the net of theft is questionable but it is the inevitable result of covering the *Moynes* situation. And it can involve the criminal law in some of the finest distinctions drawn in the civil law. It may be that many of these cases would founder from the inability to prove a dishonest intention. Yet more emphasis is placed on that element of the offence and it is undesirable that liability should turn so heavily on dishonesty.

The meaning of 'obligation'

The word 'obligation' in s 5(4) means a legal obligation.[444] It was so held in *Gilks*.[445] D placed **2.264** bets including one on a horse, Fighting Scot. Fighting Scot was unplaced and the race was won by Fighting Taffy. Because of a mistake on the part of the clerk in the betting shop, D was paid as if he had backed the winning horse and received £117.25 instead of £10.62, winnings on other races. D took the money, knowing that he was being overpaid. The trial

---

[441] [1999] 2 AC 349, followed in a number of other decisions, most recently in *Deutsche Morgan Grenfell v IRC* [2006] UKHL 49, [2007] AC 558.

[442] cf *Norwich Union Ltd, Fire Insurance Society Ltd v Price* [1934] AC 455.

[443] *Cooper v Phibbs* (1867) LR 2 HL 149. It is assumed for the purpose of this example that the contract was void.

[444] cf *Mainwaring* (1981) 74 Cr App R 99, above, para 2.228.

[445] [1972] 3 All ER 280, [1972] 1 WLR 1341, CA, criticized by *Arlidge and Parry on Fraud* (1st edn, 1984) 1.13, and in [1972B] CLJ at 202.

judge ruled that 'at the moment the money passed, it was money belonging to another'. But, in case his first ruling was wrong, the judge went on to consider s 5(4) and ruled that it was applicable if D was under an 'obligation', even though it was not a legal obligation, to repay. The Court of Appeal decided that the latter ruling was wrong: 'obligation' cannot be construed as meaning a moral or social obligation as distinct from a legal one. The court interpreted the judge's first ruling as meaning that 'the property in the £106.63 never passed to the appellant'; and they held that the ruling, so interpreted, was right.

2.265 The difficulty over s 5(4) arose because of the decision of the Court of Appeal in the civil case of *Morgan v Ashcroft*.[446] It was there held that, (i) since the Gaming Act 1845 made wagering transactions void, the court could not examine the state of accounts between a bookmaker and his client, and (ii) money paid under a mistake is recoverable only if the mistake was as to a fact which, if true, would have made the payer legally liable to pay. For both these reasons an overpayment by a bookmaker was held to be irrecoverable. Gilks, therefore, was on that analysis under no legal obligation to repay the money.[447] Of course, having regard to the decision in *Kleinwort*[448] it is now the case that a mistake of fact or law may ground a claim in unjust enrichment and so an obligation to make restitution may arise where the mistake caused the payment to be made (or other benefit to be transferred).

2.266 The decision of the court in *Gilks* that the ownership never passed was based on the decision in *Middleton*, one of the most dubious and hotly debated decisions on the old law of larceny. It is regrettable that recourse was had to such a case in interpreting the Theft Act; but, even if *Middleton* was rightly decided, its *ratio* was inapplicable to the facts of *Gilks*. It turned on the fact that the court held that there was a mistake of identity, either the identity of the payee or the identity of the post office deposit which was being repaid. In *Gilks*, there was no question of any such mistake. The clerk intended to pay the sum of money which he handed over to Gilks and to no one else. It is difficult to suppose that the bookmaker (or the plaintiff in *Morgan v Ashcroft*) could have successfully sued for conversion of the money. It is submitted that there is no doubt that the ownership in money does pass in these circumstances.

Gilks *and* Gomez

2.267 Since *Gomez*[449] it seems clear that when Gilks took the money he dishonestly appropriated property belonging to another, even if the ownership did pass to him.

2.268 The legal obligation must be to 'make restoration of the property or its proceeds or of the value thereof'. An obligation to pay the price for goods sold is not an obligation 'to make

---

[446] [1938] 1 KB 49, [1937] 3 All ER 92.

[447] It is of interest to note that where a bet is placed with the 'Tote' this problem would not arise. Such a bet is not a wager, since the Tote can neither win nor lose. The bet is an enforceable contract. An overpaid investor is no doubt under an obligation to repay: *Tote Investors Ltd v Smoker* [1968] 1 QB 509, [1967] 3 All ER 242, CA.

[448] Above, para 2.262.

[449] Above, para 2.22.

restoration'. So if V sells goods to D for £10 and, by mistake, sends a bill for £5, D does not steal if he dishonestly pays £5 and keeps the goods.[450]

The *Mens Rea* of Theft

The *mens rea* of the offence has proved only marginally less controversial than the *actus* **2.269**
reus.[451] The Crown must prove that the accused appropriated the property:

(i) dishonestly, and
(ii) with intent permanently to deprive the other of his property.

Dishonesty

As the Law Commission stated in its Consultation Paper No 155, 'in theft . . . dishonesty **2.270**
is now the principal determinant of criminality'. [452]

Inferences may be drawn from D's conduct but it is plain, and must be made plain to a jury, **2.271**
that the question is as to the state of D's mind.[453] The Act provides some further elaboration
on the elements of *mens rea*, including, importantly, s 2 which defines circumstances
in which conduct is not dishonest. In addition, By s 1(2): 'It is immaterial whether the
appropriation is made with a view to gain, or is made for the thief's own benefit.' Thus
(to take the facts of pre-Theft Act cases) if D takes V's letters and puts them down a lavatory
or backs V's horse down a mine shaft he is guilty of theft notwithstanding the fact that
he intends only loss to V and no gain to himself or anyone else. It might be thought that
these instances could safely and more appropriately have been left to other branches of
the criminal law—that of criminal damage to property for instance. But there are possible
cases where there is no such damage or destruction of the thing as would found a charge
under another Act. For example, D takes V's diamond and flings it into a deep pond. The
diamond lies unharmed in the pond and a prosecution for criminal damage would fail.
It seems clearly right that D should be guilty of theft.[454]

Dishonesty rebutted where section 2 applies[455]

By s 2 of the Act:

(1) A person's appropriation of property belonging to another is not to be regarded as dishonest— **2.272**
    (a) if he appropriates the property in the belief that he has in law the right to deprive the other of
        it, on behalf of himself or of a third person; or

---

[450] See discussion of *Lacis v Cashmarts* [1969] 2 QB 400 at 411, [1972B] CLJ at 204.
[451] On the history see the Law Commission Paper Consultation Paper No 155, Part III.
[452] Para 3.2.
[453] *Ingram* [1975] Crim LR 457, CA (defence of absent-minded taking to charge of shoplifting); *Small*
[1987] Crim LR 777, CA (D, who believes, reasonably or not, that property has been abandoned, does not
intend to appropriate property belonging to another, or permanently to deprive).
[454] The alternative would be for legislation dealing specifically with the problem by creating an offence of
denial of use of an article.
[455] See also ATH Smith, *Property Offences* (1994) ch 7; *Arlidge and Parry on Fraud* ch 1; Law Com
Consultation Paper No 155 (1999), Parts III and V; Law Com Report No 276, *Fraud* (2002), Part V.

 (b) if he appropriates the property in the belief that he would have the other's consent if the other knew of the appropriation and the circumstances of it; or

 (c) (except where the property came to him as trustee or personal representative) if he appropriates the property in the belief that the person to whom the property belongs cannot be discovered by taking reasonable steps.

(2) A person's appropriation of property belonging to another may be dishonest notwithstanding that he is willing to pay for the property.

2.273 It will be noticed that this section specifies three situations in which an appropriation of property belonging to another is *not* to be regarded as dishonest and one in which it may be. By this negative approach, the section assists somewhat in defining the meaning of dishonesty, but the section does not specify any state of mind that *must* be regarded as dishonest. The negative approach to defining dishonesty raises interesting questions about the role that the element has to play in the offence of theft generally. Dishonesty operates both as a peg on which to hang claims of an exculpatory nature—that is, as equivalent to an element of unlawfulness or lack of blameworthiness—and also as a positive element of *mens rea*, requiring proof of D's state of mind.[456] This overlap between 'dishonesty' as a state of mind (requiring a factual inquiry from the jury) and as a concept describing the wrong done (requiring a moral evaluation by the jury) is perpetuated by the case-law.

2.274 A further complexity with the element of dishonesty (beyond the law of theft per se) has been described by the Law Commission:

> In some crimes, such as conspiracy to defraud, the other elements of the offence are not *prima facie* unlawful, so dishonesty renders criminal otherwise lawful conduct. However, in deception offences the other elements of the offence, if proved, would normally be unlawful in themselves. If someone has practised a deception in order to gain a benefit their conduct is *prima facie* wrongful. Therefore dishonesty can be raised to rebut the inference that conduct was in fact wrongful . . . The former type of crime [can be described] as having a *positive* requirement of dishonesty, and the latter as having a *negative* requirement.[457]

2.275 It is regrettable that there is no statutory definition of dishonesty, particularly since the common law definition which supplements s 2 is so vague, and as noted above, dishonesty has assumed an elevated importance following the excessively broad interpretations of the *actus reus* elements of the offence.[458]

Belief in the right to deprive

2.276 D is not dishonest if he believes, whether reasonably or not, that he has the legal right[459] to do the act which is alleged to constitute an appropriation of the property of another. In spite of the courts' general insistence on reasonableness when defences of 'mistake' were

---

[456] Prof Horder describes dishonesty as a concealed excuse, 'taking the form of a morally open textured mental element', *Excusing Crime* (2003), 49.

[457] Law Com No 276, above, para 5.12. For criticism of this as unhelpful see P Kiernan and G Scanlon, 'Fraud and the Law Commission: The Future of Dishonesty' (2003) 24 Comp Law 4.

[458] cf the Law Commission's current view which is that no definition is possible: Law Com No 276, *Fraud*, above, Part V.

[459] It is irrelevant that no such right exists in law. A dictum to the contrary in *Gott v Measures* [1948] 1 KB 234, [1947] 2 All ER 609, is irreconcilable with the decision in *Bernhard* (below). The belief need not relate to a 'property' right: *Wood* [1999] Crim LR 564 and commentary.

raised, it never seems to have been doubted that a claim of right afforded a defence, even though it was manifestly unreasonable.[460] The onus is clearly on the Crown to prove a dishonest intention and, therefore, if the jury are of the opinion that it is reasonably possible that D believed that he had the right to do what he did, they should acquit.

The Act refers specifically to a right *in law*. This does not *necessarily* exclude a belief in a **2.277** merely moral right.[461] The common law, that taking another's property is not justifiable, even where it is necessary to avoid starvation,[462] suggests that even the strongest moral claim to deprive another is not enough; but, if it is now a jury question,[463] there is no law to this effect and a jury would be likely to find that a truly starving person was not dishonest.

It is made clear that a belief in the legal right of another will negative dishonesty, just as it **2.278** amounted to a claim of right under the law of larceny.[464] If D, acting for the benefit of E, were to take property from V, wrongly but honestly believing that E was entitled to it, he would clearly not be guilty of theft. Thus, in *Close*[465] an employee, paying his employer's debt in kind by taking his employer's property without consent, was apparently held not to be dishonest by a jury.

Where D specifically pleads a belief in a claim of right, the jury ought, it is submitted, to be **2.279** directed in relation to s 2 and not left to deal with the issue under the general test in *Ghosh* (below).[466] Since a belief in a claim of right should negate *mens rea* in all cases, it is arguable that this element of s 2 should have been made generally applicable throughout the Act rather than being restricted to cases of theft.

Belief that the owner would consent

It is sufficient that D holds a mistaken though genuine belief that the person to whom the **2.280** property belonged would have consented had he known of the circumstances. Thus, D will not be dishonest where he helps himself to his flatmates' milk from their fridge if he holds a belief that this would be consented to. Numerous appropriations of this nature occur every day and a specific provision dealing with the matter precludes silly prosecutions. Following *Hinks*, the issue of mistaken beliefs will be of particular importance in cases in which D claims that he was acting with the owner's consent.[467]

---

[460] *Bernhard* [1938] 2 KB 264, CCA; below, para 12.49. See recently *Terry* [2001] EWCA Crim 2979.

[461] A belief in a moral right was not a defence to larceny: *Harris v Harrison* [1963] Crim LR 497, DC. cf Williams, *CLGP* 322.

[462] 1 Hale PC 54; *Dudley and Stephens* (1884) 14 QBD 273, CCR; *Southwark London Borough Council v Williams* [1971] Ch 734 at 744. But cf the defence of 'duress of circumstances', *Conway* [1989] QB 290, [1988] 3 All ER 1025, CA, and *Smith and Hogan, Criminal Law* 314.

[463] *Ghosh* [1982] QB 1053, [1982] 2 All ER 689, CA, below, para 2.295. cf *Close* [1977] Crim LR 107.

[464] *Williams* [1962] Crim LR 111.

[465] [1977] Crim LR 107.

[466] The Court of Appeal has taken a contrary view approving a general *Ghosh* direction in *Rostron* [2003] EWCA Crim 2206, where D believed that he had a legal right to collect 'lost' golf balls. cf *Smith (Paul Adrian)* [1997] 7 Archbold News 4, CA. On charges to which s 2 does not apply *Ghosh* must perform the function: *Woods* [1999] 5 Archbold News 2, CA.

[467] See above, para 2.35. See especially Lord Hutton's dissent in *Hinks* focusing on dishonesty and the question of whether D can be convicted if he has a claim of right—consent, but not if he has a mere belief in a claim of right—under s 2(1)(a).

2.281 D's assertion that as the directing mind and will of a company he believes that the company consents to the appropriation of the corporate property is not of itself enough to bring D within s 2(1)(b).[468]

Belief that the person to whom the property belongs cannot be discovered by taking reasonable steps

2.282 Though the Act makes no reference to finding, this is obviously intended to preserve the substance of the common law [469] rule relating to finding. The finder who appropriates property commits the *actus reus* of theft (assuming that the property does belong to someone and has not been abandoned) but is not dishonest unless he believes the owner can be discovered by taking reasonable steps. This will depend on the nature of the property in question.[470]

2.283 The important change in the law of finding made by the Act has already been dealt with.[471] At common law, if D's finding was innocent (either because he did not believe that the owner could be discovered by taking reasonable steps or because he intended to return the thing to the owner when he took it) no subsequent dishonest appropriation of the thing could make him guilty of larceny; but now, in such a case, he will be guilty of theft by virtue of s 3(1).[472]

2.284 It should be stressed that the question is one of D's actual belief, not whether it is a reasonable belief. If D, wrongly and unreasonably, supposed that the only way in which he could locate the owner of property he had found, would be to insert a full-page advertisement in *The Times*, he would have to be acquitted unless that course were a reasonable one to take, which would depend upon the value of the property and all the surrounding circumstances.

2.285 While this provision is intended mainly for the case of finding it is not confined to that case and there are other instances where it would be useful. Suppose that V arranges with D that D shall gratuitously store V's furniture in D's house. V leaves the town and D loses touch with him. Some years later D, needing the space in his house and being unable to locate V, sells the furniture.[473] This is undoubtedly an appropriation of the property of another and D is civilly liable to V in conversion; but he appears to be saved from any possibility of conviction of theft by s 2(1)(c).[474] Though the purchase money probably belongs to V,[475] D's immunity under the Act must extend to the proceeds of sale.

---

[468] See *A-G's Reference (No 2 of 1982)* [1984] QB 624.

[469] *Thurborn* (1849) 1 Den 387.

[470] See eg the implausible defence in *Sylvester* (1985) CO/559/84 where D alleged that the car he was stripping of parts in a car park was abandoned and therefore s 2(1)(c) applied.

[471] Above, para 2.205.

[472] Above, para 2.08.

[473] cf *Sachs v Miklos* [1948] 2 KB 23, [1948] 1 All ER 67, CA; *Munro v Wilmott* [1949] 1 KB 295, [1948] 2 All ER 983.

[474] The bailee who disposes of uncollected goods under Sch 1 to the Torts (Interference with Goods) Act 1977 will not usually be able to rely on this provision, for he will know where the owner is; but since he is 'entitled . . . to sell the goods', it is submitted that there is no *actus reus*. See above, para 2.53.

[475] In equity, if not in law: *Taylor v Plumer* (1815) 3 M & S 562 discussed by Goode (1976) 92 LQR 360, 376 and by Khurshid and Matthews (1979) 95 LQR 79. See also *Agip (Africa) Ltd v Jackson* [1990] Ch 265, 285 and *Trustee of the Property of F C Jones & Sons (A Firm) v Jones* [1997] Ch 159. Although *Taylor v Plumer*

Where the property came to D as a trustee or personal representative and he appropriates **2.286**
it, he may be dishonest even though he believes that the person to whom the property
belongs cannot be discovered by taking reasonable steps. The point seems to be that the
trustee or personal representative can never be personally entitled to the property (unless
it is specifically so provided by the trust instrument or the will) for, if the beneficiaries
are extinct or undiscoverable, the Crown will be entitled to the beneficial interest as *bona
vacantia*. If the trustee or personal representative appropriates the property to his own use,
honestly believing that he is entitled to do so, then it is submitted that he must be acquitted.
But if he knows that he has no right to do this and that the property in the last resort
belongs to the Crown, he commits theft, from the beneficiaries if they are in fact discovera-
ble and, if not, from the Crown.

Dishonest appropriation, notwithstanding payment

Section 2(2) is intended to deal with the kind of situation where D takes bottles of milk **2.287**
from V's doorstep but leaves the full price there. Certainly D has no claim of right and he
intends to deprive V permanently of his property. Doubts had, however, arisen as to whether
this was dishonest.[476] This subsection resolves them. The mere fact of payment does not
negative dishonesty but the jury are entitled to take into account all the circumstances and
these may be such that even an intention to pay for property, let alone actual payment,[477]
may negative dishonesty. The fact of payment may be cogent evidence where D's defence
is that he believed V would have consented. D takes milk bottles from V's unattended
milk-float and leaves the price. He says that he assumed that V would have been very happy
to sell him the milk had he been there, but that he had not time to wait for V to return.
If D is believed—and the fact of repayment would be persuasive evidence—it would seem
that he has no dishonest intent. The section is important in emphasizing that D's willingness to pay the market value for appropriated property will not negate dishonesty, otherwise there would be no theft where D took V's original work of art that he had long coveted,
leaving its listed valuation price.

The Privy Council has recently confirmed that there can be a theft and dishonesty where **2.288**
the alleged act was one which was motivated in part by a desire to benefit the victim.
There is no difficulty in establishing dishonesty where there is an intention not to cause
loss. As Lord Bingham observed:

In providing that an appropriation may be dishonest even where there is a willingness to pay, [the
section] shows that the prospect of loss is not determinative of dishonesty. [478]

---

was decided by a common law court, the court was in fact applying the rules of equity: see L Smith, 'Tracing
in *Taylor v Plumer*: Equity in the Court of King's Bench' [1995] LMCLQ 240; *and Paget's Law of Banking*
(13th edn, 2006) para 19.34.

[476] cf Hawkins 1 PC c. 34, s 7; Blackstone *Commentaries* iv. 243; *Russell on Crime* 855–6.
[477] *Boggeln v Williams* [1978] 2 All ER 1061, below, para 2.293.
[478] *Wheatley and Penn v Commissioner of Police of the British Virgin Islands* [2006] UKPC 24.

Dishonesty where section 2 does not apply

2.289   Section 2 provides for three situations which do not amount to dishonesty and one situation which may. But there are many other cases where it is necessary to decide whether the defendant was dishonest and the Act gives no guidance about these. A common occurrence, with which many of the leading cases are concerned, is that of an employee who takes money from his employer's till, knowing that he is forbidden to do so but intending to replace the money as soon as he can.[479] He is charged with stealing the particular notes and coins which he took from the till and there is no doubt that he has the required intention permanently to deprive his employer of these.[480] The circumstances may vary widely—the amount may be large or small, D may believe that he will be able to repay the money almost immediately, or after some longer period or he may have just a faint hope of being able to do so one day, and his purpose in taking the money may be good or bad. But the only question in each case is whether he did so 'dishonestly'.

2.290   The meaning of this word has caused the greatest difficulty. Under the Larceny Act the taking had to be done 'fraudulently and without a claim of right'. It is not clear that the word 'fraudulently' played any important role. Indeed, a good deal of effort was expended in trying to determine what, if anything, it added to 'without a claim of right'. The CLRC in their *Eighth Report* [481] seem, surprisingly, to have overlooked this fact and to have proceeded on the assumption that the word had some large though unspecified role to play. They thought that 'dishonestly' was a better word than 'fraudulently', not because its meaning was any different, but because it is more easily understood.

'Dishonestly' seems to us a better word than 'fraudulently'. The question Was this 'dishonest?' is easier for a jury to answer than the question Was this 'fraudulent'? 'Dishonesty' is something which laymen can easily recognise when they see it, whereas 'fraud' may seem to involve technicalities which have to be explained by a lawyer.

2.291   This suggests that it is for jurors to decide whether 'this' is dishonest. Of course, it is for jurors to decide all questions of fact, including the state of mind of the defendant—what was his intention and belief, including his belief as to his legal rights. But, under the Larceny Act, it was probably for the judge to say whether that state of mind, when ascertained, was to be characterized in law as 'fraudulent'.[482] If so, the substitution of 'dishonestly' for 'fraudulently' led to an important change in the law. Possibly influenced by the above misleading passage in the Report, the Court of Appeal in *Feely*[483] held that it is for the jury in each case to decide, not only what the defendant's state of mind was, but also, subject to s 2, whether that state of mind is to be categorized as dishonest.

Jurors, when deciding whether an appropriation was dishonest can be reasonably expected to, and should, apply the current standards of ordinary decent people. In their own lives they have to decide

---

[479] *Williams* [1953] 1 QB 660, [1953] 1 All ER 1068, CCA; *Cockburn* [1968] 1 All ER 466, [1968] 1 WLR 281, CA; *Feely* [1973] QB 530, [1973] 1 All ER 341, CA.
[480] *Velumyl* [1989] Crim LR 299 and commentary.
[481] Para 39.
[482] *Williams* [1953] 1 QB 660, CCA; *Cockburn* [1968] 1 All ER 466, CA.
[483] [1973] QB 530, [1973] 1 All ER 341, [1973] Crim LR 193, CA and commentary.

what is and what is not dishonest. We can see no reason why, when in a jury box, they should require the help of a judge to tell them what amounts to dishonesty.

The court was certainly much influenced by the opinion of the House of Lords in *Brutus v* **2.292**
Cozens[484] that the meaning of an ordinary word of the English language is not a question of law for the judge but one of fact for the jury. 'Dishonestly' is such a word and so it was for the jury to attribute to it such meaning as they thought proper. A major difficulty about this view is that juries—and magistrates—are likely to give different answers on facts which are indistinguishable.[485] *Feely* at least provided a standard—that of 'ordinary decent people', as understood by the jury—against which the defendant's intentions and beliefs were to be tested. Other cases, however, went further.

In *Gilks*,[486] D agreed that it would be dishonest if his grocer gave him too much change **2.293**
and he kept it but he said bookmakers are 'a race apart' and there was nothing dishonest about keeping the overpayment in that case. The judge invited the jury to 'try and place yourselves in [D's] position at that time and answer the question whether in your view he thought he was acting dishonestly'. The Court of Appeal thought this was a proper and sufficient direction, agreeing apparently that, if D may have held the belief he claimed, the prosecution had not established dishonesty. This applied, not the standards of ordinary decent people, but the defendant's own standards, however deplorable they might be. In *Boggeln v Williams*,[487] the court expressly rejected an argument that D's belief as to his own honesty was irrelevant and held that, on the contrary, it was crucial. D, whose electricity had been cut off, reconnected the supply through the meter. He knew that the electricity board did not consent to his doing so, but he notified them and believed, not unreasonably, that he would be able to pay at the due time. It was held that the question was whether he believed that what he did was honest. A further complexity was introduced in *McIvor*,[488] where the Court of Appeal said that the test of dishonesty in conspiracy to defraud was different from that to be applied in theft.

Ghosh

The leading case is now *Ghosh*.[489] The Court of Appeal rejected the distinction between **2.294**
conspiracy and theft. The same test of dishonesty is to be applied in both. *Ghosh* itself was a case of obtaining by deception contrary to s 15 of the 1968 Act; so it is now clear that the same principle applies throughout the Theft Acts and the common law of conspiracy to defraud as well as other statutory offences in the Fraud Act 2006 and those in the Companies Acts such as fraudulent trading. There is one test of dishonesty in English criminal law.[490]

---

[484] [1973] AC 854, [1972] 2 All ER 1297, HL. The impact of the decision is now minimal—see *Paul* [1999] Crim LR 79.
[485] cf *Sinclair v Neighbour* [1967] 2 QB 279, [1966] 3 All ER 988, CA.
[486] Above, para 2.287; [1972] 3 All ER 280 at 283.
[487] [1978] 2 All ER 1061, [1978] Crim LR 242 and commentary.
[488] [1982] 1 All ER 491, [1982] 1 WLR 409, CA.
[489] [1982] QB 1053, [1982] 2 All ER 689.
[490] In some circumstances the *Ghosh* test is applicable in civil cases: *Aktieselskabet Dansk Skibsfinansiering v Brothers* [2001] BCLC 324; *Royal Brunei Airlines Sdn Bhd v Tan* [1995] 2 AC 378 and see the discussion in *Twinsectra Ltd v Yardley* [2002] 2 WLR 802, [2002] UKHL 12, particularly at paras 27–33 and 115–34, on

2.295 The test is twofold.

(i) Was what was done dishonest according to the ordinary standards of reasonable and honest people? If no, D is not guilty. If yes—

(ii) Did the defendant realize that reasonable and honest people regard what he did as dishonest? If yes, he is guilty; if no, he is not.

2.296 *Ghosh* attempts a compromise between a purely objective *Feely* type test which might be regarded as too harsh and a purely subjective test such as that in *Gilks* which would create a thief's charter. However, in seeking to achieve this compromise it introduces an unnecessary confusion in the form of the second limb. The second limb allows the accused to escape liability where he has made a mistake of fact as to contemporary standards of honesty. But why should that be an excuse? Campbell[491] cogently argues that this additional limb is superfluous if under the first limb the jury is properly directed to take account of all the circumstances. Taking the example of D who fails to pay a travel fare because he is new to the country and is accustomed to free public transport, it should not be necessary to rely on the second limb to conclude that D is not dishonest. A properly directed jury would so conclude under the first limb.

2.297 The first limb rarely gives rise to difficulties, although it can do. It was recently held that no reasonable magistrates' court could have concluded that the reasonable and honest person would not regard as dishonest the conduct of the accused manager of a tool hire shop who allowed customers to borrow items for a very short period of time for no payment (sometimes receiving a personal tip) as he would alter the company records to show that the item had been returned as faulty or incorrectly chosen.[492]

Robin Hood defences

2.298 Lord Lane CJ thought that the *Ghosh* formula would dispose of the 'Robin Hood defence', but it is not clear that it does so.[493] The defendant would have to be acquitted 'if the jury think *either* (a) that what Robin Hood did (rob the rich to feed the poor) was not dishonest *or* (b) that Robin Hood thought the plain man would not consider what he did as dishonest'. The same might be said of a more modern example, that of the member of an animal welfare association who takes beagles from a research laboratory because he knows they are being used in experiments. He would certainly not regard his own conduct as dishonest and so would escape under the rule as stated in *Gilks*. He might still do so under *Ghosh*. A jury of animal lovers would be likely to agree with him; and it might be difficult to satisfy any jury that the defendant did not believe that all right-thinking people would agree with him. Members of animal welfare organizations probably do so believe. But this surely should be theft.

---

which see MP Thompson, 'Criminal Law and Property Law: An Unhappy Combination' (2002) 66 Conv 387. R Thornton, 'Dishonest Assistance: Guilty Conduct or a Guilty Mind' [2002] 61 CLJ 524.

[491] K Campbell, 'The Test of Dishonesty in *Ghosh*' [1994] 43 CLJ 349. Campbell suggests that if the aim is to provide this hybrid test it should be: whether a reasonable jury, applying ordinary standards of honesty, is prepared to excuse D's failure to recognize that his own behaviour would be regarded as dishonest by the standards of ordinary people.

[492] *Gohill* [2007] EWHC 23.

[493] DW Elliott, 'Dishonesty in Theft: A Dispensable Concept' [1982] Crim LR 395 at 398.

One who deliberately deprives another of his property should not be able to escape liability **2.299**
because of *his* disapproval, however profound and morally justified, of the lawful use to
which that property was being put by its owner. In deciding whether a certain state of mind
should be regarded as dishonest it is not irrelevant to consider how the matter will be
regarded by the ordinary decent citizen who is the victim of the offence. The owners of the
beagles will certainly consider that their property has been stolen, even though they are
fully aware of the state of mind of the takers. The law fails in one of its purposes if it does
not afford protection to a person against what he quite reasonably regards as a straightforward case of theft.

When is a Ghosh *direction required?*

The Court of Appeal has frequently stressed that it is not necessary to give a *Ghosh* direction **2.300**
to the jury in every case. Thus, it is unnecessary where D's claim is a lack of dishonesty
owing to forgetfulness,[494] or where the question relates solely to the genuineness of D's
belief rather than D's claim that the ordinary person would not regard it as dishonest.[495]
Nor is it necessary where eg D, a shop-worker, simply denies taking the property and does
not claim for example that he borrowed it from the till.[496] If there is any evidence to suggest
that D's attitude was, 'Whatever others may think, *I* did not consider this dishonest', the
direction must be given. Where there is no such evidence it is probably unnecessary.[497]
Where this direction is necessary, the exact form of words ought to be used,[498] and a failure
to direct on this may be fatal.[499]

ECHR implications[500]

A major difficulty about the *Ghosh* formula is that juries—and magistrates—are likely **2.301**
to give different answers on facts which are indistinguishable. This creates very obvious
injustices that bring the criminal law into disrepute. It also raises the potential for challenges to the law under Article 7 of the ECHR on the basis of lack of certainty. Article 7
provides:

No-one shall be held guilty of any criminal offence on account of any act or omission which did
not constitute a criminal offence under national or international law at the time when it was
committed. . . .

---

[494] *Atkinson* [2004] Crim LR 226.

[495] *Wood* [2002] EWCA Crim 832, CA where D claimed that his trespassing into empty premises to
remove the entire stock of curtain fabric, was not dishonest since he believed it to be abandoned. cf *Rostron*
[2003] EWCA Crim 2266, where the Court of Appeal seem to restrict *Ghosh* to cases where D would have a
claim of right under s 2(1)(a). That must be wrong. Moreover, if the defendants had been aware that the golf
club on whose land they were trespassing had a legal right to the balls that was still not enough to lead to a
finding of dishonesty. They could have claimed that their behaviour was not to be regarded as dishonest by
ordinary right thinking people: then they would have been entitled to a full *Ghosh* direction.

[496] *Cobb* [2005] EWCA Crim 1549.

[497] *Price* (1990) 90 Cr App R 409 [1990] Crim LR 200; *Brennen* [1990] Crim LR 118 (handling);
Ravenshead [1990] Crim LR 398, CA; *Miles* [1992] Crim LR 657 (fraudulent trading); *Roberts* (1985) 84 Cr
App R 177; cf A Halpin, 'The Test for Dishonesty' [1996] Crim LR 289, 291.

[498] *Hyam* [1997] Crim LR 439.

[499] *Clarke* [1996] Crim LR 824.

[500] See the Law Com Paper No 155 paras 5.33–5.5.

Article 7 guarantees not only against retrospective criminalization in strict terms, but also that 'legal provisions which interfere with individual rights must be adequately accessible, and formulated with sufficient precision to enable the citizen to regulate his conduct'.[501] So vague are the elements of dishonesty under *Ghosh* that the Law Commission Paper No 155 provisionally took the view that a Home Secretary could not safely be advised to make a statement of compatibility in relation to a Bill creating a general dishonesty offence.

2.302 In the Law Commission Paper, the Commission referred to the *Sunday Times* case,[502] where in interpreting the obligations of certainty under the Convention, the Court stated that:

> the following are two of the requirements that flow from the expression 'prescribed by law'. First, the law must be adequately accessible: the citizen must be able to have an indication that is adequate in the circumstances of the legal rules applicable to a given case. Secondly, a norm cannot be regarded as a 'law' unless it is formulated with sufficient precision to enable the citizen to regulate his conduct: he must be able—if need be with appropriate advice—to foresee, to a degree that is reasonable in the circumstances, the consequences which a given action may entail.[503]

2.303 The Law Commission concluded that:

> The thrust of our analysis of dishonesty as a positive element is that, in certain circumstances, a person may not be able to foresee with any accuracy whether a proposed course of action would or would not be criminal. Seeking legal advice is not likely to take matters any further, since a lawyer's guess as to what a jury may think 'dishonest' is likely to be no better than anyone else's.[504]

2.304 In *Hashman and Harrup* [505] a case involving compatibility of bind over powers with Article 10, the Strasbourg Court's comments on the sufficiency of vague tests of liability in English criminal law raise, as Professor Ashworth has noted, support for the Law Commission's interpretation of dishonesty centred offences.[506] Subsequently, the Law Commission concluded in Report No 276, *Fraud,*[507] that the test might be compatible.[508] The Law Commission nevertheless acknowledged the force of the argument in its Report on *Fraud* by stating:

> We continue to believe that a general dishonesty offence, by not requiring as an element some identifiable morally dubious conduct to which the test of dishonesty may be applied, would fail to provide any meaningful guidance on the scope of the criminal law and the conduct which may be lawfully pursued. We do not accept the argument that inherent uncertainty is satisfactorily cured by the promise of prosecutorial discretion. That cannot make a vague offence clear and, while it might ameliorate some of the risks, it does not excuse a law reform agency from formulating a justifiable and properly defined offence. We do not believe it is for the police and prosecutors to decide the ambit of the criminal law. As the Supreme Court of the United States has said: 'A statute which either forbids or requires the doing of an act in terms so vague that men of common intelligence must necessarily

---

[501] *G v Federal Republic of Germany* 60 DR 252, 262 (1989).
[502] *Sunday Times v United Kingdom* [1979] 2 EHRR 24.
[503] Para 49.
[504] Para 5.43.
[505] (2000) 30 EHRR 24.
[506] See commentary on *Hashman and Harrup v United Kingdom* [2000] Crim LR 185 at 186.
[507] (2002) para 5.3.
[508] Hong Kong and Scotland both have general fraud offences, and both have been found to be compatible with their respective Bills of Rights.

guess at its meaning and differ as to its application, violates the first essential of due process of law.[509]

These views were echoed by the Joint Parliamentary Committee on Human Rights when scrutinizing the Fraud Bill.[510]

In relation to the offence of theft, the elements of *actus reus*—that there must be an appro-   **2.305**
priation of property belonging to another—are likely to be held to be sufficient, even after
the extensive interpretation in *Gomez* and *Hinks*, to ensure that the offence of theft is not
incompatible with Article 7. It is not yet an offence based solely on the concept of dishonesty (despite the best efforts of the House of Lords in *Morris*, *Gomez*, and *Hinks*). It has
been held at first instance that dishonesty under *Ghosh* is not itself incompatible with
Article 7.[511]

Academic critique of Ghosh

Ghosh has generated much criticism and some valuable proposals for reform.[512] Perhaps   **2.306**
the most trenchant critic of the *Ghosh* test was Professor Griew,[513] who catalogued its
numerous deficiencies. Griew suggested that the test confuses the state of mind with the
concept of dishonesty;[514] leaves a question of law to the jury[515] which may lead to inconsistent decisions with the potential for different juries to reach different verdicts on identical
facts thus presenting acute problems in respect of Article 7 of the ECHR; leads to more
trials as defendants have little to lose by pleading not guilty and hoping that the dishonesty
element is not made out; leads to longer trials as the dishonesty issue is a 'live' one in all
cases; assumes a community norm within the jury in that they must agree on the ordinary
standards of honesty; assumes that jurors are honest, or at least that they can apply ordinary
standards of honesty even if they do not adhere to them in their personal lives; and, is
unsuitable in specialized cases such as complex commercial frauds where the 'ordinary'
person is unlikely to understand the honesty or otherwise of the activities.[516]

---

[509] Para 5.28.

[510] *Joint Parliamentary Committee on Human Rights* 14th Report, para 2.25.

[511] *Pattni* [2001] Crim LR 570. And see DC Ormerod, 'Cheating the Public Revenue' [1998] Crim LR 627 and DC Ormerod, 'A Bit of a Con—The Law Commission's Proposals on Fraud' [1999] Crim LR 789.

[512] EJ Griew, 'Dishonesty—the Objections to *Feely* and *Ghosh*' [1985] Crim LR 341; DW Elliott, 'Dishonesty in Theft: A Dispensable Concept' [1982] Crim LR 395 at 398. Elliott's solution is to dispense with the word 'dishonestly' altogether but to add a new subsection (3) to s 2: 'No appropriation of property belonging to another which is not detrimental to the interests of the other in a significant practical way shall amount to theft of the property'.

[513] Author of *The Theft Acts 1968 and 1978* (7th edn, 1995) and 'Objections to *Feely* and *Ghosh*' [1985] Crim LR 341.

[514] See also K Campbell, 'The Test of Dishonesty in *Ghosh*' [1994] 43 CLJ 349, 354 criticizing *Ghosh* for confusing the state of mind and the defendant's standards of honesty.

[515] For an argument in support of leaving such issues to the jury see R Tur, 'Dishonesty and the Jury Question' in A Phillips Griffiths (ed), *Philosophy and Practice* (1985). The Law Commission provisionally concluded that 'the circumstances in which such conduct may be found to be non-dishonest cannot be cir-cumscribed by legal definition. Where dishonesty is a positive element, it *must* be open to the fact-finders to find that particular conduct is not dishonest, even if the legislation does not say so': Law Com Paper No 155 (1999), para 5.6.

[516] On the suitability of dishonesty in these cases see also DW Elliott, 'Directors' Thefts and Dishonesty' [1991] Crim LR arguing that insufficient attention has been paid to the issue of dishonesty in cases of sole traders committing theft from the company.

2.307   The CLRC view of dishonesty relied on the common sense of members of society and a consensus about the appropriate benchmarks for protecting private property. Empirical work has demonstrated that people's moral standards and interpretation of the concept of dishonesty are not as might be imagined. For example, a MORI poll for the *Sunday Times* in October 1985 found that only 35 per cent of those questioned thought it morally wrong to accept payment in cash in order to evade liability for tax.[517] Of course, it might well be that people do not generally assume that others share their own moral standards when sitting as jurors.

2.308   These criticisms are rendered all the more cogent for several reasons. First, the test applies in a great volume of cases in English courts—all those involving an element of dishonesty, which includes all Theft Act and common law conspiracy to defraud cases and many other offences under specific legislation (although it seems that dishonesty does not create enormous problems in practice).[518] Secondly, broad interpretations of the elements of *actus reus* have left dishonesty as the principal determinant of criminality in theft. As the Law Commission commented recently, 'where the conduct elements of an offence are morally neutral [as, for example, appropriation], the element of dishonesty has to do more than simply exclude specific types of conduct which, though prima facie wrongful, do not deserve to be criminal'.[519]

2.309   *Ghosh* has not been universally accepted in other jurisdictions. Before *Ghosh*, the Supreme Court of Victoria had refused to follow *Feely*, when construing the identical provision in Victorian legislation. In *Salvo*,[520] Fullagar J, with whom Murphy J seems to have agreed in substance, held that it was the duty of the judge to explain to the jury what 'dishonestly' meant; and he should tell them that it means 'with disposition to defraud, that is with disposition to withhold from a person what is his right'. There are, however, two difficulties about this interpretation. The first is that it seems to add nothing to what is expressly stated in s 2(1)(a)—that is, a person who has a claim of legal right is not dishonest—and leaves no function for the word 'dishonestly'.[521] Secondly, it seems too narrow as a matter of policy.[522] Such an approach leads to the conviction of D who, knowing that he has no right to do so, takes V's money with intent to spend it but with the certainty (in his own mind) that he will be able to replace it before it is missed, so that V will never know anything about it and suffer no detriment whatever.[523]

---

[517] M Levi, *Regulating Fraud: White Collar Crime and the Criminal Process* (1987) 6.

[518] See eg Magistrates' Association response to the LCCP 155, reported in Law Com No 276, para 5.14. And see the Commission's conclusion at para 5.18.

[519] Law Com No 155, para 5.6.

[520] [1980] VR 401. See the High Court's recent conclusion that there is no obligation for the Crown to show that D realized that his acts were dishonest by the current standards of honesty: *McLeod* [2003] HCA 24, [100].

[521] Williams, *TBCL* 730.

[522] See DW Elliott, 'Dishonesty in Theft: A Dispensable Concept' [1982] Crim LR at 406.

[523] In Australia the *Salvo* approach has been followed in *Love* (1989) 17 NSWLR 608, and *Condon* (1995) 83 A Crim R 335. In *Peters v The Queen* (1998) 192 CLR 493 the majority of the High Court distinguished *Salvo*, but declined to adopt the *Ghosh* test, preferring that the jury be directed by the standards of ordinary decent people—a test seemingly akin to *Feely*. See also *Spies* (2000) 201 CLR 603, Aus High Ct and *McLeod* [2003] HCA 24.

Reform

The Law Commission recently commented that it found the criticisms of the present law **2.310**
'compelling'.[524] It was suggested that *Ghosh* was not so much a definition as a way of coping
with the absence of a definition.[525] In light of the volume and strength of such criticisms,
it is not surprising therefore that numerous reform proposals have been advanced.[526]

One attractive solution would be a provision that a person appropriating property belong- **2.311**
ing to another *is* to be regarded as dishonest unless one of the three existing exemptions
(in s 2) apply or, fourthly—he intends to replace the property with an equivalent and
believes that no detriment whatever will be caused to the owner by the appropriation. This
would excuse the employee who 'borrows' £5 from the till when closing the shop on
Saturday afternoon, having no doubt that he will be able to replace it when he opens up on
Monday morning, only to be robbed and rendered penniless on his way home from the pub
on Saturday night. His actions would be unlawful (in civil law) although not dishonest.
It probably would not save the postmaster who 'borrows' from the post office till to keep
his ailing grocery business going, in the hope that business will improve. This proposal
goes back substantially to the explanation offered many years ago for the meaning of
'fraudulently' in the Larceny Act 1916[527] and to that made in the first two editions of this
book.[528]

This test might however be thought too severe, leaving no escape route for hard cases such **2.312**
as the parents taking food for their starving children. But perhaps the concept of dishonesty
is not the right vehicle for such cases. Suppose that the person breaks a window to get at the
food and is charged with criminal damage. The definition of criminal damage does not
require dishonesty. It would not make much sense to acquit the parent of theft and convict
instead of criminal damage. They should stand or fall together. The parent might claim he
had a 'lawful excuse' for doing the damage—that is, necessity or duress of circumstances,
general defences—and this is the right approach for theft. If dishonesty were defined
appropriately as a state of mind, exculpatory claims would be dealt with under the general
defences which are applicable equally to theft and criminal damage. It is important of
course to distinguish elements of unlawfulness and dishonesty. D may be acting unlawfully
(and aware that he is), and yet not aware that he is acting dishonestly.

---

[524] Law Commission, *Fraud and Deception* (Law Com No 155) para 5.32.
[525] ibid, 50 n.
[526] See inter alia, P Glazebrook, 'Revising the Theft Acts' [1993] CLJ 191 who provides a list of excepted
circumstances that are not dishonest. This approach is developed by A Halpin, 'The Test for Dishonesty'
[1996] Crim LR 283, 294—'1. The treatment by a person of the property of another is to be regarded as
dishonest where it is done without a belief that the other would consent to that treatment if he knew of all the
circumstances, unless the person believes that the law permits that treatment of the property. 2. The treatment
by a person of the property of another is not to be regarded as dishonest if done (otherwise than by a trustee or
personal representative) in the belief that the person to whom the property belongs is unlikely to be discovered
by taking reasonable steps'. See further, A Halpin, *Definition in the Criminal Law* (2004) 162–6.
[527] 'The Fraudulent Sub-Postmistress' [1955] Crim LR 18.
[528] 1st edn, 41–4.

2.313 Professor Elliott went so far as to suggest the removal of the element of dishonesty from the definition of theft. Elliott's solution is to dispense with the word 'dishonestly' altogether but to add a new subsection (3) to s 2:

> No appropriation of property belonging to another which is not detrimental to the interests of the other in a significant practical way shall amount to theft of the property.[529]

This solution would require legislation and that seems very unlikely. Why should the taking of £20 from Bill Gates's wallet not amount to theft?

2.314 A reconsideration by the House of Lords is, however, a practical possibility and so many diverse views have now been expressed about the concept of dishonesty, in both judgments and academic writings, that the House might well be disposed to look at the matter *de novo*.

The intention of permanently depriving the other of it

2.315 The Theft Act preserved the rule of the common law and of the Larceny Act 1916 that appropriating the property of another with the intention of depriving him only temporarily of it is not stealing.[530] English law, in general, recognizes no *furtum usus*—the stealing of the use or enjoyment of a chattel or other property. This is subject to two exceptions which are considered below in chapter 10. The first exception concerns the removal of articles from places open to the public[531] and was a creation of the 1968 Act. The second exception, insofar as it relates to motor vehicles, has existed in the Road Traffic Acts since 1935, but the extension to other 'conveyances' is new.[532] Outside these cases the law seems to remain substantially unchanged; so that, if D takes V's horse without authority and rides it for an afternoon, a week, or a month, he commits no offence under the Act and, probably, no offence against the criminal law (though a civil trespass) if he has an intention to return the horse at the end of this period.[533] There is an argument for introducing an offence to respect the value of property in terms of its immediate usefulness.

Deprivation of persons with limited interests

2.316 Theft may be committed against a person having possession or control of property or having any proprietary right or interest in it.[534] The element of permanence relates to the deprivation of V, not to the proposed benefit to D. It would seem clear, therefore, that where V has an interest less than full ownership, an intention by D to deprive him of the whole of that interest, whatever it might be, is sufficient. If, as D knows, V has hired a car from X for a month, and D takes it, intending to return it to X after the month has expired, this must be theft from V, for he is permanently deprived of his whole interest in the property, but it is not theft from X for he, plainly, is not permanently deprived. It should be stressed that the question is always one of intention; so if, in the above example, D, when

---

[529] [1982] Crim LR at 410.
[530] *Warner* (1970) 55 Cr App R 93.
[531] Section 11.
[532] Section 12, below, ch 10.
[533] *Neal v Gribble* [1978] RTR 409, below, para 10.39.
[534] Section 5(1), above, 2.183.

he took the car, believed V to be the owner, he would apparently not commit theft even though V was, in fact, deprived of his whole interest.

This is capable of producing rather odd results where the interest of the person deprived is a very small one. Z writes a letter and gives it to V to deliver by hand to X. D intercepts V and takes the letter from him. Having read it, he delivers it (as he always intended) to X. This could be theft of the letter from V (though not from Z or X) since V is permanently deprived of his possession or control of it. If the letter is taken by force or threat of force, it will be robbery from V.   **2.317**

Section 6 and the common law

The draft Bill proposed by the CLRC contained no definition or elaboration of the   **2.318**
phrase 'intention of permanently depriving'. The Committee were well aware of the existing case-law and must have assumed that it would continue to be applied. The government had other ideas and introduced a clause which, after much amendment, became s 6.[535] At common law and under the Larceny Acts the phrase was held to include the cases where—

  (i) D took V's property with intention that V should have it back only by paying for it—eg he took V's property so that, pretending that it was his own, he could sell it to V.[536]
 (ii) D took V's property intending to return it to V only when he had completely changed its substance—eg D, being employed by V, to melt pig iron, took an axle belonging to V and melted it down in order to increase his output and consequently his earnings;[537] or D wrongfully fed V's oats to V's own horses;[538] or took V's horse intending to kill it and to return the carcase.[539]
(iii) D took V's property and pawned it, intending to redeem and restore it to V one day but with no reasonable prospects of being able to do so.[540]

Section 6 was apparently intended to cover these cases and no more. But they all related,   **2.319**
inevitably, to deprivation of possession of chattels and no consideration was given to the difficulty of applying the concept of intent to deprive to things in action which, by definition, are not possessed. The section is expressed to apply only to the offence of theft.[541]

As Professor Spencer has written,[542] and the Court of Appeal was inclined to agree,[543] s 6   **2.320**
'sprouts obscurities at every phrase'. Section 6(1) provides:

A person appropriating property belonging to another without meaning the other permanently to lose the thing itself is nevertheless to be regarded as having the intention of permanently depriving the other of it if his intention is to treat the thing as his own to dispose of regardless of the other's

---

[535] See JR Spencer, 'The Metamorphosis of Section 6 of the Theft Act' [1977] Crim LR 653.
[536] *Hall* (1849) 1 Den 381.
[537] *Richards* (1844) 1 Car & Kir 532.
[538] *Morfit* (1816) Russ & Ry 307.
[539] cf *Cabbage* (1815) Russ & Ry 292.
[540] *Phetheon* (1840) 9 C & P 552; *Medland* (1851) 5 Cox CC 292. cf *Trebilcock* (1858) Dears & B 453 and *Wynn* (1887) 16 Cox CC 231 which are inconclusive on the point.
[541] Prior to the Fraud Act it was relevant in relation to s 15 obtaining by deception.
[542] Spencer, above.
[543] *Lloyd* [1985] QB 829 at 834, CA.

rights, and a borrowing or lending of it may amount to so treating it if, but only if, the borrowing or lending is for a period and in circumstances making it equivalent to an outright taking or disposal.

2.321 In *Lloyd*,[544] the Court of Appeal approved academic opinions that s 6 need be referred to in exceptional cases only and then the question for the jury should not be 'worded in terms of the generalities' of the section but be related to the particular facts. The court cited the opinion of Edmund Davies LJ,[545] that: Section 6 . . . gives illustrations, as it were, of what can amount to the dishonest intention demanded by section 1 (1). But it is a misconception to interpret it as watering down section 1', and concluded, 'we would try to interpret the section in such a way as to ensure that nothing is construed as an intention permanently to deprive which would not prior to the 1968 Act have been so construed. But before and since *Lloyd* courts have given the words of the section its wider ordinary meaning. In *Bagshaw*,[546] the Court of Appeal said that the restrictive view taken in *Lloyd* was *obiter* and that 'there may be other occasions on which s 6 applies'.

2.322 The current approach is to be that s 6 is to be given its ordinary meaning (whatever that may be) and is not necessarily restricted to the scope of the common law meaning of the concept. The concept certainly has to be applied to situations which did not arise at common law like the theft of a thing in action. It seems inevitable that it must equally apply to treating a chattel, like the refrigerator in *Bloxham*,[547] as one's own to dispose of, thus extending theft beyond anything contemplated by the CLRC who had no idea that s 6 was going to be introduced. As the Court of Appeal stated in *Fernandes*[548] the critical element of the section is satisfied whenever the accused has treated the property as his own to dispose of regardless of the other's rights.

2.323 In *Downes*,[549] the Court of Appeal held that D committed theft when, being in possession of vouchers belonging to the Inland Revenue and made out in his name, he sold them to others who, as he knew, would submit them to the Revenue so as to obtain tax advantages. The primary reason for the decision was that the document when returned would be in substance a different thing; but the court also held that s 6 was to be given its ordinary meaning—D intended to treat the vouchers as his own to dispose of regardless of the Revenue's rights.

2.324 In *Marshall* [550] D obtained part-used underground tickets and travel-cards from members of the public passing through railway barriers and resold them to other potential customers, so depriving London Underground Ltd (LUL) of the revenue it would have gained from the potential customers. D was convicted of theft of the part-used tickets from LUL. The court assumed that those tickets, though in the possession of the passengers, continued

---

[544] [1985] QB 829, [1985] 2 All ER 661, CA.
[545] *Warner* (1970) 55 Cr App R 93 at 97.
[546] [1988] Crim LR 321.
[547] (1943) 29 Cr App R 37. Above, para 2.79.
[548] [1996] 1 Cr App R 175, 188.
[549] (1983) 77 Cr App R 260, [1983] Crim LR 819, CA and commentary.
[550] [1998] 2 Cr App R 282, discussed by JC Smith, 'Stealing Tickets' [1998] Crim LR 723. For consideration of the case and offences that may have been committed see also K Reid and J MacLeod, 'Ticket Touts or Theft of Tickets and Related Offences' (1999) 63(6) J Crim Law 593.

to belong to LUL because there was a term to that effect on the reverse of each ticket. The defendants had intended to treat the tickets as their own to dispose of regardless of LUL's rights. The fact that LUL might get the ticket back eventually, albeit with the value exhausted, did not prevent a finding that D intended to deprive them permanently.

Intention permanently to deprive without causing loss

In *Chan Man-sin's* case,[551] the Privy Council held that, where a company accountant **2.325** drew a forged cheque on the company's account, there was 'ample evidence' of intention permanently to deprive the company of its credit balance, even on the assumption that D contemplated that the fraud would be discovered and the company would lose nothing. He intended to treat the balance as his own to dispose of regardless of the company's rights. *Re Osman*,[552] another case of 'theft without loss', is similar. In similar vein is *Hilton*,[553] where D, who had direct control of a bank account belonging to a charity, gave instructions for the transfer of the charity's funds to settle his personal debts, it was held that he stole the thing in action (the charity's right to payment of that sum from its bank) belonging to the charity.

Conditional intention to deprive

In *Easom*,[554] the Court of Appeal said that 'a conditional appropriation will not do'. The **2.326** difficulty of supporting this proposition is that all intention is conditional, even though the condition be unexpressed and not present to the mind of the person at that time. D picked up a woman's handbag in a cinema, rummaged through the contents, and put it back having taken nothing. The handbag was attached by a thread to a policewoman's wrist. D's conviction for stealing the handbag and the specified contents—tissues, cosmetics, etc— was quashed because D never had any intention of permanently depriving V of any of those things. It followed that he was not guilty of attempting to steal any of them. No doubt he intended to steal things which were not there—presumably money—and might have been convicted of attempting to steal on a suitably worded indictment.[555] There was no intention permanently to deprive. Consequently, he was not guilty of attempting to steal the handbag, or the specified contents either. As the chattels were rejected as soon as they were identified, it may be better to say that there was no appropriation, not even a conditional one.

In *Husseyn*,[556] DD opened the door of a van in which there was a holdall containing valua- **2.327** ble sub-aqua equipment. They were charged with attempted theft of the equipment. The judge directed the jury that they could convict if DD were about to look into the holdall and, if its contents were valuable, to steal it. The Court of Appeal, following *Easom*, held that this was a misdirection: 'it cannot be said that one who has it in mind to steal only

---

[551] Above, para 2.127.
[552] Above, para 2.112.
[553] [1997] 2 Cr App R 445, [1997] Crim LR 761 and commentary.
[554] [1971] 2 QB 315 at 319, [1971] 2 All ER 945 at 947, CA.
[555] See para 2.328 below.
[556] (1978) 67 Cr App R 131 n, [1978] Crim LR 219, CA and commentary; discussed at [1978] Crim LR 444 and 644.

if what he finds is worth stealing has a present intention to steal'. In *Re A-G's References (Nos 1 & 2 of 1979)*,[557] the Court of Appeal held these words were applicable only to an indictment which alleged an intention to steal a specific object, such as sub-aqua equipment. It would have been different if the indictment had charged an attempt to steal 'some or all of the contents of the holdall' or, in *Easom*, of the handbag. Yet, in *Husseyn*, the sub-aqua equipment *was* the contents of the holdall—there were no other contents; so, according to the court, D was not guilty of attempting to steal the equipment if it was described as such, but he was guilty if it was described as the 'contents of the holdall'. At that time it was clear law that there could be no conviction for attempting to steal a thing that was not there—it was the sub-aqua equipment or nothing.

2.328   Since the Criminal Attempts Act 1981,[558] this is no longer so. A person looking for money in an empty handbag might now be convicted of attempting to steal money. The only problem in cases of this kind is one of the form of the indictment. The formula approved in the *A-G's References* is not satisfactory because, in these cases, the defendant did not intend (or it was not proved that he intended) to steal any of the contents. But he undoubtedly intended to steal something—something which was *not* 'all or any of the contents'.[559] The indictment would be accurate if it alleged simply that D attempted to steal from the handbag, or holdall.[560] This is so whether or not there is anything there that D would have stolen. D's intention to steal anything he finds which he thinks worth stealing is a present intention to steal, at least so far as the law of attempts is concerned. The failure to specify any subject matter cannot be an objection since the 1981 Act.[561]

2.329   It is submitted that the better view is that an assumption of ownership, which is conditional because there is an intention to deprive only in a certain event, is theft. For example, D takes V's ring intending to keep it if the stone is a diamond, but otherwise to return it. He takes it to a jeweller who says the stone is paste. D returns the ring to V. It is submitted that he committed theft when he took the ring. The fact that he returned it is relevant only to sentence.

2.330   In *Easom*,[562] the court said, 'if a dishonest postal-sorter picks up a pile of letters intending to steal any which are registered, but, on finding that none are, replaces them, he has stolen nothing'. He might now be convicted of an attempt to steal registered letters. A similar problem may arise where D takes the property of V, say a ring, intending to claim a reward from V for finding it. If he intends to return the ring in any event and hopes to receive the reward, he is not guilty of stealing the ring though he is about to commit fraud by false representation. But if he intends to retain the ring unless he receives the reward, he seems to be in substantially the same situation as the taker who sells the property back to

---

[557] [1980] QB 180, [1979] 3 All ER 143, [1979] Crim LR 585, CA and commentary.

[558] *Smith and Hogan, Criminal Law* 406.

[559] cf *Bayley and Easterbrook* [1980] Crim LR 503, CA and commentary.

[560] cf *Smith and Smith* [1986] Crim LR 166, CA and commentary.

[561] Similarly with the law of burglary. Below, ch 8. It may be different where the charge is theft. A lorry-driver was held (in a civil action) not guilty of theft of the goods loaded on his lorry when he drove off intending to steal the load 'if and when the circumstances were favourable': *Grundy (Teddington) Ltd v Fulton* [1983] 1 Lloyd's Rep 16, CA; but he had assumed a right of the owner (cf *Gomez*) and the only question is whether the conditional intention was enough.

[562] Above, para 2.326.

the owner. It might be said, however, that in this example, the taker is not treating the property as his own. There are two possible answers to this: the assertion of a better right to possession might be regarded as treating the property as one's own; or, s 6 not providing an exclusive definition, this might be regarded as an analogous case falling within the same general principle.

Disposition of the property as one's own

The attribution of an ordinary meaning to the language of s 6 presents some difficulties.[563] **2.331** It is submitted, however, that an intention merely to use the thing as one's own regardless of the other's rights is not enough. It adds nothing to 'appropriates' since appropriation consists in an assumption of the right of an owner. The words 'dispose of' are crucial and are, it is submitted, not used in the sense in which a general might 'dispose of' his forces but rather in the meaning given by the *Shorter Oxford Dictionary:* 'To deal with definitely; to get rid of; to get done with, finish. To make over by way of sale or bargain, sell.'[564]

In *DPP v Lavender,*[565] however, the Divisional Court seems to have held D's intention to **2.332** treat the thing as his own, regardless of the owner's rights, as crucial and to have minimized the importance of 'to dispose of'. D surreptitiously removed two doors from another property belonging to his council landlord to replace doors in the council property he occupied. Did he not in fact treat the doors as the property of the council, like the rest of the premises he occupied? If a secretary surreptitiously swaps her typewriter for the similar model operated by a colleague (because she believes it works better), does she steal the typewriter from her employer? She may well steal it from her colleague whom she does intend to lose her limited interest for ever.

It is submitted that, on a similar basis, there is no reason why there should not be a con- **2.333** viction for theft in a case like that of the taker of the Goya from the National Gallery: 'I will return the picture when £X is paid to charity.' Substantially, the taker is offering to sell the thing back and his case is, in principle, the same as those contemplated by s 6(1). Nor should it make any difference that the price demanded is something other than money. 'I will return the picture when E (who is imprisoned) is given a free pardon'—this should be sufficient evidence of an intention permanently to deprive.

The general principle might be that it is sufficient that there is an intention that V shall **2.334** not have the property back unless some consideration is supplied by him or another; or, more generally still, unless some condition is satisfied.

Borrowing or lending

Where money or anything which is consumed by use—like petrol—is 'borrowed', the dis- **2.335** honest 'borrower' has an intention permanently to deprive even though he intends to replace the money or the article with another which is just as good. He intends to deprive

---

[563] See *Harjindel Atwal* [1989] Crim LR 293 (Judge Fricker QC) and commentary.
[564] This passage was cited in *Cahill* [1993] Crim LR 141, CA.
[565] [1994] Crim LR 297.

the owner of the specific thing he has appropriated.[566] In the case of a true borrowing it appears that there can be no theft, however dishonest the borrower may be, because, by definition, he does intend to return the specific thing taken. Yet by s 6(1), if the borrowing 'is for a period and in circumstances making it equivalent to an outright taking . . .', the borrower may be regarded as having the intention of depriving the owner permanently. This is a rather puzzling provision, because it would seem, prima facie, that borrowing cannot be an 'outright taking'. Clearly, however, this part of the subsection is intended to do something and, therefore, certain borrowings are to be treated as the equivalent of out-right takings. Once this is accepted, it is not difficult to divine the kind of borrowings which are intended to be covered: they are those where the taker intends not to return the thing until the virtue is gone out of it. D takes V's non-rechargeable battery, intending to return it to V when it is exhausted; or V's season ticket, intending to return it to V when the season is over. Similar in principle are those cases where D intends to return the thing only when it is completely changed in substance.[567]

2.336 Where property belonging to another has been entirely deprived of an essential character-istic, which has been described as its 'virtue', the matter seems reasonably clear. But what if the virtue has not been entirely eliminated—but very nearly? D takes V's season ticket for Arsenal's matches intending to return it to him in time for the last match of the season. Is this an 'outright taking' so as to amount to theft of the ticket? If it is, is it theft if D intends to return the ticket in time for two matches?—or three, four, five, or six—where should the line be drawn? The difficulty of drawing a line suggests that it should not be theft of the ticket unless D intends to keep it until it has lost *all* its virtue.[568] This means, of course, that if D takes V's car and keeps it for ten years, he will not be guilty of theft if, when, as he intended all along, he returns it to V, it is still a roadworthy vehicle, though the proportion of its original value which it retains is very small. If it can no longer be described as a car, but is scrap metal, then, if D intended to return it only when it was reduced to this state, he has stolen it.[569]

2.337 In *Clinton v Cahill* [570] the Court of Appeal in Northern Ireland construed an identical provision to conclude that D had not committed theft where she received hot water for which she had not paid. The water passed through houses, including D's as part of a district heating system before the water (by then cooled) returned to the central station. The meters on D's system were faulty and she received the hot water without paying. She was held to have no intention permanently to deprive the company of the water. Nor could she be said to have exhausted the virtue of the water—it retained some heat on its return to the station. There was no equivalent to an outright taking or disposal.

---

[566] *Velumyl* [1989] Crim LR 299.

[567] See cases cited above, para 2.318. Dicta in *Bagshaw* [1988] Crim LR 321 concerning the 'virtue' test seem inappropriate to the facts of that case.

[568] The difficulty might satisfactorily be overcome in this particular case by holding that the right to see each match is a separate thing in action, of which V is permanently deprived once that match is over. cf *Chan Wai Lam v R* [1981] Crim LR 497.

[569] cf *DPP v J* [2002] EWHC 291, holding that the magistrates were wrong to accept a submission of no case where D had taken V's headphones, snapped them, and returned them.

[570] [1998] NI 200 NICA, see *Blackstone's Criminal Practice* (2007) B4.40.

The provision regarding lending appears to contemplate the situation where D is in possession or control of the property and he lends it to another. If D knows that the effect is that
V will never get the property back again, he clearly has an intention permanently to deprive.
Similarly if D knows that, when V gets the property back again, the virtue will have gone
out of it, this is equivalent to an outright disposal. The examples of the non-rechargeable
battery, season ticket, etc[571] are applicable here, though they seem less likely to arise in the
context of lending than of borrowing.

2.338

Parting with property under a condition as to its return

Section 6(2) provides:

2.339

> Without prejudice to the generality of subsection (1) above, where a person, having possession or
> control (lawfully or not) of property belonging to another, parts with the property under a condition
> as to its return which he *may not* be able to perform, this (if done for purposes of his own and without
> the other's authority) amounts to treating the property as his own to dispose of regardless of the
> other's rights.

This is clearly intended to deal with the kind of case which gave difficulty under the old law,
where D, being in possession or control of V's goods, pawns them. If D had no intention
of ever redeeming the goods, there was no problem—he was guilty of larceny and he would
now clearly be guilty of theft, apart from s 6(2). But what if D does intend to redeem?
The answer now is that if he knows that he may not be able to do so, he is guilty of theft.
The subsection does not seem to permit of a distinction between the case where D knows
that the chances of his being able to redeem are slight and the case where he believes the
chances are high; in either case, the condition is one which he knows he may not be able
to perform.

2.340

The common law cases suggested that it was theft, notwithstanding an intention to redeem,
if the pawner had no reasonable prospects of being able to do so.[572] It is submitted,
however, that the question under the Theft Act is a purely subjective one: D must *intend* to
dispose of the property regardless of the other's rights, and s 6(2) merely describes what he
must intend. If then D is in fact *convinced*, however unreasonably, that he will be able
to redeem the property, he does not come within the terms of s 6(2) because he intends *to
dispose of it under a condition which he will be able to perform.*

2.341

This is not necessarily conclusive, however, for subsection (2) is without prejudice to the
generality of subsection (1); and it might reasonably be argued that even the pawner who
is convinced of his power to redeem intends to treat the thing as his own to dispose of,
regardless of the other's rights. This would be equally true if the pawner in fact had power
to redeem; and, since pawning is not 'lending', there is no need to prove that it was equivalent to an outright disposal. The difficulty about this interpretation is that it makes it very
difficult to see why s 6(2) is there at all; if D's disposition of property under a condition

2.342

---

[571] Above, paras 2.335–2.336.
[572] *Phetheon* (1840) 9 C & P 552; *Medland* (1851) 5 Cox CC 292. *Trebilcock* (1858) Dears & B 453 and
Wynn (1887) 16 Cox CC 231 are inconclusive.

which he is able to perform is theft under subsection (1), why refer specifically to the case of a condition which he may not be able to perform?

2.343 On the whole it would seem that the better approach is to hold that one who is certain of his ability to redeem does not have an intention permanently to deprive. Such a person, in some circumstances, may well be found by the jury not to be dishonest. For example D, a tenant for a year of a furnished house, being temporarily short of money, pawns the land-lord's clock, knowing that he will certainly be able and intending to redeem it before the year expires. A prosecution for theft of the clock should fail on the grounds both that he is not dishonest and that he has no intent permanently to deprive. The case might formerly have been dealt with as one of unlawful pawning.[573]

Abandonment of property

2.344 Early nineteenth-century cases on the taking of horses decided that there was no intent permanently to deprive, although D turned the horse loose some considerable distance from the place where he took it.[574] In the conditions of those times it might be supposed that D must have known that there was a substantial risk that V would not get his property back. This lenient attitude may be contrasted with that adopted in the pawning cases,[575] and the right course would seem to be to attach no importance to these old decisions in the interpretation of the Theft Act.

2.345 The case where the property is abandoned is not within s 6(2) for D does not part with the property under a condition. He might, however, be regarded as having an intention to treat the thing as his own to dispose of regardless of the other's rights. If D borrows the thing and then leaves it where he knows the owner or someone on his behalf will certainly find it, he clearly does not have an intention permanently to deprive. But if he abandons the thing in circumstances such that he knows that it is quite uncertain whether the owner will ever get it back or not, then it would not be unreasonable to hold that he has an intention to treat the thing as his own to dispose of regardless of the other's rights. By analogy to the pawning case discussed above, it would seem that it should be immaterial whether D believes that the chances of V's getting the property back are large or small; it is sufficient that he intends to risk the loss of V's property. In *Fernandes*,[576] Auld LJ concluded that 'section 6 may apply to a person in possession or control of another's property who dishonestly and for his own purpose deals with that property in such a manner that he knows he is risking its loss'.[577] Suppose, for example, that D, being caught in the rain when leaving a restaurant in London, takes an umbrella to shelter him on his way to the station and abandons it in the train on his arrival at Nottingham. He should be guilty of theft.[578]

---

[573] Pawnbrokers Act 1872, s 33 was repealed from 1 August 1977, and not replaced by the Consumer Credit Act 1974.

[574] *Phillips and Strong* (1801) 2 East PC 662; *Crump* (1825) 1 C & P 658; *Addis* (1844) 1 Cox CC 78.

[575] Above, para 2.341.

[576] [1996] 1 Cr App R 175.

[577] p 188.

[578] cf *Marshall* [1998] 2 Cr App R 282.

Stealing or obtaining cheques

In *Preddy*, Lord Goff noted that the cheque D obtains does belong to V but said that D 2.346
would not be guilty of stealing it because he had no intention permanently to deprive V of
it—he knew that the cheque form would, after presentation, be returned to V via his bank
(or at least be available for V's collection).[579] Since the House was not required to decide
whether D might be guilty of obtaining this item of property, it is submitted that this
was *obiter* (as well as wrong) but the Court of Appeal in *Graham*[580] treated it as ratio and
in *Clark*[581] held that it was bound by that decision. So at present a cheque form cannot be
stolen or obtained.

Things to be returned—but for a price

A problem similar to that of the cheque arises with the theft of a railway ticket or any other 2.347
ticket which entitles the holder to services or goods when he returns it.[582] If D takes the
ticket from another passenger, V, there is no difficulty. D intends to deprive V permanently
not only of the piece of paper but also of the thing in action (the contractual right to travel)
which it represents; but if he takes the ticket from the rail company intending to use it, he
may well intend to give it up at the end of the journey.[583] The rail company own the piece
of paper but they cannot own the contractual right to travel. As with a cheque,[584] it may be
said that D intends to return a different thing, a cancelled ticket with a hole punched in it;
it has lost its virtue.

An alternative explanation is that D intends that the railway company shall have the ticket 2.348
only by paying for it—through the provision of a ride on the train. That should be enough.
This explanation has the advantage that it extends to things which are intended to be
returned (but only for value) in an unchanged form. For example, D takes tokens from a
coffee shop intending to return them in exchange for his espresso. In all these cases there
is probably a conditional intention permanently to deprive in the literal sense. The ticket
and the tokens will probably not be returned at all if the taker realizes that he is not going
to receive the value they represent.

Sentencing

A person guilty of an offence of theft will be liable on conviction, on indictment, to impris- 2.349
onment for a term not exceeding seven years.

---

[579] This assumes they will all be retained for V. Modern banking practice is not to do so.

[580] [1997] 1 Cr App R 302.

[581] [2001] Crim LR 572, [2001] EWCA Crim 884. The court did not refer to the decision in *Arnold*
[1997] 4 All ER 1, 15, where the court had stated that 'there is a good reason for the application of s 6(1) if
the intention of the transferee at the time of the appropriation is that the document should find its way back
to the transferor only after all the benefit to the transferor has been lost or removed as a result of its use'.

[582] cf *Marshall* [1998] 2 Cr App R 282, above.

[583] At one time everyone knew that all tickets had to be given to the collector at the end of the journey, but,
in these days of 'open stations', this is not necessarily so. If I am travelling to King's Cross (an open station)
I expect (and intend) to retain my ticket; but if I am travelling to Leeds (a closed station), I expect (and intend)
to give it up.

[584] Above, para 2.346.

2.350   The courts have identified theft in breach of trust as being a particularly serious form of the offence where immediate custody will, save in exceptional cases, be inevitable. In *Clark*[585] the Court of Appeal reviewed the guidance given in *Barrick*[586] in light factors including the change in early release provisions, the reduction in minimum term from ten to seven years and inflation. The following factors were identified as relevant to a court's decision regarding sentence in such cases:

(a) the quality and degree of trust reposed in the offender, including his rank;

(b) the period over which the fraud or the thefts had been perpetrated;

(c) the use to which the property taken was put;

(d) the effect on the victim;

(e) the impact of the offences on the public and public confidence;

(f) the effect on fellow employees or partners;

(g) the effect on the offender himself;

(h) his own history; and

(i) those matters of mitigation special to the offender, such as illness, being placed under great strain by excessive responsibility or the like, where, as sometimes happened, there had been a long delay, say, over two years, between his being confronted with his dishonesty and the start of his trial and any help given by him to the police.

Their lordships gave the following guidelines based on the value of the sums stolen in breach of trust in contested cases:[587]

(a) where the sum stolen was not small but was less than £17,500 a range between a short custodial sentence and twenty-one months would be appropriate;

(b) where the sum stolen was between about £17,500 and £100,000 a term of two to three years' imprisonment would be appropriate;

(c) theft of between £100,000 and £250,000 would justify three to four years' imprisonment;

(d) cases involving £250,000 to £1,000,000 would justify five to nine years' imprisonment; and

(e) where the sum stolen exceeded £1,000,000 the sentence would exceed ten years.

2.351   Professional thieves will attract heavier sentences than other offenders. Also those who target vulnerable victims on the street or in their homes will face prison sentences. In November 2006, the Sentencing Advisory Panel recommended that the starting point for sentencing offenders who have stolen from an elderly or otherwise vulnerable victim should be eighteen months' imprisonment.[588] Where the theft is from the vulnerable person's home, the Panel recommended that the starting point should be thirty-six weeks and two years where there was the threat of violence.

---

[585] [1998] 2 Cr App R 137.

[586] 81 Cr App R 78.

[587] Appropriate discounts should be given where there has been a guilty plea.

[588] *Theft and Dishonesty Offences Consultation Paper*, 1 Nov 2006.

3

THE FRAUD ACT 2006

Introduction

Having received Royal Assent on 8 November 2006, the Fraud Act 2006 came into force **3.01**
on 15 January 2007.[1] It provides, for the first time a statutory 'general fraud offence'. It has
far-reaching consequences for English criminal law's approach to prosecuting dishonest
conduct. However, not all of those consequences have, it seems, been fully appreciated by
the draftsman.

The 2006 Act abolishes the eight heavily used[2] deception offences in the Theft Acts 1968 **3.02**
and 1978,[3] including that inserted post-*Preddy* by the Theft (Amendment) Act 1996.[4] The
principal replacement is the general fraud offence created by s 1 in the following terms:

(1) A person is guilty of fraud if he is in breach of any of the sections listed in subsection (2) (which
provide for different ways of committing the offence).

---

[1] Fraud Act 2006 (Commencement) Order 2006, SI 2006/3200. See also Fraud Act 2006, Sch 2, paras 2
and 3.

[2] There were 14,000 prosecutions in 2003: Hansard, HL, 22 June 2005, col 1652 (Attorney-General); for
the anticipated impact on the efficiency of prosecutions see Home Office document <http://www.homeoffice.
gov.uk/documents/cons-fraud-law-reform/Fraud_Bill_RIA.pfd>

[3] Obtaining property: 1968, s 15; Obtaining a money transfer: 1968, s 15A; Obtaining a pecuniary advantage: 1968, s 16; Procuring the execution of a valuable security: 1968, s 20(2); Obtaining services: 1978, s 1;
Securing the remission of a liability: 1978, s 2(1)(a); Inducing a creditor to wait for or to forgo payment:
1978, s 2(1)(b); Obtaining an exemption from or abatement of liability: 1978, s 2(1)(c). These offences were
examined in full in earlier editions.

[4] See the 8th edition, paras 4.60–4.64.

(2) The sections are—

    (a) section 2 (fraud by false representation),

    (b) section 3 (fraud by failing to disclose information), and

    (c) section 4 (fraud by abuse of position).

(3) A person who is guilty of fraud is liable—

    (a) on summary conviction, to imprisonment for a term not exceeding 12 months or to a fine not exceeding the statutory maximum (or to both);

    (b) on conviction on indictment, to imprisonment for a term not exceeding 10 years or to a fine (or to both).

3.03 The offence of fraud can be committed in one of three ways as proscribed by ss 2–4. Each is based on dishonest conduct against property interests, and carries a maximum ten-year sentence on indictment. Astonishingly, the 2006 Act manages to introduce a general fraud offence, use the term fraud as a label for the offences, and yet fails to provide any definition, instead producing three *descriptions* of proscribed conduct.

3.04 Liability arises by making false representations (s 2), failing to disclose information (s 3), or abusing a position of financial trust (s 4). Each form of the fraud offence is a conduct offence, complete on the accused's acts irrespective of any result caused, which represents a significant shift from the deception offences they replace. Obtaining services by deception is replaced by obtaining services dishonestly (s 11), producing a charge designed for cases where the obtaining was by wholly automated processes. Other provisions are discussed elsewhere in this edition.[5] The background to the Act is discussed more fully in chapter 1.

General matters of interpretation

3.05 The 2006 Act is a short statute designed to be unburdened by the technicality which bedevilled the old law. The Act is not a codifying Act. It is modelled largely on the Law Commission Bill attached to the *Fraud Report* No 276[6] and that document will serve as a useful interpretative tool. Indeed, given the government's refusal to define in any detail many of the core elements of the offences, the Law Commission Report may become an especially significant interpretative document.[7]

3.06 In addition to the Law Commission Consultation Paper and Report, valuable insights may be gleaned from the Home Office Consultation Paper, Home Office Paper of Responses to Consultation, and the House of Commons Research Paper 06/31.[8] Of the Parliamentary debates, the most important are probably the House of Commons Standing Committee B Debates for 20 June 2006.[9] Other documents relating to the history of the Bill have been published on the internet by the Home Office.[10] As noted, the Act leaves many core terms of the offences undefined. In most instances this is

---

[5] See on ss 6 and 7 ch 9 below.

[6] <http://www.lawcom.gov.uk/docs/lc276.pdf>

[7] On the use of explanatory notes as a method of statutory interpretation see *Montila* [2004] UKHL 50.

[8] <http://www.parliament.uk/commons/lib/research/rp2006/rp06–031.pfd>

[9] <http://www.publications.parliament.uk/pa/cm200506/cmbills/166/sc1662006.257–260.html>

[10] <http://www.homeoffice.gov.uk/documents/cons-fraud-law-reform/?version=1>

deliberate, with the Home Office explaining that the absence of definition is intended to ensure the broadest interpretation of the legislation.[11]

The language of the statute is rather odd in places and in some respects more suited to **3.07** the creation of statutory torts rather than crimes. Thus, for example, s 1 describes a person as being guilty if he is 'in breach of', and the principal offence ss 2–4 echo this by providing that 'a person is in breach of this section if . . .'. The offence of fraud will therefore be charged in one of three forms—s 1(2)(a) (fraud by false representation under s 2); s 1(2)(b) (fraud by failure to disclose under s 3); s 1(2)(c) (fraud by abuse of position under s 4). The particularity and complexity of this scheme was unnecessary. Sections 2–4 could have been free-standing offences in their own right. If nothing else it would have rendered it easier for the courts to discern sentencing principles for the very different types of offending involved in each of these sections and may have generated greater clarity in prosecution policies.

Commencement

Transitional provisions are set out in Schedule 2. Under para 3(1) of Schedule 2 the old **3.08** deception offences under the Theft Acts offences will continue to apply for any offences partly committed before 15 January 2007.

Paragraph 3(2) of Schedule 2 defines an offence as being 'partly committed' when: a rele- **3.09** vant event occurred before 15 January 2007, and another 'relevant event' occurred on or after 15 January 2007. A 'relevant event' is, for these purposes, defined in para 3(3) of Schedule 2 as 'any act, omission or other event (including any result of one or more acts or omissions) proof of which is required for conviction of the offence'. In short, only where no part of a relevant event occurred before 15 January will the 2006 Act offences apply.

Where it is unclear whether a 'relevant event' occurred before or after commencement it **3.10** will be necessary for the Crown to put alternative counts on the indictment under the 2006 Act and the previous legislation. This practice was endorsed in *Bellman*[12] where the House of Lords held that where there is prima facie evidence that a defendant has committed either crime A or crime B then both crimes may be charged and left to the jury, even though proof of crime A will establish that D cannot have committed crime B and vice versa. Where it is clear that D has committed crime A or crime B but there is no evidence to say when the crime has been committed then neither crime can be left to the jury.[13]

Jurisdiction

Background

The question of extraterritoriality was raised by the government in its 2004 Consultation **3.11** Paper. The majority of respondents favoured giving the UK courts nationality jurisdiction

---

[11] See eg the lack of definition of the term 'abuse' in s 4, below, para 3.161. In general the government were reluctant to provide a rigorous analysis of any terms.

[12] [1989] AC 836.

[13] See on this *C* [2005] EWCA Crim 3533.

but, despite this support, the government decided not to do so. This was explained in its Report:[14]

The majority favoured taking nationality jurisdiction. As one put it, in an age of globalisation, the UK should take a certain responsibility for ensuring its nationals do not exploit people in other countries whose authorities are unable to protect them. However some of those who took this view cited types of cases which can in fact be dealt with already under the Criminal Justice Act 1993. Since the implementation of Part 1 of the 1993 Act, if any act or omission proof of which is required for conviction of a crime of deception takes place in the UK, our jurisdiction will already catch the case. The wide effect of the 1993 Act is not always appreciated: it only came into effect in 1999 and its use so far has therefore been limited. . . . So, for example, no jurisdictional problem will arise in 'phishing' cases, even though the fraudster typically operates abroad. If he targets people in the UK by sending them false representations in order to obtain their personal financial details, with a view to making a gain or causing them loss, then he will be committing an offence of fraud which falls within our jurisdiction under the 1993 Act. (Whether he can be successfully detected and brought to book for that offence is, of course, a different issue.)

3.12 The government concluded that, given the provisions of the Criminal Justice Act 1993 there was inadequate justification for taking the unusual step of asserting extraterritorial jurisdiction.

The jurisdictional scope of the fraud offences

3.13 Section 2 of the Criminal Justice Act 1993 currently provides the courts with jurisdiction over fraud offences:

if any of the events which are relevant events in relation to the offence occurred in England and Wales. A 'relevant event' is defined as, 'any act or omission or other event (including any result of one or more acts or omissions), proof of which is required for conviction of the offence.'

3.14 Schedule 1 to the 2006 Act makes consequential amendments to the 1993 Act to provide for its application to all the offences in the 2006 Act. It was necessary to amend the provisions because the 1993 Act would not apply to the new 'conduct-based' 2006 Act offences if the only act within this jurisdiction was the obtaining of property: that would no longer be a 'relevant event' since it is not a requirement of the fraud offences to prove that property was in fact obtained. It was considered desirable that English courts continue to have jurisdiction over frauds when the gain or loss that the fraudster makes takes place in this jurisdiction.

D performs acts abroad and loss/gain occurs in England

3.15 The courts continue to have jurisdiction when property is fraudulently gained/lost in England or Wales, even though the conduct causing this result has taken place in another country (or countries as where D in the USA makes false representations to V in Canada causing V's London bank account to be debited). The 1993 Act provides that if any act or omission, proof of which is required for conviction of a relevant crime (a 'relevant event'), takes place here it will be capable of prosecution in England and Wales. Schedule 1 to the 2006 Act amends the 1993 Act to extend the meaning of 'relevant event' to include—

(a) if the fraud involved an intention to make a gain and the gain occurred, *that occurrence*; and

---

[14] Para 53.

(b) if the fraud involved an intention to cause a loss or to expose another to a risk of loss and the loss occurred, *that occurrence* [emphasis added].

D performs acts abroad with intent to cause loss/gain in England but no such gain/loss arises

Where, however, D performs one of the elements of the fraud offence abroad (eg making **3.16** the false representation under s 2, or abusing the financial position under s 4), but intends to make a gain which will occur in England and Wales or cause a loss in this jurisdiction, the 1993 Act (as amended by the 2006 Act) will not apply unless *there is an actual gain or loss within England and Wales*. The Act could have extended the meaning of 'relevant event' to include the making of the false representation, etc with intent rather than the result (given that these are now conduct crimes), but 'curiously'[15] did not do so.

Common Elements of the Fraud Offence

Dishonesty

The principal element of *mens rea* for the offence of fraud in each of its three forms is **3.17** that of dishonesty. The Law Commission and the Home Office intended that the *Ghosh* definition should apply, and this was confirmed repeatedly[16] in the Parliamentary debates.

If D is claiming a lack of dishonesty, the '*Ghosh* test'—(taken from *Feely*[17] and *Ghosh*[18]) **3.18** provides a two-part mixed subjective and objective test.

(a) Was what was done dishonest by the ordinary standards of reasonable and honest people? If no, not guilty; if yes, consider (b).
(b) Must D have realized that what he was doing was dishonest according to these standards? If yes, guilty.

Dishonesty is a subjective concept. The jury must assess D's actual beliefs, whether reason- **3.19** able or not. The reasonableness or otherwise of the alleged belief is relevant only to the question whether it is actually held or not.[19]

There have been powerful criticisms of the interpretation of dishonesty. It was described in **3.20** the House of Commons debates as 'tortuous'.[20] The strongest academic criticisms were voiced by Professor Griew, author of *The Theft Acts 1968 and 1978*,[21] and 'Objections to *Feely* and *Ghosh*'.[22] Griew argued that the *Ghosh* test: confuses the state of mind of the defendant with the concept of dishonesty; leaves a question of law to the jury; leads to longer trials because the issue of dishonesty will more often be a live issue; assumes a community norm of

---

[15] See *Blackstone's Criminal Practice* (2007) B5–99.
[16] See Hansard, HL Debates, 19 July 2005, col 1424 (Attorney-General); the House of Commons Research Paper 31/06, p 14; Standing Committee B, 20 June 2006, col 8 (Solicitor-General).
[17] [1973] 1 QB 530.
[18] [1982] 1 QB 1053.
[19] *Lewis* (1975) 62 Cr App R 206, [1976] Crim LR 383, CA.
[20] Hansard, HC, 12 June 2006, col 553 (Brian Jenkins MP).
[21] (7th edn, 1995).
[22] [1985] Crim LR 341.

honesty within the jury; assumes jurors are honest (or that they will adopt such a virtue when serving as jurors); leads to more trials because fewer defendants will plead guilty given the lack of definition; leads to the possibility of inconsistent decisions on identical facts; assumes 'dishonesty' has only one meaning; and is unsuitable in specialized cases especially those involving complex frauds where the jury have no appreciation of the propriety of conduct which is unfamiliar to them.[23]

ECHR compatibility

3.21 Because this question of law is left to the jury to define, it has been suggested that the *Ghosh* approach to dishonesty may also fall foul of Article 7 of the ECHR, which proscribes retrospective criminalization. This is a particular concern with an offence of fraud drafted as widely as that in ss 1–4 with no requirement for any loss or even any prejudicing of the economic interests of another. The Law Commission initially doubted the potential compliance with Article 7 of the ECHR of an offence based wholly on dishonesty,[24] and repeated that view in its final Report on *Fraud No 276*. The Fraud Act has however been confirmed by the Home Secretary and the Attorney-General as being ECHR compatible—as is required by s 19 of the Human Rights Act 1998. The Joint Parliamentary Committee on Human Rights, in its *Fourteenth Report*[25] also concluded that the new offences were compatible with the ECHR Article 7 and common law requirements of certainty:

> the new general offence of fraud *is not* a general dishonesty offence. Rather, it embeds as an element in the definition of the offence some identifiable morally dubious conduct to which the test of dishonesty may be applied, as the Law Commission correctly observed is required by the principle of legal certainty. We are therefore satisfied that, as defined in the Bill, the new general offence of fraud satisfies the common law and ECHR requirement that criminal offences be defined with sufficient clarity and precision to enable the public to predict with sufficient certainty whether or not they will be liable.[26]

The Committee did however confirm that:

> a general dishonesty offence would be incompatible with the common law principle of legality. In our view it would also be in breach of the requirement of legal certainty in Articles 5 and 7 ECHR for the same reasons.[27]

For this reason it doubted the compatibility of conspiracy to defraud.

3.22 It is worth pausing to consider what 'morally dubious' conduct over and above dishonesty renders the conduct criminal. In the s 2 offence, it is little more than making a false representation—ie lying, which might also be fairly described in many contexts at least as 'being

---

[23] See further the discussion of dishonesty in ch 2, para 2.270. One of the few supporters of the definition and its application in fraud is Scanlan: G Scanlan, 'Dishonesty in Corporate Offences: A Need for Reform' (2002) Comp Law 114, 118.

[24] See Law Com No 155, paras 5.33–5.53, and DC Ormerod [1999] Crim LR 789.

[25] <http://www.publications.parliament.uk/pa/jt200506/jtselect/jtrights/134/13402.htm>

[26] Para 2.14, emphasis added. See also the Attorney-General's statements in debate: Hansard, 19 July 2005, col 1424.

[27] ibid, para 2.12.

dishonest'. That is the 'additional' element which the Committee regards as preventing the offence being one solely of dishonesty! Similarly in s 4, the morally dubious conduct additional to dishonesty seems hard to identify, it could be something as innocuous as failing to work for an employer as hard as one might.

Claims of right

There is no equivalent to s 2 of the Theft Act 1968 and therefore, D's claims to be acting **3.23** under a claim of right are no guarantee of acquittal. Dishonesty under the Act is based solely on *Ghosh*.[28] It is submitted that this is a fundamental flaw with the section and that a claim of right is as inconsistent with dishonesty under ss 2–4 as it is for theft. If D has a claim of right to the property he should not be at risk of criminal liability.[29] For example if D lies to V in order to persuade V to return to D his own property, there should be no question of criminal liability. It is unlikely that in practice any defendant would ever be found to be dishonest under *Ghosh* in such circumstances.

Equally, it is submitted that there should be no criminal liability for the defendant **3.24** who genuinely believes he has a claim of right to the property which he seeks to gain, or indeed where D genuinely believes he has a claim of right to cause V to lose that property. It is unlikely, though not impossible, that someone in such circumstances would be found to be dishonest within the meaning in *Ghosh*. A jury might well think a person dishonest who had made a deliberately false representation even where he did so to get something to which he thought he was entitled.[30] It is doubtful that it is in the public interest to prosecute where the claim is a genuine one and substantiated by evidence.

It is submitted that a mistake of civil law giving rise to a belief in a claim of right ought **3.25** to be a defence.[31] One argument in support of such an interpretation is the desire to maintain coherence between the offence of theft and that of fraud.[32] If D believes the property to be his own, whether through a mistake of fact or a mistake of law, he has a defence if the charge is brought as theft. There are good reasons to suggest that it would be wrong that he should have no defence if the charge is brought under s 1 of the 2006 Act. If the

---

[28] Above, para 2.296. See *Melwani* [1989] Crim LR 565, CA.

[29] cf the Law Commission recommending that a claim of right ought not be a defence in all cases, No 276, para 7.66.

[30] In *Falconer-Atlee* (1973) 58 Cr App R 348 at 358, a case of theft, the judge's direction on dishonesty was held to be defective because he omitted to tell the jury that s 2(1)(a) expressly provided that a person with a claim of right was not dishonest. Yet, since D's mistake, if any, was a mistake of fact, the direction does not seem to have been necessary or, indeed, appropriate. The court in *Woolven* (1983) 77 Cr App R 231 distinguished that case, not because it was a case of theft but, apparently, on the ground that the direction in the instant case did, in effect, if not in so many words, tell the jury to acquit if they thought D might have a claim of right.

[31] The CPS has issued guidance to prosecutors stating that: 'The criminal law is not a suitable vehicle to regulate such disputes. Before a criminal charge can proceed the ownership of any property must be absolutely clear. If that ownership is in real dispute the criminal law should not be invoked until ownership has been established in the civil courts. However, circumstances will arise where the issues are clear and the offences are serious. If so, prosecution may be required in the public interest. Prosecutors should ensure that the state of affairs between the parties has not changed prior to any trial. This may affect both the public interest and the evidential test.' <http://www.cps.gov.uk>

[32] Arguably the moral wrong in the two offences is quite distinct, with theft being designed to protect property rights and the associated rights of transfer of property etc and fraud being to protect against dishonest exploitation of others. The House of Lords' broad interpretation of theft undermines such a distinction.

judge has to direct the jury expressly on the theft charge that claim of right is a defence (and it is submitted that he should), then it is desirable that he should also have to do so on the fraud charge, instead of leaving the jury to deduce this from the general *Ghosh* direction.[33]

3.26   If this interpretation is correct, D should have a defence in the following case: D's car has been obtained from him by X, who gave a cheque drawn on a bank where he had no account and who never paid the price. X has sold the car to a bona-fide purchaser, V. V refuses to give up the car to D. D, believing that he is entitled to have the car back, recovers possession by pretending to be a mechanic from V's garage collecting the car for servicing. He would be able to rely on the defence in s 2 of the 1968 Act if charged with theft, and ought therefore to be acquitted if charged with fraud contrary to s 1(2)(a) and s 2 of the Fraud Act 2006 for the false representation which he has made with intent to gain/cause loss. D is certainly guilty of a false representation; but if he genuinely believes he is entitled to possession of the car, it is submitted that the jury should be told that he is not 'dishonest' for the purposes of the section.

3.27   Probably the same result must follow where D's belief relates not to any specific property but to the repayment of debt: D, a Hungarian woman, has been V's mistress. On the termination of the relationship, V promises to pay D £100. Later he declines to do so. D is advised by a Hungarian lawyer that she is entitled to the money. By a false representation she seeks to persuade V to pay her £100.[34] In such a case there was, and no doubt is, a sufficient claim of right to negative an 'intent to steal'; and, if so, there should equally be a defence to an offence of fraud under s 1(2)(a) and s 2 for false representation.

3.28   A more difficult case is that where D intends to gain something other than the thing to which he has a claim of right. D's employer, E, cannot pay D's wages because he cannot obtain payment of a debt owed by V to E. D, by fraud, obtains some of V's property and delivers it to E, hoping thereby to enable E to procure the payment of the debt—and the means to pay D's wages. In such a case[35] Coleridge J thought that the facts negatived an intent to defraud; and in a subsequent case[36] Pollock CB put this on the ground that D must have thought he had some right to obtain the property which he did obtain. Of course, he had no right in law so to do, in which case the decision on these facts must depend on the state of D's mind in the particular case. Did he, or did he not, believe he had, or that E had, a legal right to act in this way? Looked at in this way, it would seem rather unlikely that a claim of right could often be made out. D had a claim of right to his wages; E had a claim of right to payment by V of the debt (both being actual rights) but the question is whether D had a claim of right to the particular property he obtained

---

[33] In *Parker* (1910) 74 JP 208 Ridley J held that a claim of right was no answer to a charge of demanding money upon a forged document with intent to defraud. In *Woolven*, the court thought that case was not a decisive authority against a claim of right defence under s 15; and *Parker* has been overruled by the Forgery and Counterfeiting Act 1981, s 10(2). cf *Smith and Hogan, Criminal Law* 877 and the fourth edition of this book, paras 181–3.

[34] cf *Bernhard* [1938] 2 KB 264, below, para 12.49.

[35] *Williams* (1836) 7 C & P 354. cf *Close* [1977] Crim LR 107, CA.

[36] *Hamilton* (1845) 1 Cox CC 244.

by the false representation. Few people would suppose today that they have a right to behave fraudulently to a debtor to compel him to pay his creditor.

One important consequence of the absence of an automatic and complete defence of **3.29** a claim of right is that, for example, under s 2, D's attempts to qualify his false representations with a disclaimer will not automatically lead to acquittal unless the qualification is judged sufficient to displace any degree of falsity.

In the event of a prosecution for an alleged fraud where D has a claim of right or a belief **3.30** in a claim of right, it is important that the jury is directed that dishonesty is a separate element of the offence. D may deliberately make a false representation, yet not act dishonestly.[37] The jury should always be directed that they must be satisfied that the conduct alleged under ss 2–4 as appropriate was done dishonestly.[38]

Practical implications of reliance on Ghosh

Reliance on *Ghosh* increases the chances that more cases will go to trial as defendants have **3.31** little to lose by 'trying their luck' with a jury. In terms of principle, the lack of certainty in the substantive law and inefficiency in the criminal justice system it creates render this undesirable. There is also a sting in the tail: in some cases there may soon be no jury on which D can chance his luck. The government has introduced the Fraud (Trials without a Jury) Bill 2006, which will allow for trial by High Court judge alone (cl 2(1)).[39]

With intent to gain or cause loss or to expose to a risk of loss

Section 5 defines the meaning of 'gain' and 'loss' for the purposes of ss 2–4. **3.32**

(1) The references to gain and loss in sections 2 to 4 are to be read in accordance with this section.
(2) 'Gain' and 'loss'—
    (a) extend only to gain or loss in money or other property;
    (b) include any such gain or loss whether temporary or permanent;
    and 'property' means any property whether real or personal (including things in action and other intangible property).
(3) 'Gain' includes a gain by keeping what one has, as well as a gain by getting what one does not have.
(4) 'Loss' includes a loss by not getting what one might get, as well as a loss by parting with what one has.

The definitions are essentially the same as those in s 34(2)(a) of the Theft Act 1968.[40] **3.33** Under these definitions, 'gain' and 'loss' are limited to gain and loss in money or other property. 'Property', in this context is defined as in s 4(1) of the Theft Act 1968.[41] The definition of 'property' covers all forms of property; the government was keen to ensure that

---

[37] See *Wright* [1960] Crim LR 366; *Griffiths* [1966] 1 QB 589, [1965] 2 All ER 448; and *Talbott* [1995] Crim LR 396.

[38] *Potger* (1970) 55 Cr App R 42; but see also *McVey* [1988] Crim LR 127 and commentary.

[39] This amends the controversial provision in the Criminal Justice Act 2003, s 43 which has not yet been brought into force.

[40] cf in particular their use in relation to false accounting, Theft Act 1968 s 17. They are also used in the Trade Marks Act 1994.

[41] See above ch 2.

the definition paralleled that in the Theft Act.[42] None of the special exceptions in s 4 of the 1968 apply: there can be fraud with intent to gain/cause loss of land, wild animals and flora, but they cannot be stolen.

3.34 In most cases 'an intention to gain' and an 'intention to cause loss' will go hand in hand; V's loss will be D's gain. The phrase, 'intent to cause loss' is not, however, superfluous. There may be circumstances in which D intends to cause a loss to V without any corresponding gain to D. Problems arose in some cases under the old law because the deception might cause a gain which did not correspond to a loss. In the *Guinness case*,[43] Guinness plc and Argyll Group plc were competing to take over Distillers Company plc. Both made offers partly based on their own share price and the Guinness directors entered into a fraudulent share support scheme to make their offer appear more valuable. The victims included Argyll, Distillers, their shareholders, those who bought Guinness shares at falsely inflated prices, and other indirect losers for example other companies who would have received more investment without the false enthusiasm for Guinness shares. The gains and losses were quite different.

3.35 The consequence of making the intentions alternative sufficient bases for liability is that the offences become even broader. For example, D who starts a false rumour that V is going out of business, commits the s 2 offence if he does so with intent to lead customers away from V intending V to lose or be exposed to a risk of loss and is regarded as dishonest in doing so.[44] Is such conduct properly described as fraud? There is no requirement that D seeks to gain by these actions. Similarly, D who borrows money from his neighbour and lies to avoid repayment is liable.[45]

Intention

3.36 Intention should bear its ordinary meaning, and should extend as elsewhere in the criminal law to include the foresight of a virtually certain consequence.[46] This may be significant in extending the scope of the offences. For example, it is sufficient that D makes a false representation foreseeing that it is virtually certain to cause loss to V although that is not his purpose, and although he hopes that V does not lose.

Remoteness

3.37 It should be noted that although the fraud offences are not result-based crimes, the element of intent to gain/cause loss does involve a causal link that must be established. It is '*by the*' false representation that D must intend to make the gain or cause the loss. How remote can

---

[42] See Standing Committee B, 20 June 2006, col 32 (Solicitor-General).
[43] See *Saunders* [1996] Cr App R 463, and more generally, N Kochan and H Pym, *The Guinness Affair* (1987).
[44] See No 276, para 4.13.
[45] Standing Committee, B, 22 June 2006, col 30 (Solicitor-General).
[46] See Hansard, HL, 19 July 2005, col 1414 (Attorney-General). cf the definition advanced by the House of Lords in the context of murder in *Woollin* [1998] AC 82:

(1) A result is intended when it is the actor's purpose to cause it.
(2) A court or jury *may also find* that a result is intended, though it is not the actor's purpose to cause it, when—
  (a) the result is a virtually certain consequence of that act, and
  (b) the actor knows that it is a virtually certain consequence.

D's intentions be? Suppose that D makes false representations to induce V, a wealthy banker, to marry him. Is he guilty of the s 2 offence if one intention is to enrich himself? Presumably such matters are for the jury to determine.[47]

What of the more thoughtful defence: that it is not by the false representation (under s 2) **3.38** or the failure to disclose (under s 3) or the abuse of position (under s 4) that D intends to gain/cause loss, but by some other conduct? One obvious example is where D makes a number of representations in relation to a sale: eg that a car is a genuine VW, that it has a specific mileage and that it has one careful lady owner. Can D argue that the final representation, though false, is not one by which he intended to make a gain? This may well become subsumed in a plea of honesty, but it is a distinct element of the offence and deserves to be drawn to the jury's attention. The jury will properly have regard to all the circumstances. The fact that the representation relates to a peripheral matter will not entitle the defendant to an acquittal: a proposal that the misrepresentation must be a 'material' one to qualify under s 2 was expressly rejected by the Attorney-General during the debates.[48] What is in issue then is solely a matter of D's intent. It seems to be a question of fact and degree in every case whether what was said was intended to be a misrepresentation. The jury would have to be sure that D made a representation that was untrue or misleading, and in relation to *that* representation (i) D knew it was or might have been false, and (ii) that D made the representation dishonestly, and (iii) that D, by making *that* representation, intended to make a gain/cause loss etc.

The problem may be dealt with more easily where D has made two or more false repre- **3.39** sentations. In such a case the Crown may incorporate all the representations in one count indicting the conduct as eg 'falsely representing the details of the car for sale' and rely on the two statements (original form of vehicle and previous ownership) as evidence of the dishonest intent to gain. This raises a further problem which the Act does not address—must each false representation be alleged in a separate count? There is a real likelihood that prosecutors will wrap up a number of representations in one count. In a long-running investment fraud this matter might be critical and inhibit the defendant's case, especially if he wants to run the causal intent defence. It may also give rise to a *Brown* problem:[49] six jurors might think that D is guilty because of representation A and six because of representation B.

A similar problem arises if D uses the false representation in order to secure a job, and **3.40** intends to work hard and give value for money once he is in post. In such cases D must surely foresee that it is virtually certain that his conduct in making the false representation will lead him to gain.

Claims of right

It is not necessarily a good defence that D believes he has a right to the gain or loss he **3.41** seeks. If he has such a belief, then he might not be dishonest under *Ghosh*, but he still has the intention to gain (and/or to cause loss). A may be owed £100 by B and be unable to

---

[47] The Court of Appeal seems reluctant to impose clear rules of remoteness in criminal law contexts. See eg *Kennedy No 2* [2005] EWCA Crim 785.

[48] Hansard, HL, 19 July 2005, cols 1419–20.

[49] See *Brown* (1984) 79 Cr App R 115.

get payment. Perhaps A needs the money badly and B is in a position to pay; or perhaps A can easily afford to wait and B is in difficulty. Should it be an offence for A to lie to B to get back his money? In view of the clear authority on the construction of the same expression in false accounting,[50] it seems hopeless to argue under the Fraud Act that there is in fact no gain where a person merely secures the payment of that which he is owed. 'Gain' certainly means 'profit', but the Court of Appeal has held that the element of intent to gain is satisfied by proof of an intention to 'acquire' even that property to which D is entitled. *A fortiori*, there will be a relevant intention where D genuinely though mistakenly believes that he is entitled to the gain (or to cause the loss). Such cases will be rare.

3.42   It might be argued that the definition in s 5 is too wide since it criminalizes the situation where D intends V not to get something which V might have gained, even though V was not entitled to it. For example, under s 2, if V asks D for a loan and D denies it him by saying falsely that he has no money to spare, D has made a false representation with intent to cause V not to gain that which he might[51] have obtained.[52] V has at most suffered a loss of a chance. D might avoid liability by arguing that a simple refusal, however malicious or dishonest is not a 'representation'. Any explanation which is proffered for that refusal may or may not be a representation, but it cannot be said that the representation itself was intended to cause loss or damage. Such representations are designed to ease the loss and damage caused by the refusal. D's additional/alternative saving grace is that he is probably not going to be regarded as dishonest in those circumstances.[53]

3.43   The extent of criminal liability may seem excessively broad and include making a false statement with intent to cause someone to be exposed to the risk of temporarily not being able to get that which he might otherwise have got! How will the prosecution prove the intention to cause loss by not getting what one might get? Is it enough in practice that D believes that there was a chance that V would make a gain?

Exposure to temporary loss

3.44   There is no requirement that D acts with intent to deprive V permanently of any property. It would seem to be sufficient under s 2, for example, that D makes a false representation to V with intent to cause V to lend D property[54] which D intends to return in an unaltered form. The offence comes close to criminalizing dishonest deprivation of the value of an item's usefulness. This strains the property based foundation of the offence.

Intention to expose another to a risk of loss

3.45   The offence of fraud is rendered yet wider because it is sufficient that D intends that V will be exposed to the risk of loss; there is no need for the Crown to prove that D had a more specific intention that V will lose. D who makes a false representation on his health insurance form will be liable under s 2. He intends the insurance company to be exposed to a

---

[50]   *A-G's Reference (No 1 of 2001)* [2002] Crim LR 844.
[51]   The offence would have been much tighter with a requirement that D intended that loss/gain would occur.
[52]   See GR Sullivan, 'Fraud and Efficiency in the Criminal Law' [1985] Crim LR 616.
[53]   See Standing Committee B, 20 June 2006, cols 33–5.
[54]   Even that to which D is already entitled. cf *Zemmel* [1985] Crim LR 213, and the Law Com Working Paper *Conspiracy to Defraud* (1988) para 4.4 rejecting this as a sufficient basis for criminal liability.

risk of loss, even though he desperately hopes that he will remain healthy and they will not incur actual loss.

D who makes a false statement in a job reference for V will be liable if he intends that V **3.46** will thereby not be promoted and attain the higher salary appropriate to that post.

Section 2: Fraud by False Representation

The offence created by s 1(2)(a) of the Act is incredibly broad. The offence is described in **3.47** section 2, which provides:

(1) A person is in breach of this section if he—
    (a) dishonestly makes a false representation, and
    (b) intends, by making the representation—
        (i) to make a gain for himself or another, or
        (ii) to cause loss to another or to expose another to a risk of loss.
(2) A representation is false if—
    (a) it is untrue or misleading, and
    (b) the person making it knows that it is, or might be, untrue or misleading.
(3) 'Representation' means any representation as to fact or law, including a representation as to the state of mind of—
    (a) the person making the representation, or
    (b) any other person.
(4) A representation may be express or implied.
(5) For the purposes of this section a representation may be regarded as made if it (or anything implying it) is submitted in any form to any system or device designed to receive, convey or respond to communications (with or without human intervention).

Section 1 provides that the maximum sentence on indictment is ten years. The offence **3.48** should be charged as fraud by false representation contrary to s 1(2)(a) and s 2.

The elements of the offence: **3.49**

The *actus reus* requires proof that D:

- made a representation
- which is untrue or misleading

and the *mens rea* requires proof that D:

- knew the representation was or knew that it might be false, and
- acted dishonestly, and
- with intent to gain or cause loss.

Conduct-based offence

Crucial to an understanding of the operation and scope of the offence is an appreciation **3.50** of the conduct-based nature of liability. Under the old law[55] it had to be proved that

---

[55] Even under the pre-1968 law, it was necessary to show that the false pretences *caused* the loss. cf S Farrell, N Yeo, and G Ladenburg who suggest that the 2006 Act is a return to the pre-1968 position—*Blackstone's Guide to the Fraud Act 2006* (2007) para 1.09.

D's conduct actually deceived V and caused him to do whatever act was appropriate to the offence charged—transferring property, executing a valuable security etc. Under s 2, there is no need to prove: a result of any kind; that the alleged victim or indeed any person believed any representation; that any person acted on it; that the accused succeeded in making a gain or causing a loss by the representation.

3.51 This shift from a result-based to conduct-based offence has numerous other practical implications. The principal aim is to make the offence easier to prove, and there is little doubt that in most cases this objective will be achieved. The effect is that D may be liable for the false representations even though: V knows that D's statement is false; or, V would have acted in the same way even if he had known of the falsity; or, V did not rely on the false representation but arrived at the same erroneous conclusion from his own observation or some other source; or, V did not read or hear the false statement; or the false representation is not 'a' cause, let alone 'the' cause of any action by V; there is in fact no identifiable victim.

3.52 Classic problems which recurred under the old law evaporate. For example, in *Laverty*,[56] a case under s 15 of the 1968 Act, D changed the registration number plates and chassis number plate of a car and sold it to V. It was held that this constituted a representation by conduct that the car was the original car to which these numbers had been assigned; but D's conviction for obtaining the price of the car by deception from V was quashed on the ground that it was not proved that the deception operated on V's mind. There was no direct evidence to that effect—V said he bought the car because he thought D was the owner—and it was not a necessary inference.[57] Under s 2 of the 2006 Act the offence is committed as soon as D dishonestly changes the number plate with intent to gain.

Time of commission of the offence

3.53 One of the most important consequences of the shift to a conduct-based offence is that the s 2 crime is complete before the point in time at which any person acts in response to the false representation (as would be required for a deception offence). Under the deception offences it was necessary for the Crown to establish that the deception preceded the relevant act by V. Although the 'start' date may now be more difficult to define in the particulars of the offence, it is unlikely to be material.

3.54 Not only is it important to recognize that the s 2 offence will usually be completed earlier in time than a comparable deception offence would have been, but it may also be committed later in time. Whereas under the old law D could only be liable if his deception occurred before eg the relevant property passed to him, under the s 2 offence, D can be liable if he makes a false representation after the entire proprietary interest has passed to him.

---

[56] [1970] 3 All ER 432. cf *Talbot* [1995] Crim LR 396.
[57] If the only flaw in the prosecution's case was that the representation did not influence V, the court had power to substitute a conviction for an attempt. They did not do so, possibly because there was also insufficient evidence that D intended to deceive V into buying the car by this representation. The purpose of changing the plates may well have been not to deceive the buyer, but to deceive the police, the true owner and anyone else who might identify the vehicle. It would seem that the prosecution would have been on stronger ground had they alleged that D had made a representation by conduct that he had a right to sell the car.

If, after D, a motorist, had filled his tank and the entire proprietary interest in the petrol has passed to him, he falsely convinced V the garage owner that it would be paid for by D's employer, he did not obtain the petrol *by* that deception. Under s 2, once D falsely represents to V, the cashier, that it will be paid for by his firm, he commits the offence irrespective of the fact that the property has passed.[58] He intends by that representation to cause loss to the garage.

A victimless crime?

No specific victim(s) need to be identified, because no loss needs to have been incurred **3.55** and no person needs to have believed or acted on D's representation. The fact that the accused must have acted with the intention to gain or cause loss[59] means that the offence will remain focused on the potential effect a false representation might have had on the economic interests of others.

Proof without evidence from a victim

Under the old law, the normal way of proving that a deception was relied on was to call **3.56** V to say that he had relied on it.[60] It was, however, possible for there to be a conviction without a victim giving evidence or even making a statement, as where the false representation could be proved from the documents or admissions made by the accused.[61] Under s 2 there is clearly no need to call a victim since there need be no result. In most instances, prosecutors may still prefer to call a victim or intended victim who can give unequivocal evidence of the representation being made and the surrounding circumstances which will support the allegations that it was made dishonestly, with knowledge as to its falsity and with intent to gain or cause loss. For example, in cases of high-yield investment fraud, although the offence will be committed when the accused makes the false representation regarding the rates of return on investment, the prosecution will be more effective if a victim who had invested his savings was available to testify about the operation of the scheme.

Actus reus

'Makes a representation'

Whether a representation is made is a question of fact for the jury. **3.57**

By whom a representation may be made

The offence can be committed by any 'person' who makes a false representation. Clearly this **3.58** can include a corporation where that body is responsible for the making of the representation.

---

[58] cf under the old law *Collis-Smith* [1971] Crim LR 716, CA. He may also be guilty of making off without payment which is not abolished: see ch 6 below.
[59] Above, para 3.32.
[60] *Laverty* [1970] 3 All ER 432, CA; *Tirado* (1974) 59 Cr App R 80 at 87, CA.
[61] It was, of course, always possible to prove the more onerous concept of deception by inference from other facts without direct evidence: *Tirado* (1974) 59 Cr App R 80 at 87, CA.

The most obvious example would be in the context of false representations such as a prospectus for potential investors.[62]

3.59   D will be liable for his personal representations. He might also be liable for representations of third parties which he can be said unambiguously to have adopted. For example, where a buyer tenders an article in a supermarket, knowing that the proper price has been altered by a mischievous label switcher or misapplied by a careless assistant,[63] he makes a false representation when he tenders it to the shop assistant at the cash till.

3.60   D will be liable as principal for the false representations of his agents provided he has the relevant *mens rea*[64] or he may be liable as an aider or abettor, counsellor or procurer of his agent's false representations. A representation may also be made through an innocent agent. Since there is no requirement that the representation causes a gain or loss in fact, there is nothing to prevent a prosecution where D makes a representation to X intending that the information will be passed to V, from whom D intends to gain or to whom D intends to cause loss.[65] It is important also to note the significance of the fact that it is sufficient under s 2 that D intends *either* to gain *or* to cause loss. If D offers a credit card for payment for goods in a shop, he makes a representation to the shopkeeper that payment will be made and that D has the authority to use the card.[66] If this is false but D knows/believes that the shop will be paid by the credit card company, D still commits the offence, because he is making a false representation to the shopkeeper with intent to cause loss/expose to a risk of loss the credit card company (if they pay) or the shopkeeper (if the credit card company will not pay because eg D's card is outside the expiry date and the shop ought to have refused it).[67]

When is a representation made?

3.61   Is the representation made (i) as soon as D articulates it? (ii) only if it is also addressed to something? (iii) only when it is actually perceived as such by a person ie when it is communicated? If D stands alone in the middle of an empty market and shouts 'Guaranteed solid gold watch for sale', if the watch is not solid gold and D knows that it is not, he is making a false statement, but is it a representation? Under the old law, where D had to cause V to believe the representation, the issue did not arise, because there had to be a completed communication.

3.62   It is significant that the Act uses the term 'representation' rather than 'communication'. The latter term would ordinarily imply that there was a recipient, of the statement which

---

[62] Such representations are already criminalized by the Financial Services and Markets Act 2000, s 397. The overlap seems to have been completely ignored by the legislators. For general principles of corporate liability see *Smith and Hogan, Criminal Law* ch 10.

[63] Contra, ATH Smith, *Property Offences* (1994), 17–26. cf *Dip Kaur v Chief Constable for Hampshire* [1981] 2 All ER 430, DC, [1981] Crim LR 259 and commentary, above, 2.29.

[64] cf the position in tort where an innocent principal is liable for the fraud of his agent, *Kingsnorth Trust Ltd v Bell* [1986] 1 WLR 119, CA. The agent is not liable under the Misrepresentation Act 1967 s 2(1): *Resolute Maritime Inc v Nippon Kaiji Kyokai, The Skopas* [1983] 1 WLR 857.

[65] cf in tort *Smith v Eric S Bush* [1990] 1 AC 831.

[66] See below, para 3.96.

[67] See further below para 3.96.

D made, even if that recipient ignored the statement completely. However, even that restrictive interpretation of the concept of communication cannot be asserted beyond doubt. In *DPP v Collins*[68] the House of Lords recently held that the offence under Communications Act 2003, s 127—grossly offensive communications—could be committed even if no person was in receipt of the communication. It is submitted that under s 2 of the Fraud Act 2006 there need not be a completed communication in the sense that a person must read or hear or see D's statement in order for it to constitute a representation. A representation would seem to be 'made' as soon as articulated, but in accordance with the ordinary use of the word, a representation must be made 'to' someone or something.[69] A representation could include a statement being made to the whole world.[70]

If this interpretation is correct, this could have significant repercussions for the scope of the offence. In most cases it will render the full offence complete far earlier in time. What of D, who places an advertisement containing false representations on a notice board in a new building to be opened next week. It looks like he is guilty as soon as he pins the notice up. But difficulties may arise. Consider D, who orders a textbook by writing to the publisher. If (i) when D writes he does not intend to pay, he will be liable under s 2 when he makes that false representation. If (ii) D does intend to pay when he writes his order form (and posts the order), and makes that representation, but changes his mind before V reads the order, there is, at first blush, no false representation at the time he sends it; although there is at the time it is received.[71] The representation is false when it is 'communicated'. In resolving this difficulty in interpretation, it is helpful to have regard to the Act's aim to criminalize the making of representations to a machine, and the specific provision in subsection 5 included to ensure that such conduct constitutes a representation. **3.63**

Representations to machines

The prevailing opinion under the old law was that it is not possible in law to deceive a machine.[72] It was unreal to treat an automatic chocolate machine as deceived when it was activated by a foreign coin or washer. 'To deceive is . . . to induce a man to believe that a thing is true which is false, and which the person practising the deceit knows or believes to be false.'[73] Deceit can be practised only on a human mind.[74] Where D obtained property or a pecuniary advantage as the result of some dishonest practice on a machine, without the intervention of a human mind, he could not be guilty of an obtaining offence. It was held to be larceny (and, implicitly, not obtaining by deception) to get cigarettes from a **3.64**

---

[68] [2006] UKHL 40, [2006] 1 WLR 2223.

[69] In civil law the representee must be the person to whom the representation is made or those contemplated by D that the representation might reach or those whom it did reach and who acted on it: *Swift v Winterbotham* (1873) LR 8 QB 244, 253.

[70] See *Silverlock* [1894] 2 QB 766, CCCR (fraudulent advert in newspaper).

[71] D is presumably guilty under s 3 as he has a legal duty to inform V as to his change relating to payment under the contract? What if there is an appreciable time lapse?

[72] Griew, 8–12, thinks this 'appears now to be universally accepted'. See also Williams, *TBCL* 794 and ATH Smith, *Property Offences* (1994) 11–02. *Arlidge and Parry on Fraud* 4–054, however are more doubtful. Some devices used to operate machines are now 'instruments' for the purposes of the law of forgery. Difficulties to which this may give rise are discussed in *Smith and Hogan, Criminal Law* 754.

[73] *Re London and Globe Finance Corpn Ltd* [1903] 1 Ch 728 at 732.

[74] See (1972) Law Soc Gaz 576 and Law Com Working Paper No 56, p 51.

machine by using a brass disc instead of a coin.[75] The owner of the machine intends to pass ownership and possession of the goods to anyone who inserts the proper coin.[76] There was no difference, so far as the law of theft is concerned, between operating the machine by the use of a foreign coin and causing it to disgorge its contents by the use of a screwdriver. If a trader makes a dishonest claim on the appropriate form for the repayment of VAT input tax and the claim, without being read by anyone, is fed into a computer which automatically produces a cheque for the sum claimed, this may be regarded as indistinguishable from obtaining the cigarettes by the foreign coin.[77] The clerks who feed the document into the machine and put the cheque in the envelope are innocent agents—like an 8-year-old child, told to put the foreign coin in the machine and bring home the cigarettes. Hence it was held[78] that since VAT returns are processed by computer, a person making a false return does not have an intent to deceive for the purposes of s 39(2)(a) of the Value Added Tax Act 1983.[79]

3.65 There was a similar problem where the machine did not produce goods but provided a service. If the service was dishonestly obtained without deceiving a human being, there could be no obtaining offence. If D, by using a foreign coin, operated the washing machine in V's launderette, he was not guilty of obtaining the service by deception but may be convicted of the offence of abstracting electricity, perhaps of stealing the hot water, and possibly of making off without payment contrary to 1978, s 3(1).[80] He might now commit the s 11 offence considered below.

3.66 The problem of how to criminalize the 'deception' of a machine became an acute one as businesses relied increasingly on automated facilities to pay by credit card via an automated telephone system or via the internet.[81] It is commonplace for an individual to be able to book tickets, buy insurance, or arrange services by automated dialling services. Nor is such activity restricted to the consumer context. In *Holmes*,[82] for example D faced extradition for his conduct when working as an official in a German bank. He used a co-worker's password to credit an account under his control in a Dutch bank. The banking practice, of which the court took judicial notice, was such that the transfer was not complete until

---

[75] *Hands* (1887) 16 Cox CC 188. cf *Cooper and Miles* [1979] Crim LR 42 (Judge Woods), *Goodwin* [1996] Crim LR 262, CA.

[76] Just as a news vendor who leaves papers in the street for customers to pay for and take.

[77] This may, however, amount to forgery. See Forgery and Counterfeiting Act 1981, s 10(3), discussed in *Smith and Hogan, Criminal Law* 878.

[78] According to *Arlidge and Parry on Fraud* 4–054, by the trial judge in *Moritz* (17–19 June 1981) unreported. The problem regarding VAT was dealt with by the Finance Act 1985, s 12(5), which provides, as an alternative *mens rea* to 'intent to deceive', 'intent to secure that a machine will respond to the document as if it were a true document'.

[79] Now superseded by the offence under s 72 of the VATA 1994—being knowingly concerned in the evasion of VAT. See *Hashash* [2006] EWCA Crim 2518, holding that liability for VAT can arise from a fraudulent transaction.

[80] Below, ch 6.

[81] In 2005/6 there were 42,050 recorded crimes of theft from an automatic machine or meter, although some of these will have involved someone prising open the cash box and stealing its contents. A Walker, C Kershaw, and S Nicholas, *Home Office Statistical Bulletin, Crime in England and Wales* 2005/2006 p 28, Recorded crime by offence 1996 to 2005/6 and percentage change between 2004/5 and 2005/6.

[82] [2004] EWHC Admin 2020, [2005] Crim LR 229 and commentary.

the Dutch bank received confirmation from the German bank. The process was entirely automated. In that case, the court observed that the old authorities, including in particular *Davies v Flackett*[83] were not strictly a binding authority for the proposition that deception of a machine or computer is not a deception, but accepted that the general view is that it is not possible to deceive a machine. The court regarded this as regrettable, and urged a new offence of theft or some cognate offence to deal with the problem. Section 2 and section 11 of the Act do so.

The government was clearly not confident that under s 2 a 'representation' would be inter-   **3.67**
preted to include any statements made to machines and computers as where D types in his PIN on a Chip and Pin device.[84] To ensure that such conduct is within the scope of s 2, the government introduced an amendment to s 2. Section 2(5) provides:

For the purposes of this section a representation may be regarded as made if it (or anything imply-ing it) is submitted in any form to any system or device designed to receive, convey or respond to communications (with or without human intervention).

The Home Office Explanatory Notes elaborate on the intention behind this subsection: **3.68**

fraud can be committed where a person makes a representation to a machine and a response can be produced without any need for human involvement. (An example is where a person enters a number into a 'CHIP and PIN' machine.) The Law Commission had concluded that, although it was not clear whether a representation could be made to a machine, such a provision was unnecessary (see paragraph 8.4 of their report). But subsection (5) is expressed in fairly general terms because it would be artificial to distinguish situations involving modern technology, where it is doubtful whether there has been a 'representation', because the only recipient of the false statement is a machine or a piece of software, from other situations not involving modern technology where a false statement is submitted to a system for dealing with communications but is not in fact communicated to a human being (eg postal or messenger systems).[85]

Subsection 5 is not without its difficulties. Aside from the complexity of the drafting, it   **3.69**
does not provide that a representation *is* made if anything is submitted in any form to a sys-tem; it provides only that it *may* be regarded as made. The question is still one for a jury. Difficulties also stem from the breadth of the subsection. The terms used in subsection 5 were obviously intended to provide the broadest scope of liability, but they are not unam-biguous. For example, is a document 'submitted' when the defendant saves the typing to his hard drive on the computer, or is it only 'submitted' when he sends it via email? There is a strong argument for suggesting that the document is submitted as soon as D saves it. However, if that is the case, how is it any different from D who writes his false representa-tion on a piece of paper and locks it in his safe? That would not, it is submitted look like a representation, but it is difficult to distinguish it from the case of saving data to a hard drive. Arguably the individual who has submitted it to his computer is in a position in which he may more readily communicate it, but that mere possibility does not adequately justify any difference in criminality.

---

[83] [1974] RTR 8.
[84] Hansard, HL, 14 Mar 2006, col 1108 (Attorney-General).
[85] <http://www.publications.parliament.uk/pa/cm200506/cmbills/166/en/06166x--.htm> para 17.

3.70 If the interpretation of subsection 5 is correct, it means that the offence may be committed much earlier in time, at a stage when it would not ordinarily be said that D had 'represented' anything to anyone. What of D who types his false statements into a document on his computer and proposes to send that document to V later via email. He submitted it in a form to a device designed to receive etc and commits the offence, even though it has not at that time been released from D's control. For example, suppose D intends to circulate his false sales brochure by email at 8 am the following day, and he puts his false prospectus in his 'mail waiting to be sent' box. In such a case, could D argue that he was not intending by *that representation* to make a gain or cause loss. This may seem like nothing more that an ingenious circumvention of the problem, but is it what s 2 says? It is submitted that D does intend to gain by *that* representation . . . eventually when it is sent.

3.71 Subsection 5 clearly extends the meaning of representation in cases involving 'submission to any system or device designed to receive, convey or respond to communications (with or without human intervention)', but what of those in which there is no 'submission' to such a system or device?[86] The CPS suggest that the problem will not arise: 'In practice, prosecutors are unlikely to receive a file unless the last stage was reached. If faced with a file where the final stage was earlier in the process prosecutors may wish to consider charging an attempt.'[87]

3.72 What of the case in which D simply writes his representation on a piece of paper. Has he at that time made a representation? It is submitted that subsection 5 must be regarded as informing the general interpretation of the word representation. It suggests, implicitly that there is no requirement that a representation should be addressed to anyone specifically, or to a human being, provided it is addressed to someone or something.

3.73 There will be few instances where this element of s 2 will give rise to problems in practice. If D makes a statement otherwise than to a system or device as defined in subsection 5, and it cannot be proved that it was represented to someone or something, D may nevertheless be liable for an attempted offence under s 1(2)(a) and s 2.

Attempted representation?

3.74 Since the offence can be committed as soon as D has made a false representation, there is only limited scope for a charge of attempt. Possible examples include where D, having prepared documents containing false statements, is apprehended en route to post those to V. It may be that liability for the full offence arises even earlier if D decides to make his representations via a 'system' as defined in subsection 5 discussed above.[88]

3.75 The most important circumstances in which an attempt will be charged may well be those in which D has unwittingly made a true statement. In *Deller*,[89] D induced V to purchase his car by representing (inter alia) that it was free from encumbrances, that is, that D had

---

[86] Neither term is further defined. Presumably the government was anxious not to use terminology which might become outdated or too difficult to define as eg with 'computer'. See generally, C Reed and J Angel, *Computer Law* (2003) ch 4.

[87] <http://www.cps.gov.uk>

[88] See para 3.67.

[89] (1952) 36 Cr App R 184. cf *Brien* (1903) 3 SRNSW 410; *Dyson* [1908] 2 KB 454.

ownership and was free to sell it. In fact, D had previously executed a document that purported to mortgage the car to a finance company and, no doubt, he thought he was telling a lie. He was charged with obtaining by false pretences.[90] It then appeared that the document by which the transaction had been effected was probably void in law for the technical reason that it was as an unregistered bill of sale. If the document was void the car *was* free from encumbrances— '. . . quite accidentally and, strange as it may sound, dishonestly, the appellant had told the truth'.[91] D's conviction was, therefore, quashed by the Court of Criminal Appeal, for, though he had *mens rea*, no *actus reus* had been established. Under the new law, D could be convicted of an attempted fraud as soon as he made the true representation.

Where the representation occurs

The *actus reus* requires that a representation is made, and hence the offence should be regarded as occurring in the place in which D acts in making that representation.[92] The discussion above is pertinent. A representation may be articulated and communicated at different venues. **3.76**

Representations by words, conduct, or other means

The most obvious forms of the offence will involve D's physical action in the form of oral or written representations. D satisfies the 'making' element of the offence as much by saying to a customer—'this is a genuine Chippendale chair I have for sale' as by describing the chair in like terms in his catalogue. The fraudulent doorstep seller is caught immediately.[93] **3.77**

Forms of physical conduct other than speech or writing will suffice as where D nods assent in response to the question 'Is this a genuine Chippendale chair?' In *Barnard*,[94] D went into an Oxford shop wearing a fellow-commoner's cap and gown. He induced the shopkeeper to sell him goods on credit by an express representation that he was a fellow-commoner; but Bolland B said, *obiter*, that he would have been guilty even if he had said nothing: he was making an implied representation that he was a fellow-commoner. In an Australian case,[95] the wearing of a badge was held to be a 'false pretence' when it indicated that the wearer was entitled to take bets on a racecourse. This would seem to constitute a 'representation'. Similarly, wearing a false press badge to gain entry to a sporting event or a members' tie in order to gain entry to the enclosure at Lords may constitute representations within s 2. Is it enough that D represents that he is authorized to be 'present' in a virtual place, by having logged on illicitly to a website or secure terminal? There must of course be an intention to gain or cause loss in terms of property for a completed offence under s 2. **3.78**

---

[90] Under the Larceny Act 1916, s 32. The same principles are applicable.
[91] (1952) 36 Cr App R 184 at 191.
[92] On jurisdiction see para 3.11.
[93] Home Office, *Responses to Consultation* para 13.
[94] (1837) 7 C & P 784.
[95] *Robinson* (1884) 10 VLR 131.

3.79 Most instances of s 2 will involve representations made by words spoken or contained in documents. Classic examples of conduct caught by s 2 will be false representations on mortgage application forms, or loan application forms etc. The offence is also specifically designed to criminalize 'phishing' on the internet.[96] D who posts on the internet a website purporting to be that of a bank or financial institution, encouraging account holders to reveal their passwords and confidential information will commit the offence. It does not matter that the website is ignored by everyone; the making of the false representation suffices.

Representation by omission?

3.80 In early versions of the Bill the definition of 'representation' expressly referred to the fact that it could be by 'words or conduct'[97] but there is no mention of that term in the section. Almost all representations will be by words or conduct, but Parliament's deletion of that expression from the section raises the question whether the offence might also be committed by silent inaction. A simple example of a representation by omission is provided by the CPS where D 'omits to mention previous convictions or County Court Judgements on an application form'. It seems clear that D would be falsely representing himself as being of 'good character or financial probity'.[98]

3.81 The interrelationship between ss 2 and 3 is important in this context. Section 3 of the Act expressly provides for fraud by failing to disclose. A broad reading of s 2 would overlap significantly with that section. However, s 3 is limited to cases in which the defendant is under a 'legal duty' to disclose information; a broad reading of s 2 would not be so limited. Several scenarios deserve to be considered in more detail.

3.82 If D has not actively misled V in any of the representations he has made, but realizes that V is acting under a misconception as to the facts D has expressed, D may be liable under s 1(2)(b) and s 3 if he is under a legal duty to correct V's error.[99]

3.83 If D has not actively misled V, and is *not* under a duty to correct V's error, arguably there can be no liability under s 3. D cannot be liable of course under s 2 unless there is a *false* representation. Is D making a false representation by omitting to do something to disabuse V of his own error in interpretation? It was held to be fraud in the civil law for the seller of a ship to remove her from the ways where she lay dry and where it might be seen that the bottom was eaten and her keel broken, and to keep her afloat so that these defects were concealed by the water.[100] This would seem to amount to a representation that the vessel was seaworthy. There is some conduct by D which may be construed as a representation. Suppose, however, that the ship was already in the water before any sale was in prospect. Would it be a representation for the seller to leave her there when viewed by the buyer and

---

[96] See HC Research Paper 31/06, p 12; Home Office Explanatory Notes, para 16.
[97] These were deleted by the time the Bill left the HL, see HC Bill 166, 31 Mar 2006, cf HL Bill 72, 31 Jan 2006. This followed the insertion of subs (4) and (5), which were designed to ensure that representations made to machines were caught by the provision: Hansard, HL, 14 Mar 2006, col 1107.
[98] <http://www.cps.gov.uk>
[99] See below.
[100] *Schneider v Heath* (1813) 3 Camp 506, approved by the Court of Appeal in *Ward v Hobbs* (1877) 3 QBD 150 at 162, CA.

say nothing about the defects? Under the old law there was a requirement that D deceived V by 'words *or conduct*', but no such restriction applies in s 2 of the 2006 Act.

Under the old law, in *Firth*,[101] a consultant was held to have deceived a hospital, contrary **3.84** to 1978, s 2 (1), by failing to inform the hospital that certain patients were private patients, knowing that the effect would be that they would be exempted from liability to make a payment. The court apparently regarded an omission in breach of D's duty as 'conduct' for the purposes of determining whether there was a deception.[102] In similar circumstances the courts might conclude that D was making an implied false representation, rendering him liable under s 2. It is important to emphasize that the scenarios under consideration here are those in which D is *not* under a legal duty to correct any misunderstanding by V.[103] In such a case, the question is whether it is necessary or desirable for the courts to extend the scope of criminal liability by interpreting s 2 to catch those circumstances where D is under no legal duty to correct V's misunderstanding of D's true representation.

For the sake of clarity and to keep the criminal law on a more certain footing, it is submitted **3.85** that such cases ought not to be within the scope of s 2. Liability for the failure to remedy V's misunderstanding of non-false statements ought to be restricted to that which may arise under s 3 where D has a legal duty to disclose.[104] Support for this approach derives from the early Parliamentary debates on the Bill when the Attorney-General accepted that there are occasions when:

something that most of us naturally might think of as a non-disclosure is transformed by a fiction of the law into an implicit misrepresentation. But it is a fiction; it is not how people think about it. People will frequently say, 'I was not misled because I understand that he was implicitly making this representation to me. He just did not disclose something; he was dishonest in not disclosing it; and the purpose of that was to make a gain or to do something else'. One can think of many other examples where that would be the true basis on which a charge would be laid.[105]

In the previous scenario, it was envisaged that there was a unilateral misunderstanding **3.86** by V, with no change in circumstances after D's initial representation. A different scenario is that where D makes a representation which is not false within the meaning in s 2 to V, and subsequently, to D's knowledge but not V's, circumstances change in a way that materially affects the falsity of D's original representation. If D continues to act without correcting V's (mis)understanding of the position D might be said to be impliedly making a fresh, and now false, representation. Where D is under a legal duty to disclose the change in circumstances to V (eg in a contract of insurance) he will be liable under s 3, but the question remains whether in those cases in which D is not under a legal duty, he ought to be liable under s 2.

---

[101] (1989) 91 Cr App R 217, CA, [1990] Crim LR 326, CA and commentary, criticized in *Archbold* (2007) 21–348. cf *Shama* [1990] 2 All ER 602, 1 WLR 661, CA.

[102] Such behaviour would now constitute an offence under ss 3 (if there was a legal duty to disclose) and 4 (if there was an expectation that D would not act contrary to the financial interests of the hospital).

[103] *Smith v Hughes* (1871) LR 6 QB 597.

[104] See eg *Chitty on Contracts* (29th edn, 2004) ch 5.

[105] Hansard, HL, 19 July 2005, cols 1411–12.

3.87 Under the old law, in *DPP v Ray*,[106] it was established that one who enters a restaurant and orders a meal impliedly represents that he intends to pay for the meal before leaving[107] and probably also represents, in the absence of an agreement for credit, that he has the money to pay.[108] In that case D's implied representation that he intended to pay for his meal when he entered a restaurant and sat down to dine was true when made and continued to be true until the end of the meal, but when D changed his mind and decided to leave without paying, it became false. It was, under the 1968 Act essential to prove that V acted on the false representation and that the result of V's so acting was that D obtained the property or the service as the case may be.[109] It was held that the waiter acted on the false statement by leaving the room thereby allowing D an opportunity to leave, when he would not have done so had he known the truth, that D intended to leave without paying. Lord Pearson referred to there being a continuing representation: 'By "continuing representation" I mean in this case not a continuing effect of an initial representation, but a representation which is being made by conduct at every moment throughout that course of conduct . . .'. In the scenario above (3.86) is D's conduct an initial representation of continuing effect? On that construction, D might be said, not to fall under s 2 of the 2006 Act. The position may be different if by his continued conduct D is dealing with V without informing V of any change in circumstances which materially affects the accuracy of his statement.

3.88 Might a distinction be drawn between those cases in which the material change in circumstances is one over which D has control—as where he changes his mind about a willingness to pay and those in which he has no control? Suppose, returning to the example above, that D sends an order to V for a book, promising to pay the price within ten days of delivery and that D does intend to pay when he posts the order, and makes that statement, but changes his mind before V reads the order. It was submitted above that there is a true representation when D posts the representation. If that is a correct interpretation, does D avoid liability under s 2?[110] It is likely that the courts will regard the representation in such circumstances to be a continuing one.

3.89 A further scenario to be considered is that where D makes a false representation, but at the time he makes it, he believes it to be true. It is submitted that if D discovers that the statement is false and thereafter does not seek to rectify any misunderstanding, he should be liable.[111] This conclusion is not beyond doubt because of the manner in which s 2 is drafted. At the time of making the representation, D makes a statement which is inaccurate (untrue or misleading), but it is not false under s 2 unless at that time D also knows that

---

[106] [1974] AC 370, [1973] 3 All ER 131, HL; *Nordeng* (1975) 62 Cr App R 123 at 129, CA.

[107] *DPP v Ray* [1974] AC 370 at 379, 382, 385, 388, 391, [1973] 3 All ER 131, HL.

[108] ibid, at 379, 382.

[109] It was accepted that, if D had decided only while the waiter was out of the room that he would not pay and then made off while the waiter was out of the room, he would not have committed the offence. On the particular facts, D's continued presence was essential to the prosecution's case.

[110] It will be unlikely that D would escape criminal liability altogether since he might be liable for theft, and possibly under s 3?

[111] cf *Rai* [2000] 1 Cr App R 242 under the old law where D failed to inform the council that his mother had died and allowed them to continue their installation of disability aids to which he was not entitled.

it is or might be false. The falsity of the statement contains an element of *mens rea*. If D believes he is making a true statement, then for the purposes of s 2, there is no false statement actually made. To avoid this problem, the courts will have to interpret the concept of representation as being a continuing one. Where D makes a statement which is in fact untrue or misleading and later comes to know that it is such, he can be said to be making a false statement at that later point in time. It will be at that point that he must also be found to be dishonest.

As a matter of general principle in interpretation, it is submitted that considerable cau-   **3.90**
tion should be exercised to prevent s 2 creating an undesirable extension of the criminal law where D is neither responsible nor at fault in causing V to interpret the representation in an erroneous manner nor under a legal duty to disclose the fact of V's error.

The criminal law ought to take its lead from the civil law. The maxim *caveat emptor* ought   **3.91**
to operate to restrict the scope of liability. In commercial transactions D, though under a duty to do nothing to confirm any misunderstanding by V, has no duty to correct it even though he is fully aware of it: 'the passive acquiescence of the seller in the self-deception of the buyer does not entitle the buyer to avoid the contract.'[112] This ought not to amount to a s 2 offence.

The CPS has issued important guidance on the public interest test in prosecuting frauds   **3.92**
which states that:

> The borderline between criminal and civil liability is likely to be an issue in alleged Fraud Act offences particularly those under Section 1. Prosecutors should bear in mind that the principle of *caveat emptor* applies and should consider whether civil proceedings or the regulatory regime that applies to advertising and other commercial activities might be more appropriate. Not every advertising puff should lead to a criminal conviction but it is also the case that fraudsters prey on the vulnerable. Prosecutors should guard against the criminal law being used as a debt collection agency or to protect the commercial interests of companies and organisations. However, prosecutors should also remain alert to the fact that such organisations can become the focus of serious and organised criminal offending.[113]

A representation may be express or implied—subsection 4

Subsection 4 was included late in the passage of the Bill through the House of Lords.[114] To   **3.93**
have suggested in the absence of such a provision that a 'representation' could be express but not implied would have been most unlikely to have persuaded any court. Nevertheless, subsection 4 is included for the avoidance of doubt. Express representations will rarely give rise to difficulty, at least where they relate to facts. Greater difficulty is likely to flow from the inclusion of 'implied' representations. One of the acknowledged difficulties with the old law was that it presented problems for the courts in relation to implied representations. It was established in *Ray*[115] (above) that one who enters a restaurant and orders a meal impliedly represents that he intends to pay for the meal before leaving and probably also

---

[112] *Smith v Hughes* (1871) LR 6 QB 597, above, para 2.50.
[113] <http://www.cps.gov.uk>
[114] Hansard, HL, 14 Mar 2006, col 1107.
[115] *DPP v Ray* [1974] AC 370 at 379, 382, 385, 388, 391, [1973] 3 All ER 131, HL.

represents, in the absence of an agreement for credit, that he has the money to pay.[116] A person who registers as a guest in a hotel represents that he intends to pay the bill at the end of his stay.[117] A wine waiter employed at a hotel impliedly represents that the wine he offers is his employer's, not his own.[118] A motor trader who states that the mileage shown on the odometer of a second-hand car 'may not be correct' represents that he does not know it to be incorrect.[119] A bookmaker, it is submitted, represents, when he takes a bet, that he intends to pay if the horse backed wins.[120] One who takes a taxi represents that he intends to pay, and has the means of paying, at the end of the ride.[121] A customer in a supermarket who tenders goods to the cashier represents that the price label on the goods is that which he believes to be authorized by the management.[122]

Representations and cheques

3.94   It is submitted that a person tendering a cheque impliedly makes three representations: (i) that he has an account on which the cheque is drawn; (ii) that he has authority to draw on the bank for that amount; and (iii) that the cheque as drawn is a valid order for that amount. This was the accepted orthodoxy from cases as early as *Hazelton* (1874).[123] The doubt cast on that orthodoxy in *Metropolitan Police Comr v Charles* (1976)[124] can now be safely ignored since their lordships' approach was driven by their desire to find a deception in the face of the evidence in that case. Lord Edmund-Davies in that case quoted with approval the words of Pollock B in *Hazelton*[125] that the representation is that 'the existing state of facts is such that in the ordinary course the cheque will be met'. In *Gilmartin*, the Court of Appeal thought that 'this terse but neat epitome of the representation . . . should properly be regarded as an authoritative statement of the law'.[126] It is submitted that this approach should be followed in interpreting and applying s 2.

3.95   Where the cheque is post-dated, it may be the drawer's intention to pay in sufficient funds to meet it before presentation. Alternatively, he may believe that a third party is going to pay in such funds—as where he draws a cheque, knowing that his account is overdrawn but confidently expecting that he will have an ample credit balance tomorrow when his monthly pay is paid into his account by his employer. There being no express representation, the drawer must be taken to be saying that either, (a) there are sufficient funds in the account to meet the cheque; or, (b) he intends to pay in sufficient funds; or, (c) he believes

---

[116] ibid, at 379, 382.

[117] *Harris* (1975) 62 Cr App R 28, CA.

[118] *Doukas* [1978] 1 All ER 1061, [1978] Crim LR 177, CA. The decision is to be preferred to *Rashid* [1977] 2 All ER 237, CA.

[119] *King* [1979] Crim LR 122.

[120] cf *Buckmaster* (1887) 20 QBD 182.

[121] cf *Waterfall* [1970] 1 QB 148, [1969] 3 All ER 1048, CA.

[122] cf *Morris*, above, para 2.08.

[123] LR 2 CCR 134, the source of the proposition in CS Kenny, *Outlines of Criminal Law* (19th edn, 1965 by JWC Turner) 359, adopted in *Page* [1971] 2 QB 330 at 333.

[124] [1977] AC 177, [1976] 3 All ER 112, HL.

[125] (1874) LR 2 CCR 134 at 140.

[126] (1983) 76 Cr App R 238 at 244.

that a third party will do so. Each is a representation of fact and is sufficient to constitute the offence.[127]

Credit cards and debit cards

When a person presents his credit or debit card he makes a representation (i) that he has **3.96** the authority to use that card, and (ii) that payment will be made. Under the old law problems arose because that representation had to cause the obtaining. That difficulty evaporates because the only requirement is that the representation that is made is false and D intends to gain/cause loss by that false representation.

The fact that payment will be made by the card-issuing company means that D's repre- **3.97** sentation as to payment will in most cases not be false in relation to that second representation. The debit card contains an undertaking by the bank that, if the conditions on the card are satisfied, the payment will be honoured. The position with credit cards is similar. The bank issuing the card enters into contracts with the trader, agreeing to pay the trader the sum shown on a voucher signed by the customer/confirmed by CHIP and PIN when making a purchase, provided that the conditions are satisfied. In the case of credit cards, the contract between the bank and the trader precedes the purchase by the customer, whereas in the case of the debit card the contract is made when the trader accepts the customer's cheque, relying on the card which is produced.[128] This distinction is not material for present purposes. Conditions on both types of card may be satisfied although the holder is exceeding his authority—ie the debit card-holder's bank account is over-drawn or even closed, and the credit card-holder is exceeding the credit limit which the bank has allowed him. The trader accepting either type of card will usually do so simply because the conditions on the card are satisfied. He will not know whether the customer is exceeding his authority and using the card in breach of contract with the bank. He will get his money in any event—and that is all he will be concerned with. This is neither immoral nor unreasonable. The whole object of these cards is to dispense the trader from concerning himself in any way with the relationship between the cardholder

---

[127] In *Charles* [1976] 3 All ER 112 at 116, Viscount Dilhorne said, 'Until the enactment of the Theft Act 1968 it was necessary in order to obtain a conviction for false pretences to establish that there had been a false pretence of an existing fact.' This is misleading. It is still necessary to prove a representation of an existing fact or of law: *Beckett v Cohen* [1973] 1 All ER 120, [1972] 1 WLR 1593, DC; *British Airways Board v Taylor* [1976] 1 All ER 65, HL. All that the 1968 Act did was to make clear that certain statements of fact—ie present intentions—were for the future to be treated as such. The implication of Viscount Dilhorne's statement was not accepted by Lord Diplock (p 113) or Lord Edmund-Davies (p 121) or by the court in *Gilmartin*.

[128] See *Paget's Law of Banking* (13th edn, 2006) paras 2.62–2.69. *First Sport Ltd v Barclays Bank plc* [1993] 3 All ER 789, [1993] 1 WLR 1229, CA (Civ Div), holding, Kennedy LJ dissenting, that the bank was bound even though the cheque was a forgery. Lord Roskill's opinion in *Lambie* (all their Lordships concurring) that the customer was making a contract as agent for the credit card company is powerfully criticized by Bennion, 131, NLJ 431. See also Williams, *TBCL* 779 discussing *Charles* and cheque cards: 'The card-holder is the bearer of the offer, but need no more be regarded as the bank's agent to contract than was the newspaper that carried the celebrated advertisement by the [Carbolic Smoke Ball Co], or the newsagent who sold the copy of the newspaper to [Mrs Carlill], an agent for [the smoke ball company].' (*Carlill v Carbolic Smoke Ball Co* [1893] 1 QB 256, CA, is obviously the case to which Professor Williams intended to refer.) The courts continue to treat the person producing the card as an agent with the ostensible authority of the bank but, on this issue, it is submitted that the dissenting judgment of Kennedy LJ in *First Sport Ltd v Barclays Bank plc* [1993] 3 All ER 789 at 797d–f, above, is to be preferred.

and his bank. The trader is perfectly entitled to take advantage of the facility which the banks offer him.

3.98 The fact that the payment will be made by the credit card company will rarely prevent there being a full offence because when D presents the card knowing he is lacking authority to do so—because it is not his or he is overdrawn etc—he makes a false representation. If that representation is made (impliedly), it does not matter that D intends the trader to receive payment (ie not to make a loss). D intends the bank/credit card company to be caused loss or at least to be exposed to the risk of loss. Arguably the trader will also be exposed to the risk of loss. It is by the false representation that D has authority to use the card that he intends to expose the other to a risk of loss. Arguably, D also intends to gain by keeping that which he has (s 5(3)).

3.99 If D is unaware of the banking practice whereby the trader is guaranteed to receive payment, he will make two representations: (i) a false statement that he has authority; (ii) an unwittingly true statement that payment will be made. Since he intends in making that second statement to make a false representation, he would theoretically also be liable for an attempt.

Representations as to 'fact'

3.100 Representations as to present facts will present little difficulty for the courts. If D asserts that he is selling a solid gold watch and it is, to his knowledge made of brass, he commits the offence. Greater difficulty would arise if this included making a representation as to future facts. Section 2(3) defines a representation as meaning '*any* representation as to fact . . .', but the term 'any' relates to the type of representation not the type of fact; it is designed to encourage the most expansive reading of 'representation'. It is submitted that representations as to the occurrence of future events or the existence of future facts are best seen as cases of representations as to present states of mind—as where D says he promises that payment will be made tomorrow. That is a representation as to D's present state of mind about a future event. (See below.)

Representations as to 'law'

3.101 Section 2(3) expressly provides that 'any representation' as to law will suffice, and this is a welcome provision. Representations of law should be within the terms of the offence, for example: D and V are reading a legal document and D deliberately misrepresents its legal effect. This would seem to be false representation of law since the construction of documents is a question of law. If D does so with the intent to gain or cause loss, eg by inducing V to pay money for the release of his rights, this would seem to amount to fraud contrary to s 1(2)(a) and s 2. In that case it has been assumed that the law is quite clear and definite and D knows what it is. Many legal disputes arise, of course, where the law is uncertain. In these instances it is less likely that an offence will be committed under the section. For a representation to be 'false' within s 2, not only must it be untrue or misleading, but D must know it is or might be untrue or misleading. Where there is some ambiguity as to the state of the law, D will only be making a false representation where it is untrue or misleading *and* he does not believe it to be true. Counsel often make submissions as to the law in court which do not accord with, or are in direct opposition to, the proposition which the same counsel would formulate if he were writing a textbook on the matter. The nature of his submission where the law is uncertain is governed by the interests of his client. He would not be committing an offence because it is impossible to prove that the statement is (or was at the time) false—the law, *ex hypothesi*, being uncertain. Nor would counsel be making a misleading statement, since he would never seek to mislead the court.[129]

The following proposition formulated by Street[130] for the law of the tort of deceit is prob- **3.102** ably equally true of the concept of representation in this context: 'If the representations refer to legal principles as distinct from the facts on which those principles operate and the parties are on an equal footing, those representations are only expressions of belief and of the same effect as expressions of opinion between parties on an equal footing. In other cases where the defendant professes legal information beyond that of the [claimant] the ordinary rules of liability for deceit apply.'[131]

Representations as to 'states of mind'

Section 2(3) provides that a representation as to a state of mind of any person will suffice. **3.103** A representation as to a present intention of either the accused or some other person will therefore be sufficient. Representations as to present intentions may be expressed or implied.

If D states that his intention is that he will pay V tomorrow, he is making a representation **3.104** as to his present state of mind. The Crown must of course go further and prove that the representation as to D's state of mind was false, ie it must be proved that at the time of making the representation as to the present state of mind, D knew that it was or might be false. It has long been recognized that a misrepresentation as to a present state of mind will found a civil action for deceit and this is no more difficult to prove in the criminal than in the civil case—though the standard of proof is, of course, higher. Evidence as to the circumstances in which the promise was made, or as to a systematic course of conduct by D or, of course, as to a confession are examples of ways in which a jury might be convinced beyond reasonable doubt that D was deceiving V as to his present intentions. If D, at the time of making the representation intended to carry out his promise but later changed his mind he is guilty of a breach of contract. He is also guilty under s 3 of the 2006 Act if he is under a legal duty to disclose that information.[132]

Representations as to the present intentions of another person seem to be rare. Examples **3.105** would be where an agent obtains property for his principal by representing that the principal intends to render services or supply goods, well knowing that the principal has no such intention, or where an estate agent says that a particular building society is willing to advance half the purchase price of a house, knowing that this is not so. Where the representation is as to the state of mind of another, it may be more common for the Crown

---

[129] If counsel was willing to mislead the court in a no win no fee case (CFA case), there would be an offence under s 2.

[130] J Murphy, *Street on Torts* (11th edn, 2003) ch 13.

[131] ibid, 123.

[132] Above, para 3.100.

to allege, in proving falsity, that D knew not that it was untrue but that it *might* be untrue or misleading.

Statements of opinion

3.106 A statement of opinion was not a sufficient false pretence under s 32 of the Larceny Act 1916. The leading case, *Bryan*,[133] carried this doctrine to extreme lengths. There D obtained money from V by representing that certain spoons were of the best quality, equal to 'Elkington's A', and having as much silver on them as 'Elkington's A'. These statements were false to D's knowledge.[134] Nevertheless ten out of twelve judges[135] held that his conviction must be quashed on the ground that this was mere exaggerated praise by a seller of his goods to which the statute was not intended to apply. Erle J said, 'Whether these spoons . . . were equal to "Elkington's A" or not, cannot be, as far as I know, decidedly affirmed or denied in the same way as a past fact can be affirmed or denied, but it is in the nature of a matter of opinion.' This can hardly be true, however, of the statement that the spoons had as much silver on them as "Elkington's A". This seems to be no less a (mis)representation of fact than that a six-carat gold chain is of fifteen-carat gold which was subsequently held to be a sufficient false pretence under the old law.[136] It is submitted that the second representation in *Bryan* ought now to be treated as a false representation as to fact sufficient for a conviction under s 2.

3.107 In principle it seems that statements such as those made in *Bryan* ought all to be capable of giving rise to liability under s 2. The question arises however whether they can all properly be described as representations of 'fact'. This would certainly be difficult to apply in the case of an exaggeration as to value or excessive quotation. It has been held[137] that it is a misrepresentation of fact for the accused to state 'that they [had] effected necessary repairs to a roof [which repairs were specified] that they had done the work in a proper and workmanlike manner and that [a specified sum] was a fair and reasonable sum to charge for the work involved'. The evidence showed that nothing needed to be done to the roof, what had been done served no useful purpose, and it could have been done for £5, whereas £35 was charged.

3.108 Although under the s 2 offence there is no requirement, as there was in such cases under the 1968 Act, that the representation had to be made in a situation of mutual trust between D and his customer,[138] the Crown must prove a representation as to fact or law. It might be argued that representations as to quotations could be interpreted as including an implied representation of fact that the price quoted is one reflecting only a fair profit margin. But even this strained reading will not assist in all cases. What of the vendor's description of his tenant as 'a most desirable tenant' when the rent was in arrears and, in the past, had only been paid

---

[133] (1857) Dears & B 265.
[134] D's counsel said: 'I cannot contend that the prisoner did not tell a wilful lie . . .'.
[135] Willes J *dissentiente* and Bramwell B *dubitante*.
[136] *Ardley* (1871) LR 1 CCR 301.
[137] *Jeff and Bassett* (1966) 51 Cr App R 28, CA. cf *Hawkins v Smith* [1978] Crim LR 578 ('Showroom condition throughout' a false trade description of a car which has interior and mechanical defects).
[138] *Silverman* (1987) 86 Cr App R 213, [1987] Crim LR 574, CA. Where such a relationship existed, such conduct would now also be caught by s 1(2)(c) and s 4.

under pressure? This was held by the Court of Appeal to be a sufficient misrepresentation to found an action in deceit.[139]

In a case where the facts are equally well-known to both parties, what one of them says to the other is frequently nothing but an expression of opinion. . . . But if the facts are not equally well-known to both sides, then a statement of opinion by one who knows the facts best involves very often a statement of a material fact, for he impliedly states that he knows facts which justify his opinion.[140]

A view of commercial morality very different from that of the majority of the judges in **3.109** *Bryan* now prevails and deliberate mis-statements of opinion would today be generally condemned as dishonest, no less dishonest, indeed, than mis-statements of other facts—for whether an opinion is held or not is a fact—and the law should respect the changed attitude. It may, moreover, be a significant fact that at the time *Bryan* was decided, it was not possible for the prisoner to give evidence in his own defence.[141] The question now ought to be not 'Is it a matter of opinion?' but, 'If it is a matter of opinion, was it D's real opinion?' If the opinion is not honestly held there is, in truth, a misrepresentation of fact for the accused's state of mind is a question of fact.

'False' representation

The concept of 'false representation' is well established in law and it is no surprise that **3.110** Parliament incorporated such an element as the core element of *actus reus*. Whether a representation is false usually depends on the meaning intended or understood by the parties and that too is a question for the jury, even where the statement is made in a document. Where—in this context, exceptionally—the issue is as to the legal effect of a document, it is for the judge to decide.[142]

Section 2(2)(a) provides that a representation may be false by either being 'untrue', or **3.111** 'misleading'. It is necessary for the Crown to establish as a matter of *actus reus* that the representation is false or misleading aside from any issue about D's knowledge as to its truth or otherwise. However, the states of mind of the parties are likely to be important. Indeed, rather oddly the Act provides that a statement is only false if D knows it is or knows it might be false. The definition of falsity turns not solely on the objectively discernible fact of its lack of accuracy, but on D's subjective awareness of that fact or its possibility. It would have been easier had the Act defined false representation as one which was false, and left the element of D's awareness of the falsity or likely falsity to form a separate element of *mens rea*.

---

[139] *Smith v Land and House Property Corpn* (1884) 28 Ch D 7.
[140] ibid, at 15, per Bowen LJ.
[141] In *Ragg* (1860) Bell CC 208 at 219, Erle CJ, referring to *Bryan*, said, '. . . if such statements are indictable a purchaser who wishes to get out of a bad bargain made by his own negligence, might have recourse to an indictment, on the trial of which the vendor's statement on oath would be excluded, instead of being obliged to bring an action where each party would be heard on equal terms'.
[142] *Adams* [1994] RTR 220, [1993] Crim LR 525 and commentary. (Commentary approved in *Page* [1996] Crim LR 821.) cf. *Deller*, above, para 3.75.

Untrue

3.112 The word is an ordinary English word and no doubt the courts will suggest that juries should be directed to approach it as such. The only potential difficulties in application relate to those representations made by the accused which are not wholly untrue. It should be noted that there is no requirement that the falsity relates to a material particular. Where D's representation contains one falsity, even if it relates to a peripheral matter in his dealings with V, he may be convicted subject to the jury concluding that the use of that falsity was dishonest, and that it is *by that falsity*[143] that he intended to gain or cause loss.

3.113 Where the requirement to prove that D's statement was untrue requires the prosecution to prove a negative and the affirmative fact which, if it exists, will establish the truth of the statement is within the knowledge of the accused, there may be an onus on him not to prove anything, but at least to introduce some evidence of the affirmative fact. In *Mandry and Wooster*,[144] street traders selling scent for 25p said, 'You can go down the road and buy it for 2 guineas in the big stores.' The police checked on certain stores but it was admitted in cross-examination that they had not been to Selfridges. It was held that it was not improper for the judge to point out that it was impossible for the police to go to every shop in London and that 'if the defence knew of their own knowledge of anywhere it could be bought at that price . . . they were perfectly entitled to call evidence'. Even though no evidence was called to show that the perfume was on sale at Selfridges or anywhere else, the convictions were upheld.

Or misleading

3.114 The inclusion of this alternative suggests that the draftsman intended that it constitute a distinct route to establishing falsity. The Home Office has suggested a very wide interpretation of the term misleading proposing that it means 'less than wholly true and capable of an interpretation to the detriment of the victim'.[145] Being 'untrue' and being 'misleading' are distinct behaviours. An untrue statement is one which is literally false—'this is a Chippendale chair'—when it is not a chair made by Chippendale. A statement can be misleading even though it is literally true. Common examples are where D fails to provide a comprehensive answer to a question. V asks D a car salesman 'have you had many faults reported with this model' and D replies, 'only one this year'. That may be a true statement, but is highly misleading if there were 200 faults reported the previous year.[146] To display a cheap fake with a collection of original Lowry paintings may amount to a representation that the fake is by Lowry. That action is a misleading representation even if no express statement that the fake picture is by Lowry is made.[147]

---

[143] See above para 3.55.

[144] [1973] 3 All ER 996; cf *Silverman* (1987) 86 Cr App R 213.

[145] Para 19.

[146] There is little problem in practice in saying that the misrepresentation is by something not literally true but meant to be misunderstood: *Moens v Heyworth* (1842) 10 M and W 147. There are academic debates as to which conduct is more blameworthy and whether the victim of one or the other is harmed more. One view is that the victim who is misled feels more aggrieved since he has played a part in his own loss by inferring facts which D did not expressly represent.

[147] cf *Hill v Gray* (1816) 1 Stark 434, a doubtful decision, since it is not clear that the seller induced the buyer's mistake.

Similarly with ambiguous statements, as has been held in civil law, 'if with intent to lead **3.115**
the plaintiff to act up on it [D] put forth a statement which [D] knew may bear two meanings, one of which is false to [his] knowledge and thereby the plaintiff putting that meaning on it is misled, I do not think [D] could escape by saying [the plaintiff] ought to have
put the other.'[148]

There are, arguably, important moral distinctions between the conduct of someone who **3.116**
lies outright and someone who is merely economical with the truth, allowing the hearer
to infer facts for which he must take some responsibility—*caveat auditor*![149] These distinctions find no place in the 2006 Act.

Whether a representation is misleading can be a matter of degree. Is a 'trade puff' mislead- **3.117**
ing? Does the section now criminalize utterances by street traders? Have trading standards
officers been handed excessively wide new powers? The main defence to a false representation
of selling a T shirt 'just like the one Beckham wears' may be that there was no dishonesty.[150]
The second argument that D may rely on is that he did not intend by his exaggerated banter
to cause anyone to believe him and that he did not therefore intend by that admittedly
false representation to gain or cause loss. Such arguments may sometimes be difficult to
sustain in a court remote in time and atmosphere from the theatre of a street market.

Proof of falsity

Proving whether a representation is untrue will be far easier when it relates to a fact (or law) **3.118**
that exists at the time of the making of the representation[151] than when it relates to the state
of mind of an individual. Since the requirement is that the representation is untrue, as a
matter of *actus reus*, not just that the defendant knew that it might be untrue, difficulties
may arise as regards any representation as to future facts. This is likely to arise, if at all, when
representations relate to states of mind.

If the representation is untrue, there is no explicit defence that the representation was **3.119**
made for good reason or with lawful excuse, as where D said he made the false representation in order to recover property (which he believed) belonging to him, in such a case
the defendant must rely on the claim of a lack of dishonesty,[152] and the Act does not provide
a special defence of belief in claim of right.

Note that there is no requirement that the falsity relates to a *material* particular in the **3.120**
representation.[153] If D in the course of the sale of a car made a series of honest statements
as to the age, mileage, etc of the car, but knowingly made one false statement, say that
the car having been previously driven by a 'careful lady owner', that seems sufficient to

---

[148] *Smith v Chadwick* (1884) 9 App Cas 187, 201, HL.
[149] See SP Green, *Lying, Cheating, and Stealing: A Moral Theory of White Collar Crime* (2006) 78.
[150] We are grateful to Tony Shaw QC for the example.
[151] The A-G accepted that it is implicit in the drafting of clause 2 that 'the only time at which one can
make a judgment about whether the defendant thinks his representation is, or might be, untrue, is when he
makes the representation. So if he believes it to be true at the time he makes it, he cannot have been dishonest.'
Hansard, HL, 19 July 2005, col 1420.
[152] See above para 3.26.
[153] Hansard, HL, 19 July 2005, cols 1419–20.

render him guilty of the s 2 offence. D cannot plead that he did not regard that as a material representation, but must rely on a claim of dishonesty to have that issue aired before the jury.[154] The other claim available to D is that it is not by that false representation that he intended to seal the deal and make the gain/cause the loss. But then why did he make it? This will be a particularly difficult issue to resolve where the deal is a complex commercial transaction with many hundreds of representations being made.

3.121   In many cases of complexity, the question will be whether an individual representation can fairly be examined as false when taken out of the context of the others with which it was made.

Mens rea

'Knowing that the representation is' or 'knowing that it might be' false

3.122   Knowledge is a strict form of *mens rea*. It is much stricter than 'belief', 'suspicion', 'having reasonable grounds to suspect' and even 'recklessness'.[155] However in this offence, knowledge must only be either that the representation: (i) is untrue; or (ii) is misleading; or (iii) might be untrue; or (iv) might be misleading.

3.123   In the context of representations as to existing facts, the proof of knowledge will be least difficult to establish. It will require proof, often by inference, that D possessed knowledge of the existence of the falsity of the representation. More difficult will be cases where the falsity relates to the present state of mind as to the likely existence of future facts occurring, eg 'we believe that the payment for the goods will be made to us by a creditor tomorrow and we will immediately pay you'. In many cases it will be very difficult for the Crown to establish that D knew that his present statement as to future facts was false. Even with the opportunity for the Crown to succeed on proof of knowledge that D knew that the representation might be misleading, difficulties may arise.

3.124   It is sufficient that D is shown to have known that his representation might be false. Is the offence rendered too wide by this alternative *mens rea*? D tells a customer that he has a Renoir for sale. D knows that there is a risk, as with all art, that the painting might be a fake. Does D know that the statement *might be* misleading? He will only be guilty if the painting is not in fact a Renoir (he has to make a false statement), and he was dishonest. The element of dishonesty once again serves as the principal determinant of guilt.[156] Interestingly, the Attorney-General had no difficulty with this example in Parliament:[157]

If an art dealer said, 'This is a painting by Renoir', knowing that that statement can have a huge impact on the value of the painting—but not knowing whether it is true and thinking that it might

---

[154] See also above where there is discussion of whether D can claim that he did not intend by that misrepresentation to make a gain or loss.

[155] See recently the House of Lords discussion in the context of conspiracy: *Saik* [2006] UKHL 18.

[156] Hansard, HL, 19 July 2005, col 1416 (Lord Kingsland).

[157] Nor did the Home Office in its *Response to Consultees*, observing that if it caused sellers to be more careful that was a desirable result: para 18.

be untrue—it would be for a jury to decide whether he was dishonest. If he was dishonest, I see no difficulty in saying that he is guilty of fraud in those circumstances.[158]

Is this an oversimplification? Is the Attorney-General treating as synonymous *thinking* **3.125** that a statement might be untrue or misleading[159] and *knowing* that it might be untrue or misleading. Is there a difference between these degrees of D's cognizance or mental state sufficient to render him blameworthy? Many competent art dealers will acknowledge that there is always a risk that a painting might be a forgery. If the painting in question does in fact turn out to be a forgery, a statutory representation has been made which the dealer knew might be false. The material difference between that state of mind and the Attorney-General's example is that in his example the dealer 'thought it might be untrue'. Acceptance and knowledge that a thing might be untrue is different from thinking that it in fact is or might in fact be untrue. In the former case, the dealer, while accepting that nothing can be certain in the art market, believes that his attribution is true, and therefore acts honestly. The dealer who actually thinks it might be untrue, acts dishonestly. The issue is one of dishonesty and not knowledge. A dealer who believes that his attribution in respect of this painting is true, acts honestly. He has an honest belief based upon provenance, history, his own expertise, reliance on the expertise of others, or a combination of any of these factors. The dealer who actually thinks it might be untrue, acts, it is submitted, dishonestly. It is easy to see that a person who has bought an item which has been wrongly attributed by an auction house might use the criminal law in s 2 to support his civil claim for misrepresentation.

It seems inevitable then that in practice this *mens rea* element will blur unsatisfactorily **3.126** into the element of dishonesty. The courts need to be alert to guard against reckless representations being treated as sufficient dishonest acts when the section actually requires *both* dishonesty and knowledge. The *mens rea* requirement that D 'knows' that a state of affairs 'might be' prohibited is not a unique form of *mens rea*.[160] It is not a state of mind identical to recklessness.[161] Recklessness requires proof that D was aware of the risk that the statement was false or misleading and went on to take the risk. This is a requirement that D knows that the statement might be false or misleading.

Wilful blindness

The breadth of this fault element may extend even further if the courts demonstrate **3.127** their customary willingness[162] to interpret knowledge as including 'shutting one's eyes to an obvious means of knowledge' or 'deliberately refraining from making inquiries the results of which the person does not care to have'.[163]

---

[158] Hansard, HL, 19 July 2005, col 1417. The Home Office thought likewise in its Responses to Consultation, para 17.

[159] cf the old law in which reckless deceptions sufficed: s 15(4) Theft Act 1968.

[160] cf Public Order Act 1986, s 6.

[161] See Hansard, HL, 19 July 2005, cols 1415–16.

[162] See M Wasik and MP Thompson, 'Turning a Blind Eye as Constituting *Mens Rea*' (1981) 32 NILQ 328; JL Edwards, *Mens Rea in Statutory Offences* (1955), ch 9. *Manifest Shipping Co Ltd v UniPolaris Shipping Co Ltd* [2001] UKHL 1.

[163] *Roper v Taylor's Garage* [1951] 2 TLR 284, Devlin J. See also eg *Warner v Metropolitan Police Comm* [1969] 2 AC 256, 279 (Lord Reid); *Atwal v Massey* 56 Cr App R 6, DC.

3.128 Perhaps the best-known exposition of the concept is that of Devlin J in *Roper v Taylor Garages (Exeter)*. Devlin J distinguished between actual knowledge, wilful blindness (knowledge in the second degree), and constructive knowledge (knowledge in the third degree). Devlin J thought that:

> There is a vast distinction between a state of mind which consists of deliberately refraining from making inquiries, the result of which a person does not care to have [wilful blindness], and a state of mind which is merely neglecting to make such inquiries as a reasonable and prudent person would make [constructive knowledge].[164]

3.129 Even the House of Lords has, controversially, adopted this proposition:

> It is always open to the tribunal of fact, when knowledge on the part of a defendant is required to be proved, to base a finding of knowledge on evidence that the defendant had deliberately shut his eyes to the obvious or refrained from inquiry because he suspected the truth but did not want to have his suspicion confirmed.[165]

3.130 A precise definition of wilful blindness or connivance as it is sometimes known[166] remains elusive, and could extend liability significantly in this context. The core elements appear to be a degree of awareness of the likely existence of the prohibited circumstances coupled with a blameworthy conscious refusal to enlighten oneself. Academic opinion seems united in requiring proof of more than mere suspicion.[167] Williams described it in terms of suspicion *'plus'* a deliberate omission to inquire.[168] More recently Sullivan described it in terms of 'suspicion coupled with *deliberate* failure to use *readily available* and effective means to resolve the suspicion'.[169] It is unclear what degree of awareness of risk D must hold. Is suspicion sufficient or must D hold a belief?[170] It is unclear how readily available the bases of enlightenment must be to D. Is he only wilfully blind if he can reasonably or immediately discover the truth, or is the matter one of proportionality depending on the degree of risk and the severity of the harm posed if the risk materializes? It is unclear how convinced of the outcome of investigation D must be—must it be proved as Ashworth suggests that D refrained from making inquiries because he was virtually certain that suspicion would be *confirmed*?[171] Further, it is unclear what motivation or purpose D must have in seeking to avoid the enlightenment, for his refusal to constitute wilful blindness. However described, the second limb of the test ensures that the defendant must possess more than a state

---

[164] *Roper v Taylor's Garage* [1951] 2 TLR, 284, 288.
[165] Lord Bridge in *Westminster City Council v Croyalgrange Ltd* (1986) 83 Cr App R 155 at 164, HL.
[166] *Winson* [1969] 1 QB 371, 383 (Parker LCJ).
[167] Although that was not judicially accepted in the nineteenth century: see Edwards, above n 162, 207.
[168] *CLGP* 127, para 41. In his article on *mens rea* in secondary liability, 'Complicity, Purpose and the Draft Criminal Code' [1990] Crim LR 98, he described the element as 'an attempted fraud on the law' n 4.
[169] See GR Sullivan, 'Knowledge, Belief and Culpability' in S Shute and A Simester (eds), *Criminal Law Theory: Doctrines of the General Part* (2002) 214.
[170] Glanville Williams agued that it should be 'realisation that the fact in question is probable, or at least possible above average': *CLGP* (1953), 127, para 41. The Law Commission proposed a formula based on D having 'no substantial doubt'. See Wasik and Thompson, above n. 162, 333.
[171] *Principles of Criminal Law* (5th edn, 2006) 193.

of awareness of the risk—he must demonstrate a blameworthiness[172] that justifies treating his state of mind as akin to actual knowledge.[173]

Not negligence

It is arguable that the ambiguity of the concept of wilful blindness renders it unsuitable **3.131** for application in such a serious offence. What must certainly be guarded against is any slippage into regarding as sufficient a *mens rea* test of negligence or constructive knowledge. The courts have rejected the idea that constructive knowledge is sufficient in the context of deception offences[174] and this state of negligence should have no part under the Fraud Act. It is worth noting that the government rejected as too wide *mens rea* alternatives which were proposed on consultation, including a test based on whether D had 'no reasonable grounds for believing' the representation to be true, and that he 'ought to have known' it to be false.

Knowledge and mistake of law

Where the alleged false representation is one relating to law, and D denies that he has **3.132** knowledge as to the relevant law, if that is a denial of criminal law, there is no excuse, but if D is denying a knowledge of civil law that should constitute a defence.

Dishonesty

The *Ghosh* test applies, as noted above. This is potentially problematical in the s 2 form of **3.133** the offence since the criminality turns almost exclusively on dishonesty, and the definition of that term is left to the jury to determine on a case-by-case basis. In addition, as noted, there is no guarantee of acquittal where D has a claim of right or belief in a claim of right to the property he intends to gain by his false representation.

Overlap with theft?

There was a great deal of overlap between the offences of theft and obtaining by deception **3.134** under the old law. This was a result of the House of Lords' broad interpretations of appropriation in the theft offence as discussed in chapter 2. Under the new Act there will be considerable overlap with fraud and particularly with s 2. It can be expected that prosecutors will prefer the offence of fraud because of the breadth of the *actus reus*, and the absence of any need to establish a loss or gain in fact. In addition, the fraud offence carries a higher maximum penalty than theft.

The CPS remind prosecutors that in addition the Act is of benefit in banking cases: **3.135**

The credit/debit status of any bank accounts debited is irrelevant to the Fraud Act offences. All that is in issue is the Defendant's right to use the account; it is not necessary to prove or demonstrate any consequences of fraud (though they will clearly be material to sentence, compensation and confiscation). 'Preddy' type difficulties will not arise (where the property obtained had not belonged to another); Fraud Act offences do not require an intent permanently to deprive; a charge should

---

[172] See generally, Wasik and Thompson, above n 162, 337–41.
[173] Described as 'purposeful avoidance' by W Wilson, *Criminal Law Doctrine and Theory* (2001) 167.
[174] *Flintshire CC v Reynolds* [2006] EWHC 195 (Admin).

describe what actually happened and reflect the true criminality; and the indictment should be as simple as reasonably possible.[175]

Section 3: Fraud by Failing to Disclose Information

3.136 Section 3 provides the second form of the general fraud offence introduced by section 1.

> A person is in breach of this section if he—
> (a) dishonestly fails to disclose information to another person, which he is under a legal duty to disclose, and
> (b) intends, by failing to disclose the information—
>   (i) to make a gain for himself or another, or
>   (ii) to cause loss to another or to expose another to a risk of loss.

General

3.137 The elements of this version of the fraud offence are, as with s 2, easy enough to describe. None of the elements is, however, defined in detail in the section. The *actus reus* comprises: failing to disclose information to a person; being under a *legal* duty to disclose. The *mens rea* comprises acting dishonestly, with an intention to make a gain/cause loss. It is submitted that it should be charged as fraud contrary to s 1(2)(b) and s 3. The maximum sentence on indictment is ten years.

3.138 The important overriding principle of interpretation is that criminal liability under s 3 should not be imposed where the civil law imposes no duty to speak. As has been emphasized throughout it is desirable for the criminal law to respect the civil law foundations on which the offences are created.[176] This interpretation derives explicit support from the comments of the Attorney-General in the course of debates on s 3 where he stated that 'the Government believe that it would be undesirable to create [a] disparity between the criminal and the civil law; it should not be criminal to withhold information which you are entitled to withhold under civil law.'[177]

3.139 This overriding interpretative principle is also underlined by the fact that the offence as prescribed in the Act is much narrower than original formulations proposed by the Law Commission. These included breaches of 'moral duties' or duties arising from an expectation in the mind of the person with whom D is dealing.[178] The Home Office expressly rejected these proposals as creating offences which would be too ambiguous and which would trespass on the *caveat emptor* principle.[179]

3.140 The s 3 form of fraud is firmly anchored to the civil law. This raises interesting theoretical questions about the coherence of English law's approach in dishonesty offences. In contrast to the new s 3 offence the House of Lords[180] has controversially cast off the offence

---

[175] <http://www.cps.gov.uk>
[176] See GR Sullivan, 'Fraud and the Efficacy of the Criminal Law' [1985] Crim LR 617.
[177] Hansard, HL, 19 July 2005, col 1426.
[178] Home Office *Fraud Law Reform* (2004) paras 18–22.
[179] See Home Office, *Fraud Reform Responses to Consultation* (2004) para 21–5.
[180] In *Gomez* [1993] AC 442, HL, [1993] Crim LR 304 and commentary.

of theft to float free from its civil law moorings, allowing for convictions where the property transfer has been consensual and where D obtains indefeasible title. Arguably there is no incoherence because in theft there must actually be a transfer: V must have lost property and D must have intended the loss to be permanent whereas in s 3 there need be no loss or gain, the wrongdoing is complete on D's failure to disclose. It can be suggested that there is a greater need for the criminal law to be restrained in scope by the civil law with fraud than with theft because fraud offences do not necessarily involve tangible harm to property rights, and liability turns on little more than dishonest intentions. In the case of fraud as defined in the 2006 Act the wrong committed is akin to dishonest exploitation, whereas in theft the wrong is one against property per se.[181] However, this is not entirely convincing, since it is clear that civil law concepts underpin all these dishonesty offences, and the failure to accept the consequences of this in theft remains unsatisfactory in theoretical terms at least.[182]

Overlap with section 2

This form of offence is much narrower than that under s 2, but the relationship between **3.141** the sections warrants close attention.[183] Arguably, all cases in which there is a legal duty to disclose information might be regarded as capable of prosecution as involving an implied false representation within s 2.[184] Even if the position is not this extreme, there will be considerable overlap with s 2. It is submitted that there will be many, though by no means all, s 3 cases that could be charged under s 2 by identifying an implied representation by omission. It is preferable for the charges to be brought under s 3. In principled terms this ensures an accuracy of labelling in the offence and conviction, and in practical terms it will be easier for juries to understand the wrongdoing in terms of failing to disclose.

A good example of the application of s 3 is the case of *Rai*[185] decided under the 1978 Act. **3.142** D obtained a grant from the city council to provide a bathroom for his disabled mother. Before it was installed, she died. D did not disclose this fact and allowed the work to proceed. He was convicted of obtaining services by deception. The courts regarded D as engaged in a continuing implied representation. It could be regarded in the same way under the 2006 Act and the s 2 form of fraud would apply. However, this could equally be seen as a case where D was under a duty, as a matter of civil law, to inform the council when his mother died. That would allow for a charge under s 3.

---

[181] See also the theoretical account by A Simester and GR Sullivan, 'On the Nature and Rationale of Property Offences' in RA Duff and SP Green, *Defining Crimes: Essays on the Special Part of the Criminal Law* (2006). The authors seek to identify a harm (in philosophical terms) done by a thief in terms of the damage to the regime for the recognition of property rights and the regime for property transactions.

[182] See above ch 2.

[183] See above para 3.81. See also Hansard, HL, 19 July 2005, col 1411.

[184] Provided the failure to disclose when under such a duty can be seen as synonymous with a false representation by omission.

[185] [2000] 1 Cr App R 242, [2000] Crim LR 192. The case rejects the idea that *Firth* is a general authority for a proposition that mere silence constitutes deception.

Jurisdiction

3.143 For the purposes of determining when and where the offence occurs, it appears to be committed at the point at which the failure to disclose under the duty arises.

3.144 D's duty must, it is submitted, be one arising under English law. It may arguably extend to some international law obligations to the extent that these are incorporated within domestic civil law.

Actus reus

A person

3.145 There is nothing to prevent a corporation being liable for a failure to disclose information under s 3 when the obligation is imposed by law on the corporate entity.[186]

Legal duty to disclose

Types of duty

3.146 The core element of the s 3 form of the fraud offence is the concept of 'legal duty'.[187] Unfortunately, this critical concept is not defined in the Act, nor even in the Home Office Explanatory Notes. It is necessary to turn to the Law Commission's Report for further guidance on which forms of legal duty were envisaged as being caught by the section. The Law Commission's Report on *Fraud*,[188] stated that:

> Such a duty may derive from statute (such as the provisions governing company prospectuses), from the fact that the transaction in question is one of the utmost good faith (such as a contract of insurance), from the express or implied terms of a contract, from the custom of a particular trade or market, or from the existence of a fiduciary relationship between the parties (such as that of agent and principal).
>
> For this purpose there is a legal duty to disclose information not only if the defendant's failure to disclose it gives the victim a cause of action for damages, but also if the law gives the victim a right to set aside any change in his or her legal position to which he or she may consent as a result of the non-disclosure. For example, a person in a fiduciary position has a duty to disclose material information when entering into a contract with his or her beneficiary, in the sense that a failure to make such disclosure will entitle the beneficiary to rescind the contract and to reclaim any property transferred under it.[189]

3.147 That opens an extremely broad vista of criminal liability. Some of the examples offered are already criminalized (eg the failure to disclose information in a company prospectus is criminalized by the Financial Services and Markets Act 2000).[190] Other categories will also

---

[186] For the liability of corporate officers see s 12 of the 2006 Act.

[187] The requirement of a legal duty was endorsed by the 'Rose Committee': Hansard, HL, 12 June 2006, col 536.

[188] Paras 7.28 and 7.29.

[189] For example where a person in a fiduciary position has a duty to disclose material information when contracting with a beneficiary: a failure to make such disclosure will entitle the beneficiary to rescind the contract and to reclaim any property transferred under it.

[190] One recent example is that in the case of *Butt* [2005] EWCA Crim 805 where D's duty arose from his directorship in the company making the representations about high-yield investment.

be straightforward, as eg with insurance contracts where a person fails to disclose that he has a medical condition when taking out life insurance. There may be duties that arise in equity, contract, and even in tort. Some categories will, however, be less straightforward, particularly when this involves the criminal court in an assessment of complex matters of civil law. Difficult matters of proof will arise where the question is whether a duty arises in the trade or custom or was agreed to orally etc.

Since the trigger is a 'legal' duty, the question must, it is submitted, be one of law for the judge, with the jury being directed to conclude that if they find certain facts [as identified by the judge] proved they can conclude that in law there is a duty to disclose information.[191] Several peers expressed doubts as to whether judges would struggle in explaining this issue to the jury.[192] The element was however endorsed by the 'Rose Committee'—a committee of the Senior Judiciary.[193] The Home Office rather optimistically regarded this as a 'relatively uncomplicated' requirement.[194] **3.148**

The criminal courts have demonstrated a marked reluctance to become embroiled in civil law issues in their interpretation of the Theft Acts.[195] This despite the fact that the offences in question, being specifically designed to protect property and property rights *must*, by definition, rely upon the civil law's explanation and understanding of those concepts. Under s 3, the criminal courts are statutorily obliged to have regard to the civil law. It remains to be seen whether this is a duty they accept and can fulfil without wasting vast amounts of court time bogged down in arcane points of civil law, and/or leading to confusion of jurors.[196] **3.149**

Scope of duty

The difficulties in applying the civil law are exacerbated because the civil law will be essential not only in identifying the relevant circumstances in which a duty arises, but also in assessing whether if the defendant has revealed any information, it was a sufficient disclosure to satisfy the duty imposed upon him. This will be a further matter on which the jury will require careful direction. Clearly, where the Crown can show that D has wholly failed to comply with his civil duty, he will be liable. Beyond that, where D claims that he has fulfilled the duty of disclosure it will be a matter of degree. Such issues go not only to the question of the duty and its scope, but also relate to D's dishonesty. **3.150**

Awareness of a duty?

Note that liability appears to be strict as to the existence of a duty. It is no defence for D to claim that he lacked the knowledge or awareness of the duty to disclose. Any such claims will be subsumed within the general plea of a lack of dishonesty—once again that is the element of the offence which is the principal determinant of liability. It is interesting to **3.151**

---

[191] cf the Attorney-General's view that this was a question of fact: Hansard, HL, 19 July 2005, col 1428.
[192] Hansard, HL, 19 July 2005, col 1427 (Lord Lyell of Markyate).
[193] Hansard, HL, 12 June 2006, col 536.
[194] Home Office Responses (2004) para 21.
[195] See especially *Morris* [1984] AC 320, 324.
[196] Cynics might suggest that the difficulty jurors express in understanding the civil law questions will in time be prayed in aid by the government in its campaign to remove the jury from fraud trials.

note that the Law Commission in its original proposals suggested that liability as to the existence of the duty ought not to be strict. However, that recommendation was made in the context of a range of much broader proposals, including versions of the offence which were based on a failure to fulfil moral duties or those arising by expectation between the parties. Once the government rejected those broader forms of the offence and restricted its scope to cases of breach of a legal duty, it is arguable that imposing strict liability as to the existence of such duties is less problematical. The defendant ought to be aware of his duties in civil law.

3.152   The courts' approach to this problem will be an interesting one. Despite the landmark decisions of the House of Lords in *DPP v B*[197] and *R v K*,[198] holding that there is a constitutional principle of a presumption of *mens rea* in English criminal law, the courts are willing to find that the presumption is rebutted by necessary implication. If the courts find that liability is strict as to the existence of the duty, the defendant will be able to advance a plea of a lack of awareness of the duty, and/or the scope of the obligations it imposed, within a plea of a lack of dishonesty.

Information

3.153   The duty must be one which is to disclose 'information'. That concept is not defined. It is submitted that the word is an ordinary English word and that few difficulties in interpretation should arise. It will take its meaning in part from the circumstances and terms of the duty in question.

To whom duty must be owed?

3.154   The section does not limit liability to those cases in which D is under a duty to disclose to V and fails to disclose to V. For example, D might be a company director and in breaching his duties to the company he might intend to expose to a risk of loss an investor. Again, the scope of criminal liability is determined by the particular civil law obligation imposed.

Failing to disclose

3.155   As noted, the question of whether there has been a sufficient degree of failure in disclosure may give rise to problems. The opportunity for the defence to claim that there has been adequate disclosure may well be exploited. If D has fulfilled his civil law duty in terms of the type/quantity of disclosure there should be no criminal liability. This may involve the courts in some complex issues of civil law. Particularly difficult examples might include those in which the allegation of a failure to comply with a duty which arises from the trade or custom. Such duties are less likely to be clearly prescribed and must take their form, to some extent, from the circumstances in which they arise and from the parties' expectations.

---

[197] [2002] 2 AC 428.
[198] [2002] 1 AC 462.

Mens rea

Dishonesty

As discussed above, the *Ghosh* test will apply. The element of dishonesty will be especially **3.156** important in cases where D claims that he was not aware of his duty and or that he believed that he had satisfied that duty. Arguably, the vague nature of the dishonesty test renders the offence too wide.[199]

With intent to gain or cause loss or expose to risk of loss

This element of the *mens rea* is discussed above. There is no requirement that the intention **3.157** is to cause a loss by which D gains. Nor need there be any intention for the loss to be caused to the person to whom the duty is owed.

Section 4: Fraud by Abuse of Position

The third form of the general fraud offence is perhaps the most controversial and is pro- **3.158** vided for in s 4.

(1) A person is in breach of this section if he—
    (a) occupies a position in which he is expected to safeguard, or not to act against, the financial interests of another person,
    (b) dishonestly abuses that position, and
    (c) intends, by means of the abuse of that position—
        (i) to make a gain for himself or another, or
        (ii) to cause loss to another or to expose another to a risk of loss.
(2) A person may be regarded as having abused his position even though his conduct consisted of an omission rather than an act.

Interpretation

As with ss 2 and 3 the terms of the offence are easy to describe. The *actus reus* comprises **3.159** abusing a position of financial trust and the *mens rea* comprises acting dishonestly, an intention by the abuse to make a gain/cause loss. Once again, it is lamentable that none of the terms of this form of the offence are defined in the Act. The provision met with some opposition in Parliament, being described as 'woolly'.[200] It was criticized as a 'catch all provision that will be a nightmare of judicial interpretation . . . and help bring the law into disrepute'.[201]

Jurisdiction

No consideration appears to have been given to the question of whether the relevant **3.160** question for liability is whether the abuse or the expectation arose within the jurisdiction.

---

[199] See comments of Brian Jenkins MP in Hansard, HC, 12 June 2006, col 554.
[200] Hansard, HC, 12 June 2006, col 549.
[201] Standing Committee B, 20 June 2006, col 25.

This could have given rise to some difficult questions, but the matter has been forestalled by the fact that Parliament chose to limit the jurisdictional scope of the s 1 offences as explained in paras 3.13–3.16.

Actus reus

A 'position'

3.161 Critical to understanding this offence is the concept of 'position'. Unfortunately despite repeated requests for clarification in the course of Parliamentary debates, the government refused to define with any particularity what this element of the fraud means. The most obvious interpretation of this element would be to treat it as synonymous with a requirement that D owed a 'fiduciary duty' to the other. That would have involved the criminal courts in yet more close analysis of complex civil law questions, but it would have secured certainty and ensured coherence between the civil and criminal law. Unfortunately, the government rejected this logical interpretation, being persuaded by arguments that the definition of 'fiduciary duty' would be unduly technical and would restrict the scope of the offence.[202] It preferred to allow s 4 to extend the criminal law into ambiguous territory, although, interestingly, few if any of the examples provided by government spokesmen or in government documents go beyond circumstances in which D does in fact owe a fiduciary duty. The Home Office Explanatory Notes[203] provide little assistance, simply referring the reader back to the Law Commission explanation in its *Report No 276*. The Law Commission explained the meaning of 'position' at paragraph 7.38:

> The necessary relationship will be present between trustee and beneficiary, director and company, professional person and client, agent and principal, employee and employer, or between partners. It may arise otherwise, for example within a family, or in the context of voluntary work, or in any context where the parties are not at arm's length. In nearly all cases where it arises, it will be recognised by the civil law as importing fiduciary duties, and any relationship that is so recognised will suffice. We see no reason, however, why the existence of such duties should be essential. This does not of course mean that it would be entirely a matter for the fact-finders whether the necessary relationship exists. The question whether the particular facts alleged can properly be described as giving rise to that relationship will be an issue capable of being ruled upon by the judge and, if the case goes to the jury, of being the subject of directions.[204]

3.162 This offers a very broad and ill-defined scope of liability. The Home Office gave examples of relevant 'positions' as including those where D is given access to V's premises, equipment, records, or customers.[205] They provided other obvious examples, including that of a software company employee who abused his employment position to clone software products with the intention of selling them, and employees in care homes who were

---

[202] See Standing Committee B, 20 June 2006, cols 24–7 (Solicitor-General).
[203] Para 20.
[204] Referred to in debates by the Attorney-General (Hansard, HL, 19 July 2005, col 1431) and the Solicitor-General (Hansard, HC, 12 June 2006, col 558).
[205] Para 23.

entrusted to look after the financial affairs of the elderly or disabled person and drew money for their own purposes.[206] These give no meaningful guidance on any limits of this serious offence.[207] The only other advice was that the offence applies wherever V has 'voluntarily' put D in such a position.[208] Interestingly, the government pointed to the potential for this offence to prevent frauds involving wills. The expectation is that charities will benefit by £2–3 million per annum if legacy fraud can be prevented.

As noted, the government was unwilling to accept that the scope of liability for s 4 should **3.163** be restricted to circumstances of fiduciary duties arguing that the definition of fiduciary duty was too narrow and too complex. The Solicitor-General referred to the definition of that concept provided by Millet LJ in *Bristol & West Building Society v Mothew*.[209] He said:

A fiduciary is someone who has undertaken to act for or on behalf of another in a particular matter in circumstances that give rise to a relationship of trust and confidence. The distinguishing obligation of a fiduciary is the obligation of loyalty. The principal is entitled to the single-minded loyalty of his fiduciary. This core liability has several facets. A fiduciary must act in good faith; he must not make a profit out of his trust; he must not put himself in a position where his duty and interest may conflict; he may not act for his own benefit or that of third person without the informed consent of his principal. The Solicitor General emphasised that as Millet LJ had made clear, 'He is not subject to fiduciary obligations because he is a fiduciary; it is because he is subject to them that he is a fiduciary. (p 18)

The Solicitor-General seems, with respect, to be adopting a particularly narrow view of **3.164** the concept of fiduciary duty and of the requirement that the person owes a single duty.[210] This point was raised in debates, but the Solicitor-General remained unmoved. He stated that:

The situations about which those who made representations to us were concerned were those in which someone has a relationship with such a person that supports their level of independence—situations in which there is an element of trust, but that does not extend to what Lord Justice Millett described as the 'single-minded loyalty' of the fiduciary. . . . It is on that basis that we put the wording in the clause, 'he is expected to safeguard'. Such a person is in a position where they are trusted, but it might not go as far as having a legal relationship which involves an entitlement on the part of the other person to their single-minded loyalty. The person may have loyalty to many others.[211]

It was pointed out to the Solicitor-General that he had misunderstood the concept of **3.165** fiduciary duty,[212] with regard to the use of 'single-mindedness', but following a division in the Standing Committee, an amendment which would have restricted liability to cases of fiduciary duty was rejected.

---

[206] This would also be theft—*Hopkins and Kendrick* [1997] 2 Cr App R 524; *Hinks* [2001] 1 Cr App R 18; ch 2 above.

[207] Section 4 will overlap with theft in some cases eg *Chan Man-sin v A-G for Hong Kong* [1988] 1 All ER 1 cf *A-G for Hong Kong v Reid* [1994] AC 314.

[208] No 276, para 7.37, repeated in the Home Office Consultation Paper (2004) para 23.

[209] [1998] Ch 1.

[210] J Martin, *Hanbury and Martin, Modern Equity* (17th edn, 2005) ch 6.

[211] HC Standing Committee B, 20 June 2006, col 27.

[212] See cols 27–8.

Cases of fiduciary duty

3.166   In the more obvious situations in which s 4 might be relied on, the existence of the duty will present no problem: D's civil law duties will saddle him with liability. Even in these cases, there may be practical problems with the criminal courts identifying with precision the duty, and its terms. This may pose further questions as to the functions of judge and jury. If the scope of liability under s 4 had been restricted to cases of fiduciary duty, there would have been a strong argument for saying that the judge must determine whether D's 'position' is within s 4 and to direct the jury as to what evidence of that they must find in order to convict. However, since a fiduciary duty will be a *sufficient* but not a *necessary* basis for liability, it is more questionable who has responsibility for determining D's status. The Law Commission clearly thought that whether the particular facts alleged can properly be described as giving rise to that relationship will be 'an issue capable of being ruled upon by the judge and, if the case goes to the jury, of being the subject of directions'.[213]

3.167   One area of fiduciary duty in which the s 4 offence will prove useful is that relating to secret profits. The common law had become extremely confused on this issue. In *Tarling*[214] the House of Lords held that the company directors' failure to disclose a secret profit made in breach of a fiduciary duty even if it was dishonest, did not constitute a conspiracy to defraud. In *Adams*,[215] the Privy Council held that the company director had been correctly convicted when making a secret profit. Adams seems to have gone further than Tarling by actively concealing the profits. The position was inconsistent and incoherent. Section 4 is wide enough to tackle both situations: it catches secret profiteers from the waiter who sells his bottle of wine, passing it off as one from the restaurant,[216] to the director who makes personal millions by trading company stock in breach of his fiduciary duty.

3.168   In cases involving a breach of a fiduciary duty, there may well be an overlap with s 3 where the fiduciary fails to disclose information, and/or under s 2 when there is a false representation. Note however that liability is potentially wider under s 4 because there is no need for the Crown to prove any positive act on D's part; an omission will do.

Liability in the absence of a fiduciary duty

3.169   The disturbing aspect of the s 4 offence is its potential to criminalize acts or omissions by someone who is not under a formal legal duty of a fiduciary nature. Justice criticized the offence on these grounds when it was proposed, suggesting that it 'compromised legal certainty'.[217] The Law Commission's examples, above which list the family and other voluntary arrangements as being caught, highlight the potential reach of s 4. Will the breadth of the offence open up the possibility that all sorts of trivial civil law contractual disputes

---

[213] No 276, para 7.38.
[214] (1978) 70 Cr App R 77, HL. The application of the offence in this context is discussed in the Home Office Response to Consultation Document Annex B, para 14.
[215] [1995] 1 WLR 52, PC.
[216] *Doukas* [1978] 1 All ER 1071.
[217] Briefing Document for HL, available from <http://www.justice.org.uk>.

become the subject of prosecution?[218] Concerns were expressed in Parliament that the offence would catch D who breaches a confidentiality agreement with his employer.[219]

Employee A of X Ltd will be caught by passing up an opportunity to seal a lucrative **3.170** contract so that his friend B, working for Y Ltd can take advantage.[220] D who is employed to secure three tenders for a lucrative contract and chooses instead to obtain one which turns out to be a disastrous selection will be caught. Section 4 seems to apply whether A is motivated by malice or laziness. Beyond that the scope of the offence is astonishingly wide. Its ambit lies in the hands of those defining the qualifying 'position'. To take an extreme example, what of an employee who persistently arrives late for work—arguably he occupies a position in which he is expected not to act against, the financial interests of the employer, and, abuses that position intending thereby to make a gain. Subject to a finding of dishonesty, he may be guilty. Is it sufficient that D causes V to lose merely a chance of profit?

The offence is so wide that it also has the potential to apply to financial misgovernance by **3.171** public officials. Many public officials are in a position in which they are expected to safeguard or not to act against the financial interests of another person (ie the public or the Crown). There may be overlap with offences of corruption and misfeasance in public office.[221]

Unless kept within sensible limits, the offence has the potential to elevate all sorts of **3.172** trivial contractual and familial disputes into criminal matters. The government suggested that 'something more than a breakdown of relationships' would be needed to trigger s 4, but did not elaborate on this.[222] Careful prosecuting will also be needed to ensure that the offence is not allowed to criminalize conduct which involves no civil law wrong. In those cases of non-fiduciary duty which are prosecuted, the element of dishonesty will carry a disproportionate burden in determining criminal liability. For the reasons expressed above, it is doubtful whether that ill-defined element can shoulder such a burden in an offence carrying a maximum of ten years' imprisonment.

The CPS has provided a list of examples of circumstances in which s 4 should be charged **3.173** to guide prosecutors:

- an employee of a software company who uses his position to clone software products with the intention of selling the products on his own behalf;
- where a person is employed to care for an elderly or disabled person and has access to that person's bank account but abuses that position by removing funds for his own personal use. . . .
- an Attorney who removes money from the grantor's accounts for his own use. The Power of Attorney allows him to do so but when excessive this will be capable of being an offence under Section 4;
- an employee who fails to take up the chance of a crucial contract in order that an associate or rival company can take it up instead;

---

[218] This will be a significant stick with which employers can beat employees—Mr Geoffrey Cox QC MP Standing Committee B, 20 June 2006, col 15.

[219] Standing Committee B, 20 June 2006, col 15.

[220] The CPS has issued guidance on public policy interests of prosecuting fraud and has stated that 'The criminal law should not be used to protect private confidences.'

[221] C Nichols et al, *Corruption and the Misuse of Public Office* (2006) ch 3.

[222] See Home Office, *Fraud Law Reform, Responses to Consultation* (2004), para 27.

- an employee who abuses his position in order to grant contracts or discounts to friends, relatives and associates;
- a waiter who sells his own bottles of wine passing them off as belonging to the restaurant. . . .
- a trader who helps an elderly person with odd jobs, gains influence over that person and removes money from their account. . . .
- the person entrusted to purchase lottery tickets on behalf of others—again, this will probably be theft as well but see guidance on Public Interest criteria . . .'

'Occupies'

3.174 The section applies only in relation to the positions D 'occupies'. It is clear that the 'abuse' with intent to gain or cause loss must arise while D is in occupation of that position in order for s 4 to apply. Where D has, whilst in a position of trust, obtained financial information, and then after leaving his position uses that information with intent to gain or cause loss, has the s 4 offence been committed? Arguably, the question will turn on whether D intends *at the time of the obtaining* to use the information to gain or cause loss. If he obtains the information with that intention he is abusing the position he then occupies. More difficult will be the case where D obtains such information while occupying a relevant 'position', and at the time of obtaining he has no intention by that obtaining to gain or cause loss then or in the future. Perhaps he has an intention to keep the information as a safeguard against any future allegation that he was involved in a dubious aspect of a particular deal that was being undertaken in the organization within which he occupied the position.[223] Subsequently, having left that position, D realizes that there is the potential to use the information to make a gain or cause a loss and he decides to do so. He is not at that time abusing a position which he 'occupies'. Such a person commits the offence under s 6 of the Act possession of an article for use in fraud (below) if he intends it to be used in fraud—which is of course much narrower than intending to use it for gain or to cause loss or expose to a risk of loss.

3.175 According to the Solicitor-General in the course of debates in the Standing Committee:

A person can occupy a position where they owe a duty that goes beyond the performance of a job. A contract that is entered into that obliges a person to have duties of confidentiality, perhaps, can go well beyond the time when that employment ceases. The duty may, however, still arise. The person entered into the duty at the beginning of the employment and it exists indefinitely. Therefore a person may still occupy a position in which there is a legitimate expectation. That may well, by virtue of a contract and the agreement that the employee entered into voluntarily, go beyond redundancy or the point when he leaves the post.[224]

Expectation

3.176 The scope of the concept of 'position' which D must occupy is to some extent dependent on the definition of the term 'position in which he is expected to safeguard'.[225]

---

[223] Is that an abuse? It is doubtful that a jury would regard it as such where the defendant is protecting himself against allegations that he was involved in criminal conduct by the organization; that does not sound like abuse, even though it is contrary to the interests of that organization.

[224] Standing Committee B, 20 June 2006, col 23.

[225] If the conduct is perpetrated by a public official there may be an offence of misconduct in public office.

The critical question, and one which Parliament spectacularly left unanswered, is: whose expectation counts?[226] If it is the potential victim's this could be a very wide scope of liability subject to D denying liability by way of a lack of dishonesty. If it is a test based on what D thinks his financial duties are, it might be very limited and difficult to prove. Should there be a requirement that the expectation is reasonable whether by the defendant or the victim?

Financial interests

The term is not defined. There is little doubt that the courts will be encouraged to adopt a **3.177** very wide reading. There is no restriction that the financial interests be regarded as long-term ones.

Abuse

The term 'abuse' is not defined. The Home Office makes clear in the Explanatory Notes **3.178** that it is deliberately left undefined as the term is intended to cover a wide range of conduct. Coupled with the breadth of the potential 'position' of responsibility this makes the offence extremely wide. If the positions of financial responsibility were restricted to legal duty cases the issue of abuse would be resolved by asking simply whether the defendant had breached the legal/fiduciary duty he owed.

The word is an ordinary English word and no doubt the courts will be happy to leave it **3.179** to the jury to apply on a case-by-case basis. This does nothing to promote certainty and consistency in an offence of such seriousness and ambiguity. If guidance is needed, the dictionary definitions suggest that it involves acting 'wrongly' or 'improperly' or treating in a harmful or injurious way. This may in practice serve as a useful restricting feature of this form of fraud. Jurors might not regard the offence as complete unless some loss is caused (or some gain accrued) or at least that someone is exposed to the risk of loss. Without that result, will a jury be willing to say that there has been 'abuse'?

The abuse is of the 'position', but it may be that D holds a position of financial responsibil- **3.180** ity towards B (eg the company), but acts with intent to cause loss to C (an investor) by the abuse of his position vis-à-vis B. It is notable that the original proposal contained a requirement of secrecy in D's actions of abuse,[227] but the Home Office removed this element, despite its widespread approval on the grounds that it was difficult to define and created unnecessary complication.[228]

---

[226] See the discussion in the Commons Standing Committee where it was proposed that the word 'expected' be replaced by a requirement that D had a 'fiduciary duty': HC Standing Committee B, 20 June 2006, col 11; rejected by the Solicitor-General at col 20.

[227] Indeed, the CPS said: 'In the absence of an element of secrecy, it is accepted that the new offence would probably be too wide'. However, the deletion of this requirement was supported by Lord Lloyd, Hansard, HL, 22 June 2005, col 1665.

[228] See Home Office, *Fraud Law Reform, Responses to Consultation* (2004) para 28. See also Hansard, HL, 19 July 2005, cols 1432–3; Hansard, HC, 12 June 2006, col 538; Standing Committee B, 20 June 2006, cols 28–9.

Act or omission

3.181 Section 4(2) makes clear that the offence can be committed by omission as well as by positive action. An obvious example is where D, an employee, fails to perform his duty under the contract of employment so that a rival company wins the tender at the expense of D's employer.

Mens rea

Dishonesty

3.182 The elements have been discussed above. As noted there is a very heavy burden placed on dishonesty. It would appear that liability is strict as to whether D's liability is one of occupying a position in which he is expected to safeguard the financial interests of another. D's lack of awareness that he is in such a position must be subsumed in a plea of lack of dishonesty.

3.183 It is interesting to ponder the ECHR compatibility of this form of the fraud offence. In cases in which there is no legal or fiduciary duty on the accused, it is difficult to see what additional element of conduct which is morally dubious prevents the offence being one based solely on dishonesty which as the Joint Parliamentary Committee on Human Rights recognized would be likely to infringe Article 7.[229]

Intent to gain/cause loss

3.184 One particular aspect of this element to note in the context of s 4 is that the definition of gain and loss includes intangible property which may well have a significant role to play in the context of abuse of a financial position.

3.185 There is no explicit *mens rea* requirement as to any awareness of the defendant as to the existence of the expectation that he must safeguard the financial interests of another.

Sentencing

3.186 The maximum sentences are provided by s 1(3):

> (3) A person who is guilty of fraud is liable—
>   (a) on summary conviction, to imprisonment for a term not exceeding 12 months or to a fine not exceeding the statutory maximum (or to both);
>   (b) on conviction on indictment, to imprisonment for a term not exceeding 10 years or to a fine (or to both).

3.187 As yet the government has produced no guidelines and it is expected that the courts will draw heavily upon the existing case law in relation to deception. Difficult cases might arise where the conduct prosecuted has not produced any loss or gain in fact. It can be expected that some of the cases prosecuted under s 4 may well attract significant sentences since they will by definition involve an abuse of trust.

---

[229] See above, para 3.21.

Section 11: Obtaining Services Dishonestly

Section 11 replaces the offence of obtaining services by deception in section 1 of the **3.188**
Theft Act 1978.[230] That offence is repealed. As noted above, it was increasingly apparent
that the Theft Acts failed to protect against the obtaining of services via wholly automated
processes. The Law Commission's proposal as endorsed by the Home Office was to remove
the troublesome element of deception from the offence and to place the emphasis on
dishonesty.

The section provides: **3.189**

(1) A person is guilty of an offence under this section if he obtains services for himself or another—
   (a) by a dishonest act, and
   (b) in breach of subsection (2).
(2) A person obtains services in breach of this subsection if—
   (a) they are made available on the basis that payment has been, is being or will be made for or in respect of them,
   (b) he obtains them without any payment having been made for or in respect of them or without payment having been made in full, and
   (c) when he obtains them, he knows—
     (i) that they are being made available on the basis described in paragraph (a), or
     (ii) that they might be, but intends that payment will not be made, or will not be made in full.
(3) A person guilty of an offence under this section is liable—
   (a) on summary conviction, to imprisonment for a term not exceeding 12 months or to a fine not exceeding the statutory maximum (or to both);
   (b) on conviction on indictment, to imprisonment for a term not exceeding 5[231] years or to a fine (or to both).

Interpretation

This is a result crime, and is quite distinct from the three forms of fraud offence provided **3.190**
for in ss 1–4. There must be an actual obtaining of a service.

The *actus reus* comprises (i) an act resulting in the obtaining (ii) of services (iii) for which **3.191**
payment is or will become due and (iv) a failure to pay in whole or in part. The *mens rea*
comprises (i) dishonesty (ii) knowing that the services are to be paid for or knowing that
they might have to be paid for (iii) with intent to avoid payment in whole or in part.

According to the Law Commission in its Report No 276, 'This offence would be more **3.192**
analogous to theft than to deception, because it could be committed by "helping oneself"
to the service rather than dishonestly inducing another person to provide it'.[232]

---

[230] See generally the Home Office, *Fraud Law Reform* (2004) paras 32–5; the Home Office, *Fraud Law Reform, Responses to Consultation* (2004) para 35; the Home Office Explanatory Notes, paras 34–6; the House of Commons *Research Paper* 31/06, p 17.
[231] The government rejected calls for the sentence to be a maximum of ten years consistent with ss 2–4 of the Act: Standing Committee B, 20 June 2006, col 59.
[232] Report No 276, para 8.8.

Actus reus

An act

3.193 Unusually the offence is restricted to conduct in the form of a positive act. It is made more explicit than usual that it is not possible to commit the offence by omission alone. If an unsolicited service is offered, perhaps in the mistaken belief that a customer has paid for it, no dishonest 'act' has taken place. A rather unconvincing example provided in Parliament was of D, who sits on a boat and does not alight when he hears an announcement that any-one who has not paid for the next trip should alight. It was suggested that he commits no offence under this section.[233] This restriction may be rather illusory in its practical impact. In this example there is no doubt that D commits a fraud offence under s 2 by mak-ing an implied representation by conduct that he will pay for the trip. He does so with intent to cause financial loss to the travel company and/or to gain by keeping that which he has (s 5(3)). In addition, it is difficult to see why D is not regarded as performing a positive act by sitting on the boat to take the return trip.

Obtaining

3.194 As noted this is a result crime. D's dishonest act must be a cause of the obtaining of a ser-vice. The obtaining may be for D or another. Charges alleging that D obtained from a machine will present no difficulty under s 11. In the absence of any requirement of decep-tion, the fact that no human mind is involved where the service is provided in a wholly automated process presents no problem.

Service

3.195 Service is not further defined. But the offence is restricted in that it only applies to services for which payment is required. This follows the old s 1 1978 Act offence which did not apply to gratuitous services. Some of the situations in which D obtains a service for free by making a false representation will be caught by s 2 (above). Note that ss 1–4 apply only in relation to *property* whereas s 11 applies in relation to dishonest obtaining of *services.*

3.196 As under the old law, an application for a bank account or credit card will only be caught by this offence if the service is to be paid for: *Sofroniou.*[234] What is not made clear is whether the offence extends to services which are not legally enforceable? Can the offence occur, for example, in respect of prostitution? It would seem that there is no reason why that should not be protected.[235]

3.197 The offence obviously extends well beyond the electronic 'deception' type case. It covers, for example, the case where D climbs over a wall and watches a football match with-out paying the entrance fee—such a person is not deceiving the provider of the service directly, but is obtaining a service which is provided on the basis that people will pay for it.

---

[233] The government also emphasized the need to avoid criminalizing those who received unsolicited ser-vices from unscrupulous companies: Standing Committee B, 20 June 2006, col 54.

[234] [2003] EWCA Crim 3681.

[235] *Linekar* [1995] QB 250.

But, not to cases where D watches the game from the window of a property adjoining the ground.[236]

As the Home Office explains, it also covers the situation where a person attaches a decoder **3.198** to his television to enable viewing access to cable/satellite television channels for which he has no intention of paying.[237] It was suggested that it would also catch illegally downloading music where the provision of the music constituted a service.[238]

Without payment

One major problem with the s 11 offence which does not seem to have been foreseen **3.199** is that it will be inapplicable where D obtains his service by using a credit card or debit card, and knows that although the use of the card is unauthorized, the payment will be made by the bank/issuing company. The requirement is not that D himself does not pay, but that payment has not been made at all, or in part.

In many cases where D obtains a service by use of a credit card in such circumstances he will **3.200** also obtain some element of property (eg the ticket for the travel, or entry to the theatre etc) and will therefore commit an offence under s 2 of the Fraud Act 2006 because his false representation (that he is authorized to use the card) coupled with a dishonest intention to cause either loss to the credit card company and/or expose to a risk of loss the service provider suffice for that offence. He might also be regarded as making a false representation with intention to gain by keeping what he has—ie the money he would otherwise have had to spend. Alternatively, s 6 of the 2006 Act might be used with charges of possession of the article with intent to commit fraud.

Mens rea

Dishonesty

Dishonesty has been discussed above. This is the principal *mens rea* element of the **3.201** new offence.

Knowing that payment required/might be

The additional requirement that D knows that the services are to be paid for or knows **3.202** that they might have to be paid for is a relatively strict test. Arguably, the offence is too wide in including cases where D only knows that payment might have to be made. But, if he knows that it might be the onus is surely on him to make enquiries before he engages the services, and not to act dishonestly. This form of the *mens rea* was included to deal with electronic purchasing over the internet cases where D might have alleged that he was unsure what the obligations to pay were.[239]

---

[236] Standing Committee B, 20 June 2006, col 52.
[237] See Home Office Explanatory Notes, para 36.
[238] ibid.
[239] Home Office, *Fraud Law Reform* (2004) para 35.

3.203   Other difficulties might arise where there is uncertainty over whether the knowledge is that payment will be due immediately or at some later date.

Intention that payment avoided

3.204   This requirement that D acts with intent to avoid payment in whole or in part marks a departure from the old offence under section 1 of the 1978 Act and narrows the scope of the crime.

Intends that 'payment will not be made'

3.205   The problem of the defendant who lies, but pays or knows that someone will pay has been noted above. It arises in other contexts. The Law Commission was keen to emphasize the limits of the s 11 offence in this regard and provided an example that DD, parents of D, who lie about their religion in order to get D into a private school where they will be charged and pay the full fees commit no offence under s 11.

Other Fraud Act Provisions

Section 9: fraudulent trading by sole trader

3.206   Section 9 makes it an offence for a person knowingly to be a party to the carrying on of fraudulent business where the business is not carried on by a company.[240] Non-corporate traders covered by the new offence include sole traders, partnerships, trusts, companies registered overseas, etc. This offence parallels section 458 of the Companies Act 1985 (s 993 Companies Act 2006). This extension was recommended by the Law Commission in their Report on Multiple Offending.[241] The maximum sentence for this new offence will be ten years.

Section 10: sentence for fraudulent trading by company

3.207   Section 10 increases the maximum sentence for fraudulent trading under the companies' legislation to ten years. This follows the recommendation of the Company Law Review, *Final Report: Modern Company Law for a Competitive Economy.*[242]

---

[240] See *Arlidge and Parry on Fraud* ch 2.
[241] Law Com No 277, Cm 5609, 2002.
[242] (2001) para 15.7.

4

OTHER OFFENCES INVOLVING FRAUD

False Accounting

Introduction

Section 17 of the 1968 Act replaced ss 82 and 83 of the Larceny Act 1861 and the Falsi- **4.01**
fication of Accounts Act 1875. It provides:

(1) Where a person dishonestly, with a view to gain for himself or another or with intent to cause loss
to another, —
   (a) destroys, defaces, conceals or falsifies any account or any record or document made or
       required for any accounting purpose; or
   (b) in furnishing information for any purpose produces or makes use of any account, or any
       such record or document as aforesaid, which to his knowledge is or may be misleading, false
       or deceptive in a material particular;
       he shall, on conviction on indictment, be liable to imprisonment for a term not exceeding
       seven years.
(2) For purposes of this section a person who makes or concurs in making in an account or other
document an entry which is or may be misleading, false or deceptive in a material particular, or who
omits or concurs in omitting a material particular from an account or other document, is to be
treated as falsifying the account or document.[1]

It has been suggested that the section creates six offences, although the courts have acknowl- **4.02**
edged that 'false accounting' is the appropriate way to refer to the offence no matter how
committed.[2] The offences overlap with a number of others; for example, where D falsifies
any document or record made for an accounting purpose he might also commit forgery.
But the offence under s 17 is wider than forgery. One advantage in charging this offence is

---

[1] See generally, *Blackstone's Criminal Practice* (2007), B6.6; *Archbold* (2007) 21–227.
[2] *Bow Street Magistrates, ex p Hill* (1999) 29 Nov, unreported, DC.

that it is designed not only to deal with schemes that were fraudulent from the outset but also with those that became so when, for example, a business got into financial difficulties. In addition, charges of false accounting can accurately reflect the scale of the wrongdoing without the need to deal with the complex issues of when and where property transfers (whether as bank credits or otherwise) occurred.

4.03 It remains to be seen what impact the Fraud Act 2006 will have on the frequency with which the false accounting offences are charged. There were 487 recorded offences of false accounting in 2005/6.[3] The fraud offence under s 1 of the 2006 Act has the advantage of a higher sentence (ten years) and does not require the Crown to prove that a false representation, under s 2, related to an accounting record.[4] In some instances s 3 and s 4 of the Fraud Act will also apply as where D is under a legal duty to reveal information or where he is in a position in which he is expected to safeguard V's financial interests as for example where he is the auditor or accountant.

Actus reus

4.04 The offence may be committed by any person who falsifies, etc, any document 'made or required' for an accounting purpose. It is immaterial that no one accepts or acts on the falsified document; this is a conduct offence, and requires no result caused by D's conduct. The falsification, etc, is a sufficient manifestation of the criminal intent to warrant criminalization, irrespective of whether it causes loss or results in gain for the accused.

The account or record

4.05 Account is an ordinary English word. 'Any account or any record' is wide enough to include, in addition to traditional paper accounting records, a mechanical accounting device, as in the case of a taximeter[5] or a turnstile at the entrance to a football ground.[6] Falsifying the gas meter or electricity meter would seem to be an offence within the section. A completely false set of accounts is also an account for the purposes of this section.[7] There is no doubt that the offence extends to electronic forms of accounting record. This is important given the widespread use of spreadsheets for accounting purposes and the electronic submission of accounts and even tax returns etc.

'Made or required for'

4.06 The section is confined to records or documents 'made or required for any accounting purpose'. In the context, this plainly means accounting in the financial sense. Dishonestly to falsify the odometer of a car with a view to gain would not normally be an offence under this section since the odometer of a car is not usually a record 'made or required for' any

---

[3] A Walker, C Kershaw, and S Nicholas, *Home Office Statistical Bulletin, Crime in England and Wales 2005/2006* p 28, Recorded crime by offence 1996 to 2005/06 and percentage change between 2004/5 and 2005/6.

[4] See para 3.57.

[5] cf *Solomons* [1909] 2 KB 980.

[6] *Edwards v Toombs* [1983] Crim LR 43.

[7] *Scot-Simonds* [1994] Crim LR 933.

accounting purpose. It would be otherwise, however, if the odometer reading were used to calculate a mileage allowance due to the driver for his expenses claim. It would then be indistinguishable from the taxi-meter case.

It is sufficient that the documents are made *or* required for accounting: these are disjunctive **4.07** elements of the offence.[8] Neither term is to be read restrictively, and should be given their ordinary meaning in the context and potential purpose for which the document was required, not being treated as technical terms of 'forensic accounting'.[9]

It has been held that a document may be 'required' for an accounting purpose even though **4.08** that is not its principal purpose, so long as it is required in part for an accounting purpose. In *A-G's Reference (No 1 of 1980)*,[10] it was held than an application addressed to a finance company for a personal loan to pay for goods, though not 'made' for an accounting purpose is required for one if the company intends to use the information supplied in its accounts in the event of the application being successful. The decision has been criticized[11] as going too far in holding that it is enough that the document is 'required for an accounting purpose as a subsidiary consideration'. That, however, does not seem a valid objection if the maker knows that the addressee requires it for, inter alia, an accounting purpose because he then knows that an account will be falsified if his application is accepted; but there does not appear to have been evidence that D did know this. Whether such knowledge is required is considered below.

This is certainly a controversial extension of the offence.[12] It has been persuasively sug- **4.09** gested that 'made for' refers to the purposes of the maker of the document and 'required for' to the purposes of the recipient.[13]

In terms of establishing their purpose, it appears that documents fall into two categories: **4.10** (i) those from the inspection of which a jury, with such experience and knowledge of the world as jurors may be expected to have, could be satisfied that the document was required for an accounting purpose and (ii) those from which no such inference could safely be drawn. In the second category, the prosecution must adduce evidence of the purpose of the document. The court or jury may infer from the circumstances that the document is so required[14] but only if sufficient evidence exists for this conclusion to be drawn. One of the difficulties with the offence is that jurors must not be assumed to have any specialist knowledge of accounting practice,[15] and the types of document that might be required for an accounting purpose are extremely wide ranging.

---

[8] *Baxter v Gov of HM Prison Brixton* [2002] EWHC 300 (Admin).
[9] ibid, Auld LJ [22].
[10] *A-G's Reference (No 1 of 1980)* [1981] 1 All ER 366, [1981] Crim LR 41, CA and commentary.
[11] By *Arlidge and Parry on Fraud* at 5–059 to 5–060.
[12] See *Arlidge and Parry on Fraud* para 5–060.
[13] Some support for this view is implicit in Auld LJ's judgment in *Baxter*.
[14] *Osinuga v DPP* [1998] Crim LR 216, DC; *Baxter* (above).
[15] *Sundhers* [1998] Crim LR 497.

4.11   Unfortunately, the courts have failed to adopt a consistent approach to this aspect of the offence. In *Cummings-John*[16] it was held that a 'Report on Title' was required by a building society 'for an accounting purpose'. The document was clearly required by the society in order to decide whether to grant a mortgage advance. It is not so clear that it was required for an accounting purpose. In *Okanta*[17] the court was not satisfied that a letter containing false information which induced a mortgage advance was so required. The distinction is not obvious. In *Manning*[18] it was held that it would be open to a jury to conclude that an insurer's cover note was 'required' in the terms of this section simply by looking at the document because it set out what the client owed—but it was borderline case. An insurance claim form was held to fall on the wrong side of the line.[19] A form claiming entitlement to housing benefit is a 'document made or required for' any accounting purpose: *Osinuga v DPP*.[20] Significantly, for the purposes of prosecuting high-yield investment frauds and pyramid frauds, application forms sent to a potential investor which include false statements as to the rate of return on investments may constitute a document made or required for any accounting purpose since they would be retained by the investor: 'it was the sort of document he would put in a wall safe not a waste paper basket'.[21]

4.12   Given the ambiguity with this element of the offence, it may be that prosecutors will prefer, where possible, to rely on the general fraud offence under s 1 of the 2006 Act in which no such restriction applies.

'Any accounting purpose'

4.13   The section further extends its reach to any document, so long as it is made or required for *any* accounting purpose, though the document itself is not in the nature of an account and though the falsification does not relate to figures. So if D enters in a hire-purchase proposal form false particulars relating to a company director, the case would fall within the plain words of s 17(1)(a).[22] The information in the document may be furnished for other purposes in addition to accounting. It is sufficient that accounting is *one* of the purposes for which it is required. So a hire-purchase agreement was held to be a document within the section.[23]

Destruction, etc

4.14   Some account or record must be destroyed, defaced, concealed, or falsified by D or as a result of information provided by D. It is not enough that D is cheating V, by, for example, selling his own property as V's, if that transaction is not recorded in any account.[24]

---

[16] [1997] Crim LR 660.
[17] [1997] Crim LR 451.
[18] [1998] 2 Cr App R 461, [1999] Crim LR 151.
[19] *Sundhers* [1998] Crim LR 497.
[20] [1998] Crim LR 216, cf the at first instance HH Judge Jackson in *S* [1997] 4 Archbold News 1, which must be regarded as wrongly decided. NB the specific offence under the Social Security Administration Act 1992, s 111A, inserted by the Social Security Administration (Fraud) Act 1997, s 13.
[21] *Baxter v Gov of HM Prison Brixton* [2002] EWHC 300 (Admin).
[22] *A-G's Reference (No 1 of 2001)* [2002] Crim LR 844.
[23] *Mallett* (1978) 67 Cr App R 239, CA.
[24] *Cooke* [1986] AC 909, [1986] 2 All ER 985, HL.

The courts do not seem to have provided any detailed consideration of the terms destruction, defacement, or concealment.

It is unclear to what extent the destruction of the document needs to be complete. It is sub- **4.15**
mitted that mere damage to a document will not suffice, unless that constitutes defacement. Applying the ordinary meaning of the word, damage to a document which renders
it unusable for the purposes for which it was intended constitutes destruction.[25] It is questionable whether a document that is defaced might also become a forgery under the Forgery
and Counterfeiting Act 1981.[26]

Judicial interpretations of the expression 'conceals' arise in a wide variety of cases, many **4.16**
of them involving civil law disputes as to the construction of contractual terms. Even in
those circumstances in which the expression is used in criminal proceedings, it is not clear
that any universally accepted definition has developed. The term appears in numerous
criminal statutes. Arguably the element of concealment requires some 'act' and cannot be
committed by a mere omission. The decision in *Evani*,[27] suggests that some knowing act is
required for a 'concealment' to occur. That case concerned the offence of concealing property when bankrupt. Similarly, in *Clark v Esanda Ltd*,[28] Priestly JA states that 'concealment
in the context [of a hire purchase agreement] seems to me to mean more than simply "not
communicate". To my mind it means a conscious or deliberate keeping back of material
facts.'[29] The difficulty with the argument that concealment requires a positive act is that
following general principles of construction of criminal offences, a mere omission will suffice to ground liability where the defendant is under a duty to act in a specified manner.
This is reflected in some of the case law on 'concealment' from non-criminal contexts.
For example, in *London Assurance v Mansel*,[30] Jessel MR stated that in the context of an
insurance contract:

if a man purposely avoids answering a question, and thereby does not state a fact which it is his duty
to communicate, that is concealment. Concealment properly so called means non-disclosure and . . .
it was his duty to disclose the fact if it was a material fact.

If concealment is to be based on an omission in circumstances of a duty, it is necessary for **4.17**
the prosecution to establish a clear basis for that duty, and arguably, to prove an awareness
of the responsibility to satisfy the duty. In those cases in which omissions will found liability
in criminal law, the duty is usually one expressed explicitly in a statute, or in a contract or
as a result of a special relationship.

The issue of concealment will commonly be rolled up with that of dishonesty since know- **4.18**
ing concealment commonly implies a lack of honesty.

---

[25] In the context of testamentary documents, presumptions exist as to whether the destruction of unimportant and independent part renders the rest invalid: *Leonard v Leonard* [1902] P 243 at 248 (final three
sheets useless without first two sheets destroyed).

[26] cf *Arlidge and Parry on Fraud* para 5–056.

[27] (1825) 1 Mood 79.

[28] [1984] 3 NSWLR 1.

[29] At pp 4–5.

[30] (1879) 11 Ch D 363 Jessel MR, at p 370.

Falsification

4.19　The more important issues arise in relation to falsification. Under s 17(1)(a) the offence is committed by falsification of the account etc whereas under s 17(1)(b) it is committed by *use* of a falsified account, etc. Section 17(2) provides an extended though non-exhaustive definition of falsity:

> For purposes of this section a person who makes or concurs in making in an account or other document an entry which is or may be misleading, false or deceptive in a material particular, or who omits or concurs in omitting a material particular from an account or other document, is to be treated as falsifying the account or document.

The extended meaning attaches only to documents and accounts, not records.[31]

4.20　A person making an account may, as s 17(2) makes clear, falsify it by omitting material particulars. But the courts have extended the scope of the offence much further. In *Shama*[32] D, an international telephone operator, was required to fill in for each call a 'charge ticket' which was then used for accounting purposes. He connected certain subscribers without filling in a charge ticket so that they were not charged. The prosecution could not, therefore, produce any document which they alleged to be falsified. Upholding his conviction, the court said that failure 'to complete a charge ticket by omitting material particulars from a document required for an accounting purpose' constituted the offence. But can a person who has entirely omitted to make a document which it was his duty to make properly be said to have 'omitted material particulars' from it? The omission of material particulars seems necessarily to imply the existence of a document from which those particulars are omitted. If, however, a bundle of charge sheets, handed in at the end of the day as a complete record of the day's calls, were held be a single document, then, of course, it would be falsified. But that was not the decision.

4.21　The section does not in terms require any 'duty' to account. Where there is such a duty it may be easier to bring a prosecution under s 3 of the Fraud Act 2006 for failing to disclose information which D is under a legal duty to disclose. It appears to be sufficient for s 17 that the account is in fact made with the requisite intent and is false. Where there is a duty to account, however, the extent of the duty will be relevant in determining whether the account is 'false'. If D has accounted for everything that he is obliged to account for, his omission of other items will not in itself render the account false.[33]

4.22　Subsection (2) does not provide an exclusive definition of falsification. Conduct not falling within the subsection but amounting to a falsification within the ordinary meaning of the word would be within the section. Where a turnstile operator allowed A and B to enter and

---

[31] cf *Arlidge and Parry on Fraud* para 5–062.

[32] [1990] 2 All ER 602, [1990] Crim LR 411, CA. Also criticized by *Arlidge and Parry on Fraud* 5–070, but accepted by Griew 12–03, as 'a robust decision' which avoided an absurdity. A better course might at that time have been to charge the securing of the remission of a debt or (preferably) inducing the creditor to forgo the payment of a debt, contrary to s 2 of the 1978 Act. The best course now would be to charge under s 2 of the Fraud Act 2006: when the operator handed in the forms there was presumably an implied, if not an express, representation that there was a form for each call. He would be liable if he intended to cause loss.

[33] *Keatley* [1980] Crim LR 505 (Judge Mendl) and commentary.

recorded the entry of only one of them he falsified the record, if not within the meaning of subsection (2) then within the meaning of the word, 'falsifies'.[34]

Material particular

Where the allegation is of falsification, that must relate to a material particular.[35] This aspect of the offence has also been interpreted broadly. Information is so material if it is something that matters to V in making up his mind about action to be taken on the document.[36] The omission of a name on an account application form was held to be obviously a material particular.[37] It need not be material to the accounting purpose directly. In *Mallett* the Court of Appeal approved the trial judge's description of a material particular as 'an important matter; a thing that mattered'. It was not specified to whom it must be shown to have been important. The particulars may be 'material' precisely for the purpose of auditing and detecting fraud. Thus, omitting the name of an account holder to whom unauthorized payments were to be made is a material particular since the name would have revealed instantly that the payment was unauthorized.[38] In cases of omission, it will only be possible to evaluate the materiality of the omitted particular in the context of the account as a whole.

4.23

Section 17(1)(b)

The offence under s 17(1)(b) involves *using* rather than destroying, falsifying, etc the account. The extended defintion of falsity does not apply to section 17(2).

4.24

Section 17(1)(b) is an extremely broad offence since it applies where D uses the document etc for any purpose. A document may be misleading or false within the subsection by its failure to include material particulars even though it is accurate in the sense that each statement which is contained is true.[39] It is notable that the prosecution need to show only that information in the account may be (not is) misleading or deceptive. Difficulties may arise in establishing the misleading, false or deceptive particular, and expert accounting evidence may be necessary. The elements relating to accounts and records or documents made or required for any accounting purpose are as in relation to s 17(1)(a), as are the requirements relating to falsity.

4.25

Mens rea

Under s 17(1)(a), D's *mens rea* comprises:

4.26

  (i) intentionally destroying, defacing, concealing or falsifying the document, and
  (ii) doing so dishonestly, and
  (iii) acting with a view to gain for himself or another, or with intent to cause loss to another.

---

[34] *Edwards v Toombs* [1983] Crim LR 43.
[35] If it is of destruction, etc it is the whole document or record or, presumably a relevant part.
[36] *Mallett* [1978] 3 All ER 10, [1978] 1 WLR 820, CA.
[37] *Taylor* [2003] EWCA Crim 1509.
[38] *Taylor* [2003] EWCA Crim 1509, D authorizing £73,000 payments from employer to his parents.
[39] See *Kylsant* [1932] 1 KB 442.

And in the case of s 17(1)(b), in addition:

(iv) D must act with knowledge that the document is or may be misleading, false or deceptive in a material particular.

Intentionally making the statement in the account or record

4.27 Problems can arise where D is submitting large quantities of records, and is aware that only some of them *may* be false in a material particular. In *Atkinson*[40] the defendant, a pharmacist, completed prescription forms to the pricing authority to secure repayment of prescription costs. She admitted to filling in the forms while watching TV and playing with her children. Some were false in a material particular. The trial judge directed the jury to concentrate on her dishonesty and that it was sufficient if the jury were sure that she knew it was *likely* that some of the forms were false in a material particular. The Court of Appeal regarded this as a dilution of the element of intention, coming close to mere recklessness. There must be a view to gain or intent to cause loss (below), which would not be satisfied by proof that the defendant saw the falsity of a statement as 'likely'.[41] There is a distinct requirement that D 'deliberately and intentionally' makes the statement in the account or document. It is important to keep this element separate from the question of intention to gain since there are cases in which D will act with knowledge of falsity but with no ulterior intent to gain or cause loss. This is an important element of the offence since the nature of completing records and accounts is such that there is great potential for recklessness or negligence in the recording of data. Such failings should not give rise to liability under this offence.

Mens rea *as to the accounting nature of the documents*

4.28 If the defendant is charged under s 17(1)(a) must he know that the thing he is destroying is, or may be, 'a record or document made or required for any accounting purpose'? The ordinary principles of *mens rea* suggest that such knowledge is required. In *Graham*,[42] however, the court said 'we are not for our part persuaded that knowledge of the purpose for which any record or document is made or required forms any part of the *mens rea* of the offence'. But to convict of dishonest false accounting a person who had no idea that his conduct had anything to do with accounts is to impose strict liability as to an essential element of the offence and seems objectionable. A person may be guilty of false accounting although he has no idea, perhaps reasonably so, that this is what he is doing—as for example where the document is one which requires expert evidence to show that it is required for an accounting purpose.

4.29 Since s 17(2) extends the offence to cover cases in which the statement 'is or may be' misleading, false or deceptive, it is arguable that D may be guilty if he intentionally makes statements in the account or record, knowing that they *may be false* and acts with a view to gain or intent to cause loss. The learned authors of Arlidge and Parry[43] suggest that

---

[40] [2004] EWCA Crim 303, [2004] Crim LR 226.
[41] It is acceptable to say that D intends result A (causing loss/making gain) if he does an act B (making false statement) which is likely to bring about the result A, *provided* D also has an *intention* to perform act B.
[42] (1997) 1 Cr App R 302, [1997] Crim LR 340.
[43] *Arlidge and Parry on Fraud.*

'it can hardly be intended that the subsection should apply where it is uncertain whether the proposition in question is true or false'. The conclusion is that the expression 'or may be' must relate *only* to the s 17(1)(b) offence which includes the terms 'deception' and 'misleading'.[44]

Dishonesty

Reference may be made to the discussion of this element in other crimes.[45] The courts have **4.30** relied heavily on the general element of dishonesty as the gravamen, avoiding unduly technical separation of the issues of knowledge and falsity.[46]

Familiar problems with the ambiguity of the dishonesty test arise under s 17 as elsewhere. **4.31** For example, the bookmaker's clerk may 'borrow' his employer's money to place bets (with a view to gain) and falsify the accounts to cover up his action but with every intention and expectation of replacing the money before it is missed. Is he dishonest? Only the jury in his case can tell.

In *Gohill v DPP*[47] D1 and D2 managed a plant hire shop. They had accepted 'tips' for **4.32** allowing others to use the plant for a short time without payment by recording on the company records each such short use as if the plant had not been hired at all, but had been reserved and not collected or as if the plant had been returned within the two hours that their employer permitted for the return of faulty or incorrect plant. They were charged with offences of theft and false accounting. The defendants claimed that these actions were not dishonest but were promoting customer relations. The justices were of the opinion that they could not be satisfied, beyond a reasonable doubt, that the defendants' actions had been dishonest by the ordinary standards of reasonable and honest people. The defendants were acquitted and the prosecution appealed by way of case stated. The appeal was allowed. Leveson LJ concluded that it was impossible to find that it was not dishonest by the ordinary standards of reasonable and honest people to falsify a record in this way, particularly since company policy, of which the defendants had been aware, did not permit an alteration of those records.

Claims of right?

The concept of a claim of right includes a claim to the payment of a debt, and it is unclear **4.33** whether the concept has any relevance to the dishonesty test here, as it does in s 1.[48] On one hand it can be argued that such a claim should not exclude liability for false accounting any more than it excludes liability for robbery where violence is used to get payment. The legitimacy of the end or the belief in the legitimacy of the end should not justify an illegality in the means of securing that end. This is a powerful argument when the means involve a free-standing offence such as assault (as in robbery). Similarly, in the case of false accounting, it can be argued that irrespective of D's claim of right as to the end he seeks to achieve,

---

[44] See ibid, para 5–068.
[45] Above, para 2.270.
[46] In *Atkinson* [2004] Crim LR 226 the court's suggestion that 'only lawyers would think of breaking [the *mens rea*] into component parts' is rather odd. Is this not one element of the art of statutory construction?
[47] [2007] EWHC 239.
[48] *Wood* [1999] Crim LR 564. Williams, *TBCL* 890.

the nature of the offence is such as to impose a separate obligation of honesty as to the means by which D seeks to secure that gain. If D has a genuine belief in the claim of right to the money to which he acts with a view to gain, there is no reason for his use of a false means (evidencing his dishonesty) in his attempt to attain that money.

4.34 In the *Attorney-General's Reference (No 1 of 2001)*[49] X had been charged with an offence in the USA, which attracted high-profile media coverage. A fund was established with payments from well-wishers and an appeal committee placed monies received in an account, irrespective of whether the donors expressly stated it was for X and her parents (G and S) or for the fund. G and S submitted false invoices in respect of expenses incurred in travelling to attend their daughter's trial. The judge accepted the submission that because some of the money transferred to the trust was money originally donated to G and S to use as they chose the prosecution could not prove that the amount of money that was obtained on the invoice was not the money of G and S. No claim of a belief in a claim of legal entitlement was made. It is easy to see how even though G and S had a 'view to gain' in the sense of acquiring the property (below), a jury might have found that they were not dishonest in submitting the false invoices if they believed they had a legal right to acquire the property.

A view to gain or intent to cause loss

4.35 For the purposes of the 1968 Act—

(i) 'gain' includes a gain by keeping what one has, as well as a gain by getting what one has not; and
(ii) 'loss' includes a loss by not getting what one might get, as well as a loss by parting with what one has.[50]

With a view to

4.36 The phrase 'with a view to' appears in many hundreds of statutes and it is surprising that it has not attracted much previous judicial or academic comment. Where it has been discussed, the focus has tended to be on the consequence D acts towards achieving (in this instance whether he acts with a view to 'gain').[51] The courts have acknowledged that the expression does not connote motive.[52] The academic view of the expression where it appears in offences such as blackmail has been to treat it as simply a form of intention.[53]

4.37 In *Dooley*,[54] a case on the expression in the context of indecent images possessed with a view to distribution, the trial judge regarded it as sufficient for the prosecution to prove that D acted 'with a view to' if D saw it as likely that others might access the images. The Court of Appeal rightly it is submitted rejected that as a sufficient form of *mens rea*. Foresight or

---

[49] [2002] Crim LR 844.
[50] See the discussion of these elements in connection with other crimes, below, para 12.19.
[51] See *Smith and Hogan, Criminal Law* 789–90.
[52] Per Chitty LJ in *J Lyons and Sons v Wilkins* [1899] 1 Ch 255 at 269–70, considering the offence under s 7 of the Conspiracy and Protection of Property Act 1875. See also *Bevans* (1988) 87 Cr App R 64: D's unwarranted demand with menaces for painkillers was sufficient for blackmail as he did so with a view to gain even though his motive was to alleviate pain.
[53] See, eg Williams, *TBCL* 830.
[54] [2005] EWCA Crim 3093.

awareness of a likelihood of the prohibited consequence is not equivalent to an intention that the consequence be achieved. Nor is proof of foresight of that likelihood sufficient proof that D acted 'with a view to'. The court's conclusion is that it is sufficient that D has the consequence as 'one of' the reasons for acting in that fashion.

The Court of Appeal concluded that D acts 'with a view to' a proscribed consequence even **4.38** if that is not his sole or primary purpose for acting provided it is one of his reasons. How much further does the definition of 'with a view to' extend? The court's discussion implies that 'oblique' intent will not suffice, but the question was left open.

Claim of right

In blackmail, it seems that a person may have a 'view to gain' where he is seeking nothing **4.39** more than he is entitled to—eg the payment of a debt which is due in law—but using an unwarranted threat.[55] The same is true in false accounting. In the *Attorney-General's Reference (No 1 of 2001)*[56] discussed above, G and S accepted that there was evidence that the invoice was false in the respects alleged but contended that because some of the money transferred to the trust was money originally donated to G and S to use as they chose, the prosecution could not prove that the amount of money that was obtained via the false invoice was not the money of G and S and that they had not 'gained' anything within the meaning of s 34(2)(a) because the trustees had incorporated into the trust money which in fact belonged to G and S. The judge accepted that submission and ruled that G and S should be acquitted. The Court of Appeal rejected this argument, holding that where the accused has provided false information with a view to obtaining money or other property it is not necessary for the prosecution to prove that the accused had no legal entitlement to the money or other property in question.

In *Lee Cheung Wing*,[57] the Privy Council held that D had a view to gain for the purposes of **4.40** s 17 only because he was *not* entitled to the money he sought to gain. He was an employee of a company offering facilities for dealing in futures. Employees were not allowed to use these facilities. D, in breach of his contract of employment, opened an account in the name of a friend, X. The transactions were profitable and D signed withdrawal slips in X's name. The question was whether the slips were made with a view to gain. D's defence, that he was withdrawing money to which he was entitled, was rejected on the ground that he was not entitled to the money—he would have been bound to account to his employer for a profit made by the improper use of his position as an employee.[58] The court added that an action by D to recover the profits would probably have been defeated by a plea of *ex turpi causa non oritur actio*.

Lee Cheung Wing,[59] is not a sufficiently clear and weighty authority to cast doubt on the **4.41** reasoning in the *Attorney-General's Reference* because in *Lee Cheung Wing* it was not actually

---

[55] Below, para 12.49.
[56] [2003] 1 Cr App R 8, [2002] Crim LR 844.
[57] (1991) 94 Cr App R 355, PC.
[58] He would now probably be charged under the s 4 form of the general fraud offence in the Fraud Act 2006 if the conduct occurred in England.
[59] (1991) 94 Cr App R 355, PC.

necessary to decide whether D would have been guilty had he been entitled to keep the money. It is submitted that the words should bear the meaning attributed to them in the Court of Appeal in the *Reference*.

Gain

4.42 Suppose D falsifies the accounts so as to deceive his employer into thinking that D's department is more profitable than it really is, in order to ensure that D's employment will not be terminated.[60] It may be argued that D has no view to gain in such a case, since he intends to give full economic value for the wages he receives;[61] but, whether or not this is a sound argument (and it is probably not) he perhaps has an intent to cause loss in that he knows that the effect of his deception will be that his employer will keep open an uneconomic department. This, however, is only an 'oblique' intention[62] and it is arguable that a direct intention must be proved (see above). In *Masterson*[63] the defendant's falsification of invoices in an attempt to 'improve relations with his co-directors' who were unhappy with the acquisitions he had recently made was not sufficient to constitute the necessary 'view to gain'. D knew that there was no question of losing his position and could not therefore be said even to be falsifying them with a view to retaining that 'which he had'.

4.43 Has D a view to gain or an intention to cause loss[64] where he falsifies an account in order to conceal losses or defalcations which have already occurred? In the light of s 34(2)(a) above it seems that the answer ought to be in the affirmative. At least one of the objects which D will have in view will be that of avoiding or postponing making restitution—'keeping what one has'—and preventing V from getting what he might. The Court of Appeal has said in *Eden*[65] that putting off the evil day of having to pay is a sufficient gain. In *Goleccha and Choraria*,[66] on the other hand, it was held that a debtor who dishonestly induces a creditor to forbear from suing for his debt does not have a 'view to gain' within the meaning of the section. But why does not the debtor have a view to gain by keeping what he has? A 'deed of postponement', postponing the priority of a registered charge in favour of another obligation, does 'cause loss'.[67]

4.44 If D's sole object is to avoid prosecution, it is arguable that he is not guilty of the offence. Telling lies to avoid prosecution, whether in an account or elsewhere, if it is to be a crime, would more naturally find a place in the offence of perverting the course of justice[68] than in the Theft Act. It may of course be caught by the incredibly broad terms of the Fraud Act 2006, s 2. If charged as false accounting, there may be a difficulty in proving that he intended to do more than avoid prosecution if he is penniless at least; but, if he is employed, he may find it difficult credibly to deny that one of his objects was the continuance of his

---

[60] cf *Wines* [1953] 2 All ER 1497, [1954] 1 WLR 64.
[61] See below, para 12.30.
[62] *Smith and Hogan, Criminal Law* 95.
[63] (1996) CA 94/2221/X5.
[64] Below, para 4.45.
[65] (1971) 55 Cr App R 193 at 197, CA.
[66] (1990) 90 Cr App R 241, [1990] Crim LR 865 and commentary. See also Griew 12–07, and *Arlidge and Parry on Fraud* 4–181, 4–182.
[67] *Cummings-John* [1997] Crim LR 660.
[68] *Smith and Hogan, Criminal Law* (6th edn, 1988) 751–8.

wages; and, as has been seen, this is almost certainly enough. Gain need not be D's sole object.

With intention to cause loss

As for the intention to cause loss, it is unclear whether the intent must be direct or whether **4.45** an oblique intention (where D sees a loss as virtually certain barring some unforeseen intervention) will suffice. The motives for intending to cause the loss are irrelevant. Thus, in *Leedham*[69] D was convicted when he so disliked the government ban on handguns (imposed after the Dunblane shootings) that he completed compensation forms falsely and dishonestly to cause loss to the Home Office by allowing claims for ineligible items owned by others.

Awareness of materiality?

A further element of the *actus reus* is that if the allegation is one of falsifying the document, **4.46** etc, the falsity must relate to a material particular. The question of D's knowledge or awareness of the materiality of the particular has not been the subject of detailed judicial scrutiny. In *Bowie and McVicar*[70] HH Judge Atherton ruled that it was necessary for the prosecution to establish that additional element of *mens rea*. The charges arose from the sale of the defendants' portfolio of properties, which had been let to various tenants. The details of the properties were in some cases inaccurate in recording that the rents were paid from housing benefit rather than privately by the tenants. These were false statements, and arguably material since they would affect the security of future payments. The defendants denied that they had acted 'intentionally' or 'recklessly' either as to the falsehood or the materiality of that falsehood, but were convicted.

In most cases this issue will be subsumed within the question of dishonesty. If, for example, **4.47** D makes an application for insurance and in doing so he makes a false statement as to his marital status—perhaps out of embarrassment—he knows that it is false, but is arguably unaware of the materiality of that status in enhancing the insurance rate he will be offered. Arguably, the lack of awareness or recklessness as to the materiality can be adequately addressed in the broader question of whether D is dishonest and is acting with a view to gain. The overlap is so substantial that it is difficult to envisage circumstances in which D will be able to plead simultaneously that he accepts that he was dishonest but that he lacked *mens rea* as to the materiality and should therefore be acquitted.[71]

All such cases can be prosecuted under s 1(2)(a) and s 2 of the Fraud Act 2006 where it is **4.48** sufficient that D has made a false representation with intent to gain/cause loss irrespective of the materiality of the falsity.

Section 17(1)(b)

Under the section 17(1)(b) offence, D may be guilty in furnishing information not only **4.49** where he knows that the material particular is false, but also where he knows that the

---

[69] No 200200135/Y3.
[70] Manchester Crown Court, 19 Feb 2003.
[71] cf ATH Smith, *Property Offences* (1994) 24–07a.

document *may* be false or misleading in a material particular; evidently wilful blindness suffices.

Sentencing

4.50 The maximum penalty for the offence is seven years' imprisonment (s 17(1)).

Liability of company officers for offences under section 17

4.51 Section 18 of the Act provides:

(1) Where an offence committed by a body corporate under section 17[72] of this Act is proved to have been committed with the consent or connivance of any director, manager, secretary or other similar officer of the body corporate, or any other person who was purporting to act in any such capacity, he as well as the body corporate shall be guilty of that offence, and shall be liable to be proceeded against and punished accordingly.

(2) Where the affairs of a body corporate are managed by its members, this section shall apply in relation to the acts and defaults of a member in connection with his functions of management as if he were a director of the body corporate.

Secondary liability of officers

4.52 An offence can be committed by a body corporate only through one of its responsible officers.[73] In every case where a corporation is guilty of an offence, then, there must be at least one of the officers referred to in the section who consented or connived. If he is unidentifiable, then only the corporation may be convicted; if he can be identified, he will, in the great majority of cases, be guilty of an offence under s 17 independently of s 18, either as a principal offender or as a secondary party. Connivance or an express consent to an offence, if it amounts to encouragement, would seem sufficient to found liability under the general law,[74] apart from s 18.

Liability under section 18

4.53 Section 18 extends the scope of liability wider than this:

The clause follows a form of provision commonly included in statutes where an offence is of a kind to be committed by bodies corporate and where it is desired to put the management under a positive obligation to prevent irregularities, if aware of them. Passive acquiescence does not, under the general law, make a person liable as a party to the offence, but there are clearly cases (of which we think this is one) where the director's responsibilities for his company require him to intervene to prevent fraud and where consent or connivance amounts to guilt.[75]

---

[72] References to ss 15 and 16 of the 1968 Act were deleted by the Fraud Act 2006, Sch 3.

[73] *Smith and Hogan, Criminal Law* ch 10; *Tesco Supermarkets Ltd v Nattrass* [1972] AC 153, [1971] 2 All ER 127, HL.

[74] *Smith and Hogan, Criminal Law* ch 8.

[75] CLRC, *Eighth Report*, Cmnd 2977 (1966) para 104. Notwithstanding *Wilson* [1997] Crim LR 53, applying the corresponding provision in the Insurance Companies Act 1982, s 18 (repealed by the Financial Services and Markets Act 2000 (Consequential Amendments and Repeals) Order 2001/3649, Pt 1 Art 3(1)(b)) does not create an offence and no one could be charged under it. It is submitted that it is simply an extension of the ordinary law of secondary participation which is automatically applicable.

The 'positive obligation' clearly does not go so far as to impose liability for negligence; you **4.54** cannot consent to that of which you are unaware[76] and 'connivance' involves turning a blind eye, which has usually been regarded as equivalent to knowledge.[77] Even 'passive acquiescence' has sometimes been held sufficient to found liability as a secondary party, under the general law, but probably only on the ground that inactivity was a positive encouragement to others to commit the unlawful act in question.[78] Section 18 may go a little beyond this, though that is not entirely clear and the provision does not seem yet to have been interpreted by the courts.[79]

Section 18 extends the scope of liability from that which would apply under the general **4.55** principles of secondary liability by allowing the Crown to establish that the officer 'connived' rather than knowingly aided and abetted, or that he consented—which does not require proof that the consent amounted to an aiding and abetting, etc.

Care should be taken to recognize that s 18 is a procedural mechanism for prosecuting **4.56** officers and not an offence in its own right, despite language to the contrary in the judgment of Lord Fraser of Tullybelton in *Rank Film Distributors Ltd v Video Information Centre*[80] that the respondents ran the risk of being 'guilty of criminal offences [including] an offence against s.18 of the Theft Act 1968'.

False Statements by Company Directors, Etc

Section 19 replaced s 84 of the Larceny Act 1861. It provides: **4.57**

(1) Where an officer of a body corporate or unincorporated association (or person purporting to act as such), with intent to deceive members or creditors of the body corporate or association about its affairs, publishes or concurs in publishing a written statement or account which to his knowledge is or may be misleading, false or deceptive in a material particular, he shall on conviction on indictment be liable to imprisonment for a term not exceeding seven years.

(2) For purposes of this section a person who has entered into a security for the benefit of a body corporate or association is to be treated as a creditor of it.

(3) Where the affairs of a body corporate or association are managed by its members, this section shall apply to any statement which a member publishes or concurs in publishing in connection with his functions of management as if he were an officer of the body corporate or association.

---

[76] *Re Caughey, ex p Ford* (1876) 1 Ch D 521 at 528, CA, per Jessel MR and *Lamb v Wright & Co* [1924] 1 KB 857 at 864.

[77] J Edwards, *Mens Rea in Statutory Offences* 202–5; Williams, *CLGP* 159; M Wasik and MP Thompson, 'Turning a Blind Eye as Constituting Mens Rea' (1981) 32 NILQ 324 337–41. The Draft Criminal Code also suggests that knowledge includes wilful blindness: cl 18(1)(a)—a person acts knowingly 'with respect to a circumstance not only when he is aware that it exists or will exist but also when he avoids taking steps that might confirm his belief that it exists or will exist'.

[78] *Smith and Hogan, Criminal Law* 177.

[79] cf the draconian provision in the Borrowing (Control and Guarantees) Act 1946, s 4(2), criticized by Upjohn J in *London and Country Commercial Property Investments Ltd v A-G* [1953] 1 All ER 436 at 441. The concept of 'manager' as used in s 18 was considered in *Registrar of Restrictive Trading Agreements v WH Smith & Son Ltd* [1969] 1 WLR 1460 CA (Civ Div).

[80] [1981] 2 All ER 76 at 83.

4.58 The Crown must show that the defendant is an officer of a body corporate or unincorporated association (or person purporting to act as such). By the Companies Act 2006, s 1173(1), 'officer' in relation to a body corporate includes director, manager, or secretary.

4.59 Section 19 is wider than the earlier provision in that it applies to officers of unincorporated as well as incorporated bodies—for example, the chairman of a club. It is narrower in that:

> (i) there must be an intent to deceive members or creditors, whereas the earlier provision extended to an intent to induce any person to become a shareholder or partner, or to advance money, etc;
> (ii) the written statement or account must be about the body's affairs.

4.60 Examples of the kind of case to which the section is intended to apply were provided by the CLRC: 'A prospectus might include a false statement, made in order to inspire confidence, that some well-known person had agreed to become a director. It might also include a false statement, made in order to appeal to persons interested in a particular area, that a company had arranged to build a factory in that area.'[81]

4.61 *The mens rea consists in:*

> (i) an intent to deceive;
> (ii) knowledge that the statement is or may be misleading, false, or deceptive in a material particular.

4.62 Though no intent to defraud is required, the effect seems to be much the same, since the statement must be false in a material particular. A 'particular' is hardly likely to be held to be material unless the person to whom it is addressed is likely to take action of some kind on it and, thus, almost invariably, to be defrauded in the wide meaning now given to 'fraud'.[82]

4.63 As the Criminal Law Revision Committee thought, statements made recklessly will be within the section.[83] It is enough that D knows that the statement is or may be false, etc.

4.64 The Financial Services and Markets Act 2000 s 397 creates offences for any person who makes a statement, promise, or forecast which he knows to be misleading, false, or deceptive in a material particular, or dishonestly conceals any material facts, whether in connection with a statement, promise, or forecast made by him, or otherwise, or recklessly makes (dishonestly or otherwise) a statement, promise, or forecast which is misleading, false, or deceptive in a material particular. In view of the breadth of that section, and s 2 of the Fraud Act 2006, s 19 seems largely redundant. It is surprising that it was not considered for repeal in the debates on the Fraud Act 2006.

Suppression, Etc, of Documents

4.65 Section 20(1) provides:

> (1) A person who dishonestly, with a view to gain for himself or another or with intent to cause loss to another, destroys, defaces or conceals any valuable security, any will or other testamentary

---

[81] CLRC, *Eighth Report*, Cmnd 2977 (1966) para 105.
[82] *Welham v DPP* [1961] AC 103, [1960] 1 All ER 805, HL.
[83] CLRC, *Eighth Report*, Cmnd 2977 (1966) para 104.

document or any original document of or belonging to, or filed or deposited in, any court of justice or any government department shall on conviction on indictment be liable to imprisonment for a term not exceeding seven years.

The offence is triable either way.

Section 20(1)[84] replaced an elaborate group of offences in ss 27–30 of the Larceny **4.66**
Act 1861. These offences had been little used and the Criminal Law Revision Committee
had doubts as to whether any part of them should be retained, but s 20(1) was included
because 'It seemed to us that it might provide the only way of dealing with a person who,
for example, suppressed a public document as a first step towards committing a fraud but
did not get so far as attempting to commit the fraud.'[85]

The main constituents of the offence—dishonesty and with a view to gain—are considered **4.67**
in connection with other offences above.[86]

Which documents are covered?

Valuable security

Section 20(3) provides that: **4.68**

For purposes of this section . . .[87] 'valuable security' means any document creating, transferring,
surrendering or releasing any right to in or over property, or authorising the payment of money or
delivery of any property, or evidencing the creation, transfer, surrender or release of any such right,
or the payment of money or delivery of any property or the satisfaction of any obligation.

Valuable security is widely defined and includes a crossed cheque.[88] In *Benstead and Taylor*,[89] **4.69**
it was held that an irrevocable letter of credit was a 'valuable security' within the meaning
of the subsection, apparently on the ground that it was a document creating a right in
property. This is a questionable interpretation of the provision. The words, 'any right to,
in or over property', seem to assume some existing property, a right to, in, or over which is
created, transferred, surrendered, or released. In the case of a letter of credit there is no
existing property to, in, or over which a right is created. The letter of credit creates a right,
but it is not a right to, in, or over property. It is no answer to say that the thing in action
created by the letter of credit is itself property because the subsection does not include
a document creating property.[90] If the decision is taken to its logical conclusion, any written contract is a valuable security because, being an enforceable contract, it creates a thing
in action.

---

[84] Section 20(2) of the Theft Act 1968 created a very important offence of 'procuring the execution of a valuable security'. This was repealed by the Fraud Act 2006.

[85] CLRC, *Eighth Report*, Cmnd 2977 (1966) para 106.

[86] As to 'dishonestly', see above, para 2.270; 'with a view to gain' and 'with intent to cause loss', see above, paras 4.35–4.45.

[87] Words repealed by the Fraud Act 2006.

[88] *Cooke* [1997] Crim LR 436. Probably also a 'payable order' issued by a government department: *Graham* [1997] 1 Cr App R 302 at 325–6.

[89] (1982) 75 Cr App R 276, [1982] Crim LR 456, CA, and commentary.

[90] cf ATH Smith, *Property Offences* (1994) 24–17.

4.70 It was held in *King*[91] that a 'CHAPS' (Clearing House Automated Payment System) order was a valuable security, even though the primary 'executor' (for an offence under the now repealed s 20(2)) was the defendant himself, because it was also signed by bank officials and their signatures were obtained by deception. This was decided before the House of Lords decision in *Kassim* and, though their lordships accepted it as right, it is not clear that this conclusion is correct.[92]

4.71 In *Bolton*,[93] the judge's direction that a telegraphic transfer of funds was capable of being a valuable security was held to be wrong in the absence of any evidence of how such a transfer works. In *Manjdadria*,[94] it was held that neither the telegraphic transfer nor the computerized ledger account of the solicitors making it was a valuable security. There was no document authorizing a money transfer.[95] The court was somewhat sceptical about *King*, which was described as 'a case in which perhaps the extreme boundaries of a valuable security were canvassed'.[96]

4.72 Documents 'authorising the payment of money' which would include cheques and bills (and probably a letter of credit) are expressly included. But promissory notes (which were expressly mentioned in the 1858 Act) neither create any right in existing property nor 'authorize' the payment of money. Clearly promissory notes ought to be valuable securities but this badly drafted subsection seems to exclude them.

4.73 The wide definition of valuable security renders this offence available in a diverse range of circumstances and it is rather surprising that it is not often prosecuted. Presumably, the evidential difficulties in establishing the destruction etc of the document lie behind this.

Will or 'testamentary document'

4.74 The determination of whether a document falls within the protection of this section is, it is submitted, a question of law, and not a matter of the terminology used by either the victim or defendant.[97]

Government documents

4.75 It should be noted that the subsection does not apply to local government documents, the CLRC being of the opinion that these were adequately protected by existing statutory provisions.

---

[91] [1992] QB 20, [1991] 3 All ER 705.

[92] The bank officials might be compared to the witnesses to a promisor's signature on a promissory note. Such witnesses do not 'execute' the note. Perhaps the counter-signature of the bank officials had a more substantive effect on the validity of the CHAPS order, rendering them more than mere witnesses.

[93] (1991) 94 Cr App R 74.

[94] [1993] Crim LR 73.

[95] *Peter Weiss v Government of Germany* [2000] Crim LR 484, DC, explaining *Manjdadria*.

[96] In *Nolan* [2003] EWHC 2709, having regard to these cases, the court accepted that a printout of a transfer to the defendant's account was a valuable security.

[97] cf *Hawksby v Kane* (1913) 47 ILT 96, X's use of the term 'deed', did not preclude the court treating it as a testamentary document.

The prohibited conduct

Destroys, defaces or conceals

These are, it is submitted, ordinary English words, and should be interpreted as such.[98]   **4.76**
They are considered above in the context of s 17.

Related offences

The Proceeds of Crime Act 2002 creates offences including that under s 327: concealing,   **4.77**
disguising, converting, or transferring criminal property or removing it from the
jurisdiction.[99]

---

[98] cf ch 1.
[99] See below para 13.161.

5

CONSPIRACY TO DEFRAUD[1]

Introduction

This common law offence is one of the most controversial in English criminal law, and **5.01** there has been sustained pressure for its abolition.[2] It is incredibly broad, vague, and criminalizes conduct by two or more that would not be criminal or even involve a civil wrong when performed by an individual. It has been repeatedly suggested that it offends against the principles of legality, certainty, and fair warning.[3] The most recent calls for abolition come from academic commentators, the Law Commission, Liberty, Customs and Excise,[4] and even by Law Lords in the course of debates in the House of Lords.[5] The Law Commission commented that the offence is 'so wide that it offers little guidance on the difference between fraudulent and lawful conduct'.[6] Even the Home Office has acknowledged that

---

[1] See ATH Smith, *Property Offences* (1994) ch 19; *Arlidge and Parry on Fraud* ch 2; R Sutton and L Dobbs (eds), *Fraud Law, Practice and Procedure* (2004) ch 3. For a historical account see T Hadden, 'Conspiracy to Defraud' [1996] CLJ 248. See for a typically thought-provoking review of the problems presented by this offence JC Smith, 'Fraud and the Criminal Law' in P Birks (ed), *Pressing Problems in the Law* (1995) i. 49.

[2] See for discussion the Law Commission Working Papers No 56 (1974) and LH Leigh (1975) 38 MLR 320; Law Commission Working Paper No 104 (1988) and ATH Smith, 'Conspiracy to Defraud' [1988] Crim LR 508; Law Com Report No 228, *Conspiracy to Defraud* (1994) and JC Smith, 'Conspiracy to Defraud: Some Comments on the Law Commission's Report' [1995] Crim LR 209. The Law Commission offered a defence of its approach: S Silber, 'The Law Commission, Conspiracy to Defraud and the Dishonesty Project' [1995] Crim LR 461, and see JC Smith, Letter [1995] Crim LR 519.

[3] See below 5.02

[4] See the Home Office, *Fraud Law Reform, Responses to Consultation* (2004).

[5] See especially debates on 22 June, 19 July 22 Nov 2005, and 14 Mar 2006.

[6] Law Com Report No 276, *Fraud* (2002) para 1.6.

the offence is 'arguably unfairly uncertain and wide enough potentially to encompass sharp business practice'.[7]

5.02 The Commission's conclusion was that the offence should be abolished, to be replaced by the three specific forms of fraud offence.[8] Indeed, the Law Commission went so far as to describe the continued existence of the offence as 'indefensible'.[9] Similarly, during the Parliamentary debates on the Fraud Bill, there were powerful calls for abolition. For example, Lord Lloyd of Berwick, a former Law Lord stated that:

> I have an instinctive dislike, and I think that many judges have, of these catch-all offences such as conspiracy to defraud. Of course, as the noble and learned Lord the Attorney-General has pointed out, it makes it easier for prosecutors, but that surely is the whole danger. It seems to me that offences of such generality, and so amorphous as conspiracy to defraud, offend against one of the more fundamental principles of our judicial system: the principle of legal certainty. How can anyone know whether they are guilty of a conspiracy to defraud until it is too late as far as they are concerned?[10]

The offence was described as 'repellent',[11] 'constitutionally' defective,[12] and as so broad that it 'risk[ed] bringing the law into disrepute'.[13]

5.03 In the face of such overwhelming criticism,[14] the Home Office recommended that although the new Fraud Act offences will cover most if not all of the conduct currently caught by conspiracy to defraud, nevertheless the common law offence should be retained—as a safeguard against lacunae being revealed in the new scheme. The future of the offence is considered below.[15]

5.04 The advantages and dangers of the use of conspiracy to defraud are clearly encapsulated in the following statement taken from the inquiry initiated by the Attorney-General following the collapse of the Jubilee Line case:[16]

> Conspiracy to defraud at common law is an extremely useful weapon for a fraud prosecutor and frequently a course of offending cannot be adequately reflected in an indictment without recourse to it. For example, such a charge avoids the difficulties associated with 'specimen' counts of substantive offences. Not surprisingly, it is frequently used and is the main charge in most SFO prosecutions. However, it can sometimes be resorted to in an attempt to sidestep significant difficulties in the proof of any substantive offence and bridge the gaps in an investigation which has failed to prove more specific offences of dishonesty. Furthermore, as happened in this case, the use of the charge, because of

---

[7] See Home Office, *Fraud Law Reform: Consultation on Proposals for Legislation* (2004), para 6. <http://www.homeoffice.gov.uk/docs3/fraudlawreform.html>. For comment, see P Binning, 'When Dishonesty is not Enough' (2004) 154 NLJ 1042.

[8] See also Law Commission Report No 228, *Conspiracy to Defraud* (1994).

[9] *Fraud*, Law Com No 276 (2002) para 1.4.

[10] Hansard, HL, 22 June 2005, col 1665.

[11] Mr Heath MP, Hansard, HC, 12 June 2006, col 561.

[12] Lord Kingsland, Hansard, HL, 14 Mar 2006, col 1111.

[13] Chris Bryant MP, Hansard, HC, 12 June 2006, col 565.

[14] Academic support is offered by G Scanlan, 'Dishonesty in Corporate Offences; A Need for Reform' (2002) Comp Law 114, 117.

[15] Para 5.65.

[16] *R v Rayment and Others* (2001) CCC.

its great breadth, can make potentially relevant a very large body of documentary and other evidence which would not be relevant or admissible in relation to specific statutory offences.[17]

Statutory and common law conspiracies

Conspiracy was a misdemeanour at common law for many centuries. It was classically **5.05** defined[18] as an agreement to do an unlawful act or a lawful act by unlawful means. The word 'unlawful' was used in a broad sense to include not only all crimes triable in England, even crimes triable only summarily, but also at least (i) fraud, (ii) the corruption of public morals, (iii) the outraging of public decency, and (iv) some torts. In this respect it went far beyond the other inchoate offences of incitement and attempt, where the result incited or attempted must be a crime.

Following comprehensive review by the Law Commission in the 1970s,[19] an offence of **5.06** statutory conspiracy was enacted in the Criminal Law Act 1977, and most forms of the common law conspiracy were abolished. Section 1(1) of the 1977 Act creates the offence of statutory conspiracy. It provides in effect that it is a conspiracy to agree to commit *any* offence. On a literal reading this would mean that it dealt with common law conspiracies to defraud etc, but s 1(1) is subject to the following provisions of Part I of the Act. These include s 5(1) and (2) which[20] provide:

(1) Subject to the following provisions of this section, the offence of conspiracy at common law is hereby abolished.
(2) Subsection (1) above shall not affect the offence of conspiracy at common law so far as relates to conspiracy to defraud.

The 1977 Act, as originally enacted, caused great difficulty and controversy over the rela- **5.07** tionship between statutory conspiracy and conspiracy to defraud at common law. Eventually the House of Lords decided in *Ayres*[21] that if the alleged agreement would involve the commission of an offence it must be indicted as a statutory conspiracy to commit that offence under the 1977 Act and not as a conspiracy to defraud. Statutory conspiracy and conspiracy to defraud were held to be mutually exclusive. This presented difficulties for prosecutors. Indictments and convictions for conspiracy to defraud had to be quashed because it was discovered that the carrying out of the agreement necessarily involved the commission of some offence, however trivial. The House substantially modified the effect of *Ayres*, as generally understood, in the decision in *Cooke*.[22] That decision brought new difficulties.[23]

---

[17] *Review of the Investigation and Criminal Proceedings Relating to the Jubilee Line Case* (2006) para 11.88.
[18] By Lord Denman in *Jones* (1832) 4 B & Ad 345 at 349. But a few years later in *Peck* (1839) 9 Ad & El 686 at 690 he declared, 'I do not think the antithesis very correct'.
[19] Law Commission, *Report on Conspiracy and Criminal Law Reform* No 76 (1976).
[20] As amended by the Criminal Justice Act 1987.
[21] [1984] AC 447, [1984] 1 All ER 619. On this see GR Sullivan [1985] Crim LR 615.
[22] [1986] AC 909, [1986] 2 All ER 985.
[23] See [1987] Crim LR 114 and *Levitz* (1989) 90 Cr App R 33, [1989] Crim LR 714, where Bingham LJ pointed out that the problems apply to conspiracies entered into between the coming into force of the 1977 Act and 20 July 1987 when s 12 of the Criminal Justice Act 1987 took effect—by now (2007) none is likely to be outstanding.

These are now of historical interest only because of the enactment of s 12 of the Criminal Justice Act 1987.

5.08 Section 12 of the Criminal Justice Act 1987 restored the full scope of conspiracy to defraud at common law:

(1) If—
  (a) a person agrees with any other person or persons that a course of conduct shall be pursued; and
  (b) that course of conduct will necessarily amount to or involve the commission of any offence or offences by one or more of the parties to the agreement if the agreement is carried out in accordance with their intentions,
the fact that it will do so shall not preclude a charge of conspiracy to defraud being brought against any of them in respect of the agreement.

Present relationship between statutory and common law conspiracies

5.09 Statutory conspiracy and conspiracy to defraud are no longer mutually exclusive. An agreement to commit a crime involving fraud or dishonesty is both a statutory conspiracy (to commit a Theft Act or a Fraud Act offence) and a conspiracy to defraud. The prosecutor will frequently have a choice[24] which should be exercised in accordance with the guidance in the Code for Crown Prosecutors issued by the Director of Public Prosecutions under s 10(1) of the Prosecution of Offences Act 1985,[25] and the Attorney-General's guidance of 2007 issued to ensure appropriate use of conspiracy to defraud after the Fraud Act 2006 came into force.[26]

5.10 The Attorney-General's guidelines provide that:

In selecting charges in fraud cases, the prosecutor should consider:
• whether the behaviour could be prosecuted under statute—whether under the Fraud Act 2006 or another Act or as a statutory conspiracy;
• whether the available statutory charges adequately reflect the gravity of the offence.
• Statutory conspiracy to commit a substantive offence should be charged if the alleged agreement satisfies the definition in section 1 of the Criminal Law Act 1977, provided that there is no wider dishonest objective that would be important to the presentation of the prosecution case in reflecting the gravity of the case.[27]

5.11 This echoes the statement made in the Report of the inquiry into the Jubilee Line Fraud:

The charging of conspiracy to defraud needs therefore to be carefully considered in each case, not only to ensure that it is good in law, but also so as to anticipate the consequences of its use for the length and manageability of any ensuing trial. *Conspiracy to defraud should only be used in preference to substantive offences when it can clearly be shown that the available substantive offences are significantly*

---

[24] In the recent case of *Mohammed* [2004] EWCA Crim 678, the Court of Appeal was prepared to uphold a conviction on an erroneous charge of conspiracy to defraud contrary to s 1 of the 1977 Act.
[25] See *Archbold* (2007) at paras 1–262 and 1–263. See further <http://www.cps.gov.uk>
[26] See below Appendix 8.
[27] Available from <http://www.lslo.gov.uk>

inadequate to reflect the real and demonstrable criminality of the case, as revealed unequivocally by the evidence gathered.[28] (Emphasis added.)

Conspiracy to Defraud Defined

It is an offence triable only on indictment to agree to defraud, whether or not the fraud **5.12** amounts to a crime or even a tort. There are two versions of the offence of conspiracy to defraud:

(i) agreeing dishonestly to prejudice another's economic interests; or
(ii) agreeing to mislead a person with intent to cause him to act contrary to his duty.

Agreeing dishonestly to prejudice another's economic interests

This is the most commonly used form of the offence. It extends the reach of the criminal **5.13** law beyond the scope of even the extraordinary reaches of theft or the general fraud offence. It goes further even than statutory conspiracies to commit those offences.

Scott v MPC

It was stated by the House of Lords in the leading authority of *Scott v Metropolitan Police* **5.14** *Comr*[29] that:

> . . . it is clearly the law that an agreement by two or more by dishonesty to deprive a person of some-thing which is his or to which he is or would be or might be entitled and an agreement by two or more by dishonesty to injure some proprietary right of his, suffices to constitute the offence of conspiracy to defraud.[30]

In *Wai Yu-Tsang v The Queen*,[31] Lord Goff, giving the judgment of the Board, described the **5.15** offence in much the same way, including by way of example, but not as an essential ingredi-ent, an intention or contemplation of deceit of the potential victim:

> . . . it is enough for example that . . . the conspirators have dishonestly agreed to bring about a state of affairs which they realise will or may deceive the victim into so acting, or failing to act, that he will suffer economic loss or his economic interests will be put at risk. It is however important in such a case . . . to distinguish a conspirator's intention (or immediate purpose) dishonestly to bring about such a state of affairs from his motive (or underlying purpose). The latter may be benign to the extent that he does not wish the victim or potential victim to suffer harm; but the mere fact that it is benign does not prevent the agreement from constituting a conspiracy to defraud . . .'.[32]

In *Scott*, D agreed with the employees of cinema owners that in return for payment, they **5.16** would abstract films without the consent of their employers, or of the owners of the copy-right, in order that D might make copies infringing the copyright, and distribute them for profit. It was held that D was guilty of a conspiracy to defraud. It was held to be immaterial

---

[28] *Review of the Investigation and Criminal Proceedings Relating to the Jubilee Line Case* (2006) para 11.88.
[29] [1975] AC 819, [1974] 3 All ER 1032.
[30] Per Viscount Dilhorne at 1039.
[31] [1992] 1 AC 269, PC, [1992] Crim LR 425.
[32] At 279H–280B.

that no one was deceived. The offence is one of defrauding. Although the well-known definition of 'defraud' by Buckley J in *Re London and Globe Finance Corpn Ltd*,[33] includes a reference to deceit ('to defraud is by deceit to induce a course of action'), there can be fraud without deceit. For example, larceny was an offence which had to be committed 'fraudulently', but deceit has never been a necessary ingredient of theft.

5.17 The majority of the authorities relied on in *Scott* were in fact conspiracies to steal or to do acts which included theft, though the defrauding was not necessarily confined to theft. The great majority of agreements to defraud in this category will be agreements to commit offences under the Theft Acts and under the Fraud Act 2006 but clearly there are cases amounting to fraud within the definition in *Scott* that are not agreements to commit substantive offences.

5.18 Senior judges have acknowledged the potential unfairness and undesirability of this breadth:

> Viscount Dilhorne's words [in *Scott*], if taken as a comprehensive definition of the offence of conspiracy to defraud, inevitably embrace conspiracies to commit a multitude of other specific offences, as, for example, robbery, burglary, theft, obtaining by deception, [now repealed] most offences of forgery, and a formidable list of minor offences created by statute, many of them summary offences only, in which an element of fraud is involved—in short every offence of which the ingredients include (a) dishonesty and (b) either some injury to private proprietary rights or some fraud upon the public. This category of offences, of which the examples given above are by no means exhaustive, must cover a very wide band of the entire spectrum of crime. The only other band of comparable importance would seem to be offences against the person.[34]

Agreement

5.19 There must be an agreement between two or more conspirators.[35] In all cases, the *actus reus* is the agreement which, of course, is not a mere mental operation, but must involve spoken or written words or other overt acts. If D repents and withdraws immediately after the agreement has been concluded, he is guilty[36] and his repentance is a matter of mitigation only. This is the crucial distinction between inchoate offending and liability for encouraging and assisting.[37]

5.20 There is no requirement for the agreement necessarily to involve the commission of any substantive offence. It is in this respect that the common law conspiracy to defraud is much wider than the statutory conspiracy under s 1 of the 1977 Act which requires D1 and D2 to have agreed on a course of conduct which will necessarily involve the commission of a substantive criminal offence if it was carried it out in accordance with their intentions.

---

[33] [1903] 1 Ch 728 at 732, 733.
[34] *Ayres* (1984) 78 Cr App R 232, HL, per Lord Bridge at 240.
[35] See generally on the requirement for an agreement the discussion in *Smith and Hogan, Criminal Law* ch 12.
[36] As in the *Bridgewater Case*, unreported, referred to by Lord Coleridge CJ in the *Mogul Steamship Case* (1888) 21 QBD 544 at 549.
[37] See generally *Smith and Hogan, Criminal Law* ch 12.

Parties to the agreement

A company may be convicted of an offence of conspiracy to defraud.[38] It must be proved **5.21**
that D conspired with another but the other need not be identified.[39] If the managing
director of a company resolves to perpetrate an illegality in the company's name, but com-
municates this to no one, there is no conspiracy between him and the company. To allow
an indictment would be to 'offend against the basic concept of a conspiracy, namely an
agreement of two or more to do an unlawful act it . . . would be artificial to take the view
that the company, although it is clearly a separate legal entity can be regarded here as a separate entity or a separate mind . . .'.[40]

No need for acts to be performed by conspirators

In a statutory conspiracy it is expressly provided that the contemplated offence is to be com- **5.22**
mitted 'by one or more of the parties to the agreement'.[41] In *Hollinshead*,[42] the Court of Appeal
held that this was a restatement of the common law, so the same principle applied to conspiracy to defraud: the contemplated fraud must be one which is to be perpetrated by one
of the parties to the agreement in the course of carrying it out. But complete execution of
the agreement to sell the black boxes in that case would not defraud anyone. The parties
contemplated that the fraud would be carried out by other persons, not yet ascertained,
who would buy the boxes and use them to defraud the electricity suppliers. The court
therefore quashed the convictions for conspiracy to defraud—but they were restored by the
House of Lords. The House held that the 'purpose' of the defendants was to cause economic loss to the electricity suppliers. This is difficult to understand. Their purpose was to
make a profit by selling the devices to the (as they thought) middleman. Presumably they did
not care what happened to the boxes after that. If they had been accidentally destroyed in a
fire, they would not consider that their enterprise had failed. On the contrary they might
have been pleased at the prospect of selling some more. The House seems to have been much
influenced by the fact that the boxes were 'dishonest devices' with only one 'purpose', which
was to cause loss. But 'purpose' is here used in the sense of 'function'. An inanimate thing
cannot have a 'purpose' (any more than it can be 'dishonest') in the sense in which that
word is used in the law of conspiracy. However that may be, *Hollinshead* seems to broaden
the law of conspiracy to defraud to include the case where the defendants contemplate that
the execution of their agreement will enable some third party to perpetrate a fraud.

Dishonesty

A core element of the offence is the requirement that the conspirators acted dishonestly. **5.23**
In the recent case of *Norris v USA*, Auld LJ referred to the fact that dishonesty is 'the critical

---

[38] *ICR Haulage Co Ltd* [1944] KB 551, CCA.
[39] *Phillips* (1987) 86 Cr App R 18, discussed [1988] Crim LR at 338.
[40] *McDonnell* [1966] 1 QB 233, [1966] 1 All ER 193 (Nield J). cf *ICR Haulage Co* [1944] KB 551.
A conviction might ensue if D agrees with his company in his capacity as a person responsible for the acts of
another corporation rather than as the person responsible for his company: see the Canadian cases cited in
McDonnell.
[41] Criminal Law Act 1977, s 1(1)(a). See *Smith and Hogan, Criminal Law* 362.
[42] [1985] 1 All ER 850 at 857, see further *Smith and Hogan, Criminal Law* 370. Arguably such conduct is
an incitement or conspiracy to abstract electricity.

constituent of the offence—and has been since at least the mid twentieth century'.[43] The Home Office accepted that the element of dishonesty is 'left to do all the work'.[44]

5.24 The test for dishonesty is now agreed to be the usual objective/subjective test provided for in *Ghosh*:[45]

(a) was what was done dishonest by the ordinary standards of reasonable and honest people? If no, not guilty; if yes,

(b) must the defendant have realized that what he was doing was dishonest according to those standards?

5.25 There was earlier controversy about what 'dishonesty' means in this context. In *Landy*[46] the court appeared to think that the ultimate test was whether the *defendant* thought his conduct dishonest. In *McIvor*[47] the court reiterated this view, holding that the test in theft is different; but, shortly afterwards in *Ghosh*[48] it was held that the same test should be applied in conspiracy to defraud as in theft. The standard of honesty is that of ordinary decent people and D is dishonest if he realizes he is acting contrary to that standard. In theft, D is not dishonest if he believes he has a right to do the act in question and this must also apply in conspiracy. If, however, he knows for example, that no 'ordinary decent company director' would take the risk in question, then he knows that the risk is an unjustifiable one and it is dishonest for him to take it.[49] The test proposed in *Sinclair*[50] accords with this. If *no* director could have believed the risk was justified, it follows that the defendant did not; but it would seem right that the jury should be directed that they must find this is so.

5.26 Concerns have been raised as to whether the offence remains compatible with the guarantee against retrospective criminalization in Article 7 of the ECHR.[51]

Agreement to deprive V of property

5.27 Following *Scott*, one of the ways in which the offence can be committed is by an agreement dishonestly to deprive the victim of property. The crime is complete upon the agreement (as with all conspiracies) and hence it is irrelevant that there is in fact no loss actually incurred. Where V is in fact induced to part with something of economic value, he is probably defrauded even if he receives the profit on the investment in precisely the terms represented by the conspirators.[52] Their liability turns almost exclusively on the dishonesty and

---

[43] [2007] EWHC 71 [60].

[44] Home Office, *Fraud Law Reform* (2004) para 4.

[45] *Feeley* [1973] 1 QB 530; *Ghosh* [1982] 1 QB 1053, CA, above, para 2.270.

[46] [1981] 1 All ER 1172 at 1181.

[47] [1982] 1 All ER 491, [1982] 1 WLR 409.

[48] [1982] QB 1053, [1982] 2 All ER 689. See *Cox and Hodges* [1983] Crim LR 167 and commentary (fraudulent trading).

[49] For a remarkable difference of opinion in the House of Lords as to whether there was evidence of dishonesty, see *Tarling v Government of the Republic of Singapore* (1978) 70 Cr App R 77, and JC Smith, 'Theft Conspiracy and Jurisdiction: Tarling's Case' [1979] Crim LR 220.

[50] [1968] 3 All ER 241, (1968) 52 Cr App R 618.

[51] See para 5.50.

[52] *Potger* (1970) 55 Cr App R 42, CA.

the preparedness to induce V to take an economic risk without being aware of the true circumstances and consequences.

Agreement to imperil V's property interests

Under *Scott*, it is also sufficient to constitute a conspiracy to defraud that the conspirators   **5.28**
agree dishonestly to induce the victim to take an economic risk which he would not have
taken but for their deception.[53] It is irrelevant that they have agreed on a scheme which will
not lead to any loss to their intended victim; it is sufficient that it will put at risk the economic interests of the victim. It is no defence that the scheme did in fact produce the profit
for the victim that they had promised. Nor is it any defence to a charge of conspiracy to
defraud that the conspirators believed that the speculation into which they were inducing
V to invest was a good one and that V had a good chance of making a profit. All of these
issues will be matters relevant to the central issue of dishonesty.

Agreement to deprive V of that to which he might be entitled

It seems to be sufficient that the agreement will be to deprive V of that to which he might   **5.29**
be entitled. In *Tarling v Government of the Republic of Singapore*[54] the House of Lords held
by a majority that the intention of company directors to make and retain a secret profit for
which they would have been accountable to the shareholders was not evidence of an intention to defraud.[55] In *Adams v R*[56] the court seems to have been of the view that, even if the
agreement to make and retain the secret profit is not an offence, the agreement to take positive steps to conceal it is.[57] Such conduct would now be an offence under s 4 of the Fraud
Act 2006.[58]

Intention to defraud

If a person is defrauded when he is 'prejudiced', conspirators clearly have a sufficient *mens*   **5.30**
rea if it is their purpose to cause that prejudice by carrying out their agreement. There
are dicta to the effect that direct intention in the form of a purpose is required, but in *Wai*
Yu-tsang the Privy Council thought this too restrictive and that it is enough that the parties
have *agreed to cause* the prejudice. If they have agreed to cause it, that is, to defraud, they
intend to defraud, and it is immaterial that defrauding is not their purpose.

In the light of these principles the *Attorney-General's Reference (No 1 of 1982)* (the 'whisky-label   **5.31**
case')[59] is a doubtful decision. The defendants were charged with conspiracy to defraud
X Co by causing loss by unlawful labelling, sale, and supply of whisky, falsely purporting to
be 'X label' products. The agreement was made in England but the whisky was to be sold

---

[53] *Allsop* (1976) 64 Cr App R 29, [1976] Crim LR 738, CA and commentary; cf *Hamilton* (1845) 1 Cox
CC 244; *Carpenter* (1911) 22 Cox CC 618.
[54] (1978) 70 Cr App R 77, [1978] Crim LR 490. See also the Home Office, *Fraud Law Reform, Responses
to Consultation*, (2004) para 15.
[55] See, however, JC Smith, 'Theft, Conspiracy and Jurisdiction: Tarling's Case' [1979] Crim LR 220 at
225–6.
[56] [1995] 1 WLR 52, PC.
[57] See commentary [1995] Crim LR 561, 562.
[58] See para 3.158.
[59] [1983] QB 751, [1983] 2 All ER 721, [1983] Crim LR 534 and commentary.

in Lebanon. The *ratio decidendi* was that the trial judge had rightly held that he had no jurisdiction to try the indictment because the contemplated crime in Lebanon (obtaining by deception from the purchasers of the whisky) would not have been indictable in England (see now below on jurisdiction). One reason for holding that there was no conspiracy to defraud X Co was that this was not the 'true object' of the agreement. Damage to X Co would have been 'a side effect or incidental consequence of the conspiracy and not its object'.[60]

5.32 This must now be considered in the light of the decision of the House of Lords in *Cooke*.[61] British Rail stewards boarded a train, equipped with their own food which they dishonestly sold to passengers, instead of that provided by their employers, intending to keep the proceeds of sale for themselves. They were probably guilty in law of going equipped to cheat the passengers and, when they sold food to them, of obtaining the price by deception.[62] Whether this was so or not, the House had no difficulty in holding that they were guilty of conspiracy to defraud British Rail. It is true that the House was preoccupied with the problem of distinguishing *Ayres*, the 'whisky-label case' was not cited, and it does not appear that it was argued that the loss to British Rail was 'a side effect or incidental consequence'. Nevertheless, it is clear that this was a case where the object of the conspirators was to make a profit out of the customers, not to defraud British Rail.

5.33 Lord Lane CJ must have been right in the 'whisky-label case'[63] when he said that, 'it would be contrary to principle, as well as being impracticable for the courts, to attribute to defendants constructive intentions to defraud third parties based on what the defendants should have foreseen as probable or possible consequences.' Constructive intentions are to be abhorred; but presumably the House in *Cooke* thought that a jury could properly find that the defendants must have known that their conduct would, inevitably, cause loss to British Rail. If so, it was right to hold that they *intended* to defraud British Rail and it should be immaterial that this was not their purpose.

Sufficient that conspirators intend to put V's interests at risk

5.34 If the conspirators know that the effect of carrying out the agreement will be to put V's property at risk, then they intend prejudice to V and, if they are dishonest, they are guilty of conspiracy to defraud him. This is so notwithstanding that it turns out that V's property is unimpaired, or even that he makes a profit out of the transaction. A clear example would be where the conspirators agree to take V's money without his consent and then bet with it on a horse with odds at 20 to 1. They have agreed to defraud him and the conspiracy is not undone even if the horse wins and, as they intended throughout, they pay half the winnings into his bank account.

---

[60] [1983] 2 All ER 724. But in *Governor of Pentonville Prison, ex p Osman* (1990) 90 Cr App R 281 at 298 it was held, distinguishing the whisky-label case, that a conspiracy to deprive V of dollars in the United States was only the means to effecting the 'true object' of the conspiracy which was the defrauding of V in Hong Kong. The distinction is not blindingly obvious.

[61] [1986] AC 909, [1986] 2 All ER 985, [1987] Crim LR 114.

[62] Now of fraud contrary to ss 1 and 2 of the Fraud Act 2006.

[63] [1983] 2 All ER at 724.

This, it is submitted is the best explanation of *Allsop*.[64] The judgment is difficult because of **5.35** its reliance on two dicta of Lord Diplock which were mutually inconsistent and have both since been disapproved; but the decision on the facts is readily explicable. D was a 'sub-broker' for a hire-purchase finance company, V. His function was to introduce prospective hire-purchasers who wished to acquire cars. In collusion with others, he filled in application forms with false statements about the value of the cars and the payment of deposits so as to cause V to accept applications for hire-purchase finance which, otherwise, they might have rejected. He expected and believed that the transactions he introduced would be duly completed, so that V would achieve their contemplated profit to the advantage of all concerned, including D who got his commission. His defence was that he did not intend V to suffer any pecuniary loss or be prejudiced in any way. The court found that V was defrauded when he was induced to do the very acts which D intended him to do. V paid an excessive price for cars and advanced money to persons who were not as creditworthy as they were alleged to be. This not merely put him at risk of being defrauded, but actually defrauded him: 'Interests which are imperilled are less valuable in terms of money than those same interests when they are secure and protected'.[65] The result intended by D was, in law, the defrauding of V; and V was in law defrauded. It is wholly immaterial whether D would have regarded that result as 'fraud'. If he did not, he was making a mistake of law.

According to this explanation D intended to prejudice V. The facts admitted of no other **5.36** interpretation. But the judge had directed the jury that they could convict if they were satisfied that D realized that his conduct was *likely to lead* to the detriment or prejudice of V. If this is taken literally, it is sufficient that D is reckless (in the *Cunningham/G* sense[66]) whether prejudice—that is, defrauding—occurs. It is submitted that this would be going too far and take common law conspiracy out of line with statutory conspiracy.

In *Wai Yu-tsang* the Privy Council expressed a reluctance 'to allow this part of the law to **5.37** become enmeshed in a distinction, sometimes artificially drawn between intention and recklessness'; but they then said, of *Allsop* and the instant case, that it is enough that:

the conspirators have dishonestly agreed to bring about a state of affairs which they realize will *or may* [authors' italics] deceive the victim into so acting, or failing to act, that he will suffer economic loss or his economic interests will be put at risk.

The use of the words, 'or may', admit recklessness as a sufficient *mens rea*—it is enough that **5.38** the parties have taken a conscious risk of causing prejudice. This was probably not necessary to the decision since the trial judge had directed the jury that D was guilty if he knew what he had done 'would cause detriment or prejudice to another'. It is a stark contrast to the position under the statutory conspiracy offence which requires proof that a crime will necessarily occur if the actions are carried out in accordance with the conspirators' intentions.

---

[64] (1976) 64 Cr App R 29.
[65] (1976) 64 Cr App R at 32.
[66] *G* [2004] AC 1034 in which the House of Lords held that the *mens rea* of recklessness was satisfied only on proof that D personally foresaw the risk and went on unreasonably to take it.

Risk taking and dishonesty

5.39   The intention to defraud is readily discernible in *Allsop* where there could be no question of V believing he had any right to do what he did. More difficult is the case where company directors take a risk with the company's property, perhaps hoping to make a large profit and so benefit the shareholders. If the risk taken was such that 'no director could have honestly believed it was in the interest of that company that the risk should be taken',[67] then the company is defrauded. Whether a risk is unjustifiable is a question of judgement and a matter of degree. There is no clear dividing line between right and wrong, such as was crossed in *Allsop* when false statements were made or in *Wai Yu-tseng* where the dishonouring of cheques was concealed in a bank account. Whether the risk is so grave that no director could believe it justified is equally a matter of judgement and degree. Conspiracy to defraud thus lacks the precision that we should normally look for in any offence, and certainly in one of this seriousness.

Proof of intention

5.40   The intention to defraud must always be proved. Thus, the use abroad of a stolen cheque book and cheque card is capable of being fraud on a bank in England because the effect is to cause the bank in England to meet its legal or commercial obligation to honour the cheque; but, if D is charged with conspiracy to defraud the bank, the jury must be directed that he appreciated that his conduct would have this effect.[68]

Agreement to deceive V to act contrary to public duty

5.41   The proposition in *Scott* is not an exclusive definition of conspiracy to defraud. It is confined to economic prejudice; but a person is also defrauded if he is deceived into acting contrary to his public duty.[69] So it would be a conspiracy to defraud if DD agree by deception to induce a public official to grant an export licence,[70] or to supply information[71] or to induce a professional body to accept an unqualified person as a member,[72] assuming, in each case, that it was the duty of the person so deceived not to do as asked in the actual circumstances of the case.

5.42   If the public official is persuaded by means other than deception—for example, bribes or threats—to act contrary to his duty, he is obviously not defrauded and the agreement is not a conspiracy to defraud unless it can be said that those affected by the breach of duty have been defrauded—for example, those persons about whom the confidential information is disclosed or, more likely, perhaps, the official's superiors whose duty to keep the information secret has been vicariously violated. Most conspiracies to pervert the course of justice consist in agreements to deceive a public official so that he acts contrary to his duty and are conspiracies to defraud.

---

[67] *Sinclair* [1968] 3 All ER 241, (1968) 52 Cr App R 618.
[68] *McPherson and Watts* [1985] Crim LR 508.
[69] *Welham v DPP* [1961] AC 103, [1960] 1 All ER 805. *Welham* was followed in *Terry* [1984] AC 374, [1984] 1 All ER 65, HL. (D, who uses an excise licence belonging to another vehicle intending to cause police officers to act on the assumption that it belongs to his vehicle, has an intention to defraud, even though he intends to pay the licence fee.)
[70] *Board of Trade v Owen* [1957] AC 602, [1957] 1 All ER 411.
[71] *DPP v Withers* [1975] AC 842, [1974] 3 All ER 984.
[72] *Bassey* (1931) 22 Cr App R 160, CCA.

Public officials?

Some of their lordships in *Withers*[73] thought that this principle was strictly confined to **5.43** public officials, and did not extend to the case, for example of a bank manager deceived into breaking his contractual duty.[74] However in *Wai Yu-tsang v R*[75] the Privy Council said that the cases concerned with public duties are not to be regarded as a special category but as examples of the general principle that conspiracy to defraud does not require an intention to cause economic loss. The Board, disapproving Lord Diplock's more restrictive statement in *Scott*,[76] preferred the broad propositions of Lord Denning—'If anyone may be pre-judiced in any way by the fraud, that is enough'—and Lord Radcliffe, who agreed with Lord Denning and used similar language, in *Welham*.[77] The result is an astonishingly wide offence.

Jurisdiction over conspiracy to defraud[78]

An agreement in England or Wales to carry out a fraud abroad is not indictable at common **5.44** law in England or Wales as a conspiracy to defraud. This is now regulated by s 5(3) of the Criminal Justice Act 1993 which provides that, where the conspiracy would be triable in England but for the fraud which the parties had in view not being intended to take place in England and Wales, a person may be guilty of conspiracy to defraud if:[79]

(a) a party to the agreement constituting the conspiracy, or a party's agent, did anything in England and Wales in relation to the agreement before its formation, or

(b) a party to it became a party in England and Wales (by joining it either in person or through an agent), or

(c) a party to it or a party's agent, did or omitted anything in England and Wales in pursuance of it.

Indicting conspiracy to defraud

The courts have reiterated the need for greater care in the framing of indictments for con- **5.45** spiracy to defraud, in particular making clear a distinction between the agreement alleged and the reasonable information given in respect of it.[80]

In *Landy*,[81] the Court of Appeal identified two principal reasons for the prosecution's obli- **5.46** gation to provide specificity in the indictment: to enable the accused to know the case against him and to fix the prosecution case on a particular course so that it could not

---

[73] 1975] AC 842, [1974] 3 All ER 984.
[74] On the broad interpretation of public duty in the offence of misconduct in public office, see *A-G's Reference (No 3 of 2003)* [2004] EWCA Crim 868.
[75] [1991] 4 All ER 664 at 670, PC.
[76] [1975] AC 819 at 840–1. But the court in *Wai* made no reference to *Withers* [1975] AC 842, decided by the same judicial committee at the same time as *Scott*, where Lords Simon and Kilbrandon agreed with Lord Diplock.
[77] [1961] AC 103 at 133 and 124 respectively.
[78] See generally M Hirst, *Jurisdiction and the Ambit of the Criminal Law* (2001) 175–8.
[79] Hirst argues that s 5(3) should be charged separately from and in addition to conspiracy to defraud, p 178.
[80] *K* [2004] EWCA Crim 2685, [2005] Crim LR 298.
[81] [1981] 1 All ER 1172, (1981) 72 Cr App R 237.

unfairly change tack during the trial. Specificity is also needed for the jury to return verdicts which can be properly understood for sentencing, and to avoid problems of double jeopardy, particularly in prosecutions alleging frauds over lengthy periods. In prosecutions for conspiracy to defraud, an offence renowned for its breadth and lack of definition, the need for specificity is at its highest for all the reasons identified, and also to assist in keeping the trial manageable. In *Landy*[82] the court proposed a model of how an indictment should be drawn for the facts of that case. The words italicized illustrate these points: causing and permitting the Bank to make *excessive* advances to *insubstantial* and *speculative* trading companies incorporated in Liechtenstein and Switzerland, such advances being *inadequately* guaranteed and without *proper* provision for payment of interest.[83]

5.47 The obligation identified in *Landy* does not alter the fundamental difference between the ingredients of the offence as contained in the indictment, which the prosecution must prove, and the further particulars provided. Whether the particulars are elevated to the status of ingredients depends on the charge involved. With conspiracy, the essential ingredient of the offence is the agreement. If the particulars provide detail of the manner in which the *agreement* was implemented they do not form part of the ingredients of the offence. There may of course be cases where the particulars relate not to the implementation, but to the form of the agreement itself, in which case they become part of the ingredients of the offence alleged and must be proved by the prosecution.[84] This method of indicting conspiracy to defraud, distinguishing between the essential ingredient of the agreement and the other particulars of implementation from which jurors are invited to infer dishonesty etc. was commended in *K*.[85]

5.48 In *K*, the Court of Appeal held that it is only necessary to specify in detail in the indictment the agreement, and not how the participants intended individually to go about (or had gone about) defrauding V. Where the prosecution provides further particulars to clarify the allegations, these do not form part of the ingredients of the offence in the indictment unless they relate to the *agreement* not the method of implementation and as such there need not be jury unanimity on them.[86] The court suggested, helpfully it is submitted, that indictments for conspiracy to defraud:

should identify the agreement alleged with the specificity necessary in the circumstances of each case; if the agreement alleged is complex, then details of that may be needed and those details will . . . form part of what must be proved. If this course is followed, it should then be clear what the prosecution

---

[82] [1981] 1 All ER 1172, (1981) 72 Cr App R 237.
[83] [1981] 1 All ER at 1179.
[84] *Bennett* [1999] EWCA Crim 1486.
[85] [2005] 1 Cr App 408.
[86] ibid; cf *Fussell* [1997] Crim LR 812. JCS in his comment on *Fussell* had questioned the distinction drawn in *Hancock* [1996] 2 Cr App R 554 and suggested that if the accused 'had been charged with the offences of obtaining property by deception and obtaining services by deception, which was the substance of the allegations, the case would have been indistinguishable from *Brown*' (1984) 79 Cr App R 115. *K*, rightfully it is submitted, regards that criticism as misplaced. The analogy with the deception cases is an imperfect one since, as explained above, the particulars in *Brown* (and deception cases) provide details on the essential ingredient—D's representation and its effect. The true force of the criticism in that commentary lies in the excessive breadth of the offence of conspiracy to defraud and the fact that its breadth allows the prosecution to succeed where the jury are 'satisfied in a general way that the appellants were a dishonest lot, up to no good'.

must prove and the matters on which the jury must be unanimous: see *Bennett* [1999] EWCA Crim 1486. Further particulars should be given where it is necessary for the defendants to have further general information as to the nature of the charge and for the other purposes identified by Lawton LJ in *Landy*. Such further particulars form no part of the ingredients of the offence and on these the jury do not have to be unanimous, as this court correctly decided in *Hancock*.

The Crown is entitled to allege several fraudulent transactions in a single count if the trans-   **5.49**
actions were all related to the same dishonest agreement.[87]

Article 7(1) of the European Convention on Human Rights[88]

As has been noted above, the offence is heavily dependent on the concept of dishonesty,   **5.50**
and as has been emphasized in a number of chapters in this book, that test is one lacking in certainty.[89] Concerns were raised by Liberty and the Joint Parliamentary Committee on Human Rights as to whether the offence was compatible with Article 7 of the ECHR which prohibits criminal laws which lack sufficient certainty. Article 7 provides: 'No-one shall be held guilty of any criminal offence on account of any act or omission which did not constitute a criminal offence under national or international law at the time when it was committed . . .'

The English courts have held that Article 7, 'while providing a salutary reminder, has not   **5.51**
effected any significant extension of or change to the "certainty" principle long understood at common law.'[90] This suggests there will be no lowering of the high threshold of which a domestic court would have to be satisfied before concluding that a common law offence (particularly one of the longevity and pedigree of conspiracy to defraud) was so uncertain as to be contrary to law. Similarly, the Strasbourg Court has been reluctant to hold that English common law offences which have evolved through judicial decision making in the classic declaratory tradition of the common law are so uncertain as to be incompatible with Article 7 ECHR.[91]

Nevertheless, the challenge to the Article 7 compatibility of the offence seems inevitable.   **5.52**
The Law Commission acknowledged the force of the argument in its Report on *Fraud* by stating:

We continue to believe that a general dishonesty offence, by not requiring as an element some identifiable morally dubious conduct to which the test of dishonesty may be applied, would fail to provide

---

[87] *Mba* [2006] EWCA Crim 624.

[88] See generally R Clayton and H Tomlinson, *The Law of Human Rights* (2000) ch 11.257; J Simor and B Emmerson (eds), *Human Rights Practice* (2004) ch 7.

[89] See para 2.302.

[90] *Mirsa and Srivastava* [2005] 1 Cr App R 21, 18. The court described it as reflecting a well-understood 'principle of domestic law, that conduct which did not contravene the criminal law at the time when it took place should not retrospectively be stigmatised as criminal, or expose the perpetrator to punishment', p 11.

[91] See *Handyside v United Kingdom* (1976) 1 EHRR 737; *Sunday Times v United Kingdom* (1979) 2 EHRR 245; and *SW and CR v United Kingdom,* all considered by the Court of Appeal in *Misra and Srivastava* [2005] 1 Cr App R 21 (common law offence of gross negligence manslaughter) and by the House of Lords in *Goldstein and Rimmington* [2006] 1 AC 459 (common law offence of public nuisance). cf *Hashman & Harrup v United Kingdom* (1999) 30 EHRR 241, at [38], where the court held, at paras 38–40, that conduct simply characterized as 'wrong' as *contra bonos mores* (the blowing of a hunting horn and hallooing to disrupt a hunt) was insufficiently specific to amount to conduct 'prescribed by law' so as to justify restriction by way of a binding-over order under Article 10(2) on the right to freedom of expression.

any meaningful guidance on the scope of the criminal law and the conduct which may be lawfully pursued. We do not accept the argument that inherent uncertainty is satisfactorily cured by the promise of prosecutorial discretion. That cannot make a vague offence clear and, while it might ameliorate some of the risks, it does not excuse a law reform agency from formulating a justifiable and properly defined offence. We do not believe it is for the police and prosecutors to decide the ambit of the criminal law. As the Supreme Court of the United States has said:

> A statute which either forbids or requires the doing of an act in terms so vague that men of common intelligence must necessarily guess at its meaning and differ as to its application, violates the first essential of due process of law.[92]

5.53 These views were echoed by the Joint Parliamentary Committee on Human Rights which when scrutinizing the Fraud Bill concluded:[93]

> notwithstanding that other broad common law offences have so far survived legal challenge on the ground that they lack legal certainty, we remain concerned that the common law offence of conspiracy to defraud is a general dishonesty offence and as such is not compatible with the common law and ECHR requirements of legal certainty for the reasons given above. In light of the strength of this concern, we urge the Government to reassess the issue on receipt of the Law Commission's report on encouraging and assisting crime, and not to await the outcome of the review of the operation of the new Act in several years' time.

5.54 A challenge seems most likely if the conspiracy to defraud offence is used in a case where it amounts to an allegation of an agreement to act dishonestly, even though that action would not constitute an agreement to perform a criminal offence.[94] The Attorney-General is alert to the likelihood of such a challenge and stated in a letter to the Joint Committee on Human Rights that:[95]

> In view of the ECHR case law . . . I would be sanguine about dealing with any challenge that might arise. . . . To date there have been no successful Article 7 challenges to conspiracy to defraud. However, the High Court has ruled that the common law offence of cheating the public revenue is compliant with Article 7 (see *R v Pattni* (13th November 2000)) even though it is heavily reliant on the element of dishonesty. Further, other broad offences have been found to be compatible with Article 7, for example, the Court of Appeal have recently held that the common law offence of gross negligence manslaughter is sufficiently certain (see *R v Misra* [2004] EWCA Crim 2375). Accordingly, I do not consider that conspiracy to defraud fails to meet the requirements of Article 7.

5.55 The Attorney's confidence was no doubt boosted by the decision of the Administrative Court in the extradition case of *Norris v USA*.[96] In the course of that case the court was required to address the question whether the conspiracy to defraud charges laid in an alleged price-fixing scheme were contrary to Article 7. Auld LJ rejected the defence submission that reliance on conspiracy to defraud based on the vague notion of dishonesty

---

[92] Para 5.28.
[93] Para 2.25.
[94] The challenge to the offence of cheat on this basis failed in *Pattni* [2001] Crim LR 570.
[95] *Fourteenth Report*, Appendix 2b.
[96] [2007] EWHC 71. The issue for the court was whether the English common law offence of conspiracy to defraud is capable of application to price fixing, so as to constitute an extradition offence within s 137 of the 2003 Act.

would breach the principles of clarity and ascertainability required by Article 7 and the common law.

Auld LJ concluded that: **5.56**

This is not a case of broadening the scope of a highly specific common law offence. Whether the Law Commission or academics like it or not, the broad umbrella offence of conspiracy to defraud is and has been for a long time part of our law. The same goes for the broad and variously factually applicable element of dishonesty, which is the heart of that offence, one of conspiracy to defraud another in the *Welham* and *Wai Yu-Tsang* senses, namely an agreed intent to practise a fraud on another, an offence, as I have said, expressly preserved by section 5(2) of the Criminal Law Act 1977, notwithstanding the new statutory offence of conspiracy to commit an offence that it created by section 1(1). No change to the offence, whether of principle or of detail is involved in allowing for its application to a conspiracy to commit a species of dishonest conduct, whatever its form, that a jury could view as dishonest and potentially damaging to another.

The use of conspiracy to defraud in novel circumstances

The Article 7 challenge is particularly likely should the Crown rely on conspiracy to defraud   **5.57** in a case in which the agreement does not represent an agreement to commit a substantive criminal offence, and the Crown is seeking to criminalize the alleged conduct for the first time by use of the conspiracy to defraud offence. In addition to the specific Article 7 argument, reliance would in such a case be placed on the comments of the Court of Appeal in *Zemmel*[97] and the House of Lords in *Jones*.[98]

In *Zemmel* the defendants dishonestly induced an American exporter to ship goods on   **5.58** credit and extend the time allowed for payment. There was no intention permanently to default on the debt: they were dishonestly playing for time. Logically this form of agreement amounted to a conspiracy to defraud.[99] At that time, such conduct was also an offence contrary to s 16(2) of the Theft Act (obtaining a pecuniary advantage by deception). However, that section had been severely criticized for its potential to overcriminalize.[100] Parliament subsequently replaced s 16(2) with a narrower offence requiring an intention to make permanent default: Theft Act 1978 s 2(1)(b). That 1978 reform should not have had any effect on the common law position of conspiracy to defraud the dishonest agreement to obtain a temporary extension of credit should have remained indictable as a conspiracy to defraud. However, the Court of Appeal rejected that argument.[101]

The court accepted that the distinct 'purpose' of part of the conspiracy was 'one which   **5.59** involved the commission of acts which constituted no offence known to the law'. It stated that the Crown's position was effectively that 'by a side wind the common law has suddenly

---

[97] (1985) 81 Cr App R 279, CA.
[98] [2006] UKHL 16.
[99] Being recognized as such by the Law Commission, *Criminal Law: Conspiracy to Defraud*: Working Paper No 104, paras 4.4 et seq.
[100] Capturing behaviour such as telling lies to extend a period of credit ('the cheque is in the post').
[101] See *Arlidge and Parry on Fraud* 2-026–2-028 in which it is argued that Parliament tends simply to ignore the common law, which continues intact.

re-emerged to reinstate or create as a crime that which Parliament thought it right to take off the statute book as a crime. We cannot accept that.'[102]

5.60   *Zemmel* was considered in the Law Commission's Report on *Fraud* which stated that the court's 'reasoning may apply more broadly, although it would probably need to be clear that parliament had consciously decided that the conduct in question should not be criminal, rather than merely failing to make provision for it'.[103]

5.61   In *Jones*, a case dealing with the applicability of international law in criminal cases in England, their lordships expressly stated that criminal law can only be extended by Parliament. The English common law does not permit the creation of new offences nor applying existing offences to activity previously regarded as outside the remit of the criminal law. Lord Bingham stated that:

> it is for those representing the people of the country in Parliament, not the executive and not the judges, to decide what conduct should be treated as lying so far outside the bounds of what is acceptable in our society as to attract criminal penalties. One would need very compelling reasons for departing from that principle.[104]

The House of Lords also stated that:

> Where Parliament has defined the ingredients of an offence, perhaps stipulating what shall and shall not be a defence, and has prescribed a mode of trial and a maximum penalty, it must ordinarily be proper that conduct falling within that definition should be prosecuted for the statutory offence and not for a common law offence which may or may not provide the same defences and for which the potential penalty is unlimited.[105]

5.62   However, the argument to restrict the scope of conspiracy to defraud to those circumstances in which it has previously been prosecuted has recently been firmly rejected by the Administrative Court. The particular form of conduct that had not been previously charged as a conspiracy to defraud involved the dishonest agreement between suppliers, to fix prices or limit production. Such anti-competitive cartels are now proscribed by a series of specific offences introduced by the Enterprise Act 2002.[106] The Serious Fraud Offence has however commenced a prosecution in which the allegation is of price fixing before the Enterprise Act came into force, and in which the offence charged is conspiracy to defraud. The allegation is that the conspirators routinely sold product to their customers pursuant to their agreement to avoid price competition. In effect, that the conspirators defrauded their customers by requiring that they pay higher prices than they might otherwise have paid had there been no conspiracy.

---

[102] At p 284.
[103] Law Com No 276: Cm 5560.
[104] [2006] UKHL 16 [29].
[105] [30].
[106] Sections 188–202 create offences involving agreements to fix prices, limit production or supply, rig bids, etc where the agreement is a horizontal one between providers. For detailed analysis see C Harding and J Joshua, 'Breaking up the Hardcore' [2002] Crim LR 933; M Furse and S Nash, 'Partners in Crime—the General Cartel Offence in UK Law' (2004) Int Company and Commercial Law Review 138; K MacDonald and R Thompson, 'Dishonest Agreements' (2003) Competition Law Journal 94.

In *Norris*, noted above, Auld LJ rejected the argument reliant on *Zemmel* that the use of   **5.63**
conspiracy to defraud in such circumstances was contrary to Article 7 and the common law
principles of legal certainty.[107] His lordship stated that

> while there has, as yet, been no reported price-fixing case prosecuted as one of dishonesty in our
> courts, it is difficult to see why any such agreement involving dishonesty or other fraud should not
> amount to a common law criminal conspiracy to defraud, as expressly preserved by section 5(2) of
> the Criminal Law Act 1977. At its broadest, such an offence consists of any conduct 'dishonestly to
> do any act prejudicial to another' (*Smith and Hogan*[108]) or any agreement between two or more per-
> sons dishonestly to prejudice or to risk prejudicing another's right, knowing that they have no right
> to do so . . . This is not, therefore, a case of the court introducing by a side-wind a crime that
> Parliament had declined to recognise, as in *R v Zemmel*. . . . Nor is it a case of an impermissible
> attempt to charge conduct with a common law offence when it lacks an essential ingredient for such
> an offence, as in the public nuisance case of *R v Rimmington*.'[109]

His lordship concluded that the SFO were merely resorting to the broad common law
offence of fraud, 'the centre-piece of which is dishonesty capable of manifestation in all
sorts of ways'.

It may therefore be extremely difficult to argue that conspiracy to defraud cannot be used   **5.64**
in such circumstances even where Parliament has created a statutory offence that covers in
whole or in part the same ground as that covered by conspiracy to defraud (eg where the
Fraud Act now covers conduct previously covered by the common law offence), and has not
expressly abolished the common law.[110] Since the government retained the offence on the
basis that it may be necessary to deal with forms of fraud that have not been foreseen and
protected against with the Fraud Act, the use of conspiracy to defraud in novel circumstances is effectively endorsed by Parliament.

Retention of conspiracy to defraud with the Fraud Act 2006

The Law Commission in its Report No 276 catalogued those forms of conduct which   **5.65**
would, if the offence were abolished, cease to be criminal. This was of course prior to the
enactment of the Fraud Act 2006. Similar lists had appeared in earlier Law Commission
papers on conspiracy to defraud.[111] These are discussed in penetrating style by JC Smith in
his article in the *Criminal Law Review* in which he suggests the examples drawn upon reveal
that the Law Commission was 'scraping the barrel'.[112]

The circumstances for conspiracy to defraud included: deception which obtains a benefit   **5.66**
which does not count as property, services, or any of the other benefits defined in the Theft
Acts; deception which causes a loss and obtains a directly corresponding gain, where the

---

[107] The court was influenced by Sir Jeremy Lever QC and John Pike, 'Cartel Agreements, Criminal
Conspiracy and the Statutory "Cartel Offence"' (2005) 26 ECLR ii 70–7.

[108] *Criminal Law: Cases and Materials* (7th edn) 370–3. It is unclear why his lordship chose to rely on an
out-of-date edition of the cases book rather than the recent edition of the text book.

[109] [81] per Auld LJ.

[110] cf Auld LJ at [89].

[111] See n 2 above and the articles referred to therein.

[112] See n 2 above, p 217.

two are not the same property (other than a transfer of funds between bank accounts);[113] deception which causes a loss and obtains a gain where the two are neither the same property nor directly correspondent;[114] deception which does not obtain a gain, or cause a loss, but which prejudices another's financial interests;[115] conduct involving a view to gain or an intent to cause loss, but not deception;[116] obtaining a service by giving false information to a machine;[117]deception to gain a temporary benefit;[118] deceptions which do not cause the obtaining of a benefit;[119] making a secret gain or causing a loss by abusing a position of trust or fiduciary duty;[120] dishonestly failing to fulfil a contractual obligation;[121] deception for a non-financial purpose; fixing' an event on which bets have been placed[122] and, dishonestly infringing another's legal right.

5.67   In view of the breadth of offences created under the Fraud Act 2006, very few of these situations will now be chargeable only as conspiracy to defraud. The Home Office suggested possibly only the last two.[123] In respect of those that are, it is questionable whether they ought to be criminal at all: hence the Law Commission's 2002 Report recommendation that conspiracy to defraud should be abolished.[124] Indeed, the Law Commission went so far as to describe the continued existence of the offence as 'indefensible'.[125] The Home Office had also stated: 'if we achieve a proper and full definition of fraud there should be no need for a fall back offence of this kind.'[126] Perhaps this is an implicit recognition of the weakness of the Fraud Act.

5.68   On consultation by the Home Office the majority of those who responded on this point were opposed to abolition of the offence.[127] The government's main concern was whether abolition would affect the ability to prosecute multiple offences and the largest and most serious cases of fraud. Many consultees felt that it was wise to see how the new statutory offences worked in practice before abolishing conspiracy to defraud. The government therefore decided to reject the Law Commission recommendation for abolition and to retain the common law offence alongside the new Fraud Act offences.

5.69   A number of further attempts to abolish the offence were made, unsuccessfully in the Lords and Commons during the course of the Fraud Bill passing through Parliament.[128] So keen

---

[113] Now an offence under ss 1(2)(a) and 2 of the Fraud Act 2006 or an inchoate thereof.
[114] Ditto.
[115] Ditto.
[116] Ditto.
[117] Now an offence under s 11 Fraud Act 2006.
[118] Now an offence under ss 1(2)(a) and 2 Fraud Act 2006.
[119] Now *possibly* an offence under s 2 of the Fraud Act 2006 or an inchoate thereof.
[120] Now an offence under s 4 of the Fraud Act 2006 or an inchoate thereof.
[121] Now possibly an offence under s 3 of the Fraud Act 2006.
[122] See now the Gambling Act 2005, s 42.
[123] Home Office, *Fraud Law Reform* (2004) para 38.
[124] See also Law Commission Report No 228 *Conspiracy to Defraud* (1994).
[125] *Fraud* Law Com No 276 (2002) para 1.4.
[126] Home Office, *Fraud Law Reform* (2004) para 37.
[127] See Home Office, *Fraud Law Reform, Responses to Consultation* (2004).
[128] eg '(1) The common law offence of conspiracy to defraud is abolished for all purposes not relating to offences wholly or partly committed before the commencement of this Act.
(2) An offence is partly committed before the commencement of this Act if—

were some to see the conspiracy to defraud offence abolished that there were suggestions of a sunrise clause—prospectively repealing the offence in three years' time, thereby leaving the government the opportunity to reverse that provision before it came into effect if it became apparent that the conspiracy offence was necessary. These sunrise clauses were all rejected by the government.

The Attorney-General's arguments for retention

There appear to be six main arguments for retention of the offence of conspiracy to defraud **5.70** despite the incredible breadth of the Fraud Act offences. The Attorney-General sent a letter to the opposition spokesman in the Lords, Lord Kingsland, apparently setting out further arguments, but this has not been published.[129] A number of these arguments are drawn directly from the debates, others were advanced by the Attorney-General in a letter to the Joint Parliamentary Committee on Human Rights,[130] and unusually the Explanatory Notes discuss why the offence was retained.[131]

(a) The risk of unforeseen lacunae

The principal argument for retention seems to be that abolition might leave an unforeseen **5.71** lacuna in the law. In short, that it would be too 'risky' or 'rash'.[132] The government drew support for this argument from the conclusion of the 'Rose Committee.'[133] Although that committee's report has not been published, the Attorney-General quoted its conclusion that:

> It would be risky to repeal common law conspiracy to defraud as it can be the most effective charge in a case where multiple defendants are engaged in a fraudulent course of conduct. There are limitations on the law of statutory conspiracy, which has had something of a chequered history. All the judges present at the meeting agreed the Bill should not repeal common law conspiracy to defraud.[134]

This decision, reached by such an eminent committee, was sufficient to persuade even the **5.72** doubting Law Lords who had in earlier debates been committed to abolition. With respect, the argument is not conclusive. As the Law Commission recognized in its 2002 Report:

> To retain conspiracy to defraud on the ground that it might occasionally prove useful in such a case would in our view be an excess of caution. Since it is not practicable to identify all such cases in

---

(a) a relevant event occurs before its commencement, and
(b) an other relevant event occurs on or after its commencement.
(3) "Relevant event" in relation to an offence, means any act, omission or other event (including any result of one or more acts or omissions) proof of which is required for conviction of the offence.'

[129] This fact is revealed in HC Research Paper 31/06, p. 21.
[130] <http://www.publications.parliament.uk/pa/jt200506/jtselect/jtrights/134/13405.htm> Appendix 2b.
[131] This was commended by the Joint Parliamentary Committee on Human Rights in its 14th Report, para 2.26.
[132] See Home Office, *Fraud Law Reform, Responses to Consultation* (2004) paras 39–45.
[133] A gathering of senior judges chaired by the former Vice-President of the Court of Appeal Criminal Division.
[134] HL Debates, 14 Mar 2006, cols1113–16. A portion of the letter from Rose LJ to the A-G is published by the A-G as an appendix to his response to the Joint Parliamentary Committee on Human Rights: Fourteenth Report Appendix 2b <http://www.publications.parliament.uk/pa/jt200506/jtselect/jtrights/134/13405.htm>

advance, it would mean that we could never be in a position to abolish conspiracy to defraud . . . The advantages of abolishing it, in our view, greatly outweigh any possible advantage that might accrue from retaining it alongside the new offences which we recommend.[135]

5.73 That argument must apply with even greater vigour now that the Home Office have added the very wide offences in sections 6 and 7[136] which were not within the Law Commission's recommendations.

(b) Conspiracy to defraud a necessity in certain cases

5.74 The Attorney-General identified a number of circumstances in which it was claimed that the conspiracy to defraud offence would be necessary, even with the availability of the new fraud offences and the opportunity to charge statutory conspiracies to commit those new offences.

5.75 An example of a case in which the conduct could only be prosecuted as conspiracy to defraud would, according to the Attorney,[137] be 'where a person allows his bank account to be used by a third party as a vehicle in the transfer of funds (typically from overseas) which form part of a conspiracy to defraud'. Since the prosecution might not be able to establish that the defendant 'knew' the details of the fraud it might be difficult to establish a statutory conspiracy. It is unclear why this is not an offence under section 2 of the Fraud Act 2006—the defendant has made a false representation about the use of the account and has done so with a view to gain or cause loss. Even if this not an offence under s 2, it would seem to be covered by the Law Commission's latest proposed inchoate offence of assisting/ encouraging in its Report No 300, *Inchoate Liability for Assisting and Encouraging Crime*.[138]

(c) The 'Hollinshead' *argument*

5.76 One specific and repeated example of the need for conspiracy to defraud to prevent a lacuna in the law was that based on the case of *Hollinshead*.[139] There were also concerns that because of the limitations on the scope of statutory conspiracy meant that certain types of secondary participation in fraud might still only be caught by the common law charge.

5.77 In *Hollinshead* D1 and D2 conspired to manufacture 'black box' devices that were then used to help third parties avoid paying for electricity. They were charged with conspiring to aid, abet, counsel, or procure persons unknown to commit the offence of evading liability by deception and, alternatively, with conspiracy to defraud. They were convicted of conspiracy to defraud. The House of Lords held that the manufacturers could not be found guilty of statutory conspiracy to commit the offence of obtaining the electricity by use of those devices because they were not involved in the actual abstraction of electricity.

---

[135] Para 9.4.

[136] See below in ch 9.

[137] In his letter to the Joint Committee on Human Rights 2006, Appendix 2b.

[138] <http://www.lawcom.gov.uk/docs/lc300.pdf>. These are now being taken forward in the Serious Crime Bill 2007, cll 54–60.

[139] [1985] AC 975.

The House of Lords held that they had been rightly convicted of conspiracy to defraud because they manufactured and sold the devices for the dishonest purpose of enabling the devices to be used to the detriment of electricity boards. The decision has been heavily criticized.

The Attorney-General pointed out that the case 'illustrates the problem that people may be involved in conspiring to do something but not in the substantive offence because that is done by a third party who is outside the conspiracy'.[140] As Lord Goodhart was quick to point out in response, the argument is not a strong one since the new offence in s 7 will adequately cover such conduct'.[141] The Attorney's concern that despite the availability of that new charge there would be difficulties because the principal offender would face different charges is, it is submitted, not one of any substance in this instance. **5.78**

In Report No 300, *Inchoate Liability for Assisting and Encouraging Crime*,[142] the Law Commission confirms, having discussed *Hollinshead*, that its proposed offence of encouraging or assisting in crime would meet the potential lacuna were conspiracy to defraud abolished: **5.79**

We recommended the abolition of conspiracy to defraud in our Report on Fraud,[143] . . . accepting that this could create a lacuna in cases where a person *assisted* in a fraud.[144] The cl 2(1) offence of encouraging or assisting a crime would address this lacuna should conspiracy to defraud be abolished. It would also cover the type of situation addressed . . . in our Report on Fraud,[145] where D is an assister on the fringe of a conspiracy, but does not know the details of what the protagonists are planning. D would be liable under cl 2(1) on the basis of the offence he anticipated, regardless of what anyone else intended to do.[146]

(d) The practical advantages in using conspiracy to defraud

The Attorney-General was also keen to point out that there were many cases in which the use of the conspiracy to defraud charges, although not necessary, would render a prosecution far easier than if charges were brought under the 2006 Act. These are generally cases in which the overall picture of criminality can best be presented by charging conspiracy to defraud. The Attorney-General gave examples in his letter to the Joint Parliamentary Committee. These included cases where the prosecution involved 'evidence of several significant but different kinds of criminality; several jurisdictions; different types of victims, eg individuals, banks, web site administrators, credit card companies; organised crime networks'.[147] **5.80**

A particular example was provided involving a 'standard large scale "credit card scam"'. **5.81**

Over a period of time, A, B, C and others unknown: dishonestly obtain credit card numbers held abroad; dishonestly gain access to legitimate credit card balance checking services and select

---

[140] HL Debates, 14 Mar 2006, cols 1113–16.
[141] ibid.
[142] <http://www.lawcom.gov.uk/docs/lc300.pdf>
[143] Law Com No 276 at 83–4.
[144] (p 100, n 14).
[145] n 15 of p 101.
[146] n 139 para 3.17.
[147] Appendix 2b.

individual card holders with large amounts of credit available; conduct biographical research to gather sufficient personal information about compromised cardholders to be able to impersonate them; take over accounts, impersonating the account holders, changing the billing address and obtain duplicate cards (A does this); produce counterfeit identity documents then used to rent accommodation, internet 'office space' and to open bank accounts (B does this); use the accounts to purchase expensive goods which are then delivered to the accommodation addresses (C does this). After the passage of the Fraud Bill it will be possible to prosecute A, B and C for substantive offences under that legislation but they have no 'common purpose' that links them together under any single provision either of the Fraud Bill or of any of the Theft Acts. As a result, the indictment against them would have to contain hundreds of separate counts; it is also almost inevitable that A, B and C would be tried separately. In those separate trials much of the evidence in one case would be deemed inadmissible in another. The new evidential rules on bad character, contained in the Criminal Justice Act 2003, might allow the introduction of additional evidence, but it would have to be given in each separate trial and the considerations would be different in each case. On the other hand, if the case were prosecuted as a conspiracy to defraud the indictment would consist of one precise, clear and short count alleging that the defendants: '. . . conspired together and with others to defraud banks, credit card providers and their customers by obtaining personal banking details; dishonestly using such information to effect changes of billing addresses; dishonestly obtaining goods and services; exposing banks to a liability to compensate account holders in the sums withdrawn'.[148]

5.82 The example does, of course, demonstrate the advantage of the offence. The Attorney confirmed to the Joint Parliamentary Committee that there is no evidence that the common law offence of conspiracy to defraud is being used inappropriately. There are 'fewer than 7% of all defendants in fraud cases being prosecuted under the common law offence.'[149] It might be asked if there is no inappropriate use of the offence, why is the government committed to its abolition?

5.83 Consultees of the Home Office also raised concerns about the 'serious practical' difficulties in prosecuting multiple offences and the largest/most serious cases of fraud. Neither of these arguments seems compelling. As for the multiple offences problem, s 17 of the Domestic Violence Crime and Victims Act 2004 provides a solution, and it was only the government's tardiness, in the face of repeated requests for implementation from the Court of Appeal[150] and the House of Lords,[151] which prevented this solution being available earlier.[152] As for the largest frauds, it is unclear whether the concern is with the number of offenders (but there is no obvious advantage for the conspiracy to defraud over the substantive or statutory conspiracy) or the time scale (no advantage is obvious over the statutory conspiracy) or the amount allegedly lost (the new fraud offences carry the same maximum sentence as conspiracy to defraud).

---

[148] Appendix 2(b): Letter from Rt Hon The Lord Goldsmith QC, Attorney-General, to the Chair, re Fraud Bill.

[149] Para 2.23.

[150] See *Ali* [2005] EWCA Crim 87.

[151] *Saik* [2006] UKHL 18.

[152] It was brought into force 8/01/2007, Domestic Violence, Crime and Victims Act 2004 (Commencement No 7 and Transitional Provision) Order 2006, SI 2006/3423.

(e) The Law Commission Paper on assisting and encouraging

A final argument advanced by the government for the retention of conspiracy to defraud **5.84** was that the offence would be reviewed imminently in the Law Commission's (then forthcoming) Report on assisting and encouraging crime.[153]

In this latest Report No 300, *Inchoate Liability for Assisting and Encouraging Crime*,[154] the **5.85** Law Commission has now offered a proposal which would meet the government's concerns identified above and confirms that its proposed offence of assisting in crime would meet the potential lacuna were conspiracy to defraud abolished.

Conclusion

The government proposes to reassess whether there is a continuing need to retain conspir- **5.86** acy to defraud in the light of the operation of the new offences.

John Smith was right as usual when he wrote in 1995:

5.87

For almost 25 [read now 35] years the Commission, in a series of papers, has expressed the opinion that there is no place in the criminal law for an offence of conspiring to do an act which is not a criminal offence. If this state of the law is offensive, it looks as if we shall have to go on being offended by it for some considerable time yet.[155]

Sentencing

A person convicted of a common law conspiracy was liable to imprisonment and a fine at **5.88** the discretion of the court; but under the Criminal Justice Act 1987, s 12, conspiracy to defraud is now punishable with a maximum of ten years' imprisonment.

A person convicted of a statutory conspiracy is liable to a sentence of imprisonment for a **5.89** term not exceeding the maximum provided for the offence which he has conspired to commit.[156] Where the conspiracy is to commit more than one offence, the maximum is the longer or longest of the sentences provided for. Where the offence is triable either way the maximum for conspiracy is the maximum provided for conviction on indictment.

The power to impose a fine without limit is unaffected by the 1987 Act. Section 3(1) pro- **5.90** vides the general power of the Crown Court, under what is now the Powers of Criminal Courts (Sentencing) Act, to impose a fine in lieu of or in addition to dealing with the offender in any other way. A conspiracy to commit an offence punishable with a maximum fine of £100 is thus punishable with a fine without limit except, of course, that it must not be unreasonable in all the circumstances.

---

[153] The Law Commission Report, which has now been published <http://www.lawcom.gov.uk/docs/lc300.pdf> is not focused on conspiracy to defraud at all. It mentions the term only eleven times, in three paras in the entire report.

[154] <http://www.lawcom.gov.uk/docs/lc300.pdf>

[155] [1995] Crim LR 209.

[156] Criminal Law Act 1977, s 3(3).

6

MAKING OFF WITHOUT PAYMENT

The Theft Act 1978,[1] s 3(1) provides: **6.01**

Subject to subsection (3) below, a person who, knowing that payment on the spot for any goods supplied or service done is required or expected from him, dishonestly makes off without having paid as required or expected and with intent to avoid payment of the amount due shall be guilty of an offence.

Background

This section is 'intended to create a simple and straightforward offence'.[2] It deals with cases   **6.02** such as that of the customer in the restaurant or at the petrol station who departs without paying but it is not possible to prove that he had a dishonest intention permanently to deprive the owner at the time when he received the food or the petrol as the case may be.[3] In *DPP v Ray*,[4] such a case was held to be the offence of evading a debt by deception contrary to s 16(2)(a) (now repealed) of the 1968 Act; but the deception found by the court was of a highly artificial character and in many other similar cases it would be impossible to discern any deception at all. These activities might now be dealt with as fraud contrary to s 2 of the Fraud Act 2006. D could be said to be making a false representation and it would not matter whether this was at the time of his act of receiving the food/petrol etc. This would be less artificial than the reasoning in *DPP v Ray*. Whereas under the old deception offences D could only be liable if his deception occurred before eg the relevant property passed to him, under the s 2 offence, D can now be liable under s 2 if he makes a false representation after the entire proprietary interest has passed to him. It follows that if,

---

[1] See CLRC Working Paper, *Section 16 of the Theft Act* (1974) and *Thirteenth Report* (1977); G Syrota, 'Annotations to Theft Act 1978' in *Current Law Statutes* 1978; (1978) 42 MLR 301, 304. *Blackstone's Criminal Practice* (2007), B5.68; *Archbold* (2007) 21–349.

[2] Per Pill LJ in *Vincent* [2001] 1 WLR 1172, CA.

[3] If he had such an intention he is guilty of theft: *Gomez* [1993] AC 442, HL, para 2.22. These are the only two examples of the use of s 3 provided in the CPS guidance: <http://www.cps.gov.uk>

[4] [1974] AC 370, [1973] 3 All ER 131.

after D, a motorist has filled his fuel tank and the entire proprietary interest in the petrol has passed to him, he falsely represents to V, the cashier, that it will be paid for by his firm, he commits the offence under s 2.[5]

6.03　The offence under s 3 of the 1978 Act creates an exception to the general principle that it is not an offence dishonestly to avoid the payment of a debt.[6] This might be thought to pose a potential problem of over-criminalizing. The exception is, however, limited and understandable. In the ordinary case a dishonest debtor (who can be traced) can be coerced into payment via civil remedies without resort to criminal sanctions; where bilking is involved it is usually a matter of enforcement on the spot or never since the person becomes difficult if not impossible to trace.

Actus reus

Makes off

6.04　It is the dishonest departure from the spot which is the offence. An attempt to depart from the spot is an attempt to commit it. 'The spot' will usually, but not necessarily, be the premises of the creditor. It may be a place on the highway on which the news vendor has his stall selling papers, or where the mechanic has repaired D's car in expectation of immediate payment. In *McDavitt*,[7] it was held that the spot was a restaurant and that D, who had made for the door, might be convicted, not of the full offence, but of an attempt to commit it. The words in *Brooks and Brooks*,[8] 'passing the spot where payment is required', suggest that the spot is the cash point rather than the restaurant, so that D would be guilty of the full offence if he were stopped between the cash point and the door. In *Moberly v Allsop*,[9] it was held that a traveller on the London Underground was still 'on the spot' when going through the exit barrier at his destination. 'The spot' may change. In the case of a taxi-ride it is the agreed destination; but if D, the passenger, declines to pay at that point and the driver thereupon drives him towards the police station, D commits the offence if he alights and makes off en route.[10] The requirement and expectation of payment of the fare due continue throughout the journey so it seems that the 'spot' is in motion.

6.05　Can the offence be committed after D has left the spot without any dishonest intention? He absent-mindedly walks out of the restaurant without paying his bill. As soon as he is outside the door, he realizes what he has done, but continues on his way, intending to avoid payment. Possibly his innocent departure becomes a dishonest making off at that moment. If, on the other hand, he arrives home before he realizes that he has not paid, he is clearly incapable of committing the offence.[11]

---

[5]　cf under the old law *Collis-Smith* [1971] Crim LR 716, CA.
[6]　See further G Treitel, 'Contract and Crime' in P Glazebrook (ed), *Reshaping the Criminal Law* (1978) 89.
[7]　[1981] Crim LR 843.
[8]　(1982) 76 Cr App R 66 at 70, CA.
[9]　(1992) 156 JP 514.
[10]　*Aziz* [1993] Crim LR 708, CA.
[11]　cf *Drameh* [1983] Crim LR 322.

An offence committed on leaving the premises probably continues so long as D can be said to be 'making off' in the ordinary meaning of those words. If D is fleeing from the restaurant down the street, he is doing just that. **6.06**

The phrase 'makes off' has a pejorative connotation, lacking in such verbs as 'leaves' or 'departs'. It means 'decamps', and is clearly apt in the case of a person who slips away secretly or runs or drives off at top speed. The phrase can hardly be limited to departure in haste.[12] It could surely also apply to a dishonest customer who, by force or threats of force, compelled a waiter to stand aside and allow him to go. It has been argued that making off is departing without the creditor's consent but this also is too narrow without, at least, some qualification. For example, at the end of a long taxi-ride, D says he is just going into the house to get the fare and disappears into the night, never to return.[13] This conduct must be caught by the offence.[14] Again, if D tells a restaurateur that he has forgotten his wallet and gives a false name and address ('Sir George Bullough, St James's Square') and is allowed to go, there is authority for saying that he goes with consent; but the case seems clearly to fall within the mischief at which the section is aimed.[15] **6.07**

John Spencer[16] argues cogently that makes off means 'disappearing: leaving in a way that makes it difficult for the debtor to be traced'. This would cover the dishonest taxi-passenger and the impersonator. It would also apply to D, who leaves a cheque signed in a false name. It would not apply to the regular customer of known address who gets away by stealth, force, or fraud, or to the person who leaves a worthless cheque with his true name and address. These persons are certainly avoiding payment of a debt but the intention behind the section was not to make the debtor liable to arrest and punishment merely because he defaulted. The mischief at which it was aimed was the escape without trace of the 'spot' debtor. Spencer's argument that the applicability of the offence turns on the traceability of the bilker has force, but is not easy to square with the language of s 3. It can lead to some illogical results. For example, assume that F is V's best customer of many years' standing. One day F determines not to pay and decamps from the premises via the toilet window. All the elements of the offence appear to be present unless it is to be said that F did not make off. It may puzzle us all to wonder why F should have thought that he could get away with his conduct but he seems clearly to have made off. A customer in a wheelchair would surely make off if he decamps without paying though he does not at all fancy his chances of out-pacing the restaurateur.[17] If the untraceability of D was the touchstone of the offence, it is arguable that the offence would then fail to protect the proprietor (for example, the restaurant owner) who knows who D is, but is unlikely to pursue D's small debt via the civil courts.[18] **6.08**

---

[12] cf Bennion [1980] Crim LR 670, ATH Smith, *Property Offences* (1994) 644–5.

[13] cf *Drameh* [1983] Crim LR 322.

[14] It would also seem to be an offence under s 2 of the Fraud Act 2006 of making a false representation with intent to cause loss.

[15] D has again committed the offence under s 2 of the Fraud Act 2006 by making the false representation.

[16] [1983] Crim LR 573.

[17] For further views on this difficult aspect of the offence see Williams, *TBCL* 878; F Bennion, Letter, 'The Drafting of Section 3 of the Theft Act 1978' [1980] Crim LR 670; Letters [1983] Crim LR 205, 574; Griew, paras 13–16.

[18] See Griew paras 13–16.

The CLRC[19] regarded the purpose of the offence as a wider one of protecting legitimate business.

6.09 On a natural interpretation, s 3 does not mean that D does not make off if he gives a correct identification but E does make off it he gives a false one. Suppose in the latter case that V orders a taxi for E and bids him a cheery farewell from the hotel lobby. Can it really be said that E has made off?[20] If, however, V permits D to leave the spot where payment is required for a purely temporary purpose (for example to answer a telephone call or to collect his wallet from his overcoat which he has deposited in the cloakroom) expecting him to return to settle up, it is submitted that D commits the offence if he then decamps.[21] In such cases V has not consented to D leaving without paying, quite the contrary, he has consented to D facilitating payment.[22] But, the offence is not committed if the supplier consents to D's leaving permanently without payment, even if the consent was obtained by fraud, as where D deceives V into accepting postponement of payment.[23] Payment in such a case is not required or expected at *that* time.

Goods supplied or service done

6.10 The words 'goods[24] supplied or service done' might be taken to suggest that the supply or service must precede the requirement of payment; but in *Moberly v Allsop*[25] it was held that the traveller on the London Underground committed the offence on passing the exit barrier although payment was required and expected before the journey began. No doubt the requirement continues in the case of a passenger who has avoided payment of the fare and he is certainly expected to pay before he leaves the premises.

6.11 It is not sufficient that D has become indebted unless that debt arose from the supply of goods or the doing of a service.

Supply

6.12 A shoplifter who carries off the shopkeeper's property is liable to pay the price but, if the shop is not a self-service store, no goods have been 'supplied' to him and he does not commit this offence when he makes off. It is submitted, however, that a self-service establishment is different and that goods are 'supplied' by V to D where V has made them available to be taken and they are taken by D.[26] If it were not so, the section would fail to cover those

---

[19] Cmnd 6733, para 19.

[20] cf *Hammond* [1982] Crim LR 611, para 6.21. This case must be doubted.

[21] See *Vincent*, para 12.

[22] D may also be liable under s 2 of the Fraud Act 2006 as he has made a false representation with intent to cause loss.

[23] *Vincent* [2001] Crim LR 488, [2001] 2 Cr App R 150, [2001] EWCA Crim 295, CA. A charge under s 2 of the Fraud Act 2006 would be appropriate. See also *Evans v Lane* (1984) CO/137/84, CA.

[24] As defined in s 34 of the 1968 Act, applicable to the 1978 Act by s 5(2).

[25] (1992) 156 JP 514, para 6.04.

[26] Griew 13–07 thinks goods exposed for sale are not goods supplied. Certainly; but is this not an offer to supply which becomes 'supply' when the goods are removed? Griew agrees, 13–08, that permitting the use of a tennis court or a boat is a 'service done' and this seems indistinguishable in principle. See also Williams, *TBCL* 878 and ATH Smith, 'Shoplifting and the Theft Acts' [1981] Crim LR 590, who argues that the self-service shop is different from the self-service petrol station. There is a 'supply' in the latter case because the motorist acquires ownership on taking the petrol, but ownership does not pass when the shoplifter takes goods.

cases at which it is primarily aimed. The customer who honestly fills up his car and then dishonestly makes off has been 'supplied' with petrol. Even after *Gomez*,[27] he is probably not guilty of theft because there is no 'property belonging to another' when he forms the dishonest intention. If he was dishonest from the start, he stole the petrol but it is submitted that he is also guilty of making off. Any argument that he could not at the same moment steal and be supplied is untenable. The sale of goods in *Gomez* did not cease to be a sale (or supply) of goods because the House decided that it was also theft. There is a substantial overlap of theft contrary to the 1968 Act, s 1 with the 1978 Act, s 3.

Services

There is no definition of goods or of service. 'Service' is not the same as the extended meaning of 'services' which was contained in s 1 of the 1978 Act.[28] It has been suggested by Professor Williams[29] that, '[t]he tenant of an unfurnished flat or house who bilks his landlord of the rent has not obtained a service'. It is submitted, however, that the landlord, whether of furnished or unfurnished premises, does supply a service to his tenant but that the tenant is not guilty of the offence for the second reason offered by Professor Williams: 'and anyway there is no requirement in an ordinary lease that the rent be paid on the spot'. The CLRC was anxious that the non-payment of rent should not become a criminal offence. The letting of goods is clearly the supply of goods or a service which is presumably why Williams distinguishes unfurnished premises. **6.13**

The service must be 'done', presumably by V or his agents. Is a service 'done' where D takes advantage of a proffered facility? For example, he parks his car in an unmanned car park and leaves by lifting up the barrier and driving off without paying. Probably the custody of the car by the proprietor of the park while it was left there would be regarded as a 'service done'. It might be otherwise, however, if D were to leave his car in a street parking bay and drive off without putting money in the meter. The highway authority could not be said to have custody of the car, but it is arguable that the provision of a parking space on the highway is a service. Even so that case is more appropriately dealt with under the relevant traffic and parking regulations. **6.14**

Payment 'on the spot'

Section 3(2) provides: 'For the purposes of this section "payment on the spot" includes payment at the time of collecting goods on which work has been done or in respect of which service has been provided.' **6.15**

It is not clear that this provision is really necessary. The cases to which it applies are probably adequately covered by the words of subsection (1). It is made clear beyond all doubt that D may commit the offence where he makes off with his clothes which have been cleaned, his shoes which have been repaired or his car which has been serviced. The existence of **6.16**

However the transfer of possession or custody may constitute 'supply': cf *Greenfield* (1983) 78 Cr App R 179 n, [1983] Crim LR 397, CA (supplying drugs).

[27] [1993] 1 All ER 1, [1993] Crim LR 304, HL, para 2.22.
[28] See on that *Sofroinou* [2003] EWCA Crim 3681, and ch 4 in earlier editions of this work. Section 1 was repealed by the Fraud Act 2006.
[29] *TBCL* 879.

subsection (2) may, however, cast doubt on another type of case. D makes off without paying the hand car-wash attendant who has cleaned his car. Work has been done on the goods but D was not 'collecting' them. 'Collecting' seems to imply that D is acquiring possession of the goods. He has never parted with possession of his car. Similarly where D calls a mechanic to repair his car which is broken down by the roadside. In no sense does the motorist 'collect' his car when he drives off. It is submitted that these cases, though not within s 3(2), are adequately covered by s 3(1). If so, subsection (2) is indeed superfluous.

Unenforceable debts

6.17 Section 3(3) provides: 'Subsection (1) above shall not apply where the supply of the goods or the doing of the service is contrary to law, or where the service done is such that payment is not legally enforceable.'

6.18 The CLRC explained this provision on the ground that 'the new offence is essentially a protection for the legitimate business'.[30] The offence is thus not committed where D makes off from a prostitute's flat, a brothel, a disorderly house, an obscene performance in a night-club, or a drug-pedlar's premises without paying for the principal service or goods provided therein. If some goods or services have been legitimately provided—for example, drinks in the night-club—the answer will depend on whether the vice of the principal service infects collateral transactions, which it may do where it amounts to illegality but should not do where the principal transaction is merely void, as in the case of a wager in a betting shop.

6.19 Where the transaction is 'contrary to law', there is no distinction between goods and a service, but where it is merely 'not legally enforceable', services only are affected. Thus subsection (3) applies where there is a merely void contract for services—for example, the wager—but it seems that it does not apply where there is a merely void contract for the supply of goods. If an impecunious minor has her hair done at the most expensive salon in London and walks off without paying it seems she commits no offence under s 3[31] because the service done was not 'necessary' and payment for it is unenforceable. If, however, the same impecunious minor dines on caviar and champagne she may be guilty of making off without payment even though—as is most probable—these expensive items cannot be proved to be necessities for her. There is nothing contrary to law in supplying non-necessary goods to a minor.[32] A seller may properly do so if he chooses but he will not be able to recover the price. Since goods and not services are involved, it is immaterial that payment is not legally enforceable.

Without having paid as required or expected

6.20 It is implicit in s 3 that V requires or expects payment on the spot and that the payment is due in fact and law. If a taxi-driver, in the course of a journey, commits a breach of contract

---

[30] *Thirteenth Report*, para 19. For a general review of the relationship and consideration of s 3 see G Trietel, 'Contract and Crime' in C Tapper (ed), *Crime, Proof and Punishment: Essays in Memory of Sir Rupert Cross* (1981) 81.

[31] She may commit an offence under the Fraud Act 2006, ss 1 and 2 if she is held to have made a representation by her conduct that she will pay and she intends to gain property or cause a loss of property.

[32] cf P Rowlands, 'Minors: Can they Make off without Payment' (1981) JP 410.

entitling his passenger to rescind the contract, the passenger does not commit an offence by making off.[33] Where the money is due, does a person who gives a worthless cheque in 'payment' of the debt commit the offence?[34] The issue was previously of little importance because D would have been guilty of the more serious offence under s 2(1)(b) of the 1978 Act. (The offence would now be one under s 2 of the Fraud Act 2006 if D makes a false representation that the cheque will be honoured and his intention is to gain or cause loss in terms of property.)

In the one reported case[35] in which the matter has arisen the judge ruled that the offence **6.21** under s 3 was not committed because a worthless cheque was not the same as counterfeit money and that D was not making off because he departed with V's consent. The true answer may well be that D is guilty because he has not paid 'as required or expected'. V requires and expects payment in legal tender or by a good cheque. Payment by a worthless cheque no more satisfies his requirement or expectation than payment in counterfeit money. If, however, the cheque is backed by a cheque card, then, depending on the conditions of its issue, D may have paid as required or expected although his authority to use the card has been withdrawn or even if it has been stolen.[36] Similarly with payment by credit card.[37] If the bank is bound to honour the cheque or card, a question of civil law, V has been paid.

As noted above, the s 3 offence is not committed if the supplier consents to D's leaving **6.22** without payment, even if the consent was obtained by fraud, as where D deceives V into accepting postponement of payment.[38] Payment in such a case is not 'required or expected' at *that* time. This is an offence under s 2 of the Fraud Act 2006 if D is intending to gain, or cause loss of, property.

Mens rea

The offence requires that D should make off (i) dishonestly; (ii) knowing that payment on **6.23** the spot is required or expected from him; and (iii) with intent to avoid payment.

Dishonestly[39]

D must be dishonest when he makes off. He may have been dishonest from the start (in **6.24** which case he will also be guilty of theft) or have formed the dishonest intention only after the goods were supplied or the service done. Whether D was dishonest or not is a question for the jury but it seems clear that he could not be held to be dishonest if he believed that payment was not due (even though required and expected by V) because, for example, the goods supplied or service done was deficient in some fundamental respect. If D were

---

[33] *Troughton v Metropolitan Police* [1987] Crim LR 138, DC.
[34] G Syrota, 'Are Cheque Frauds covered by Section 3 of the Theft Act 1978' [1980] Crim LR 413.
[35] *Hammond* [1982] Crim LR 611 (Judge Morrison).
[36] cf *First Sport Ltd v Barclays Bank plc* [1993] 3 All ER 789, CA (Civ Div).
[37] cf *Re Charge Card Services Ltd* [1988] 3 All ER 702, [1988] 3 WLR 764, CA.
[38] *Vincent* [2001] Crim LR 488, [2001] 2 Cr App R 150, [2001] EWCA Crim 295, CA. See also *Evans v Lane* (1984) CO/137/84, CA.
[39] Paras 2.270–2.315.

prepared to leave his name and address, that would be cogent evidence of honesty whereas secret departure or flight would be strong evidence of dishonesty. If D is E's guest in a restaurant and E leaves without paying, D will probably be liable to pay, at least for his own food, unless it ought to have been clear to the restaurateur that E was contracting to pay for both meals.[40] If D makes off, his criminal liability will depend on whether he believed he had no legal liability to pay the bill. His mistake of law might negative dishonesty.[41]

Knowing that payment on the spot . . . is required or expected from him

6.25 Clearly D is not guilty if he wrongly supposes that the goods have been supplied or the service done on credit and that he is going to receive a bill through the post; or if, for example, he is under the impression that his firm has arranged to pay his hotel bill. D's belief that he has been given credit, whether reasonable or not, is inconsistent with the *mens rea* required. Is 'payment on the spot . . . required or expected' where the trader has indicated in advance that he will accept payment by credit card? He is no longer entitled to require or expect payment in cash. It now seems clear that the answer is yes. Acceptance by the trader of the credit card discharges the liability of the debtor [42] so he pays as required or expected, either by paying cash or by signing the sales voucher. If he dishonestly makes off without doing either, he commits the offence.

6.26 A similar question arises when V has indicated that he will take a cheque. Here the debtor's obligation is discharged only conditionally on the cheque being honoured but, in modern usage, a cheque is frequently treated as the equivalent of cash.[43] It is common to speak of payment by cheque. Presumably then, the trader who is willing to take a cheque (whether or not backed by a cheque card) requires or expects payment on the spot.

With intent to avoid payment

6.27 It is now settled that an intention permanently to avoid payment is required. An intention to delay or defer payment is not enough.[44] In *Allen*[45] D had left a hotel without settling his bill and the trial judge directed the jury that all that was required was an intention to make default at the time payment was required. The Court of Appeal held, however, that an intention to make permanent default was required because s 3 required both (i) a making off without paying on the spot; and (ii) an intent to avoid payment. In view of the requirement in (i), (ii) made sense only if permanent default was intended. The House of Lords endorsed this view and drew further support for it by reference to the fact that the CLRC had intended permanent default to be necessary.[46]

---

[40] *Lockett v A & M Charles Ltd* [1938] 4 All ER 170.
[41] cf *Brooks and Brooks* (1982) 76 Cr App R 66, CA.
[42] '. . . the word "payment" in itself is one which, in an appropriate context, may cover many ways of discharging obligations . . .': *White v Elmdene Estates Ltd* [1960] 1 QB 1, [1959] 2 All ER 605 at 610–11, per Lord Evershed MR.
[43] *D and C Builders Ltd v Rees* [1965] 3 All ER 837 at 843, per Winn LJ.
[44] *Allen* [1985] AC 1029, [1985] 2 All ER 641, HL, criticized by Griew 12–18.
[45] [1985] AC 1029, [1985] 2 All ER 641, [1985] Crim LR 739.
[46] Cmnd 6733, para 18.

The Home Office has recently rejected a reform proposal which would have extended **6.28** the offence to include cases where D acts with intent to 'defer' payment.[47] The proposals emanated from garage owners who complained of individuals who, having filled their cars with fuel, claimed to have left their wallets at home and promised to pay at a later date. In such a case, if D is lying about that intention, and the owner consents to D's departure, D will not be liable under s 3 of the 1978 Act; he will be liable for an offence under s 2 of the Fraud Act 2006. As the Home Office accepted, where D makes no false representation and leaves his address he leaves with V's consent and no offence is committed under s 2 of the 2006 Act or s 3 of the 1978 Act. This is a civil law debt and ought to be dealt with as such.[48]

Sentencing

By s 4 the offence, which is triable either way, is punishable on summary conviction by **6.29** imprisonment and/or a fine not exceeding the prescribed maximum (presently £5,000), and on indictment by imprisonment for a term not exceeding two years and/or a fine.

Aggravating features will include the value of the sum evaded and the degree of planning **6.30** involved: *Foster*.[49] Where the offence is dealt with summarily assistance is provided by the Magistrates' Courts Guidelines (2004).[50]

There is provision to make a restitution order under Powers of Criminal Courts **6.31** (Sentencing) Act 2000 s 148.

---

[47] See Home Office, *Fraud Law Reform* (2002).
[48] Para 45.
[49] (1994) 15 Cr App R (S) 340.
[50] See *Blackstone's Criminal Practice* (2007) B5.71.

7

ROBBERY

Robbery was a common law offence and was never defined in the Larceny Acts. A definition **7.01** is now contained in s 8(1) of the Theft Act 1968:[1]

A person is guilty of robbery if he steals, and immediately before or at the time of doing so, and in order to do so, he uses force on any person or puts or seeks to put any person in fear of being then and there subjected to force.

Both robbery and assault with intent to rob, contrary to s 8(2), are punishable with life imprisonment.

The offence is prevalent. In 2005/6 there were 98,204 recorded robberies.[2] **7.02**

Robbery: an aggravated form of theft

Robbery is an aggravated form of stealing. Proof of the commission of theft is essential **7.03** to secure a conviction. Surprisingly, the court in *Forrester*[3] treated as open the question whether the word 'steal' in s 8 is to be regarded as subject to the definition of theft in s 1. It is submitted that there is no doubt that it is to be so regarded and that whenever the Act refers to 'theft', 'thief', 'steal', or 'stolen' it is referring to theft contrary to s 1. If it were otherwise there might be difficulty in treating theft as an 'included offence' on an indictment for robbery for the purposes of s 6(3) of the Criminal Law Act 1967.

It follows from the fact that theft is an element of robbery that robbery is not committed **7.04** unless every element of theft can be proved. Accordingly, it is not robbery if D has a claim of right to the property which he takes by force, even if he knows he has no right to use

---

[1] See generally A Ashworth, 'Robbery Reassessed' [2002] Crim LR 851; J Andrews, 'Robbery' [1966] Crim LR 524; Griew ch 3; ATH Smith, *Property Offences* (1994) ch 14; *Archbold* (2007) 2-85; *Blackstone's Criminal Practice* (2007) B4.46.

[2] A Walker, C Kershaw, and S Nicholas, *Home Office Statistical Bulletin, Crime in England and Wales* 2005/2006 p 28, Recorded crime by offence 1996 to 2005/6 and percentage change between 2004/5 and 2005/6.

[3] [1992] Crim LR 792.

force, because the claim of right negatives dishonesty and therefore theft.[4] The prosecutor has the option of charging offences against the person as appropriate. Similarly, where D lacks the intention permanently to deprive V but uses or threatens force to 'borrow' V's property, there is no theft and no robbery.

7.05 It is necessary to prove that there has been an appropriation[5] of the property of another by force or threat of force. The wider concept of appropriation approved in *Gomez*[6] and *Hinks*[7] has a correspondingly broadening effect on robbery. Taking hold of the property with intent to steal it is enough, whereas under the Larceny Act this might have constituted only an attempt. If D snatched at a woman's earring but failed to detach it from her ear,[8] the robbery would be complete. Where a handbag is dragged by force from a woman's grasp so that it falls to the ground, there is an appropriation and a robbery: *Corcoran v Anderton*[9] where the court thought (and *Gomez* now confirms) that forcible tugging at the handbag would have been a sufficient appropriation, even if the woman had managed to retain control.[10] If D were pursuing V with intent to take his wallet by force and V were to throw away the wallet in order to escape,[11] this would not be theft until D did some act to appropriate the wallet; but, even before he did so, he might be guilty of attempted robbery, for his pursuit of V would probably be more than a merely preparatory act and he might also be guilty of an assault with intent to rob.

7.06 The appropriation must normally be by 'taking' since it is difficult to imagine realistic situations in which robbery might be effected by other modes of appropriation.[12] One possibility is where a bailee refuses to return property to the owner, and backs this refusal with a threat of force. It is unclear whether D can be said to have completed a robbery where he issues a threat to V and demands that V hand over his property and V is in the process of doing so, but D has not yet touched it, or secured control or any other rights of an owner over it.[13] A safer course is to charge an attempted robbery or blackmail in such circumstances. It is doubtful whether frequent recourse to the offence of assault with intent to rob will be necessary given the availability of a charge of attempted robbery.

Use or threat of force

7.07 The use, or the threat of the use, of force against the person is the aggravating factor which elevates a theft to a separate sphere of criminality producing an offence of a qualititatively

---

[4] *Skivington* [1968] 1 QB 166, [1967] 1 All ER 483 (a case under the Larceny Act); *Robinson* [1977] Crim LR 173, CA. In *Forrester* (above) D admitted that he had no claim of right; but a person without a claim of right is not necessarily 'dishonest'.

[5] See para 2.08.

[6] [1993] AC 442, para 2.22.

[7] [2001] 2 AC 241, para 2.35.

[8] cf *Lapier* (1784) 1 Leach 320 (held robbery, because the earring was detached).

[9] (1980) 71 Cr App R 104, CA.

[10] ibid, 108.

[11] cf Hale 1 PC 533. It is different if the wallet is thrown down at D's instruction for then he has assumed the rights of the owner.

[12] See Andrews, n 1 above, for possible instances.

[13] cf *Briggs* [2004] Crim LR 495, CA. cf *Farrell* (1787) 1 Leach 332 n. D apprehended before V handed over the property.

distinctive and more serious character. Robbery is not an offence of violence per se.[14] It has been argued that the offence is otiose since it always involves theft and an offence against the person. Despite the overlap, it is submitted that a specifically labelled offence of robbery is desirable, not least because in cases of a threat, unless the threat is to kill, the offence against the person likely to have been committed will only be that of assault.[15] In addition, robbery allows for a higher sentence than theft and most offences against the person. In short, the whole is greater than the sum of the parts.

Force

The term 'force' was preferred by the CLRC to 'violence', which was used in the Larceny **7.08** Act 1916 to designate an aggravated form of robbery. Though the difference, if any, between the words is an elusive one, it is probable that 'force' is a slightly wider term. Thus it might be argued that simply to hold a person down is not violence but it certainly involves the use of force against the person. Force denotes any exercise of physical strength against another whereas violence seems to signify a dynamic exercise of strength as by striking a blow. In *Dawson*,[16] it was held that, where D nudges V so as to cause him to lose his balance and enable D to steal, it is a question of fact for the jury whether the nudge amounts to 'force'.[17] It is submitted that it would be better if the law gave an answer to the question—preferably in the affirmative. It is submitted that no jury could reasonably find that the slight physical contact that might be involved where D picks V's pocket would amount to a use of force.[18]

If D causes a substance to come into contact with V, in an effort to incapacitate V in order **7.09** to facilitate theft, then it is submitted that D would be guilty of robbery. An example would be where D pumps a noxious gas into a bank causing the occupants to be overcome by the fumes and D then steals from them while they are incapacitated. He has caused a substance to be brought into contact with the victim and in this sense his actions are no different from shooting a bullet at V to steal from him. It is submitted that there is no requirement that V needs to be aware that D is using force on him—as where D creeps up behind V and knocks him unconscious before stealing his wallet, or where D points a gun at V who unknown to D is blind.

Threat of force

A threat of force may be implied as well as express. So long as D intends V to understand that **7.10** force will be used against him if he seeks to prevent the theft, the offence is accomplished

---

[14] *Baker* [2000] Crim LR 700, CA.

[15] Ashworth, n 1 above, 863. Strictly speaking there is no need for an assault since the victim need not 'apprehend immediate personal violence'; a battery will suffice. For this reason, assault is not available as an alternative offence: *Tennant* [1976] CLY 133. It might be argued that the allegation of robbery impliedly includes one of assault and that assault is therefore an alternative within the scope of s 6(3) of the Criminal Law Act 1967, as interpreted in *MPC v Wilson* [1984] AC 242.

[16] [1976] Crim LR 692, CA, and commentary.

[17] See Williams, *TBCL* 825, suggesting a distinction based on 'gentle force' used to take by stealth as opposed to force used to overcome resistance. See also Griew, para 3–05; ATH Smith, *Property Offences* (1994) para 14–10.

[18] See eg *Monaghan and Monaghan* [2000] 1 Cr App R (S) 6, CA where 'jostling' to pick V's pockets was charged as theft.

by the threat of force.[19] Where D threatens V with force unless V complies with D's demands (eg to accompany him) and at a later stage D takes property from an unresisting V, D may be convicted of robbery if he intends, and V understands, the threat to continue, even though D's original threats were not made for the purpose of immediately taking V's property.[20] This might be a common occurrence where D threatens V and subsequently D escorts V to an ATM and V withdraws cash to hand over to D. It is irrelevant whether V is in fear since it is sufficient that D acts so as to 'seek to put V in fear'.[21]

Force/threat of force in order to steal

7.11 The force must be used or threatened in order to steal.[22] So, if D is attempting to commit rape on V and she offers him money to desist, which he takes, he is not guilty of robbery (even assuming that there is theft of the money) whether he in fact desists or continues and completes the rape.[23] Similarly if D knocks V down out of revenge or spite and, having done so, decides to take, and does take, V's watch, he does not commit robbery. Such cases can, however, be adequately dealt with by charging rape or an offence under the Offences Against the Person Act 1861, as well as theft.[24]

Force against the person

7.12 At common law the prosecution had to prove that D's force was directed against V's person in order to overpower him or make him give up the property.[25] It was not enough that force was used on the property, rather than the person, to get possession of it, as where force was used to detach V's watch chain from his waistcoat pocket. The CLRC[26] did not intend to alter this rule—it was not their intention to turn 'bag-snatching' into robbery—but the rule was not spelt out in their Draft Bill or in the 1968 Act. In *Clouden*,[27] where D wrenched V's shopping basket out of her grasp and ran off with it, the Court of Appeal held that 'the old distinctions have gone' and that it was rightly left to the jury to say whether D used 'force on any person' in order to steal. Thus the bag-snatcher will usually be guilty of robbery—because 'snatching' will involve some force on the person—whereas the pickpocket usually will not because he acts with stealth, not force.

7.13 Though the Act omits the word 'wilfully', which was included in the Draft Bill proposed by the CLRC,[28] it is submitted that the force or threat must be used intentionally or at least recklessly; so that for D accidentally to cause V to fall and injure himself while picking

---

[19] See eg *Grant v CPS* (2000) unreported, 10 Mar, QBD.

[20] *Donaghy and Marshall* [1981] Crim LR 644 (Judge Chavasse).

[21] *R and B v DPP* (2007) The Times, 27 March.

[22] *Shendley* [1970] Crim LR 49, CA. If the jury are satisfied that D stole, but not satisfied that he used force for the purpose of stealing, they should acquit of robbery and convict of theft. Failure to direct the jury on this point renders the conviction unsafe: *West* (1999) 14 Sept, CA, unreported.

[23] cf *Blackham* (1787) 2 East PC 555, 711.

[24] *Harris* (1998) The Times, 4 Mar; *James* [1997] Crim LR 598.

[25] *Gnosil* (1824) 1 C & P 304.

[26] *Eighth Report*, Cmnd 2977, para 65.

[27] [1987] Crim LR 56, CA, following *Dawson and James* (1976) 64 Cr App R 170, CA.

[28] CLRC, *Eighth Report*, Cmnd 2977 (1966), para 102.

his pocket or accidentally to cut V while slitting his pocket to get his money would not be robbery.

Immediately before or at the time

The force or threat must be used immediately before or at the time of stealing, and, in the case of a threat, it must be of force 'then and there'. Thus there can be no robbery or attempted robbery by letter or telephone, except in the most unlikely circumstances—for example, D telephones V and informs V that if V does not hand over certain property to E (D's innocent agent who has called at V's house) D will detonate an explosive charge under V's house. Where the threats seek to secure a transfer of property at some time in the future the proper charge would be blackmail, contrary to s 21.[29] **7.14**

Immediately before

'Immediately before' must add something to 'at the time of' the theft. The approach taken in some Australian decisions—'no intervening space or lapse of time or event of any significance'[30]—may be too restrictive. Clearly if a gang overpowers V, the security guard at the main gate of a factory, this would be a use of force immediately before the theft, although many minutes might elapse before the gang reaches the part of the factory where the safe is housed.[31] And it can make no difference that V is not present in the factory at all; it would be robbery where some members of the gang by force detain V at his home while their confederates open the safe in the factory many miles away. It does not seem to be possible to put any particular temporal limit on 'immediately'. All the circumstances have to be considered including the time when, and the place where, the force was used or threatened in relation to the theft. The guiding principle seems to be that force converts theft into robbery only when its use or threat is in a real sense directly part of the theft, and is used in order to accomplish the theft. **7.15**

It is not enough that D gets V to part with property by threatening to use force on a separate and future, occasion. This may well amount to blackmail but the fact that V is intimidated or frightened is not in itself enough for robbery unless he is put in fear of being 'then and there' subject to force. In *Khan*,[32] the victim, at D's request, withdrew cash from his bank to hand over to D. V stated that he was in fear that D would be attacked by X, a violent man to whom D claimed to be in debt. V claimed that he feared that if X beat up D, D would then come and beat up him, V. The Court of Appeal quashed D's robbery conviction: there was no evidence that V feared that he would be subjected then and there to force. But suppose a gang by threats of force persuade V, the factory security guard, to stay away from work the following evening, and on that evening they steal from the factory uninterrupted. At the time of the theft the threat of force still operates on V's mind; he stays at home because he is afraid of what will happen if he goes to work. This does not seem to amount to robbery. At the time of the theft V is not put in fear of being 'then and there' subjected to force. **7.16**

---

[29] See ch 12 below.
[30] *Stanichewski* [2001] NTSC 86.
[31] It would surely be open to the jury so to find. cf *Hale* (1978) 68 Cr App R 415, [1979] Crim LR 596, CA.
[32] [2001] EWCA Crim 923.

7.17 To use force when a theft has been, but is no longer being, committed—for example, in order to escape—does not constitute robbery. This raises the question which arises in other contexts under the 1968 Act of how long a theft continues.[33] It is submitted that this question should receive a uniform answer throughout the Act. In the context of robbery, *Hale*[34] decides that, where D has assumed the ownership of goods in a house, the 'time of' stealing is still continuing while he is removing the goods from the premises so that he is guilty of robbery if he uses force to get away with the goods.

An assumption of the rights of an owner describes the conduct of a person towards a particular article. It is conduct which usurps the rights of the owner. To say that the conduct is over and done with as soon as he lays hands upon the property, or when he first manifests an intention to deal with it as his, is contrary to common-sense and to the natural meaning of words. A thief who steals a motor car first opens the door. Is it to be said that the act of starting up the motor is no more a part of the theft?[35]

Whether D is guilty of robbery if he uses force when running down the garden path or driving off in the getaway car are, it seems, questions which the court will leave to the common sense of the jury.[36] Was D still 'on the job'?[37] There comes a point when no reasonable jury could find the thief to be still in the course of stealing and this must surely be not later than the time when the expedition is complete. Thus, where D has already gained access to V's car, and locked himself in, and V is only threatened by D's driving at him to escape, the theft might be said to be continuing and a robbery committed.[38] But, if, having taken property from V without using or threatening force, D is subsequently stopped by a police officer in the street outside and knocks him down in order to avoid arrest this would not amount to robbery.

7.18 Where an act of force has occurred after the theft is over, it would, of course, be proper to charge D both with theft and with the appropriate crime under the Offences Against the Person Act 1861. Where a mere threat has been used after the theft is over this will generally not constitute a separate offence unless it is a threat to kill,[39] because a threat to do some lesser degree of harm is not an offence unless it amounts to an assault, an attempt to commit an aggravated assault, or possibly a public order offence. There may be merit in extending the offence to include force or the threat of force 'immediately after' a theft.[40] This would resonate with the existing underlying approach which is that robbery offers protection against the use of force in the dishonest acquisition of property.

7.19 Force used to retain possession of property not obtained by force would not ordinarily be thought of as robbery.[41] Even on a broad view the use of force is neither at the time

---

[33] Above, para 2.103.
[34] (1978) 68 Cr App R 415, CA, criticized by ATH Smith, *Property Offences* (1994) paras 14–31 to 14–32. *Hale* is unaffected by *Gomez: Lockley* [1995] Crim LR 656, CA.
[35] Eveleigh LJ, 418.
[36] ibid.
[37] *Atakpu* [1994] QB 69, [1993] 4 All ER 215, CA.
[38] *Hayward v Norwich Union Insurance Ltd* [2000] Lloyd's Rep IR 382. Whether the offence is one of theft or robbery may be of special significance for V's insurance claim: see generally M Wasik, 'Definitions of Crime in Insurance Contracts' [1986] J Bus Law 45.
[39] Offences against the Person Act 1861, s 16.
[40] Griew, para 3–08.
[41] *Harman's Case* (1620) 2 Roll Rep 154.

of, nor in order to commit, the theft.[42] D may be convicted of handling stolen goods contrary to s 22 of the 1968 Act if he has handled the goods other than in the course of the robbery. [43]

Force or threat against a third person

It is clear that, under the Theft Act 1968, force used against any person will constitute **7.20** robbery when it is used in order to commit theft. Similarly a threat to use force against any person aimed at putting that person in fear of being then and there subjected to force is enough. So if D, being about to commit theft from V, is interrupted by a passer-by, X, and repels X's attempt to interfere, either by actual force or the threat to use force, he is guilty of robbery if he completes the theft. It is immaterial that no force or threat is used against V from whom the theft is committed. It would seem that in such a case the indictment would properly allege robbery from V, for clearly there was no robbery from X.

The case put above may be an extension of the common law of robbery; but there is another **7.21** respect in which the Act may have narrowed the law. Suppose that D threatens V that, if V will not hand over certain property to D, D will use force on X. This was probably robbery at common law.[44] It is difficult if not impossible, however, to bring such a case within the words of the Act since D does not seek to put any person in fear of being then and there subjected to force in order to commit theft. He does not put V in such fear because the threat is to use force on X. He does not put X in fear because the threat is not addressed to him (unless of course X is in fear because of the nature and circumstances of the threat which make X fear that D will use violence against anyone who frustrates his purpose). Such cases should again be treated as blackmail contrary to s 21.

It might be different in the example put in the previous paragraph if the threat were **7.22** addressed to X as well as to V or overheard by X.[45] If it were D's object to cause X to intercede with V to hand over the property, so as to save himself from D's threatened force, this would be robbery. It does not therefore amount to robbery where D hands V, a bank teller, a note which reads 'I have a gun pointed at a customer'.[46] If D reads the note aloud, that is sufficient for robbery since the customer, X, is in fear.

At common law, the theft had to be from the person or in the presence of the victim. **7.23** In *Smith v Desmond*[47] the House of Lords, reversing the Court of Criminal Appeal,[48] put a wide interpretation upon this rule, holding that it was satisfied if the force or threat of force was used on a person who had the property to be stolen in his immediate personal care and protection. D was therefore guilty of robbery when he overpowered a night-watchman and a maintenance engineer in a bakery and then broke into a cash office some distance away

---

[42] cf Cmnd 2977, para 65.

[43] *Fernandez* [1997] 1 Cr App R 123, CA.

[44] *Reane* (1794) 2 East PC 734 at 735–6, per Eyre CB, *obiter*.

[45] See eg *Canelhas Comercio Importacao e Exportacao v Wooldridge* [2004] EWCA Civ 984 (insurance claim where jeweller's son kidnapped and attached to bomb to force father to release stock).

[46] *Taylor* [1996] 10 Archbold News 2, CA. cf *Reane* (1794) 2 Leach 616. Unless of course the bank teller fears from D's actions that he will also be subjected to immediate force.

[47] [1965] AC 960, [1965] 1 All ER 976, HL.

[48] [1964] 3 All ER 587, CCA.

and stole from a safe. Though the victims did not have the key to the office or the safe they were in the building to guard its contents which were, therefore, in their immediate personal care and protection.

7.24 Such a case is obviously within the terms of the Theft Act. Indeed, it follows from what has been said above that there is no longer any necessity to prove that the property was in the care and protection of the victim of the force or threat. It is enough that the force or threat was directed against any person so that, if in *Smith v Desmond* the persons overpowered had been mere passers-by who happened to have interfered with D's plans, this would be enough under the Theft Act, though not at common law.

CPS guidance on prosecuting

7.25 The CPS provide as examples of when a charge of robbery would be appropriate:

- When a handbag or mobile phone is forcibly snatched from a person's grasp.
- When an 11 year old hands over a small amount of money following threats of significant violence made by an older and physically larger youth.
- When no force is used or threatened but a weapon is produced or made visible to the victim (on the basis of an implied threat).
- When a car is taken using force or the threat of force and the evidence supports the inference that the offender did not intend the victim to recover the car intact (e.g. the car is not recovered; or is recovered but seriously damaged or burnt out).

The CPS examples when it would not be appropriate to charge robbery are:

- When a bag has been taken from off the shoulder of a victim without any force being used or threatened on the victim.
- When a shoulder strap is cut and the victim is unaware of this until after the handbag has been stolen.

Sentencing

7.26 The maximum penalty is life imprisonment. Robbery is a specified violent offence within Schedule 1 to the Criminal Justice Act 2003. Sentences are high; on average the highest of the dishonesty-based offences. Some commentators, notably Ashworth, have argued that the offence is too broad and that for a more proportionate sentencing regime it ought to be subdivided so as to differentiate the gravity of the threat or the level of violence involved.[49]

Sentencing Guidelines 2006

7.27 In 2006 the Sentencing Guidelines Council issued guidelines on robbery. The guidelines apply to offenders convicted of robbery sentenced on or after 1 August 2006. Five categories of robbery were identified based on sentencing ranges and previous guidance. They are:

1. Street robbery or 'mugging'
2. Robberies of small businesses

---

[49] See A Ashworth, 'Robbery Reassessed' [2002] Crim LR 851.

3. Less sophisticated commercial robberies
4. Violent personal robberies in the home
5. Professionally planned commercial robberies.

The 2006 guidelines concentrate only on street robbery, robbery of small businesses, and **7.28** small-scale commercial robberies. For each of the three categories, three levels of serious-ness are defined based on the extent of force used or threatened: Level 1—Threat and/or use of minimal force; Level 2—Use of weapon to threaten and/or use of significant force; Level 3—Use of weapon and/or significant force and serious injury caused. The relative seriousness of each offence will be determined by the following factors:

• Degree of force and/or nature and duration of threats
• Degree of injury to the victim
• Degree of fear experienced by the victim
• Value of property taken.

The 2006 guidelines provide that for an adult first time offender convicted after pleading **7.29** not guilty the starting point would be twelve months' custody if there is a threat or use of minimal force, rising to four years if a weapon was used or injury caused, rising further to eight years if there is serious physical injury.

Street robbery or 'mugging'
In recent years the sentencing of street robbers has attracted considerable controversy. **7.30** A review of the important sentencing decisions was provided by Lord Woolf CJ in *A-G's Reference (Nos 4 and 7 of 2002) (Lobban)*.[50]

Robberies of small businesses
The 2006 guidelines consider within this category a 'small shop or post office, petrol station **7.31** or public transport/taxi facility which may well lack the physical and electronic security devices available to banks or building societies and larger businesses'. Offences in this sentencing category tend not to be committed by professional criminals and typically do not involve injury.

Less sophisticated commercial robberies
This category covers a wide range of locations, extent of planning and degree of violence **7.32** including less sophisticated bank robberies or where larger commercial establishments are the target but without detailed planning or high levels of organization.

Other categories

Robbery in the home
The 2006 guidelines do not apply to violent personal robberies in the home. Heavy sentences **7.33** are imposed, particularly in cases where the homes of the vulnerable are targeted.[51]

---

[50] [2002] 2 Cr App R (S) 345.
[51] *Pegg and Martin* [1996] 2 Cr App R (S) 346.

Professionally planned commercial robberies

7.34   The most serious category of offending relates to professional armed robberies. The 2006 guidelines do not apply to this category of robbery. In *Turner*[52] a sentence of fifteen years' imprisonment was held to be the appropriate starting point for armed robberies where the target is a bank, a postal van, or security van.

Aggravating and mitigating features

Aggravating

7.35   The 2006 Sentencing Guidelines specify as aggravating factors particularly relevant to robbery: the degree of force or violence; use of a weapon; the vulnerability of the victim; the number involved in the offence and roles of offenders; the value of the items taken; whether the offence is committed at night/in hours of darkness; whether the offender wore a disguise. Others include the use of a real/loaded firearm, the discharge of the firearm, the sophistication of the planning, and the fact of multiple offences.

Mitigating

7.36   The 2006 Sentencing Guidelines specify as mitigating factors: the fact that the act was unplanned/opportunistic; that the offender had a peripheral involvement; the voluntary return of property taken; personal mitigation. Others include a plea of guilty, the youth of the offender, the absence of injury to victims, and the fact of an offender acting alone.[53]

7.37   The authorities seem to show that when an offender is sentenced there is a focus on the offence or offences charged and that previous offending is less important in robbery than elsewhere. The exception is when the previous offending involves robbery or other offences of violence.

---

[52] [1975] 61 Cr App R 89–91, CA; these are likely to be revised upwards to reflect current attitudes to the offence: *Adams and Harding* [2002] 2 Cr App R (S) 274.
[53] *Gould* [1983] 5 Cr App R (S) 67 and *Daly* [1981] 3 Cr App R (S) 340.

8

BURGLARY AND RELATED OFFENCES

Burglary

The law relating to burglary and other breaking offences contained in the Larceny Act   **8.01**
1916, ss 24–7, was unnecessarily complex and involved excessively technical distinctions
between a 'bewildering series of offences'.[1] The Theft Act 1968 effected a considerable simplification of the law. The Act eliminated entirely the concept of 'breaking', which was a
requisite of burglary, and most forms of house-breaking under the Larceny Act. 'Breaking'
was a highly technical term on which there was a great deal of case-law and it no longer
served a useful purpose in the definition of the offences. The 1968 Act also got rid of the
distinction between breaking 'in the night' and breaking 'in the day' which was the most
conspicuous difference between the old offences of burglary and house-breaking. It eliminated from the definition the concept of 'dwelling house' which had its own difficulties.
However, the Criminal Justice Act 1991 has subsequently amended the law by providing
for a higher penalty when burglary is committed in respect of 'a dwelling', and the effect of
this is considered below.

---

[1] CLRC, *Eighth Report*, Cmnd 2977 (1966) para 69. See generally on the old law JC Smith and B Hogan,
Smith and Hogan, Criminal Law (1st edn, 1965) 397–401.

8.02 The offence of burglary is provided in s 9 of the Act, as amended by the Criminal Justice Act 1991 and the Sexual Offences Act 2003:

(1) A person[2] is guilty of burglary if—
  (a) he enters any building or part of a building as a trespasser and with intent to commit any such offence as is mentioned in subsection (2) below; or
  (b) having entered any building or part of a building as a trespasser he steals or attempts to steal anything in the building or that part of it or inflicts or attempts to inflict on any person therein any grievous bodily harm.
(2) The offences referred to in subsection (1) (a) above are offences of stealing anything in the building or part of a building in question, of inflicting on any person therein any grievous bodily harm[3] and of doing unlawful damage to the building or anything therein.
(3) A person guilty of burglary shall on conviction on indictment be liable to imprisonment for a term not exceeding—
  (a) where the offence was committed in respect of a building or part of a building which is a dwelling, fourteen years;
  (b) in any other case, ten years.
(4) References in subsection (1) and (2) above to a building and the reference in subsection (3) above to a building which is also a dwelling, shall apply also to an inhabited vehicle or vessel, and shall apply to any such vehicle or vessel at times when the person having a habitation in it is not there as well as at times when he is.

8.03 The offence is prevalent. There were a total of 645,118 recorded offences of burglary in 2005/6, including burglaries in a dwelling and aggravated burglaries.[4]

8.04 It seems there are at least four forms of burglary. The effect of subsection 3, as inserted by the Criminal Justice Act 1991 appears to be that burglary in a dwelling becomes a separate offence.[5] If the higher penalty is to be available the indictment must allege, and the prosecution must satisfy the jury, that the premises burgled constitute a dwelling. It continues to be necessary to distinguish between 'dwellings' and other buildings for the purposes of ascertaining whether magistrates' courts have jurisdiction.[6] Paragraphs (a) and (b) of s 9(1) create separate offences. The effect of subsection 3 is that each paragraph now creates two

---

[2] In *Deutsche Genossenschaftsbank v Burnhope* [1996] 1 Lloyd's Rep 113, 123, the majority of the HL found that, on the facts of that case, the company in question had not committed a burglary; however, Lord Steyn, dissenting, had no doubt that a company could commit burglary—as where a company chairman dishonestly instructs an innocent employee to enter V's warehouse and remove valuables.

[3] The offence of burglary by entering with intent to rape was repealed by the Sexual Offences Act 2003, Sch 7, para 1. Section 63 of that Act creates a much broader offence of trespass with intent to commit a sexual offence which is considered, para 8.86.

[4] A Walker, C Kershaw, and S Nicholas, *Home Office Statistical Bulletin, Crime in England and Wales 2005/2006* p 28, Recorded crime by offence 1996 to 2005/6 and percentage change between 2004/5 and 2005/6.

[5] *Courtie* [1984] AC 463, HL. The escape-from-*Courtie* route taken in *DPP v Butterworth* [1995] 1 AC 381, HL (that *Courtie* applies unless a contrary Parliamentary intent is apparent) does not seem open here.

[6] Magistrates' Courts Act 1980, Sch 1, para 28(c). Burglary comprising the commission of, or an intention to commit, an offence triable only on indictment and a burglary in a dwelling where any person in the dwelling was subjected to violence or the threat of violence are triable on indictment only: Magistrates' Courts Act 1980, Sch 1, para 28; *MacGrath* [2003] EWCA Crim 2062, [2004] Crim LR 142 and comment; *Practice Direction (Criminal Proceedings: Consolidation)* [2002] 1 WLR 2870, para 51. The offence is triable only on indictment where it is an allegation of D's third domestic burglary after 1999. See below, para 8.66.

offences (in a dwelling or not, as the case may be) so there are four offences in all. It has been decided[7] that a person charged with an offence under s 9(1)(b) may be convicted of an offence under s 9(1)(a) because (however contrary to the facts this may seem to be) the allegation of an offence under s 9(1)(b) is held to include an allegation of an offence under s 9(1)(a).

Actus reus

Enters

Determining whether there has been an entry has proved more difficult than might be **8.05** envisaged. The common law rule was that the insertion of any part of the body, however small, was a sufficient entry. So where D pushed in a window pane and the forepart of his finger was observed to be inside the building, that was enough.[8] This produced a broad but clear approach to the offence. The Act gives no express guidance and it seems to have been assumed in Parliament that the common law rules would apply.[9] The courts have, however, adopted inconsistent approaches and sought to qualify the rule.

In *Collins*,[10] D, naked but for his socks, had climbed up a ladder on to a bedroom window **8.06** sill, as a trespasser and with intent to rape, when the woman in the bedroom invited him in. It was not clear whether he was on the sill outside the window or on the inner sill at the moment when he ceased to be a trespasser and became an invitee. Edmund Davies LJ said that there must be 'an effective and substantial entry' as a trespasser to constitute burglary. This suggests that it is no longer enough that any part of the body, however small, is intruded; but it is not clear what 'effective and substantial' means.[11] The insertion of an arm may be 'effective' if it is long enough to reach property and remove it. In *Brown*,[12] there was a sufficient entry where D's feet were on the ground outside a shop and the top half of his body was inside the broken shop window, as if he was rummaging for goods displayed there. The court said that the word 'substantial' did not materially assist but the entry must be 'effective' and here it was. D was presumably in a position to steal. But in *Ryan*[13] D became trapped by the neck with only his head and right arm inside the window. His argument that his act was not capable of constituting an entry because he could not have stolen anything was rejected. This is surely right.[14] It cannot have been the intention of the legislature that D must have got so far into the building as to be able to accomplish his unlawful purpose. The person intent on committing grievous bodily harm is guilty of

---

[7] *Whiting* (1987) 85 Cr App R 78, CA applying *Wilson and Jenkins* [1984] AC 242, [1983] 3 All ER 448, HL. *Whiting* is criticized by JC Smith, at [1987] Crim LR 473 and by ATH Smith, *Property Offences* (1994) para 28–08. See also the CLRC, *Eighth Report*, Cmnd 2977 (1966) para 76.

[8] *Davis* (1823) Russ & Ry 499.

[9] Hansard, House of Lords, Official Report, vol 290, cols 85–6.

[10] [1973] QB 100 at 106, [1972] 2 All ER 1105 at 1111, CA.

[11] cf Griew, 4-18 commenting that 'too much was made of this unelaborated dictum from an extempore judgment'.

[12] [1985] Crim LR 212, CA.

[13] (1995) 160 JP 610, [1996] Crim LR 320, CA.

[14] Note the *obiter* statements of Lord Lane CJ in *Watson* (1989) 89 Cr App R 211, 214, that the burglary occurred with D's 'foot crossing the threshold or windowsill'.

burglary when he enters through the ground floor window though his victim is on the fourth floor. Thus it seems that the act need be neither an 'effective' nor a 'substantial' entry. *Ryan* decided, not that D *had* 'entered' but only that there was evidence on which a jury could find that he had. It is, however, in principle unsatisfactory that it should be left to a jury to decide whether there is an entry when all the necessary facts are established. What possible criteria can they apply? This can only increase the likelihood of inconsistent verdicts in what is a serious offence.

8.07 At common law, if an instrument was inserted into the building *for the purpose of committing* the ulterior offence, there was an entry even though no part of the body was introduced into the building. So it was enough that hooks were inserted into the premises to drag out the carpets,[15] or that the muzzle of a gun was introduced with a view to shooting someone inside.[16] It would amount to an entry if holes were bored in the side of a granary so that wheat would run out and be stolen by D,[17] provided that the boring implement emerged on the inside. On the other hand, the insertion of an instrument *for the purpose of gaining entry* and not for the purpose of committing the ulterior offence, was not an entry if no part of the body entered.[18] If D bored a hole in a door with a drill bit for the purpose of gaining entry, the emergence of the point of the bit on the inside of the door was not an entry.

8.08 Even if the courts are willing to follow the common law in holding that the intrusion of any part of the body is an entry, they may be reluctant to preserve these technical rules regarding instruments, for they seem to lead to outlandish results. Thus it seems to follow from the common law rules that there may be an entry if a stick of dynamite is thrown into the building or if a bullet is fired from outside the building into it.[19] What then if a time bomb is sent by parcel post? Has D 'entered', even though he is not on the scene at all?—perhaps even being abroad and outside the jurisdiction? Yet this is hardly an 'entry' in the 'simple language as used and understood by ordinary literate men and women' in which the Act is said to be written.[20] Perhaps a restriction may be read into the approach so that D must be present at the scene, or 'on the job'.

8.09 There is, however, a cogent argument in favour of the common law rules being applied which may be put as follows. If D sends a child, under the age of 10, into the building to steal, this is obviously an entry by D,[21] through an 'innocent agent', under ordinary principles. Suppose that, instead of a child, D sends in a monkey. It is hard to see that this should not equally be an entry by D. But if that point be conceded, it is admitted that the insertion of an animate instrument is an entry; and will the courts distinguish between animate and inanimate instruments? Unless they will, the insertion of the hooks, or the use of a remote controlled robotic device etc, must also be an entry.[22]

---

[15] (1583) 1 Anderson 114.
[16] 2 East PC 492.
[17] *State v Crawford* 46 LRA 312 (1899) (Alabama).
[18] *Hughes* (1785) 1 Leach 406; but cf *Tucker* (1844) 1 Cox CC 73.
[19] Hawk PC c 17, s 11; 2 East PC 490; contra, 1 Hale PC 554.
[20] Above, para 1.10 n 11.
[21] 1 Hale PC 555; *Smith and Hogan, Criminal Law* 167-8.
[22] Transvestites who hooked dresses worth £600 through letter boxes of shops pleaded guilty to burglary in a metropolitan magistrates' court: *Daily Telegraph*, 4 Mar 1979. See also *Richardson and Brown* [1998]

If D puts a child under 10 through the window, so that the child may open a door and **8.10** admit D who will himself steal, it is by no means so clear that the innocent agency argument is open; and the common law rule regarding instruments would suggest it is not an entry; since the child is being used to gain entry and not to commit the ulterior offence.[23] In the light of these considerations, it is submitted that the best course is to assume the continued existence of the common law rules.

The CPS provides the rather unhelpful advice that: 'When there are any factual difficulties **8.11** with the degree of entry, consideration should be given to charging another offence, for example theft.'

As a trespasser

Trespass is a legal concept and resort must be had to the law of tort in order to ascertain its **8.12** meaning.[24] This is yet another example of the criminal offences under the Theft Act 1968 turning on the technical definitions of the civil law. In tort, it would appear that any intentional, reckless, or negligent entry into a building is a trespass if the building is in fact in the possession of another and either that person does not consent to the entry or the person entering lacks a specific legal right to enter. A person entering property exercising a legal power of entry, such as a police officer conducting an authorized search under warrant, will not be a trespasser whether the occupier consents or not. Entry with the consent of the occupier cannot be a trespass. This begs a number of questions—Who is entitled to consent? To what are they entitled to consent? What is the effect of a mistake as to the identity or purpose of the entering party? What must the burglar know about his status as a trespasser?

Effective consent?

In all cases of burglary it must be shown that D entered the building as a trespasser, although **8.13** evidence from the occupier in person is unnecessary.[25] In *Collins*,[26] it was held that, whatever the position in the law of tort, an invitation by the occupier's daughter to enter her bedroom and have intercourse with her, without the knowledge or consent of the occupier, precluded trespass for this purpose. Suppose, however, that the occupier's daughter or servant invites her lover into the house to steal the occupier's property. This ought to be burglary if the lover realizes, as he surely must, that the daughter or servant has no right to invite him in for this purpose. Where the invitation is issued by a member of the household,

---

2 Cr App R (S) 87 (burglary by use of mechanical digger to remove ATM from bank wall); *Sang* [2003] EWCA Crim 2411, going equipped for burglary with fishing rod bound with sellotape at its end to extract car keys through letterboxes.

[23] Williams, *TBCL* 840 suggests that the use of the child is theft or attempted theft rather than burglary in any event since the owner would not be alarmed by the appearance of the child. This assumes that the offence is designed to protect the occupier's personal safety and privacy, which is arguably only one of its functions. For an academic analysis of the types of wrongdoing included in burglary see B Mitchell, 'Multiple Wrongdoing and Offence Structure' (2001) 64 MLR 393; GR Sullivan and A Simester, 'On the Nature and Rationale of Property Offences' in RA Duff and SP Green (eds), *Defining Crimes* (2005) 168, 192.

[24] WVH Rogers, *Winfield and Jolowicz on Torts* (17th edn, 2006) ch 13.

[25] *Maccuish* [1999] 6 Archbold News 2, CA.

[26] [1973] QB 100 at 107, [1972] 2 All ER 1105 at 1111, CA; para 8.06. cf *Robson v Hallett* [1967] 2 QB 939; [1967] 2 All ER 407 (invitation by occupier's son effective until withdrawn by occupier).

it is submitted that the question is whether the accused knew that, or was reckless whether, the invitation was issued without authority.

8.14 In *Jones and Smith*,[27] where the occupier's son had a general permission to enter the house, entry with an accomplice, and with an intention to steal, constituted burglary. The accused had knowingly exceeded the permission. It is perhaps noteworthy that it was a case 'where [DD] took elaborate precautions, going there at dead of night'; and that, even if the son's entry was covered by the general permission, this would scarcely extend to the entry of his accomplice; and, if the accomplice's entry was unlawful, the son abetted it. Williams[28] argues that *Jones and Smith* is wrongly decided, being inconsistent with *Collins*,[29] because Collins also exceeded the permission since he entered intending to use force if necessary to have sex. But as the girl saw him to be 'a naked male with an erect penis' it seems clear that she invited him in for the purpose of sexual intercourse, that he knew he was so invited, and that any intention to rape must have lapsed.[30]

8.15 The cases highlight a number of problems. First, that the question of trespass cannot in criminal law be divorced from the question of *mens rea*. D might, in civil law, be a trespasser because the invitation is issued by one without authority or whose authority does not extend to permitting entry for the particular purpose, yet not be liable for burglary as he lacks knowledge or recklessness as to whether he is entering without proper authority. The second problem highlighted is that burglary protects against a number of harms—the trespass and infringements of privacy and the ulterior harms—and the interests being protected may be those of different individuals.[31]

Mistakes and consent?

8.16 In *Collins*, the invitation to enter was issued under a mistake as to the man's identity: she thought he was her boyfriend. It is submitted that, if he had known of the woman's mistake, he would have intentionally entered as a trespasser. Mistake as to identity, where identity is material, generally vitiates consent. Mistake by the person entering is no defence to an action in tort; so that, if D on a very dark night were to enter the house next door in mistake for his own, this would be regarded as an intentional entry and a trespass. This would apparently be so even if D's mistake was a reasonable one, *a fortiori* if it were negligent as, for example, if he made the mistake because he was drunk. It is established, however, that it is not sufficient (though it is necessary) that D is a trespasser in the civil law. In the criminal law he must be shown to have *mens rea*. If he is charged under s 9(1)(a), it must appear that, when he entered, he knew the facts which caused him to be a trespasser or at least that he was reckless whether those facts existed.[32] A merely negligent entry, as where D enters

---

[27] [1976] 3 All ER 54, [1976] 1 WLR 672, CA.
[28] *TBCL* 846-50.
[29] Para 8.06.
[30] cf Mason J in *Barker* (1983) 7 ALJR 426 at 429: '. . . The foundation for this conclusion (sc, that of Williams) is too frail.'
[31] Burglary does not require that the ulterior offence should concern the occupier. If D and E, squatters, occupy V's house, it would amount to burglary were D to steal E's wallet or to inflict on E grievous bodily harm.
[32] *Collins* [1973] QB 100 at 104–5, [1972] 2 All ER 1105 at 1109–10. 'Reckless' is used in the *Cunningham* ([1957] 2 QB 396) sense. See *Smith and Hogan, Criminal Law* 106-7.

another's house, honestly but unreasonably believing it to be his own, should not be enough. So too, D's belief in a right to enter the house of another should lead to acquittal, for then D has no intention to enter as a trespasser. Suppose that D, being separated from his wife, wrongly believes that he has a right to enter the matrimonial home of which she is the owner-occupier and does enter with intent to inflict grievous bodily harm upon her. Even if he is in law a trespasser it is submitted that he is not a burglar.[33] His ignorance is not of the criminal law (for that would avail him of no defence), it is a mistake as to his status in civil law. In the case where D's mistake as to his status on entry is as a result of voluntary intoxication, the question ought to be whether he would have made that mistake if sober.[34]

If D's entry is involuntary, he is not a trespasser and cannot be guilty of burglary. So if he **8.17** is dragged against his will into V's house and left there by his drunken companions and he steals V's vase and leaves, this is not burglary. If, however, D had intentionally entered the building, believing it to be his own house and committed theft on discovering the truth, it appears from the previous paragraph that he would have committed theft after entering as a trespasser and thus committed the *actus reus* of burglary. In this case it seems that D has *mens rea* as well, for burglary under s 9(1)(b) is committed, not at the time of entry, but when the ulterior crime is committed; and at that time, he knows that he has entered as a trespasser.[35]

Entry for a purpose outside the scope of the licence to enter

It seems to be entirely clear that where D gains entry by deception he enters as a trespasser. **8.18** There is no need to distinguish between a licence which is void and one which is merely voidable[36] because entry under either is a trespass. For example, D gains admission to V's house by falsely pretending that he has been sent by the BBC to examine the radio in order to trace disturbances in transmission. The old law went so far as to hold[37] that this was a constructive 'breaking'. That is no longer an issue and there can be no doubt that it constitutes a trespassory entry. This is acknowledged by the routine prosecution of 'distraction' burglars who deceive vulnerable (usually elderly) occupiers into allowing them entry by purporting to represent a utility company and then once on the premises stealing therein.

The authorities, however, go much farther than this, establishing that a person who has a **8.19** limited authority to enter for a particular purpose enters as a trespasser though he practises no deception, if he has an unlawful purpose outside the scope of his authority. In *Taylor v Jackson*,[38] D had express permission to go on V's land and hunt for rabbits. He went there

---

[33] The CPS guidance observes that: 'Complications may arise when a spouse or partner who has been excluded from the former matrimonial home returns there and takes property. When the issue of trespass is or may be difficult to prove, you should consider charging theft or attempted theft. Remember that the DPP's consent is required for such cases.' <http://www.cps.gov.uk>

[34] Griew 4-07; cf *Irwin and Richardson* [1999] Cr App R 392, CA.

[35] The common law doctrine of trespass *ab initio* has no application to burglary under the Theft Act: *Collins* [1973] QB 100 at 107, [1972] 2 All ER 1105 at 1111, CA. See the second edition of this work at paras 377–8.

[36] See earlier editions of this book, eg fourth edition, paras 338–9.

[37] *Boyle* [1954] 2 QB 292, [1954] 2 All ER 721.

[38] (1898) 78 LT 555.

to hunt for hares and the Divisional Court held that this was evidence of trespass in pursuit of game, contrary to the Game Act 1831, s 30. In *Hillen and Pettigrew v ICI (Alkali) Ltd*,[39] members of a stevedore's gang employed to unload a barge were held to be trespassers when they placed kegs on the hatch covers, knowing that this was a wrong and dangerous thing to do. They were, therefore, not entitled to damages when the hatch covers collapsed and they were injured. Lord Atkin said:

> As Scrutton LJ has pointedly said: 'When you invite a person into your house to use the staircase you do not invite him to slide down the banisters.'[40] So far as he sets foot on so much of the premises as lie outside the invitation or uses them for purposes which are alien to the invitation he is not an invitee but a trespasser, and his rights must be determined accordingly. In the present case the steve-dores knew that they ought not to use the covered hatch in order to load cargo from it; for them for such a purpose it was out of bounds: they were trespassers.

8.20   In *Farrington v Thomson and Bridgland*,[41] an Australian court held that a police officer who entered a hotel for the purpose of committing a tort was a trespasser. The tacit invitation to the public to enter the hotel did not extend to persons entering for the purpose of commit-ting a tort or a criminal offence. In *Barker*,[42] the High Court of Australia (Murphy J dissenting) held that D committed burglary where, having been asked by his neighbour, V, to keep an eye on V's house while V was on holiday and told the whereabouts of a concealed key in case he needed to enter, D entered in order to steal. 'If a person enters for a purpose outside the scope of his authority then he stands in no better position than a person who enters with no authority at all.'[43]

8.21   One decision goes against this view. In *Byrne v Kinematograph Renters Society Ltd*,[44] Harman J held that it was not trespass to gain entry to a cinema by buying tickets with the purpose, not of seeing the film, but of counting the patrons. It is submitted that this decision is against the weight of authority and should not be followed.

8.22   It seems to follow that a person who enters a shop for the *sole* purpose of shoplifting is a burglar, though two of the majority in *Barker* thought otherwise. In their view, a person with a permission to enter, not limited by reference to purpose, is not a trespasser merely because he enters with a secret unlawful intent; and the shopkeeper's invitation is not so limited: 'the mere presence of the prospective customer upon the premises is itself likely to be an object of the invitation and a person will be within the invitation if he enters for no particular purpose at all'.[45] It is doubtful, however, if the shopkeeper's invitation can be said

---

[39] [1936] AC 65, HL.
[40] *The Carlgarth* [1927] P 93 at 110, CA.
[41] [1959] ALR 695, [1959] VR 286 (Smith J). See also *Gross v Wright* [1923] 2 DLR 171.
[42] (1983) 7 ALJR 426.
[43] Per Mason J at 429.
[44] [1958] 2 All ER 579 at 593; distinguished in *Jones*, para 8.14, and by Mason J in *Barker* (1983) 7 ALJR 426 at 429 on the ground that 'the invitation by the lessee of the cinema to the public to enter the cinema was in very general terms and could on no view be said to be limited in the way in which was contended'.
[45] Brennan and Deane JJ (1983) 7 ALJR at 436. See also Williams, *TBCL*, 'a person who has a licence in fact to enter does not become a trespasser by reason of his criminal intent', 846. See further 846–9; PJ Pace, 'Burglarious Trespass' [1985] Crim LR 716; ATH Smith, 'Shoplifting and the Theft Acts' [1981] Crim LR 586. In terms of sentencing, a burglarious shoplifter should be sentenced in accordance with shoplifting sentencing guidelines rather than burglary guidelines: *Creed* [2005] EWCA Crim 215.

to extend to those who enter for the *sole* purpose of shoplifting. There is no need to strain to exclude them. It is only in the exceptional case that it will be possible to prove the intent at the time of entry—as where there is evidence of a previous conspiracy, or system, or preparatory acts such as the wearing of a jacket with special pockets. Such an entry may be no more than a merely preparatory act to stealing and so not attempted theft; but it ought to be possible, where there is clear evidence, to make an arrest. Few would object to the conviction of burglary of bank robbers who enter the bank flourishing pistols, for they are clearly outside the invitation extended by the bank to the public. A person who enters a shop for the sole purpose of murdering the manager is surely a trespasser; and the case of the intending thief is no different in principle.

This extension of the law beyond what was intended by the CLRC[46] is significant in terms **8.23** of the number of people potentially at risk of prosecution for burglary. The interpretation in *Jones and Smith* underlines the fact that the scope of burglary has shifted from an act of 'breaking' and entering—one of manifest illegality—to include acts of illicit entry where the principal element of blameworthiness lies in D's criminal intent.[47] The cumulative effect of the extension in *Jones* with that of recent decisions in theft considered in chapter 2 above must also be considered. Consider the case of D, an antiques dealer who calls on a gullible old lady with the intention of tricking her into selling him her priceless heirloom for a gross undervalue (fraud by false representation[48] but seemingly also theft[49]). D could be guilty of burglary. The decision in *Jones and Smith* does, however, have the advantage of focusing on *mens rea* and reducing the reliance within the offence on the technicalities of the civil law of trespass.[50]

It has been suggested by one commentator that to keep the *Jones and Smith* extension of **8.24** burglary within desirable limits a distinction might be drawn between buildings that are open to the public and others,[51] but such a distinction might create an unnecessary layer of technicality. Buildings are increasingly commonly quasi-public[52] (as for example in large shopping centres) and this might produce further doubts as to the ability of the tort of trespass to provide a sufficiently clear foundation for the offence in this context. Another possible limitation to the *Jones and Smith* extension is to accept that D enters as a trespasser where he has the intention to commit the particular offence he then goes on to commit, but not otherwise—as where D enters with an intent to commit theft but then commits damage instead. This would seem to be a rather unhelpful limitation.

The fact that buildings are increasingly commonly quasi-public does generate interesting **8.25** questions as to the potential uses to which the burglary charge might be put. If a shop-keeper issues a ban on a particular individual, D, from his store, D is clearly a trespasser if

---

[46] See CLRC, *Eighth Report*, Cmnd 2977 (1966) para 35.
[47] See G Fletcher, *Rethinking Criminal Law* (1977) 128.
[48] Fraud Act 2006, s 2.
[49] See para 2.22.
[50] A Ashworth, *Principles of Criminal Law* (5th edn, 2006) 395.
[51] ATH Smith, *Property Offences* (1994) para 28–14, referring to the American Model Penal Code, s 221.1.
[52] See K Gray and S Gray, 'Civil Rights, Civil Wrongs and Quasi-public Space' [1999] 1 EHRLR 46, discussed in the breach of the peace case, *Porter v MPC* (1999) 20 Oct, CA Civ Div, unreported.

he enters. What if the owners of a shopping complex accede to the requests of the individual shop owners within the complex by banning D, a persistent shoplifter, from the entire complex? Is D a burglar as soon as he enters the complex, subject to the *mens rea* being proved?

8.26 The CPS provides rather misleading advice in its guidance to prosecutors on this area. It is suggested that

> When an accused has been formally barred from shop premises, the circumstances, which have resulted in the accused being excluded, may not be admissible in evidence on the basis that they result from alleged previous misconduct by the accused. If you form the view that the facts, which led to the accused being excluded, are unlikely to be admitted in evidence, or that it cannot be proved that the defendant knew about the notice, you should consider charging theft or attempted theft. The sentence for such a burglary would be unlikely to be more than for theft. The exclusion notice could be drawn to the court's attention when sentencing for theft. When the issue of trespass is or may be difficult to prove, you should consider charging theft or attempted theft.

Following the introduction of the bad character provisions in the Criminal Justice Act 2003 there is a strong likelihood that evidence of the misconduct which has led to D being barred from the premises will be admitted under ss 101(1)(c) or 101(1)(d).

8.27 It should be noted that a person who enters under a legal right—usually in the exercise of a statutory power—does not commit trespass, but where that person enters with an intention to steal, damage, or cause grievous bodily harm, contrary to the scope of the legal power under which he enters, he enters as a trespasser. If however he enters under the power, lacking any intent to act outside its scope, and once he has entered commits one of the ulterior offences, there is no burglary.[53]

Who is the victim of the burglary?

8.28 Trespass is an interference with possession. Burglary is therefore committed against the person in possession of the building entered. Where the premises are let, the burglary is committed against the tenant and not against the landlord. The landlord could commit burglary of the premises, the tenant could not. Even if the tenant is only a tenant at will, he may maintain trespass. On the other hand, '[t]he guest at a hotel will not ordinarily have sufficient possession of his room to enable him to sue in trespass.'[54] It has been held that, where a servant occupies premises belonging to his master for the more convenient performance of his duties as servant, he cannot maintain an action for trespass against the master.[55] That was a decision of over a century and a half ago, and it is questionable whether the social conventions underpinning that decision apply with the same force. In such a case it is, of course, necessary to look at the precise terms of the arrangement between the parties; if the servant has been given exclusive possession, he and not the master is the victim of a trespass. And it does not necessarily follow that, because the servant in a particular case may not maintain trespass against the master, he cannot do so against third parties.[56]

---

[53] cf Griew 4-08.
[54] J Murphy, *Street on Torts* (11th edn, 2003) 74-6.
[55] *Mayhew v Suttle* (1854) 4 E & B 347; *White v Bayley* (1861) 10 CBNS 227.
[56] Though in *White v Bayley* (above, n 55) Byles J thought, *obiter*, that an action could not have been maintained by the servant against a stranger (10 CBNS at 235).

The position of a lodger depends on the precise terms of his contract. If he has exclusive **8.29** possession so that he can refuse entry to the landlord then, no doubt, he may maintain trespass. Many lodgers, however, do not have such possession and in such cases an unauthorized entry by a third party is a trespass against the landlord. It seems to follow that burglary is not committed where a hotelier enters the room of a guest, even though the entry is without the guest's consent and with intent to steal; and that, depending on the terms of the contract, the same may be true in the case of a master entering premises occupied by his servant for the purposes of his employment and a landlord entering the rooms of his lodger.

It seems that an indictment will lie although it does not allege that the building was the **8.30** property of anyone. Whereas the Larceny Act 1916 required that the breaking and entering be of the dwelling house *of another*, there is no such expression in the Theft Act.[57] The requirement of trespass means that evidence must be offered that someone other than the accused was in possession. If that is all that is necessary, evidence that A or B was in possession should suffice—it is equally a trespass in either event. But if a statement of ownership is required in the indictment, 'A or B' will hardly do. It is submitted, therefore, that it should be sufficient that the indictment alleges that D trespassed in a building without alleging who is the owner of the building.

Any building or part of a building

The meaning of 'building' in various statutes has frequently been considered by the courts. **8.31** Clearly the meaning of the term varies according to the context and many things which have been held to be buildings for other purposes will not be buildings for the purpose of the Theft Act—for example, a garden wall, a railway embankment, or a tunnel under the road. According to Lord Esher MR, its 'ordinary and usual meaning is, a block of brick or stone work, covered in by a roof'.[58] It seems clear, however, that it is not necessary that the structure be of brick or stone to be a building within this Act. Clearly all dwelling houses are intended to be protected and these may be built of wood; while 'the inhabited vehicle or vessel' which is expressly included is likely to be built of steel or of wood. More helpful is the view of Byles J that a building in its ordinary sense is 'a structure of considerable size and intended to be permanent or at least to endure for a considerable time'.[59]

To be a building, the structure must have some degree of permanence. A substantial portable **8.32** structure may be a building[60] but probably not a tent even though it is someone's home.[61]

---

[57] See JN Adams, 'Trespass under the Theft and Firearms Act' (1969) 119 NLJ 655.
[58] *Moir v Williams* [1892] 1 QB 264, CA.
[59] *Stevens v Gourley* (1859) 7 CBNS 99 at 112. For other descriptions, see *Stroud's Judicial Dictionary*, ed D Greenberg (7th edn, 2006) i. 323.
[60] Contrast *B and S v Leathley* [1979] Crim LR 314 (Carlisle CC) and *Norfolk Constabulary v Seekings and Gould* [1986] Crim LR 167 (Norfolk CC). In the former it was held that a freezer container detached from its chassis, resting on railway sleepers, and used to store frozen food, was a building; while in the latter it was held that two similar containers, still on their wheeled chassis, remained vehicles though they were, as in the first case, being used by a supermarket to provide temporary storage space. cf *King* [1978] 19 SASR 118 (walk-in freezer could be a building).
[61] See CLRC, *Eighth Report*, Cmnd 2977 (1966) para 78. This is certainly questionable in the case of, for example a substantial marquee housing many facilities. cf *Storn* (1865) 5 SCR (NSW) 26. A tent or marquee would obviously only be capable of being burgled when erected.

It is again a question of the meaning of the word in the language of ordinary literate men; and this perhaps suggests that a telephone kiosk is not a building.[62] If it is, the wreckers of these places are probably burglars.

8.33 The outbuildings of a house seem to be buildings for the purpose of the Act so that burglary may be committed in a detached garage, a wooden toolshed, or a greenhouse. Similarly, farm buildings such as a stable, cow-byre, pigsty, barn or silo, and industrial buildings such as factories, warehouses, and stores, fall under the same category. Other cases are more difficult.[63] It is not uncommon for trespassers to enter unfinished buildings and do damage. If they enter with intent to cause damage by fire or explosion are they now guilty of burglary? An unfinished building was a building within s 6 of the Malicious Damage Act 1861.[64] Why not for the purposes of burglary? Clearly there is a difficult question as to the point in its erection at which a structure becomes a building. In *Manning*,[65] Lush J said: '. . . it is sufficient that it should be a connected and entire structure. I do not think four walls erected a foot high would be a building.' In that case all the walls were built and finished and the roof was on. It may be that a roof will be thought necessary for a structure to be a building under the present Act, for it clearly was not intended to extend to a walled garden, yard, or paddock. On the other hand there are many substantial open air structures which ought to be protected against burglars. What if D breaks into Lords intent on damaging the pitch? Is this burglary or mere criminal damage? It has been held in a different context that 'a mere structure or superstructure composed of a steel and concrete frame [as yet] having no roof' could constitute a building.[66] Conversely, the question can be asked, what if there is a roof but no walls, as in the case of a bandstand?[67]

8.34 There is no obvious answer to borderline cases such as this but they are likely to be rare. It is likely that a court would hold, following *Brutus v Cozens*,[68] that 'building' is an ordinary word the meaning of which is 'a matter of fact and degree' to be determined by the trier of fact. The judge must at least rule whether there is evidence on which a reasonable jury could find the structure to be a building. As with the concept of entry, the fact that an essential element of burglary is left to be determined by the trier of fact can only lead to inconsistency and uncertainty in the law.

The extent of a 'building' and its 'parts'

8.35 Under the old law, the entry had to be into a particular dwelling house, office, shop, garage, etc. A single structure might contain many dwelling houses—for example a block of flats—many offices, shops, or garages. If D broke into Flat 1 with intent to pass through it, go upstairs and steal in Flat 45, the breaking and entering of Flat 1 was neither burglary nor

---

[62] Although it probably constitutes a 'structure' for the purposes of s 63 of the Sexual Offences Act 2003, para 8.86.

[63] There is authority that a structure is capable of being a 'building' notwithstanding that it is 'implanted within another building': *Royal Exchange Theatre Trust v The Commissioners* [1978] VATTR 139.

[64] *Manning and Rogers* (1871) LR 1 CCR 338.

[65] ibid, 341.

[66] *R v Ealing London Borough Council, ex p Zainuddain* [1994] 2 PLR 1, 4 per Tucker LJ.

[67] Held to be a building for the purpose of a private act regulating the provision of public entertainments in buildings: *A-G v Eastbourne Corpn* (1934) 78 Sol Jo 633, CA.

[68] [1973] AC 854, [1972] 2 All ER 1297, HL.

house-breaking for D did not intend to commit a felony therein.[69] It was probably not even an attempt, not being an act of more than mere preparation to the intended crime. If D broke into a flat above a jeweller's shop with intent to break through the ceiling and steal in the shop, he could be convicted of burglary in the flat only if it could be said that he broke and entered the flat with intent to commit a felony therein, namely to break and enter the shop.[70] The difficulty about this argument is that while the breaking may reasonably be said to have occurred in the flat, the entering, strictly speaking, took place in the shop. On that view, there was no intent to commit a felony in the flat and it was not, therefore, burglary or house-breaking to break and enter it.

The effect on this situation of the Theft Act depends on what is the extent of a 'building'. **8.36** In its ordinary natural meaning, this term could certainly include a block of flats. If that meaning be adopted, D's entering Flat 1 as a trespasser with intent to pass through it, go upstairs and steal in Flat 45 is an entry of a building as a trespasser with intent to steal therein—that is, it is burglary. Similarly, the intending jewel thief would be guilty of burglary when he entered the flat above the jeweller's shop as a trespasser. The effect would be to make the full offence of what was previously, at the most, an attempt, and probably was only an act of preparation. There seems no good reason, however, why the law should not be extended in this way. On the contrary, there is everything to be said for enabling the police to intervene at the earliest possible moment to prevent such offences; and for forestalling defences such as 'I had no intention to steal in the flat—I was only using it as a passage to another flat which I never reached.' It is submitted, therefore, that the word 'building' should be given its natural meaning.

Part of a building

It is sufficient if the trespass takes place in part of a building so that one lodger may commit **8.37** burglary by entering the room of another lodger within the same house, or by entering the part of the house occupied by the landlord. A guest in a hotel may commit burglary by entering the room of another guest. A customer in a shop who goes behind the counter and takes money from the till during a short absence of the shopkeeper would be guilty of burglary even though he entered the shop with the shopkeeper's permission. The permission did not extend to his going behind the counter. It is enough that there is a defined area within the building into which D was not permitted to go and that he knew this when he entered the area or when he stole or attempted to steal, etc, within the area. It is not necessary that the building be permanently divided into parts. A temporary physical division is enough if it clearly marks out a part of the building into which D is not allowed to go. In *Walkington*,[71] there was a moveable, three-sided, rectangular counter in a shop. It was held that the rectangle bounded by the three sides of the counter was capable of being 'part' of the building. A customer who entered the area with intent to steal from the till on the counter was held to have knowingly entered that part of the building as a trespasser and to be guilty of burglary. In many modern open-plan stores, cash tills are not separated off from the

[69] cf *Wrigley* [1957] Crim LR 57.
[70] cf comment on *Wrigley* [1957] Crim LR 57.
[71] [1979] 2 All ER 716, [1979] Crim LR 526, CA.

shopping area but constitute a computer terminal on a table surrounded by merchandise. This cannot constitute a part of a building.[72]

8.38 Other problems arise over the scope of a 'part of a building'. Take a case put by the Criminal Law Revision Committee.[73] D enters a shop lawfully,[74] but conceals himself on the premises until closing time and then emerges with intent to steal. When concealing himself he may or may not have entered a part of the building to which customers are not permitted to go; but even if he did commit a trespass at this stage, he may not have done so with intent to commit an offence in that part of the building into which he has trespassed. For example, he hides in a cleaner's cupboard of a department store, intending to emerge and steal items of food from the shop displays. Entering the cupboard, though a trespass committed with intent to steal, is not burglary, for he has no intent to steal in the part of the building which he has entered as a trespasser. When he emerges from the cupboard after the shop has closed, he is a trespasser and it is submitted that he has entered a part of the building with intent to steal. He is just as much a trespasser as if he had been told in express terms to go, for he knows perfectly well that his licence to remain on the premises terminated when the shop closed.[75]

8.39 Suppose, however, having entered lawfully, he merely remained concealed behind a display in the main hall of the store. This was not a trespass because he had a right to be there. When he emerged and proceeded to steal, still in the main hall of the store, was he entering another part of the building? It is submitted that every step he took was 'as a trespasser', but it is difficult to see that he entered any part of the building as a trespasser; the whole transaction took place in a single part of the building which he had entered lawfully.

8.40 It would seem that the whole reason for the words 'or part of a building', is that D may enter or be in part of a building without trespass and it is desirable that he should be liable as a burglar if he trespasses in the remainder of the building with the necessary intent. It is submitted that the building need not be physically divided into 'parts'. It ought to be sufficient if a notice in the middle of a hall stated, 'No customers beyond this point'. These considerations suggest that, for present purposes, a building falls into two parts only: first, that part in which D was lawfully present and, second, the remainder of the building. This interpretation avoids anomalies which arise if physical divisions within a building are held to create 'parts'.[76]

8.41 Suppose, however, that D is lawfully in Flat 1, and that he can get to Flat 45 where he intends to steal only by trespassing into Flat 2. Suppose he is apprehended in Flat 2. He is guilty of burglary only if he can be shown to have intended to steal in 'the part of the building in question'. If Flat 2 is a separate part, he had no such intention and his act is probably

---

[72] *Walkington* (1979) 68 Cr App R 427, 434.

[73] CLRC, *Eighth Report*, Cmnd 2977 (1966) para 75.

[74] That is, without intent to steal; para 8.52.

[75] The CLRC thought, 'The case is not important, because the offender is likely to go into a part of the building where he has no right to be, and this will be a trespassory entry into that part.' But he has no right to be in any part of the building after closing time and the only question, it is submitted, is whether he went into another part.

[76] See para 8.37; Griew 4–24, n 49, finds this interpretation 'desirable but strained' and rejects it.

too remote to constitute an attempt to enter Flat 45. But it is very odd that entering Flat 1 (from outside where D lawfully was) as a trespasser with intent to steal in Flat 45 should be burglary, and entering Flat 2 as a trespasser (from Flat 1 where D lawfully was) with intent to steal in Flat 45 should be nothing. It is therefore submitted that, as physical divisions are unnecessary to create 'parts', so the existence of such divisions is insufficient to create them. If the building is divided into the part into which D may lawfully go and the part into which he may not, then Flats 2 and 45 are in the same 'part' of the building and D is guilty of burglary as soon as he enters Flat 2.

8.42 Is a row of terraced houses a single building?[77] Suppose D breaks into No 1, climbs into the rafters and makes his way above No 3, intending to continue to No 33, descend into the house and steal therein. Has he already committed burglary? It is difficult to discern any satisfactory principle by which this case can be distinguished from those of the block of flats and the flat above the shop considered above. In both the block of flats and the terrace a series of dwelling houses are contained within a single structure and it cannot matter that the arrangement is horizontal rather than vertical. It is true that there is internal communication between the flats; but it can hardly be said that the block of flats would cease to be 'a building' because access to them was confined to an external staircase. In policy and in principle there seems to be no reason why 'building' should not include the whole terrace.[78]

Inhabited vehicle or vessel

8.43 The obvious cases which are brought within the protection of burglary by this provision are a caravan or a houseboat which is someone's home. There seems to be no reason whatever why a home should lack the ordinary protection of the law because it is mobile. 'Inhabited' implies, not merely that there is someone inside the vehicle, but that someone is living there. My sports car is not an inhabited vehicle because I happen to be sitting in it when D enters against my will. The caravan or houseboat which is a person's home is, however, expressly protected, whether or not he is there at the time of the burglary. He may, for example, be away on his holidays.

8.44 The provision is not free from difficulty. Some people own 'dormobiles' or motorized caravans which they use for the ordinary purposes of a car during most of the year but on occasions they live in them, generally while on holiday. While the vehicle is being lived in, it is undoubtedly an inhabited vehicle. When it is being used for the ordinary purposes of a car, it is submitted that it is not an inhabited vehicle. The exact moment at which the dormobile becomes an inhabited vehicle may be difficult to ascertain. Is it when the family

---

[77] In *Hedley v Webb* [1901] 2 Ch 126, Cozens-Hardy J held that two semi-detached houses were a single building for the purpose of determining whether there was a sewer within the meaning of the Public Health Act 1875, s 4. In *Birch v Wigan Corpn* [1953] 1 QB 136, [1952] 2 All ER 893, CA, the Court of Appeal (Denning LJ dissenting) held that one house in a terrace of six was a 'house' within the meaning of s 11(1) and (4) of the Housing Act 1936 and not 'part of a building' within s 12 of that Act. But, since the sections were mutually exclusive, the house could not be both a 'house' and 'part of a building' for the purpose of the Act. Otherwise, Denning LJ would have been disposed to say that the house was both and Romer LJ also thought that 'for some purposes and in other contexts two "houses" may constitute one building'.
[78] cf Griew 4-23.

has loaded it with their belongings before departing on their holiday? When they take to the road on their journey to the seaside? When they park the vehicle at the place where they intend to sleep? Or when they actually go to sleep in the vehicle? It can hardly be later than that. Since the vehicle is not really distinguishable from any other family car going on holiday until it reaches its destination, it probably becomes 'inhabited' when it reaches the place at which it is to be used as a home. But does it then cease, for the time being, to be inhabited, if the family go for a spin in it next day? Is it burglary if a thief enters it in the car park of the swimming pool where they have gone for a swim? Similar problems arise when the holiday is concluding. If the answer tentatively suggested above regarding the beginning of the holiday is correct, then it ought to follow that when the vehicle embarks on its homeward journey, after the last night on which it is intended to sleep in it, it then ceases to be inhabited.[79]

8.45 Problems may also arise in connection with boats as living accommodation. Ships where the passengers or crew sleep aboard are clearly covered. The person who trespasses into a passenger's cabin on the *Queen Elizabeth II* in order to steal is clearly guilty of burglary.[80]

8.46 Difficult problems of *mens rea* may arise. According to ordinary principles, D should not be convicted unless he knew of the facts which make the thing entered 'a building' in law. Suppose D enters a dormobile parked by the side of the road. If he knew that V was living in the vehicle, there is no problem. But what if he did not know? In principle it would seem that he ought to be acquitted of burglary, unless it can be shown that he was at least reckless whether anyone was living there or not; and this seems to involve showing that the possibility was present to his mind.

Dwelling

8.47 Since the Criminal Justice Act 1991, it has become crucial to identify whether the building entered is a dwelling, rendering the offence a 'domestic burglary' for sentencing purposes. This issue is discussed below.

Mens rea

Intention to enter as a trespasser; or knowledge of having trespassed

8.48 As pointed out above,[81] it must be proved on a charge under s 9(1)(a) that D intended[82] to enter, knowing of the facts which, in law, made his entry trespassory; or, at least, being reckless whether such facts existed; and, on a charge under s 9(1)(b), that, at the time of committing the ulterior offence, D knew of or was subjectively reckless as to the facts which

---

[79] Query the protection for the unoccupied boat or caravan, which is visited and lived in only during holidays. Is this capable of being burgled? See ATH Smith, *Property Offences* (1994) para 28–39 (no); Williams, *TBCL* 841 (yes); Griew 4–27 (no).

[80] Presumably, in such a case, the trespass is committed against the owners since, under modern conditions, they, and not the master, are in possession of the ship: *The Jupiter (No 3)* [1927] P 122 at 131; affirmed [1927] P 250, CA. The passengers would seem to be in the same situation as the guests in a hotel. See para 8.28.

[81] See para 8.16.

[82] Burglary is a crime of specific intent for the purposes of the law in relation to intoxication: *Durante* [1972] 1 WLR 1612.

had made his entry a trespass. If, in a case under either paragraph, D sets up an honest belief in a right to enter, it should be for the Crown to prove the belief was not held.

The ulterior offence

It must be proved that D, either —   **8.49**

(a) entered with intent [83] to commit one of the following offences:
    (i) stealing,
    (ii) inflicting grievous bodily harm,
    (iii) unlawful damage to the building or anything therein; or
(b) entered and committed or attempted to commit one of the following:
    (i) stealing,
    (ii) inflicting grievous bodily harm.

It is unclear whether the availability of the charge of burglary under s 9(1)(b) where D has   **8.50**
entered the building as a trespasser and then committed or attempted to commit theft or grievous bodily harm is a recognition of the difficulty the prosecution might face in proving that D held the relevant intention at the time of the entry, or whether it is to reflect the aggravated nature of the theft/grievous bodily harm given that it is committed by a trespasser in a building.[84]

For some time the law of burglary was bedevilled by the ruling in *Husseyn*,[85] that 'it cannot   **8.51**
be said that one who has it in mind to steal only if what he finds is worth stealing has a present intention to steal'; but in *A-G's References (Nos 1 and 2 of 1979)*[86] these difficulties were substantially eliminated. It is now clear that, for the purposes of burglary, a person who enters intending to steal only if he finds something he thinks worth stealing has a sufficient *mens rea*. He may be interested only in money, which may or may not be on the premises, or in a particular item which may or may not be there. He has a sufficient intention to steal. The problem of *Husseyn* lingers on only in one rare type of case—where D intends to steal a specific thing only if he decides that the specific thing is worth stealing. He intends to take V's necklace—but only if, on examining it, he finds the pearls are real and not paste. *Husseyn* was distinguished, not overruled, and it seems that it continues to apply to this case. The result is strange. An intention to steal anything at all that comes to hand, if it is worth stealing, is an intention to steal; but an intention to steal a specific thing, if it is worth stealing, is not.[87]

Stealing

This clearly means theft, contrary to s 1. So an entry with the intention of dishonestly using   **8.52**
electricity contrary to s 13 is not burglary.[88] Nor is it enough to prove that D has entered

---

[83] For an example of a conviction being quashed owing to the use of the word 'recklessness' in this context, see *A v DPP* [2003] EWHC 1676 (Admin).
[84] Griew prefers the former, para 4-28.
[85] (1978) 67 Cr App R 131 n at 132.
[86] [1980] QB 180, [1979] 3 All ER 143, CA; above, para 2.327.
[87] cf commentaries on *Walkington* [1979] 2 All ER 716, [1979] Crim LR 526 and *A-G's References (Nos 1 and 2 of 1979)* [1980] QB 180, [1979] Crim LR 585.
[88] *Low v Blease* [1975] Crim LR 513; para 11.01.

with intent to commit an offence under the 1978 Act or the Fraud Act 2006. Prior to the Fraud Act 2006, and the abolition of the deception offences, there was considerable overlap between those offences and theft. From the decision of the House of Lords in *Gomez*,[89] D's intention to obtain property (other than land) by deception was also an intention to steal. For example, D, who entered V's 'trade only' warehouse by falsely representing that he is in the trade, induces V, by a further deception, to sell him a television set at trade prices. His intention to obtain by deception was an intention to steal; and his obtaining the set was theft; so he might also have been convicted of burglary under either s 9(1)(a) or 9(1)(b). A trespasser who receives stolen goods in the building is a burglar, either as a party to the continuing theft by others or by the theft he commits himself.[90]

Inflicting grievous bodily harm

8.53   The intention to inflict grievous bodily harm in s 9(1)(a) must be an intention to commit an offence. The offence in question would be causing grievous bodily harm with intent to do so, contrary to s 18 of the Offences Against the Person Act 1861. It is arguable that s 23 of that Act may also be a qualifying offence since it involves administering or causing to be administered poisons or noxious substances so as thereby to endanger life or *inflict* grievous bodily harm.

8.54   Section 9(1)(b), however, does not use the word 'offence' but simply requires that D inflicts or attempts to inflict on any person in the building any grievous bodily harm. The omission of the word 'offence' is in fact a legislative accident;[91] but in *Jenkins*[92] the Court of Appeal held that the infliction need not amount to an offence of any kind. They gave this example:

> An intruder gains access to the house without breaking in (where there is an open window for instance).[93] He is on the premises as a trespasser and his intrusion is observed by someone in the house of whom he may not even be aware, and as a result that person suffers a severe shock, with a resulting stroke . . . Should such an event fall outside the provisions of s. 9 when causing some damage to property falls fairly within it?

This is a question (in its context) plainly expecting the answer, no'. It is submitted that the right answer is an emphatic 'yes'. Otherwise a person may become guilty of burglary in consequence of a wholly unforeseen and unforeseeable event. The analogy with damage to property is misplaced. Causing damage to property does not fall within the provisions of s 9(1)(b). There must be an actual intention to cause damage at the time of the trespassory entry. This requires a *mens rea* which is wholly absent in the example put by the court. The House of Lords allowed the appeal[94] in *Jenkins* but on a different point and no allusion was made to the interpretation by the Court of Appeal of s 9(1)(b). The case, therefore,

---

[89]   Para 2.22.

[90]   *Gregory* (1982) 77 Cr App R 41, [1981] Crim LR 229 and commentary.

[91]   See JC Smith, 'Burglary under the Theft Bill' [1968] Crim LR 367 and commentary on *Jenkins* [1983] 1 All ER 1000, [1983] Crim LR 386, CA.

[92]   [1983] 1 All ER 1000, at 1002. cf *Watson* (1989) 139 NLJ 866, CA. (Death caused after entry is caused in the course of committing an offence under s 9(1)(a).)

[93]   The relevance of the absence of breaking is obscure.

[94]   [1984] AC 242, [1983] 3 All ER 448, [1984] Crim LR 36 and commentary.

stands as an authority—but, it is submitted, a bad one. When para (b) is read in the context of s 9(1) and (2) it is reasonably clear that the infliction of bodily harm required must be an offence—in effect, under s 18 or s 20 (and arguably s 23) of the Offences Against the Person Act 1861.[95]

Whether or not this interpretation of para (b) is correct, it is now established that a jury **8.55** may acquit D of burglary contrary to s 9(1)(b) and convict him on the same count of inflicting grievous bodily harm contrary to s 20 of the 1861 Act—the latter offence is included in the former for the purposes of s 6(3) of the Criminal Law Act 1967.

What if D enters with intent to murder? It would be very strange if an entry with intent to **8.56** inflict grievous bodily harm amounted to burglary, and an entry with intent to murder did not. It is submitted that the greater includes the less and that an intention to kill, whether by inflicting physical injuries or by poisoning, is enough.

Unlawful damage to the building or anything therein

The damage intended must be such that to cause it would amount to an offence. It is an **8.57** offence under s 1 of the Criminal Damage Act 1971, intentionally or recklessly to destroy or damage any property belonging to another.[96]

Arguably s 9(1)(b) ought to be extended to create an offence of burglary where D enters **8.58** as a trespasser and subsequently when in the building, forms the intention to damage property and does so therein. The basis for the restriction of the s 9(1)(b) offence to theft and violence to the exclusion of property damage is not obviously clear.

Object of ulterior offence must be 'therein'

Is it necessary that the object of the ulterior crime be in the building before the trespassory **8.59** entry? In other words, is it burglary if D drags V into a barn with intent to rob, or inflict grievous bodily harm on him?[97] Similarly, it might be asked what of D who enters with the aim of removing a piece of property to damage it outside. Must it be proved only that in relation to the building or part thereof the property was 'therein' or that the damage would occur 'therein'? The words of the section do not supply a clear answer, but the purpose of the offence—the protection of persons and things in a building—suggests that the crime does not extend to these cases.

Burglary in Respect of a Dwelling

As noticed above[98] burglary in respect of a dwelling, whether contrary to 9(1)(a) or 9(1)(b) **8.60** of the Act, now appears to be a separate offence—a new aggravated form of burglary. Arguably, this represents a return to the origins of the offence being a crime against

---

[95] If this offence is included within s 9(1)(b), that form of the offence of burglary might be a basic intent offence, but cf *Heard* [2007] EWCA Crim 125.

[96] See *Smith and Hogan, Criminal Law* ch 24.

[97] See S White, 'Lurkers, Draggers and Kidnappers' (1986) 150 JP 37, 56.

[98] Above, para 8.04.

'habitation',[99] and has significance in labelling the conduct appropriately. The only constituent of the offence that requires consideration is 'dwelling'; but it must be looked at in respect of both *actus reus* and *mens rea*.

Actus reus

8.61 'Dwelling' is not defined but it presumably means substantially the same as 'dwelling house' in the former offence of burglary at common law and under the Larceny Acts[100]—a building or, now, a vehicle or vessel, in which someone lives as his home. Where the places are different, a person dwells in that place where he sleeps, not that where he spends his waking hours. A building, such as a block of flats, may contain many dwellings. A hotel room is probably not a dwelling unless the particular inhabitant does live there as his home. Premises which have become a dwelling will not cease to be one because of the temporary absence of the inhabitants, provided that at least one of them intends to return. A person normally dwells in the place where he sleeps; but he may have more than one dwelling as where he has a flat in London and a house in the country. The dormobile considered in para 8.44, above, will probably be a dwelling while the family is living in it, but will cease to be a dwelling when they stop doing so.

Mens rea

8.62 As 'dwelling' is an aggravating element in the offence warranting a higher maximum sentence of imprisonment, it should, in principle, import a requirement of *mens rea*. A person who commits burglary in a dwelling should be convicted only of simple burglary if he believed that no one lived there. But, in principle and by analogy to the construction of 'as a trespasser' in *Collins*,[101] recklessness should be enough. If D entered knowing that someone might be living there, and someone was, he should be guilty of burglary in respect of a dwelling.

Sentencing

8.63 On conviction for a domestic burglary after 30 November 1999 if D has two convictions on separate occasions for domestic burglaries, both of which were committed after 30 November 1999, and s/he was 18 or over at the date of commission of the third burglary, D is liable to a minimum term of imprisonment for a period of three years under the provisions of s 111 Powers of Criminal Courts (Sentencing) Act 2000.

---

[99] E Christian (ed), *Commentaries on the Laws of England*, by Sir William Blackstone (17th edn, 1830) iv. 220.

[100] *Smith and Hogan, Criminal Law* (1st edn, 1965) 399; *Russell on Crime* 826. cf Public Order Act 1986, s 8: ' "dwelling" means any structure or part of a structure occupied as a person's home or as other living accommodation (whether the occupation is separate or shared with others) but does not include any part not so occupied, and for this purpose "structure" includes a tent, caravan, vehicle, vessel or other temporary or movable structure.' Cf Terrorism Act 2000, s 121: ' "dwelling" means a building or part of a building used as a dwelling, and a vehicle which is habitually stationary and which is used as a dwelling . . .'

[101] Para 8.06, above.

Domestic burglary

Domestic burglary has always been regarded as a serious offence by the courts.[102] In the case of *McInerney; Keating*[103] the Court of Appeal gave guidance as to sentencing levels in domestic burglary cases. The guidance relates to convictions after trial and categorizes offences according to the level of seriousness. The fact of a guilty plea would, of course, give rise to an appropriate discount.[104]

8.64

The Court of Appeal in *McInerney* influenced by the Sentence Advisory Panel's proposals, categorized burglary offences as follows: (i) low-level domestic burglaries; (ii) a domestic burglary displaying most of the features of a standard domestic burglary;[105] (iii) a standard domestic burglary which additionally displays any one of the 'medium relevance' factors;[106] and, (iv) a standard domestic burglary which additionally displays any one of the 'high relevance' factors.[107] Categories (ii)–(iv) above involve the concept of a 'standard domestic burglary'. A 'standard domestic burglary' would have the following features: (i) committed by a repeat offender, (ii) would involve the theft of electrical goods, (iii) the theft of personal items, (iv) damage as a result of the break-in, (iv) some turmoil in the house, (v) no injury or violence, but some trauma caused to the victim.

8.65

Medium-level aggravating features are:

8.66

  (i) a vulnerable victim, although not targeted as such,
  (ii) the victim was at home (whether day-time or night-time burglary),
 (iii) goods of high value were taken (economic or sentimental),
 (iv) the burglars worked in a group.

High-level aggravating features are:

  (i) force used or threatened against the victim,
  (ii) victim injured (as a result of force used or threatened),
 (iii) the especially traumatic effect on the victim, in excess of the trauma generally associated with a standard burglary,
 (iv) professional planning, organization or execution,[108]
  (v) vandalism of the premises, in excess of the damage generally associated with a standard burglary,
 (vi) the offence was racially aggravated,
(vii) a vulnerable victim deliberately targeted (including cases of 'deception' or 'distraction' of the elderly).

---

[102] See *Brewster* [1998] 1 Cr App R 220 at 225 per Lord Bingham CJ.
[103] [2003] 1 Cr App R 36.
[104] Where s 111 of the Powers of Criminal Courts (Sentencing) Act 2000 applies the maximum discount is limited to 20 per cent of the determinate sentence of at least three years.
[105] See 8.60.
[106] See 8.66.
[107] See 8.66.
[108] The number of offences for which an offender falls to be sentenced may indicate that he is a professional burglar, which is a high-level aggravating feature.

8.67 In *McInnery*, the court agreed with the Panel that mitigating factors should include:

 (i) a first offence,
 (ii) nothing, or only property of very low value, is stolen,
 (iii) the offender played only a minor part in the burglary,
 (iv) there is no damage or disturbance to the property.

It was also observed that the fact that the crime was committed on impulse, the offender's age or state of health, physical or mental, evidence of genuine remorse, response to previous sentences, and ready cooperation with the police would be capable of being mitigating features in a case of domestic burglaries.

8.68 The Court of Appeal noted the starting points recommend by the Panel in relation to the each of the four categories identified above.[109] Whilst accepting that a community sentence would generally be appropriate in cases involving low-level domestic burglaries, the court rejected the stepped approach to sentencing proposed by the Panel and suggested that a community sentence should be the starting point for cases where the court would otherwise be considering a starting point of up to eighteen months' imprisonment.

Non-domestic burglary

8.69 The maximum penalty for burglary other than from a dwelling is ten years' imprisonment on indictment, six months or a fine not exceeding the statutory maximum, or both, summarily (s 9(4)). Burglary of a non-dwelling is regarded as slightly less serious than domestic burglaries.

Aggravated Burglary

8.70 By s 10 of the Theft Act:

(1) A person is guilty of aggravated burglary if he commits any burglary and at the time has with him any firearm or imitation firearm, any weapon of offence, or any explosive; and for this purpose —
  (a) 'firearm' includes an airgun or air pistol and 'imitation firearm' means anything which has the appearance of being a firearm, whether capable of being discharged or not; and
  (b) 'weapon of offence' means any article made or adapted for use for causing injury to or incapacitating a person, or intended by the person having it with him for such use; and
  (c) 'explosive' means any article manufactured for the purpose of producing a practical effect by explosion, or intended by the person having it with him for that purpose.
(2) A person guilty of aggravated burglary shall on conviction on indictment be liable to imprisonment for life.

8.71 The reason given by the Criminal Law Revision Committee for the creation of this offence is that 'burglary when in possession of the articles mentioned . . . is so serious that it should in our opinion be punishable with imprisonment for life. The offence is comparable with robbery (which will be so punishable). It must be extremely frightening to those in the building, and it might well lead to loss of life.'[110]

---

[109] See above, para 8.42.
[110] CLRC, *Eighth Report*, Cmnd 2977 (1966) para 80.

The articles of aggravation

'Firearm' is not defined in the Act, except to the extent that it includes an airgun or air **8.72** pistol. It is possible that the courts will seek guidance as to the meaning of this term from the definition in the Firearms Act 1968, s 57(1). The expression is given a wide meaning in that Act, however, and it does not necessarily follow that it should bear a similarly wide meaning in the Theft Act. Thus the definition includes any component part of a firearm, but the natural meaning of the term does not include parts. If I have the body locking pin of a Bren gun in my pocket, no one would say I was carrying a firearm. As the statutory definition has not been incorporated in the Theft Act, which could easily have been done, it is submitted that the word should not be given a meaning any wider than that which it naturally bears; and that, therefore, the term 'imitation firearm' should be similarly limited.[111]

The definition of 'weapon of offence' is slightly wider than that of 'offensive weapon' in **8.73** s 1(4) of the Prevention of Crime Act 1953. It would seem that (i) articles made for causing injury to a person, (ii) articles adapted for causing injury to a person, and (iii) articles which D has with him for that purpose are precisely the same as under the 1953 Act.[112] Thus, (i) would include a rifle, or bayonet, a revolver, a cosh, knuckleduster, dagger, or flick-knife;[113] (ii) would include razor blades inserted in a potato, a bottle broken for the purpose, a chair leg studded with nails; and (iii) would include anything that could cause injury to the person if so desired by the person using it—a sheath-knife, a razor, a shotgun, a sandbag, a pick-axe handle, a bicycle chain or a stone.[114] To these categories, however, s 10(1)(b) adds (iv) any article made for incapacitating a person, (v) any article adapted for incapacitating a person, and (vi) any article which D has with him for that purpose. Articles made for incapacitating a person might include a pair of handcuffs and a gag; articles adapted for incapacitating a person might include a pair of socks made into a gag, and articles intended for incapacitating a person might include sleeping pills to put in the night-watchman's tea, a rope to tie him up, a sack to put over his head, pepper to throw in his face, and so on.

In the cases of (i), (ii), (iv), and (v) the prosecution need prove no more than that the article **8.74** was made or adapted for use for causing injury or incapacitating as the case may be. In the cases of (iii) and (vi) clearly they must go further and prove that D was carrying the thing with him with the intention of using it to injure or incapacitate, not necessarily in any event, but at least if the need arose. It is not necessary to prove that D intended to use the article in the course of the burglary. It is enough that he had it with him for such use on another occasion.[115]

---

[111] A defendant's fingers positioned under a coat to resemble a firearm could not be considered to be an imitation firearm for the purposes of the Firearms Act 1968, s 17. One could not possess one's fingers, they are part of oneself: *Bentham* [2005] UKHL 18.
[112] *Smith and Hogan, Criminal Law* 582.
[113] *Gibson v Wales* [1983] 1 All ER 869, DC; *Simpson* [1984] Crim LR 39, CA.
[114] *Harrison v Thornton* [1966] Crim LR 388.
[115] *Stones* [1989] 1 WLR 156, CA, criticized by NJ Reville, 'Mischief of Aggravated Burglary' [1989] 139 NLJ 835. cf *Allamby* [1974] 3 All ER 126, [1974] 1 WLR 1494, CA.

8.75 The definition of 'explosive' closely follows that in s 3(1) of the Explosives Act 1875 which, after enumerating various explosives, adds:

> . . . and every other substance, whether similar to those above mentioned or not, used or manufactured with a view to produce a practical effect by explosion or by a pyrotechnic effect . . .

It will be observed that the definition in the Theft Act is narrower. The Explosives Act, if read literally, is wide enough to include a box of matches—these produce a 'pyrotechnic effect'; but it seems clear that a box of matches would not be an 'explosive' under the Theft Act.

8.76 The main difficulty about the definition—and this is unlikely to be important in practice—lies in determining the meaning of 'practical effect'. Perhaps it serves to exclude fireworks which, so it has been said in connection with another Act, are 'things that are made for amusement',[116] but if the thing is intended to produce 'a practical effect', it is immaterial that it was not manufactured for that purpose and that it is incapable of doing so. What then of the distress flare which can be fired from a gun?

At the time of commission of burglary

8.77 It must be proved that D had the article of aggravation with him at the time of committing the burglary. Where the charge is one of entry with intent (s 9(1)(a)) this is clearly at the time of entry. Where the charge is one of committing a specified offence, having entered (9(1)(b)), it is at the time of commission of the specified offence.

8.78 Burglary is not aggravated merely because a weapon is used against the occupier outside the building or is held by an accomplice in a getaway car.[117] If D, having entered as a trespasser, is armed when he commits the specified offence, he is then guilty of aggravated burglary,[118] though he entered unarmed and whether or not he intended to commit a specified offence at the time of entry. If he did have such an intention, he is guilty of both simple and aggravated burglary. An armed person who discards his weapon before entry can be guilty of no more than simple burglary. An armed person who enters as a trespasser but without intent and discards his weapon before committing a specified offence is guilty only of simple burglary.[119] Whether D who arms himself only to escape, having already completed the burglary (for example, by stealing), is guilty of the aggravated offence is debatable.[120] By analogy with the court's approach in *Watson*,[121] and the courts' willingness to treat theft act offences as continuing[122] it is likely that the offence would be held to have been committed.

---

[116] *Bliss v Lilley* (1862) 32 LJMC 3, per Cockburn CJ and Blackburn J; but Wightman J thought that a fog-signal was a 'firework'. For the definition of firework see now the regulations made under s 1 of the Fireworks Act 2003.
[117] *Klass* [1998] 1 Cr App R 453, CA.
[118] *O'Leary* (1986) 82 Cr App R 341, CA.
[119] cf *Francis* [1982] Crim LR 363, CA.
[120] See ATH Smith, *Property Offences* (1994) para 28–61.
[121] *Watson* (1989) 89 Cr App R 211, CA.
[122] *Atakpu* (1994) 98 Cr App R 254, CA 2.104.

Has with him

This phrase denotes a narrower concept than possession. A burglar who leaves a gun locked   **8.79**
up at home when he sets out on his night's work is in possession of the gun but plainly
does not have it with him. It has been held that the phrase, as used in the Firearms Act 1968,
s 18 (1), 'imports an element of propinquity' but is not to be read as 'to have immediately
available'.[123] D need not be carrying the article: *Pawlicki*.[124] In that case there was held to
be sufficient evidence—the question is one of fact—that D had guns 'with him', with
intent to commit a robbery, when they were in a car fifty yards from an auction room which
was alleged to be the scene of a planned robbery. The court stated that it was adopting
a 'purposive approach'. The purpose of the Firearms Act might be held to be different from
that of the Theft Act; but the decision is persuasive. If D had entered the auction room as a
trespasser, it is arguable that he might have been convicted of aggravated burglary.[125] Under
legislation in Northern Ireland similar to s 10, it was held,[126] before *Pawlicki*, that it must
be proved that D entered, or was on the premises, as an armed man, so that a burglar who
left his pistol in a car across the road would not be guilty of the offence. Where D1 enters
a building with D2 as trespassers with intent to inflict grievous bodily harm on a person
therein and D1 knows that D2 carries a firearm, D1 has that firearm with him and both are
guilty under s 10.[127]

It was held in *Cugullere*,[128] where the weapon may have been inserted in D's van without   **8.80**
his knowledge, that the words in the Prevention of Crime Act 1953 mean '*knowingly* has
with him'. It is certainly arguable that the court was concerned only with that minimum
mental element which is necessary to constitute possession. But in *Russell* [129] it was held in
a reserved judgment that the court in *Cugullere* was 'applying the general principle of
responsibility which makes it incumbent on the prosecution to prove full *mens rea*' in the
sense that D must be proved to have known that he had the thing which is an offensive
weapon. It was held that, where D had known of the weapon but had completely forgotten
its existence, he was to be treated as if he had never known it was there at all. *Russell* was misunderstood in *Martindale* [130] which was followed by *McCalla*,[131] holding it to be no defence
to having a cosh that D had picked it up a month ago, put it in the glove compartment of
his car, and forgotten about it. *McCalla* was followed on similar facts in *Wright*.[132] The prevailing view, therefore, is that the offence is one of strict liability; but the better opinion is
that *Russell*, though treated as overruled, should be regarded as the binding authority.[133]

---

[123] In respect of the Firearms Act offence, it has been held that the question of propinquity is to be
approached in a commonsense way. A person could not therefore be said to 'have with him' a firearm two or
three miles away: *Bradish* [2004] EWCA Crim 1341, (2004) 148 SJ 474, CA.
[124] [1992] 3 All ER 902, CA explaining *Kelt* [1977] 3 All ER 1099, CA.
[125] Professor ATH Smith thinks not: *Property Offences* (1994) 28–54. cf Griew, 4–43.
[126] *Murphy, Lillis and Burns* [1971] NI 193.
[127] *Jones* [1979] CLY 411.
[128] [1961] 2 All ER 343 at 344.
[129] (1984) 81 Cr App R 315, [1985] Crim LR 231, CA.
[130] [1986] 3 All ER 25, (1986) 84 Cr App R 31, CA.
[131] (1988) 87 Cr App R 372, CA.
[132] [1992] Crim LR 596, CA.
[133] See commentary on *Wright* [1992] Crim LR 596.

8.81 In the recent case of *Jolie*[134] D was found in possession of a knife in a car he was driving and claimed that he had forgotten it was there although he admitted putting it there as he had used it to start the broken ignition. Kennedy LJ suggested that in the cases of *McCalla*, *Martindale*, and *Buswell* it had been clear that the article had remained under D's control. His lordship suggested that the jury should be directed that they may find possession if either D was aware of the presence of the weapon or he was responsible for putting it where it was mislaid. Similarly as in *Glidewell* [135] where a taxi-driver discovered weapons left by a passenger, and forgot to remove them because he was busy.

8.82 As regards the relevant *mens rea* as to the offensiveness of the weapon, in *Densu*[136] counsel abandoned an argument before the Court of Appeal that the ruling of the trial judge was wrong insofar as it suggested that the proof that D has with him an offensive weapon is satisfied on proof that D knew that he had the weapon (a baton) with him but did not know that it was a weapon. The prevailing view is that liability is strict. In principle (though neither *Cugullere* nor *Russell* decides this) it should be necessary to prove that D knew that the thing had those characteristics which make it an offensive weapon within the meaning of the Act. The question is not merely one of possession, as in the law relating to possession of controlled drugs,[137] but of *mens rea*. It does not seem right that no fault should be required with respect to the element which converts a ten or fourteen-year offence into one carrying life imprisonment.[138]

8.83 It has been decided under the Prevention of Crime Act 1953, in effect overruling earlier decisions, that a person carrying an inoffensive article for an innocent purpose does not become guilty of having an offensive weapon with him merely because he uses that article for an offensive purpose.[139] The 1953 Act is directed against the carrying of articles intended to be used as weapons, not against the use of an article as a weapon. It was to be expected that the same construction would be put upon the similar words of s 10 of the Theft Act, but in *Kelly*[140] it was held that D, who had used a screwdriver to effect an entry, became guilty of aggravated burglary when he used it to prod V in the stomach. The court purported to apply the ordinary meaning of the words of the subsection; but they seem indistinguishable in this respect from the words of the Prevention of Crime Act; and the same considerations of policy seem applicable to the two provisions. *Kelly* seems a dubious decision.

---

[134] [2003] EWCA Crim 1543, [2003] Crim LR 730.
[135] (1999) 163 JP 557.
[136] [1998] 1 Cr App R 400.
[137] *Warner v Metropolitan Police Comr* [1969] 2 AC 256, [1968] 2 All ER 356, HL.
[138] It must, however, be noted that, under the Firearms Act 1968, it is unnecessary to prove that D knew the thing he used was a firearm within the meaning of the Act.
[139] *Dayle* [1973] 3 All ER 1151.
[140] (1992) 97 Cr App R 245, [1993] Crim LR 763 and commentary.

It has also been held under the 1953 Act that no offence is committed where a person **8.84** arms himself with a weapon for instant attack on his victim;[141] but, if *Kelly* is right, it seems that that decision can hardly apply to s 10. So if D is interrupted in the course of stealing after a trespassory entry, and picks up an inkstand (or any object) and throws it with intent to cause injury, he will thereby become guilty of aggravated burglary. He could be adequately dealt with by a second count charging whatever offence against the person he has committed; and it is submitted that this is the proper course. On the other hand, if D picked up a stone outside the house to use as a weapon if he should be disturbed after entry, the subsequent burglary would properly be held to be aggravated. Here D has armed himself before an occasion to use violence has arisen; and the stone is a weapon of offence.

Sentencing

Sentences are generally high, especially where the victim is vulnerable. In *O'Driscoll*,[142] **8.85** which seems to have obtained the status of a guideline case, a sentence of fifteen years was upheld.

Trespass with Intent to Commit a Sexual Offence

Section 63 of the Sexual Offences Act 2003 introduces a new offence to replace burglary **8.86** with intent to rape.[143]

(1) A person commits an offence if—
    (a) he is a trespasser on any premises,
    (b) he intends to commit a relevant sexual offence on the premises, and
    (c) he knows that, or is reckless as to whether, he is a trespasser.
(2) In this section—
    'premises' includes a structure or part of a structure;
    'relevant sexual offence' [is all those in that Part of the Act];
    'structure' includes a tent, vehicle or vessel or other temporary or movable structure.

The offence is significantly wider in a number of respects than the form of burglary it **8.87** replaces. Any trespass is sufficient and there is no need to prove a trespassory *entry*. The trespass may arise as a result of D exceeding permission as regards the purpose for which entry was granted or exceeding permission in terms of the areas or parts of premises entered. The trespass relates to 'premises', which is wider than the concept of a building or part of a building.[144] It is a term used in many statutes, including criminal ones, and

---

[141] *Ohlson v Hylton* [1975] 2 All ER 490; *Giles* [1976] Crim LR 253; *Bates v Bulman* [1979] 3 All ER 170, (1979) 68 Cr App R 21; *C v DPP* [2002] Crim LR 322.

[142] (1986) 8 Cr App R (S) 121.

[143] See generally P Rook and R Ward, *Sexual Offences: Law and Practice* (2004), 393.

[144] 'Structure' is a term used in numerous statutes, but its interpretation is heavily dependent on context. A recent example is the Criminal Justice and Police Act 2001, where s 66 provides: ' "premises" includes any vehicle, stall or moveable structure (including an offshore installation) and any other place whatever, whether or not occupied as land'. Section 48 of the RIPA 2000 similarly provides that 'premises' includes any vehicle or moveable structure and any other place whatever, whether or not occupied as land. This suggests that structure is wider than building.

is usually widely construed.[145] Technically it could extend to all areas of land which could be the subject of a lease. This will include open spaces (fields and parks). The concept of 'structure' is widely defined: it will include a car or van and presumably a telephone kiosk or such.

8.88 As with s 9(1)(a) there is no need for the ulterior (sexual) offence to occur, indeed, there is no need for any intended victim to be on the premises. This is a form of inchoate offence.

8.89 The list of ulterior offences to which this section applies is much wider than purely rape, as under the old law; it extends to all those in Part 1 of the 2003 Act. These include rape, sexual penetration, sexual assault, causing a person to enagage in a sexual act, child sex offences, and many more.[146]

8.90 As with burglary, the *mens rea* of the offence requires that D have knowledge or subjective recklessness[147] as to the facts that render him a trespasser and proof that D intended to perform the relevant sexual offence.

Sentencing

8.91 The offence is triable summarily or on indictment and has a maximum penalty of ten years. The Sentencing Advisory Panel[148] suggests that the main factors determining the seriousness of a preparatory offence are—

- the seriousness of the intended offence (which will affect both the offender's culpability and the degree of risk to which the victim has been exposed);
- the degree to which the offence was planned;
- the degree of determination of the offender;
- how close the offender came to success;
- the reason why the offender did not succeed i.e. was it a change of mind or did someone or something prevent him from continuing?
- any physical or psychological injury suffered by the victim;
- the vulnerability of the victim (but where the victim's vulnerability is an integral feature of the offence, as in meeting a child following sexual grooming etc, this should not be treated as an additional aggravating factor).

8.92 The Panel recommended that the starting point sentences ought to be:

- five years' custody—where the intent is to commit assault by penetration or rape and the victim is an adult;
- eight years' custody—where the intent is to commit assault by penetration or rape and the victim is a child under 16.

---

[145] For example, in the Criminal Law Act 1977, 'premises' means any building, any part of a building under separate occupation, any land ancillary to a building, the site comprising any building or buildings together with any land ancillary thereto: s 12(1)(a).

[146] See *Smith and Hogan, Criminal Law* ch 17.

[147] This is one of the few offences in the Act that includes a reckless *mens rea* element.

[148] *Sentencing Guidelines on Sexual Offences: Consultation Paper* (2004).

- where the intended sex offence was other than rape or assault by penetration—a lower starting point of three years is suggested where the intended victim is an adult; five years where the intended victim is a child.

Early cases on sentencing for the s 63 offence include *Fulton*[149] in which on a plea, the Court of Appeal substituted a sentence of two years' imprisonment where D had forced his way into the house of a 60-year-old woman and forced her to watch him masturbate.[150] **8.93**

After completion of the manuscipt the Sentencing Guidelines Council have issued final guidance on sexual offences (May 2007). In relation to s 63, the recommended starting point for a trespass with intent to commit rape or penetration is 4 years and for other cases 2 years.[151] **8.94**

---

[149] [2006] EWCA Crim 960.
[150] See also *C* [2006] EWCA Crim 1024 and *Ralston* [2005] EWCA Crim 3279.
[151] See further <http://www.sentencing-guidelines.gov.uk/docs/0000_SexualOffencesAct1.pdf>

9

GOING EQUIPPED AND POSSESSION OF ARTICLES TO COMMIT FRAUD

Introduction

Many of the offences in the Theft Acts and Fraud Act have been criticized for their consid- **9.01**
erable breadth particularly in view of the generally wide interpretations that have been
adopted by the courts. Thus, for example, it is possible for D to be convicted of theft from
the moment that he touches an item or acts in a way that assumes any single right of
an owner, provided he has the proscribed state of mind.[1] Similarly, it is possible for D to
be convicted of burglary where he has only entered as a trespasser with a proscribed intent.[2]
With fraud, the entire basis of the new Act is that the offences are committed without
proof of any consequential loss to the victim, without proof of an intention permanently
to deprive, nor even any proof of an effect on the victim's state of mind or any imperilling
of his economic interests. The making of, for example, a false representation with the
dishonest intent suffices for a conviction. The breadth of these offences is obvious. Couple
that with the availability of charges of attempted theft or fraud where D need only be
shown to have gone beyond an act of mere preparation, and it will be obvious that the reach
of the criminal law in this area is vast. It may seem somewhat surprising then for the
Acts to contain offences which criminalize conduct of a more preliminary nature than
even attempt.

The Theft Act 1968 introduced an offence of 'going equipped', which was based on the **9.02**
preliminary offences found in the Larceny Acts. This singles out as a separate wrong worthy

---

[1] See the discussion of *Gomez* [1993] AC 442 and *Hinks* [2001] 2 AC 241 above, para 2.22.
[2] See s 9(1)(a) above.

of criminalization the conduct of a person who is in the process of preparing himself to commit the relevant offences—theft, burglary (and when originally enacted cheat) by possessing articles to do so. The offence is qualified by a requirement that the defendant must have at least left his home, although there is no need for him to be on his way to commit the offence at the time he is found in possession of the offending articles.

9.03 The Fraud Act 2006, s 6 goes further still by criminalizing the possession or control of items for fraud even where that possession is exclusively within the accused's own home. It is a strikingly wide offence not only because it criminalizes conduct of an even more preliminary nature than attempted fraud or going equipped, and in doing so infringes the respect for a persons' privacy in the home, but also because it is capable of applying to entirely innocuous articles such as a computer and a printer, or a pen and paper. It is no exaggeration to say that unless the courts construe the offence in a narrow fashion by reading in *mens rea* the entire adult population may be committing the offence.

Going Equipped[3]

9.04 By s 25(1) and (2) of the Theft Act:

(1) A person shall be guilty of an offence if, when not at his place of abode, he has with him any article for use in the course of or in connection with any burglary, theft or cheat.

(2) A person guilty of an offence under this section shall on conviction on indictment be liable to imprisonment for a term not exceeding three years.

9.05 This offence replaced the more complicated provisions contained in the Larceny Act 1916, s 28. The 1916 Act was directed chiefly against, though it was not limited to, preparatory acts in contemplation of offences of breaking and entering.[4] Section 25 is expressed to be directed against acts preparatory to:

(i) burglary contrary to s 9, Theft Act 1968
(ii) theft contrary to s 1, Theft Act 1968[5]
(iii) taking a conveyance, contrary to s 12 Theft Act 1968.[6]

There were 4,388 recorded offences of going equipped in 2005/6.[7]

---

[3] See JK Bentil (1979) 143 JP 47.
[4] CLRC, *Eighth Report*, Cmnd 2977 (1966) para 69.
[5] The offence as originally enacted included acts preparatory to deception under s 15 of the Theft Act 1968. That provision gave rise to some difficult interpretation in practice, all of which is discussed in the 8th edn of this work—see *Rashid* [1977] 2 All ER 237, [1977] Crim LR 237, CA, and commentary *Doukas* [1978] 1 All ER 1061, [1978] Crim LR 177, CA; *Cooke* [1986] AC 909, [1987] Crim LR 114, HL and commentary. The Fraud Act 2006 provides an entirely new offence, below para 9.27, to replace the application of the s 25 offence to deception.
[6] By s 25(5), 'theft' in this section includes an offence of taking under s 12(1).
[7] See A Walker, C Kershaw, and S Nicholas, *Home Office Statistical Bulletin, Crime in England and Wales* 2005/2006 p 29, Recorded crime by offence 1996 to 2005/6 and percentage change between 2004/5 and 2005/6.

'Going' equipped

The cross-heading, 'Possession of house-breaking implements, etc', and the side note, **9.06**
'Going equipped for stealing, etc', indicate that the offence, like s 28 of the Larceny Act
1916 which it replaced, is aimed primarily at a person who sets out on an expedition
equipped with jemmy, skeleton keys, and such like. *Re McAngus*,[8] an extradition case, however, held that there was evidence of the offence when undercover agents said that D had
agreed to sell them counterfeit clothing and shown them shirts, wrongly bearing an
American brand name, in a bonded warehouse. If D intended to sell the shirts to unsuspecting buyers, he was certainly 'equipped' for criminal deception and, when visiting
the warehouse, he was not at his place of abode. If he had been hawking the shirts from door
to door, it would have been a straightforward case; but D did not 'go' anywhere with
the articles.[9]

The side-note is not part of the section but might now be considered as a legitimate aid **9.07**
to statutory construction[10] and it might be taken to show that 'going' is the essence of
the offence.[11] Presumably it would have made no difference if the shirts had been kept in
D's own warehouse which does not seem substantially different from keeping them
at home. There is the further difficulty[12] that McAngus had no intention to deceive[13]
the agent buyers, so that the case cannot be rightly decided unless he intended to sell
some of the shirts to other, innocent, buyers. But, even if he did, it seems extraordinary
that he should commit the offence by the mere act of showing his wares to—as he
thought—accomplices.

Actus reus

Any article

The *actus reus* consists in the accused having with him any article. Clearly the article need **9.08**
not be made or adapted for use in committing one of the specified offences. It is sufficient
that the *mens rea* is proved in respect of the article, that is, that the accused intended to
use it in the course of, or in connection with, one of the specified offences. Thus, it might
be a tin of treacle, intended for use in removing a pane of glass; a diving suit to allow D
to steal golf balls from a lake on a course;[14] a pair of gloves to be worn so as to avoid leaving
fingerprints; a collecting box marked 'Oxfam' when the possessor did not represent
that organization; and so on.[15] The *actus reus* is extremely broad and places an enormous
emphasis on the relevant *mens rea*.

---

[8] [1994] Crim LR 602, DC and commentary.
[9] This is an interesting contrast to the s 6 offence below.
[10] *M* [2004] UKHL 50, [2005] Crim LR 479. cf R Munday, 'Bad Character Rules and Riddles: 'Explanatory Notes' and True Meanings of s 103(1) of the Criminal Justice Act 2003' [2005] Crim LR 337.
[11] As the long title showed that 'carrying' was the essence of the offence under the Prevention of Crime Act 1953.
[12] See Griew 16–08.
[13] At that time this was one of the forms of the offence (prior to the Fraud Act 2006).
[14] *Rostron* [2003] All ER (D) 269 (Jul).
[15] See the recent conviction in *Sang* [2003] EWCA Crim 2411 where D had a fishing rod with a magnet attached by sellotape so that he could fish car keys through letterboxes of their owners.

9.09 There may occasionally be difficulty in deciding what is an 'article'. Does it include black-ing on the face to prevent recognition, or 'Bostik' on the fingers to prevent fingerprints? Having regard to the mischief at which the section is aimed, it is arguable that a substance so applied to the body, remains an 'article'.

9.10 There would seem to be no need for the courts to read across from s 8 of the Fraud Act 2006 to include within the definition of article 'electronic data' (below, para 9.54). Any person who has left his abode with electronic data for use in a theft or burglary—perhaps an electronic device to deactivate a security sensor, or to open an electronic security coded door—would necessarily be carrying it on some disc or device in tangible form which would therefore fall within the definition of article as generally accepted in s 25.

9.11 The offence of going equipped is clearly very wide in its scope. But there must be some limits. Thus D can hardly be committing an offence because he is wearing his trousers when on his way to do a burglary. Yet he intends to wear them while he is committing the burglary and would not dream of undertaking such an enterprise without them.[16] Similarly, he can hardly be committing an offence by wearing his shoes or any other item of everyday apparel, even wearing a hooded top is not yet criminal. Yet it is stated above that gloves for the avoidance of fingerprints would entail liability. This suggests that the article must be one which D would not be carrying with him 'but for' the contemplated offence. If it is something which he would carry with him on a normal, innocent expedi-tion, it should not fall within this section.[17] So there might be a difference between a pair of rubber gloves and a pair of fur-lined gloves which D was wearing to keep his hands warm on a freezing night, even though he did intend to keep them on so as to avoid leav-ing fingerprints. The latter pair of gloves is hardly distinguishable, for this purpose, from D's overcoat which seems to fall into the same category as his trousers. If D is carrying a pair of plimsolls in his car to facilitate his cat-burgling, this seems a plain enough case; but what if he has simply selected his ordinary crepe-sole shoes for wear because they are less noisy than his hobnails? Arguably, the 'but for' analysis is too simplistic. What of D who picks up his gloves with a view to avoid leaving finger prints at a burglary that he is about to commit, but on opening his front door sees that it is snowing and would ordi-narily have picked up his gloves on seeing snow outside? There is no difference between wearing the woolly gloves, for a dual purpose, and wearing rubber gloves for a sole purpose. In both cases, D wears the gloves in order to avoid detection.

9.12 It has been held that being in possession of a driving licence and other documents belong-ing to another, with intent to obtain a job that would give an opportunity to steal, is too remote from the intended theft to constitute the offence.[18] This would now constitute an offence under s 6 of the Fraud Act 2006, below.

---

[16] cf Mr Collins para 8.06.
[17] See Williams, *TBCL* 853–4.
[18] *Mansfield* [1975] Crim LR 101, CA.

Has with him

The expression 'has with him', is the same as in s 10(1) of the Act[19] and similar problems   **9.13**
of construction arise. Questions as to D's knowledge of the nature of the thing can hardly
arise here, since it must be proved that he intended to use it in the course of or in connection with a specified offence. No doubt D has an article with him if it is in his immediate
possession or control; so that he will be guilty if the article is only a short distance away
and he can take it up as he needs it; as where a ladder has been left in a garden by an accomplice and D enters the garden intending to use the ladder to make an entry. If the article
is found in D's car some distance from the scene of the crime this will be evidence that
D was in possession of the article when driving the car.

It might reasonably be expected that this phrase would be construed in the same manner   **9.14**
as the same phrase in s 1 of the Prevention of Crime Act 1953.[20] If the gist of that offence
is the *carrying* of the weapon, so under s 25 the gist of the offence, as indicated in the side-
note, is '*Going equipped* for stealing'; so that picking up some article for use in committing
a theft immediately before, or in the course of, doing so, would not constitute the offence.
Dayle supports this opinion, but *Kelly* [21] is against it. Moreover, in *Minor v DPP*[22] it was held,
in response to a question posed by magistrates, that the s 25 offence could be committed when D was in possession of the equipment only at the time of or after preparatory
acts and within a very short time of the intended theft. This suggests that D is guilty of
an offence under s 25 when he picks up a stone which he intends to use to break a window
in order to steal. It is submitted that, properly construed, the section does not apply to
that case.

If a number of defendants are charged jointly with going equipped it must be proved that   **9.15**
all the members of the enterprise knew of the existence of the articles and had the common
purpose to use those articles in the specified offence.[23]

When not at a place of his abode

No offence is committed by being in possession of house-breaking implements in one's   **9.16**
own home. The CLRC regarded this as an important limitation of the offence. The offence
is, however, committed as soon as D steps from his house into the street carrying the article
with intent. Though the offence is primarily aimed at persons who have started out to commit crime, it extends well beyond that. It may be committed by possession of an article
at a place of employment or, indeed, at any place other than D's place of abode. While a
burglar's car is in his garage at home he is probably not committing an offence, both because
the articles are at his place of abode and because he does not have them with him. Where
a person had no home but his car, it was held that the car was his 'place of abode' only when

---

[19] See above.
[20] Above.
[21] Cases discussed in para 8.83, above.
[22] (1987) 86 Cr App R 378, [1988] Crim LR 55 and commentary where it is pointed out that it is difficult
to see how the facts of the case raised the question posed.
[23] *Reader, Connor and Hart* (1998) 7 Apr 1998, CA unreported.

it was on a site where he intended to abide. While it was in transit he was committing the offence.[24]

Use in the course of or in connection with

9.17   It is not necessarily a defence that D did not intend to use the article while actually committing the contemplated crime. If, for example, he intended to use it only in the course of making his escape after the commission of the offence, this would be enough, being use 'in connection with' the offence. Similarly, if he intended to use the article while doing preparatory acts.

9.18   The offence is directed at acts preparatory to the offences specified. It is not an offence under the section merely to be in possession of articles which *have been* used in the course of or in connection with one of the offences.[25] A person concealing or disposing of articles which have been so used may be guilty of an offence under s 4 of the Criminal Law Act 1967.[26]

Mens rea

9.19   The *mens rea* for the offence would appear to consist in:

   (i) knowledge that one possesses the article; and
   (ii) an intention that the article be used in the course of or in connection with either of the specified crimes.

9.20   D must have it in mind that, when he uses the article, he will do so with the intention required by any one of the specified crimes. In *Ellames*,[27] the court expressed the opinion that it is not necessary to prove that D intended to use the article in the course of or in connection with any specific burglary or theft; it is enough that he intended to use it for some burglary or theft. Although the Committee[28] stated that they regarded the offence as a preparatory one 'in contemplation of a particular crime', the dictum in *Ellames* seems to be right. It is supported by the use of the word 'any'. If a person sets out with a jemmy looking for a suitable house to break into, he has the article with him for use in the course of a burglary and it should not be a defence that he has not yet decided which house to break into. His conditional intention is enough. If D is equipped with car keys, having it in mind to steal anything from the cars which he thinks is worth stealing, he ought to be guilty, notwithstanding *Husseyn*.[29] The court in *Ellames*[30] also thought it enough that D intended the article to be used by another. There is nothing in the section to require that the contemplated use shall be by the accused himself.

---

[24] *Bundy* [1977] 2 All ER 382, CA. cf *Kelt* [1977] 3 All ER 1099, [1977] Crim LR 556 and commentary.
[25] *Ellames* [1974] 3 All ER 130, CA. cf CLRC, *Eighth Report*, Cmnd 2977 (1966) para 150. cf *Allamby* [1974] 3 All ER 126, CA.
[26] *Smith and Hogan, Criminal Law* 165.
[27] [1974] 3 All ER 130 at 136, CA.
[28] Report, para 150.
[29] (1978) 67 Cr App R 13, CA, above, para 2.327. But *Lyons v Owen* [1963] Crim LR 123 suggests the contrary.
[30] [1974] 3 All ER 130 at 136, CA.

Proof

Section 25 (3) provides: **9.21**

Where a person is charged with an offence under this section, proof that he had with him any article made or adapted for use in committing burglary or theft shall be evidence that he had it with him for such use.[31]

This is probably no more than enactment of the general rules regarding proof of intent.[32] **9.22**
The jury may take this fact into account but it is entirely for them to say what weight, if any, is to be attached to it. If D offers no explanation then the jury may be told that there is evidence upon which they may find that he had the necessary intent; but it is submitted that they should be told so to find only if satisfied beyond reasonable doubt that he in fact had that intent.[33] If D does offer an explanation then the jury should be told to acquit if they think it may reasonably be true and to convict only if satisfied beyond reasonable doubt that the explanation is untrue.[34]

Where the article in question is not made or adapted for use in any specified offence,[35] **9.23**
mere proof of possession without more will not amount to prima facie evidence—ie the case will have to be withdrawn from the jury. But, in certain circumstances, possession of articles not made or adapted for committing offences may amount to very cogent evidence of intent.[36] It is a question of law for the judge, at what point proof of other incriminating circumstances amounts to a case fit for submission to the jury.

Sentencing

The s 25 offence is triable either way and is subject to a maximum sentence of three years' **9.24**
imprisonment on indictment. Although there are no guideline cases, aggravating features will include the degree of sophistication of the contemplated offence together with the use of specialized equipment.

In the case of *Ferry*[37] sentences of twelve months for the prime mover and six months **9.25**
for the second defendant were upheld in a case where telephone boxes were targeted. The defendants were stopped with a cordless drill, screwdrivers, surgical gloves, and a map pinpointing the location of various telephone boxes—some of which had been interfered with. The defendants had relevant convictions for offences of dishonesty.

If the s 25 offence contemplates the theft or taking of motor vehicles then the court has the **9.26**
discretion to disqualify the defendant from driving.[38]

---

[31] As amended by the Fraud Act 2006, Sch 1, para 8.
[32] cf Criminal Justice Act 1967, s 8. For this reason the Home Office chose to omit an equivalent in the Fraud Act 2006, s 6: Home Office, *Fraud Law Reform, Responses to Consultation* (2004) para 47.
[33] cf the case where the alleged receiver is proved to have been in possession of recently stolen property and offers no explanation: *Abramovitch* (1914) 11 Cr App R 45.
[34] The decision in *Patterson* [1962] 2 QB 429 that the onus of proof under Larceny Act 1916, s 28 was on the accused, was based on the express wording of that section and is entirely inapplicable to s 25.
[35] cf *Harrison* [1970] Crim LR 415, CA.
[36] Griew 16–14, 16–15.
[37] [1997] 2 Cr App R (S) 42.
[38] Road Traffic Offenders Act, Sch 2.

Possession of Articles for Fraud

9.27 The scope of the criminal law's proscription of acts merely preparatory to the commission of acquisitive crime is taken to a wholly new level by s 6 of the Fraud Act 2006 which provides:

(1) A person is guilty of an offence if he has in his possession or under his control any article for use in the course of or in connection with any fraud.

(2) A person guilty of an offence under this section is liable—

    (a) on summary conviction, to imprisonment for a term not exceeding 12 months or to a fine not exceeding the statutory maximum (or to both);

    (b) on conviction on indictment, to imprisonment for a term not exceeding 5 years or to a fine (or to both).

9.28 This is a disturbingly wide new offence. The Law Commission in its 2002 Report, *Fraud*, had proposed simply to replace that form of the s 25 offence which covered going equipped with implements for 'deception'[39] with one covering going equipped for 'fraud'.[40] That form of the offence would have been subject to the restrictions relating to the defendant being absent from his abode etc., as discussed above. The Home Office in its consultation exercise in 2004 proposed much wider reform, stating that: 'section 25 merits reconsideration because the offence is outdated in relation to its application to fraud offences. Its restriction to possession of relevant articles outside of the defendant's "place of abode" is unhelpful in relation to modern frauds which can easily take place from home computers.'[41]

9.29 The Home Office went on to explain its desire for an offence of mere possession of eg computer software for use in 'the course of or in connection with' a fraud.[42] One particular concern was the widespread use of software to read credit cards, and the impact this has on the volume of fraud and more generally the public's fear of fraud and of 'identity theft'.[43] The proposal had barely a page of explanation devoted to it.

9.30 The rapid developments in information technology, the prevalence of the personal computer and their impact on the ease with which a fraud can be committed from any venue, including the home, do present new problems for the law. A new offence may be desirable to deal with the risks posed. The problem is that the Home Office has not provided a

---

[39] Confusingly termed 'cheat' in s 25 of the 1968 Act.

[40] See Law Commission, *Fraud* (2002), Draft Bill, 'In section 25 (going equipped for burglary, theft or cheat)— (a) in subsections (1) and (3) for "cheat" substitute "fraud", and (b) in subsection (5) for "and 'cheat' means an offence under section 15(1) of this Act" substitute "and 'fraud' means fraud contrary to section 1 of the Fraud Act 2002".'

[41] Para 39.

[42] Para 41.

[43] The Home Office explained the target included articles which are specifically 'made or adapted' for committing frauds. 'Examples cited by police are the computer programme "creditmaster IV" which generates (genuine) credit card numbers on request; computer templates for producing blank utility bills; and draft letters in connection with "advance fee" frauds. Such items have no known legitimate use, so in their case it is reasonable to provide that mere possession of such articles is evidence that they were intended "for use in the course of or in connection with" fraud.' At para 42.

very convincing rationale for the offence in the extremely broad form in which it has been enacted. Rather surprisingly, the proposal from the Home Office was welcomed by almost all the consultees![44]

It is submitted that the argument that s 6 needed to extend to possession within the home **9.31** because so much fraud could be committed from the home is not as compelling as it might at first seem. There are now extremely wide offences (ss 2–4) of the 2006 Act with which to prosecute frauds. The fraudster who works from home is caught by those provisions just as easily as anyone else. Similarly, the fraudster who has *attempted* to commit frauds from his home will be caught. Section 6 extends to those who have not yet even attempted. But is it likely that the police or other investigative agencies will search a property and discover articles for use in fraud unless they already have evidence that a person within he property is committing such offences?

Section 6 may turn out to be a powerful weapon in prosecuting the peripheral players in **9.32** major frauds. If the key players are prosecuted under ss 2–4 or for conspiracy to defraud, there will be many who have assisted in some way who could be more easily prosecuted under s 6 than for assisting or encouraging or conspiring.

The going equipped offence as discussed above is limited in two significant ways: (a) the **9.33** offence cannot be committed by possession of the materials at the defendant's abode, thereby respecting the unique privacy rights attaching to that space, (b) the s 25 offence is designed to deal with the defendant who has set out to commit the specified wrong—albeit this might be mere preparation and hence not an attempt, nevertheless, it does require evidence that the accused has a degree of proximity to the offence although the defendant need not be on his way to commit a crime at that moment and need not have distinguished a target.

Actus reus

An article

As noted above, the concept of article has been given a wide reading under the s 25 offence.[45] **9.34** The 2006 Act provides a yet broader defintion of the term in s 8.

(1) For the purposes of—
    (a) sections 6 and 7, and
    (b) the provisions listed in subsection (2),[46] so far as they relate to articles for use in the course
        of or in connection with fraud,
'article' *includes* any program or data held in electronic form.[47]

The Home Office Explanatory Notes state that: **9.35**

Examples of cases where electronic programs or data could be used in fraud are: a computer program can generate credit card numbers; computer templates can be used for producing blank utility bills;

---

[44] Home Office *Fraud Law Reform, Response to the Consultation* (2004) para 46.
[45] See ibid, para 50.
[46] Offences of having in possession under PACE etc.
[47] Emphasis added. See on the wide interpretation of the concept of article in the Terrorism Act 2000, s 57 to include electronic data the case of *M* [2007] EWCA Crim 218; cf *Rowe* [2007] EWCA Crim 635.

computer files can contain lists of other peoples' credit card details or draft letters in connection with 'advance fee' frauds.[48]

9.36 There is no requirement that the program or data is designed exclusively for fraud. Any word processing or spreadsheet program is capable of being used to produce false invoices or false utility bills. Any email software is capable of sending false representations and thus for committing frauds under s 2, and so on. It is difficult to see any restriction on the concept of article which might limit the offence. A printer and computer, or even a humble pen and paper are articles and capable of being used in the course of or in connection with fraud and are capable of being possessed.

A person

9.37 The offence is designed primarily to tackle the *individual* but would seem also on the application of general principles of interpretation to apply to corporate defendants. The company director who is aware of the DVD copying machine or the software for producing false bills etc which is loaded onto the company's computers may render the company liable.

Has in his possession

9.38 The concept of possession has given rise to problems for the courts, particularly in relation to drugs offences.[49] Possession is a neutral concept, not implying any kind of blame or fault but experience, especially in the old law of larceny, has shown that, when it becomes the determinant of guilt, it tends to acquire a refined and artificial meaning of great complexity.

9.39 There is no requirement that the articles are held in possession in any particular venue. Any article in the possession of the person whether at home, in public, or at work is capable of satisfying this element of the offence. The term applies to the possession of tangible items such as a deck of marked cards or false die and clearly extends to possessing data on a computer such as software to create false utility bills or for skimming credit cards.

9.40 Whereas the concept of possession has created few problems with the going equipped offence, it might be suggested that this is in part at least because the offence only applies where D is not at his abode. That restriction makes it more likely that the articles will be on D's person or in very close proximity to him for the offence to be triggered. With the offence under s 6, there is no such restriction. A person might be said to have in his possession many thousands of articles around his home and workplace.

Personal possession?

9.41 One issue which the courts may well be called on to resolve under s 6 is whether it is possible for D to be in possession through an agent or intermediary? Does D have in his possession the software held on his teenage son's computer? Does the employer possess

---

[48] Para 26.

[49] See generally R Fortson, *Misuse of Drugs, Offences, Confiscation and Money Laundering* (5th edn, 2005).

all the software loaded onto each of his employees' computers? Such cases might more naturally be thought to be cases of control by D, if at all. There is, however, nothing in the section to require the possession to be exclusive to D. In the context of the theft offence, in *Turner (No 2)*,[50] the court refused to qualify the words possession or control in any way. There appears to be no obvious basis for the courts to take a restrictive interpretation.[51] The question therefore arises: what limits on liability are there. Does D possess the articles for fraud when they lie outside the jurisdiction? Does D possess the article in the form of data if it is stored only on a server outside the jurisdiction and accessible via the internet? If so, does D possess all that software or data on the internet to which he has instant access? Surely not. What about the case where D takes an annual subscription to an electronic product, which can be used in fraud, stored on a server outside the jurisdiction, which by virtue of his subscription he can access from the UK? Might he have possession of an article, through the internet, for use in connection with fraud?

Knowing possession?

One way of restricting the scope of the concept of possession in this context would be for the courts to read in an element of *mens rea*. If it must be shown that the accused intended that the article be used in the course of fraud, as it is to be hoped and anticipated the courts will confirm, this will obviously impose a natural limitation on the scope of the offence as a whole, although it will do nothing to restrict the scope of the concept of possession. Is it appropriate or necessary therefore for the courts to read in a further element of *mens rea* that the accused 'knew' that he had the article in his possession? **9.42**

One view is that there is no need to do so, since the requirement of *mens rea* as to the intended use of the article will be a sufficient safeguard against the conviction of an innocent person for possessing articles which are *capable* of being used for fraud. An alternative view is that even though an additional *mens rea* element that D must *know* he is in possession of articles which he intends will be used for fraud is not necessary, it is nevertheless desirable since s 6 is so wide in its reach.[52] The defendant who intends that the article will be used for fraud is almost inevitably likely to 'know' that it is in his possession, but not always. What of the accused who is party to a gang of would-be fraudsters and is aware of a device that the gang has could be used for fraud, and he intends that it should be used for their proposed fraud, but is unaware that he possesses it—perhaps because it has been left in his garage by the gang. From such examples, it is certainly arguable that an element of knowing possession is desirable in the construction of the section. **9.43**

In construing the concept of possession and its *mens rea*, it is unclear to what extent the courts might usefully and legitimately draw upon the jurisprudence regarding the concept of possession and its interpretation in other contexts. In the unlikely event that the courts **9.44**

---

[50] [1971] 2 All ER 441, [1971] Crim LR 373, discussed by JC Smith [1972B] CLJ at 215–17.

[51] cf other statutes in which specific provision is made eg Misuse of Drugs Act 1971, s 37(3): 'For the purposes of this Act the things which a person has in his possession shall be taken to include any thing subject to his control which is in the custody of another.'

[52] The House of Lords has made very clear its position against strict liability offences unless Parliament has expressly or by necessary implication displaced the presumption of mens rea: *B v DPP* [2000] AC 428.

refuse to read in the element of intention as to use, then there would be a greater similarity with the offences of drug possession where there is also no obligation on the Crown to establish any intent to use etc. The CPS suggest in their guidance that it is 'probable' the courts are likely to draw on the case-law on possession of drugs. In that context the courts have held that D must 'know' that he is in possession of something which is, in fact, a controlled drug.[53]

9.45   If it must be proved that D 'knew' that he possessed the article that is alleged to be for use in fraud, particular difficulties may arise in the case of electronic data. (See para 9.54 below.) Even in cases of tangible articles problems may arise. What of the defendant who claims that he was unaware of the credit card cloning machine being stored in his son's bedroom or his office storeroom? In the drugs context, in *Lewis*[54] it was held that the judge had not misdirected the jury by telling them that the tenant of a house might be found to be in possession of articles (drugs) found on the premises although he did not know they were there, provided he had had an opportunity to find out that they were. But this seems to go too far.[55] It is submitted that D does not possess 'articles' for use in fraud if the Crown can only establish that he had an opportunity to discover that they were on his property.

Knowledge of the fraudulent 'nature' of the article

9.46   If the courts do apply an element of *mens rea* and require proof that D must know he has the thing which he is alleged to possess, the question arises whether there is a further element which must be established—that D must know or comprehend the *nature* of the article?[56] What if D knows of the existence of the software that he possesses, but not its function? On one view, he is still in possession, a position akin to the container cases in drugs law.

9.47   It is submitted that this should not pose any great problems for the courts. If there is a requirement that the defendant intends that the article be used for fraud, it will be very rare for the accused to be able to raise a plausible plea of this type. Where the Crown have established his intention as to fraudulent use, it will be possible but unlikely that D did not also know of the nature of the article. In contrast, if D lacks *any* understanding as to the nature of the article and its use, he must also lack an intention that it be used for fraud.

9.48   Nor is any serious practical problem posed if the Crown establish D's intention that the article be used for fraud, but if D claims that he wrongly believed that the article can be used for fraud in one particular manner when it can in fact only be used for fraud in a different manner: D remains liable because the Crown must only establish a general intention as to its use.

---

[53] *Warner v Metropolitan Police Comr* [1969] 2 AC 256, *Boyesen* [1982] AC 768, and *McNamara* (1988) 87 Cr App R 246; *Lambert* [2002] 2 AC 545. This allows the gang member at para 9.44 a defence.

[54] (1987) 87 Cr App R 270, [1988] Crim LR 517 and commentary.

[55] 'First of all man does not have possession of something which has been put into his pocket or into his house without his knowledge': *McNamara* (1988) 87 Cr App R 246 at 248.

[56] *Boyesen* [1982] AC 768, [1982] 2 All ER 161. (It is immaterial how minute the quantity is provided only that it amounts to something and D knows he has it.)

The defendant who intends that the article be used for fraud and who knows that he is **9.49**
in possession of that article commits the offence, irrespective of whether he knows the precise nature of the article.

In many cases, a claim of a lack of knowledge as to the nature of the article will be bound **9.50**
up with a claim of a lack of intention that the article be used for fraud. For example,
if D claims that he thought the computer programme was a scanning device to assist in
uploading photographs onto a computer and it is in fact a sophisticated device for creating
electronic signatures, he will lack the relevant intention and the knowledge.

A further issue which may arise, and one which was less likely in the s 25 offence, because **9.51**
of the likelihood that D would have physical control of the item at the time, is whether
D has possession of an article which he has forgotten about. D might have an article capable of use in fraud, intend when purchasing it that it be used for fraud, but then decide
to hide it away in his cellar. Does he commit the offence if it is still there years later?

In theft, the courts have held that a person remains in possession of articles on land which **9.52**
he owns, even if he is unaware that the articles are on the land.[57] That broad interpretation is of course to provide the maximum protection to the owner against theft of his property, different considerations of policy and principle apply in determining the scope of
the possession by the accused. It is possible that the courts might draw upon the jurisprudence in the drug context, where it is clear that a person is still in possession of something
even if he has forgotten about it.[58] Many other possession offences contain an express
defence of having reasonable grounds for the possession or a reasonable excuse,[59] and such
defences provide the accused with a peg on which to hang the plea of having forgotten
about the presence of the proscribed article. However, this offence seems distinguishable.
The prosecution merely need to prove that D had possession and the relevant intent
at some stage. If D asserts that he had forgotten that he had the article, by implication he
is admitting knowing possession at some earlier time. If the prosecution can establish that
at that stage he had the relevant intention he will be guilty.

Possession of electronic data

Where the article is electronic data on a computer (perhaps one of many thousands of **9.53**
items on D's office machine), proving possession may be more difficult for the Crown.
The Crown's task will be even harder if the courts interpret the provision as requiring proof
that D 'knew' he had possession of the article.

What of a case where D claims to have deleted the relevant data or software and therefore **9.54**
not to have it in his possession even though an IT expert could recover the material from
D's computer? This argument as a basis for denial of possession was accepted in the case
of *Porter*[60] in the context of possession of indecent images of children. The Court of Appeal

---

[57] *Woodman* [1974] QB 754, [1974] 2 All ER 955, CA.
[58] *Martindale* [1986] 1 WLR 1042, following *Buswell* [1972] 1 WLR 64; cf Russell (1984) 81 Cr App
R 315.
[59] See eg the Prevention of Crime Act 1953.
[60] cf *Porter* [2006] EWCA Crim 560, [2006] Crim LR 748.

held that 'if a person cannot retrieve or gain access to an image, in our view he no longer has custody or control of it. He has put it beyond his reach just as does a person who destroys or otherwise gets rid of a hard copy photograph.'[61] It is questionable whether that is a faithful analogy. It is not as if D has burnt the hard copy photograph, rather he has put the hard copy in a safe and thrown away the key. Someone with the relevant skills can allow him to access it. Similarly, someone who has deleted the data from his computer could still be said to be in control of it in the sense that he possesses the machine on which it is stored and controls access to it, even if that access must be by another (more skilled) person. It is arguable that a charge of controlling such an article would be better suited in these circumstances. Again, the fact of deletion proves that D possessed the article pre-deletion and if it can be shown he had the relevant intent at that stage he is guilty.

'Control'

9.55 Use of the words possession *or* control must suggest that Parliament intended them to be capable of applying differently. The CPS guidance suggests that the phrase is intended to suggest something 'looser' than the concept of 'absolute possession under POCA'.[62] Possession is intended to mean merely having custody of the article and the word 'or' does not extend the meaning of possession, but signifies that 'under his control' is a discrete, alternative version of the offence.

9.56 Again the distinction between this offence and the type of conduct proscribed by going equipped is obvious. With the s 25 offence, the requirement that D 'has *with* him' the article brings with it a more explicit element of D's proximity to the article. That element is not implicit in the requirement that D has the article under his control.

9.57 How far does the concept of control extend in this context? Does D control his teenage son's computer? Does D control all material that is present on any of D's premises, or in his car etc? To what extent can D be said to be in control of an article which he cannot access instantly? In some offences in which the concept of having control of an article is used, the scope of the control is defined by the nature of the article or the illegal uses to which it is to be put. Given the breadth of the definition of article, there is no such implicit restriction in this offence. The courts might follow the interpretation in relation to electronic articles at least, in the offences under RIPA 2000,[63] in which the Court of Appeal held that a person has a right to control where he has the ability to authorize and forbid use.[64]

9.58 There is no obvious way in which 'control' will be limited by the courts to incorporate some requirement of D's physical proximity to or ease of access to the article. In the absence of any such limitation, the question arises whether any geographical limit can be placed

---

[61] [21].

[62] <http://www.cps.gov.uk>

[63] Section 1(6) of that Act provides: 'The circumstances in which a person makes an interception of a communication in the course of its transmission by means of a private telecommunication system are such that his conduct is excluded from criminal liability under subsection (2) if—(a) he is a person with a *right to control* the operation or the use of the system; or (b) he has the express or implied consent of such a person to make the interception.'

[64] *Stanford* [2006] EWCA Crim 258.

on the concept in this context. Does D control the articles in his safety deposit box, or locked in his safe many miles away? If so, does it matter that the articles are in D's safe in Liechtenstein rather than in London? It does not seem to be an abuse of language to say that someone sitting at a computer terminal in London can be in control of data on his own server in the USA which he intends to be used to send false representations to the UK with intent to cause loss to the recipients. In *Ex p Levin*,[65] an extradition case, the court thought that the fact that a computer operator was physically in Russia was of far less significance than the fact that he was looking at and operating on magnetic discs in the USA: he had committed theft in the USA and could be extradited to that country. That again prompts the question—can D be in control of data which is instantly accessible to him because it is posted on the internet. It is submitted that this would be going too far. The courts may be able to avoid such a broad reading by concluding that material/data etc stored on a site to which D does not have the ability to regulate access is not within his control. If D controls the website, he can regulate access to the data and can be said to be in control of it.

D may still be said to be in control of data where his intention for it to be used in fraud **9.59** is remote in time. For example where D's intention is that data in his possession or under his control may one day in the future be used for fraud if he can successfully design and construct the software.

Knowing control?

As with the element of possession, there is a question mark over whether the Crown must **9.60** show that D knows he is in control of the article. As above, if the courts read in the element of intention that the article be used for fraud, there is arguably no need or desirability in including a further element of *mens rea* that D knew he was in control of the article. The defendant who intends that the article will be used for fraud is almost inevitably likely to know that it is under his control. But, as noted above, it is possible for D to be aware of the existence of an article for use in fraud, intend that it be used for such, but believe that it is under the control of an associate.

The courts have construed the concept of control in s 5 of the Theft Act 1968 in a wide **9.61** fashion such that a person may be in 'control' of property, even though unaware of its presence.[66]

Electronic data

Special problems may arise in proving that D was in control of electronic data. Although **9.62** 'article' extends to electronic data, it is submitted that D does not control something if it is available instantly on the internet via his computer, unless it is on a website to which D can regulate access.

As with the concept of possession, D will have a strong argument that he no longer has **9.63** control of data if he has deleted from his computer to the extent that he does not have the

---

[65] *Governor of Brixton Prison, ex p Levin* [1997] QB 65, [1997] 3 All ER 289, DC.
[66] *Woodman* [1974] QB 754 at 758.

immediate capability to access that data, even though it is capable of being retrieved by an IT expert.

'For use in the course of or in connection with'

9.64 This form of words is identical to that under the s 25 offence. The offences of fraud are so wide that the items which might be used in connection with such activities are endless. As with the s 25 offence, it is not necessarily a defence that D did not intend to use the article while in the physical commission of the contemplated crime. If, for example, he intended to use it only in the course of covering his tracks after the commission of the offence, this would be enough, being use 'in connection with' the offence. Similarly, if he intended to use the article while doing preparatory acts, the offence would be committed.

'Any fraud'

9.65 This clearly extends to offences under ss 2–4 of the 2006 Act. Presumably it also extends to ss 9 and 11. Is it limited to frauds under the Act? Is conspiracy to defraud caught as well? If the offence of fraudulent trading by a non-corporate business is caught (Fraud Act 2006, s 9), is the Companies Act 1985 s 458 offence of fraudulent trading by a corporation also caught? Is it restricted to the commission of the offence as principal or as an accessory or conspirator?

9.66 It is submitted that the offence does not extend to articles for use in connection with all dishonest offences. Some support for this is derived from the refusal of the Home Office in its responses to consultation to extend the proposal to include possession of articles for use in theft.[67]

9.67 The s 25 offence catches going equipped to commit burglary and theft, the s 6 offence covers those possessing articles for at least the offences under the Fraud Act. Charges of attempt are available where the conduct is more than merely preparatory to the commission of these and all the other dishonesty related offences (except taking without the owner's consent, which is also covered by specific provision). It is submitted therefore that there is no need for the s 6 offence to be construed as being of broader application.

9.68 Logically, the use must relate to future use. Past illicit use can be evidence of a current intention as to future use.

Mens rea

9.69 The section makes no reference to *mens rea*.[68] The Home Office Explanatory Notes suggest that 'A general intention to commit fraud will suffice.'[69] It is submitted that this

---

[67] Para 49.
[68] For criticism see Justice, 'Briefing for the Fraud Bill House of Lords Committee', para 18–21; and debates in Parliament: Hansard, HL Committee, 19 July 2005, col 1451; Hansard, HC, Standing Committee B, 20 June, cols 38–42; DC Ormerod, 'The Fraud Act 2006—Criminalising Lying' [2007] Crim LR 192.
[69] [25].

interpretation *must* be adopted by the courts to prevent the entire population being at risk of prosecution for the possession of pens paper etc.[70]

In *Ellames*[71] construing the s 25 offence the court said that: **9.70**

In our view, to establish an offence under s 25(1) *the prosecution must prove that the defendant was in possession of the article, and intended the article to be used* in the course of or in connection with some future burglary, theft or cheat. But it is not necessary to prove that he intended it to be used in the course of or in connection with any specific burglary, theft or cheat; it is enough to prove a general intention to use it for some burglary, theft or cheat; we think that this view is supported by the use of the word 'any' in s 25(1). Nor, in our view, is it necessary to prove that the defendant intended to use it himself; it will be enough to prove that he had it with him with the intention that it should be used by someone else.

A number of arguments can be marshalled in support of this interpretation. First, the **9.71** Home Office had made clear in its response to consultation that the prosecution

should have to prove a general intention that the article be used by the possessor (or someone else) for a fraudulent purpose, though they should not have to prove intended use in a particular fraud.'[72]

The Home Office intention is clearly for this offence to follow the *mens rea* of the s 25 offence.[73] Secondly, the Attorney-General[74] and Solicitor-General[75] confirmed that the offence was not one of strict liability. Although they declined to amend the provision by the simple insertion of a requirement that D is in possession 'with intent that the article will be used for fraud', the Law Officers both confirmed that it was the government's intention that the *mens rea* as laid down in *Ellames* would be 'attracted' by the use in s 6 of the same language as that in s 25 of the 1968 Act.[76] It is unfortunate that the amendment was rejected. The courts are naturally cautious in interpreting statutes by using analogous language from a different Act, particularly where the surrounding words are not identical. As a matter of principle, it would be preferable for the offence to have included specific *mens rea* requirements as to both knowledge of possession or control as well as an intention that the article will be used in the course of or in connection with fraud.

It is possible that the courts will interpret s 6 as including one or both of two further ele- **9.72** ments of *mens rea*:

(a) that the accused 'knows' that he is in possession or control of the article
      and/or

---

[70] In its original proposal the Home Office had implicitly envisaged a strict liability offence of pure possession. This follows from the discussion in para 43 of the Consultation document where it is explained that maximum sentencing powers will have to distinguish between 'simple possession where no intention can be proved . . . and possession with intent to commit a fraud.'

[71] [1974] 3 All ER 130.

[72] Paras 46–52.

[73] See *Ellames* [1974] 3 All ER 130 (above).

[74] Hansard, HL, 19 July 2005, col 1452; Hansard, HL, 22 June 2005, col 1674.

[75] Hansard, HC, 12 June 2006, cols 541–2.

[76] See the Solicitor-General's acceptance that he was making a '*Pepper v Hart*' statement to this effect: Standing Committee B, 20 June 2006, col 45. See also the Home Office Explanatory Notes, para 25. The CPS guidance clearly assumes that *Ellames* will apply: <http://www.cps.gov.uk>

(b) that the accused 'knows' of the nature of the article in his possession or control.

These are discussed above at paras 9.42 and 9.47.

Defences

9.73 Note that there is no defence of lawful excuse or lawful authority. The Home Office in its responses to consultation regarded this as unnecessary given the *mens rea* requirement—which is unfortunately not spelled out on the face of the statute. The investigative agency which possesses such materials as a part of an undercover operation etc will be protected by the lack of *mens rea* and/or by the absence of any public interest in prosecution.[77] The Home Office explanation for the absence of such a defence was that the 'dishonesty test' would protect those in undercover operations.[78] This seems to demonstrate a fundamental misunderstanding of s 6, which contains no dishonesty element.

Inchoate liability

9.74 It seems strange to contemplate an inchoate form of an offence of this nature, but it seems possible in principle.

Attempts

9.75 Where D seeks to purchase a device for use in fraud from a state agent in a sting operation, a charge of attempt might be appropriate.

9.76 However, it is submitted that it is not necessary to fall back on the use of an attempt charge where there is a potential impossibility problem.[79] The full offence seems to be committed. For example, D is proved to be in possession of an article which he thinks will be able to clone credit cards, but which is in fact a useless piece of software which will be incapable of doing so. He is in possession of an article and he intends that the article will be used for fraud. He commits the full offence, even though it would be impossible for the article to be used to commit fraud.

Conspiracy

9.77 There seems no reason in principle why D1 and D2 cannot be liable for agreeing to make/purchase etc (and therefore to possess or control) articles for use in fraud. The statutory conspiracy would be charged under s 1 of the Criminal Law Act 1977. The *mens rea* for that offence would require proof that D1 and D2 knew or intended that the article would be for use in fraud. It may be that charges under s 7 are also more appropriate in some of these cases.

Incitement

9.78 D, who sells articles for use in fraud, could be charged with a common law offence of inciting[80] E to possess an article for use in fraud contrary to s 6 of the Fraud Act 2006, but

---

[77] Paras 47–8.

[78] Home Office, *Fraud Law Reform, Responses to Consultation* (2004) para 48.

[79] See *Smith and Hogan, Criminal Law* 420.

[80] The offence is likely to be abolished and replaced by statutory offences of encouraging or assisting as proposed in the Serious Crime Bill 2007, cll 54–60, building on the recommendations of the Law Commission in its Report No 300 (2006).

it is submitted that all such cases ought to be charged under the specific statutory offence provided by s 7 (considered below).

Sentence

The Home Office explained that the Home Office had anticipated a differential in sentencing between offences of simple possession and possession with intent. In the event, the either way offence created by s 6 is subject to a maximum of five years' imprisonment on indictment. **9.79**

Making or Supplying Articles for use in Frauds

Section 7 of the Fraud Act 2006

Section 7 provides for a further broad offence: **9.80**

(1) A person is guilty of an offence if he makes, adapts, supplies or offers to supply any article—
    (a) knowing that it is designed or adapted for use in the course of or in connection with fraud, or
    (b) intending it to be used to commit, or assist in the commission of, fraud.
(2) A person guilty of an offence under this section is liable—
    (a) on summary conviction, to imprisonment for a term not exceeding 12 months or to a fine not exceeding the statutory maximum (or to both);
    (b) on conviction on indictment, to imprisonment for a term not exceeding 10 years or to a fine (or to both).

The forms of the offence

It is submitted that there are in fact several distinct versions of the offence contained in s 7. **9.81**
There are obviously differences between making, adapting, supplying, and offering to supply. There are also important differences between s 7(1)(a) which requires that the article *is*[81] for use in connection with fraud and s 7(1)(b) where there is no requirement that the article is so designed etc provided D intends it to be used. Section 7(1)(b) is in that respect much wider, and that difference may be important particularly where the charges allege supply/offer to supply.[82] In a different respect s 7(1)(b) seems narrower than s 7(1)(a), being restricted to articles for use in the commission of fraud, whereas s 7(1)(a) is wider—encompassing use in connection with fraud. Whether the courts will be willing to draw such a distinction remains to be seen.

This is far from being the straightforward offence that the government proposed. The **9.82**
Home Office had suggested that the offence would extend only to cases where the article was 'specifically designed to commit fraud or where the manufacturer knows the article is to be used to commit frauds.'[83] Clearly the offence extends much wider than this. It suffers

---

[81] Otherwise there could be no knowledge that it is for such use: *Montila* [2005] UKHL and *Saik* [2006] UKHL 18.
[82] If the allegation is that D made or adapted the article it is likely to be caught by s 7(1)(a) in any event.
[83] *Responses to Consultation* (2005) para 52.

from the same defects of overlapping and over-particularity that complicated the deception offences in the 1968 and 1978 Acts.[84]

Background

9.83 This offence was proposed for the first time by the Home Office in its Consultation Paper in 2004. The government suggested that it was necessary to introduce a broad ranging offence of this nature in order to 'strengthen compliance' with the EU Framework Decision of 28 May 2001 on combating fraud and counterfeiting of non-cash means of payment. Article 4 of that Decision requires Member States to criminalize the intentional and fraudulent making, receipt, sale, transfer, or possession of computer programs for the purpose of committing fraudulent electronic transfers of funds.[85]

Scope of offence

9.84 The only example of its operation provided in the Explanatory Notes to the Act is that where 'a person makes devices which when attached to electricity meters cause the meter to malfunction. The actual amount of electricity used is concealed from the provider, who thus makes a loss.'[86] Such conduct was capable of being prosecuted as conspiracy to defraud where there was more than one actor involved in the agreement. In *Hollinshead*,[87] DD agreed to sell to X 'black boxes', devices for altering electricity meters to show that less electricity had been used than was the fact. They expected X to resell the devices to consumers of electricity for use in defrauding the electricity supplier. Upholding the conviction for conspiracy to defraud, the House implicitly decided that there was no statutory conspiracy and therefore that an agreement to aid and abet the consumers to commit an offence against the suppliers was not a statutory conspiracy.[88]

9.85 Clearly, s 7 has potential to apply to a much wider range of circumstances. It will catch the software manufacturer who produces programs such as 'Creditmaster IV' and others which are designed solely for criminal purposes. In that respect it is a welcome addition to the prosecution's armoury.

9.86 There seems to be no doubt that the section could apply to the corporate defendant. The company producing blank cards for use in credit card cloning, or designing software for the production of phishing sites etc are all caught.

---

[84] The variations include that D (i) makes an article knowing it is designed or adapted for use in the course of or in connection with fraud; (ii) D adapts an article knowing it is designed or adapted for use in the course of or in connection with fraud; (iii) D supplies an article knowing it is designed or adapted for use in the course of or in connection with fraud; (iv) D offers to supply knowing it is designed or adapted for use in the course of or in connection with fraud; (v) D makes an article intending it to be used to commit, or assist in the commission of, fraud; (vi) D adapts an article; intending it to be used to commit, or assist in the commission of, fraud; (vii) D supplies an article intending it to be used to commit, or assist in the commission of, fraud; (viii) D offers to supply an article intending it to be used to commit, or assist in the commission of, fraud.

[85] Home Office *Law Reform Consultation Paper* (2004) para 44.

[86] Para 27.

[87] [1985] 1 All ER 850 at 858.

[88] See commentary on *Hollinshead* [1985] Crim LR 653 at 656.

The offence has obvious advantages over charges that might otherwise be brought to com- **9.87** bat such conduct. A statutory conspiracy to commit fraud contrary to s 1(1) of the Criminal Law Act 1977 and s 1 of the Fraud Act 2006, or conspiracy to defraud would be possible charges, but these would require two individuals: this offence allows for the conviction of the lone producer. Similarly, the offence has advantages over the charges of being an aider and abetter to the use of such devices, since those charges require proof that the fraud related offence was committed.

There are already in existence very specific crimes to deal with particular examples of this **9.88** type of behaviour—eg s 126 Communications Act 2003: possessing or supplying appara- tus for dishonestly obtaining telecommunications services etc.[89] Section 7 merely creates general, though very wide, forms of the offence.

Actus reus

Any article

The definition of article has been considered above, para 9.34. By virtue of s 8, it inclu- **9.89** des electronic data. The scope of the *actus reus* is extremely broad. An allegation based on articles 'designed or adapted for' use in fraud will be relatively narrow but will still encompass eg computer software for credit card cloning etc. In comparison, if the allega- tion is that the article is 'intended for use in' fraud and it was made or supplied or offered for supply, the offence extends much wider and could include innocuous articles such as mobile phones. Prosecutors have to be alert to the correct formulation of the charges.

It is notable that where this form of offence is used elsewhere in criminal legislation, **9.90** Parliament has extended it by making clear that the making etc of the article is criminalized if it can be used in the prohibited manner 'whether by itself or in combination with another article or other articles'.[90] No such extension appears on the version in s 7, but it seems clear that the offence is committed irrespective of whether the article is capable of being used by itself or in combination with other articles.

As noted above at para 9.81 where the charge is laid under s 7(1)(a), it is necessary that the **9.91** Crown establish that the article *is* designed or adapted for use in fraud. The article must be such in order for D to know that it is such.

'Makes'

This is an ordinary English word, and in this context is used in the sense of 'manufactures'. **9.92** It should not give rise to many difficulties in application. Where D has made the article, it will be most likely that he also knows that it is designed for or adapted for use in fraud and the charge will be under s 7(1)(a). In that case the Crown would have to establish that the article is designed or adapted for use in fraud. It is possible however that D has made some article which is not designed or adapted for fraud, but which he nevertheless intends

---

[89] See also the Mobile Telephones (Re-programming) Act 2002, s 2.
[90] See Misuse of Drugs Act 1971, s 9A inserted by Drugs Trafficking Offences Act 1986, s 34(1).

to use for that purpose. This would fall under s 7(1)(b) and could extend as widely as eg the making of paper which D intends to use to print false cheque forms.

9.93 Where the allegation involves electronic data, the courts might draw upon the interpretation of the word 'makes' from the offences dealing with indecent images of children. In that context it has been held that D makes an image when he downloads it to his computer cache from the internet.[91] If such an interpretation is adopted under s 7, it will broaden the offence considerably. The individual who downloads software, even if he does not then adapt it or alter it or use it, may be liable if the Crown can establish either: (i) that it was designed or adapted for use in fraud (s 7(1)(a)) eg credit card cloning software; or (ii) even if it is entirely innocuous software such as a spread sheet programme, that D intended to use it for the commission of fraud (s 7(1)(b)).

'Adapts'

9.94 This seems equally uncontroversial. It is a term which may have been chosen with the application of this offence to electronic data in mind. To describe the action of creating software or other electronic data as 'making' an article would be an unnatural use of that word (unless the courts adopt the interpretation in the previous para in which case downloading constitutes making). Moreover, it will often be the case that the defendant has not created the software from scratch but has changed a form of software which has pre-existing legitimate uses and has 'adapted' it for fraudulent use. There is no requirement that the article which D adapts must have been in his possession, ownership, or control.

9.95 As with the individual who 'makes' the article, it is most likely that the individual who has adapted the article will have done so knowing that it is designed or adapted for fraud. In that case the appropriate charge will be under s 7(1)(a). In the rare circumstances where D adapts an article such that it does not become adapted for use in the course of or connection with fraud, but D intends it to be used in the commission of fraud, the charge must be under s 7(1)(b). D who adapts a pen to write in a very fine script with intent to use that pen to alter ledgers commits the offence under s 7(1)(b), but would seem also to commit the offence under s 7(1)(a). There will be considerable overlap unless the courts construe the expression in the 'course or connection' with fraud differently from 'in the commission' or 'assisting in the commission of'.

'Supplies'

9.96 This is a term which, like possession, has created difficulties for the courts in a number of contexts. However, given that in this context we are dealing with the supply of articles for illegal purposes, it is unlikely that the courts will take a restrictive or unduly technical approach to the term. In the leading case on the interpretation of this term in the Misuse of Drugs Act, *Maginnis*,[92] the House of Lords held that the word 'supply' is to be interpreted by reference to the 'ordinary natural meaning of the word together with any assistance which may be afforded by the context'.

---

[91] *Atkins v DPP* [2000] 1 WLR 1427.
[92] [1987] AC 303; See Fortson, n 49 above.

The word 'supply', in its ordinary natural meaning, conveys the idea of furnishing or providing to another something which is wanted or required in order to meet the wants or requirements of that other. It connotes more than the mere transfer of physical control of some chattel or object from one person to another. No one would ordinarily say that to hand over something to a mere custodier was to supply him with it. The additional concept is that of enabling the recipient to apply the thing handed over to purposes for which he desires or has a duty to apply it.[93]

It is unlikely that the courts will need to become embroiled in the difficulties arising **9.97** from the interpretation of the term 'supply' in the drugs offences where there is a transfer from A to B for a short period. In such cases the Court of Appeal has concluded that a supply only occurs where there is a transfer for the benefit of the transferee rather than the transferor.[94]

There is no restriction that the supply has to be for money or money's worth or that it **9.98** is restricted to commercial supply.[95] D handing over a blank credit card to his friend for free is as guilty as the commercial provider of software programs for eg decoding satellite television boxes.

Where D is alleged to have supplied an article, the prosecutor will have to exercise consi- **9.99** derable care over the selection of the charges. If D has supplied the article and knows that it is designed or adapted for use in fraud the correct charge is under s 7(1)(a). That charge will only be available where the article supplied is actually designed or adapted for use in fraud. Where the articles are not designed or adapted for fraud, the charges will have to be brought under s 7(1)(b), and that charge will be available only where D has the intention that the articles are used for fraud.

'Offers to supply'

This expression is also one with which the courts will be familiar from the Misuse of Drugs **9.100** Act 1971 ss 4(1)(b) and 4(3)(a). It seems likely that the courts will follow the interpretation developed under that Act, and an offer will therefore be capable of being made by words or conduct. Whether the words or conduct amount to an offer will be a question of fact. Further, it will not be necessary for the accused making the offer to have in his possession or control the article he is offering to supply. The manufacturer, or someone acting as his agent, who has yet to make the articles in question may be liable for offering to supply them.[96] Whether D intends to perform the act of supplying he is offering will be irrelevant; the offence is complete as soon as an offer to supply is made.[97]

The offence may be committed whether or not D genuinely intends to supply the articles. **9.101** D who makes an offer to sell credit card cloning software to X with the intention of defrauding X by taking X's money and not supplying the goods may commit the offence.[98]

---

[93] Lord Keith at p 309.
[94] *Dempsey* (1985) 82 Cr App R 291, CA.
[95] cf s 1(4) of the Video Recordings Act 1984 where an extended definition makes this clear.
[96] *Mitchell* [1992] Crim LR 723; *Haggard v Mason* [1976] 1 WLR 187.
[97] *Gill* (1993) 97 Cr App R 215.
[98] And a s 2 Fraud Act offence!

9.102   Perhaps most importantly, as an overriding principle, the courts have held that this is not
an area in which it will be helpful to refer to principles of contract law in determining
whether there is an offer.[99]

9.103   Where the article is one designed or adapted for use in fraud and D knows that, his offer to
supply it will be caught under s 7(1)(a). D's knowledge as to that fact is what matters; there
is no need to show that D is aware/intends that the recipient intends to use it for fraud.[100]
Where D merely has an intention that the articles he offers to supply will be used in the
commission of fraud, he commits the s 7(1)(b) offence, irrespective of whether the articles
are in fact designed or adapted for fraud. Again, there is no need for the Crown to prove
that D has any intent or knowledge of the offeree's *mens rea*. In this respect the offence is
more strict than even incitement where D's liability turns in part on his *mens rea* as to the
incitee's likely criminality.

In the course of or connection with any fraud

9.104   This expression suggests a very broad scope of application. It would seem to include articles
not only for use in performance of the actual elements of the fraud offence, but also articles
for use in preparation and/or concealment of the offence.

To commit or assist in the commission of

9.105   In contrast to the expression 'in the course of or connection with' this expression seems to
be more restricted. A reasonable argument can be advanced that the expression denotes the
elements of the fraud offence, and does not extend to the acts preparatory or ancillary to
that offence whether before or after its commission.

For use in 'any fraud'

9.106   As with the s 6 offence, it is unclear whether the offence can be committed where the 'fraud'
offence is one which is proscribed by common law (conspiracy to defraud) or by legislation
other than the Fraud Act 2006. Are articles for use in a conspiracy to defraud caught? The
Home Office's use of the example based on *Hollinshead* suggests that the s 7 offence does
apply to conspiracy to defraud. Whether the s 7 offence extends further and applies, for
example, to supply of articles for use in the commission of other dishonesty offences generally and in specific fraud-based offences such as those under the Taxes Management Act
and the Value Added Taxes Act remains to be seen.

---

[99] *Dhillon* [2000] Crim LR 760.
[100] cf eg the offence under s 125 of the Communication Act 2003 in which it is an offence to possess or
supply apparatus knowing or believing that the intentions of the person to whom it is supplied are to dishonestly obtain etc communication services. See similarly the requirement of *mens rea* in s 126(3)(b) of the
Mobile Telephone (Re-programming) Act 2002 and that in the Telecommunications (Fraud) Act 1997.

Mens rea

Section 7(1)(a)

'Knowing' that it is designed or adapted for such use

This is a relatively strict *mens rea* requirement. Knowledge involves a state of mind of true **9.107**
belief. As the House of Lords has recently acknowledged in *Montila*:

> A person may have reasonable grounds to suspect that property is one thing (A) when in fact it is
> something different (B). But that is not so when the question is what a person knows. A person can-
> not know that something is A when in fact it is B. The proposition that a person knows that some-
> thing is A is based on the premise that it is true that it is A.[101]

The Crown must establish that the article which D has made, adapted, supplied, or offered **9.108**
to supply is designed or adapted for use in the course of or in connection with fraud.
In addition, the Crown must prove that D knew that the article was designed or adapted
for such use. There is no requirement that D intends or believes or knows that the person
to whom the article is supplied or offered will commit any fraud offence. The CPS suggest,
with some optimism, that the 'use to which the article can be put is likely to provide sufficient evidence of the defendant's state of mind.'[102]

It is difficult to see how the doctrine of wilful blindness has any application in the context **9.109**
of design, although it is possible in the context of adaptation. There is no doubt that the
courts have for several centuries[103] demonstrated a willingness to interpret knowledge as
including 'shutting one's eyes to an obvious means of knowledge' or 'deliberately refraining
from making inquiries the results of which the person does not care to have'.[104] Even the
House of Lords has, controversially, adopted this proposition:

> It is always open to the tribunal of fact, when knowledge on the part of a defendant is required to be
> proved, to base a finding of knowledge on evidence that the defendant had deliberately shut his eyes
> to the obvious or refrained from inquiry because he suspected the truth but did not want to have his
> suspicion confirmed.[105]

Section 7(1)(b)

Intending it to be used to commit or assist in committing

The section 7(1)(b) offence is available where D makes, adapts, supplies or offers to supply **9.110**
any article, whether it is designed or adapted for use in fraud or not, with the intention that
the article will be used in the commission of fraud or to assist in the commission of fraud.

Intention here will presumably include not only direct intention in the sense of purpose, **9.111**
but also an oblique intention where the defendant sees the use of the article for fraud as
virtually certain.

---

[101] [2005] UKHL 53.
[102] <http://www.cps.gov.uk>
[103] See the discussion of the early case-law in JL Edwards, *Mens Rea in Statutory Offences* (1955), ch IX,
'The Criminal Degrees of Knowledge in Statutory Offences', 194.
[104] *Roper v Taylor's Garage* [1951] 2 TLR 284 Devlin J. See also eg *Warner v Metropolitan Police Comr*
[1969] 2 AC 256 at 279, per Lord Reid; *Atwal v Massey* 56 Cr App R 6, DC.
[105] Lord Bridge in *Westminster City Council v Croyalgrange Ltd* (1986) 83 Cr App R 155 at 164, HL.

9.112 It is submitted that it is not necessary that D intends that the person to whom he supplies or offers to supply the article will act with *mens rea*.

Sentencing

9.113 This is an either way offence and the maximum sentence following conviction on indictment is ten years' imprisonment. There is, as yet, no guidance available as to how the courts will approach sentencing s 7 offences, but it seems clear that the heavier sentence will be reserved for offences involving large-scale commercial supply.

10

OFFENCES OF TEMPORARY DEPRIVATION OF PROPERTY

Background

It has been seen that an intention permanently to deprive is an essential constituent of **10.01** theft, as it was of larceny. The CLRC considered the matter and came down against either (i) extending theft to include temporary deprivation, or (ii) creating a general offence of temporary deprivation of property.

The former course seems to the Committee wrong because in their view an intention to return the property, even after a long time, makes the conduct essentially different from stealing. Apart from this either course would be a considerable extension of the criminal law, which does not seem to be called for by an existing serious evil. It might moreover have undesirable social consequences.

Quarrelling neighbours and families would be able to threaten one another with prosecution. Students and young people sharing accommodation who might be tempted to borrow one another's property in disregard of a prohibition by the owner would be in danger of acquiring a criminal record. Further, it would be difficult for the police to avoid being involved in wasteful and undesirable investigations into alleged offences which had no social importance.[1]

---

[1] CLRC, *Eighth Report*, Cmnd 2977 (1966) para 56. The CLRC had not included a clause in the Draft Bill.

10.02 The question whether temporary deprivation should be criminal attracted more attention than any other issue, both in and out of Parliament, during the passage of the Theft Bill;[2] but the government stuck firmly to the view expressed by the Committee. In two instances, the Committee found that there was a case for making temporary deprivation an offence, though not theft. These two cases are the subjects of this chapter.

Removal of Articles from Places Open to the Public

10.03 By s 11 of the Theft Act:

(1) Subject to subsections (2) and (3) below, where the public have access to a building in order to view the building or part of it, or a collection or part of a collection housed in it, any person who without lawful authority removes from the building or its grounds the whole or part of any article displayed or kept for display to the public in the building or that part of it or in its grounds shall be guilty of an offence.

For this purpose 'collection' includes a collection got together for a temporary purpose, but references in this section to a collection do not apply to a collection made or exhibited for the purpose of effecting sales or other commercial dealings.

(2) It is immaterial for purposes of subsection (1) above, that the public's access to a building is limited to a particular period or particular occasion; but where anything removed from a building or its grounds is there otherwise than as forming part of, or being on loan for exhibition with, a collection intended for permanent exhibition to the public, the person removing it does not thereby commit an offence under this section unless he removes it on a day when the public have access to the building as mentioned in subsection (1) above.

(3) A person does not commit an offence under this section if he believes that he has lawful authority for the removal of the thing in question or that he would have it if the person entitled to give it knew of the removal and the circumstances of it.

(4) A person guilty of an offence under this section shall, on conviction on indictment, be liable to imprisonment for a term not exceeding five years.[3]

10.04 Section 11 undoubtedly owes its existence to one particular and very unusual case—the removal from the National Gallery of Goya's portrait of the Duke of Wellington. The portrait was returned after a period of four years. There was evidence that the taker tried to make it a condition of his returning it that a large sum should be paid to charity. It has been argued above[4] that this should constitute a sufficient intent to deprive, but the accused was acquitted of larceny of the portrait, though convicted of larceny of the frame which was never recovered. The CLRC referred to two other cases, both of a very unusual nature.

an art student took a statuette by Rodin from an exhibition, intending, as he said, to live with it for a while, and returned it over four months later. (Meanwhile the exhibitors, who had insured the

---

[2] See Samuels 118 NLJ 281; Hadden 118 NLJ 305; Smith 118 NLJ 401; Parl Debates, Official Report (HL) vol 289, cols 1305–25, 1480–5, vol 290, cols 51–71, 1390–421, vol 291, cols 59–71; (HC) Standing Committee H, cols 3–18. For further consideration, see G Williams, 'Temporary Appropriation should be Theft' [1981] Crim LR 129.

[3] See generally *Archbold* (2007) 21–136; *Blackstone's Criminal Practice* (2007) B4.82; ATH Smith, *Property Offences* (1994) ch 8.

[4] See para 2.334.

statuette, had paid the insurance money to the owners, with the result that the statuette, when returned, became the property of the exhibitors.)[5] Yet another case was the removal of the coronation stone from Westminster Abbey.

It may well be doubted whether these instances amounted to a case for the creation of a   **10.05**
special offence but the government acted on the Committee's suggestion and produced a clause which, after much debate and amendment, became s 11. The object of the section is to protect things which are put at hazard by being displayed to the public. Where, however, the purpose of the display is 'effecting sales or other commercial dealings', it was thought reasonable to expect the person mounting the exhibition to bear the resulting risks and to take adequate precautions against them.

It is questionable why special protection should be provided for the temporary deprivation   **10.06**
of this category of items in such specific circumstances when the temporary removal of non-exhibited property of individuals or companies will commonly be a cause of much greater concern, and pose the risk of much greater financial hardship to the victim.

Actus reus

The public must have access to a building

The contents of a building will not be protected where only a particular small class of per-   **10.07**
sons is permitted to have access; as where the owner opens the building to the members of a club, school, or similar body.[6] It does not matter that the public are required to pay for the privilege of access, nor whether the purpose of imposing the charge is merely to cover expenses or to make a profit.[7] But the access must be to a building or part thereof.[8] So if D removes a statuette displayed in the open in a municipal park this would not be within the section.[9] If, however, the park consists of a building and its grounds, and the public have access to the building in order to view, D's removal of the statuette would be within this section.

The public must have access to a building 'in order to view'

The purpose is that of the invitor, not the invitee.[10] If the public have access to the building   **10.08**
for this purpose, then articles in the grounds are protected. If the public do not have access to the building or have access only for some purpose other than viewing, articles in the grounds[11] to which they do have access in order to view are not protected. If an exhibition of sculpture is put on in the grounds of a house, it will not be an offence to 'borrow' an item unless the public are also invited into the house for the purpose of viewing. If one piece of

---

[5] If this had been foreseen by the taker then he might have been held to have an intention permanently to deprive; but this kind of foresight could probably only be attributed to a lawyer!

[6] But the exclusion of a particular class, for example, the exclusion of children from an exhibition considered unsuitable for them, would not prevent access being public access.

[7] But see para 10.21.

[8] Reference should be made to the discussion on burglary ch 8.

[9] cf the discussion in relation to burglary, para 8.31.

[10] *Barr* [1978] Crim LR 244 (Deputy Judge CS Lowry).

[11] A word described by Griew as 'pleasantly untechnical', 5-06.

sculpture is displayed in the hall, then the fifty pieces in the grounds will also be protected. If, however, the public are invited into the house only for some purpose other than viewing—for example, to have tea—none of the articles will be protected. The public might have access to a building (a shopping precinct or arcade for example) where collections are from time to time exhibited in the lanes connecting the shops; but in such circumstances access exists in order to shop and access to view the collection is only incidental to that shopping purpose. If, however, the collection is housed in a cordoned off part of the precinct and access is given to that part specifically so that the collection may be viewed, it would be within the protection of s 11.

10.09   Normally, no doubt, D will have entered the building in consequence of the owner's invitation[12] to the public to view. But, so long as the public have access to view, D may commit the offence although he entered as a trespasser or although he is the owner's guest and is temporarily residing in the building. It is possible that the courts will interpret the phrase 'in order to' in a more restrictive fashion than that of 'intending to'. The former suggests a purposive element.

The article must be 'displayed or kept for display'

10.10   The offence proscribes the removal of *any* articles displayed or kept for display, and is not confined to works of art. 'Displayed' means exhibited in the sense in which an art gallery exhibits a painting. A cross placed in a church solely for devotional purposes is not 'displayed'.[13] If D, while touring the art gallery, removes the fire extinguisher, he commits no offence against this section. If the article is in a store, it may be 'kept for display' though not presently displayed. The coronation stone in Westminster Abbey (something which the CLRC expressly considered)[14] is clearly for this purpose an article displayed to the public though it is not a work of art.

Requirement of removal if article is displayed in a building

10.11   If it is displayed in the grounds of the building, it must be removed from the grounds. Presumably it would be enough to take the article from the grounds into the building. If D is apprehended in the course of removing the article either from the grounds or the building then, no doubt, he is guilty of an attempt.

The thing taken must be an article

10.12   The meaning of the word depends on its context. The expression, 'any article whatsoever', in the Public Health Act 1936 was held not to include a goldfish, the court evidently taking the view that the word did not cover animate things.[15] On the other hand, a horse has been held to be an article for the purposes of a local Act dealing with exposure for sale at a market.[16] Bearing in mind the mischief at which the section is aimed, it is submitted that,

---

[12] *Barr* [1978] Crim LR 244 (Deputy Judge Lowry) and commentary.
[13] *Barr*, above.
[14] Cmnd 2977. cf *Barr* [1978] Crim LR 244, CA.
[15] *Daly v Cannon* [1954] 1 All ER 315, [1954] 1 WLR 261.
[16] *Llandaff and Canton District Market Co v Lyndon* (1860) 8 CBNS 515.

if the other conditions are satisfied, any thing is protected, from an elephant in the London Zoo to a flower growing in the grounds of a stately home to which the public have access. The word 'article' has been given an extended meaning in the Fraud Act 2006, s 8 to include electronic data. It is submitted that no such extended meaning should be applied in this context. It will be most unusual for a person to be regarded as 'removing' electronic data from display from a building. The appropriate charges for someone who causes a computerized display etc to be removed from view lie under the Computer Misuse Act 1990.[17]

Timing of offence[18]

Where the article is in the building or its grounds as forming part of, or being on loan for exhibition with, a collection intended for permanent exhibition to the public, the offence may be committed at any time. A collection is 'intended for permanent exhibition to the public' if it is intended to be permanently available for exhibition to the public. It may be so intended though the pictures are exhibited in rotation and kept in store when not exhibited.[19] So the offence may be committed during the night when the building is closed, or on Sunday, even though the public are not admitted on Sunday, or in the middle of a month when the building is closed for renovation. Where this condition is not satisfied, then the article is protected only on a day when the public have access to the building. If V opens his stately home to the public only on Easter Monday, then for the duration of that day only, articles displayed to the public in the building or its grounds are protected by the section. If D hides in the building until after midnight and removes an article on Tuesday he commits no offence under this section. **10.13**

This serves to illustrate how unduly complex the provision is as a result of its being tailored to meet such a particular mischief. It underlines the fact that the offence is driven in part by a desire to criminalize the abuse of trust of those given access to public exhibitions.[20] **10.14**

Scope of protection of offence

If the public are admitted to view the building or part of it, then anything displayed is protected. If they are not admitted to view the building or part of it, then articles are protected only if a collection or part of a collection is displayed. Where a cathedral is open to the public to view and D removes an article which is displayed there, it is immaterial whether a collection is displayed or not. The term 'collection' was used because it helps to indicate the intended purpose of the section—to protect articles assembled as objects of artistic or other merit or of public interest. It seems clear that it is not necessary that the contents should have been brought together for the purposes of exhibition in order to amount to a collection. If that were so, the contents of the stately home would be excluded from protection, for they were brought together for the edification of the collector, not for exhibition. **10.15**

---

[17] See *Smith and Hogan, Criminal Law* ch 25.
[18] Section 11(2).
[19] *Durkin* [1973] QB 786, [1973] 2 All ER 872, CA.
[20] See Griew para 5–08.

It is no doubt sufficient that articles are preserved together. A single article could hardly constitute 'a collection'; but, if it were on loan from a collection, might it not be 'part of a collection'? A single article, not forming part of a collection, which was displayed to the public, would not be protected unless the public were admitted to view the building in which it was housed, as well as the article. Thus, if it were exhibited in a prefab hut, it would not be protected, but it might be otherwise if the surroundings were more elegant.

Scope of protection for exhibitions[21]

10.16   If the public are admitted to view a collection made or exhibited for the purpose of effecting sales or other commercial dealings, the articles will not be protected. If the public are admitted to view the building, it would seem that articles will be protected even though they do form part of an exhibition for the purpose of effecting sales or commercial dealings. This will be so even where the public are admitted for the dual purpose of viewing the building and the collection; when the public are admitted to view a building, any article which is displayed is protected.

10.17   The definition of 'collection' excludes not only commercial art galleries but also shops, salerooms, and exhibitions for advertising purposes. Had it not been for this limitation, it is obvious that the scope of the section would have been immensely wider than is necessary to deal with the narrow class of cases at which the provision is aimed. Of course, a particular collection may be protected if the conditions of the section are satisfied, even though it is housed in a saleroom, as where Christie's gave an exhibition in their saleroom of articles which had been purchased from them and were lent by public galleries all over the world.

10.18   It seems odd that the law draws this distinction between exhibitions for commercial and non-commercial purposes. The reason for this restriction upon the offence was to avoid creating an unduly wide offence, involving a very substantial exception to the general principle that temporary deprivation should not be criminal.[22] It would have meant, for example, that a removal from the premises of an ordinary commercial bookseller would have been an offence. In addition, since the section protects things at risk because they are on display to the public, it is reasonable for that risk to be borne by the commercial exhibitor.

10.19   As it stands the limitation applies only where the collection is made or exhibited for *the purpose*[23] of sale or other commercial dealings. If then a commercial bookseller, for the purpose of encouraging local art, arranges exhibitions in a room of his bookshop to which the public are admitted, the removal by D of the paintings, or of any other article displayed or kept for display in his premises, would fall within the section whether or not it was available for sale.

---

[21] Section 11(1).

[22] The clause as originally drafted would have excluded not only the case where the public was invited to view the contents for a commercial object, but also where the public was invited to view the building for a commercial object. The latter limitation was removed; cf para 10.16.

[23] Presumably it is the dominant one that matters.

Application where articles displayed are for sale

It is a question of the purpose of the exhibitor in inviting the public to attend whether they **10.20** are for sale. Thus, it is clear that the pictures displayed at the Royal Academy exhibitions are protected, even though they are for sale. Neither sale nor any other commercial dealing is the purpose of the Royal Academy in mounting the exhibition—though it may be the purpose of individual artists. There may be a difficult question where the exhibition has a dual purpose. Perhaps this is a case where it would be proper to have regard to the dominant purpose.

It is also clear that articles do not lose the protection of the section because a charge is made **10.21** for admission with the object of making money in excess of the cost of upkeep. The sale or commercial dealing which is contemplated is one which is consequent upon the viewing of the exhibition.

Mens rea

The *mens rea* of the offence is an intention to remove the article, knowing that there is no **10.22** lawful authority for doing so and that the owner would not have authorized removal had he known of the circumstances. This closely follows the *mens rea* required for taking conveyances under s 12. If the building were on fire and D removed a picture from it, he might well suppose that V would have authorized him to remove the picture had he known of the circumstances. The onus is, of course, on the Crown, once D has laid a foundation for such a defence, to prove beyond reasonable doubt that D did not so believe.

As with s 12 (below), 'dishonesty' is *not* a constituent of the offence. Where students bor- **10.23** row some article for the purpose of a 'rag' other charity event, it might be debatable whether they are dishonest or not; but the question need not be considered on a charge under s 11; it is enough that they know that the removal is not and would not have been authorized by the owner had he known of it.

Sentencing

There are few instances of s 11 being prosecuted and no reported sentencing guidelines. **10.24** As a matter of principle the relevant factors will include: the value of the item; whether damage was caused to that or other items in removal; whether the item was at risk of damage; the duration of the removal; the reasons for the removal; and whether there was loss consequent upon its absence from the display.

Taking a Motor Vehicle or Other Conveyance Without Authority[24]

Section 12 of the 1968 Act replaced the offence under s 217 of the Road Traffic Act 1960. **10.25** Section 12(1) provides:

Subject to subsections (5) and (6) below, a person shall be guilty of an offence if, without having the consent of the owner or other lawful authority, he takes any conveyance for his own or another's use

---

[24] See generally *Wilkinson's Road Traffic Encyclopaedia* (21st edn, 2003) ch 15; *Archbold* (2007) para 21.42; *Blackstone's Criminal Practice* (2007) B4.100.

or, knowing that any conveyance has been taken without such authority, drives it or allows himself to be carried in or on it.

10.26 An offence under this section was originally triable either way and punishable on indictment with three years' imprisonment but, by s 37(1) of the Criminal Justice Act 1988, it is now triable only summarily and punishable by a fine not exceeding level 5 on the standard scale, or by six months' imprisonment, or by both. When a jury acquits of theft of a conveyance it may convict of an offence under s 12, whereupon the offender is punishable as he would have been on summary conviction.[25] Proceedings under s 12 cannot be commenced after the end of a period of three years from the date on which the offence was committed, and six months after the date on which sufficient evidence to justify the proceedings comes to the knowledge of the prosecutor.[26]

10.27 The offence is one commonly committed. In 2005/6 there were 203,560 instances of theft of or unauthorized taking of a motor vehicle.[27]

10.28 Section 12 appears to create two offences and it is convenient to treat them separately.[28]

Taking a Conveyance

Actus reus

Takes

10.29 A person 'takes' if he assumes possession or control of the conveyance and moves it or causes it to be moved.[29] It does not matter how small the movement is. One who fails to move a car which he intends to take is not guilty of an attempt since this is a summary only offence, but the Criminal Attempts Act 1981, s 9 creates a specific offence of interference with a motor vehicle with the intention that an offence under s 12(1) shall be committed. Where a vehicle is taken but possession is then abandoned and then resumed, there is a second taking when the vehicle is moved again.[30] If a vehicle is taken by X without the consent of the owner, V, and D, being unaware that the vehicle has been so taken, takes it from X without X's consent, D is guilty of taking it without the consent of V.[31]

---

[25] For the position in the magistrates' court see *R (H) v Liverpool City Youth Court* [2001] Crim LR 487.

[26] Vehicles (Crime) Act 2001, s 37(1).

[27] A Walker, C Kershaw, and S Nicholas, *Home Office Statistical Bulletin, Crime in England and Wales 2005/2006* p 28, Recorded crime by offence 1996 to 2005/6 and percentage change between 2004/5 and 2005/6.

[28] It is possible to jointly charge under s 24(1) of the Magistrates' Court Act 1980 two people with 'driving' and 'allowing to be carried on a conveyance': *Re Allgood* [1996] RTR 26.

[29] *Bogacki* [1973] QB 832, [1973] 2 All ER 864. *Webley v Buxton* [1977] QB 481, [1977] 2 All ER 595. It is not enough that movement is caused accidentally: *Blayney v Knight* (1975) 60 Cr App R 269, DC. A fingerprint on the internal rear view mirror is not sufficient evidence of possession or taking: *Chief Constable of Avon and Somerset v Jest* [1986] RTR 372.

[30] *DPP v Spriggs* [1994] RTR 1, [1993] Crim LR 622, DC. cf *Starling* [1969] Crim LR 556, CA.

[31] Commentary on *Spriggs* [1993] Crim LR 622, above. If necessary, reliance may be placed on the doctrine of transferred malice: *Smith and Hogan, Criminal Law* 113. If D, knowing that the vehicle has been taken by X, drives the vehicle with X's consent, he is guilty, not of taking, but of driving a taken vehicle: para 10.52.

The Theft Act omits the words 'and drives away' which were in the Road Traffic Acts.[32] The **10.30** object of this omission was not to bring the mere acquisition of possession within the ambit of the offence but to include the case where the conveyance is removed without being 'driven' or, in the case of an aircraft 'flown', a boat 'sailed', and so on. So the offence was committed where a man took an inflatable rubber dinghy from outside a lifeboat depot, put it on a trailer and drove it away.[33] The essence of the offence is not stealing a ride but depriving the owner, though only temporarily, of his conveyance.[34] However, the requirement of a physical taking demonstrates that the offence does not protect against deprivation generally. Thus, where D intentionally hides V's car keys, depriving V of the use of the vehicle, he does not commit the offence under s 12.[35]

In the Larceny Acts the word 'takes' connoted merely the acquisition of possession and the **10.31** requirement of 'asportation' rested upon the further words, 'and carries away'. In *Bogacki*,[36] it was held that, because 'takes' is not a synonym of 'uses', it imports a requirement of some degree of movement of the conveyance. A courting couple, occupying the back seat of a parked car as trespassers do not 'take' it. If D takes possession of V's motorized caravan and lives in it for a month without moving it he does not commit this offence. This is not unreasonable. It is not different in substance from making use of V's bungalow. The section is, after all, concerned with conveyances and the essence of a conveyance is that it moves.

Where an employee has control, in the course of his employment, of a vehicle belonging to **10.32** his employer, possession of the vehicle in law remains in the employer and the employee's control is known as custody. If the employee, without authority, so alters the character of his control of the vehicle that he can no longer be regarded as holding it as employee but rather for his own purposes, he 'takes' by assuming possession in the legal sense.[37] If, in the middle of the working day, he were to decide to drive his employer's van away for a fortnight's holiday, he would 'take' it as soon as he departed from his authorized route with intent to control the vehicle for his own purpose. On the other hand, a lorry-driver who diverted briefly from his authorized route merely to visit a favourite café would probably continue to hold the vehicle as employee. The journey, though by an unnecessarily roundabout route, might still be in substance the journey he was employed to make. It is a question of degree. In *McKnight v Davies*,[38] a lorry-driver was held guilty when, instead of returning the lorry to his employer's depot, as was his duty, he drove it to a public house, drove three men to their homes, back to another pub and then to his house, returning the vehicle to the

---

[32] The words were included in the Bill presented to Parliament but deleted so as to cover eg the case of a boat which is towed away: HL Deb, vol 291, col 106.

[33] *Bogacki* [1973] QB 832, [1973] 2 All ER 864.

[34] According to the Criminal Law Revision Committee, under the old law, 'the essence of the offence is stealing a ride' (*Eighth Report*, Cmnd 2977 (1966) at para 84); but there was more to it than that, as appears if the offence is compared with that of unlawful riding on public transport, where the authority is not deprived of the vehicle.

[35] The *actus reus* of theft does not of course require a physical moving of the vehicle.

[36] N 33.

[37] *McKnight v Davies* [1974] RTR 4, [1974] Crim LR 62, DC.

[38] *Mowe v Perraton* [1952] 1 All ER 423, DC, appears to be wrongly decided.

depot the following morning. *McKnight* was applied in *McMinn v McMinn*[39] to a case where the person who had originally been authorized to drive the vehicle (his employer's van) was alleged to have taken it by allowing someone else to drive it whom he knew did not have the employer's permission to drive it.

10.33 While a deviation in the course of the working day raises a question of degree, it seems clear that when the working day is over and the driver resumes control over the vehicle for a purpose of his own, he commits the offence.[40]

10.34 It is clear that a hirer in possession of a conveyance under a hire-purchase agreement cannot commit the offence because he is the 'owner' for this purpose.[41] Other bailees, however, may commit the offence. A bailee, unlike a servant, has possession of the thing entrusted to him; yet if he operates the conveyance after the purpose of the bailment has been fulfilled, that subsequent use may be held to amount to a taking, though he has never given up possession. In *McGill*,[42] D borrowed a car to take his wife to the station on the express condition that he brought it straight back. He did not return it that day and the following day drove it to Hastings. It was held that his use of the car after the purpose of the borrowing was fulfilled constituted a taking. Once the conveyance has been taken by D, however, subsequent movement of it does not constitute a fresh taking,[43] unless he has abandoned and then resumed possession; though it may be an offence under the second limb of the section.[44]

10.35 The requirement of the Road Traffic Act that the vehicle be 'driven away' led to some very subtle distinctions. It was held that, for example, a vehicle was not being driven where D released the handbrake so that it ran down a hill or where it was being towed or pushed by another vehicle. It would seem that there is a taking in each of these cases and convictions would now be possible, if the other constituents of the offence were present.[45]

For his own or another's use[46]

10.36 The CLRC considered the essence of the offence they proposed in their draft bill to be 'stealing a ride' but material amendments were made to the draft bill in Parliament which affect the nature of the offence. The words 'and drives away' were omitted from the draft bill and the words 'for his own or another's use' were inserted. These words were intended to exclude from the offence one who let the conveyance run away, or float away, out of malice.

---

[39] [2006] EWHC 827.
[40] *Wibberley* [1966] 2 QB 214, [1965] 3 All ER 718.
[41] Section 12(7)(b).
[42] [1970] RTR 209, 54 Cr App R 300, CA. See commentaries at [1970] Crim LR 291 and 480 and *Whittaker v Campbell*, para 10.44.
[43] *Pearce* [1961] Crim LR 122.
[44] Para 10.52.
[45] In *Roberts* [1965] 1 QB 85, [1964] 2 All ER 541, the court thought it 'possible' that D's releasing the handbrake and allowing the vehicle to run down the hill amounted to a taking. It would clearly be sufficient taking for the purposes of larceny—suppose D had had an intention permanently to deprive, as by allowing the vehicle to run over a cliff into the sea; and it is thought that the requirements of this section should not be more stringent.
[46] See S White, 'Taking the Joy out of Joy-Riding' [1980] Crim LR 609.

In *Bow*,[47] the Court of Appeal thought 'use' meant 'use as a conveyance'; but the actual taking need not involve the use of the conveyance at all—as in *Pearce*[48] where the conveyance, a rubber dinghy, was carried away on a trailer. An intention to use in the future may be enough and the court may have fairly assumed that D intended to use the dinghy for its normal purposes. If, however, he had intended to use it only as a paddling pool for his children he would not (according to *Bow*) have been guilty of the offence, though the injury to the owner would have been the same.

In *Bow*,[49] D parked a vehicle in a private lane, allegedly for the purpose of poaching. V, a **10.37** gamekeeper, blocked his exit with a Land-Rover and sent for the police. When V declined to move the Land-Rover, D got into it, released the handbrake and coasted 200 yards to allow his vehicle to be driven away. D's appeal, on the ground that he did not take the Land-Rover 'for his own use', was dismissed: the taking necessarily involved the use of the Land-Rover 'as a conveyance' and D's motive—to remove an obstruction—was immaterial. If D had pushed the vehicle without getting into it, the answer would presumably have been different. Thus in *Stokes*,[50] there was held to be no 'use' where D, as a joke, pushed V's parked car around the corner so as to make V believe that it had been stolen. It would have been an offence, apparently, if D had got into the car while it was moved; but, even on those facts, or the actual facts of *Bow*, it seems doubtful whether the taking is properly regarded as 'use as a conveyance'; for the purpose of the taking is not to convey any person or thing.[51] But to push a car with the intention of subsequently going for a ride in it is taking it for use as a conveyance.[52]

Conveyance

By s 12(7)(a) of the Act: **10.38**

'conveyance' means any conveyance constructed or adapted for the carriage of a person or persons whether by land, water or air, except that it does not include a conveyance constructed or adapted for use only under the control of a person not carried in or on it, and 'drive' shall be construed accordingly.

Thus conveyances for the carriage of goods are excluded, but only where the conveyance **10.39** has no place for a driver. A lorry is clearly within the protection of the Act, since it is constructed for the carriage of at least one person. A goods trailer (which may contains many thousands of pounds of merchandise), however, would not be so protected, nor a barge with no provision for a passenger. A vehicle, such as some lawnmowers, which is operated by a person walking beside it, is expressly excluded. A horse-drawn carriage

---

[47] (1977) 64 Cr App R 54, [1977] Crim LR 176, CA and commentary.
[48] [1973] Crim LR 321, CA. cf *Dunn and Derby* [1984] Crim LR 367.
[49] (1976) 64 Cr App R 54, [1977] Crim LR 176, CA.
[50] [1983] RTR 59, [1982] Crim LR 695, CA.
[51] *Bow* is also open to criticism on the ground that V had no right to detain D: Williams, *TBCL* 721–2. Presumably he had no right to detain D's vehicle either.
[52] *Marchant and McCallister* (1984) 80 Cr App R 361, CA following *Pearce*. The jury convicted of an attempt although the evidence was that DD had pushed it two or three feet which amounts to the full offence.

is clearly a conveyance, but a horse is not.[53] A conveyance evidently means something that is manufactured. Moreover, it has been held that attaching a halter or bridle to the horse is not 'adapting' it but only making it easier to ride.[54]

10.40 The elimination of the requirement of 'driving' may bring within the section (or, at least, the first part of it) certain conveyances which otherwise would be outside it—that is any conveyance with accommodation for a passenger or passengers which has no means of self-propulsion and so cannot be driven but must be towed.[55]

10.41 Pedal cycles are expressly excluded by s 12(5):

Subsection (1) above[56] shall not apply in relation to pedal cycles; but, subject to subsection (6) below,[57] a person who, without having the consent of the owner or other lawful authority,[58] takes a pedal cycle for his own or another's use, or rides a pedal cycle knowing it to have been taken without such authority, shall on summary conviction be liable to a fine not exceeding [level 3 on the standard scale].'[59]

In 2005/6 there were 113,206 such offences recorded.[60]

Without having the consent of the owner or other lawful authority

10.42 If the owner had not given his consent at the time of the taking, the offence is committed. It is no defence that the owner later declares that he would have given consent had he been asked.[61] It is not necessary to identify the owner provided it can be established that whoever it was there was no consent. Thus, where D admitted that he did not have the consent of the owner for taking a bicycle, and admitted that it did not belong to him, he was rightly convicted.[62]

Consent by threats

10.43 It would seem clear that a consent extracted by intimidation would not amount to a defence.[63]

Consent by fraud

10.44 In *Whittaker v Campbell*,[64] the Divisional Court held that a consent obtained by fraud is consent for the purposes of the section even though it might not be so regarded in other

---

[53] *Neal v Gribble* [1978] RTR 409, [1978] Crim LR 500.
[54] ibid. See commentary [1978] Crim LR 500–1.
[55] *Pearce* [1973] Crim LR 321.
[56] Above, para 10.25.
[57] Below, para 10.49.
[58] Below, para 10.48.
[59] For a case under this section see *Sturrock v DPP* [1996] RTR 216.
[60] A Walker, C Kershaw, and S Nicholas, *Home Office Statistical Bulletin, Crime in England and Wales* 2005/2006 p 149, Recorded crime by offence 1996 to 2005/6 and percentage change between 2004/5 and 2005/6.
[61] *Ambler* [1979] RTR 217.
[62] *Sturrock v DPP* [1996] RTR 216.
[63] *Hogdon* [1962] Crim LR 563.
[64] [1984] QB 318, [1983] 3 All ER 582, [1983] Crim LR 812 and commentary.

branches of the law, such as the law of contract. D found a driving licence belonging to E and obtained the hire of a motor vehicle from V by producing the licence and representing that he was E. The *ratio decidendi* is that, even if this was a mistake of identity so fundamental as to preclude the existence of a contract between D and V, it did not 'vitiate' V's consent to D's taking the car. The court recognized that it might have decided the case on a narrower ground, ie that V was dealing with the person in his presence, D, believing that his name was E and that he was the owner of the licence produced—errors, not as to identity but as to attributes, which would result in a merely voidable contract with D.[65] It is submitted that, in a true case of mistaken identity—which will be rare—there is no consent in fact and the law should not say there is.

Suppose that V has two friends, E, in whom he has the utmost confidence, and D whom **10.45** he would not trust with a tricycle. When V is away from home, D telephones, says he is E, and asks for permission to borrow V's car. V, addressing him as E, tells him where to find the keys. If D then takes the car, it is submitted that he does so without the consent of the owner.[66] Apart from principle, the *ratio* (though not the facts) of *Whittaker v Campbell* is difficult to reconcile with *McGill*[67] but gains some support from *Peart*.[68] D induced V to lend his van, for a payment of £2, by representing that he wanted to drive to Alnwick and would return the van by 7.30 pm. Instead, as presumably he intended all along, he drove to Burnley where he was found at 9 pm. It was held that there was no taking; the misrepresentation did not vitiate V's consent. The court reserved the question whether a misrepresentation can ever be so fundamental as to vitiate consent for the purposes of this crime. By reason of the direction given to the jury by the trial judge, the Court of Appeal had to consider the position at the time when the van was borrowed in the afternoon: 'There was no issue left to [the jury] whether, in this particular case, there could have been a fresh taking . . . at some time after it was originally taken away at 2.30 pm. The consent which has to be considered is thus a consent at the time of taking possession of the van with licence to drive and use it.'[69] It seems then that even if he did not commit an offence at the time of the taking he would, like the defendants in *McGill* and *McKnight v Davies*,[70] have done so as soon as he departed from the Alnwick road and set course for Burnley.

There is, however, a difference. In *McGill* and *McKnight v Davies* there was no evidence **10.46** that the defendants had the unauthorized use in mind when they obtained possession but that proof was not lacking in *Peart*—D frankly admitted it—and it is submitted the case ought to be reconsidered. Given the use for a journey to which V had consented, D *took* it

---

[65] *Chitty on Contracts* (29th edn 2004), ch 8.

[66] An argument on these lines is said by ATH Smith (*Property Offences* (1994) 9–23) to involve a fallacy because 'The person who is deceived intends to deal both with the owner of the voice and with the person he has in mind . . . since he believes that these two persons are one and the same.' However, the one person whom V has in mind is certainly E and no one else.

[67] [1970] RTR 209, CA.

[68] [1970] 2 QB 672, [1970] 2 All ER 823, CA.

[69] [1970] 2 All ER 823 at 824. It seems surprising that the proviso which was then available to the Court of Appeal was not applied.

[70] Above, para 10.32.

for a journey for which no consent was given. As a practical matter of evidence it will often be necessary to prove a departure from the stated use in order to prove that D intended to use the vehicle in other than the authorized way but this cannot affect the substantive criminal law.

10.47   If, when a conveyance has been borrowed for a particular purpose, it is 'taking' to use it for a quite different purpose after the declared purpose has been fulfilled, it is difficult to see why it is not 'taking' to use it immediately for a purpose quite different from that declared. It is submitted that *McGill* is to be preferred to *Peart*. If D gets V's permission to drive V's car around the corner to buy a newspaper and immediately drives off on the Monte Carlo rally, it is submitted that this is properly regarded as a taking without consent. *Peart* and *Whittaker v Campbell* were distinguished by the Court of Appeal (Civ Div) in *Singh v Rathour (Northern Star Insurance Co Ltd, third party)*.[71] A borrower of a vehicle, being aware of an implied limitation as to the purpose for which it was to be driven, did not have the consent of the owner to drive it for a purpose outside that limitation and consequently was not insured in respect of such driving.

10.48   'Other lawful authority' would apply to the removal of a vehicle, in accordance with a statutory power, eg where the vehicle has been parked in contravention of a statutory prohibition, or in a dangerous situation, or in such circumstances as to appear to have been abandoned. It would also cover any removal of a vehicle in pursuance of a common law right such as that of abating a nuisance,[72] or of a contractual right such as that of a letter under a hire-purchase agreement to resume possession in certain circumstances.

Mens rea

10.49   Section 12(6) provides:

> A person does not commit an offence under this section by anything done in the belief that he has lawful authority to do it or that he would have the owner's consent if the owner knew of his doing it and the circumstances of it.

10.50   Once D has raised the issue, the prosecution must prove that he did not believe that he had lawful authority or that he would, in the circumstances (presumably the circumstances which D believed to exist) have had the owner's consent.[73]

10.51   If an unlicensed and uninsured garage employee who has driven a customer's car asserts that he believed he had lawful authority to do so, it must be left to the jury to decide whether they are satisfied that he had no genuine belief that the owner had consented, or would have consented, to his doing so.[74] The more unreasonable the alleged belief, the more likely is the jury to be satisfied that it was not really held.

---

[71] [1988] 2 All ER 16, [1988] 1 WLR 422, CA. See J Birds, 'Consent of the Owner under a Motor Policy' [1998] J Bus Law 421.
[72] cf *Webb v Stansfield* [1966] Crim LR 449.
[73] *MacPherson* [1973] RTR 157, [1973] Crim LR 457, CA; *Briggs* [1987] Crim LR 708, CA.
[74] *Clotworthy* [1981] RTR 477, [1981] Crim LR 501, CA.

Driving or Allowing Oneself to be Carried by a 'Taken' Conveyance

Actus reus

Where a conveyance has been unlawfully taken, D does not commit an offence of 'taking' **10.52**
by driving with the consent of the taker or allowing himself to be carried in or on the taken
conveyance.[75] Special provision was made to meet this case in the Road Traffic Act 1962,
s 44 and reproduced in s 12 of the Theft Act. At least one offence, separate and distinct from
taking a conveyance, is created; and there are two such offences if driving[76] and allowing
oneself to be carried cannot be regarded as alternative modes of commission of a single
offence. Such an offence is hereafter in this chapter designated a 'secondary offence'.

Driving a 'taken' vehicle

A person who drives a taken vehicle with the consent of the taker is guilty of the secondary **10.53**
offence of driving the taken vehicle. He is not guilty of the primary offence of taking, probably because possession of the conveyance, though unlawful, is now in the taker, not the
owner. Where, however, a person drives a taken vehicle without the consent of the taker,
the position is less clear.

If (a) he is unaware that the vehicle has been taken, he cannot be guilty of the secondary **10.54**
offence, so, if he is not guilty of the primary offence, he gets off scot-free. That can hardly
have been Parliament's intention. Unlike the person who drives with the consent of the first
taker, he is assuming possession of the vehicle and he is certainly doing so without the consent of the person entitled to possession, the owner. The owner, not the first taker, is the
victim of the offence.

If (b) he is aware that the vehicle has been taken and he drives it without the consent of the **10.55**
taker (or, of course, the owner) he too must (if (a) above is right) be guilty of the primary
offence, for he too is assuming possession without the consent of the owner. Yet it is clear
that he is guilty of the secondary offence. Assuming that there are indeed two offences, can
he be guilty of both? Or does his plain guilt of the secondary offence imply that he cannot
be guilty of the primary offence?

This speculation is prompted by the decision in *DPP v Spriggs*.[77] But that case is rela- **10.56**
tively straightforward. The first taker abandoned the car and thus gave up possession of it.
It thereupon either reverted to the possession of the true owner or was in no one's possession. In either event D, when he drove the car, was assuming possession of, and therefore
'taking' the car and committing the primary offence.

---

[75] *Stally* [1959] 3 All ER 814, [1960] 1 WLR 79; *D (infant) v Parsons* [1960] 2 All ER 493, [1960] 1 WLR
797.

[76] 'Driving' now includes the activity of a person who sets in motion and controls an aircraft, hovercraft,
boat, or any other conveyance: s 12(7)(a). It is conceivable that the old technicalities of what is 'driving' might
arise again here. It is submitted that D is driving when he is in or on the vehicle and is in control of its forward
or backward motion. cf *Wallace v Major* [1946] KB 473, [1946] 2 All ER 87; *Saycell v Bool* [1948] 2 All ER
83; *Shimmell v Fisher* [1951] 2 All ER 672; *Spindley* [1961] Crim LR 486; *Roberts* [1965] 1 QB 85, [1964]
2 All ER 541; *Arnold* [1964] Crim LR 664.

[77] [1993] Crim LR 622.

Allowing oneself to be carried

10.57 If, when D allows himself to be carried, he is aiding and abetting the taking of the convey-ance, he may be convicted of the primary offence as a secondary party. But if the 'taking' has come to an end, the primary offence has ceased and it is no longer possible to aid and abet it. Moreover, 'allow' is probably a word of wider ambit than 'aid, abet, counsel or procure'. If D allows himself to be driven by a person who, as he knows, would drive the car whether D was there or not, he may neither assist or encourage, nor intend to assist or encourage, the driver.[78] He is not aiding and abetting the driving but he is allowing himself to be carried. The fact that D allows himself to be carried is some evidence of secondary participation in the driving offence, but no more.[79]

10.58 It has been held that a person is not 'carried' in a conveyance merely because he is present in it. Carriage imports some movement. A person is not carried in a stationary boat though he is borne by its buoyancy.[80] It would presumably be no different where the boat rises or falls with the waves or the tide. This is not distinguishable from the movement of a station-ary car on its shock absorbers as people get in or out. The slightest vertical motion of a hovercraft, however, should suffice. D does not 'allow' himself to be carried in a taken vehi-cle merely by agreeing to take a ride and sitting in the vehicle. He does so only when the vehicle moves off.[81] If, in the course of the journey a passenger learns for the first time that a vehicle has been unlawfully taken, he is, it seems, under a duty to require the driver to put him down as soon as he reasonably can.[82]

10.59 'Drives' similarly seems to import movement. One who starts up a vehicle and engages the gear has reached the stage of an attempt but has not yet committed the offence.[83] It might be argued that there is a distinction between 'drives' and 'driving'. The latter has been exten-sively defined.[84] Arguably, those offences involving 'driving' are concerned with the physi-cal manner of D's activity, and with whether D has a sufficient degree of control over the vehicle to be responsible for it/liable if not in a fit state. In contrast, 'drives' in the context of this section is concerned with whether there is movement by D's control. It is submitted that the distinction is not one which is persuasive and that a consistent interpretation ought to be adopted.

10.60 In *DPP v Alderton*[85] merely sitting in the car with the engine on, gear engaged, and the wheels spinning was held to be 'driving'. In *Planton v DPP*,[86] D stopped his vehicle on a causeway, awaiting an opportunity to cross at the low tide. D claimed he was not 'driving'

---

[78] cf *Smith and Hogan, Criminal Law* ch 8.
[79] *C (a minor) v Hume* [1979] Crim LR 328. cf *D (infant) v Parsons* [1960] 2 All ER 493; *Boldizsar v Knight* [1980] Crim LR 653.
[80] *Miller* [1976] Crim LR 147, CA. Similarly, presumably, where D climbs up a rope into a tethered hot air balloon.
[81] *Diggin* (1981) 72 Cr App R 204, [1980] Crim LR 656, CA and commentary.
[82] *Boldizsar v Knight* [1980] Crim LR 653, where D pleaded guilty to allowing himself to be carried.
[83] cf the broader interpretation of driving—the 'use of the driver's controls for the purpose of directing the movement of the vehicle': *MacDonough* [1974] QB 448.
[84] *Blackstones Criminal Prctice* (2007) C.1.8.
[85] [2004] RTR 367.
[86] [2001] EWHC 450 (Admin).

for the purposes of a drink driving offence since his vehicle was not moving. The Divisional Court held that he was driving: a driver who had stopped at traffic lights was in a similar position but was still driving. It seems to be a question of fact and degree whether a cessation of movement has been so long that it could not reasonably be said that a person was still driving.

The secondary offence is intended to deal with persons other than the original taker, but is **10.61** not expressly limited to such persons. Unless such a limitation is to be implied, the taker appears to commit another offence on each subsequent occasion when he drives the vehicle or allows himself to be carried in or on it. Where the original taking is not an offence because of lack of *mens rea*, a subsequent driving of it may make the taker liable. For example, D takes V's car, wrongly supposing that V consents to his doing so. The car has been taken without V's consent but no offence has been committed. Having learned that V does not consent to his having the car, D continues to drive it. He appears to commit the offence though it is arguable that a 'taken' conveyance is one taken with *mens rea*.

Mens rea[87]

It must be proved that D *knew* that the conveyance had been taken without authority when **10.62** he drove it or allowed himself to be carried in or on it as the case may be. The vehicle must actually have been taken; one cannot know a thing to be so, unless it is so.[88] 'Wilful blindness' would probably be enough as in the case of other statutes.[89] Such a state of mind is dangerously close to that of belief that the conveyance had been so taken. The Criminal Law Revision Committee thought that belief was not knowledge for the purpose of the old law of receiving[90] and made special provision for that state of mind in the offence of handling.[91]

It is inevitable that comparison will be made between s 12(1) and s 22, with the implication **10.63** that belief will not do in the case of s 12. However, knowledge is clearly distinct from belief and only that stricter form of *mens rea* will suffice in this offence.[92]

Taking a conveyance has been held to be a crime of basic intent so that evidence of intoxica- **10.64** tion is not relevant as tending to show that D lacked *mens rea*.[93] Arguably, where D's belief as to the consent of the owner is based on a mistake induced by voluntary intoxication he can rely on that mistake.[94]

---

[87] See the article by S White [1980] Crim LR 609.
[88] See the discussion of the House of Lords of the concept of knowledge in *Saik* [2006] UKHL 18.
[89] *Smith and Hogan, Criminal Law* 290; JL Edwards, *Mens Rea in Statutory Offences* (1955), 202–5; Williams, *CLGP* 159.
[90] CLRC, *Eighth Report*, Cmnd 2977 (1966), para 134.
[91] See s 22(1).
[92] cf *Saik* [2006] UKHL 18, accepting the crucial difference between knowledge and belief.
[93] *MacPherson* [1973] RTR 157, CA; *Gannon* (1988) 87 Cr App R 254, CA. For a contrary view see White, above n 87.
[94] By analogy with the decision in *Jaggard v Dickinson* [1981] QB 527, DC, decided under s 5(2) of the Criminal Damage Act 1971, which uses similar terms. See Griew 6.20. Glanville Williams is heavily critical of *Gannon*, 'Two Nocturnal Blunders' (1990) 140 NLJ 1564.

Sentence

10.65 The maximum penalty is six months' imprisonment and/or a fine not exceeding level 5. No guideline case has been delivered.

Aggravated Vehicle-taking

10.66 The so-called 'joyrider' (or 'twocker') under s 12 is liable to relatively limited punishments. The taker is additionally liable for any offence involved in taking the vehicle (most obviously criminal damage caused in making access to the conveyance and in interfering with the locks and the electrics in order to get it started) and the driver, whether or not he is the original taker, is liable for any offence committed whilst driving the vehicle (for example, driving whilst uninsured, careless driving, dangerous driving).

10.67 It might be thought therefore that s 12 was entirely adequate to deal with the taker, those who subsequently drive the taken conveyance, and (by the ordinary application of the principles of secondary liability) those who allow themselves to be carried in or on it. In the normal case the fine of £5,000 and/or six months' imprisonment would seem adequate. In the abnormal case where the driver drives dangerously, or kills whilst driving dangerously, a count can be added for that and again the punishment (imprisonment in this case) would seem to be adequate. But the abnormal case became not so abnormal in the early 1990s. The taking of motor vehicles increased to an extent that it was described as epidemic. As the activity increased, so did the risks. Youngsters (usually male) use the vehicles they have taken to demonstrate their driving 'skills' or become involved in high-speed chases when pursued by the police. The hazards of either are obvious. Even in the face of this epidemic, it might be argued that s 12 and the range of driving offences and ordinary criminal charges for damage and injury inflicted were adequate in the sense that the activity would always be capable of being punished and the penalties provided seemed appropriate.[95]

10.68 There was an additional problem, in many cases the taking was performed by a group, and the vehicle was then damaged or injury inflicted, but it was difficult to prove whether it was D or E or F who damaged the vehicle or caused the injury. One or more of them was able to claim that the damage was done before he joined the enterprise. And where, as not infrequently happens, the vehicle is found burned out, all three would say that this must have been done by someone else after they had abandoned the vehicle. Public concern at the risks of death and injury to the person and damage to property caused by so-called 'joyriders' led to the enactment of the Aggravated Vehicle-Taking Act 1992.[96]

10.69 This Act inserts after s 12 of the Theft Act 1968 a new s 12A which creates an aggravated form of the offence under s 12, punishable on indictment with imprisonment

---

[95] It is not suggested that the answer or solution lies in the penalty, merely that the penalty is adequate in relation to the crime. The answer lies in foolproof (or is it expert-proof?) immobilizing devices.

[96] See JN Spencer, 'The Aggravated Vehicle Taking Act 1992' [1992] Crim LR 69.

for two years or, if death is caused, fourteen years.[97] A person is guilty of the new offence if:

(i) He committed an offence under s 12 (the 'basic offence') in relation to a mechanically propelled vehicle.[98] This element of the offence requires proof of the *mens rea* as discussed above.

(ii) After the vehicle was unlawfully taken (whether by him or another[99]) and before it was recovered it was driven, or injury or damage was caused, in one or more of the following circumstances:

    (a) the vehicle was driven dangerously (as defined in s 1(7) of the 1992 Act) on a road or other public place;

    (b) owing to the driving of the vehicle an accident occurred by which injury was caused to any person;[100]

    (c) owing to the driving of the vehicle an accident occurred by which damage was caused to any property other than the vehicle;

    (d) damage was caused to the vehicle. It is a defence for the defendant to prove either:

        (i) that the driving, accident or damage in (a), (b), (c), or (d) above occurred before he committed the basic offence; or

        (ii) that he was neither in, nor in the immediate vicinity of, the vehicle when that driving, accident or damage occurred.

10.70 Section 12A is a peculiar provision in that, once the basic offence has been committed, liability for the aggravated offence depends simply on whether something—(a), (b), (c), or (d) above—happens. Anyone who commits the basic offence takes the chance that, without his doing anything more, he may become liable for the aggravated offence. Under (b) it is not necessary to prove that the vehicle was being driven dangerously; and it has been held that 'owing to the driving of the vehicle' does not imply any fault in the driving of the vehicle. If, when the car is being driven with perfect care, a child runs in front of it and is inevitably injured, it seems that this has occurred 'owing to the driving of the vehicle'.[101]

10.71 Under (d) the damage need not be caused by the driving and may apparently be caused by some third party. D may have merely allowed himself to be carried in the taken vehicle (the basic offence). If he is then standing beside it (in the 'immediate vicinity' of it) when a third party runs into it and damages it, it appears that he commits the aggravated offence. This is strict liability of the most severe kind and difficult to justify in principle. The message to the 'joyrider' is that he acts at his peril and if anything goes wrong, it will end not in joy but tears.

---

[97] Criminal Justice Act 2003, s 285. Since there are different sentencing regimes for cases involving death, the section creates two offences and it is important that an indictment reflects that: *Sherwood* [1995] RTR 60.

[98] The offence does not apply to conveyances more generally.

[99] 'A passenger may be liable even though the passenger has protested at the driving which has caused damage to the vehicle': *Dawes v DPP* [1995] 1 Cr App R 65 at 72 per Kennedy LJ. See also *Wiggins* [2001] RTR 37 on the sentencing implications in such cases.

[100] If D has used the car as a weapon, he will still be caught by the section 'Accident' includes deliberate causing of injury: *B* [2005] 1 Cr App R 140.

[101] *Marsh* [1997] Crim LR 205.

10.72 The activity known as 'car jacking'—where D causes V to stop his car and D then forcibly ejects V from the car and drives V's vehicle away—is more appropriately prosecuted by offences of theft, robbery, offences against the person, etc. In particular, in cases where V is caused to stop by D's minor collision with V's vehicle, after which D then seizes V's vehicle, aggravated vehicle taking will not be a suitable charge because the damage will have occurred prior to the taking.

10.73 It is unclear whether an attempt to commit aggravated vehicle taking is an offence. The s 12A offence requires proof of the basic offence under s 12 which is triable summarily only (and therefore cannot be the subject of an attempt charge), but the s 12A offence itself is triable either way. It is submitted that in an appropriate case a charge of attempt would be available, as where D is apprehended trying to break into a high powered vehicle and admits that his intention was to take it for an evening's 'racing' against his friends' cars.[102]

Sentence

10.74 On indictment, the maximum penalty is two years or a fine or both. The maximum penalty, is fourteen years where it is proved that, in circumstances falling within s 12A(2)(b), the accident caused the death of the person concerned.

10.75 On summary conviction the maximum penalty is imprisonment not exceeding six months or a fine not exceeding the statutory maximum or both.

10.76 Disqualification is obligatory, as is licence endorsement. Between 3 to 11 penalty points may be imposed.[103]

10.77 The leading case remains that of *Bird*,[104] where Taylor LCJ stated that

> In our judgment the most important of [the paragraphs of subsection (2)], in judging the gravity of the case, is paragraph (a), that the vehicle was driven dangerously on a road or other public place, for that concerns the culpability of the driver, whereas the incidents and the severity of any injury or damage under paragraphs (b), (c) and (d) are to some extent a matter of chance. However, the fact that Parliament has fixed a maximum of five years' imprisonment for death, as opposed to two years for injury, shows that the extent of the physical harm done is an aggravating feature, if only to reflect public reaction to maiming or death caused by bad driving. Accordingly the aggravating features of this offence will be primarily the overall culpability of the driving: how bad it was and for how long and, to a lesser extent, how much injury or damage, or both, was caused. Where drink has played a part, no doubt this will affect the dangerousness of the driving. But where it is a major factor, it will often be the subject of a separate charge. As in other cases, a guilty plea showing contrition will be a mitigating feature. The youth of the defendant, however, will be less significant in this type of case than in others, by way of mitigation, because the Aggravated Vehicle-Taking Act 1992 is primarily aimed at young offenders amongst whom this type of activity has become so prevalent.[105]

---

[102] Wilkinson (above, n 24) asserts that an attempt is possible, relying on pre-Criminal Attempts Act 1981 authority: para 15.27.

[103] Road Traffic Offenders Act 1988, ss 28, 96, and 97 and Sch 2.

[104] [1993] RTR 1, 5.

[105] See also *Evans* (1994) 15 Cr App R (S) 137.

11

ABSTRACTING ELECTRICITY AND
RELATED OFFENCES[1]

Abstracting Electricity

The Larceny Act of 1916 made special provision for the stealing of electricity; electricity is **11.01** not capable of being taken and carried away, it could not therefore fall within the protection of the general offence of larceny. The Theft Act 1968 replaced the requirement of asportation, with one of mere appropriation. It might have been possible to have applied the concept of appropriation without incongruity to the abstraction of electricity, but the unique nature of electricity was thought to call for a special provision.[2] It has been held that electricity is not 'property' within s 4 of the 1968 Act and that it is not appropriated by switching on the current.[3] It seems rather surprising that in the twenty-first century when jurors all have an understanding of what electricity is[4] and how it might be appropriated dishonestly, the law retains a special form of offence to cover this wrongdoing. It may be an offence that could be readily disposed of and electricity treated as property as are gas and water.[5]

Section 13 of the 1968 Act provides: **11.02**

A person who dishonestly uses without due authority, or dishonestly causes to be wasted or diverted, any electricity shall on conviction on indictment be liable to imprisonment for a term not exceeding five years.

The offence is triable either way. There were 1,301 recorded cases of the offence in 2005/6.[6]

---

[1] See Griew 2.162–2.165; Williams, *TBCL* 736–7; ATH Smith, *Property Offences* (1994) ch 12; *Archbold* (2007) 21–165; *Blackstone's Criminal Practice* (2007) B4.112.

[2] See CLRC, *Eighth Report*, Cmnd 2977 (1966) para 85.

[3] *Low v Blease* (1975) 119 Sol Jo 695, [1975] Crim LR 513. It has been held by the House of Lords that electricity is a 'noxious thing' for the purposes of the Firearms Act 1968 s 5: *Flack v Baldry* [1988] Crim LR 610.

[4] One explanation for the different treatment of electricity by comparison with other utilities such as gas and water is that it is a form of power.

[5] *White* (1853) 169 ER 696 (gas); *Ferens v O'Brien* (1883) 11 QBD 21 (water).

[6] A Walker, C Kershaw, and S Nicholas, *Home Office Statistical Bulletin, Crime in England and Wales 2005/2006* p 28, Recorded crime by offence 1996 to 2005/6 and percentage change between 2004/5 and 2005/6.

Scope of the offence

11.03   The offence would be committed by an employee who dishonestly used his employer's electrically operated machinery without authority; by a householder who, having had his electricity supply cut off, dishonestly[7] reconnected it or who bypassed the meter; and by a tramp who, having trespassed into a house to obtain a night's shelter, turned on the electric fire to keep himself warm.[8]

11.04   The tramp who turned on the fire would not be guilty of burglary, since abstracting electricity is not one of the ulterior offences specified in s 9(1)(b).[9] Yet, oddly, it would seem that if the fire were a gas fire, he would be guilty of theft and so the tramp would be a burglar. Not a very happy result, but one that could be easily remedied by the extension of burglary to include the commission or intended commission of other ulterior offences (perhaps even extending only to a list of those under the Theft Acts).

Uses

11.05   If the tramp found the electric fire already burning, would he 'use' the electricity by warming himself in front of it? It is thought not. 'Use' implies some consumption of electricity which would not occur but for the accused's act.[10] It is not necessary to prove that there has been any tampering or interference with the meter.[11] If squatters switch on the electricity, not intending to pay for it, they use it dishonestly. Suppose that D subsequently joins them and enjoys the heat and light provided. He appears to be a party to the dishonest use which is taking place.

11.06   Where D1 and D2 are sharing accommodation, it is not sufficient to prove that a meter has been improperly disconnected and that either person is the registered consumer; nor that the disconnection must have been done either by D1 or by D2 unless it can be shown that they were acting in concert.[12] A person who knew that a meter had been disconnected to avoid payment would, prima facie, commit an offence each time he switched on an electrical apparatus; but it would be for the jury or magistrates to decide whether he did so dishonestly.

Dishonestly

11.07   The partial definition of dishonesty in s 2 of the 1968 Act does not apply. The test of dishonesty in *Ghosh* does.[13] Although it has been held in cases of electricity meter tampering

---

[7] *See Boggeln v Williams* [1978] 2 All ER 1061, above, para 2.288 and *Ghosh*, above, para 2.270.

[8] It has been successfully prosecuted where, eg, D has entered premises and called a premium rate sex chat line: *P* (2000) 11 Aug, CA, No 0003586 Y5. It is often used as a means by which the police can arrest 'squatters'.

[9] Above, para 8.49.

[10] This sentence was approved in *McCreadie and Tume* (1992) 96 Cr App R 143, CA.

[11] ibid. In *Harrison* [2001] EWCA Crim 3427, D was the occupier who continued to use the electricity knowing it was bypassing the meter having found that guests had tampered with it. There was no finding that D tampered with the meter, merely that he used it. The case is readily distinguishable from the tramp example on the further basis that D had a duty to pay the costs, it being his property which was being supplied.

[12] *Collins and Fox v Chief Constable of Merseyside* [1988] Crim LR 247, DC, and commentary; *Swallow v DPP* [1991] Crim LR 610.

[13] *Melwani* [1989] Crim LR 565, CA. See para 2.270.

that the defendant must be shown to have an intention not to pay, this is too generous to the defence; it is one factor to be considered in the overall question of dishonesty.[14] The offence is narrower than that under the Larceny Act since it is firmly based in the category of dishonesty offences whereas its predecessor could be committed 'maliciously or fraudulently'.

Wastes or diverts

It is enough under s 13 that D dishonestly causes electricity to be wasted or diverted; he **11.08** need not be shown to have made any use of the electricity for himself. An employee who out of spite for his employer puts on all the lighting and heating appliances in the office would commit the offence if found to be dishonest.

Abstracting 'without due authority'

Concerns were raised as to the liability of D who obtains the benefit of the use of the elec- **11.09** tricity by fraud. In debates on the 1968 Act, Lord Airedale put the case[15] of a woodworking company allowing sea scouts to use their electrically operated machinery and D obtaining the use of the machinery by falsely stating that he is a sea scout. Lord Airedale thought D might escape because he had obtained authority, albeit by false pretences, and was therefore not acting 'without due authority'. One answer to this might be that some meaning should be given to the word 'due'; and that, while D was acting with actual authority, he was not acting with 'due' authority, since the authority was voidable on the ground of fraud. The Fraud Act 2006[16] renders the problem less significant than it may have been. In some instances the appropriate charge will be one of obtaining services dishonestly under s 11 of the Fraud Act 2006, provided the services are to be paid for.[17]

Sources of electricity protected

There is nothing in the section to suggest that the electricity must come from the mains **11.10** supply from the electricity supply company.[18] For example, the electricity generated by V's wind turbine or solar panels can be abstracted dishonestly by V's neighbour tapping into V's power cables. More importantly, it is probable that D commits the offence if he borrows V's torch, portable radio, or laptop and depletes the batteries, whether recharge-able or not.

What of D who takes an electrically powered 'environmentally friendly' car. There seems to **11.11** be no reason why the s 13 offence is not committed in such circumstances. What if the vehicle is a part battery powered/part engine powered machine?[19] Is the s 13 offence committed by the dishonest 'borrower' of a conveyance, such as a petrol or diesel powered car, which consumes electricity from the battery when it is operated? If so, we have the

---

[14] See *Collins and Fox v Chief Constable of Merseyside* [1988] Crim LR 247; Griew 2–164.
[15] Parl Debates, HL, vol 190, col 154.
[16] Ch 3.
[17] See the discussion at para 3.188.
[18] The UK Revenue Protection Association, estimates that every year £340 million of gas and electricity is stolen from UK energy companies. <http://www.ukrpa.co.uk>
[19] See para 10.52.

incongruous result that the—merely incidental—use of the electricity is a more serious offence than the use of the vehicle as a whole.[20] It might be argued that if, as will usually be the case, the alternator is working properly and the battery is charging properly, there will be as much electricity stored in it at the end of the journey as the beginning; and that, therefore, the use is not dishonest. An analogy might be drawn with the case where D takes V's coins, intending permanently to deprive him of them but to replace an equivalent sum from D's own money, not causing any injury to V.[21] It is not a fair analogy, however. In the case of the coins, the replacements are D's property; in the case of the electricity, the replacement is generated by the use of V's petrol and V's machinery and belongs to V as much as the electricity consumed. It seems likely, therefore, that the dishonest borrower of a motor vehicle (or motor boat, aircraft, etc) does commit an offence against s 13.[22]

Charging guidance

11.12   The CPS[23] provides as examples of cases in which it is appropriate to charge abstracting electricity: when a device is fitted to an electricity meter so that the meter gives a false reading; when the electricity supply to a house is reconnected without the consent of the electricity company; when the electricity supply to a house bypassed the meter. The circumstances in which it is suggested to be inappropriate to charge abstraction of electricity: when an unauthorized telephone call has been made from a telephone belonging to another person.[24]

Sentencing

11.13   The maximum penalty under s 13 is five years on indictment; six months or a fine not exceeding the statutory maximum, or both, summarily. The courts have been explicit in issuing deterrent sentences for this offence when committed by evading payment for mains supply. In *Hodkinson*,[25] the offender pleaded guilty to abstracting electricity by having fitted a device to the electricity meter at his home, which caused the meter to give a false reading. Bristow J commented that:

> In the judgment of this court deliberately stealing electricity in this way is an offence which calls for deterrent treatment when caught. In the circumstances of this case this court has come to the conclusion that the necessary deterrent element would be sufficiently dealt with by a sentence of one month's immediate imprisonment, accompanied by a fine of £750.

---

[20] This incongruity has always been present with regard to the petrol which is consumed.

[21] Paras 2.336–2.339.

[22] This incongruity would not have arisen under the draft Bill proposed by the Criminal Law Revision Committee, since the draft clause contained the words, 'with intent to cause loss to another'. These words were excised by the House of Lords.

[23] <http://www.cps.gov.uk/legal/section8>

[24] A charge contrary to s 125 or 126 Telecommunications Act 2003 is usually more appropriate.

[25] (1980) 2 Cr App R (S) 331, CA.

Hodkinson was followed in *Western*,[26] where a short deterrent custodial sentence was approved.

In *Harrison*,[27] the court observed that **11.14**

> This is quite a serious criminal offence and is not to be taken lightly. After all, law-abiding members of the public have to pay their public utility bills and some people, such as retired folk or lone parents, find difficulty in doing so because of their limited means.[28]

There are numerous instances of the offence being prosecuted in relation to large-scale **11.15** cannabis cultivation where the cost of running the cultivation equipment would otherwise be very high.[29]

Dishonest Telephone Use

The corresponding provision in the Larceny Act was sometimes used to deal with those **11.16** who dishonestly used a telephone and this would seem to be perfectly possible under the Theft Act s 13. For example, the employee who dishonestly uses his employer's telephone for his own private purposes would seem to be in no different situation from the employee who uses any other electrically operated machine. The same must be true of mobile telephones. The phones operate on batteries providing electricity, and the use of the phone involves the abstraction of that electricity.

Section 125 of the Communications Act 2003 creates an offence of dishonestly obtain- **11.17** ing an electronic communications service with intent to avoid payment of a charge applicable to the provision of that service.[30] The offence is triable either way, with a maximum penalty, on conviction on indictment, of imprisonment for a term not exceeding five years or a fine or both and, on summary conviction, of imprisonment for a term not exceeding six months or a fine not exceeding the statutory maximum or both.[31] It would seem right to rely on this offence, rather than the Theft Act, whenever it is available but, for cases which do not fall within s 125 there seems to be no reason why s 13 should not be invoked.

It is also an offence under s 126(1) of the Communications Act for a person to have in his **11.18** possession or under his control anything which may be used for obtaining an electronic communications service, with intent.[32]

---

[26] (1987) 9 Cr App R (S) 6.
[27] [2001] EWCA Crim 3247.
[28] [6] per HH J Rant QC. See also *Buckley and Buckley* [2004] EWCA Crim 78, where the losses were claimed to be in the region of £29,000.
[29] See eg *Owens* [2006] EWCA Crim 1061; *Ferris* [2006] EWCA Crim 720; *Hodgson and Barnes* [2003] EWCA Crim 2185; *Nicholls* [2002] EWCA Crim 752; *Snowden* [2002] EWCA Crim 923.
[30] Section 125(2) restricts the scope of s 125 so that it is not an offence to obtain a service mentioned in the Copyright Designs and Patents Act 1988, s 297(1), namely to receive a programme included in a broadcasting or cable programme service provided from a place in the United Kingdom with intent to avoid payment of any charge applicable to the reception of the programme.
[31] Section 125(3).
[32] Section 126(2) also provides an offence for a person to supply or offer to supply anything which may be so used, where he knows or believes that the intentions of the person supplied or offered fall within s 126(3).

11.19 Parliament has also created specific offences to deal with dishonesty in relation to particular conduct involving electronic equipment including, for example, receiving programmes broadcast via satellite and cable,[33] and reprogramming mobile phone SIM cards.[34] The offences in ss 6 and 7 of the Fraud Act 2006 will also apply in many such cases.[35]

---

[33] See the Copyright Designs and Patents Act 1988, s 297(1) and s 297A inserted by the Conditional Access (Unauthorized Decoders) Regs 2000, SI 2000/1175.

[34] Mobile Telephones (Re-programming) Act 2000.

[35] Ch 9.

12

BLACKMAIL

Actus reus	12.02
Mens rea	12.16
Sentencing	12.51

'Blackmail'[1] is the name which was commonly given to the group of offences contained in   **12.01**
ss 29–31 of the Larceny Act 1916.[2] That term was officially adopted for the first time as the
name of the offence which replaces these unsatisfactory and 'obscure'[3] sections of the
Larceny Act. Section 21(1) of the 1968 Act provides:

A person is guilty of blackmail if, with a view to gain for himself or another or with intent to cause
loss to another, he makes any unwarranted demand with menaces; and for this purpose a demand
with menaces is unwarranted unless the person making it does so in the belief—
   (a) that he has reasonable grounds for making the demand; and
   (b) that the use of the menaces is a proper means of reinforcing the demand.

It is triable only on indictment. In 2005/6 there were 1,646 recorded offences of blackmail.[4]

Actus reus

The *actus reus* consists in a demand with menaces; and the two problems here are to deter-   **12.02**
mine the meaning of the expressions, 'demand' and 'menaces'.

Demand

Under the Larceny Act, the demand had to be for 'any property or valuable thing'[5] or some-   **12.03**
thing capable of being stolen[6] or for an appointment or office of profit or trust.[7] The Theft

---

[1] CLRC, *Eighth Report*, Cmnd 2977 (1966) paras 108–25; Griew ch 14; ATH Smith, *Property Offences*
(1994) ch 15.
[2] See the historical account in W Winder, 'The Development of Blackmail' (1941) 5 MLR 21; G Williams,
'Blackmail' [1954] Crim LR 7.
[3] CLRC, *Eighth Report*, Cmnd 2977 (1966) para 108.
[4] A Walker, C Kershaw, and S Nicholas, *Home Office Statistical Bulletin, Crime in England and Wales*
2005/2006 p 29, Recorded crime by offence 1996 to 2005/6 and percentage change between 2004/5 and
2005/6.
[5] Sections 29 and 31(a).
[6] Section 30.
[7] Section 31(b).

Act is not so limited. Section 21(2) provides: 'The nature of the act or omission demanded is immaterial, and it is also immaterial whether the menaces relate to action to be taken by the person making the demand.' In effect, this is limited by the requirement that the demand be made with a view to gain or intent to cause loss[8] so that the change in the law is probably slight. In the vast majority of cases, the blackmailer will be demanding money or other property, intending both a gain to himself and a loss to another. It is clearly intended that the demand for a remunerated appointment or office[9] be covered, though whether such a case satisfies the requirement of view to gain or loss requires further consideration.[10] It would seem, however, that a demand for an unremunerated office, which would formerly have been an offence, would now, prima facie, not be. For D to threaten a person he believed to have influence in these matters, if that person did not procure D's appointment as Lord Lieutenant of the County, or Chairman of the Trustees of the British Museum, would appear no longer to be an offence of blackmail. The limitation would seem to reflect a general policy of limiting the provisions of the Act to the protection of economic interests. Had there been no such limitation, the section would have extended to such cases as that where D demands with menaces that V shall have sexual intercourse with him—a case which is obviously outside the scope of an enactment dealing with 'theft and similar or associated offences' and which is provided for by other legislation.[11] Many academic arguments have been advanced that the offence can be viewed as an offence protecting more than economic interests, and in particular that it protects privacy.[12] A wealth of academic literature, beyond the scope of this work, has sought to identify the harm or interest being protected by the offence of blackmail.[13]

12.04 In other respects, the 1968 Act extended the scope of the law. To demand with menaces that a person abandon a claim to property or release D from some legal liability of an economic nature now constitute blackmail. To demand with menaces that V discontinue divorce proceedings would not, however, be within the section.[14]

12.05 Whereas under s 29 of the Larceny Act the demand had to be in writing, it is quite immaterial whether the demand under s 21 of the Theft Act be oral or written. As was the case under the old law, it is likely that there may be a demand although it is not expressed in words, 'a demand may be implicit or explicit'.[15] It is probably enough that 'the demeanour

---

[8] See below, para 12.33.

[9] CLRC, *Eighth Report*, Cmnd 2977 (1966) para 117.

[10] Below, para 12.33.

[11] Sexual Offences Act 2003, s 4. Bizarrely, the offence of procuring sexual intercourse by threats (Sexual Offences Act 1956, s 2) was not replaced in the 2003 Act. See generally, *Smith and Hogan, Criminal Law* ch 17. There are unreported instances of convictions for blackmail in these circumstances (e.g. *Downer* (2000) 17 Oct CA), but these must be erroneous.

[12] P Alldridge, 'Attempted Murder of the Soul: Blackmail, Privacy and Secrets' (1993) 13 OJLS 368.

[13] See inter alia, 'Blackmail—A Symposium' (1993) 141(5) U Pa L Rev and L Katz, *Ill-gotten Gains: Evasion, Blackmail, Fraud, and Kindred Puzzles of the Law* (1996). For recent English literature see W Block, 'The Logic of the Argument of Legalising Blackmail' [2001] Bracton LJ 61; W Block and R McGee, 'Blackmail as a Victimless Crime' [1999] Bracton LJ 24.

[14] cf where D demands with menaces that V settle a divorce on terms favourable to D: *St Q* [2002] 1 Cr App R (S) 440. What if D made a demand with a view to V discontinuing the divorce proceedings so that D would avoid paying higher maintenance?

[15] *Clear* [1968] 1 QB 670, [1968] 1 All ER 74 at 77, CA.

of the accused and the circumstances of the case were such that an ordinary reasonable man would understand that a demand . . . was being made upon him . . .'.[16] There may also be a demand although it is couched in terms of request and obsequious in tone;[17] D's humblest form of request may be a demand.[18] The addition of the menace is sufficient to show that it is truly a demand that is made. The demand can take any form. The essence of the matter is that D's communication to V, however phrased, conveys to V the message that a menace will materialize unless V complies with the demand. D may be guilty of blackmail where, for example, he apprehends V in the act of stealing and, without any formal demand, makes it clear to V that if he pays D money he will hear no more of the matter.[19] But, whether express or implied, there must actually be a demand. If, having caught V in the act of stealing, D receives and accepts an unsolicited offer to buy his silence, D would not be guilty of blackmail. Whether an utterance amounts to a 'demand' seems to depend on whether an ordinary literate person would so describe it.[20]

An oral demand would appear to be made as soon as it is uttered, though unheard by the person addressed. A demand may be made through an intermediary.[21] If D dispatches an intermediary, other than the Post Office, bearing a demand, whether written or oral, it is questionable whether it could be held to be 'made' until delivered.[22] The test would seem to be whether D has done, personally or through an agent, the final act necessary in the normal course to result in a communication. The Post Office, though sometimes treated as such, is not an agent in any real sense. The posted letter is as irrevocable as the bullet expelled from a gun. Any emissary other than the Post Office, whether he carries a demand or not, may be recalled; so the principal has, as yet, not demanded. **12.06**

A demand is made when and where a letter containing it is posted; and it probably continues to be made until it arrives and is read by the recipient.[23] Presumably the same is true of email communications, with the demand being complete once sent. The offence is, of course, complete irrespective of V's compliance with the demands or otherwise. It has been argued that the wide interpretation of demand means that there is no room for a crime of attempted blackmail,[24] although there are hypothetical scenarios of D being intercepted on his way to the post etc. Treating the full offence as committed before the demand has been communicated, emphasizes that the gravamen of the offence is the *making* of unwarranted demands per se. **12.07**

---

[16] *Collister and Warhurst* (1955) 39 Cr App R 100 at 102.

[17] *Robinson* (1796) 2 East PC 1110; *Studer* (1915) 11 Cr App R 307.

[18] cf *Robinson* (1796) 2 East PC 1110, where the words 'Remember, Sir, I am now only making an appeal to your benevolence' were held in the circumstances capable of importing a demand. In *Miah* [2003] 1 Cr App R (S) 379, D sent videos of child pornography to Vs with a return address and then contacted Vs informing them that their fingerprints were on the videos and 'urging' them or 'inviting' them to call a telephone number. D pleaded guilty and no issue arose as to whether these invitations to call the number were a 'demand'.

[19] cf *Collister and Warhurst* (1955) 39 Cr App R 100, CCA: 'the demeanour of the accused' was sufficient.

[20] *Treacy v DPP* [1971] AC 537 at 565, [1971] 1 All ER 110 at 124, HL, per Lord Diplock.

[21] *Thumber* (1999) No 199900691, 29 Nov, CA.

[22] See Griew, 12–11 to 12–15, and the discussion by Lord Reid (dissenting) in *Treacy* [1971] AC 537 at 550 and [1971] 1 All ER at 111. See PJ Pace, 'Demanding with Menaces' (1971) 121 NLJ 242.

[23] ibid. cf *Baxter* [1972] 1 QB 1, [1971] 2 All ER 359, CA.

[24] See *Moran* (1952) 36 Cr App R 10, 12, cf JL Edwards, 'Criminal Attempts' (1952) 15 MLR 345.

12.08   To post a letter containing a demand with menaces in England addressed to V in Germany amounts to an offence in England: *Treacy v DPP*.[25] To post the letter in Germany addressed to V in England is an offence triable here. According to Lord Diplock the offence is triable here even if the letter does not arrive in England. If he was right, there will be no problem for the prosecutor.[26] If he was wrong, then resort must be had to the 1993 Act. Blackmail is a Group A offence under the 1993 Act. Under s 2 of the Criminal Justice Act 1993, provided an essential element of the offence occurs within England and Wales the English courts will have jurisdiction. Proof of the arrival of the letter in England is 'an event . . . proof of which is required for the conviction of the offence'—a 'relevant event'[27]—so D will be triable here for the full offence if the letter arrives and for an attempt if it does not. The only potential difficulty for the courts is in identifying whether a relevant act has occurred.[28]

Menaces

12.09   The Criminal Law Revision Committee stated:[29]

> We have chosen the word 'menaces' instead of 'threats' because, notwithstanding the wide meaning given to 'menaces' in *Thorne*'s case . . . we regard that word as stronger than 'threats', and the consequent slight restriction of the scope of the offence seems to us right.

It is reasonably clear, then, that it was the intention that the old law should be preserved here. In the case referred to, *Thorne v Motor Trade Association*,[30] Lord Wright said:

> I think the word 'menace' is to be liberally construed and not as limited to threats of violence but as including threats of any action detrimental to or unpleasant to the person addressed. It may also include a warning that in certain events such action is intended.

12.10   In view of the breadth of this definition, it is apparent that any restriction imposed by the use of the word 'menaces' rather than 'threats' must be slight. In most cases, there is no need to spell out the meaning of the word to a jury, since it is 'an ordinary English word which a jury could be expected to understand'.[31]

12.11   Where D makes a demand with a 'menace' that would cause a person of ordinary fortitude to succumb, V's refusal to accede to the demand cannot relieve D of liability. There can be a menace even if V is not intimidated. Thus, D may be guilty of blackmail where he

---

[25] See n 20 followed in the High Ct in Australia in *Austin* (1989) 166 CLR 669.

[26] Rose LJ followed this approach in *Smith (No 1)* [1996] 2 Cr App R 1. See also *Smith (Wallace) (No 4)* [2004] EWCA Crim 631.

[27] Above, para 2.04. There is a potential problem in that s 4 of the 1993 Act refers to a 'communication' within the jurisdiction. Blackmail does not require the demand/menace to be communicated, it is sufficient that D makes such a demand with menaces. cf the view of Lords Reid and Morris dissenting in *Treacy*.

In relation to a Group A or Group B offence—(a) there is an obtaining of property in England and Wales if the property is either despatched from or received at a place in England and Wales; and (b) there is a communication in England and Wales of any information, instruction, request, demand or other matter if it is sent by any means—(i) from a place in England and Wales to a place elsewhere; or (ii) from a place elsewhere to a place in England and Wales.

[28] See generally, M Hirst, *Jurisdiction and the Ambit of the Criminal Law* (2001) 167.

[29] CLRC, *Eighth Report*, Cmnd 2977 (1966) para 123.

[30] [1937] AC 797 at 817, HL.

[31] *Lawrence* (1971) 57 Cr App R 64.

threatens to assault V unless V pays him money, though V is in no way frightened and squares up to D with the result that D runs away.[32]

However, a threat does not amount to a menace unless 'it is of such a nature and extent **12.12** that the mind of an ordinary person of normal stability and courage might be influenced or made apprehensive so as to accede unwillingly to the demand'.[33] If the threat is 'of such a character that it is not calculated to deprive any person of reasonably sound and ordinarily firm mind of the free and voluntary action of his mind,'[34] then it does not amount to a menace; but it has been said this doctrine should receive 'a liberal construction in practice',[35] that is, the court should be slow to hold that the threat would not influence an ordinary person. If the threat is one of so trivial a nature that it would not influence anybody[36] to respond to the demand, it is certainly reasonable to say that it is not a menace. A letter from a student rag committee to shopkeepers offering to sell 'indemnity posters' reading 'these premises are immune from all rag 73 activities whatever they may be' has been held not to amount to a menace.[37] It would no doubt have been different if the 72 rag activities had been of such a nature as to cause apprehension in ordinary shopkeepers.

The doctrine is satisfactory enough, then, where the person to whom the demand is **12.13** addressed is a person of normal stability and courage, but it has been said that 'persons who are thus practised upon are not as a rule of average firmness'.[38] Suppose that V is a weak-minded person, likely to be swayed by a fanciful or trivial threat which an ordinary person would ignore; and that this is known to the threatener. It is submitted that the threat should be regarded as a menace; and that to hold the contrary would be hardly more reasonable than to say that robbery was not committed because the victim allowed himself to be overcome by a degree of force which a courageous person would have successfully resisted.[39] In *Garwood*,[40] it was held to be a misdirection to tell the jury, in the case of an exceptionally timid victim, that it was immaterial that an ordinary person would not have been influenced, unless they were also told that they must be satisfied that D knew of that exceptional timidity.

Whether a threat amounts to a menace within this principle appears, at first sight, to be **12.14** an objective question to be answered by looking at the actual facts of the case. It appears from *Clear*,[41] however, that the question is to be answered by reference to the facts known

---

[32] cf *Moran* [1952] 1 All ER 803 n, CCA.
[33] *Clear* [1968] 1 QB 670, [1968] 1 All ER 74, CA.
[34] *Boyle and Merchant* [1914] 3 KB 339 at 345, CCA.
[35] *Tomlinson* [1895] 1 QB 706 at 710, per Wills J; *Clear* (above) at 80.
[36] cf *Tomlinson* (above) per Wills J; *Boyle and Merchant* [1914] 3 KB 339 at 344.
[37] *Harry* [1974] Crim LR 32 (Judge Petre).
[38] *Tomlinson* [1895] 1 QB 706 at 710, per Wills J. The vulnerability arises not from physical weakness or timidity but from the position of risk of the victim. A recent illustration is of businessmen being charged extortionate prices for champagne ordered in Soho clubs and threatened with violence if they fail to pay. The perpetrators are rarely charged since the businessmen are unwilling to admit their presence in the clubs: *The Observer*, 29 Feb 2004.
[39] cf the view of ATH Smith, *Property Offences* (1994), who suggests that the proper test is what effect the threat would have on the ordinary person: para 15–17.
[40] [1987] 1 All ER 1032, [1987] Crim LR 476, CA.
[41] Above, para 12.11 [1968] 1 All ER 74 at 80, CA.

to the accused, if these are different from the actual facts—that, in effect, the question is one of intention. In that case, D had received a subpoena to appear as a witness in an action in which V was the defendant. D demanded money from V with a threat that, if the money were not paid, he would alter the statement he had made to the police and so cause V to lose the action. V was quite unmoved by this threat since the action was being defended by his insurers and, if the action succeeded, it was they and not he who would pay. D's blackmail conviction was upheld. It might be said that, in the actual circumstances of the case, the words used could not influence a person of normal stability and courage; but the court appears to have held that regard must be had, not to the actual circumstances, but to the circumstances as they appeared to the person making the demand:

> There may be special circumstances unknown to an accused which would make the threats innocuous and unavailing for the accused's demand, but such circumstances would have no bearing on the accused's state of mind and of his intention. If an accused knew that what he threatened would have no effect on the victim it might be different.[42]

12.15 It is submitted, therefore—and *Garwood*[43] appears to confirm—that there is a sufficient menace if, in the circumstances known to the accused, the threat might:

(i) influence the mind of an ordinary person of normal stability and courage, whether or not it in fact influences the person addressed; or
(ii) influence the mind of the person addressed, though it would not influence an ordinary person.

It is assumed, of course, that in both cases there is an intention to influence the person addressed to accede to the demand by means of the threat.

Mens rea

12.16 The *mens rea* of blackmail comprises a number of elements:

(1) An intention to make a demand with menaces.[44]
(2) A view to gain for himself or another, or intention to cause loss to another.
(3) Either:
   (a) no belief that he has reasonable grounds for making the demand, or
   (b) no belief that the use of the menaces is a proper means of reinforcing the demand.

12.17 It is clear that the onus of proof of each of these elements is on the Crown; but it is enough to establish (1) and (2) and *either* (3)(a) or (3)(b). It may well be that, once the Crown has introduced evidence of elements (1) and (2), an evidential burden is put upon the accused as regards (3); that is, he must introduce some evidence of his belief of both (a) and (b), whereupon it will be for the Crown to prove that he did not believe one, or the other, or both. Where, on the face of it, the means used to reinforce the demand are improper, and D does not set up the case that he believed in its propriety, the jury need not be directed on the point.[45] It will be noted that whether or not a demand is 'unwarranted' is primarily a

[42] ibid.
[43] Above, para 12.13.
[44] Above.
[45] *Lawrence* (1971) 57 Cr App R 64.

question of the accused's belief, as to which no one is better informed than he; and the phraseology of the section—'a demand with menaces is unwarranted unless . . .'—suggests that it is for the accused to assert that his demand was warranted. Where, however, D does not set up such a defence, but the evidence is such that a jury might reasonably think he had the beliefs in question, it is the duty of the judge to direct the jury not to convict unless satisfied that he did not have the beliefs or one of them.[46]

An intention to make a demand with menaces

It is difficult to envisage circumstances in which difficulties with this aspect of the *mens rea* will arise in practice. One possibility is where D is intoxicated to such an extent that he lacks the *mens rea*. Since the offence is one of specific intent a successful plea of voluntary intoxication will lead to acquittal.[47] A further possibility is where D acts entirely in jest and believes that his joke is not a demand.

12.18

A view to gain or intent to cause loss

'Gain' and 'loss' are defined by s 34(2)(a) of the Theft Act:

12.19

'gain' and 'loss' are to be construed as extending only to gain or loss in money or other property, but as extending to any such gain or loss whether temporary or permanent; and

    (i) 'gain' includes a gain by keeping what one has, as well as a gain by getting what one has not; and

    (ii) 'loss' includes a loss by not getting what one might get, as well as a loss by parting with what one has.

12.20

As has already been noted,[48] this definition limits the offence to the protection of economic interests. Without it, the scope of s 21—demanding with menaces the performance of any act or omission—would have been very wide indeed and would certainly have extended far beyond 'theft and similar or associated offences' which it was the object of the 1968 Act to revise. In most cases, the blackmailer is trying to obtain money to which he knows he has no right and there will be no doubt about his view to gain. It is clearly not necessary, however, that there should be evidence of a direct demand for money or other property. It is enough that D's purpose in demanding the act or omission, whatever it may be, is gain or loss in terms of money or other property. Suppose that D demands with menaces that V should marry him. If V is an heiress and D's object is to enrich himself, he is guilty of blackmail. A person who, to ease his pain, demands a morphine injection from his doctor at pistol-point has a view to gain. The drug is unquestionably property and it is immaterial that D's motive is relief of pain rather than economic gain and that the drug is injected into his arm rather than put in his hand.[49] A similar demand for medical treatment, such as a massage, is not blackmail unless, possibly, it involves, and D knows it involves, the use of some oil or cream on his body.

---

[46] 'It is always the duty of the judge to leave to the jury any issue (whether raised by the defence or not) which, on the evidence in the case, is an issue fit to be left to them:' *Palmer* [1971] AC 814, [1971] 1 All ER 1077 at 1080, PC, per Lord Morris.

[47] *Majewski* [1977] AC 443.

[48] Above, para 12.03.

[49] *Bevans* (1987) 87 Cr App R 64, [1988] Crim LR 236, CA.

12.21   It is, however, arguable that there is no sufficient view to gain or intent to cause loss where the gain and loss are merely incidental to a service which is the real object of the demand. Where D demands to be driven in V's car, does he have a view to gain or intent to cause loss in respect of the petrol? To charge blackmail would have the same artificiality as to charge the 'joyrider' (see chapter 10) with theft of the petrol; but that does not necessarily rule out the charge as a matter of law. It is enough that the acquisition of money or other property is one of several objects which D has in mind in making the demand.[50]

12.22   'With a view to' is therefore wider than a requirement that D has the gain as his primary purpose or sole purpose. It is not as wide as a test of 'oblique intent', whereby D may be found to have intended to gain if his purpose was a different consequence and he realizes that gain is a virtually certain outcome if he achieves that other result. The requirement is that D acts with 'a view to' and this requires that he has 'gain' as at least one of his objectives. Thus, if D is so consumed with desire for the heiress that he would have made exactly the same demand with menaces even if she had been a pauper, but knows that the marriage will be profitable, he may be liable if that was 'one of his reasons' for acting.

12.23   The gain or loss must be in money or other property so it is probable that, though obtaining services by dishonesty is now an offence,[51] obtaining them by threats is not, though D is enriched thereby.

12.24   Where it is a case of causing loss rather than making a gain, 'intent' is specifically required and this is likely to be construed to require a purposive intent or desire that loss should ensue. D demands with menaces that V should jump into a muddy pool. D's object is that V, who has offended him, should suffer discomfort and humiliation. As D foresaw, V's clothes are ruined by immersion in the pool and so he suffers a loss. It is probable that D is not guilty.

Belief in a right to the gain

12.25   It is not necessarily a good defence that D believes he has a right to the gain. If he has such a belief, then he certainly believes that he has reasonable grounds for making the demand, but it will be recalled that this does not cause the demand to be warranted unless it is coupled with a belief that the use of the menaces is a proper means of reinforcing the demand. Section 21 does not use the word 'dishonestly' which, in ss 1, 17, and 20, ensures that a claim of right to the property is a defence. It is clear that the Criminal Law Revision Committee intended that the offence might be committed where D had both a claim of right and an actual right to the property which he intended to acquire.[52]

A may be owed £100 by B and be unable to get payment. Perhaps A needs the money badly and B is in a position to pay; or perhaps A can easily afford to wait and B is in difficulty. Should it be black-mail for A to threaten B that, if he does not pay, A will assault him; or slash the tyres of his car; or tell people that B is a homosexual, which he is (or which he is not); or tell people about the debt and anything discreditable about the way in which it was incurred? On one view none of these threats should be enough to make the demand amount to blackmail. For it is no offence merely to utter

---

[50] *Dooley* [2005] EWCA Crim 3093, [2006] Crim LR 544. The court in considering a different offence refers with approval to the suggested definition in *Smith and Hogan, Criminal Law* 807.

[51] Fraud Act 2006, s 11, above, para 3.188.

[52] CLRC, *Eighth Report*, Cmnd 2977 (1966) para 119.

the threats without making the demand (unless for some particular reason such as breach of the peace or defamation); nor would the threat become criminal merely because it was uttered to reinforce a demand of a kind quite different from those associated with blackmail. Why then should it be blackmail merely because it is uttered to reinforce a demand for money which is owed? On this view no demand with menaces would amount to blackmail, however harsh the action threatened, unless there was dishonesty. This is a tenable view, though an extreme one. In our opinion it goes too far and there are some threats which should make the demand amount to blackmail even if there is a valid claim to the thing demanded. For example, we believe that most people would say that it should be blackmail to threaten to denounce a person, however truly, as a homosexual unless he paid a debt. It does not seem to follow from the existence of a debt that the creditor should be entitled to resort to any method, otherwise non-criminal, to obtain payment. There are limits to the methods permissible for the purpose of enforcing payment of a debt without recourse to the courts. For example, a creditor cannot seize the debtor's goods; and in *Parker*[53] it was held that a creditor who forged a letter from the Admiralty to a sailor warning him to pay a debt was guilty of forgery notwithstanding the existence of the debt.

This has given rise to much discussion in academic journals over whether there is a 'paradox' in the offence: while it is lawful for D to make a demand for payment of a debt owed by V and it is lawful for D to expose, or threaten to expose conduct about which V is likely to be embarrassed, it is an offence of blackmail to perform the two in combination. Academics have advanced a diverse range of theories in an attempt to justify the inclusion of the offence of blackmail in a coherent and principled code of criminal law.[54] **12.26**

In practical terms, the CLRC's stated objective was that blackmail might occur where D **12.27** had both a claim of right and an actual right to the property he demanded with menaces. Acts of Parliament do not always carry out the intention of those who frame them, and it has been argued that the use of the words 'with a view to gain' will defeat the object of the Committee in this case:[55] 'There is surely no gain or loss where a person merely secures the payment of that which he is owed.' The argument might be elaborated as follows: 'If I liquidate a just debt, I suffer no economic loss. In my personal balance sheet, the amount of cash in hand on the credit side is reduced, but this is offset by a corresponding reduction on the debit side in the item "sundry creditors".'[56] If the debtor has suffered no economic loss it follows that the creditor has acquired no economic gain for, while his cash in hand will increase, his credit balance under 'sundry debtors' will diminish. If 'gain in money or other property' means economic enrichment, then it is arguable that D has no view to gain when he demands that to which he is entitled.

The answer turns on the meaning of the word 'gain'. That word has frequently been the **12.28** subject of interpretation in other statutes.[57] The meaning given to a word in one statute is

---

[53] (1910) 74 JP 208.

[54] See for discussion *Smith and Hogan, Criminal Law* ch 20.

[55] B Hogan, 'Blackmail: Another View' [1966] Crim LR at 476.

[56] RN Gooderson [1960] CLJ 199 at 205, discussing the meaning of 'fraud' in relation to *Welham v DPP* [1961] AC 103, [1960] 1 All ER 805, HL.

[57] Particularly the Companies Acts and Factories Acts. See D Greenberg (ed), *Stroud's Judicial Dictionary* (7th edn 2006) 1094 under 'gain'. See also Obscene Publications Act 1964 and *Blackpool Chief Constable v Woodhall* [1965] Crim LR 660.

by no means conclusive as to that which it should bear in another; but it may give some guidance. 'Gain' certainly might mean 'profit'[58] and if that is its meaning in the Theft Act, then the argument in the preceding paragraph seems a sound one. On the other hand, Jessel MR has said ' "Gain" means exactly acquisition . . . Gain is something obtained or acquired.'[59] Though he found that there was a profit, and therefore a gain, in that case, it would seem that he did not think that gain was necessarily to be equated with profit. If then, 'gain' includes acquisition, whether at a profit or not, the difficulty disappears. A person may properly be said to have acquired that which he is entitled to have, if he secures ownership or possession of it. Apart from the intentions of the Committee which have been quoted above, the Act itself suggests that this is the right view, (a) through the omission of the word 'dishonestly', which would have imported a defence of claim of right, (b) because s 21 requires not merely a belief that D is entitled to the thing demanded but also a belief that the use of the menaces is proper, and (c) because 'gain' is defined to include 'getting what one has not'. It is submitted, therefore, that 'gain' includes the acquisition of money or other property whether it is due in law or not.[60] This view appears to be accepted by the courts.[61]

12.29 It has been held that 'getting hard cash as opposed to a mere right of action is getting more than one already has'.[62] It should be noted that it may also be a summary offence to harass a debtor where the debt is due.[63]

Intention to return an economic equivalent

12.30 If the view expressed in the preceding paragraphs is wrong, similar problems arise where D intends to restore to V an economic equivalent of the alleged gain which he has in mind. As a starting point, suppose that D wishes to acquire a particular 50p piece belonging to V which has a sentimental value for both V and D. D demands of V with menaces that he exchange the desired 50p piece for another. Obviously D intends to acquire the 50p piece but he does not intend to make any profit in terms of money.[64] If there were no view to gain in this situation, many cases would be excluded from the section which it is reasonably clear that it is intended to cover. If D demands with menaces that he be employed, he may have every intention of doing a good day's work and earning his wages.[65] The runner who, by menaces, gains admission to a race may have every intention of supplying a first-class performance which will be worth as much or more in terms of money to the organizers of the meeting as any prize he may win. The gambler who, by menaces, causes

---

[58] 'Any gain consequent on death' in the New Zealand Law Reform Act 1939 means 'any increase in financial resources', per Ostler J in *Alley v Alfred Bucklands & Sons Ltd* [1941] NZLR 575.

[59] *Re Arthur Average Association for British, Foreign and Colonial Ships, ex p Hargrove & Co* (1875) 10 Ch App 542 at 546.

[60] cf *Lawrence* (1971) 57 Cr App R 64, CA, where it appears that D believed the debt to be due.

[61] See *Attorney-General's Reference (No 1 of 2001)* [2002] EWCA Crim 1768.

[62] *Parkes* [1973] Crim LR 358 (Judge Dean); cf *Parkes* [1974] Crim LR 320, CA.

[63] Administration of Justice Act 1970, s 40. *Smith and Hogan, Criminal Law* 809.

[64] Of course, the problem under consideration would not arise if the coin had a higher market value than its nominal value. cf *Moss v Hancock* [1899] 2 QB 111.

[65] Lord Denning has expressed the view that, in such a case, there is no intention to cause economic loss to the employer: *Welham v DPP* [1961] AC, 103 at 131, HL. It follows that the employee has no intention to make an economic gain.

the bookmaker's clerk to let him bet on credit may have every intention of paying up if the horse backed loses—he is prepared to pay the full economic value of the chance he has bought. In each of these examples, D has a view to the acquisition of money or other property—his wages, the prize, the winnings—and in each case it is submitted that he is guilty of blackmail.

12.31 If the argument advanced here is correct, the same principle must govern 'loss'. D intends V to suffer a loss if he intends him to be deprived of particular money or property, though he may also intend that V be fully compensated in economic terms.

Temporary gain and loss

12.32 The intention permanently to deprive—which is an essential ingredient of theft and robbery—is not a requisite of blackmail. Suppose that D by menaces causes V to let him have a car on hire for a week. If D intends to return that car at the end of the week, he cannot be guilty of theft or of robbery.[66] He has, however, a view to a temporary gain, which is sufficient under s 21, and he is guilty of blackmail. This may seem strange, but it is consistent with the theory that it is the method of obtaining the property—the demand with menaces—which is the gist of the offence and not the unlawful profit made or contemplated by D or the corresponding loss to V. As we have seen, D may even be demanding property which he is entitled to have.

Intent to cause loss

12.33 In most cases 'a view to gain' and an 'intent to cause loss' will go hand in hand; V's loss will be D's gain. The phrase, 'intent to cause loss' is not, however, superfluous. There may be circumstances in which D intends to cause a loss to V without any corresponding gain to D. If V has written his memoirs and D demands with menaces that V destroy them, D has an intent to cause loss but no view to gain. Another instance would be the case where D demands with menaces that V dismiss X from a remunerated office or employment or that V should not promote X. D intends to cause X a loss (by not getting what he might get)[67] and it is immaterial whether D has in view any gain to himself or another. Likewise where D demands with menaces that V resign his own appointment, or not apply for, or refuse promotion.

Gain by keeping and loss by not getting

12.34 A view to gain includes an intention to keep what one has; and intent to cause a loss includes causing another not to get what he might get.[68] Thus if D owes V £10 and, by menaces, he induces him to accept £5 in full satisfaction, he has caused a gain and a loss within the meaning of s 21.

12.35 If D, knowing that V is in financial difficulties and in urgent need of money, takes advantage of this situation in order to induce V to accept a lesser sum in satisfaction, he may be in danger of conviction of blackmail. D can hardly say, to any effect, that he had reasonable grounds for making the demand if he knew the larger sum was due; and in that case it is

---

[66] Above, para 2.316.
[67] Above, para 12.30.
[68] Section 34(2)(a)(i) and (ii), above, para 12.30.

immaterial whether the use of the menaces is a proper means of reinforcing the demand. The Court of Appeal has taken the view that it is 'intimidation' and holding a creditor 'to ransom' to say, 'We cannot pay you the £480. But we will pay you £300 if you will accept it in settlement. If you do not accept it on those terms you will get nothing. £300 is better than nothing.'[69] This suggests that that court, at least, would regard such pressure on a creditor as a 'menace'. In *Ford Ag Werke AG v Transtec Automotive (Campsie) Ltd*[70] Jacobs J concluded that the suppliers' receivers demanding a higher price from Ford for parts, knowing that Ford had no stocks of that part, may have constituted a demand with menaces, but that there was no evidence of the *mens rea*.

Remoteness

12.36 Where a number of intermediate steps are required between the act caused by D's menace and the acquisition by him of any gain, problems of remoteness may arise. If D gains admission to an Inn of Court by menacing the Under-Treasurer,[71] is he guilty of an offence under the section? If he intends ultimately to practise and thereby to earn fees it would seem that his action is taken with a view to gain—that is one of his reasons for acting and following *Dooley*, (above) that suffices. But if he has no intention to practise and merely wants the prestige of the barrister's qualification it is difficult to see that he can have committed the offence. It must appear that D had as one of his reasons the possibility of using his qualification to earn money.

12.37 What, then, if D menaces the headmaster of the public school with a view to gaining admission for his newly-born son? If D believes that the only advantage of education at that school is that it will produce a more cultured person with a greater capacity for the enjoyment of life than education in a state school, he has no view to gain. If, however, he believes and is motivated by his belief that his son will (in about twenty years' time) have a greater earning power, is it to be said that he has a view to gain? Literally he does. Yet the gain is so distant in time and subject to so many contingencies that its connection with the demand with menaces may be thought too remote. A stronger case is that of a candidate for a university examination who menaces the examiner with a view to passing or getting a better-class degree than he would otherwise obtain. Most candidates have an eye on their earning capacity and this might be prima facie evidence of a view to gain. It would certainly seem to be one of their reasons for acting.

Unwarranted demands[72]

12.38 Whether a demand is 'warranted' or not appears to be exclusively a question of the accused's belief. Theoretically a demand with menaces may be unwarranted, although D is entitled to recover the property demanded and the menace is a perfectly proper means of enforcing the demand. Suppose V has stolen and disposed of D's picture. D threatens to report him

---

[69] *D & C Builders v Rees* [1966] 2 QB 617 at 625, CA, per Lord Denning MR. The problem of threats in contractual negotiation is not new. See the cases of *Denyer* [1926] 2 KB 258, and *Hardie and Lane Ltd v Chilton* [1928] 2 KB 306.

[70] [2001] BCC 403.

[71] cf *Bassey* (1931) 22 Cr App R 160.

[72] See Williams, *TBCL* 829–8.

to the police unless he pays D £1,000. D believes the picture is only worth £100; so he does not believe that he has reasonable grounds for making the demand. The picture is in fact worth £1,000, so he does actually have reasonable grounds. D who has looked up an out-of-date law book believes that it is the offence of compounding a felony to accept any consideration for not disclosing a theft; so he does not believe that the use of the menace is a proper means of enforcing the demand. But by the Criminal Law Act 1967, s 5(1) it is lawful to accept reasonable compensation for making good the injury or loss caused by a relevant offence,[73] in consideration for not disclosing it. The use of the menaces then—or so it seems—is a proper means of reinforcing the demand. Looking at the facts objectively, D has done nothing wrong; but he is guilty of blackmail.

It does not seem likely that this will be a serious issue in practice. Where D's conduct is **12.39** objectively innocent, it is unlikely that a prosecution will ever be instituted. If it is, the onus of proof on the Crown will be very difficult to satisfy. The usual way of satisfying the jury that D did not have the beliefs referred to in s 21(1)(a) and (b) will be by showing that no reasonable person could have held such a belief. For example, if D says that he believed that he had reasonable grounds for demanding £1,000 from his neighbour in return for not disclosing to the neighbour's wife that her husband had committed adultery, it is safe to assume, in the absence of some extraordinary circumstances, that the jury will disbelieve him and be satisfied beyond reasonable doubt of his guilt.[74] They will be so satisfied because they will feel that no person in his right mind could entertain such a belief for a moment.[75] If then, D's beliefs are entirely reasonable, the normal mode of proof fails; and, in the absence of some confession by D as to his belief in the unreasonableness of his demand, or the impropriety of his threat, conviction will be impossible.

The problem that does arise is the converse. That is, the grounds for making the demand **12.40** were not reasonable but D asserts that he believed they were; the use of the menaces is not a proper means of reinforcing the demand but D asserts that he believed it was. The question for the jury then appears to be simply whether D is speaking the truth. Juries have to determine this question often enough; but the difference about this case is that it is not a question of the accused's belief in fact, but the accused's belief in standards.

This provision of the Act has been criticized by a judicial writer:[76] **12.41**

If a defendant has acted disgracefully by making a certain demand reinforced by threats of a particular kind, I see no injustice in holding him responsible in a criminal court, even though he may have acted according to his own standard in these matters. On the other hand I see some danger to our general standards of right and wrong, if each man can claim to act according to his own, however low that standard may be. That is one objection. Another is the difficulty of the jury's ascertaining the defendant's standard, so that it may be decided whether in the case before them he acted

---

[73] As substituted by the Serious Organised Crime and Police Act 2005, s 111, Sch 7 pt 3, para 40(1), (3)(a).
[74] See eg in *Kewell* [2000] 2 Cr App R (S) 38 V owed a debt to D but there was little difficulty in establishing that D knew it was improper to threaten to reveal embarrassing but consensually taken photos of V taken during their period of cohabitation.
[75] The ultimate question is as to the state of mind of the accused person and this should always be stressed to a jury.
[76] Sir Bernard MacKenna, 'Blackmail: A Criticism' [1966] Crim LR 467 at 472.

in accordance with it. A man whose standard is below the general may fail in a particular case to observe even his own standard in which event he would, I suppose, be punishable under clause 17 [now section 21]. But are questions of this kind triable?

12.42   If no regard whatever were paid to external standards, the crime of blackmail would virtually disappear. It is almost invariably a premeditated offence. By the accused's own standards, it is something which he might do, whatever others might think. It is his belief at the time of making the demand which is relevant. If he should later admit that his conduct was unreasonable or improper, this is probably because he knows full well that people generally regard it as unreasonable or improper. It would be unreasonable to attribute to Parliament an intention to enact an offence which would be a dead letter. It was certainly not the intention of the Committee. If we look first at the question of the propriety of the threat, some clear guidance as to their intentions can be found in the Report.[77] Some care was devoted to the choice of the word 'proper':

> we chose the word 'proper' after considering 'legitimate' or 'fair' instead. Any of the three words would, we think, be suitable. 'Fair' would provide a good test for a jury to apply. It might also be a little more favourable to the accused, because the jury might think that, even if the accused behaved improperly the prosecutor behaved so badly that it was fair that he should be treated as he was. There seems little difference between 'legitimate' and 'proper'. On the whole, 'proper' seems the best word. 'Proper' directs the mind to consideration of what is morally and socially acceptable, which seems right on a matter of this kind; 'legitimate' might suggest that it is a purely legal question whether the accused had a right to utter the menaces.

This passage clearly shows that it was intended that the jury should apply a standard and that the standard should be 'what is morally and socially acceptable'.

12.43   We are, of course, concerned with D's beliefs in the matter, not the jury's. Once D's belief has been ascertained, it has to be decided whether it fits the words of the section. The word 'proper' has to be given a meaning. According to this interpretation then, the test is: 'Did the accused person believe that what he threatened to do was morally and socially acceptable?' The effect might be illustrated by considering the effect on the case, decided under the Larceny Act, of *Dymond*.[78] D wrote to V alleging that he had indecently assaulted her and adding, 'I leave this to you to think what you are going to do, paid or get summons . . . If you dont send to and apologise I shall let everybody knowed in the town it [*sic*].' Her conviction was upheld by the Court of Criminal Appeal holding that an honest belief in 'reasonable cause' for making the demand, as opposed to reasonable cause in fact, was not a defence. Probably a jury would take the view that Miss Dymond's conduct was, by their standards, morally and socially unacceptable; but the question would be whether she knew that it was morally and socially unacceptable. In the circles in which Emily Dymond moved it may well be that the advice of the neighbours was: 'If he won't pay up, you ought to summons him and tell everyone.' If these were the only standards known to Emily, she ought to be acquitted.

---

[77] Para 123.
[78] [1920] 2 KB 260.

This is not to say that the standards of the small social group to which D belongs will neces-   **12.44**
sarily govern in every case. D may belong to a terrorist organization, the members of which
think it right to demand money as the price of releasing a hostage in order to further their
political ends. The conduct may be morally and socially acceptable within the small group;
but it is safe to assume that these are not the only standards known to D. He is well aware
that, in English society generally, such conduct is morally and socially unacceptable; and it
must be the known standards of English society generally which apply.

This appears to have been the interpretation adopted in the only reported case on the   **12.45**
section so far to reach the Court of Appeal. In *Harvey Uylett and Plummer*,[79] V had obtained
£20,000 from D by deception. He had promised to supply D with a large quantity of cannabis but had no intention of carrying out this illegal promise. D may well have thought
he had reasonable grounds for demanding the return of the money; but he reinforced
his demand with threats to kill or maim or rape. The judge directed that, as a matter of
law, these threats could not be 'proper'. The Court of Appeal agreed that 'no act which
was not believed to be lawful could be believed to be proper within the meaning of the
subsection'; but it should have been left to the jury to decide whether D knew that what
he was threatening to do was a criminal act.[80] Since the threats were to do acts 'which any
sane man knows to be against the laws of every civilised country' the Court of Appeal
applied the proviso (as was then still possible).

A person might not realize that the acts he is threatening to do are crimes. It is lawful to use   **12.46**
or threaten reasonable force to recover property which is wrongfully withheld. A person
who misjudged what is reasonable might be threatening to commit a crime without realiz-
ing it and so might rightly be held to believe to be 'proper' what was in fact unlawful. It is
difficult to imagine that anyone brought up in England could fail to know that killing,
maiming, or raping is an unlawful way of recovering property; but a person coming from
a land where cutting off the hands of thieves is commonplace might not realize that his
threat to cut off a thief's hand, if his property was not returned, was unlawful; and so might
rightly be held to believe that the threat was proper.[81]

Even if D does not know that it is unlawful to threaten another with a dagger in order to   **12.47**
compel the payment of a debt,[82] a jury might well find that he knew that it was a socially
and morally unacceptable way of compelling the wages clerk to pay his wages. If so, D,
though not guilty of robbery or attempted robbery, would be guilty of blackmail. In many
cases of blackmail the threat is to do something not amounting to a crime. Here the exclusive test must be whether D knew that the threat in the circumstances would be condemned
as improper by the community generally.

---

[79] (1981) 72 Cr App R 139, [1981] Crim LR 104, CA.

[80] Even if there is only one conceivable answer to the question, 'Did D know that what he was threatening
to do was unlawful?' it must still be left to the jury: *Stonehouse* [1978] AC 55, [1977] 2 All ER 909, HL.

[81] The view that what is known to be unlawful cannot be believed to be 'proper' was advocated in the
fourth edition of this book but is criticized by Williams, *TBCL* 836–7, pointing out flaws in the logic of the
court in *Harvey*. *Lambert* [1972] Crim LR 422 (Deputy Circuit Judge Arnold) must now be regarded as a
doubtful decision, though it appears that in *Harry* [1974] Crim LR 32 the prosecution conceded that *Lambert*
was correct.

[82] cf *Skivington* [1968] 1 QB 166, [1967] 1 All ER 483, CA; above, para 7.04.

12.48 D's plea might very well be accepted in the following cases. D, a bookmaker, being unable to obtain payment of a wagering debt due from V, another bookmaker, threatens to report V to Tattersalls if he does not pay up. D threatens V that she will tell V's wife of their immoral relationship if V does not pay her the money he promised for her immoral services. D threatens that he will warn his friends against doing business with V if V does not pay up a statute-barred debt.

12.49 A similar test might be applied to determine whether D believed he had reasonable grounds for making the demand. If he had a claim of legal right then, clearly, he believed he had reasonable grounds for making the demand. A woman who believed, wrongly but on the advice of a Hungarian lawyer, that she was entitled to money promised to her as the price of her past immoral services, would have a good defence.[83] If she knew that she had no legal right, she might nevertheless believe that the man was under a moral obligation to compensate her, and a jury could find that she believed that she had reasonable grounds for her demand. Similarly where D demands money won on a wager with V, though he knows that wagers are unenforceable in law, or demands payment of a statute-barred debt, being aware of the statute of limitations.

12.50 If this view is accepted, the law is certainly lacking in precision; but this is a branch of the law in which precision is not easily obtainable. From the point of view of justice, however, the law seems unexceptionable. The defendant is not to be held liable unless it is proved that he knew he was doing something which he ought not to do, in the broad sense described, either in making the demand, or in making the threat. Moreover, it is very similar in effect to the interpretation now put upon dishonesty by *Ghosh*.[84]

Sentencing

12.51 The maximum penalty for the offence is fourteen years (s 21(3)). Sentences for the offence are severe with a substantial deterrent element.[85] The Court of Appeal described the offence as being 'one of the ugliest' in the criminal calendar.[86] The range of conduct covered by the offence is vast and the sentences reflect this.

Threats to publish embarrassing material

12.52 Sentences of up to four years are not excessive in this context. Relevant factors include whether the material is fabricated, and whether the accused believes he is recovering a debt.

12.53 In *Miah*,[87] four years was upheld as not excessive where M had pleaded guilty to eleven counts of blackmail and one of perverting the course of justice when he had sent to company directors child pornography videos. When the victims returned the videos (about half did), M contacted them saying that their fingerprints were on the cassettes and that he

---

[83] *Bernhard* [1938] 2 KB 264, [1938] 2 All ER 140.
[84] Above, para 2.270.
[85] *Davies* [2004] 1 Cr App R (S) 209.
[86] *Hadjou* (1989) 11 Cr App R (S) 29.
[87] [2003] 1 Cr App R (S) 379.

would reveal this. Demands for £5,000 were made.[88] The sentence will be lower where D has a belief that he is recovering a debt. In *Kewell*,[89] in an attempt to recover monies owed to him from his ex partner, after other methods of request had failed, K threatened to reveal intimate photos taken with her consent during their cohabitation. D, pleaded guilty and expressed remorse. The Court of Appeal substituted a term of eighteen months with one of twelve months. Three years was said to be appropriate in *Stone*,[90] where the offender took part in homosexual activities with the victim and then demanded sums of money under the threat of disclosing the victim's behaviour to the police.

Debt collecting

Sentences vary dramatically depending on whether the accused is recovering a debt by improper means, whether weapons or threats of violence are used.   **12.54**

---

[88] See also *Daniels* [2002] 1 Cr App R (S) 443 letters falsely alleging that D had had homosexual contact with V and threatening to expose this to V's partner unless paid £3,000. Two years on a plea where D had serious depressive illness.

[89] [2000] 2 Cr App R (S) 38.

[90] (1989) 11 Cr App R (S) 176.

13

HANDLING STOLEN GOODS AND RELATED OFFENCES

Handling Stolen Goods

English law provides a specific offence of handling and has, since the nineteenth century, treated this conduct as an independent crime rather than one of being an 'accessory after the fact' to theft.[1] The offence created by s 22 replaced both the indictable offences under the Larceny Act 1916, s 33 and the summary offences under the Larceny Act 1861, s 97. Section 22 provides: **13.01**

(1) A person handles stolen goods if (otherwise than in the course of the stealing) knowing or believing them to be stolen goods he dishonestly receives the goods, or dishonestly undertakes or assists in their retention, removal, disposal or realisation by or for the benefit of another person, or if he arranges to do so.

(2) A person guilty of handling stolen goods shall on conviction on indictment be liable to imprisonment for a term not exceeding fourteen years.[2]

---

[1] J Hall, *Theft Law and Society* (2nd edn, 1952), 55–8. A point echoed by A Simester and GR Sullivan, 'The Nature and Rationale of Property Offences' in R Duff and S Green, *Defining Crimes: Essays on the Special Part* (2005) 192.

[2] *Smith and Hogan, Criminal Law* ch 22; Griew ch 15; ATH Smith, *Property Offences* (1994) ch 30; CLRC, *Eighth Report,* Cmnd 2977 (1966), paras 127–32; *Blackstone's Criminal Practice* (2007) B4.127; *Archbold* (2007) 21–270. For criticism of the present law see by DW Elliott, 'Theft and Related Problems—England, Australia and the USA Compared' (1977) 26 ICLQ 110, 135–44.

13.02 The incidence of handling seems to be dropping significantly. In 1996 there were 37,888 recorded offences, and in 2005–6 only 12,715.[3] This difference may be accounted for by the increased use of money laundering offences, but the statistics suggest that only a small number of money laundering crimes are recorded.[4] Other explanations may include: the reduction in the price of goods that tended to be fenced eg TVs, videos DVDs etc; fewer armed robberies of jewellery stores etc (because of tougher sentences) and greater access to second hand goods at reasonable prices through e-bay and similar schemes.

Actus reus

13.03 The *actus reus* is drafted in extremely broad terms, resulting in an offence that can be committed in many different ways.[5] In particular two core elements of the offence are broad ones: the concept of stolen goods carries an extended meaning, and there is no requirement that the handler ever comes into physical possession of the stolen goods.

Stolen goods

13.04 By s 34(2)(b):'"goods", except in so far as the context otherwise requires, includes money and every other description of property except land, and includes things severed from the land by stealing.'

13.05 This definition is narrower than the definition of 'property' for the purposes of theft in s 4(1).[6] Since, however, land generally is excluded from theft by s 4(2), the effect seems to be that, with small exceptions to be discussed below, the property which can be the subject of handling is co-extensive with that which can be the subject of theft.

13.06 If the information or indictment specifies that the goods were stolen from a specific entity, the prosecution is obliged to prove that issue, if the ownership by the entity is integral to the case.[7]

Things in action

13.07 Things in action are expressly mentioned in s 4(1) and not in s 34(2)(b). They must, however, be included in the words 'every other description of property except land'. The remaining question is whether the context of s 22 requires the exclusion of things in action. The context would require that interpretation if s 22 were confined, like the old law, to receiving. Receiving connoted taking possession or control of a physical thing and was wholly inapplicable to a thing in action. However, handling, as defined in s 22, is not confined to receiving, but may be committed by retention, removal, disposal, or realization, words which are apt to include dealing with a thing in action. A possible construction is that 'property' includes things in action for all forms of handling other than receiving; but the

---

[3] A Walker, C Kershaw, and S Nicholas, *Home Office Statistical Bulletin, Crime in England and Wales* 2005/2006 p 28, Recorded crime by offence 1996 to 2005/6 and percentage change between 2004/5 and 2005/6.

[4] ibid, 1130 in 2005/6.

[5] *Nicklin* [1977] 1 WLR 403.

[6] Above, para 2.130.

[7] *Iqbal v DPP* [2004] All ER (D) 314 (Oct).

better view probably is that things in action may also be received. 'Receive' is not an inappropriate word to apply to the assignee of a thing in action. 'Receive' necessarily had a limited meaning under the Larceny Acts because larceny could be committed only of tangible things. In the context of the 1968 Act, with its broader concept of stealing, a wider meaning is appropriate.

In *A-G's Reference (No 4 of 1979)*,[8] the Court of Appeal had no doubt that things in action **13.08** were capable of being handled and did not distinguish between one form of handling and another. A gave D a cheque drawn on an account into which she had paid stolen funds. It was held that D was guilty of handling where 'part of the balance in the thief's account is transferred to the credit of the receiver's [D's] account . . .'.[9] But *Preddy*,[10] now establishes that the balance is not 'transferred'. A new thing in action is created which belongs to D and has never been in the hands of a thief or handler and so is not stolen. *A-G's Reference (No 4 of 1979)* no longer provides a satisfactory precedent in this regard. Reliance must now be placed on s 24A (below).

In *Forsyth*[11] the court had no doubt that there could be an offence of handling of a thing in **13.09** action. F was convicted of handling goods which were stolen because it was held that they represented goods stolen in London. The 'goods' alleged to be stolen were a thing in action, £400,000 of a balance in PPI's account at the M bank in London. N was alleged to have stolen it on October 17, 1989 by ordering the transfer of that sum, via other banks, to the X bank in Geneva. F collected that sum, less commission, in cash from the X bank and deposited it with the Y bank also in Geneva. On her instructions, the Y bank transferred £307,000 to a bank in England and F brought back the balance (after commission) of £88,050 in cash to England. It was alleged she dishonestly handled (i) the thing in action of £307,000 and (ii) £88,050 in cash by undertaking or assisting in the retention, removal, etc., of this property. The court held that the credit balances remained under the control of N and could be handled by the appellant.[12]

The only difficulty in construing 'stolen goods' as including things in action is the assump- **13.10** tion in s 34(2)(b) that 'goods' bears a variable meaning and it is not easy to discern any other possible variation. It may be that the draftsman used the words, 'except in so far as the context otherwise requires', out of an abundance of caution. Alternatively, the phrase may apply to s 23 which is concerned with 'any goods which have been stolen or lost'. It is difficult to conceive of a 'lost' thing in action.

Reported cases of handling a stolen thing in action are rare. Examples include A's obtaining **13.11** a negotiable cheque by fraud and negotiating it to D. Where E, an executor, dishonestly sells to F a copyright which belongs to a beneficiary under the will, F is not guilty of handling though he knows all the facts, because his participation is 'in the course of the

---

[8] [1981] 1 All ER 1193, (1980) 71 Cr App R 341, CA.
[9] [1981] 1 All ER 1193 at 1198. cf Law Com No 243, 36–8. The court thought there was much to be said for the view that the *cheque* given by A to D was stolen goods as representing the goods originally stolen with s 24 (2)(a) but this view seems untenable. See para 13.22 below and cf Griew 15–06, para (iii).
[10] [1996] AC 815.
[11] [1997] 2 Cr App R 299, [1997] Crim LR 581 and commentary.
[12] See further para 13.11 below.

stealing'—since the stealing consists in the sale.[13] The copyright is, however, stolen goods in F's hands. If D then assists F to dispose of, or realize, the copyright for F's benefit, D is guilty of handling and F is presumably guilty of aiding and abetting him in handling. Where a thief pays stolen money into a bank account he no longer owns any money, but is owed a debt by the bank.[14] The debt is a thing in action—and it is stolen. If D assists the thief to retain the 'money in the bank' he will be guilty of handling the thing in action.

Land

13.12 A 'thing', attached to or forming part of the land, can be stolen by virtue of s 4(2)(b) and can always be the subject of handling since the stealing necessarily involves severance of the thing in question. A fixture or structure which is stolen contrary to s 4(2)(c), on the other hand, may or may not be severed from the land. Only if it is severed can it be the subject of handling. If E, an outgoing tenant, dishonestly sells to D, the incoming tenant, a fixture belonging to V, D cannot be guilty of handling (whether or not his act is in the course of stealing) if the fixture is not severed; nor, of course, is F guilty of handling if he, knowing all the facts, takes over the premises, including the fixture, from D; yet he has knowingly taken possession of a stolen fixture.

13.13 Land which is stolen contrary to s 4(2)(a) will rarely be capable of being handled since the kind of conduct contemplated by s 4(2)(a) will not normally involve severance.

13.14 Land may be the subject of obtaining by fraud and blackmail. Again, severance may or may not take place and handling is possible only if it does so.

Meaning of 'stolen'

13.15 By s 24(4):

For purposes of the provisions of this Act relating to goods which have been stolen (including subsections (1) to (3) above) goods obtained in England or Wales or elsewhere either by blackmail or [, subject to subsection (5) below by fraud (within the meaning of the Fraud Act 2006)][15] shall be regarded as stolen; and 'steal', 'theft' and 'thief' shall be construed accordingly.

By 24(5):

Subsection (1) above applies in relation to goods obtained by fraud as if—
(a) the reference to the commencement of this Act were a reference to the commencement of the Fraud Act 2006, and
(b) the reference to an offence under this Act were a reference to an offence under section 1 of that Act.

By s 24A(8):

References to stolen goods include money which is withdrawn from an account to which a wrongful credit[16] has been made, but only to the extent that the money derives from the credit.

---

[13] But cf *Pitham and Hehl*, above, para 2.65. If the receiving is in the course of the stealing F is, of course, guilty of aiding and abetting the theft.

[14] This point seems to have been overlooked in *Pitchley* (1972) 57 Cr App R 30, CA, below, para 13.70. cf *Forsyth* [1997] Crim LR 581.

[15] Words substituted by the Fraud Act 2006, Sch 1 para 6, in force from 15 Jan 2007.

[16] See s 24A (dishonestly retaining a wrongful credit), below, para 13.126.

And by s 24(1):

The provisions of this Act relating to goods which have been stolen shall apply whether the stealing occurred in England or Wales or elsewhere, and whether it occurred before or after the commencement of this Act, provided that the stealing (if not an offence under this Act) amounted to an offence where and at the time when the goods were stolen; and references to stolen goods shall be construed accordingly.

Thus goods are 'stolen' for the purposes of the Act[17] if:

13.16

(i) they have been stolen contrary to s 1 of the Theft Act 1968;[18]
(ii) they have been obtained by blackmail contrary to s 21 of the Theft Act 1968;
(iii) they have been obtained by fraud contrary to s 1 of the Fraud Act 2006;
(iv) they consist of money dishonestly withdrawn from a wrongful credit; or
(v) they have been the subject of an act done in a foreign country which was:
    (a) a crime by the law of that country and which
    (b) had it been done in England, would have been theft, blackmail or fraud contrary to s 1 or s 21 of the Theft Act 1968 or s 1 of the Fraud Act 2006.[19]

In terms of the jurisdictional scope of the offence, it is now the case that if T steals property in, for example, Spain by performing an act that is theft in Spanish law[20] but would not be theft if performed in England, and D, in England, handles that property with *mens rea*, D can be convicted of handling under s 22.[21]

The 'theft' must be proved

Though s 22 does not say so expressly, it is now established that the goods must have been stolen in fact.[22] It is not sufficient that D believed them to be 'stolen' if they were not. If, because of a mistake of fact (or, possibly, of civil law[23]) D wrongly believed the goods to be stolen he might, since the Criminal Attempts Act 1981, be convicted of an attempt to handle. If D says he knew the goods were stolen because E told him so, this is excellent evidence of *mens rea* but it is not evidence that the goods were stolen in fact.[24] An admission based on hearsay is of no more value than the hearsay itself. The statement made by E in this example is a hearsay statement under ss 114 and 115 of the Criminal Justice Act 2003 since it is a 'statement not made in oral evidence in the proceedings' and thus 'admissible as

13.17

---

[17] For a comparison with the law under the Larceny Act 1916, see editions of this book before the fifth edition—fourth edition, paras 386–8.

[18] See commentary on *Forrester* [1992] Crim LR 792, 794–5.

[19] Handling is a Group A offence for the purposes of the Criminal Justice Act 1993. See generally, M Hirst, *Jurisdiction and the Ambit of the Criminal Law* (2001), 180 et seq.

[20] This will have to be proved and cannot be presumed: *Ofori and Tackie (No 2)* (1994) 99 Cr App R 223; *Okolie* [2000] All ER (D) 661, The Times, 15 May. See *Blackstone's Criminal Practice* (2007) B4.133.

[21] The question whether D commits theft in England if he performs acts in eg Greece amounting to theft under Greek law and transports the goods to England, is considered above, para 2.103 *Atakpu* [1994] QB 69; and GR Sullivan and C Warbrick, 'Territoriality, Theft and *Atakpu*' [1994] Crim LR 650. D who commits theft abroad and returns to England with it commits an offence of money laundering contrary to s 329 of the Proceeds of Crime Act 2002.

[22] *Haughton v Smith* [1975] AC 476, [1973] 3 All ER 1109 at 1112, 1119, and 1124, HL.

[23] *Smith and Hogan, Criminal Law* 421.

[24] *Porter* [1976] Crim LR 58; *Marshall* [1977] Crim LR 106; *Lang v Evans (Inspector of Police)* [1977] Crim LR 286; *Hack* [1978] Crim LR 359; *Overington* [1978] Crim LR 692, CA.

evidence of any matter stated if, but only if' it falls within one of the exceptions. Section 115 provides that a 'statement is any representation of fact or opinion made by a person by whatever means' and that 'references to a statement or to a matter stated are to be read as follows. . . . (3) A matter stated is one to which this Chapter applies if (and only if) the purpose, or one of the purposes, of the person making the statement appears to the court to have been—(a) to cause another person to believe the matter, or (b) to cause another person to act or a machine to operate on the basis that the matter is as stated.' Clearly it is E's purpose, or one of them to cause D to believe that the goods are stolen or at least to act on that basis.

13.18 It is a misdirection to tell the jury that they are entitled to take such an admission into account, except as evidence of *mens rea*.[25] D's admission of facts which he himself perceived is, however, direct evidence of those facts which might amount to evidence from which a jury could infer that the goods were stolen. Thus D's admission that he bought goods in a public house at a ridiculously low price is evidence that the goods were stolen. Similarly, where a television set is bought in a betting shop or where a publican buys cases of whisky from a lorry-driver.[26] The conduct of a person who offers a bag of jewellery to a stranger for £2,000 and then accepts £100 for it suggests strongly, as a matter of common sense, that the jewellery is stolen.[27] However, the seller's conduct in this and similar cases goes to show only that he believed the goods to be stolen. His express statement to that effect would be hearsay as noted above. His statements as to the low price and his actions in dealing in such circumstances are implied statements that the goods are stolen and *may* also be inadmissible hearsay. At common law, the courts were slow to recognize that conduct which is not intended to be assertive was hearsay, but the House of Lords did so in *Kearley*.[28] Following the reversal of that decision by s 115 of the Criminal Justice Act 2003[29] only if the seller's purpose (or one of them) was to cause the buyer to believe the matter stated—that the goods were stolen—would his conduct constitute a hearsay statement.

13.19 If the alleged thief is not guilty, the handler cannot be convicted for there are no stolen goods for him to handle. So if the alleged thief turns out to have been under the age of 10, or insane[30] at the time of the alleged theft, then the goods appropriated cannot be stolen goods and there can be no conviction for handling them.[31] If D believed that the thief was 10, he might be convicted of an attempt to handle. Whatever his belief as to the 'thief's' age, the appropriate charge for him when the thief is under 10 would be theft of the goods.[32]

13.20 If the appropriator of the goods is guilty of theft, it is submitted that the goods appropriated may be the subject of handling although the appropriator is immune from prosecution

---

[25] *Hulbert* (1979) 69 Cr App R 243, CA.
[26] Example put by Lawton LJ in *McDonald* (1980) 70 Cr App R 288, CA.
[27] *Korniak* (1983) 76 Cr App R 145, CA.
[28] [1992] 2 All ER 345, HL.
[29] See *Singh* [2006] 2 Cr App R 12.
[30] See *Farrell* [1975] 2 NZLR 753.
[31] *Walters v Lunt* [1951] 2 All ER 645, thus remains good law.
[32] Above, para 2.96.

by reason, for example, of diplomatic immunity.[33] The thief could be prosecuted for the theft if diplomatic immunity were waived. The handler may be convicted whether that immunity is waived or not—unless, of course, he too is entitled to diplomatic immunity.

It must be proved, as against an alleged handler, that another person (T) was guilty of steal-   **13.21** ing the goods. The fact that T has been acquitted of stealing the goods is no bar to the prosecution of the handler and is, indeed, inadmissible in evidence.[34] But the fact that T has been convicted of stealing the goods is now admissible[35] and, when it is admitted, T must be taken to have committed the theft unless the contrary is proved. If D claims that T did not steal the goods—that T was wrongly convicted—it is for him to prove it on a balance of probabilities.

When goods cease to be stolen

By s 24(3) of the Act: **13.22**

But no goods shall be regarded as having continued to be stolen goods after they have been restored to the person from whom they were stolen or to other lawful possession or custody, or after that person and any other person claiming through him have otherwise ceased as regards those goods to have any right to restitution in respect of the theft.

It is obvious that goods which have once been stolen cannot continue to be regarded as   **13.23** 'stolen' so long as they continue to exist thereafter. A line must be drawn somewhere; and the Act draws it in the same place as did the common law. Though the word 'restored' seems inappropriate to the case where the goods are taken into possession by the police, the Court of Appeal has held that the subsection applies to that case.[36] So if the stolen goods are taken from the thief by the owner or someone acting on his behalf, or by the police, and subsequently returned to the thief so that he may hand them over to a receiver, the receiver will not be guilty of handling because the goods are no longer stolen goods.[37]

Difficult questions may arise over whether goods have in fact been 'restored to the person   **13.24** from whom they were stolen or to other lawful possession or custody'. It cannot be enough that V (the owner or his agent) knows that D has stolen the goods and follows D to his destination so that the handler can be caught red-handed;[38] nor that V marks the goods and

---

[33] cf *Dickinson v Del Solar* [1930] 1 KB 376; *AB* [1941] 1 KB 454; *Madan* [1961] 2 QB 1, (1961) 45 Cr App R 80.

[34] This seems a little unfair, but the Crown can rerun the evidence of theft (comforting themselves on the basis that the first jury got it wrong).

[35] Police and Criminal Evidence Act 1984, s 74(1) and (2); *O'Connor* (1986) 85 Cr App R 298 at 302, CA; *Robertson* [1987] QB 920, (1987) 85 Cr App R 304 at 310, 311, CA; *Barnes* [1991] Crim LR 132 and *Cross and Tapper on Evidence* (10th edn, 2004) 126–8.

[36] *Re A-G's Reference (No 1 of 1974)* [1974] QB 744, [1974] 2 All ER 899, CA. Was it the inappropriateness of the word 'restored' which led some members of the House of Lords in *Haughton v Smith* [1975] AC 476, [1973] 3 All ER 1109 to doubt whether it had properly been conceded that the goods in that case had ceased to be stolen? Perhaps the word 'reduced' would be better.

[37] cf *Dolan* (1855) Dears CC 436; *Schmidt* (1866) LR 1 CCR 15; *Villensky* [1892] 2 QB 597.

[38] In *Haughton v Smith* [1975] AC 476, [1973] 3 All ER 1109, where the police accompanied the driver of a van containing stolen goods to its destination in order to trap the handler, Lords Hailsham and Dilhorne questioned whether the prosecution was right to concede that the goods had been restored to lawful custody.

keeps them under observation.[39] More difficult is *King*,[40] where a parcel containing the stolen goods (a fur coat) was handed by E, the thief, to a policeman who was in the act of examining the contents when the telephone rang. The caller was D, the proposed receiver. The policeman discontinued his examination, D was told to come along as arranged, he did so and received the coat. It was held that D was guilty of receiving stolen goods on the ground that the coat had not been reduced into the possession of the police—though it was admitted that there was no doubt that, in a few minutes, it would have been so reduced, if the telephone had not rung. Presumably the same result would follow under the Theft Act. The case has, however, been subjected to criticism. It is easy to see that if the police are examining a parcel to see whether it contains stolen goods they do not take possession or even custody of the contents until they decide that this is what they are looking for.[41] In *King*, however, E had admitted the theft of the coat and produced the parcel. One might have expected, therefore, that the policeman had in fact made up his mind to take charge of it before the telephone rang. The decision presumably proceeds on the assumption that he had not done so.

13.25 The Court of Appeal has affirmed[42] that the question is one of the intention of the police officer. An officer correctly suspected that goods on the back seat of a car were stolen. He removed the rotor arm from the car, kept observation until D appeared and got into the car, and then questioned him. It was held that the jury ought to have been asked to consider whether the officer had decided before D's appearance to take possession of the goods or whether he was of an entirely open mind, intending to decide when he had questioned D. Possession[43] requires both an intention to possess and some act of possession. To immobilize a car is not the same thing as to take possession of it or its contents.

13.26 It is now quite clear that the goods may cease to be stolen in the case where the police are acting without the authority of the owner for they are clearly in 'other lawful possession or custody' of the goods.[44] Indeed, it would seem to be enough that the goods fall into the possession of any person provided that person intends to restore them to the person from whom they were stolen.

13.27 Section 24(3) also provides that the goods lose their character of stolen goods if the person from whom they were stolen has ceased to have any right of restitution in respect of the theft. Whether a 'right to restitution' exists is a question of civil law. A person whose goods have been wrongfully converted under the Torts (Interference with Goods) Act 1977 does not have a right to have those goods restored to him. He has a right to damages but it is

---

[39] *Greater London Metropolitan Police Comr v Streeter* (1980) 71 Cr App R 113, CA. Even if the owner does resume possession, the goods may be stolen again when the thief continues to deal with them: ibid, at 119.

[40] [1938] 2 All ER 662, CCA.

[41] cf *Warner v Metropolitan Police Comr* [1969] 2 AC 256, [1968] 2 All ER 356, HL.

[42] *Re A-G's Reference (No 1 of 1974)*, above, fn 1.

[43] For the purposes of s 24(3) possession *or control* suffices. Arguably in both the above cases the police officer had at least control of the goods but control, like possession, must involve an intention to take charge.

[44] cf the dictum of Cresswell J in *Dolan* (above) that goods retained their stolen character in this situation. Presumably the police in *King* were acting with the owner's authority. The point is not discussed, but it would seem likely that the theft had been reported to the police by the owner.

in the discretion of the court whether to order the goods to be delivered to him.[45] It is quite clear that s 24(3) is not intended to be confined to those cases in which a court would exercise its discretion to order the goods to be returned to V. In the criminal proceedings, it would be impossible to identify such cases and it is submitted that the subsection is applicable to all cases in which V could succeed in a civil action based on his proprietary interest in the thing, whether in conversion or for the protection of an equitable interest. The words 'any right to restitution' might have been better if replaced with a phrase such as 'any legal or equitable right'.

The provision seems to have been intended to bear a yet wider meaning. The Criminal Law Revision Committee explained it as follows:[46] **13.28**

> This is because, if the person who owned the goods when they were stolen no longer has any title to them, there will be no reason why the goods should continue to have the taint of being stolen goods. For example, the offence of handling stolen goods will . . . apply also to goods [obtained as a result of a fraud[47]]. If the owner of the goods who has been [defrauded] chooses on discovering the [fraud] to ratify his disposal of the goods he will cease to have any title to them.

It is clear that 'title' is here used in a broad sense to include a right to rescind. The Committee **13.29** clearly has in mind a case where property passes from V to D when the goods are obtained by fraud. In such a case, V, strictly, has no 'title' and his right to recover the goods (or, much more likely, their value) will only arise on his rescinding the contract.[48] Such a potential right, it is submitted, is clearly a 'right to restitution' within the Act.

Because of the exceptional breadth of the offence of theft as discussed above, particularly in **13.30** the light of the decision in *Hinks*[49] it is possible for T to be guilty of theft where he has dishonestly acquired goods by way of an *inter vivos* gift. T will in such a case have appropriated the goods even though he has the donor's consent. The property T has appropriated and 'stolen' will not be stolen goods for the purposes of s 24(3) because the donor will have no right to restitution.

Goods will cease to be stolen in the following cases: **13.31**

(i) E obtains goods by fraud from V. There is a voidable contract of sale. On discovering the fraud, V ratifies the contract. D, not knowing of the ratification, receives the goods believing them to be stolen. D is not guilty of handling.
(ii) E obtains goods by fraud from V. There is a voidable contract of sale. E sells the goods to F, a bona-fide purchaser for value without notice of the fraud. F gets a good title.[50] He delivers the

---

[45] Torts (Interference with Goods) Act 1977, s 3. See generally, WVH Rogers, *Winfield and Jolowicz on Tort* (17th edn, 2006) para 17–27.
[46] CLRC, *Eighth Report*, Cmnd 2977 (1966) para 139.
[47] The CLRC's example concerned the offence of deception under s 15 of the Theft Act 1968, since repealed.
[48] cf above, para 2.52 where it is argued, in relation to s 5(4), that a person holding property under a voidable title is not 'under an obligation to make restoration' until the transaction under which he obtained the property is rescinded.
[49] [2000] 4 All ER 833, [2001] Crim LR 162 and commentary.
[50] Sale of Goods Act 1979, s 23.

goods to D who knows they have been obtained by, but was not a party to, the fraud.[51] D is not guilty of handling.[52]

(iii) V entrusts his goods to E, a mercantile agent. E dishonestly and in breach of his agreement with V, sells the goods to F who is a bona-fide purchaser for value without notice of E's dishonesty. This is theft (and fraud contrary to section 1(2)(c) Fraud Act 2006) by E but F gets a good title to the goods.[53] D receives the goods knowing that they have been dishonestly appropriated by E. D is not guilty of handling.

(iv) V delivers a motor vehicle to E under a hire-purchase or conditional sale agreement. Before the property in the vehicle has passed to E, he dishonestly sells it to F, a bona-fide purchaser for value without notice of the agreement and who is not a 'trade or finance purchaser' as defined in s 29 (2) of the Hire-Purchase Act 1964. This is theft by E but F gets a good title to[54] the vehicle. (This is an exception to the normal principle that a vendor cannot convey to a purchaser better title to the property than he has himself acquired.) D receives the vehicle knowing that it has been dishonestly appropriated by E. He is not guilty of handling.

13.32 In all the cases considered in the previous paragraph, D will be guilty of attempted handling if he believes the goods to be stolen because he is unaware of the facts which have caused them to cease to be stolen. If he is aware of those facts but fails to appreciate their effect in law, he is probably not guilty.[55]

Goods representing those originally stolen may be stolen goods

13.33 By s 24(2) of the Act:

For purposes of those provisions reference to stolen goods shall include, in addition to the goods originally stolen and parts of them (whether in their original state or not)—

(a) any other goods which directly or indirectly represent or have at any time represented the stolen goods in the hands of the thief as being the proceeds of any disposal or realisation of the whole or part of the goods stolen or of goods so representing the stolen goods; and

(b) any other goods which directly or indirectly represent or have at any time represented the stolen goods in the hands of a handler of the stolen goods or any part of them as being the proceeds of any disposal or realisation of the whole or part of the stolen goods handled by him or of goods so representing them.

---

[51] cf *Peirce v London Horse and Carriage Repository* [1922] WN 170, CA; *Robin & Rambler Coaches Ltd v Turner* [1947] 2 All ER 284.

[52] F is not guilty of theft even if he realizes the goods have been obtained by fraud before he sells them to D: s 3(2) above. Nor, of course, is D.

[53] Factors Act 1889, s 2.

[54] Hire Purchase Act 1964, s 27; Consumer Credit Act 1974, Sch 4, para 22. Section 27 of the Hire Purchase Act provides: 'where a motor vehicle has been bailed . . . under a hire purchase agreement . . . and, before the property in the vehicle has become vested in the debtor, he disposes of the vehicle to another person . . . [who is] a private purchaser [who has purchased] the motor vehicle in good faith without notice of the hire purchase . . . agreement . . . that disposition shall have effect as if the creditor's title to the vehicle has been vested in the debtor immediately before that disposition.' Section 29(4) defines the debtor as, for present purposes, the person to whom the vehicle is bailed. See *Shogun Finance Ltd v Hudson* [2003] UKHL 62, [2004] 1 AC 919, considering such a case in which title did not pass to F because the hire-purchase company were held not to have contracted with the fraudster, but with the real person under whose identity he was posing. See also C Elliott, 'No Justice for Innocent Purchasers of Dishonestly Obtained Goods' [2004] J Bus Law 381.

[55] *Smith and Hogan, Criminal Law* 420–2.

The effect of the interpretation put upon the corresponding provision in the Larceny Act **13.34**
1916 (s 46(1)) was that anything into or for which the stolen goods were converted or
exchanged, whether immediately or otherwise, acquired the character of stolen goods.
Thus if A stole an Audi car from V and exchanged it with B for a BMW; B exchanged the
Audi with C for a Citroën; and A exchanged the BMW with D for a Daimler, all four cars
would now be stolen goods even though B, C, and D might be innocent. And if A, B, C,
and D each sold the car he had in his possession, the proceeds of each sale (as well as the
cars) would be stolen, as would any property purchased with the proceeds. Thus the stolen
goods might be multiplied to an alarming extent. The provision did not seem to give rise
to any difficulty in practice and it seems that it was very rarely invoked; but it was clearly
undesirable to re-enact a provision with such far-reaching theoretical possibilities. Section
24(2) imposes a limitation upon the possible multiplication of stolen goods.

The Criminal Law Revision Committee stated of s 24(2):[56]   **13.35**

It may seem technical; but the effect will be that the goods which the accused is charged with handling must, at the time of the handling or at some previous time, (i) have been in the hands of the
thief or of a handler, and (ii) have represented the original stolen goods in the sense of being the
proceeds, direct or indirect, of a sale or other realisation of the original goods.

The difference between the old law and that under the 1968 Act is, of course, that a disposi- **13.36**
tion or realization of the stolen goods by a person who is neither a thief nor a handler (ie by
one who is in fact appropriating or handling the goods but who has no *mens rea*) no longer
causes the proceeds to be stolen.

The effect is best explained by example. Suppose D steals an Audi car and subsequently that **13.37**
car passes, by way of sale or exchange or otherwise, through the hands of E, F, and G. The
Audi remains stolen until such time as it ceases to be stolen by virtue of s 24(3) (that is, until
the Audi is restored to the owner or other lawful custody or until the owner ceases to have
a right to restitution in respect of it). It follows that until such time any person acquiring
the Audi may be convicted of handling it, if he acquires it knowing or believing it to be
stolen. It is not necessary for every person in the chain to have been a handler for the Audi
to remain stolen. So, where the person acquiring the Audi, say G, acquires it from F, knowing or believing it to be stolen, G handles it even though F's acquisition of the car did not
constitute handling by F because he, F, acquired it innocently.

The position with regard to the *proceeds* of stolen goods is different. Assume that D, the **13.38**
thief, exchanges the stolen Audi with E for a BMW. The BMW is now notionally stolen for
the purposes of the offence because it directly represents the proceeds of the stolen Audi
in the hands of the thief, D. Assume that E was aware that the Audi was stolen and he
exchanges it with F for a Citroën. The Citroën is now notionally stolen because it represents
the proceeds of the stolen Audi *in the hands of the handler*, E. Assume, then, that D sells the
BMW to H who buys in good faith for £5,000. The BMW now ceases to be stolen goods
as V has no right to restitution and (unlike with actual stolen goods in the example of the
Audi with G and F above) once *notionally* stolen goods cease to be stolen goods they cannot

---

[56] CLRC, *Eighth Report*, Cmnd 2977 (1966) para 138.

revert to being notionally stolen because they are subsequently acquired by someone who is aware of their provenance. The £5,000 in D's hands, however, *is* notionally stolen because it indirectly represents the proceeds of the stolen Audi in the hands of the thief and a recipient of all or part of that £5,000 would, if aware of its provenance, be guilty of handling.

13.39 If D *innocently* receives stolen goods and converts them into another form—for example, he buys a car with stolen money, or pays stolen money into a bank—the property in the changed form is not stolen; and the dishonest retention of it by D is not handling,[57] nor is it theft if value was given for the goods.[58] In the case where he pays the money into his bank, however, he may now commit the offence of dishonestly retaining a wrongful credit; and money which he dishonestly withdraws from the account will be stolen goods.[59]

13.40 Thus, in the example in para 13.32, if B, C, and D were innocent (i) the Audi would continue to be stolen throughout unless V ceased to have any right to restitution of it in respect of the theft;[60] (ii) the BMW would be stolen goods since it directly represented the goods originally stolen *in the hands of the thief* as the proceeds of a disposition of them;[61] (iii) the Citroën would not be stolen since B was neither a thief nor a handler; (iv) the Daimler would be stolen since it indirectly represented the stolen goods *in the hands of the thief;* and the proceeds of sale of the Daimler would also be stolen goods; but the proceeds of sale of the Audi, the BMW, and the Citroën would not, since they came into the hands of C, D, and B respectively, none of whom was a thief or a handler.

13.41 Where goods are stolen in such circumstances that the property does not pass, s 24(2) probably makes no difference: any goods notionally stolen by virtue of that subsection are probably also 'stolen' by virtue of other provisions in the Act, read in the light of the rules of common law and equity under which an owner can trace his property when it is converted into another form. But where the goods are 'stolen' in such circumstances that the property passes to the 'thief', the subsection has a potentially wider effect. The reasons for this are examined in the fourth and earlier editions of this work.[62]

Payments of stolen monies into bank accounts

13.42 Difficult questions may arise where a thief or handler pays stolen money or a stolen cheque into his bank account.

13.43 Does the balance represent stolen goods 'in the hands of' the thief? In the difficult case of *Forsyth*[63] T stole funds in a company's bank account and transferred them to a series of other banks in which he had accounts. It was held that 'in the hands of' means 'in the possession or control of' and therefore that the new credit balances remained under T's control.

---

[57] The point seems to have been overlooked in *Pitchley* (1973) 57 Cr App R 30, [1973] Crim LR 705, CA. cf Griew 15–23. See also *Forsyth* [1997] 2 Cr App R 299, [1997] Crim LR 581.

[58] Above, para 2.93.

[59] Theft Act 1968, s 24A, below, para 13.126.

[60] Section 24(3), above, para 13.22. cf *Forsyth* [1997] Crim LR 581.

[61] Because a car representing stolen money is stolen goods, an action by one who conspired to steal the money will fail: *ex turpi causa non oritur actio*: *Solomon v Metropolitan Police Comr* [1982] Crim LR 606 (Milmo J).

[62] See the fourth edition, paras 401–4.

[63] [1997] 2 Cr App R 299, [1997] Crim LR 589 and additional commentary, 755, and above, para 3.09.

This renders the offence even wider. The balances were new property, distinct from that stolen,[64] but they 'represented' that stolen money and, 'being in the hands of' the thief, were accordingly stolen goods. More difficult to follow is the court's assumption that the actual banknotes withdrawn, on T's instructions, by D from one of the accounts were also stolen, so that D was guilty of handling them when she took physical possession of them. The notes belonged exclusively to the bank and had never been in the hands of a thief or handler until D received them and therefore could not have been stolen under s 24(2). If A pays stolen money into a bank account and, in payment of a debt he owes to B, gives B a cheque drawn on that account, B, if he cashes the cheque, does not receive stolen money. The actual cash in the shape of pound coins in the hands of the bank is not stolen goods. B is not the thief, nor is he receiving stolen goods. He is not guilty of handling. Nor is it permissible to argue that B is a handler and therefore that the goods are stolen because they are in his hands. That is a circular argument.

In that example, however, B is acting on his own behalf. In *Forsyth* D was acting as agent for **13.44** T, the original thief. For the reason given above, D (it is submitted) was not *receiving* stolen goods. But, because D, unlike B in the example, was acting as agent for the thief, the cash, though physically in D's hands, was, in law, 'in the hands of' T—that is, it 'indirectly represented the stolen goods in the hands of the thief' (s 24(2)(a))—and was therefore stolen goods. D was not a receiver of stolen goods—the cash became stolen only when she received it. She then had stolen goods in her hands. That is not an offence; but she then went on to assist in the retention, etc, of the stolen goods for the benefit of T; and that is the offence of handling. See now the offence under s 24A below.

What if the account is one in which there is a credit balance? If it is a new account or one **13.45** with a zero balance then the stolen money or cheque has been converted into an identifiable thing in action, ie the right to recover an equivalent sum from the bank, which is therefore also 'stolen'. If, however, the account already has a credit balance, representing money lawfully acquired by the holder, the question is whether the owner of the stolen money retains any proprietary interest in the mixed fund.[65] If he does not, it seems impossible to say that he has any 'right to restitution' in respect of the theft: the stolen money or cheque has ceased to exist and nothing remains which can be the subject of handling. If, however, the theft was a breach of trust, the fiduciary relationship between trustee and beneficiary would enable the latter to trace his money into the mixed fund so that he would have a proprietary interest in it, sufficient, it is submitted, to amount to a right to restitution within the meaning of s 24(3). The portion of the mixed fund representing the stolen property would then be stolen goods. Where the theft does not amount to a breach of a fiduciary relationship, the position is more doubtful;[66] but the courts have indicated some readiness to recognize the existence of the interests of victims of thefts in mixed funds.[67] If a person is under an obligation to V to 'retain and deal' with property under s 5(3) it seems logical that V has 'a right to restitution'.

---

[64] *Preddy* [1996] AC 815.
[65] See J Martin, *Hanbury and Martin, Modern Equity* (17th edn, 2005) 3.022.
[66] ibid, and [1981] Crim LR at 52–3.
[67] *Governor of Brixton Prison, ex p Levin* [1997] QB 65, [1996] 4 All ER 350, 364–5, HL.

13.46 If the victim of the theft can trace into the mixed fund, 'the correct rule appears to be that the beneficiary [ie the victim of the theft] may claim a charge upon any part of the fund which he can identify as being part of the mixed fund.'[68] The effect is, where D steals £100 from V and pays it into his bank account which has a credit balance of £100—

(a) if he draws out £100 and dissipates it, the remaining £100 belongs in equity to V and is stolen goods; but

(b) if he draws out £100 and invests it in premium bonds and then dissipates the remaining £100, the premium bonds belong in equity to V and are stolen goods.

When bank credits cease to be stolen

13.47 If the goods have ceased to be stolen no one can thereafter be convicted of handling them as stolen goods, whatever his intention or belief. If the parties intend and believe the payment to represent the stolen property, even though it does not do so in law, it is possible that they might, since the Criminal Attempts Act 1981, be convicted of an attempt to handle.[69] Assuming that the credit balance in the account of the thief or handler does represent stolen property, is a cheque, drawn on it and intended to enable D to obtain a transfer of part of the credit balance, or of cash, stolen goods?[70] If the delivery of the cheque operated as an assignment of part of the debt represented by the bank balance then the answer would be in the affirmative; but it is clear that it does not so operate.[71]

When proceeds of stolen goods cease to be stolen

13.48 It has already been seen that stolen goods cease to be stolen when the conditions laid down by s 24(3) are fulfilled. What then, is the position of goods which have been stolen notionally under s 24(2)? Do they cease to be notionally stolen when the goods which they represent cease to be stolen? They must do so when the original goods are restored to the possession of the owner, for then the right to restitution of the proceeds lapses. Do the proceeds also cease to be stolen when the owner loses his right to restitution of the original goods? It seems clear that the answer must be in the negative. If it were otherwise, s 24(2) would be almost completely ineffective. Suppose that A obtains a car by fraud from V. The contract of sale is voidable, so that A gets ownership of the car. He sells it to B who knows all the facts and who resells it to C who is bona fide and without notice of A's dishonesty. C gets an unimpeachable title to the car, ie V's right to restitution of it is lost and it ceases to be stolen goods. A then gives the proceeds of the sale to D who knows all the facts. This is just the situation in which it might be desirable to rely on s 24(2) but it would not be possible to do so if the money (notionally stolen, as the proceeds of the car) ceased to be stolen on the car's so ceasing. It is submitted, therefore, that the money does not cease to be stolen. It continues to be stolen until the conditions specified in s 24(3) are satisfied in respect of it.

---

[68] J Martin, *Hanbury and Martin, Modern Equity* (17th edn, 2005) 3.022 *Clowes (No 2)* [1994] 2 All ER 316, 335–6, CA.

[69] The case is quite analogous to *Haughton v Smith* [1975] AC 476, HL which is reversed by the Act.

[70] The question was raised in *A-G's Reference (No 4 of 1979)* (1981) 71 Cr App R 341 at 349. The court was inclined to think it did but it was unnecessary to decide the point.

[71] *Schroeder v Central Bank of London Ltd* (1876) 34 LT 735.

Section 24(3) may be applicable to 'stolen' proceeds since the person from whom the origi- **13.49**
nal goods were stolen may assert a right to restitution as against the proceeds. Suppose that
a thief used stolen money to purchase a necklace from a bona-fide seller so that the right
to restitution of the money was lost and it ceased to be stolen. Suppose further that the
necklace had been given to D who knew all the facts. The necklace would be stolen by virtue of s 24(2).[72] V would have a right to restitution in respect of it and there would be room
for the application of s 24(3) in that this right might be lost in the various ways[73] in which
the right to restitution of the original goods might be lost. Additionally, it would be lost
if the original property were restored to the possession of the owner, since he could not
recover the value of his property twice.

To sum up, it is submitted that: **13.50**

1. Goods notionally stolen as being the proceeds of other stolen goods do not necessarily cease to be
   notionally stolen when the original stolen goods cease, by virtue of s 24(3), to be stolen.
2. Goods notionally stolen cease to be notionally stolen when the conditions of s 24(3) are satisfied
   in respect of those goods.
3. Goods notionally stolen are usually also actually stolen.

Forms of handling

The term 'handling' was adopted because 'receiving'—the only way of committing the **13.51**
offence under s 33(1) of the 1916 Act—is now one of several (at least eighteen) ways in
which the new offence can be committed. As the section has been interpreted by the House
of Lords in *Bloxham*,[74] these are:

(i) Receiving the goods.
(ii) Undertaking the retention, removal, disposal, or realization of the goods for the benefit of
another person.
(iii) Assisting in the retention, removal, disposal, or realization of the goods by another person.
(iv) Arranging to do (i), (ii), or (iii).

Although in *Bloxham* Lord Bridge stated that, 'It is, I think, well settled that this subsection **13.52**
creates two distinct offences but no more than two', it is submitted that the subsection
creates only one offence[75] which may be committed in a variety of ways. What was well settled before *Bloxham* was that, where the evidence justified it, the proper practice was to
have one count for receiving (or perhaps arranging to receive) and a second count for all the
other forms of handling.[76] In law, however, the subsection created only one offence. Thus
in *Nicklin*[77] it was held that an indictment alleging unparticularized handling is not defective. If, as Lord Bridge suggested, the subsection creates two offences, the indictment would
have been bad for duplicity. The dictum is incorrect.

---

[72] It would also be stolen independently of s 24(2).
[73] Above, paras 13.22 and 13.31.
[74] [1983] 1 AC 109, [1982] 1 All ER 582, HL.
[75] *Griffiths v Freeman* [1970] 1 All ER 1117, [1970] 1 WLR 659.
[76] *Willis and Syme* [1972] 3 All ER 797, CA; *Deakin* [1972] 3 All ER 803, CA.
[77] [1977] 2 All ER 444, CA.

13.53 If D is charged only with receiving, he may not be convicted on that indictment of some other form of handling;[78] and vice versa. Since receiving is 'a single finite act' each receipt of stolen goods is a separate offence and, therefore, a single count for receiving a quantity of goods found in D's possession will be bad for duplicity if the receipt took place on more than one occasion.[79] The other forms of handling include 'an activity which may be continuing'; so that a single count may encompass goods which have been received on a number of different occasions.[80] The word, 'retention', in particular, would be apt to include a large quantity of goods found in D's possession and perhaps received by him over a long period of time. In order to obtain a conviction under the single count it would of course be necessary to prove, not merely that D received the goods, but that he was retaining them for the benefit of another person, or that he was assisting another person in retaining them.

13.54 Particulars should be given so as to enable the accused to understand the ingredients of the charge he has to meet.[81] The maximum number of counts for a single instance of handling in the ordinary case is two.[82]

Receiving

13.55 All forms of handling other than receiving or arranging to receive are subject to the qualification that it must be proved that D was assisting another person or acting 'for the benefit of another person'.[83] If there is no evidence of this—as will frequently be the case—then it must be proved that D received or arranged to receive the goods and evidence of no other form of handling will suffice. The Act does not define receiving in any way and it must be assumed that all the old authorities remain valid.

13.56 It must be proved, then, that D took possession or control of the stolen property or joined with others to share possession or control of it. 'Receiving' the thief who has the goods in his possession does not necessarily amount to receiving the goods. If the thief retains exclusive control, there is no receiving.[84] There may, however, be a joint possession in thief and receiver, so it is unnecessary to prove that the thief ever parted with possession—it is sufficient that he shared it with the alleged receiver. In *Smith*,[85] it was held that a Recorder had correctly directed a jury when he told them that if they believed 'that the watch was

---

[78] *Nicklin* [1977] 2 All ER 444, [1977] Crim LR 221, CA. The CPS state in their charging considerations: 'When it is not clear whether the offence committed was by way of receiving stolen goods or by way of undertaking or assisting in the retention, etc, of the property, it is permissible to charge both forms of handling in one charge. If, on the other hand, it is clear that the accused could only have handled the stolen goods in one form, then only that particular limb of section 22 should be charged.'

[79] *Smythe* (1980) 72 Cr App R 8, CA. cf *Skipp*, above, para 2.28 (overruled, but still relevant on this issue).

[80] The CPS Charging Advice is to use one charge if the property came from several thefts (or burglaries, etc) but was all received on one occasion. 'If a number of items of property have been received by the accused on different occasions, you should have a separate charge for each occasion, unless: i. There is a continuous series of closely linked offences, and it is not possible to show the dates or amounts of individual receipts ii The evidence of receiving the goods on separate occasions comes from the defendant, and it is not accepted from the prosecution.'

[81] *Sloggett* [1972] 1 QB 430, [1971] 3 All ER 264, CA.

[82] *Ikpong* [1972] Crim LR 432, CA.

[83] Below, 13.79.

[84] *Wiley* (1850) 2 Den 37.

[85] (1855) Dears CC 494.

then in the custody of a person with the cognizance of the prisoner, that person being one over whom the prisoner had absolute control, so that the watch would be forthcoming if the prisoner ordered it, there was ample evidence to justify them in convicting . . .'. Lord Campbell CJ said that if the thief had been employed by D to commit larceny, so that the watch was in D's control, D was guilty of receiving. In such a case D was an accessory before the fact to larceny and today he would be guilty of theft. If the facts were as put by Lord Campbell, when did D become a receiver? As soon as the theft was committed? If so, we have the extraordinary result that D became guilty of both theft and receiving at the same moment. But, if this moment is not selected, it is difficult to see what other is appropriate. This may, however, appear less anomalous under the 1968 Act than under the old. Virtually all handling is now theft, so it is the general rule that the two offences are committed simultaneously. In the ordinary case, however, the offence is handling because there has been a previous theft. The peculiarity of this problem under discussion is that there has been no previous theft; and it may be, therefore, that the requirement that the handling be 'otherwise than in the course of the stealing', would prevent D from being guilty of handling until he did some act amounting to that offence, after the theft was complete.

As is clear from *Smith*, actual manual possession by D need not be proved. It is enough **13.57** if the goods are received by his servant or agent with his authority.[86] The receipt may be for a merely temporary purpose such as concealment from the police.[87] It is unnecessary that the receiver should receive any profit or advantage from the possession of the goods. If D took possession of the goods from the thief without his consent, this was formerly only larceny (from the thief) and not receiving.[88] There seems to be no reason why it should not be both theft and handling under the Act, since it is clear that the two offences can be committed by one and the same act.

It continues to be essential for the judge to give a careful direction as to possession or con- **13.58** trol.[89] If the only evidence against D is that he ran away on being found by the police in a house where stolen property had been left, there would appear to be no case to leave to a jury. Likewise where the evidence is consistent with the view that D went to premises where stolen goods were stored with the intention of assuming possession, but had not actually done so;[90] or where the only evidence of receiving a stolen car is that D's fingerprint was found on the driving mirror.[91] The mere fact that the stolen goods were found on D's premises is not sufficient evidence. It must be shown that the goods had come either by invitation or arrangement with him or that he had exercised some control over them.[92] D is not necessarily in possession of a stolen safe simply because he assists others in trying to open it.[93]

---

[86] *Miller* (1854) 6 Cox CC 353.
[87] *Richardson* (1834) 6 C & P 335.
[88] *Wade* (1844) 1 Car & Kir 739.
[89] *Frost and Hale* (1964) 48 Cr App R 284.
[90] *Freedman* (1930) 22 Cr App R 133.
[91] *Court* (1960) 44 Cr App R 242.
[92] *Cavendish* [1961] 2 All ER 856. cf *Lloyd* [1992] Crim LR 361, CA.
[93] *Tomblin* [1964] Crim LR 780.

Arranging to receive

13.59 D's preparations to receive, not yet amounting to an attempt to do so because they are merely preparatory, may nevertheless constitute a sufficient 'arrangement'. The goods must be stolen at the time the arrangement is made. D must know or believe the goods to be stolen. If his belief is mistaken, the full offence is not committed but he may be guilty of an attempt to commit it. An agreement to handle goods to be stolen in the future may be a conspiracy to handle but it is not handling even when the goods are actually stolen.[94] The crime is complete as soon as the arrangement is made. It is not undone if D repents or does nothing to carry out the arrangement, or it becomes impossible of performance. So in a case like *King*[95] (with the officer inspecting the fur coat) it might now be possible to get a conviction for handling by showing that the arrangement was made while the goods were still stolen. It is odd that the offence is committed both by arranging to receive and by actually doing so. Is it two offences or one continuing offence? The latter view is preferable, for *Griffiths v Freeman*[96] by no means solves all the problems of duplicity. Most arrangements will involve agreement with another. An arrangement with an innocent person will be enough. If the other knows the goods are stolen, there will usually be a conspiracy.

Undertaking and assisting

13.60 Handling can be committed by retention, removal, disposal, or realization in one or other of two ways.

First, the offender may himself undertake the activity for the benefit of another person. Secondly, the activity may be undertaken by another person and the offender may assist him. Of course, if the thief or an original receiver and his friend act together in, say, removing the stolen goods, the friend may be committing the offence in both ways.[97]

13.61 Some examples drawn from the old law will illustrate the kind of case to which the law extends:

(i) D negotiates the sale to F of goods which he knows to have been stolen by E. D is never in possession or control of the goods.[98] He has undertaken the disposal and realization of stolen goods.

(ii) D assists E to lift from a van a barrel of gin which he knows to have been stolen by E or another. Even if he never has possession or control[99] he has assisted the removal of the stolen goods.

(iii) D's 11-year-old son, E, brings home a bicycle which he has stolen. D assists in its retention if (a) he agrees that E may keep the bicycle in the house, or (b) he tells the police there is no bicycle in the house, or (c) he gives E a tin of paint so that he may disguise it.

(v) D lights the way for E to carry stolen goods from a house to a barn so that E may negotiate the sale of the goods. D has assisted in the removal of the goods.[100]

---

[94] *Park* (1987) 87 Cr App R 164, [1988] Crim LR 238, CA, disapproving a tentative suggestion in the fifth edition of this book, para 4.03.
[95] Above, para 13.24.
[96] Above, para 13.52.
[97] *Bloxham* [1983] 1 AC 109, [1982] 1 All ER 582 at 585, HL, per Lord Bridge.
[98] cf *Watson* [1916] 2 KB 385.
[99] *Gleed* (1916) 12 Cr App R 32; *Hobson v Impett* (1957) 41 Cr App R 138.
[100] *Wiley* (1850) 2 Den 37.

It has been held that where a seller employs a subcontractor to make goods which are **13.62** delivered to the buyer, the seller may be guilty of handling by assisting in the realization of stolen goods if, knowing or believing the materials to have been stolen, he pays the subcontractor for the goods.[101] The buyer of stolen goods may be assisting in the realization of them but is not 'undertaking' the realization.[102]

Merely to use goods knowing them to be stolen does not in itself amount to assisting in **13.63** their retention. D did not commit the offence by using a stolen heater and battery charger in his father's garage,[103] nor by erecting stolen scaffolding in the course of a building operation.[104] Nothing was done with the purpose, or with the effect, of assisting in retention. According to *Kanwar*,[105] 'something must be done by the offender, and done intentionally and dishonestly, for the purpose of enabling the goods to be retained'. However, it was held to be sufficient in that case that D told lies to protect her husband who had dishonestly brought the stolen goods into the house. She knew that, if the deception succeeded, the effect would be that her husband would be enabled to retain the goods.

A person does not 'assist' in the disposition of stolen property merely by accepting the **13.64** benefit of the disposition. There must be proof that D gave help or encouragement. In *Coleman*,[106] D knew that his wife was using money which she had stolen to pay solicitors' fees relating to the purchase of a flat in the couple's joint names. That did not in itself amount to assisting though it was evidence from which a jury might infer that he had assisted by telling his wife to use the stolen money or agreeing that she should do so.

It was said in *Kanwar* that, 'The requisite assistance need not be successful in its object.' But **13.65** does one who attempts to assist and fails 'assist'? This seems to involve reading the section as if it read, 'does an act with the purpose of assisting'. The would-be assister who fails to assist in any way would surely be more properly convicted of an attempt.

Arranging or undertaking to assist

Far-reaching though the extension of the law to undertaking and assisting is, the Act goes **13.66** further. A mere arrangement to do any of the acts amounting to undertaking or assisting is enough. D simply agrees or prepares to negotiate the sale of stolen goods, to lift down the barrel of stolen gin or to do any act for the purpose of enabling E to retain, remove, or dispose of the goods. Nothing more is required.

Handling by omission

'Receiving', 'undertaking', and 'arranging' all suggest that an act of some kind is required. **13.67** It is difficult to envisage any of these forms of handling being committed by omission. It is, however, possible to assist another by inactivity; but this will not constitute an offence except in the rather rare case where the law imposes a duty to act.

---

[101] *Tamm* [1973] Crim LR 115 (Judge R David).
[102] *Bloxham* at 585, disapproving a statement by Phillimore LJ in *Deakin* [1972] 3 All ER 803 at 808, CA.
[103] *Sanders* (1982) 75 Cr App R 84, CA.
[104] *Thornhill* unreported; discussed in *Sanders*, above.
[105] [1982] 2 All ER 528, (1982) 75 Cr App R 87.
[106] [1986] Crim LR 56, CA.

13.68   In *Brown*,[107] it was held that D's mere failure to reveal to the police the presence of stolen goods on his premises did not amount to assisting in their retention. (Nor did his advice to the police to 'Get lost'.) Clearly the thief was in fact assisted by D's silence in the sense that D's omission to disclose the truth delayed the finding of the stolen goods. There is, however, no duty to give information to the police.[108] No doubt the answer would have been different if D had not merely refused information but had told lies.[109]

13.69   The court thought that D's conduct was evidence that D was permitting the goods to remain and thereby assisting in their retention. It would obviously be an act of assistance for D, expressly or tacitly, to give a thief permission to keep stolen goods on D's premises. The court's remarks (and, indeed, decision for they applied the proviso to uphold the conviction[110]) seem to go farther and suggest that it would be enough if D did not communicate with the thief at all but simply allowed stolen goods which had been placed on his premises to remain there. This comes very close to making the mere omission to remove goods or report their presence an offence. But the result is perhaps reasonable. If a lorry-driver were to observe that his mate had secretly inserted some stolen goods in the lorry and were then to drive the lorry to its destination without comment, there would be no difficulty in saying that he had assisted in the removal of the goods. Where the goods are planted on static premises, the assistance consists in the maintenance of the premises where the goods lie and the exclusion of strangers, just as in the lorry case it consists in driving the lorry.

13.70   The dicta in *Brown* were followed in *Pitchley*.[111] D's son stole £150 and on 5 November gave it to D to look after for him. D may not have known the money was stolen when he received it and, on 6 November, he paid it into a savings bank account. On 7 November D learnt that the money was stolen. He did nothing about it. He was indicted for handling the sum of £150 between 5 and 11 November. The prosecution case was that he either received the money dishonestly or assisted dishonestly in its retention. The court thought that the word 'retain' in the section bears its dictionary meaning—'keep possession of, not lose, continue to have'.[112] D, by permitting the 'money' to remain under his control, was retaining it,[113] and was guilty. He was, it appears, under a duty to withdraw 'the money' and return it to its owner. But the stolen money in fact had ceased to exist and it appears that the thing in action which replaced it was not 'stolen' because D was neither a thief nor a handler at the time of the 'realization'.[114] It is thus very doubtful whether Pitchley was

---

[107]   [1970] 1 QB 105, [1969] 3 All ER 198, CA.

[108]   Refusal to answer a constable is not an obstruction in the course of his duty: *Rice v Connolly* [1966] 2 QB 414, [1966] 2 All ER 649; *Smith and Hogan, Criminal Law* 549. Although cf recently the decision of the Admin Court in *Sekfali v DPP* [2006] EWHC 894.

[109]   This probably is obstruction of the police: *Rice v Connolly* (n 108, above); *Mathews v Dwan* [1949] NZLR 1037.

[110]   A power since repealed.

[111]   (1973) 57 Cr App R 30, [1972] Crim LR 705, CA, and commentary thereon.

[112]   'The meaning of the word "retention" in the section is a matter of law in so far as the construction of the word is necessary', per Cairns LJ at 57 Cr App R 37. cf *Feely*, above, para 2.292.

[113]   But is 'retaining' (as distinct from undertaking the retention) an offence? If D alone retains, it is odd to describe him as assisting in retention. D's conduct might have been better described as undertaking the retention, but he was not dishonest when he 'undertook'.

[114]   See Griew 15–23, n 62; Williams, *TBCL* 873: above, para 13.39.

rightly convicted. A better charge would have been theft. The thing in action, being the proceeds of the stolen money, probably continued to belong to V; and D, by keeping it as owner, appropriated it: s 3(2).

The courts have emphasized that charging and jury directions should be kept simple where **13.71** these issues arise.[115] It is often a sensible course for alternative counts of theft and handling to be left to the jury.

Otherwise than in the course of the stealing

Recall that s 22 defines the offence: 'A person handles stolen goods if (otherwise than in the **13.72** course of the stealing) . . .' Almost every handling is also stealing[116] but the stealing here referred to is the stealing which caused the goods to be stolen goods before the alleged handling. If D was a party to that theft, his participation in it cannot be the offence of handling stolen goods. The provision was necessary to keep handling within proper bounds. Without it, virtually every instance of theft by two or more persons would also have been handling by one or other or, more likely, both of them.[117]

In the fifth edition of this book it was stated that 'whatever the form of handling alleged, it **13.73** must be proved that it was done 'otherwise than in the course of the stealing'. In *Cash*,[118] the court said this statement 'might be unhappily worded'. It is a general principle that the judge must direct the jury as to all the elements of an offence[119] but in *Cash* it was held that 'where in reality [D] had to be acquitted if he could not be shown to be a handler', the words, 'otherwise than in the course of the stealing', have little importance and the jury should not even be told about them. Perhaps these words, being in parentheses in s 22, are regarded as an exception to, or exemption from, rather than an element of, the offence; so that it is for D to introduce sufficient evidence to raise a doubt whether he received the goods in the course of the stealing, or even (though this seems unlikely) to prove on the balance of probabilities that he did so receive them.[120] The case envisaged is one where, in the opinion of the judge, no reasonable jury could be satisfied beyond reasonable doubt that D, the alleged handler, was the thief—it is, in his judgment, handling or nothing. But, even if no reasonable jury could be satisfied beyond reasonable doubt that D was the thief, they might think it quite possible, or even probable, that he was. If the matter were left to them, they would not be satisfied beyond reasonable doubt that D received the goods

---

[115] See *Bosson* [1999] Crim LR 596.

[116] But even with the excessively broad definition of appropriation, not all handling is theft—an arrangement to do something might not be theft.

[117] The CPS Charging advice is that 'when the evidence is such that the accused could be either a thief or a handler of stolen goods it is permissible to charge both offences. Both charges, however, should only be preferred when there is a real and not a fanciful possibility that the evidence might support one rather than the other.'

[118] [1985] QB 801, [1985] Crim LR 311, CA and commentary.

[119] *McVey* [1988] Crim LR 127.

[120] Section 101 of the Magistrates' Courts Act 1980 provides that the onus of proof is on a defendant to an information or complaint who relies on an exception, exemption, etc and the House of Lords in *Hunt* [1987] AC 352, [1987] 1 All ER 1 held that the section is a statement of the common law which applies in trials on indictment; but, in fact, the application of the supposed principle is haphazard, inconsistent and, in serious offences, rare. See JC Smith, 'The Presumption of Innocence' (1987) 38 NILQ 223.

otherwise than in the course of the stealing and they would acquit; but because they are not told about this provision they will convict. This seems wrong. It is certainly exceptional for the prosecution to have to prove that D is not guilty of an offence,[121] but this seems to be what Parliament has provided.

13.74 In *Cash*, stolen goods were found in D's possession on 25 February. The property was stolen (by a burglar) not later than 16 February. It was held that it was not open to the jury to infer that D was the burglar rather than a receiver. Perhaps the evidence was insufficient to satisfy the jury beyond reasonable doubt that D was the burglar but may they not, given the opportunity, have thought that it was reasonably possible, if not probable, that he was the burglar? Is it unheard of for burglars to retain possession of the stolen property for nine days? In *Greaves*,[122] it was held that the judge had properly left it open to the jury to convict of burglary where the time lapse was seventeen days.

13.75 In *Wells*,[123] the Court of Appeal went as far as to say that *Cash* applies in any case in which there is no evidence to be left to the jury suggesting that D was a burglar/thief. *Cash* was described as a decision which makes 'entirely good sense'.[124]

13.76 There are at least four possible scenarios for D's recent possession in these cases—(i) that he is the thief, (ii) that he took part in the theft and received the goods in the course of it, (iii) that he was implicated in the theft and only received his proceeds later, (iv) that he was not involved in the theft and received the stolen goods at a later date.[125] If all that can be proved by the prosecution beyond a reasonable doubt is that D was in possession with a dishonest state of mind, how can handling be satisfactorily established?

The duration of stealing

13.77 The duration of 'the course of the stealing' depends on the extent to which appropriation is a continuing act.[126] As has been observed, one case involving handling, *Pitham and Hehl*,[127] suggested that appropriation is an instantaneous act, concluded at the moment the goods are stolen. If this were right, the words 'in the course of the stealing' would be rendered nugatory. It is submitted that, in the light of *Hale*[128] and *Atakpu*,[129] cases concerned with robbery and theft respectively, *Pitham* must be wrongly decided in this respect. *Atakpu* adopts the transaction test—was the thief still 'on the job'?

13.78 This does not, of course, solve all the problems. A thief is likely to be held to be on the job while he is in a building which he has entered for the purpose of stealing and from which he intends to remove the stolen goods. But is he still in the course of theft as he walks down the garden path with the swag? as he drives home? and as he shows it to his wife in the

---

121 But see *McMonagle v Westminster City Council* [1989] Crim LR 455, DC.
122 (1987) The Times, 11 July, discussed *Archbold* (2007) 21–127, 128. *Cash* was also distinguished in *Bruce* [1988] VR 579. Failure to add alternative theft counts can be fatal to the indictment *Suter* [1997] CLY 1339 (Judge Bull Guildford CC).
123 [2004] EWCA Crim 79.
124 Para 1.
125 See M Hirst, 'Guilty but of what' (2000) 4 E & P 31.
126 Above, para 2.103.
127 (1977) 65 Cr App R 45, CA above, para 2.75.
128 (1978) 68 Cr App R 415, CA above, paras 2.106 and 7.15.
129 [1994] QB 69, [1993] 4 All ER 215, above, para 2.104.

kitchen? It does not necessarily follow that the theft is still in the course of commission because the stolen property has not yet been removed from the premises on which it was stolen. The thief may have completed his part of 'the job', leaving it to others to take possession of the goods. Arguably, in such a case, E is no longer in the course of stealing. If so, some of the old cases on larceny are no longer in point. Thus in *Atwell and O'Donnell*,[130] goods were left in the warehouse in which they had been stolen for some time thereafter and the court held that it was a continuing transaction as to those who joined in the plot before the goods were finally carried away from the premises. Presumably until this occurred, the larceny was incomplete. It does not necessarily follow that the course of stealing under the Theft Act continues so long. If E appropriates goods in his employer's warehouse and conceals them so that they may be taken by D who comes to the warehouse a week later, is it to be said that D's taking is in the course of the stealing? Surely not.[131]

By or for the benefit of another person

Each of the nouns, 'retention', 'removal', 'disposal', and 'realization' is governed by the words 'by or for the benefit of another person'.[132] It must therefore be proved that: **13.79**

(a) D undertook or arranged the retention, removal, disposal, or realization *for the benefit of another person*; or
(b) D assisted or arranged the retention, removal, disposal, or realization *by another person*.[133]

There can hardly ever have been a thief who did not retain, remove, dispose of, or realize the stolen goods, and the qualification created by the italicized words prevents all thieves from being handlers as well. The italicized words are an essential part of the offence and the indictment must allege that the handling was 'by or for the benefit of another person'.[134] The thief may himself be guilty of handling (by undertaking) if he himself retains, removes, etc, the goods for the benefit of another person. It would seem to be immaterial that the other person is guilty of no offence and even unaware of what is going on.   **13.80**

In *Bloxham*,[135] it was held that a purchaser, as such, of stolen goods is not 'another person' within the meaning of the section. Sellers usually sell for their own benefit, not the benefit of the purchaser but, even if the sale could be described as for the purchaser's benefit, it would not, in the opinion of Lord Bridge, be within the ambit of the section. This is to give a special meaning to 'another person', the limits of which are not clear. Griew lucidly summarizes the interpretation—something will be for the benefit of another when it is 'an act done on behalf of another person; it is an act that the other might do himself'.[136]   **13.81**

---

130 (1801) 2 East PC 768.
131 The CPS Charging Advice is that 'when the accused is in possession of property that has been stolen over a period of time and there is insufficient evidence to show that the accused was the thief, you should consider charging both theft and handling.'
132 *Sloggett* [1972] 1 QB 430, [1971] 3 All ER 264 at 267, CA.
133 cf Blake, 'The Innocent Purchaser and Section 22 of the Theft Act' [1972] Crim LR 494 arguing that there is no need that the third party benefits if he retains, removes, realizes, or disposes.
134 *Sloggett* [1972] 1 QB 430, [1971] 3 All ER 264, CA.
135 Above, para 13.51.
136 Paras 15–22. Spencer suggests, 'the requirement that the act be "for the benefit of another'" serves no intelligible purpose unless it limits the offence to those who act on another's behalf. 'The Mishandling of Handling' [1981] Crim LR 682 at 685.

13.82 In *Bloxham*, D in good faith purchased a stolen car for £1,300. Eleven months later, suspecting the truth, he sold it for £200 to a person unknown who was prepared to buy it without documents. D was charged with handling by undertaking or assisting in the realization of the car for the benefit of the buyer. A submission of no case to answer was rejected, whereupon he pleaded guilty. His conviction was upheld by the Court of Appeal who thought that the buyer's use of the car, for which he had paid less than its true value, was a benefit to him. Maybe it was; but it seems a travesty to say that the sale was for his benefit. The House of Lords quashed the conviction. The buyer was not 'another person'. In fact, of course, he was 'another person'; but the sale was certainly not effected 'on his behalf'.

13.83 *Bloxham* was distinguished in *Tokeley-Parry*[137] where D was charged with undertaking or assisting in removal by E, whom he had procured to smuggle stolen antiquities from Egypt.[138] An argument that D and E were one person was firmly rejected. E was 'another person' in fact and in law. In *Roberts*[139] it was held that, if A and B are jointly charged in one count with an act of handling 'by or for the benefit of another', the other must be some person other than A or B. This seems logical if, indeed, only one act, jointly done by A and B, is alleged.[140] A might, however, arrange the disposition of the goods *by* B; and B might undertake the disposition *for the benefit of* A. In that case both have committed an offence under s 22 and there is no need to show that any third person was involved.

Conspiracy to handle

13.84 As s 22 creates only one offence (*pace* Lord Bridge in *Bloxham*) an indictment for conspiracy to handle contrary to s 22, not particularizing the form of handling, is good. It is not an allegation of conspiracy to commit crime X *or* crime Y. An agreement by A and B that B would, for example, dispose of the goods for the benefit of A is, notwithstanding *Roberts*, a conspiracy. A and B have agreed that B will commit the offence of handling, and that is enough. If B does dispose of the goods as agreed, he commits the offence under s 22; and, obviously A has counselled or procured him to do so. They are both guilty of the same offence. There seems to be every reason, *pace* the court in *Roberts*, why A and B should be jointly charged with committing it.

Innocent receipt and subsequent retention with *mens rea*

13.85 If D receives the stolen goods either believing them not to be stolen or knowing them to be stolen but intending to return them to the true owner he commits no offence. Suppose he subsequently discovers the goods to be stolen or decides not to return them to the true owner or disposes of them. He has, presumably dishonestly, undertaken the retention of or

---

[137] [1999] Crim LR 578. It is questionable how this was for the benefit of anyone other than D.

[138] See also the offends in the Dealing in Cultural Objects (Offences) Act 2003—'acquiring, disposing of, importing or exporting tainted cultural objects, or agreeing or arranging to do so'.

[139] (9 July 1993, unreported); see *Slater and Suddens* [1996] Crim LR 494, CA, and see *Gingell* [2000] 1 Cr App R 88.

[140] Although why this should only apply if they are jointly charged is less logical, see R Harrison, 'Handling Stolen Goods for the Benefit of Another' (2000) 64 J Crim L 156.

has disposed of stolen goods knowing them to be stolen. Whether he is guilty of an offence depends on a number of factors.[141]

Where D does not get ownership of the goods[142]

If D gives value for the goods: **13.86**

(a) D retains or disposes of the goods for his own benefit. This is not theft because of s 3(2);[143] nor is it handling by undertaking, assisting, or arranging since it is not for the benefit of another. D might be guilty of handling by aiding and abetting the receiving by the person to whom he disposes of the goods, if that person has *mens rea*.

(b) D retains or disposes of the goods 'for the benefit of another person'—whatever that means. This is not theft (s 3 (2)) but is handling.

If D does not give value: **13.87**

(a) D retains or disposes of the goods for his own benefit. This is theft but not handling unless it amounts to aiding and abetting receipt by another.

(b) D retains or disposes of the goods 'for the benefit of another person'. This is theft and handling.

Where D gets ownership of the goods[144]

If D gives value for the goods: **13.88**

(a) Retention or disposal of the goods cannot be theft, since V has no property in the goods, nor handling since V has lost his right to restitution,[145] his right to rescind being destroyed on the goods coming into the hands of D who was a bona-fide purchaser for value.

If D does not give value: **13.89**

(a) Again this cannot be theft, since V has no property in the goods, but it may be handling since V's right to rescind and secure restitution of his property is not extinguished by the goods coming into the hands of one who does not give value. It will be handling if this is so and D either aids and abets a guilty receipt by another or disposes of the goods 'for the benefit of another person'.

Handling by the thief

The common law rules regulating the liability of a thief to a charge of receiving goods feloniously stolen by him were complicated by the distinction between principals and accessories. **13.90**

That distinction[146] was abolished in 1967 and all participants in a crime are now classed as principals.[147] The effect is that any thief may be convicted of handling the goods stolen by **13.91**

---

[141] The CPS Charging Advice is that a theft charge is more appropriate if the defendant did not know or believe the goods to be stolen when he received them but, later discovered they were stolen and then dishonestly kept, or otherwise appropriated them.

[142] The normal situation where goods are stolen.

[143] Above, para 2.93.

[144] Because the rogue obtained them by fraud and acquired a voidable title or because of some exception to the *nemo dat* rule.

[145] Above, para 13.29.

[146] See the third edition of this book, para 405.

[147] Criminal Law Act 1967, s 1.

him by receiving them—if the evidence warrants this conclusion[148] and proves that he handled, or aided and abetted the handling of, goods, otherwise than in the course of the theft which caused the goods to be stolen. In the majority of cases the thief can only be guilty of handling by receiving where he aids and abets the receipt by another. Since he is already in possession or control, he cannot receive as the principal offender. In some circumstances, however, a thief might be convicted of handling the stolen goods by receiving them as the principal offender. For example, D steals goods and, in the course of the theft, delivers them to E. Two days later E returns the goods to D.

Mens rea

Knowledge or belief

13.92 It must be proved that D handled the goods, 'knowing or believing them to be stolen goods', ie that he knew or believed the goods to be stolen at the time when he received them or did such other act as is alleged to amount to handling.[149] The test is subjective. The fact that any reasonable man would have known that the goods were stolen is evidence, but no more, that D knew or believed that this was so.[150]

13.93 There is some difficulty about the function of the words, 'or believing'. The law of receiving stolen goods under the Larceny Acts used the word 'knowing' alone. To say that a person 'knows' a thing to be so implies that it is so.[151] To say that he 'believes' it to be so means that he thinks it is (or, perhaps, probably is) so, whether it is in fact so or not.[152] It might have been supposed that 'believing' was introduced to extend the law to cover one who received the goods believing them to be stolen when they were not. It has already been noticed that this interpretation was considered and rejected by the House of Lords in *Haughton v Smith*.[153]

13.94 The CLRC intended the words 'or believing' to extend the *mens rea* of the offence. They said:[154]

It is a serious defect of the present law that actual knowledge that the property was stolen must be proved. Often the prosecution cannot prove this. In many cases indeed guilty knowledge does not exist, although the circumstances of the transaction are such that the receiver ought to be guilty of an offence. The man who buys goods at a ridiculously low price from an unknown seller whom he meets in a public house may not know that the goods were stolen, and he may take the precaution of asking no questions. Yet it may be clear on the evidence that he believes that the goods were stolen.

---

[148] *Dolan* (1976) 62 Cr App R 36 at 39, CA, where this passage was followed. cf *Stapylton v O'Callaghan* [1973] 2 All ER 782.

[149] *Brook* [1993] Crim LR 455, CA.

[150] *Stagg* [1978] Crim LR 227, CA; *Brook* [1993] Crim LR 455, CA.

[151] See *Saik* [2006] UKHL 18.

[152] For academic analysis see in particular E Griew, 'Consistency, Communication and Codification— Reflections on Two *Mens Rea* Words' in P Glazebrook (ed), *Reshaping the Criminal Law* (1978) 57; S Shute, 'Knowledge and Belief in the Criminal Law' in S Shute and A Simester (eds), *Criminal Law Theory: Doctrines of the General Part* (2002) 171; GR Sullivan, 'Knowledge, Belief and Culpability', ibid 207; AR White, *Misleading Cases* (1991) 133.

[153] [1975] AC 476 at 485; above, para 13.17.

[154] CLRC, *Eighth Report*, Cmnd 2977 (1966) 64.

In such cases the prosecution may fail (rightly, as the law now stands) for want of proof of guilty knowledge.

It seems clear that they intended to include the concept of 'wilful blindness' which is often **13.95** held by the courts to be included in the word 'knowing' standing alone. But, if this was their intention, it has not been achieved. Wilful blindness postulates that D has a strong suspicion that something is so and consciously decides not to take steps which he could take to confirm or deny that fact.[155] But the courts have constantly said that, for the purposes of s 22, suspicion is not to be equated with belief.[156] It is a misdirection to tell the jury that it is enough that D, 'suspecting that the goods were stolen deliberately shut his eyes to the consequences'.[157]

What, if anything, then, does 'believing' add? According to *Hall*:[158] **13.96**

A man may be said to know that goods are stolen when he is told by someone with first-hand knowledge (someone such as the thief or the burglar) that such is the case. Belief, of course, is something short of knowledge. It may be said to be the state of mind of a person who says to himself: 'I cannot say I know for certain that these goods are stolen but there can be no other reasonable conclusion in the light of all the circumstances, in the light of all that I have heard and seen.'

But this seems to be merely a distinction between two sources of D's knowledge or belief: **13.97** if D had direct evidence, he knows, if he has circumstantial evidence, he believes. This section requires a distinction between two states of mind, not two modes of arriving at the same state of mind. The case suggests that if D had direct evidence, he knows; if he has mere circumstantial evidence, he believes, but, it would surely be more accurate to describe knowledge in terms of the accuracy of the belief, not the directness of the evidence leading to the belief. As Shute has recently suggested, the distinctions between the two concepts are twofold: knowledge constitutes a true belief, and belief includes acceptance of the proposition in question whereas knowledge does not.[159]

In *Forsyth*[160] the court said that the judgment in *Hall* is 'potentially confusing'.[161] In *Moys*[162] **13.98** the court confirmed simply that the question whether D knew or believed that the goods were stolen is a subjective one and that suspicion, even coupled with the fact that D shut his eyes to the circumstances, is not enough. D may be left in varying degrees of certainty whether he has been told by the thief or deduced the fact from his own observation.

---

[155] See paras 3.126–3.129.

[156] *Grainge* [1974] 1 All ER 928, CA. cf *Woods* [1969] 1 QB 447, [1968] 3 All ER 709, CA; *Ismail* [1977] Crim LR 557, CA and commentary. cf Griew paras 15–29 to 15–33, Williams, *TBCL* 39–36, *Spencer* [1985] Crim LR 101. See also G Williams, 'Handling, Theft and the Purchaser Who Takes a Chance' [1985] Crim LR 432.

[157] *Griffiths* (1974) 60 Cr App R 14, CA. *Atwal v Massey* [1971] 3 All ER 881, DC, is definitely misleading on this point and seems to have misled the judge in *Pethick* [1980] Crim LR 242, CA where it was said that suspicion, 'however strong', does not amount to knowledge.

[158] (1985) 81 Cr App R 260 at 264, [1985] Crim LR 377; criticized in *Forsyth* [1997] Crim LR 581.

[159] P 194. See the House of Lords' recognition of the difference between knowledge and belief in *Saik* [2006] UKHL 18.

[160] A *Hall* direction is not necessary in every case—*Toor* (1987) 85 Cr App R 116.

[161] It is the second part of *Hall* that present a problem: *Adinga* [2003] EWCA Crim 3201.

[162] (1984) 79 Cr App R 72, CA.

If both processes cause D to be certain that the goods are stolen, there is no difference in his state of mind. What seems to be implied in *Hall* is that the person with direct information is certain and the person with circumstantial evidence is nearly certain. But it would be dangerous so to direct a jury because 'near certainty' is strong suspicion and that is not enough. It is unclear whether it is sufficient that D considers the likelihood that the goods are stolen to be 'virtually certain'; presumably not. It is clearly not enough for D to believe that the goods are 'probably' stolen.[163]

13.99 In general, however, it seems that a judge cannot be wrong if he simply directs the jury in accordance with the words of the section and offers no elaboration or explanation of 'believing'.[164] Of course, it may be that the jury will then apply the word as if it included wilful blindness, but no one will ever know.

Knowledge of what?

13.100 It is sufficient that D knows or believes that the goods, whatever they are, are stolen. His knowledge or belief need not extend to the identity of the thief, or the owner,[165] or the nature of the stolen goods.[166] If D knows he is in possession of a box containing stolen goods, it is no defence that he does not know what the contents are and is shocked to discover that the box contains guns; nor would it be a defence that he believed the box contained stolen watches.[167] Equally, it is enough for D to know or believe that the goods are stolen in the extended meaning that term has under s 34. Thus, it does not matter that D believed the goods to be the product of blackmail when they were in fact the product of a theft. As elsewhere, it is not necessary for D to know the criminal law: it is sufficient that D has knowledge or belief as to the facts and conduct of the thief that renders it criminal.

Dishonesty

13.101 D may receive goods knowing or believing them to be stolen and yet not be guilty if, for example, he intends to return them to the true owner or the police.[168] A claim of right will amount to a defence, but it will be difficult to establish such a claim where D knows or believes the goods to be stolen except in the case put above, where he intends to return the goods to the owner. Whether there is dishonesty is presumably now a question of fact for the jury in each case, as in theft.[169]

---

[163] *Reader* (1977) 66 Cr App R 33, 36, CA. For consideration of whether this ought to be a sufficient *mens rea* see J Spencer, 'Handling, Theft and the Mala Fide Purchaser' [1985] Crim LR 92 at 95–6; G Williams, 'Handling, Theft and the Purchaser who takes a chance' [1985] Crim LR 432 at 435; J Spencer, 'Handling and Taking Risks: A Reply to Professor Williams' [1985] Crim LR 440.

[164] *Reader* (1977) 66 Cr App R 33, CA; *Harris* (1987) 84 Cr App R 75, CA; *Toor* (1986) 85 Cr App R 116, [1987] Crim LR 122, CA.

[165] *Fuschillo* [1940] 2 All ER 489; but it may be necessary to name the owner where the property is of a common and indistinctive type: *Gregory* [1972] 2 All ER 861, CA. See recently *Webster* [2002] EWCA Crim 1346.

[166] *McCullum* (1973) 57 Cr App R 645, CA.

[167] ibid at 649–50. An argument that D was not in possession of the contents because he was mistaken as to their nature would probably fail because he knew there was 'something wrong' with the goods: *Warner v Metropolitan Police Comr* [1969] 2 AC 256 at 308, [1968] 2 All ER 356 at 390, HL.

[168] cf *Matthews* [1950] 1 All ER 137.

[169] *Feely* [1973] QB 530, [1973] 1 All ER 341, CA.

Proving theft and handling

The general principles of evidence in criminal cases apply to the proof of offences under the **13.102** Theft Act as they apply to other crimes. This is not the place to examine those rules but their application to some Theft Act offences has created special problems and an exposition of the substantive law which did not examine these matters would be incomplete.

Declarations for lost goods

One way in which the Act seeks to facilitate proof that handled goods were stolen is by the **13.103** use of statutory declarations by witnesses to 'loss' of goods in the post.

Theft Act 1968, s 27:

(4) In any proceedings for the theft of anything in the course of transmission (whether by post or otherwise), or for handling stolen goods from such a theft, a statutory declaration made by any person that he dispatched or received or failed to receive any goods or postal packet, or that any goods or postal packet when dispatched or received by him were in a particular state or condition, shall be admissible as evidence of the facts stated in the declaration, subject to the following conditions:—

(a) a statutory declaration shall only be admissible where and to the extent to which oral evidence to the like effect would have been admissible in the proceedings; and

(b) a statutory declaration shall only be admissible if at least seven days before the hearing or trial a copy of it has been given to the person charged, and he has not, at least three days before the hearing or trial or within such further time as the court may in special circumstances allow, given the prosecutor written notice requiring the attendance at the hearing or trial of the person making the declaration.

(5) This section is to be construed in accordance with section 24 of this Act; and in subsection (3)(b) above the reference to handling stolen goods shall include any corresponding offence committed before the commencement of this Act.

The 'doctrine of recent possession'

Where D is found in possession of, or dealing with, property which has recently been **13.104** stolen, a jury may be directed that they may infer that he is guilty of an offence if he offers no explanation or if they are satisfied beyond reasonable doubt that any explanation he has offered is untrue. They are not bound so to infer and should be directed to do so only if satisfied beyond reasonable doubt that D was in fact guilty of the particular offence. The onus of proof remains on the Crown throughout. Whether D offers an explanation or not, the jury must not convict unless they are sure that he committed the offence in question.[170]

These principles are sometimes misleadingly referred to as 'the doctrine of recent posses- **13.105** sion'. The 'doctrine' is nothing more than the application to this constantly recurring situation of the ordinary principles of circumstantial evidence. Sometimes the correct inference will be that D was the thief (or robber or burglar if the goods were stolen in the course of

---

[170] *Abramovitch* (1914) 11 Cr App R 45; *Aves* (1950) 34 Cr App R 159; *Hepworth and Fearnley* [1955] 2 QB 600.

a robbery or burglary), sometimes that he was a handler. If the lead is stolen off the church roof at midnight and D is found dragging it across a field at 1 am, this is very cogent evidence that he stole the lead from the roof. If it is found in his backyard the next day and he offers no explanation,[171] or an explanation which is shown to be untrue, as to how he came by it, this is slightly less cogent evidence that he was the thief but very persuasive that he either stole it or received it knowing it to be stolen. As the time lengthens between the theft and discovery of D's connection with the stolen property, the weight of the evidence diminishes but it will vary according to the nature of the property stolen and other circumstances. One relevant circumstance will be the nature of D's conduct in relation to the goods, but the same principles apply whether D is charged with receiving or with one of the other forms of handling. So in *Ball*,[172] it was held that there was evidence of handling otherwise than by receiving where D assisted the thief in physically handling stolen goods and accompanying him on an expedition to sell the stolen property.

Mutually destructive alternative counts

13.106 Because of the impossibility of predicting which inference the jury will decide to be the right one, the prosecution may find it convenient to include two counts, count 1, say, for robbery and count 2 for receiving the goods which were stolen in the course of that robbery. These two counts are mutually contradictory. If D is guilty of robbery he came by the goods in the course of the stealing and therefore cannot be guilty of the alleged handling;[173] but, if he is guilty of handling, he received the goods otherwise than in the course of the stealing and is not guilty of robbery. On count 1 the prosecution are alleging that D received the goods in the course of the theft. On count 2 they are alleging that he did not receive the goods in the course of the theft. It is established[174] that it is lawful to include two such 'mutually destructive' counts in an indictment where there is a prima facie case on each count.

13.107 The difficulty which then arises is that a jury may be quite certain that the defendant was either the thief or a receiver but not satisfied beyond reasonable doubt that he was the one rather than the other. Indeed, it may be that there is no evidence on which they could possibly be satisfied that he was the one rather than the other. In that case, it appears that neither offence is proved beyond reasonable doubt and the only proper course is a complete acquittal—a conclusion satisfactory to no one but the accused.

13.108 A solution which has been adopted in some jurisdictions, following *Langmead* (1864),[175] is to direct the jury that, if they are satisfied beyond reasonable doubt that D was either the thief or a receiver, they may convict of the offence which they think more probable—ie it is enough that they are satisfied on a balance of probabilities that D was the thief, or that he

---

[171] Note that inferences at trial might be drawn under ss 34–8 of the Criminal Justice and Public Order Act 1994 for the failure. See generally, C Tapper, *Cross and Tapper on Evidence* (10th edn, 2004). The court must be careful not to apply the inference in such a way as to reverse the burden of proof: *Camara v DPP* (2003) All ER (D) 264 (Oct).
[172] (1983) 77 Cr App R 131, [1983] Crim LR 546, CA.
[173] Section 22(1), above.
[174] *Bellman* [1989] 1 All ER 22, [1989] 2 WLR 37, HL.
[175] (1864) Le & Ca 427.

was the receiver. As the jury is unlikely to find that the evidence is exactly evenly balanced, this is a practical solution, and one that should be Article 6(2) compliant.[176] It was, however, rejected by the Privy Council in *A-G of Hong Kong v Yip Kai-foon*.[177] D was charged with robbery and with handling the goods stolen. The Privy Council, following *Cash*,[178] held that the jury had been rightly directed to consider the robbery charge first. Once they had decided that they were not sure that D was guilty of robbery, he was to be presumed to be innocent of the theft of the goods and it followed that any handling that occurred took place 'otherwise then in the course of the stealing' so there was no need for more than a passing reference to those words. This is a novel use of the presumption of innocence against a defendant. Because the jury are not satisfied beyond reasonable doubt that D was guilty of theft it is apparently to be conclusively presumed that he was not guilty of that offence. If the jury are satisfied that he was guilty of one offence or the other, it follows inevitably that he was guilty of handling. But this is arbitrary. The outcome depends on which offence the jury consider first, and it becomes critical for the jury to be directed carefully as to the order in which they approach the verdicts.[179] More fundamental objections are that the approach treats the acquittal as proof of innocence and may offend Article 6(2) of the ECHR.[180]

Charging handling and aiding and abetting theft

A person guilty of handling stolen goods almost inevitably dishonestly appropriates, or aids **13.109** and abets the appropriation, of property belonging to another and so is guilty of theft as well. In *Devall*,[181] where D was charged in two counts with stealing a generator and handling the stolen generator, the Court of Appeal approved, *obiter*, of the judge's direction to the jury that they could convict on an alternative basis of such 'a second appropriation'. D had equally stolen the goods and committed the theft charged whether he was the original thief or a thief-by-handling. But the court suggested that there should be a separate count giving particulars of the second appropriation. There is a difficulty about this. If the jury cannot decide whether D was the thief or a handler, they cannot be satisfied that he was guilty on the first count; and they cannot be satisfied that he was guilty on the second count. We are no farther forward.

A single wide count of theft

An alternative is a single count of theft drawn in sufficiently wide terms to cover both the **13.110** first and second appropriations. This solution was found attractive by the Court of Appeal

---

[176] If the approach was applied more widely it would pose problems particularly where more than two alternatives are left, leading to possible conviction of an offence of which the jury are not even sure D is probably guilty. See further M Hirst 'Guilty but of what' (2000) 4 E & P 31.

[177] [1988] AC 642, [1988] 1 All ER 153, followed in *Foreman* [1991] Crim LR 702 and *Ryan and French v DPP* [1994] Crim LR 457, DC; but see commentaries thereon.

[178] Above, paras 13.72–13.74.

[179] *Fernandez* [1997] 1 Cr App R 123.

[180] See Hirst, above, n 176.

[181] [1984] Crim LR 428. cf *Falconer-Atlee* (1973) 58 Cr App R 348, CA and *Japes* [1994] Crim LR 605, CA.

in *More*[182] and seems in effect to have been the solution adopted in *Shelton*.[183] There seems to be no particular difficulty about alleging that D committed theft between two specified dates—the dates of the theft and of D's being found in possession. But it is not a case where it is merely uncertain on which day a particular act was done. Two distinct acts are envisaged and the prosecution are saying that D committed the one or the other. It has been held that it is not sufficient to prove that D attempted to pervert the course of justice either (a) by making false allegations, or (b) by resiling from those allegations at an ensuing trial.[184] This is very close to the case envisaged and the decision may be a fatal objection. Perhaps legislation is the only satisfactory solution to the problem.

Previous convictions

13.111 Because of the difficulty of proving guilty knowledge, the Larceny Act provided for the admission of certain evidence on a receiving charge which would not be admissible in criminal cases generally. The Theft Act has corresponding but somewhat different provisions. By s 27(3):

> Where a person is being proceeded against for handling stolen goods (but not for any offence other than handling stolen goods), then at any stage of the proceedings, if evidence has been given of his having or arranging to have in his possession the goods the subject of the charge, or of his undertaking or assisting in, or arranging to undertake or assist in, their retention, removal, disposal or realisation, the following evidence shall be admissible for the purpose of proving that he knew or believed the goods to be stolen goods—
>
> (a) evidence that he has had in his possession, or has undertaken or assisted in the retention, removal, disposal or realisation of, stolen goods from any theft taking place not earlier than twelve months before the offence charged; and
>
> (b) (provided that seven days' notice in writing has been given to him of the intention to prove the conviction) evidence that he has within the five years preceding the date of the offence charged been convicted of theft or of handling stolen goods.

13.112 Whereas under (b) the previous conviction must have occurred within five years preceding the offence charged, the possession, etc under (a) must have occurred 'not earlier' than twelve months before the offence charged. The possession, etc which is admissible under (a) may have taken place later than the offence charged.[185]

13.113 The section has been strictly construed. Paragraph (a) allows proof of the fact of possession of stolen goods and probably of their description but not of the circumstances in which D came into possession of them.[186] Under paragraph (b) it was formerly held that not even the description of the goods is allowed: 'the prosecution is not permitted to go further than to relate the fact of conviction for handling stolen goods and where and when'. However in *Hacker*[187] the House of Lords held that paragraph (b) must now be read with s 73(2) of the Police and Criminal Evidence Act 1984 (PACE) which provides that a certificate of

---

[182] (1987) 86 Cr App R 234 at 238.
[183] [1986] Crim LR 637.
[184] *Tsang Ping-Nam* [1981] 1 WLR 1462.
[185] *Davis* [1972] Crim LR 431, CA.
[186] *Bradley* (1980) 70 Cr App R 200, CA; criticized in [1980] Crim LR 173.
[187] [1994] 1 All ER 45, [1994] 1 WLR 1659, HL.

conviction on indictment which is admitted to prove the conviction must give the substance and effect of the indictment. As was stated in the Court of Appeal and repeated by Lord Slynn, '[The jury] might, quite sensibly, take the point that if it was handling of a stolen motorcar it might be quite different from handling of half a pound of sugar.'

It appears to be assumed that the conviction is evidence that the convicted person com-   **13.114**
mitted the offence. By s 74(3) of PACE the person proved to have been convicted is taken
to have committed the offence until the contrary is proved but only where the evidence
is relevant for a reason other than to show that the accused has a disposition to commit
the kind of offence with which he is charged. It is not clear whether the reason for the
admissibility of a conviction under s 27 is to show the disposition of the accused to handle
stolen goods.

Section 27 and the bad character under Criminal Justice Act 2003

It appears that these provisions supplement the statutory rules governing the admissibility   **13.115**
of previous misconduct.[188] Thus a handling of goods stolen earlier than twelve months
before the handling now charged might be admissible under s 101 of the Criminal Justice
Act 2003.[189] So too might a conviction of theft or handling after the date of the offence
charged or more than five years before it.[190]

Section 27(3) imposes limitations upon admissibility which do not exist in s 101 of the   **13.116**
Criminal Justice Act 2003. The section applies only where handling is the only offence in
issue.[191] The evidence in question may not be given until after some evidence of the *actus
reus* has been given; and evidence admissible under (b) may not be given without seven
days' notice in writing of intention to tender it. Although evidence has been given of the
actus reus—for example that D was in possession—D may dispute that fact. Evidence
admitted under s 27(3) may not be considered on the question whether D was in possession. It is admissible for one purpose only—to prove the knowledge or belief[192] that the
goods were stolen.[193] Since proof of possession also requires proof of a mental element,
these questions may become virtually indistinguishable.

In *Wilkins*,[194] evidence was given that stolen goods were found in D's garden and behind   **13.117**
a drawer in her bedroom. This was evidence that she was in possession, permitting the
admission of evidence under s 27(3). Her defence was that the articles had been put there
without her knowledge, that she did not know they were there, and, accordingly, that she
was never in possession. Since the judge's direction failed to make clear that the evidence
could be taken into account only on the issue of guilty knowledge or belief that the goods

---

[188] See ss 98–112 of the Criminal Justice Act 2003. It was held that the section did not conflict with the old common law position on admissibility: *Davis*, para 13.112 above.

[189] Or in some odd cases at common law if s 98(a) applies. C Tapper, *Cross and Tapper on Evidence* (10th edn, 2004) 440–2; *Blackstone's Criminal Practice* (2007) F12.39.

[190] See *Adenusi* [2006] EWCA Crim 1059.

[191] *Gardner v New Forest Magistrates Court* (1988) 5 June, unreported.

[192] Not dishonesty: *Duffas* (1994) 158 JP 224.

[193] It may be received by the judge in his consideration of a half-time submission: *Adinga* [2003] EWCA Crim 3201.

[194] [1975] 2 All ER 734, CA.

were stolen, the convictions were quashed. Where there is a danger that the jury may think the evidence relevant to some other issue, the judge might be wise to exercise his discretion to exclude the evidence.

13.118 The evidence of previous convictions might be admitted under s 101(1) of the Criminal Justice Act 2003 as important explanatory evidence (101(1)(c)); in relation to propensity to commit the offence in question (101(1)(d)) or some aspect of the offence (101(1)(d)) as evidence of untruthfulness (101(1)(d) which is not the same as dishonesty); as evidence to rectify a false impression that D may have made (101(1)(f)); and in response to a character attack on a witness (101(1)(g)). Subject to the statutory criteria for notice being complied with, the statutory criteria for admissibility being met in s 101 and to the exercise of judicial discretion in ss 101 and 103 (where appropriate) and to s 78 of PACE in all cases, the evidence can be admitted in a wider range of circumstances and be put to a wider range of uses than under s 27(3).

13.119 Section 27(3) may now be an unnecessary provision. The Law Commission has called for its abolition.[195]

Procedure

13.120 By 27(1):

Any number of persons may be charged in one indictment with reference to the same theft, with having at different times or at the same time handled all or any of the stolen goods, and the persons so charged may be tried together.

If £500 is stolen from a bank and the thief, on separate occasions, hands £100 to each of five persons, all five may be tried together for handling the stolen money, though they have no connection with one another except through the thief.

13.121 By s 27(2):

On the trial of two or more persons indicted for jointly handling any stolen goods the jury may find any of the accused guilty if the jury are satisfied that he handled all or any of the stolen goods, whether or not he did so jointly with the other accused or any of them.

13.122 Under the rule in *DPP v Merriman*[196] where two persons are jointly charged with committing the same act and it emerges that they were not acting in concert, each may be convicted of committing the act independently. The subsection goes further in that it allows conviction not only where there is separate participation in a single act but where there are different acts in relation to the same stolen goods. In *French*,[197] D received stolen goods and took them to E's shop where E received them. It was held that they were properly jointly indicted, although the handlings were quite separate and the case against each must be considered separately.

---

[195] See Law Commission, *Evidence of Bad Character in Criminal Proceedings* (2001) Cm 5257, paras 4.13–4.23, 11.53–11.55.
[196] [1973] AC 584, [1972] 3 All ER 42, [1972] 3 WLR 545, HL.
[197] [1973] Crim LR 632, CA.

Sentencing

It will be noted that the maximum sentence is twice that available for theft. This reflects the **13.123** desire to deter the professional 'fence' so that the market for stolen goods will thereby diminish and the incidence of theft will decrease.[198] It is this same philosophy that lies behind the far-reaching and draconian Proceeds of Crime Act 2002 under which dealing with the proceeds of criminal activity, not just stolen goods, becomes criminal. In practical terms the substantial differences between the sentencing of large-scale professional fencing and, for example, receipt of low-value goods for personal use[199] raises questions about whether the handling offence ought to be subdivided so as to better reflect the type of criminality involved. This overgeneralization and failure to provide adequate differentiation in the offence has long been the subject of criticism.[200]

In *Webbe and others*[201] the Court of Appeal were persuaded that it would be helpful to issue **13.124** guidelines for sentences in handling cases. In doing so they adopted proposals contained in advice given to the court by the Sentencing Advisory Panel. In his judgment Lord Justice Rose adopted the nine key aggravating factors identified by the Panel. They are as follows:

1. The closeness of the handler to the primary offence. (We add that closeness may be geographical, arising from presence at or near the primary offence when it was committed, or temporal, where the handler instigated or encouraged the primary offence beforehand, or, soon after, provided a safe haven or route for disposal.)
2. Particular seriousness in the primary offence.
3. High value of the goods to the loser, including sentimental value.
4. The fact that the goods were the proceeds of a domestic burglary.
5. Sophistication in relation to the handling.
6. A high level of profit made or expected by the handler.
7. The provision by the handler of a regular outlet for stolen goods.
8. Threats of violence or abuse of power by the handler over others, for example, an adult commissioning criminal activity by children, or a drug dealer pressurizing addicts to steal in order to pay for their habit.
9. As is statutorily provided by s 151(2) of the Powers of Criminal Courts (Sentencing) Act 2000, the commission of an offence while on bail.

The Court of Appeal also felt able to adopt the general mitigating features identified by the sentencing panel. Those features included:

1. Low monetary value of the goods,
2. The offence being a one-off offence,

---

[198] *Shelton* (1986) 83 Cr App R 379; *Tokeley-Parry* [1999] Crim LR 578 (deterring removal of antiquities from Egypt).

[199] See generally the Sentencing Advisory Panel, *Handling Stolen Goods* (2001) and *Archbold* (2007) 21–279a. Low monetary value goods received for handler's own use will attract a modest fine or conditional discharge. For analysis of the activities of the professional handler see CB Klockars, *The Professional Fence* (1975).

[200] See DA Thomas, 'Form and Function in Criminal Law' in P Glazebrook (ed), *Reshaping the Criminal Law* (1978) 23–4.

[201] [2002] 1 Cr App R (S) 22.

3. The offence committed by an otherwise honest defendant,

4. The fact that there is little or no benefit to the defendant, and

5. The fact of voluntary restitution to the victim.

13.125 The court additionally felt it right that general mitigating features such as personal mitigation, ready cooperation with the police, previous convictions, especially for offences of dishonesty, and, as statutorily provided by s 152 of the Powers of Criminal Courts (Sentencing) Act 2000, a timely plea of guilty should be weighed 'in the balance by a sentencing court.

Dishonestly Retaining a Wrongful Credit

13.126 Section 24A of the Theft Act 1968 (inserted by s 2 of the Theft (Amendment) Act 1996) provides:

(1) person is guilty of an offence if—
   (a) a wrongful credit has been made to an account kept by him or in respect of which he has any right or interest,
   (b) he knows or believes that the credit is wrongful, and
   (c) he dishonestly fails to take such steps as are reasonable in the circumstances to secure that the credit is cancelled.
(2) References to a credit are to a credit of an amount of money.[202]

The offence is punishable under s 24A on indictment with imprisonment for ten years.

13.127 The effect is that D1, a thief, who has credited to his account a wrongful credit commits an offence if he does not take steps within a reasonable time to divest himself of his ill-gotten gains. The provision is not, of course, aimed at him but at D2, where D1 has procured the crediting, not of his own, but of D2's account. If this was done with D2's connivance, D2 would be guilty as a secondary party to D1's original offence which generated the proceeds which were credited to D1's account. There would be no need to invoke s 24A. Suppose, however, that the credit was made without D2's connivance. One day D2 finds that an unexpected credit has been made to his account. As soon as he knows or believes that the credit has been made in such circumstances as amount to an offence he comes under a duty to divest himself of this unforeseen windfall. If he fails to do so within a reasonable time he commits the offence. It is an offence of omission,[203] rather like theft where s 5(4) applies. Whereas, however, s 5(4) requires D to intend to 'make restoration' of the property, s 24A(1)(c) merely requires him to cancel the credit. Does he do this merely by withdrawing the money to spend on riotous living? It seems not.

13.128 In *Lee*,[204] the Court of Appeal addressed the question of whether a wrongful credit is cancelled within s 24. The appellant relied on a passage in the previous edition of *Smith and Hogan* to the effect that if D withdraws the money to spend for his own benefit, he cancels the credit and might escape liability under s 24A—'if the draftsmen meant

---

[202] As amended by the Fraud Act 2006, Sch 1.
[203] The argument of the Law Commission that this is necessary is found in Law Com No 243 at 39.
[204] [2006] EWCA Crim 156.

"make restoration" he should have said so—but, by section 24A(8), the money withdrawn is stolen goods so he will be guilty of receiving stolen goods.' The Court of Appeal rejected this submission noting that if it were correct it would lead to a 'surprising conclusion, since it is clear from the terms of the section itself that the offence consists in retaining the credit rather than taking reasonable steps to cancel it'. The conclusion was that 'the word "cancelled" as used in section 24A(1)(c) means cancelling the original credit so as to achieve the same effect as if it had not been made in the first place. In many cases that will be achieved by a corresponding debit reversing the original entry in the account.'[205]

13.129 The Act extends to other conduct which was not an offence even before the decision of the House of Lords in *Preddy*. Section 24A (2A)[206] provides:

(2A) A credit to an account is wrongful to the extent that it derives from
   (a) theft
   (b) blackmail
   (c) fraud (contrary to section 1 of the Fraud Act 2006); or
   (d) stolen goods.

13.130 So D2 may be guilty of the offence if:

   (i) D1 steals money and pays it into D2's account;
  (ii) D1 obtains money by blackmail and pays that money into D2's account;
 (iii) D1 obtains money by fraud and pays that into D2's account;
  (iv) D1 receives stolen money and pays it into D2's account.

13.131 In each of these cases the credit in D2's account is a new item of property—a thing in action belonging to D2—which has never been 'in the hands' of a thief or handler and so is not 'stolen goods' within s 24(2). D2 is not guilty of handling by retaining it. Now, however, he commits an offence under s 24A(1) if he dishonestly fails to cancel 'the wrongful credit' within a reasonable time. Cancelling according to *Lee* means cancelling it as if it had never been made and not simply withdrawing that amount. In any event, s 24A(8) provides that any money which is withdrawn from a wrongful credit will be stolen goods and subject to the general law of handling so D2 may commit an offence under s 22.

13.132 An incidental effect is that the thief, blackmailer, or handler who pays the proceeds of his offence into his own account commits another offence when he fails to take reasonable steps to cancel the credit. This is so because the Law Commission thought: 'It would be difficult, if not impossible, to devise a simple way of excluding the case where A dishonestly secures a credit to his own account, while including the case where A dishonestly secures a credit to B's.'[207] The Commission comforted themselves with the consideration that there was already an enormous degree of overlap in the existing offences under the Theft Acts.

13.133 Section 24A(5) provides that it is immaterial whether an account is overdrawn before or after a credit is made. So if D2's account is overdrawn to the tune of £100 when a wrongful

---

[205] [22].
[206] As inserted by the Fraud Act 2006.
[207] Law Com No 243, paras 6.16–6.17.

credit of £50 arrives, he is under a duty, somehow, to get his overdraft restored to its former level.

13.134 There is no provision corresponding to s 24(3)[208] (stolen goods cease to be 'stolen' when they are restored to lawful custody or when the owner and any others claiming through him have ceased to have any right to restitution of the goods). Nor is there any exemption for the bona-fide purchaser such as is to be found in s 3(2).[209] Suppose that D sells his car in good faith to A who pays him with stolen money. After learning that the money was stolen D spends it. He did not commit any offence before the enactment of s 24A. He still commits no offence if A paid him in cash and he spends the cash. But if D paid the cash into his own bank account, or if he was paid by a cheque which he has paid into that account, he has received a wrongful credit and it appears that he will (subject to proof of dishonesty) commit an offence under s 24A when he spends the money, because he has failed to take reasonable steps to disgorge. That would create not only an unsatisfactory anomaly but also a conflict with the civil law. A transferee of stolen currency for value and without notice gets a good title: *Miller v Race*.[210] The money, whether in cash or in the bank, is surely his to dispose of as he chooses. How then can he be guilty of a crime by doing so?

13.135 It may be that a court will think it necessary to read into s 24A(1)(c) some such qualification as 'except where no person has any right to restitution of the credit,' on the ground that Parliament could not have intended to change, or create a conflict with, such a fundamental rule of the civil law. This would introduce a limitation to the same effect as that relating to stolen goods generally in s 24(4).

13.136 The Fraud Act also makes the following substitutions in s 24:

(2) In subsection (7), for 'subsection (4)' substitute 'subsection (2A)'.
(3) For subsection (9) substitute—
'(9) "Account" means an account kept with—
(a) a bank;
(b) a person carrying on a business which falls within subsection (10) below; or
(c) an issuer of electronic money (as defined for the purposes of Part 2 of the Financial Services and Markets Act 2000).
(10) A business falls within this subsection if—
(a) in the course of the business money received by way of deposit is lent to others; or
(b) any other activity of the business is financed, wholly or to any material extent, out of the capital of or the interest on money received by way of deposit.
(11) References in subsection (10) above to a deposit must be read with—
(a) section 22 of the Financial Services and Markets Act 2000;
(b) any relevant order under that section; and
(c) Schedule 2 to that Act;
but any restriction on the meaning of deposit which arises from the identity of the person making it is to be disregarded.

---

[208] Above, para 13.22.
[209] Above, para 2.93.
[210] (1758) 1 Burr 452.

(12) For the purposes of subsection (10) above—
    (a) all the activities which a person carries on by way of business shall be regarded as a single business carried on by him; and
    (b) "money" includes money expressed in a currency other than sterling.'

The Attorney-General explained the amendments in debates in Parliament,[211] where he described them as technical amendments to expand the existing definitions to protect electronic money accounts which are increasingly prevalent—some £137 million of emoney being in circulation in the UK economy. **13.137**

Advertising Rewards for Return of Goods Stolen or Lost[212]

It is a summary offence to advertise publicly for the return of stolen or lost goods, using any words to the effect that no questions will be asked, or no inquiries made, or that any money paid for the goods will be repaid.[213] The history of this provision goes back to 1828. Until the Common Informers Act 1951 it was not punishable in criminal proceedings but was enforceable by any person who sued in debt for the sum of £50 which the defendant forfeited for every offence—'a penal action'. The 1951 Act abolished penal actions and provided that conduct formerly subject to this procedure should be an offence punishable on summary conviction by a fine (now a fine not exceeding level 3 of the standard scale). After some hesitation, the CLRC decided to keep the offence as 'advertisements of this kind may encourage dishonesty'.[214] In *Denham v Scott*,[215] it was held that the offence is one of strict liability so that the advertising manager of a free weekly newspaper in which such an advertisement appeared was guilty, as the controlling mind of the company for the purpose of publication, although he had not inspected the advertisement before it was published and did not know it had appeared. In light of the House of Lords' recent stance against interpreting provisions as imposing strict liability, the authority should be treated with caution.[216] **13.138**

Money Laundering[217]

In a series of complex statutes over the last two decades the government has sought to combat serious crime by targeting not just the offenders, but those who assist in the disposal of criminal proceeds. The legislative response to serious and organized crime has involved specific money laundering offences and a raft of measures providing for confiscation, assets recovery, civil recovery, and restraint proceedings. In some respects the offences of money **13.139**

---

[211] Hansard, HL, 31 Jan 2006, col 183.
[212] See JC Smith, 'Rewards for the Return of Lost or Stolen Property' in N Palmer, *The Recovery of Stolen Art* (1998).
[213] 1968 Act, s 23.
[214] CLRC, *Eighth Report*, Cmnd 2977 (1966) para 144.
[215] (1983) 77 Cr App R 210, [1983] Crim LR 558, DC.
[216] See *DPP v B* [2000] 2 AC 428; *R v K* [2002] 1 AC 462.
[217] See generally, A Mitchell, S Taylor, and K Talbot, *On Confiscation and the Proceeds of Crime* (2002) ch 9; *Archbold* (2007) ch 33; *Blackstone's Criminal Practice* (2007) B.22; and for a more theoretical account see P Alldridge, *Money Laundering Law* (2003) ch 9.

laundering share a similar rationale to handling: to target those who render criminal activity profitable rather than the person committing the substantive crime himself. However, the
money laundering offences are concerned not just with stolen goods but with criminal
proceeds more generally. The legislation has been driven by the international treaty obligations, and these are frequently relied upon by the courts as an aid to interpretation.[218]
In addition, offences relating to money laundering and disclosure of information have been
extended in response to the terrorist threat and in an effort to cut off terrorist funds.[219]

13.140   The Drug Trafficking Offences Act 1986, Criminal Justice Act 1993, and then the Drug
Trafficking Act 1994 provided a series of offences which criminalized entering into or
being concerned in an arrangement involving the retention, acquisition, use possession, etc
of criminal proceeds or the proceeds of drug crime.[220] This strict division between laundering 'drug' money and 'other criminal proceeds' created significant practical problems, as
when D admitted that he thought that he was involved in something suspicious but was
not sure what. Unless the Crown could establish that he knew or suspected it was drug
money *or* that he suspected it was proceeds of non-drug crime he would be acquitted. This
led to complex indictments alleging that D laundered either drug and/or other property.
Even greater complexity arose in prosecutions for conspiracies of these offences.[221]

13.141   Part 7 of the Proceeds of Crime Act 2002 (POCA) remedies some of these problems but
creates offences of a no less draconian nature. The legislation is extremely technical and
cannot be dealt with in detail in this work. This section offers only an overview of the three
principal offences.[222]

The Proceeds of Crime Act 2002[223]

13.142   Part 7 of the Act[224] introduces three sections which create at least nine offences replacing
the separate categories of offence relating to drug and non-drug crime.[225] The Terrorism
Acts contain separate offences dealing with laundering the proceeds of terrorist activity.
The offences under the Act are only a small part of the overall scheme to protect against
money laundering. There are important additional Money Laundering Regulations 2003[226]

---

[218] See *M* [2005] Crim LR 479, [2004] UKHL 53.
[219] New offences were included in the Anti-Terrorism, Crime and Security Act 2001. Laundering the
proceeds of terrorist activities was criminalized by the Prevention of Terrorism (Temporary Provisions)
Act 1989, Terrorism Act 2000, Pt 3.
[220] For an excellent review of some of the problems under the old law see J Fisher and J Bewsey, 'Laundering
the Proceeds of Fiscal Crime' (2000) JIBL 11.
[221] See *El Kurd* [2001] Crim LR 234; *Hussain* [2002] Crim LR 407.
[222] The offences are supplemented by the important provisions in the Money Laundering Regulations
2003, SI 2003/3075.
[223] See references in E Rees and A Hall, *Blackstone's Guide to the Proceeds of Crime Act 2002* (2003);
R Fortson, *Misuse of Drugs: Offences Confiscation and Money Laundering* (5th edn, 2005); *Mitchell, Taylor and
Talbot on Confiscation and Proceeds of Crime* (2005) ch 8.
[224] In force only from 24 Feb 2003: The Proceeds of Crime Act 2002 (Commencement No 4, Transitional
Provisions and Savings) Order 2003, SI 2003/120.
[225] Criminal Justice Act 1988, ss 93(2), 93A, 93B and Drug Trafficking Act 1994, ss 49, 50, 51.
[226] SI 2003/3075. The Regulations were also introduced to ensure the UK had implemented Directive
2001/97/EC of the European Parliament and of the Council of 4 December 2001 amending Council Directive
91/308/EEC on prevention of the use of the financial system for the purpose of money laundering.

which place duties on specified individuals to ensure processes exist to detect and report money laundering in their institution or business dealings. These regulations include criminal penalties for failure to comply. There is also a number of international and EU regulations dealing with money laundering.

This chapter deals only with the principal English offences in POCA. These principal offences apply only where the alleged money laundering activity began on or after 24 February 2003 irrespective of whether the predicate offence occurred before that date.[227]   **13.143**

Criminal property

The offences in POCA relate to dealings with 'criminal property'. Section 340 is therefore central to their operation. Section 340(3) provides that: **13.144**

. . . property is criminal property if
(a) it constitutes a person's benefit from criminal conduct or it represents such a benefit (in whole or part and whether directly or indirectly), and
(b) the alleged offender knows or suspects that it constitutes or represents such a benefit.

Property

Property is extremely widely defined in s 340(9) as being all property wherever it is situated including: money; all forms of property, real or personal, heritable or moveable; and things in action and other intangible or incorporeal property.   **13.145**

The extensive scope of this definition means that D can be liable for one of the offences in ss 327–9 where his transfer/concealment etc relates to his own ill-gotten gains.   **13.146**

By subsection 10:   **13.147**

(a) property is obtained by a person if he obtains an interest in it;
(b) references to an interest, in relation to land in England and Wales or Northern Ireland, are to any legal estate or equitable interest or power;
(c) . . .
(d) references to an interest, in relation to property other than land, include references to a right (including a right to possession).

Benefit

Subsection (5) provides that 'a person benefits from conduct if he obtains property as a result of or in connection with the conduct.' And subsection (8) 'if a person benefits from conduct his benefit is the property obtained as a result of or in connection with the conduct.'   **13.148**

Criminal conduct

By s 340(2) Criminal conduct is conduct which: **13.149**

(a) constitutes an offence in any part of the United Kingdom, or
(b) would constitute an offence in any part of the United Kingdom if it occurred there.

---

[227] Article 3, Proceeds of Crime Act 2002 (Commencement No 4, Transitional Provisions and Savings) Order 2003, SI 2003/120 as amended by Article 14, Proceeds of Crime Act 2002 (Commencement No 5, Transitional Provisions, Savings and Amendment) Order 2003, SI 2003/333.

And by s 340(4):

(4) It is immaterial—
    (a) who carried out the conduct;
    (b) who benefited from it;
    (c) whether the conduct occurred before or after the passing of this Act.

13.150 'Criminal conduct' includes the accused's own criminal conduct and conduct abroad that is not an offence under any UK law but which would be such an offence if committed somewhere in the UK.

Prior criminal conduct

13.151 There must be criminal conduct prior to the money laundering offence as alleged and the Crown must prove that offence, but there is no requirement that a conviction for the predicate offence has already been secured.[228] The Crown can prove the predicate offence in the course of the money laundering prosecution. The CPS Guidance suggests that if a person can be charged with both a predicate offence and money laundering then a careful exercise of prosecutorial discretion is required especially in relation to s 329.

13.152 In *Louizou*[229] the defendants appealed the judge's ruling that one of the ways in which the Crown would be entitled to put its case would be that where property had been transferred for a criminal purpose, it would become 'criminal property' within the meaning of s 340. The prosecution sought to prove that the property became criminal within the meaning set out in s 340 because of, and at the time of, the criminal transfer. This is clearly not what the statute intended. The offence (under s 327 in that case) involves, inter alia, transferring criminal property. It is not an offence of criminally transferring property. The prosecution must prove that the property is criminal property within s 340 at the time of or immediately before the acts alleged to constitute the transfer etc.

13.153 The Crown's more sophisticated attempt to extend the meaning of criminal property was also rightly rejected. That argument proceeded on the basis that if A and B had formed a conspiracy to launder proceeds, and a transfer of the proceeds then occurred, the transfer related to property that was already criminal—being related to the existing conspiracy. As the court rightly points out, it is at that time of transfer not criminal property under s 340 since it did not constitute anyone's benefit from criminal conduct.

13.154 However, in the course of delivering judgment, the Court of Appeal gave an example which was likely to confuse the clear ruling delivered.

Suppose I [Clarke LJ] receive pay as a judge in cash, that cash is not criminal property. Suppose I use that money to pay Hughes J for a car which I know he has stolen. In that event I, of course, commit the offence of receiving goods knowing them to be stolen. I do not, however, commit the offence of transferring criminal property because the property I am transferring, namely the money which I earned as a judge, is not criminal property. Of course, in the hands of Hughes J as the seller of the stolen car, the cash is criminal property because it constitutes 'a person's benefit from criminal conduct' within section 340(3)(a) which he knows suspects constitutes such a benefit within section

---

[228] This was confirmed by the Court of Appeal in *Sabaharwal* [2001] 2 Cr App R (S) 81.
[229] [2004] EWCA 1579.

340(3)(b). Does Hughes J commit an offence under section 327(1)? The answer is plainly no, because he has not concealed, disguised, converted or transferred criminal property. He has simply received what is now criminal property and retained it. Section 327(1) does not create an offence of receiving criminal property.

Hughes J certainly does not commit an offence in relation to the cash received since that did not, at the time of/immediately before transfer, constitute criminal property. But does not Hughes J commit an offence under s 327 by his transfer of the criminal property (the stolen car which directly represents the benefit of his crime)? What is more, if Clarke LJ knows that Hughes J has stolen the car, by purchasing it from him, Clarke LJ commits a money laundering offence by assisting Hughes J in the commission of a money laundering offence, namely the transfer of the stolen car.

In the subsequent case of *Gabriel*,[230] the Court of Appeal provided further important clari- **13.155** fication of the Crown's responsibilities in proving that the property was property derived from criminal conduct:

In our judgment it is a sensible practice for the prosecution, as was done in *Louizou*, either by giving particulars, or at least in opening, to set out the facts upon which it relies and the inferences which it will invite the jury to draw as proof that the property was criminal property. In doing so it may very well be that the prosecution will be able to limit the scope of the criminal conduct alleged.[231]

Common elements of the offences

Suspicion

The *mens rea* requirements are astonishingly wide, being based on mere suspicion. There is **13.156** no requirement to prove dishonesty. Such a low level of *mens rea* is remarkable for offences of such seriousness.

In *Da Silva*[232] the judge directed the jury that 'to suspect something, you have a state of **13.157** mind that is well short of knowing that the matter that you suspect is true. It is an ordinary English word . . . the dictionary definition of "suspicion" [is] an act of suspecting, the imagining of something without evidence or on slender evidence, inkling, mistrust'.[233] The Court of Appeal upheld the conviction concluding that the word 'suspect' and its affiliates was that the defendant had to think that there was a possibility, which was more than fanciful, that the relevant facts existed. A vague feeling of unease would not suffice; however, the statute did not require that the suspicion had to be 'clear' or 'firmly grounded and targeted on specific facts', or based upon 'reasonable grounds'.

Where a judge felt it appropriate to assist the jury with the word 'suspecting', a direction **13.158** along those lines would be adequate and accurate. The only possible qualification was whether, in an appropriate case, a jury should also be directed that the suspicion had to be

---

[230] [2006] EWCA Crim 229.
[231] [29].
[232] [2006] EWCA Crim 1654.
[233] Taken from *Mitchell, Taylor and Talbot on Confiscation and Proceeds of Crime* (2005).

of a settled nature; a case might, for example, arise in which a defendant had entertained a suspicion in the above sense but, on further thought, had honestly dismissed it from his or her mind as being unworthy or as contrary to such evidence as existed or as being outweighed by other considerations. In such a case a careful direction to the jury might be required; however, before such a direction was necessary there would have to be some reason to suppose that the defendant had gone through some such thought process.

13.159 This interpretation is consistent with earlier pronouncements including notably that of Lord Devlin in *Hussien v Chang Fook Kam*:[234]

> Suspicion in its ordinary meaning is a state of conjecture or surmise where proof is lacking: 'I suspect but I cannot prove'. Suspicion arises at or near the starting point of an investigation of which the obtaining of prima facie proof is the end.[235]

13.160 The court's interpretation of suspicion has been held to apply in the civil law relating to this offence: *K Ltd v National Westminster Bank plc*.[236]

Section 327

13.161 By section 327:

> (1) A person commits an offence if he—
> (a) conceals[237] criminal property;
> (b) disguises criminal property;
> (c) converts criminal property;
> (d) transfers criminal property;
> (e) removes criminal property from England and Wales or from Scotland or from Northern Ireland.

Subsection 2 provides important qualifications to the scope of the offence by excluding from liability (i) a person who has made an authorized disclosure under section 338; or, (ii) intended to do so and had a good reason for not doing; or, (iii) a person who knows, or believes on reasonable grounds, that the relevant criminal conduct occurred in a particular country or territory outside the United Kingdom, and was not, at the time it occurred, unlawful under the criminal law then applying in that country or territory, and is not of a description prescribed by an order made by the Secretary of State.

13.162 The broad scope of the offence is obvious. Read strictly, it appears that the section creates five different offences, and on that basis the indictment should specify which to avoid being bad for duplicity. This could create undue complexity, and it may be that the section is

---

[234] [1970] AC 942 at 948.
[235] See also the definition suggested in the JMLSG 2006 Guidance at para 7.9 'A degree of satisfaction and not necessarily amounting to belief but at least extending beyond speculation as to whether an event has occurred or not'; and 'Although the creation of suspicion requires a lesser factual basis than the creation of a belief, it must nonetheless be built upon some foundation.'
[236] [2006] EWCA Civ 1039.
[237] By subsection (3) 'Concealing or disguising criminal property includes concealing or disguising its nature, source, location, disposition, movement or ownership or any rights with respect to it.'

treated, as with handling, as creating a single offence that can be committed in one of a number of ways.[238]

Section 328

Section 328:

13.163

(1) A person commits an offence if he enters into or becomes concerned in an arrangement which he knows or suspects facilitates (by whatever means) the acquisition, retention, use or control of criminal property by or on behalf of another person.

Subsection 2 provides exclusion from liability in circumstances similar to those in s 327(2) considered at para 13.161 above.

13.164

Section 328 creates only one offence of entering into or becoming concerned in an arrange-ment which he 'knows or suspects facilitates (by whatever means) the acquisition, reten-tion, use or control of criminal property by or on behalf of another person.' It is has been held that this extraordinarily broad offence does not cover the ordinary conduct of litiga-tion by professions.[239]

13.165

The purpose of the section was explained by Laddie J in *Squirrell Ltd v National Westminster Bank plc*:[240]

13.166

The purpose of s. 328(1) is not to turn innocent third parties like [banks] into criminals. It is to put them under pressure to provide information to the relevant authorities to enable the latter to obtain information about possible criminal activity and to increase their prospects of being able to freeze the proceeds of crime. To this end, a party caught by s. 328(1) can avoid liability if he brings himself within the statutory defence created by s. 328(2). . . .'

In *Bowman v Fels*[241] the Court of Appeal examined whether the phrase 'enters into or becomes concerned in an arrangement' could encompass the ordinary conduct of legal proceedings. It concluded that on a proper interpretation s 328 was not intended to cover or affect the ordinary conduct of litigation by legal professionals, including any steps taken by legal professionals in the litigation from the issue of proceedings and the securing of injunctive relief or a freezing order up to its final disposal by judgment. Brooke LJ said:[242]

13.167

It is . . . not intended to cover or affect the ordinary conduct of litigation by legal professionals. That includes any step taken by them in litigation from the issue of proceedings and the securing of injunctive relief or a freezing order up to its final disposal by judgment. We do not consider that either the European or the United Kingdom legislator can have envisaged that any of these ordinary activities could fall within the concept of 'becoming concerned in an arrangement which . . . facili-tates the acquisition, retention, use or control of criminal property.

There is no doubt that this is an extremely wide offence, but is it wide enough to cover, in *one* substantive count, the conduct of a number of defendants who have made repeated

13.168

---

[238] cf *Griffiths v Freeman* [1970] 1 ALL ER 1117.
[239] *Bowman v Fels* [2005] EWCA Civ 328.
[240] [2006] 1 WLR 637 at [16].
[241] [2005] EWCA Civ 226.
[242] [83].

transfers etc? If D1 transfers property for X, and D2 in a separate transaction converts different property for X, and D3 does likewise etc, is it possible to indict X, D1, D2, and D3 in one count under s 328? These facts would obviously allow for three substantive offences under that section. In each transaction, the relevant defendant and X enter into an arrangement which they know/suspect facilitates the use of criminal property by another. But, when engaged in his transaction with X, can D1 be said to be 'entering or concerned in an arrangement' in which D2 and D3 are concerned? Can X be indicted in the same count given that X is 'another' under the terms of this section? Is the conduct properly described as an 'arrangement' or more accurately as a series of arrangements? It is submitted that, applying the logic of *Bowman v Fels*,[243] it is the latter.[244]

13.169 What must D1 know or suspect? It is submitted that it is not enough that D1 knows he is entering into an arrangement with X, unless he also knows that that arrangement involves others, but that it is not necessary for him to know the identities of those others.

Section 329

13.170 Section 329 creates three offences of acquisition, use, and possession of criminal property.

> (1) A person commits an offence if he—
>   (a) acquires criminal property;
>   (b) uses criminal property;
>   (c) has possession of criminal property.

13.171 Subsection 2 provides exclusion from liability in circumstances similar to those in s 327(2) considered at para 13.161 above.

13.172 Section 329(3) provides a further specific defence where a person has acquired, used, or had possession of the criminal property for adequate consideration.[245]

> (3) For the purposes of this section—
>   (a) a person acquires property for inadequate consideration if the value of the consideration is significantly less than the value of the property;
>   (b) a person uses or has possession of property for inadequate consideration if the value of the consideration is significantly less than the value of the use or possession;
>   (c) the provision by a person of goods or services which he knows or suspects may help another to carry out criminal conduct is not consideration.

Sentence

13.173 A person guilty of an offence under ss 327 to 329 will be liable on conviction, on indictment, to imprisonment for a term not exceeding fourteen years, or to a fine, or both.[246] On summary conviction the maximum penalty is a term of imprisonment not exceeding six months, or a fine of £5,000, or both.[247]

---

[243] [2005] EWCA Civ 226.
[244] cf the discussion of whether there is one general 'wheel conspiracy' or a series of individual ones in cases such as *Griffiths* [1966] 1 QB 589, *Smith and Hogan, Criminal Law* 365.
[245] Section 329(2)(c).
[246] Section 334(1)(b).
[247] Section 334(1)(a).

Charging Money Laundering or Handling?

The overlap between the offences in the Proceeds of Crime Act and the offence of handling **13.174** seem obvious at one level. They are both regimes designed to deter the predicate criminal conduct or at least to ensure that those who perform such conduct will have a more difficult time in disposing of their ill-gotten gains and to deter those who engage in disposing of such gains. Questions have been raised about the extent to which the money laundering offences have rendered the handling offence obsolete.

There would certainly be advantages for the prosecutor in charging money laundering if **13.175** there is the degree of overlap envisaged by some commentators. There is no need to prove that D was dishonest, nor that he 'knew or believed' that the property in question was stolen goods. Mere suspicion is enough for money laundering. Money laundering also has the advantage of capturing the conduct of the thief himself, who under s 22 and following *Bloxham* cannot be convicted of handling unless he does so 'for the benefit of another'. Moreover, there are no difficulties in money laundering charges if the goods were allegedly stolen abroad.[248]

The CPS clearly takes the view that there is a degree of overlap. Its guidance suggests that if **13.176** it is possible to charge money laundering or handling stolen goods then money laundering may be more appropriate if 'either a defendant has possessed criminal proceeds in large amounts or in lesser amounts, but repeatedly and where assets are laundered for profit.'[249] The learned authors of *Blackstone's Criminal Practice* also assert that the offences overlap,[250] suggesting that 'a money laundering offence will often be much easier to establish than any Theft Act offence.'

However, other eminent commentators have taken a different view. James Richardson, in **13.177** *Criminal Law Week*[251] describes the use of money laundering in cases which involve the 'common or garden handler' is a 'flagrant misuse of legislation':

the money laundering legislation, in all its guises, was not intended to deal with the activities of persons who go out and commit front-line criminal offences (robbers, burglars, drug dealers, *etc.*); it was intended to deal with those who operate with a veneer of respectability, under cover of which they clean up (launder) the proceeds of the activities of the front line criminals.

He goes on to suggest that the money laundering offences do not apply in such a case, because, he argues, for the handler to be guilty of an offence under s 329 of POCA he must acquire 'criminal property'. Although s 340(9) provides that 'property' is 'all property',

---

[248] If handling is charged it is necessary to prove the foreign law see *Ofori* (1994) 99 Cr App R 223 above. SOCPA 2005, s 102, will, once in force, ensure that D will not ordinarily be guilty of any of the principal money laundering offences where he knows, or believes on reasonable grounds, that the relevant 'criminal' conduct occurred (or is occurring) in a country or territory outside the UK, and is not (or was not at that time) criminal under the applicable local law.

[249] <http://www.cps.gov.uk>

[250] B22.14.

[251] (2007) 19 Feb.

so would include the stolen car and TV set, s 340(10) it is argued curtails the scope of that definition. Section 340(10) provides:

(a) property is obtained by a person if he obtains *an interest* in it;

(b) references to an interest, in relation to land in England and Wales or Northern Ireland, are to any legal estate or equitable interest or power;

(c) ...

(d) references to an interest, in relation to property other than land, *include* references to a right (including a right to possession). (Emphasis added.)

13.178   Richardson argues that:

for the purposes of Part 7 of the 2002 Act [see s 340(1)], the thief only 'obtains' the property he steals if he acquires an interest in it. Subsection (10) makes it absolutely plain that 'interest' in this context must be some form of lawful interest. A thief acquires no legal or equitable interest whatsoever in the property he steals. The stolen property in his hands at least is not, therefore, 'criminal property'.

13.179   However, this seems to involve an unusually restrictive interpretation of the provision. First, it is clear that the thief would acquire possession of the property. That is treated, in the law of theft at least, as a proprietary interest. There is no explicit requirement in s 340(10) that the thief must obtain a legal interest, otherwise than in cases involving land—hence the particular reference to that in para (b). Furthermore, para (d) merely provides that a right to possession is *included* within the concept of an 'interest' in personal property. It is not an exhaustive definition of what might constitute an interest, and does not preclude mere possession from also being included within the concept of an 'interest in property'. Paragraph (d) actually extends the section rather than narrowing it. It provides that even if all that D obtains is a right to possession without obtaining possession in fact, that is sufficient to amount to an interest and hence for that to constitute criminal property.

14

PROCEDURE AND ENFORCEMENT

Case Management

Preparatory hearings

A system allowing for preparatory hearings before trial was recommended by the Roskill **14.01** Fraud Trials Committee[1] and was introduced only for serious fraud cases in the Criminal Justice Act 1987. Section 7 permits a judge to order a preparatory hearing in cases where the 'evidence on an indictment reveals a case of fraud of such seriousness or complexity that substantial benefits are likely to accrue from a hearing before the jury are sworn'. An order for a preparatory hearing may be made on the application of a party or of the judge's own motion (s 7(2)), and the procedure for applying is set out in Criminal Procedure Rules (hereinafter 'Crim PR'), part 15.

This new form of hearing replaced the pre-trial review which was considered unsatisfactory **14.02** not least because it was not part of the trial and judicial rulings made at pre-trial review were not binding. Preparatory hearings are treated as part of the trial and begin with the arraignment of the defendant.[2] There must be a valid indictment before the preparatory hearing occurs, otherwise there can be no arraignment. These hearings are aimed at (a) identifying issues which are likely to be material to the determinations and findings which are likely to be required during the trial; (b) if there is to be a jury, assisting their comprehension of those issues and expediting the proceedings before them; (c) assisting the judge's management of the trial; or (d) considering questions as to the severance or joinder of charges.

---

[1] The Report of the *Fraud Trials Committee* para 6.25. See M Levi, 'The Future of Fraud Prosecutions and Trials: Reviewing Roskill' [1986] Comp Law 139; M Zander [1986] Crim LR 423.
[2] Section 8 Criminal Justice Act 1987, s 8.

14.03   At these hearings the judge has the power to make binding rulings on issues of law and evidence and powers to identify, simplify, and narrow the issues in dispute. The judge can order the prosecution to prepare and serve a 'case statement' setting out the principal facts, names of witnesses, exhibits, and propositions of law that it will be relying upon. The prosecution should also indicate any documents or other matters that in its view should be agreed by the defendant.[3] Save in exceptional circumstances, the same judge should conduct both the preparatory hearing and the proceedings in front of the jury.[4]

14.04   The Criminal Procedure and Investigation Act 1996[5] extended the power of the court to make binding rulings in *all cases* on any question as to the admissibility of evidence and any other question of law at any point after the case arrives at the Crown Court. The provisions in the 1996 Act for preparatory hearings follow very closely those contained in the Criminal Justice Act 1987 on which they were based.

14.05   Rulings made at a preparatory hearing will take effect at the trial, subject to two qualifications. First, an appeal against the order or ruling can be taken forthwith to the Court of Appeal (Criminal Division), but only with the leave of the judge or the Court of Appeal.[6] The preparatory hearing can continue meanwhile, but the jury cannot be sworn until after the appeal is determined or abandoned.

14.06   Not all rulings in a preparatory hearing can be the subject of an interlocutory appeal. An interlocutory appeal will only be available if the decision relates to the admissibility of evidence or question of law relating to the case (s 9(3)(b)(c)). On the Court of Appeal's view, it must have been made for one of the purposes specified in s 7(1)(a)–(d), namely: identifying issues which are likely to be material to the verdict of the jury; assisting their comprehension of such issues; expediting the proceedings before the jury; or assisting the judge's management of the trial.[7] This interpretation of s 9 as being subordinate to s 7 restricts the scope of the interlocutory appeal considerably.[8] It is doubted by the House of Lords in *H* (below).

14.07   In determining whether any particular ruling is subject to appeal, care must be taken to distinguish the mere exercise of judicial discretions which are not 'questions about law' and not appealable unless fundamentally flawed.[9]

---

[3] See *Re Case Statement made under section 9 of the Criminal Justice Act 1987* (1993) 97 Cr App R 417.

[4] *Hedworth* [1997] 1 Cr App R 421.

[5] Sections 28–38.

[6] Section 9(11) Criminal Justice Act 1987 and the Criminal Justice Act 1987 (Preparatory Hearings) (Interlocutory Appeals) Rules 1988 (SI 1988/1700) allow for interlocutory appeals in serious fraud cases and ss 35 and 36 of the Criminal Procedure and Investigations Act 1996 cover the position regarding interlocutory appeals in other long, complex, or serious cases.

[7] See *Gunawardena* [1990] 1 WLR 703; *Van Hoogstraaten* [2003] EWCA Crim 3642.

[8] The many decisions and their inconsistencies are examined by A Jones, 'The Decline and Fall of the Preparatory Hearing' [1996] Crim LR 460, in which the author demonstrates how the Court of Appeal's interpretation has 'stifled' the procedure.

[9] See eg *Smithson* [1995] Crim LR 913. Difficulties may arise, for example over whether the ruling on severance is a judgment 'about law' under s 9(3), or merely a discretionary ruling.

The House of Lords has recently emphasized that the statutory purposes expressed in s 7(1) **14.08** enabling a judge to order a preparatory hearing to be held should be given a broad and purposive construction. But a judge should not order a preparatory hearing where the court has adequate powers to decide the matters in dispute before the trial took place. A majority of their lordships held that having regard to the purpose underlying preparatory hearings there was no sense in limiting the type of interlocutory applications that could be made at a preparatory hearing. The House of Lords noted that 'the case law had become a maze through which it was now impossible to find a coherent path. The court should instead take a chainsaw to the impenetrable thicket of interpretation that had grown up and should start again.'[10]

Interlocutory appeals should be resolved swiftly and oral application should be made to **14.09** the trial judge within two days of the date of the order complained against. Secondly, the order or ruling can be varied or discharged by the judge at the trial.[11]

Prosecution appeals

The Crown have powers of appeal in preparatory hearings, and also against terminating **14.10** rulings at trial. Part 9 of the Criminal Justice Act 2003 extended the appeal rights of prosecutors to challenge points of law made by trial court judges in the Crown Court at any time up until the summing up. Section 58[12] of the Act allows for appeals to be made against terminating rulings.[13] but extends to any ruling in which the Crown is prepared to inform the court of their agreement that if leave to appeal is refused or if the prosecution abandons the appeal the defendant is acquitted. This preparedness to accept an acquittal if the appeal is lost/abandoned is the limiting factor of the section. The prosecution define, in effect, what is a terminating ruling.

The Fraud Protocol

On 22 March 2005 the Lord Chief Justice issued a protocol dealing with the 'Control and **14.11** Management of Heavy Fraud and other Complex Cases'.[14] The protocol is designed to aid the judiciary in its ongoing struggle to manage serious fraud and other complex criminal trials, many of which are by general agreement too long and costly. The protocol aims to promote pro-active judicial case management from the moment a case arrives at the Crown Court. Active management of the case is identified by the Criminal Procedure Rules on Case Management as the means by which the overriding objective of the just disposal of criminal cases can be achieved.[15] To that end the early designation of a trial judge, a sensible

---

[10] *H* [2007] UKHL 7, [2007] Crim LR (Sept) and commentary.

[11] Section 9(10) Criminal Justice Act 1987 also see *Stannard* [1965] 2 QB 1; *Beck* [1982] 1 WLR 461, CA.

[12] Section 62 allows for appeals against evidentiary rulings but is not yet in force.

[13] These include, for example, a stay of proceedings; successful plea of *autrefois acquit* or *autrefois convict*; a ruling on unfitness to plead; a ruling of no case to answer. It does not apply to the Attorney-General's grant of a *nolle prosequi*; unsolicited jury verdicts; rulings made during the summing up; a ruling to discharge the jury; quashing a count on the indictment: *Thompson* [2006] EWCA Crim 2849.

[14] Appendix 7; <http://www.dca.gov.uk/criminal/procrules_fin/contents/pd_protocol/pd_protocol.htm>. See D Kirk, 'Fraud Trials a Brave New World' (2005) 69 J Crim L 508.

[15] Criminal Procedure Rules on Case Management Part 1 Rule 1.1 and Part 3 Rule 3.2.

allowance for judicial reading time and focused Plea and Case Management Hearings are encouraged.

14.12   Looking to apply the principles set out in the 2005 protocol the Presiding Judges of the South Eastern Circuit issued a practice direction relating to 'Heavy' fraud trials.[16] The direction dictates that all trials involving allegations relating exclusively to money laundering or fraud, estimated to last either six weeks or more, and committed or sent to London Crown Courts should go to Southwark Crown Court as the London receiving court. The direction provides that either the committing magistrates or the receiving Crown Court should deal with the case at a first hearing in accordance with proforma directions documents.[17] These documents invite orders to be made which should facilitate an effective first case management hearing. These orders include the preparation of a draft indictment, a prosecution case summary, and if necessary provisional opening, together with a core bundle of documentary exhibits.

The Criminal Procedure Rules

14.13   The most important of the changes to case management generally arise from the introduction of the Criminal Procedure Rules. The Criminal Procedure Rules on Case Management identify active management of the case as an essential prerequisite to achieving the overriding objective of dealing with criminal cases justly.[18] Under the rules, active case management includes inter alia the early identification of the real issues, early identification of the needs of witnesses monitoring the progress of the case and compliance with directions. Clearly these rules will have an impact on the way that all trials, no matter how long complex or serious, including those for dishonesty offences, are going to be conducted.

Fraud trials without a jury

14.14   There have long been concerns about the ability of the jury to cope with complex and voluminous information,[19] and the nature of many complex frauds renders these concerns more acute than elsewhere in the law.[20] The Roskill Committee on *Fraud Trials* examined the problem and concluded:

---

[16] Practice Direction issued on 10 May 2006.

[17] '"Heavy Fraud"—Southwark Crown Court—First Case Management Hearing (Magistrates)' and 'Heavy Fraud'—Southwark Crown Court—First Case Management Hearing (Sent Cases—Preliminary Hearings)'

[18] Rules 1.1 and 3.2.

[19] On the scope to assist the jury by, for example, visual aids and proper preparation of documentation see *Fraud Trials Committee* (1986) ch 9. See also Lord Devlin, 'Trial by Jury for Fraud' (1986) OJLS 311–21.

[20] Research into the decision making of juries suggests that juries *are* competent to make decisions, including decisions in complex cases. See TM Honess, M Levi, and EA Charman, 'Juror Competence in Processing Complex Information: Implications from a Simulation of the *Maxwell* Trial' [1998] Crim LR 763. See more recently, S Lloyd Bostock 'The Jubilee Line Jurors: Does Their Experience Strengthen the Argument for Judge-Only Trial in Long and Complex Fraud Cases?' [2007] Crim LR 255, reporting on empirical research with interviews conducted with eleven of the jurors from the Jubilee Line trial, concluding that concerns regarding juror competence are unfounded. See also W Young, 'Summing up to Juries in Criminal Cases: What Jury Research Says about Current Rules and Practice' [2003] Crim LR 665, and M Levi, 'Frauds on Trial: What is to be Done' (2000) Comp Law 54.

we do not find trial by a random jury a satisfactory way of achieving justice in cases as long and complex as [many fraud trials]. We believe that many jurors are out of their depth.[21]

Consequently, the Committee recommended that for complex fraud cases, the jury should be abolished and trial should take place before a 'Fraud Trials Tribunal'.[22] The Committee admitted that the foundation for this recommendation was flimsy because it was unable to obtain accurate evidence to suggest 'that there has been a higher proportion of acquittals in complex fraud cases than in fraud cases or other criminal cases generally'.[23]

14.15 The main arguments against allowing juries to hear complex frauds are that:[24] they lack experience in commercial matters; the subject matter is too complex; the trials are too long leading to unrepresentative juries; the jury places additional strain on all parties; judges and experts would deal with cases more expeditiously; judges and experts could give reasons for their decision; trial without jury would result in a reduction in the cost flowing from a more expeditious process. The arguments for retention of the jury trial in fraud cases include: the fundamental institution of a jury trial; the very high public confidence in juries; the randomness of jury selection; the jury's ability to determine issues of dishonesty; the absence of evidence of jury incompetence in such cases; the fact of a jury causing matters to be explained more clearly; the protection they offer to the judge from suggestions of bias. The empirical work carried out, which is limited by the fact that formal jury research is prohibited, has not supported the assumption that the jury is unable to deal with the subject matter, but has highlighted the need for more assistance to the jury in the decision-making process.[25]

14.16 The Home Office/Lord Chancellor's Department returned to the question in 1998, issuing a Consultation Document[26] questioning whether an alternative to the jury trial should be available in cases of serious and complex fraud. The paper considered the arguments for alternatives to the traditional jury trial and examined how suitable cases for an alternative trial process would be identified and segregated from the mainstream. The four alternatives to the orthodox jury trial that were considered were:

(i) specialist juries in which the jury members were screened for suitability, or where selection would occur from a specially selected pool of suitable jurors;
(ii) judges sitting without jurors but possibly with a panel of judges;
(iii) a Roskill Committee—style tribunal of judge with a small panel of specially qualified members;
(iv) trial by single judge with a jury assisting in making key decisions—the judge would produce a document to clarify the issues for a jury.

14.17 The Criminal Courts Review—'*The Auld Report*'—(2001) also made recommendations relating to juries in fraud trials. It was observed that:

---

[21] *Fraud Trials Committee* (1986) para 8.35.
[22] Para 8.51.
[23] Para 8.35.
[24] See Auld, *The Criminal Courts Review* (2000) ch 5, para 182.
[25] See in particular S Lloyd Bostock, above, n 20.
[26] *Juries in Serious Fraud Trials*, Feb 1998.

The [problem] is not just a matter of expense and toil flowing from the use of procedures peculiar to jury trial in such difficult cases. The remorseless increase in the length of such trials over recent years has become a severe intrusion on jurors' working and private lives. It cannot be good for them or for justice.[27]

14.18 Having reviewed the options for such a tribunal proposed by the *Roskill Committee*, *Auld* favoured the composition of a judge and lay members.[28] Specifically, it recommended that as an alternative to jury trial in serious and complex fraud cases, the trial judge should be able to order that the trial occurs without a jury, being heard instead by the judge alone (if the defendant wishes) or by the judge sitting with lay members.[29] It was recommended that the category of cases to which such a direction might apply should be 'frauds of seriousness or complexity within ss 4 and 7 of the Criminal Justice Act 1987' and both parties would have a right of appeal against the decision to have trial without a jury. There would be a panel of specially nominated judges trying such cases and a panel of experts, established and maintained by the Ministry of Justice with lay members selected for trials. At the trial the judge would be the arbiter of law, procedure, evidence and sentence; with all of the panel acting as judges of fact.[30]

The Criminal Justice Act 2003

14.19 Section 43 of the Criminal Justice Act 2003, which is not yet in force, will enable the prosecution to apply for a serious or complex fraud trial on indictment in the Crown Court to proceed in the absence of a jury.

14.20 An application made under s 43 must be determined at a preparatory hearing within the meaning of the Criminal Justice Act 1987[31] (s 45(2)), at which the parties must be given the opportunity to make representations with respect to the application (s 45(3)).[32] The court would need to be satisfied that the length or complexity (or both) of the trial is likely to make it so burdensome upon the jury that the interests of justice require serious consideration to be given to conducting the trial without a jury (s 43(5)).

14.21 Where the court is satisfied[33] of these issues, it has the discretion to order that the trial should be conducted without a jury, but such an order requires the approval of the Lord Chief Justice or a judge nominated by him (s 43(4)). The judge is required to consider whether there is anything that can reasonably be done to make the trial less complex and lengthy.

---

[27] Ch 5, para 173.

[28] Ch 10, para 191.

[29] Ch 10, para 192. See also the work of Penny Darbyshire appended to the Review. Note also the New Zealand Law Commission Report 69, *Juries in Criminal Trials* (2001), and its recommendation that in all, save 'high tier', offences a judge should be empowered to order trial by judge alone in cases likely to exceed 30 days (p 54).

[30] See D Corker, 'Trying Fraud Cases without Juries' [2002] Crim LR 283.

[31] Section 43(4) substitutes paras (a) to (c) of s 7(1) of the 1987 Act (above), redefining the purposes for preparatory hearings as: (a) identifying issues which are likely to be material to the determinations and findings which are likely to be required during the trial; (b) if there is to be a jury, assisting their comprehension of those issues and expediting the proceedings before them; and (c) determining an application by the prosecution for a trial to be conducted without a jury.

[32] Part 15 of the Criminal Procedure Rules 2005 (as inserted by the Criminal Procedure (Amendment) Rules 2006) makes special provision for s 43 applications.

[33] Presumably it is the Crown's burden?

In so doing the court is not to regard as reasonable any measures that would *significantly*[34] disadvantage the prosecution by the severing of an indictment or by the exclusion of relevant and important evidence simply on jury management grounds.

As far as the actual conduct of a trial without a jury is concerned, the court will have all the **14.22** powers, authorities, and jurisdiction which the court would have had if the trial had been conducted with a jury including determining any question and making any finding required of a jury.[35]

If the judge convicts a defendant, he must, under s 48(5)(a) give 'a judgment which states **14.23** the reasons for the conviction at, or as soon as reasonably practicable.' This ensures that the procedure is compatible with Article 6 of the ECHR.

Search for Stolen Goods

Power to issue a warrant or authority to search premises for stolen goods is given by s 26 of **14.24** the 1968 Act.[36] Only a policeman may be authorized to search, though the information may be sworn by any person.[37] Other enactments authorizing the issue of search warrants to persons other than police officers are expressly preserved. In any such Act a reference to stolen goods shall be construed in accordance with s 24 of the Theft Act.[38] The power of search includes goods which have been obtained by blackmail and by deception.

There is an obvious overlap between the search powers in s 8 of PACE and s 26. The overlap **14.25** must have been recognized when s 8 was created, since that section repealed only specific parts of s 26. In some ways s 8 is broader since it is not restricted to a search for stolen goods.[39] A detailed review of the powers of search and seizure lies beyond the scope of this work.[40]

Section 26 is not limited to a power to search for and seize goods to return them to their **14.26** rightful owner; it includes a general power to search and seize stolen goods whether identified in the warrant or not.[41] Once the justice is persuaded by whoever was applying for the warrant that there was reasonable cause to believe that any person had in his custody or possession or on his premises any stolen goods, he might grant a warrant to search for and seize such property. Once the warrant is issued the person authorized under it can enter the premises and seize not only such property as might have been identified, whether generally

---

[34] Presumably then some steps will be reasonable even if *some* disadvantage would be caused to the prosecution?

[35] Section 48(3).

[36] Below, para 14.26.

[37] On the paucity of information on which warrants are commonly issued under s 26, see V Bevan and K Lidstone, *The Investigation of Crime* (2nd edn, 1996) 102, reporting that 61% of s 26 warrants were issued on application 'as a result of information received'.

[38] See s 32(2)(b).

[39] And can therefore include a search for incriminating papers, which s 26 cannot: see also *R v Reading Justices, ex p South West Meat Ltd* [1992] Crim LR 672.

[40] See R Stone, *Entry, Search and Seizure* (4th edn, 2005).

[41] *R v Chief Constable of Kent, ex p Cruikshank* [2002] EWCA Civ 1840.

or otherwise in the warrant, but also any other property which the person entering the premises believed to be stolen.[42]

Restitution

14.27   Section 148 of the Powers of Criminal Courts (Sentencing) Act 2000 provides a summary procedure whereby the court before which a person is convicted of certain offences may order that the property concerned be restored to the owner.[43] This procedure is modelled on its predecessor under the now repealed s 28 Theft Act 1968. [44] Before the 1968 Act, conviction might affect the title to goods. This is no longer so.[45] Who is the owner of property is a question for the civil law and the fact that there has been a conviction of any criminal offence with respect to the property is irrelevant, so far as title is concerned.

14.28   Section 148(1) provides:

This section applies where goods have been stolen, and either—
  (a) a person is convicted of any offence with reference to the theft (whether or not the stealing is the gist of his offence); or
  (b) a person is convicted of any other offence, but such an offence as is mentioned in paragraph (a) above is taken into consideration in determining his sentence.

14.29   By s 148(2):

Where this section applies, the court by or before the offender is convicted may on the conviction (whether or not the passing of sentence is in other respects deferred), exercise any of the following powers—
  (a) the court may order anyone having possession or control of the stolen goods to restore them to any person entitled to recover them from him; or
  (b) on the application of a person entitled to recover from the person convicted any other goods directly or indirectly representing the stolen goods (as being the proceeds of any disposal or realisation of the whole or part of them or of goods so representing them), the court may order those other goods to be delivered or transferred to the applicant; or
  (c) the court may order that a sum not exceeding the value of the stolen goods shall be paid, out of any money of the person convicted which was taken out of his possession on his apprehension, to any person who, if those goods were in the possession of the person convicted, would be entitled to recover them from him;
and in this subsection 'the stolen goods' means the goods referred to in sub-section (1) above.

---

[42] Contrast the wording of s 42(1) of the Larceny Act 1916.
[43] Police have no power to retain property seized from the accused solely in anticipation of a compensation, forfeiture, or restitution order being made: *Malone v Metropolitan Police Comr* [1980] QB 49, [1979] 1 All ER 256, CA.
[44] For a historical account see JK Macleod, 'Restitution under the Theft Act' [1968] Crim LR 577.
[45] Section 31(2).

Stolen goods

'Goods' are defined in s 34(2)(b), which is considered above.[46] 'Stolen' bears the same **14.30** meaning as in s 24(4)[47] and thus extends to goods obtained by blackmail or by fraud, money dishonestly withdrawn from an account to which a wrongful credit has been made, to the extent that the money derives from the credit.

Conviction

The court's power arises on a conviction, or a taking into consideration, 'of any offence **14.31** with reference to the theft[48] (whether or not the stealing is the gist of his offence)'. The convictions would include handling the stolen goods, robbery, burglary, and aggravated burglary. The two latter offences do not necessarily involve theft/stolen goods and it would, of course, be necessary for the court to be satisfied on the evidence admissible under s 148(5),[49] that a theft of the goods which were the object of the burglary had in fact been committed. It is not necessary that the conviction should be an offence against the Act. It might be, for example, a conviction of assisting a relevant offender under s 4(1) of the Criminal Law Act 1967[50] or of concealing a relevant offence under s 5(1) of that Act; of conspiracy or an attempt to commit theft where there is proof that the theft was actually committed; or of a forgery done for the purpose of committing the theft in question.

Against whom the order may be made

An order under s 148(2)(a), can be made against anyone having possession or control of **14.32** the goods. An order under s 148(1)(b) may be made only against the person convicted.

In whose favour the order may be made

An order may be made in favour of any person who is entitled to recover the goods from **14.33** the person in possession or control (para (a)) or who would be entitled to recover the goods if they were in the possession of the person convicted (para (c)); and any applicant[51] entitled to recover the proceeds of the stolen goods from the person convicted (para (b)).

As has been pointed out above,[52] it is only in exceptional cases that the owner of goods has **14.34** a literal right to recover them, even from a thief, in civil law. Generally his remedy is an action in conversion in which he will be awarded damages. It is submitted that, as with 'right to restitution', so also 'entitled to recover' must be given a broad interpretation to extend to cases in which the claimant would be able to succeed in an action based upon his proprietary rights in the thing in question. This would therefore extend to a case in which the ownership has passed to the rogue under a voidable transaction which the owner has rescinded.

---

[46] See para 13.04.
[47] Above, para 13.15.
[48] That is, the theft, blackmail, fraud, or wrongful credit.
[49] Below, para 14.44.
[50] As amended by the Serious Organized Crime and Police Act 2005, Sch 7(3) para 40.
[51] *Thibeault* (1983) Cr App R 201, CA which related to an order made under s 28 Theft Act 1968.
[52] In discussing the meaning of 'a right to restitution' in s 24(3); para 13.22.

14.35 The person entitled to recover will generally be the victim of the theft or someone standing in his shoes, as his executor, administrator, or trustee in bankruptcy. If the victim has received compensation for the loss of the stolen goods under an insurance policy, then the insurance company may be subrogated to his rights.[53] If the victim had not the best right to possession of the goods (as, for example, if he himself had stolen them from another) the person with that right is the person entitled.

The property in respect of which the order may be made

14.36 The property in respect of which the order may be made is as follows:

> Section 148(1)(a): such of the goods[54] which have been stolen as are in the possession or control of the person against whom the order is made.
> Section 148(1)(b): such of the proceeds of the goods which have been stolen as are in the possession or control of the person against whom the order is made.
> Section 148(1)(c): any money of the person convicted which was taken out of his possession on his apprehension, not exceeding the value of the stolen goods.

14.37 Two questions arise here. The first relates to the meaning of 'taken out of his possession on his apprehension'. This is not confined, as might have been supposed, to money which is taken from D's person when he is arrested. In *Ferguson*,[55] it was held to include money in a safe deposit box at Harrods, of which D had the key, which was properly appropriated by the police as the suspected proceeds of the theft, ten days after D's arrest. This decision seems to attribute to 'possession' its legal rather than its popular meaning but the court said that it was 'difficult to think of a clearer case of money being in the possession' of the accused and that, giving '"on his apprehension" a commonsense meaning', the money was so taken. If the money had been deposited in a bank account, the result would have been different since D would have been only a creditor of the bank and not in possession. It seems then that money at D's home or in his car is in his possession for this purpose.

14.38 Presumably the taking must be lawful. The police have no right to seize money which they do not reasonably believe to be the proceeds of a crime or evidence of its commission. It is submitted that money unlawfully seized, though literally taken from the accused on his apprehension, could not be used to compensate the victim. The provision may thus work somewhat capriciously. Money wrongly but reasonably suspected to be the proceeds of the theft may be taken and used to compensate, but other money in the possession of the accused may not. It is odd that a wrong, though reasonable, suspicion should make the difference.

14.39 Any provision containing the word 'possession' is likely to present problems. In *Parker*,[56] D apparently threw away a wallet containing money shortly before his arrest, and this was found in a garden by the police the following day; the court refused to answer the question whether the money was taken from his possession on his apprehension. On one view,

[53] *Church* (1970) 55 Cr App R 65 at 71.
[54] cf s 34(2)(b), above, para 13.04.
[55] [1970] 2 All ER 820, CA.
[56] [1970] 2 All ER 458, CA.

he had abandoned possession by throwing the wallet away; but so to hold would seem to depart from the broad 'commonsense' view taken in *Ferguson*.[57]

Finally, the money must be 'money of the person convicted' so that if, as in *Ferguson*, any doubt is raised as to D's ownership of the money, no order may be made. **14.40**

The second problem concerns the extent to which D may be required to make compensa- **14.41** tion. Section 148(1)(c) says to the extent of 'a sum not exceeding the value of the first mentioned goods'—ie the goods which have been stolen. This presents no difficulty where D is convicted of the theft. He may, however, be convicted of an offence 'with reference to the theft' and his participation may relate only to a small part of the stolen property. For example, it may be proved that £1,000 was stolen from a bank and that D dishonestly received £10 of that money which was taken from him when he was arrested. On a literal reading, it would seem that D might be ordered to pay £990 out of other money taken from him on his arrest which was not the proceeds of the theft. However, in *Parker*,[58] the court held that, whatever the proper construction of the section:

If a man is charged with handling stolen goods and the whole of the goods in respect of which he has been convicted are recovered, then it must, we hold, be an incorrect exercise of any discretion which exists under the section to make him pay compensation in addition in respect of other goods which are not the subject of a charge against him.

Compensation to a third party

By s 148(4): **14.42**

Where the court on a person's conviction makes an order under subsection (2)(a) above[59] the court on a person's conviction makes an order under paragraph (a) for the restoration of any goods, and it appears to the court that the person convicted—
  (a) has sold the goods to a person acting in good faith, or
  (b) has borrowed money on the security of them from a person so acting,
the court may order that there shall be paid to the purchaser or lender, out of any money of the person convicted which was taken out of his possession on his apprehension, a sum not exceeding the amount paid for the purchase by the purchaser or, as the case may be, the amount owed to the lender in respect of the loan.

Thus if D has stolen a necklace from V and pawned it with X for a loan of £100, on D's **14.43** conviction, X may be ordered to restore the necklace to V and be compensated out of the money taken from D on his apprehension. The provision is confined to money taken from D on his apprehension so X will have no remedy under s 148 if D, when apprehended, is wearing a gold watch but carrying no money, though he has large sums in his bank. X, may, however, be compensated by an order made under s 35 of the Powers of Criminal Courts Act 1973.[60]

---

[57] 54 Cr App R 410, CA.
[58] [1970] 2 All ER 458 at 462 to 463.
[59] See above, para 14.29.
[60] See generally *Blackstone's Criminal Practice* (2007) E11.1.

When an order should be made

14.44   It is provided by s 148(5)[61] that:

> The court shall not exercise the powers conferred by this section unless in the opinion of the court the relevant facts sufficiently appear from the evidence given at the trial or the available documents, together with admissions made by or on behalf of any person in connection with any proposed exercise of the powers . . .

14.45   Section 148(6) defines 'available documents' for the purposes of s 148(5).[62] In order to make an order under the section the court must be satisfied on the evidence given at the trial that an order should be made.[63] The court may not embark on a new inquiry at the end of the trial.

14.46   The court is never bound to make an order under s 148; when the condition in s 148(5) is satisfied it is a matter for the discretion of the court. Clearly, however, when the relevant facts do sufficiently appear, an order should generally be made unless there is a real dispute as to the title to the goods. Even when the facts are absolutely clear the question of entitlement to the goods may involve difficult questions of law. Where they have been transferred to a third party, many of the subtleties of the old law of larceny by a trick and false pretences may arise. If there is any real dispute or any doubt as to title, then an order should not be made; the parties should be left to their civil remedies. Only in the plainest cases, where there is no doubt of fact or law, should an order be made.[64]

> In practice the power will be exercisable only where there is no real dispute as to ownership. It would seriously hamper the work of the criminal courts if at the end of a trial they had to investigate disputed titles.[65]

14.47   As Lord Hoffmann stated in the House of Lords in *Re Norris:*[66]

> it is well established that these powers of restitution are only to be used where there is no disputed civil law right or similar issue which needs to be determined (*eg* s 148(5) of the Act of 2000). If there is such an issue, the proper course for the Crown Court to take is to leave the relevant person interested to pursue his or her civil remedy in the civil courts: *Ferguson* (1970) 54 Cr App R 410 and *Calcutt* (1985) 7 Cr App R (S) 385. The English system of criminal justice does not itself confer any civil jurisdiction upon the criminal courts and it takes a clear and express provision in a statute to achieve that result.

---

[61]   This section mirrors the earlier s 28(4) Theft Act 1968.

[62]   By subsection (6), 'In subsection (5) above "the available documents" means—(a) any written statements or admissions which were made for use, and would have been admissible, as evidence at the trial; and (b) such written statements, depositions and other documents as were tendered by or on behalf of the prosecutor at any committal proceedings.'

[63]   The trial concludes when sentence is passed—*Church* (1970) 55 Cr App R 65, CA.

[64]   *Ferguson* [1970] 2 All ER 820, CA; *Calcutt and Varty* 7 Cr App R (S) 385, CA. In *Calcutt* Woolf J observed, 'the criminal courts are not the appropriate forum in which to satisfactorily ventilate complex issues as to the ownership of such money or goods. In cases of doubt it is better to leave the victim to pursue his civil remedies or, alternatively, to apply to the magistrates' court under the Police (Property) Act 1897'.

[65]   CLRC, *Eighth Report*, Cmnd 2977 (1966) para 164: 'it would probably be impracticable (as well as being undesirable) that an order should be made in any but straightforward cases'.

[66]   [2001] UKHL 34.

Exercise of more than one power

The question may arise as to whether the court may exercise more than one of its powers   **14.48**
in respect of the same theft.[67] Though paras (a), (b), and (c) of s 148(2) are expressed in
the alternative, s 148(3) contemplates that an order may be made against the thief under
both (b) and (c). The situation contemplated is that where the thief has disposed of the
goods for less than their true value. If power is exercised under (b) to award these proceeds
to the applicant, the balance may be made up from money taken from D on his apprehension. Normally, where the power under (a) is exercised to restore the goods to the owner,
no further compensation will be required. If, however, only a part of the goods can be
restored by exercising power (a), there seems to be no reason why power (b) or (c) should
not be exercised in relation to the remainder.

Where V gets the whole of his goods back under (a) but they are damaged, he might suc-   **14.49**
ceed in an application for compensation under (c). The court might also exercise its power
under s 130 of the Powers of Criminal Courts (Sentencing) Act 2000.[68] There seems to be
nothing to prevent the court exercising these various statutory powers on the same occasion
and in combination if it thinks it just to do so.

Where D has succeeded in passing a good title to a bona-fide purchaser (B), and the court,   **14.50**
in the exercise of power (a), consequently orders possession to be given to B, may it then
exercise power (c) in favour of the original owner, A? This is the converse of a more usual
situation expressly provided for in s 148(4)[69] where the bona-fide purchaser gets no title
and consequently is ordered to surrender the goods to A. It is submitted that the above
question should be answered in the affirmative. If the goods were in the possession of D, A
'would be entitled to recover them from him'. The superior right of B would not defeat an
action by A against D. A therefore satisfies the condition in para (c), and it seems entirely
right that he should be compensated out of money taken from D where D has succeeded
in depriving him of his title to the goods. The situation will probably rarely arise, since
it will not often be absolutely clear that D has passed a good title to B; and where there is
a doubt, the court must refrain from making orders.[70]

Enforcement of an order

The Act makes no provision for the enforcement of orders made under s 148. Under the   **14.51**
Magistrates' Court Act 1980, s 63(3):

Where any person disobeys and order of a magistrates' court made under an Act passed after 31st
December 1879 to do anything other than the payment of money or to abstain from doing anything the court may—
   (a) order him to pay a sum not exceeding £50 for every day during which he is in default or a sum
       not exceeding £5,000 or
   (b) commit him to custody until he has remedied his default or for a period not exceeding
       2 months;

---

[67] cf Macleod [1968] Crim LR at 586–7.
[68] Below, para 14.57.
[69] Above, para 14.42.
[70] Above, para 14.43.

but a person who is ordered to pay a sum for every day during which he is in default or who is committed to custody until he has remedied his default shall not by virtue of this section be ordered to pay more than £1,000 or be committed for more than 2 months in all for doing or abstaining from doing the same thing contrary to the order (without prejudice to the operation of this section in relation to any subsequent default).

The effect of an order

14.52 The Act contains no provision similar to that in the Police (Property) Act 1897, protecting the person in whose favour an order is made against claims to the property on the expiration of six months from the order.[71] It is submitted that an order should have no effect whatever on the rights under the civil law of any claimant to the property, except possibly where those rights consist in a merely possessory title.[72]

14.53 It may frequently happen that a magistrates' court is in a position to order the return of the property under the Police (Property) Act, and, when this is so, the court should make it clear whether this is the provision under which it is acting since there is the difference in effect referred to.[73]

Appeal

From an order in the Crown Court

14.54 An order under s 148 is appeallable under the provisions of s 30[74] of the Criminal Appeal Act 1968:

(2) The Court of Appeal may by order annul or vary any order made by the court of trial for the restitution of property to any person, although the conviction is not quashed; and the order, if annulled, shall not take effect and, if varied, shall take effect as so varied.

(3) Where the House of Lords restores a conviction, it may make any order for the restitution of property which the court of trial could have made.

From an order in the Magistrates' Court

14.55 Section 108 of the Magistrates' Courts Act 1980 gives a right of appeal against sentence to the Crown Court and sentence includes (with inapplicable exceptions) 'any order made on conviction'. This clearly gives a right of appeal to the convicted person against an order made under s 148. Both the convicted person and a third party against whom an order has been made might appeal by way of case stated to the High Court on a question of law or jurisdiction, under s 111(1) of the Magistrates' Courts Act which applies to any person aggrieved by an order.

---

[71] Below, para 14.60.
[72] cf *Irving v National Provincial Bank Ltd* [1962] 2 QB 73, [1962] 1 All ER 157, CA.
[73] Moreover the order under s 148 of the PCC(S) Act 2000 does not take effect if the conviction is quashed (below, para 14.56) whereas that under the Police (Property) Act is quite unaffected by the quashing of any conviction since the power does not depend upon the existence of a conviction, but only of a charge.
[74] Substituted by Criminal Justice Act 1988 s 170, Sch 8 para 16, Sch 15 para 28.

Suspension of orders made on indictment

Under s 30(1) of the Criminal Appeal Act 1968, as amended, the operation of an order for **14.56** the restitution of property to a person made by the Crown Court shall be suspended, unless the court direct to the contrary in any case in which, in their opinion, the title to the property is not in dispute. The suspension is until 'disregarding any power of a court to grant leave to appeal out of time there is no further possibility of an appeal on which the order could be varied or set aside'.

Other powers to award compensation

Under the Powers of Criminal Courts (Sentencing) Act 2000

Section 130 of the Powers of Criminal Courts (Sentencing) Act 2000 provides that a court **14.57** by or before which a person is convicted of any offence may, instead of, or in addition to, dealing with him in any other way and whether on application or otherwise, make an order requiring the offender to pay compensation for any personal injury, loss, or damage resulting from that offence or any other offence which is taken into consideration in determining the sentence or make payment for funeral expenses or bereavement in respect of a death resulting from any such offence, other than a death due to an accident arising out of the presence of a motor vehicle on a road.[75] The court can move of its own motion to make an order without application from the victim. The court is required to have regard to the offender's means so far as they appear or are known to the court. In the Crown Court there is no other limit but in a magistrates' court the maximum for one offence is £5,000.[76] Enforcement of confiscation orders is undertaken by the magistrates' courts.[77]

Deprivation

Section 143 provides: **14.58**

(1) Where a person is convicted of an offence and the court by or before which he is convicted is satisfied that any property which has been lawfully seized from him, or which was in his possession or under his control at the time when he was apprehended for the offence or when a summons in respect of it was issued—
    (a) has been used for the purpose of committing, or facilitating the commission of, any offence, or
    (b) was intended by him to be used for that purpose,
the court may (subject to subsection (5) below) make an order under this section in respect of that property.

---

[75] Section 130(2) provides 'Where the person is convicted of an offence the sentence for which is fixed by law or falls to be imposed under ss 109(2), 110(2) or 111(2) above, subs (1) above shall have effect as if the words "instead of or" were omitted'. For the principles to be applied in determining whether an order should be made, see *Kneeshaw* [1975] QB 57, [1974] 1 All ER 896, CA; *Oddy* [1974] 2 All ER 666, CA; *R v Horsham Justices, ex p Richards* [1985] 1 WLR 986.
[76] Section 131 Powers of Criminal Courts (Sentencing) Act 2000.
[77] The maximum terms of sentences to be imposed in default is set out in the Magistrates' Courts Act 1980 Sch 4.

(2) Where a person is convicted of an offence and the offence, or an offence which the court has takenintoconsiderationindetermininghissentence,consistsofunlawfulpossessionofpropertywhich—

    (a) has been lawfully seized from him, or

    (b) was in his possession or under his control at the time when he was apprehended for the offence of which he has been convicted or when a summons in respect of that offence was issued,

the court may (subject to subsection (5) below) make an order under this section in respect of that property.

14.59 An order made under s 143 deprives the offender of his rights, if any, in the property to which it relates, and the property shall (if not already in their possession) be taken into the possession of the police. [78] The court may make a deprivation order in addition to any other form of penalty although the court will as always have an eye to totality.[79] The court will not make a deprivation order where to do so would result in unusual hardship.[80]

Under the Police (Property) Act 1897

14.60 Where any property has come into the possession of the police in their investigation of a suspected offence, a magistrates' court may, under s 1(1) of the Police (Property) Act 1897, make an order for the delivery of the property to the person appearing to be the owner, or, if the owner cannot be ascertained, make 'such order with respect to the property as to the magistrate or court may seem meet'. The procedure should be used only in straightforward cases, where there is no difficulty of law.[81] The word 'owner' is to be given its ordinary, popular meaning;[82] so that a jeweller to whom a ring has been handed for valuation and who, suspecting it to be stolen, has given it to the police, is not 'the owner'. Though no one with a better title has appeared, somewhere (presumably) there is a person who 'owns' the ring in the ordinary popular sense. No order may be made in favour of the jeweller.[83]

14.61 The property must not be restored to the person who is the owner in the popular sense if it appears that there is some person with a better right to immediate possession, such as a person with a valid lien on the property. It was so held in *Marsh v Police Comr*,[84] though the court declined to decide whether the lienor was the 'owner' for this purpose. According to *Raymond Lyons* case,[85] he is not. The curious result is that where another person has a better right to possession than the owner, no order can be made in favour of either claimant. Moreover, the magistrates cannot exercise the discretion given to them by the section where 'the owner cannot be ascertained', because the owner is ascertained. It is submitted that, notwithstanding *Raymond Lyons* case, if it is wrong to deliver[86] to the

---

[78] Section 143(3).
[79] Section 143(4).
[80] See *Tavernor* unreported, 4 Apr 1974; *Bucholz*, 10 May 1974.
[81] *Raymond Lyons & Co Ltd v Metropolitan Police Comr* [1975] QB 321, [1975] 1 All ER 335. On the procedure see also *R v Uxbridge Justices, ex p MPC* [1981] 1 WLR 112 and on appeal [1981] QB 829.
[82] See *Chief Constable of West Midlands v White* (1992) 157 JP 222.
[83] ibid.
[84] [1945] KB 43, [1944] 2 All ER 392, CA.
[85] Above, para 14.60.
[86] On the requirement of delivery as opposed to making available see *Price v Dobson* [2006] EWHC 1017 (Admin).

owner in the strict sense where there is another with a better right to possession, this can only be because the owner in the strict sense is not 'the owner' for the purpose of the Act; and that it should follow that 'the owner' is the person with the best right to possession.[87]

It is provided by s 1(2) of the Police (Property) Act 1897 that an order made under s 1(1) **14.62** does not affect any person's right to bring legal proceedings within six months of the order to recover the property from the person to whom it has been delivered under the order of the court; but on the expiration of those six months, the right shall cease.

An order may, however, affect the onus of proof: *Irving v National Provincial Bank Ltd*[88] **14.63** where it was held that, in the absence of any evidence as to the ownership of the money, the defendant bank's title arising from an order made under the Act was superior to that of the claimant from whose possession the money had been taken by the police; the onus was on the claimant and not on the defendant to establish actual ownership in the money. It is submitted that this provision should defeat the title only of one who might have asserted a better right to possess before the magistrates' court. If, for example, D steals a car from V and, on D's conviction, the magistrates order that it be returned to V, the rights of X, from whom V had the car on hire or hire purchase, should not be affected. If, after the expiration of six months, X seeks to recover the car in accordance with the terms of the contract he should not be debarred from doing so by the order made under the Act.[89] Even thus limited, the provision could lead to arbitrary and unjust interference with civil rights. Suppose that the court makes an order in favour of V from whom goods have been stolen. The goods had been the subject of an earlier theft from X. More than six months after the order, X discovers that the goods are in the possession of V. His right to recover them would appear to be barred. It is not obvious why V should have this windfall arising out of the dishonest intervention of a third party.

It has been held by a metropolitan magistrate that 'property' includes anything into or for **14.64** which the property has been converted or exchanged by analogy to s 46(1) of the Larceny Act 1916.[90] It is submitted that this was the correct decision, though it would be better to rely on the common law concerning ownership[91] than on the analogy of a criminal statute. Difficult questions might arise where the property has been converted into a more valuable thing by the expenditure of skill and labour.[92] In *Chief Constable of West Yorkshire v Singh*[93] it was held that the police may if appropriate be ordered to pay a sum of money equivalent to the value of the items (perishable consumables sold by the assumed owner).

---

[87] Howard argues that the property must in all cases be awarded to the owner in the strict sense; [1958] Crim LR 744. A forfeiture order made by the Crown Court under Powers of Criminal Courts (Sentencing) Act 2000 does not determine the issue of the ownership of the property: *R v Chester Justices, ex p Smith* [1978] RTR 373, [1978] Crim LR 226, DC decided under Powers of Criminal Courts Act 1973, s 43.

[88] [1962] 2 QB 73, [1962] 1 All ER 157, CA.

[89] cf the view of Stone, n 36 above, para 2.124.

[90] (1959) 123 JPJ 640.

[91] *Taylor v Plumer* (1815) 3 M & S 562.

[92] See Torts (Interference with Goods) Act 1977, s 6.

[93] 3 November 1997, QBD.

14.65   The Theft Act no longer provides that the 1897 Act shall apply to any property seized by the police under the authority of s 26 of the Theft Act.[94] Such property appears to be covered by the amended words of s 1(1) of the 1897 Act.

Husband and Wife[95]

14.66   Under the Larceny Act 1916, a husband could steal from a wife and vice versa only if, at the time of the theft, either, they were not living together or the property was taken with a view to their ceasing to live together. So where a wife took her husband's property and gave it to her lover, the lover was not guilty of receiving stolen goods.[96] This rule was abolished by s 30(1) of the 1968 Act which also applies to the 1978 Act[97] and provides:

This Act shall apply in relation to the parties to a marriage, and to property belonging to the wife or husband whether or not by reason of an interest derived from the marriage, as it would apply if they were not married and any such interest subsisted independently of the marriage.

The effect is that wives and husbands can steal, or commit any other offence under the Acts in relation to, the property of each other.

Proceedings instituted by injured spouse

14.67   The proceedings may be instituted by the injured spouse. The 1968 Act, s 30(2) provides:

Subject to subsection (4) below, a person shall have the same right to bring proceedings against that person's wife or husband for any offence (whether under the Act or otherwise) as if they were not married, *and a person bringing any such proceedings shall be competent to give evidence for the prosecution at every stage of the proceedings.*[98]

14.68   This subsection is not confined to offences under the Acts but applies to 'any offence'. Thus, for example, a wife may prosecute her husband for stealing or damaging the property of a third party, for an offence against the person of a third party, or for perjury; and in any such prosecution the wife will become a competent witness for the prosecution.

Restrictions on prosecution

14.69   The 1968 Act, s 30(4) provides:

(4) Proceedings shall not be instituted against a person for any offence of stealing or doing unlawful damage to property which at the time of the offence belongs to that person's wife or husband or civil partner, or for any attempt, incitement or conspiracy to commit such an offence, unless the proceedings are instituted by or with the consent of the Director of Public Prosecutions:
Provided that—
   (a) this subsection shall not apply to proceedings against a person for an offence—
      (i) if that person is charged with committing the offence jointly with the wife or husband or civil partner;

---

[94] Section 26(4) was repealed by the Criminal Justice Act 1972, s 64(2), Sch 6, Part II.
[95] CLRC, *Eighth Report*, Cmnd 2977 (1966) paras 189–99.
[96] *Creamer* [1919] 1 KB 564.
[97] 1978, s 5(2).
[98] The italicized words are to be repealed as from a day to be appointed by the Youth Justice and Criminal Evidence Act 1999 s 67(3) and Sch 6.

(ii) if by virtue of any judicial decree or order (wherever made) that person and the
wife or husband are at the time of the offence under no obligation to cohabit; [or]

(iii) an order (wherever made) is in force providing for the separation of that person
and his or her civil partner.[99]

Where it is a case of stealing or the doing of unlawful damage by one spouse to the proper- **14.70**
ty of the other, consent is required whether the proceedings are to be instituted by the
aggrieved spouse or by a third party.[100] Outside these cases, however, no consent is required
whether the proceedings be instituted by the aggrieved spouse or by a third party. If a
wife alleges, or a third party alleges, that her husband has blackmailed her, wounded her,
or raped her, no consent is required. Presumably consent will be required on a robbery
charge since this is within 'any offence of stealing'. It is not obvious why this clause (which
was not in the draft Bill produced by the Criminal Law Revision Committee) should
be thus limited.

Proviso (a)(i) is not very clear. It is a proviso to a subsection dealing with a case of a person **14.71**
who steals or damages his spouse's property; and so one would expect a proviso to qualify
the rule that such a person cannot be prosecuted except with the consent of the Director.
That is, the natural meaning of 'that person' in the proviso is the person who has stolen or
damaged the property of his wife or husband.

If that be correct, proviso (a)(i) deals with the case where the husband and wife are **14.72**
jointly charged with theft of or criminal damage to property which belongs to one of
them. This looks a little curious; but it will be recalled[101] that it is perfectly possible for
a person to be convicted of stealing his own property where some third person has a
proprietary interest in it. Suppose that a husband has pawned his watch. While his wife
engages the pawnbroker's attention, he secretly takes the watch back again. Proceedings
may be brought against the couple without the consent of the Director. It is very reasonable
that consent should not be necessary in this case; and perhaps the proviso is required
because the proceeding, literally, is for an offence of stealing property belonging to the
husband.

The position would seem to be much the same in the case of criminal damage. Generally **14.73**
a man may damage property which is his own with impunity, no matter how barbarous
his action may be. But if another has a proprietary interest in the property, this would surely
be an offence. For example, D has mortgaged a valuable painting to V by bill of sale. If
he deliberately destroys the painting, he is surely guilty of an offence of criminal damage.
If then, his wife destroys the painting with his connivance, they may both be prosecuted
without consent.

If this interpretation is correct, it follows that if, in the above examples, the wife had taken **14.74**
the watch and destroyed the painting, without the husband's connivance, the Director's
consent would have been required, for proceedings instituted by V. This looks strange

---

[99] As amended by the Civil Partnership Act 2004, Sch 27 para 27(3).
[100] *Withers* [1975] Crim LR 647.
[101] Above, para 2.190.

because, though it is the husband's property which is destroyed, the offence is committed against a third party.

14.75 Moreover, property may 'belong' to one of the spouses, at least for the purposes of theft,[102] although the ownership in the strict sense is in a third party. Suppose that H has a satellite TV box on hire or hire purchase from V. If his wife, W, sells the satellite box without H's consent, it is clearly right that he should have to get consent to prosecute her for stealing from him. The same should apply if she smashes the box and he alleges that she has criminally damaged his property. On the other hand, it looks distinctly odd that V has to get the consent of the Director to prosecute W; but that appears to be the effect.

14.76 It may well be that the proviso was not actually intended to deal with this situation at all, but to apply to the case where D, a third party, assists H to steal or destroy W's property and D and H are prosecuted jointly. It may be intended to say that, in those circumstances, no consent shall be required so far as the proceedings against D are concerned. If that is the intention, the proviso is not strictly necessary because D is not within the main part of the subsection. It would mean, moreover, that consent would still be necessary for the proceedings against H; so that joint proceedings would still have to wait on consent. That would not be very sensible; so probably the better course (if not the only proper course) is to assume that the proviso means what it says. In that event, the situation envisaged in this paragraph is the same as if the proviso did apply to it. No consent is required so far as D is concerned (because he is not a person charged with an offence against his wife's property) but consent is required so far as H is concerned. There must either be separate trials or the Director's consent obtained.

14.77 Proviso (a)(ii) means that if H and W have been judicially separated or if a non-molestation order has been made[103] and one of them steals or damages the other's property, proceedings may be brought without the consent of the Director, whether they were in fact living together at the time of the offence or not. If the parties have merely separated in pursuance of an agreement, the Director's consent is required even if they are in fact living apart at the time of the alleged offence.

Privilege

14.78 Section 31 of the 1968 Act provides that an individual may not claim a right to privilege against self-incrimination to avoid answering questions in 'proceedings for the recovery or administration of any property, for the execution of any trust or for an account of any property or dealings with property'[104] or otherwise comply with any order made in any such proceedings.

---

[102] See s 5, above, para 2.189.
[103] *Woodley v Woodley* [1978] Crim LR 629, DC.
[104] Section 31(1)

Section 31(1) reads: **14.79**

A person shall not be excused, by reason that to do so may incriminate that person or the [spouse or civil partner] of that person of an offence under this Act—

    (a) from answering any question put to that person in proceedings for the recovery or administration of any property, for the execution of any trust or for an account of any property or dealings with property; or

    (b) from complying with any order made in any such proceedings;

but no statement or admission made by a person in answering a question put or complying with an order made as aforesaid shall, in proceedings for an offence under this Act, be admissible in evidence against that person or (unless they [married or became civil partners after the making of the statement or admission) against the spouse or civil partner] of that person.

    (2) Notwithstanding any enactment to the contrary, where property has been stolen or obtained by fraud or other wrongful means, the title to that or any other property shall not be affected by reason only of the conviction of the offender.

Section 13 of the Fraud Act 2006 introduces a provision which closely resembles section 31(1).   **14.80**
Section 13 provides:

(1) A person is not to be excused from—

    (a) answering any question put to him in proceedings relating to property, or

    (b) complying with any order made in proceedings relating to property,

on the ground that doing so may incriminate him or his spouse or civil partner of an offence under this Act or a related offence.

    (2) But, in proceedings for an offence under this Act or a related offence, a statement or admission made by the person in—

    (a) answering such a question, or

    (b) complying with such an order,

is not admissible in evidence against him or (unless they married or became civil partners after the making of the statement or admission) his spouse or civil partner.

    (3) 'Proceedings relating to property' means any proceedings for—

    (a) the recovery or administration of any property,

    (b) the execution of a trust, or

    (c) an account of any property or dealings with property,

and 'property' means money or other property whether real or personal (including things in action and other intangible property).

Under s 13 a person is protected from incriminating himself or his spouse or civil partner   **14.81**
for the purposes of offences under the Act *and related offences*, while nonetheless being obliged to cooperate with certain civil proceedings relating to property. The section extends beyond s 31(1) applying as it does to offences under the Fraud Act and 'related offences'.[105]

Related offence

The scope of this term is important in defining the scope of the protection but it is left   **14.82**
undefined in the Act. The question arises whether it extends the scope of the section only

---

[105] Section 13(4) defines related offences as (a) conspiracy to defraud and (b) any other offence involving any form of fraudulent conduct or purpose.

to those offences in which 'fraud' is a formal element required to be proved by the Crown or whether 'related offences' include others which might legitimately be described as involving fraud. It is submitted that the narrower view ought to be adopted.

14.83 This view is supported to some extent by the debates in Parliament. There was a proposed amendment to the clause adding the words 'that the Secretary of State may by order prescribe' to the end of clause 13(4) so that it would have read:

> on the ground that doing so may incriminate him or his spouse or civil partner of an offence under this Act or a related offence that the Secretary of State may by order prescribe.

14.84 The Solicitor-General rejected this amendment on the grounds that it would involve considerable difficulty drawing up a comprehensive list of offences. He stated:

> As drafted, in our view, clause 13 makes clear that the offences under discussion are those involving any form of fraudulent purpose or conduct. That provides the right degree of specification for the context. We should bear in mind that the clause addresses the needs of civil justice and not to be deprived of evidence in property proceedings on the grounds that the answers and documents given may incriminate the person who gives them.
>
> At the stage when someone is giving answers, the matter of whether an answer or a document discloses a fraud under the Bill, or some other type of fraud, may not be clear. It is likely that it will only be clear that his answers might show that some form of fraud has taken place. That might be a fraud that could be prosecuted under the Bill, or possibly under section 458 of the Companies Act, VAT legislation or tax law. We should not tie the law to a specific list of offences which might leave gaps in which a person who does not want to answer questions, might say that it may or may not fit into a particular list.
>
> We want any form of fraudulent purpose or conduct to be covered by that provision. . . . We would have to list everything in order to make sure that we do not give a loophole, that someone could use not to answer questions in a civil case.
>
> We could put the Social Security Acts on the list and all the offences that could be characterised as fraud. However, it would be much simpler, more straightforward and understandable for individuals and for the court, to know that we have a generalised definition in the Bill. Ultimately, it will be a matter for the judge in the trial as to whether a party to civil proceedings can refuse to answer questions on grounds of self-incrimination. It is the judge who has to decide whether clause 13 should apply or not and clause 13 exemption applies. Judges are perfectly capable of applying clause 13. Our approach is better than the specific list of offences that the amendment suggests. A specific list would add to a great deal more confusion. It might also encourage persons who wish to refuse to answer questions to find a loophole. Something might not be on the list, which they might have cause to fear, and they might not want to incriminate themselves.

14.85 The Solicitor-General was clearly of the opinion that s 13 catches all offences where fraudulent conduct or a fraudulent purpose forms one element of the offence.

Retrospectivity

14.86 Section 13 should be construed so that it only applies where the related offences were committed after the coming into force of the Act. If s 13(1) stood alone then the removal of the right to self-incrimination could only have applied to offences committed after the Act came into force because s 13(1) refers to offences under the Act which, by definition, can only be committed after the Act came into force. The question then is whether related offences in s 13(4) extend to offences committed before the Act came into force. This is a provision depriving a person of such a fundamental right as the right to claim privilege against self-incrimination and is to be strictly construed.[106]

There is strong presumption against interpreting a statute as taking away the right of silence,[107] coupled with a strong presumption that penal statutes are not to be interpreted retrospectively.[108] These principles all militate against an interpretation of s 13 which removes the right to claim the privilege against self-incrimination in relation to offences allegedly committed before s 13 came into force. **14.87**

---

[106] *Sociedade Nacional de Combustiveis de Angola UEE v Lundqvist* [1991] 2 QB 310, 337, construing s 31 of the Theft Act 1968.

[107] *R v Director of the Serious Fraud Office, ex p Smith* [1993] AC 1, 40.

[108] See *L'Office Chefifien Des Phosphates v Yamashita-Shinnihon Steamship Co Ltd* 1994] 1 AC 486, 494.

APPENDICES

APPENDIX 1

Theft Act 1968

1968 c.60

CONTENTS

---

¹ Repealed by the Fraud Act 2006.

An Act to revise the law of England and Wales as to theft and similar or associated offences, and in connection therewith to make provision as to criminal proceedings by one party to a marriage against the other, and to make certain amendments extending beyond England and Wales in the Post Office Act 1953 and other enactments; and for other purposes connected therewith. [26th July 1968]

BE IT ENACTED by the Queen's most Excellent Majesty, by and with the advice and consent of the Lords Spiritual and Temporal, and Commons, in this present Parliament assembled, and by the authority of the same, as follows:—

DEFINITION OF 'THEFT'

Basic definition of theft

1. —(1) A person is guilty of theft if he dishonestly appropriates property belonging to another with the intention of permanently depriving the other of it; and 'thief' and 'steal' shall be construed accordingly.
(2) It is immaterial whether the appropriation is made with a view to gain, or is made for the thief's own benefit.
(3) The five following sections of this Act shall have effect as regards the interpretation and operation of this section (and, except as otherwise provided by this Act, shall apply only for purposes of this section).

'Dishonestly'

2. —(1) A person's appropriation of property belonging to another is not to be regarded as dishonest—
    (a) if he appropriates the property in the belief that he has in law the right to deprive the other of it, on behalf of himself or of a third person; or
    (b) if he appropriates the property in the belief that he would have the other's consent if the other knew of the appropriation and the circumstances of it; or
    (c) (except where the property came to him as trustee or personal representative) if he appropriates the property in the belief that the person to whom the property belongs cannot be discovered by taking reasonable steps.
(2) A person's appropriation of property belonging to another may be dishonest notwithstanding that he is willing to pay for the property.

'Appropriates'

3. —(1) Any assumption by a person of the rights of an owner amounts to an appropriation, and this includes, where he has come by the property (innocently or not) without stealing it, any later assumption of a right to it by keeping or dealing with it as owner.
(2) Where property or a right or interest in property is or purports to be transferred for value to a person acting in good faith, no later assumption by him of rights which he believed himself to be acquiring shall, by reason of any defect in the transferor's title, amount to theft of the property.

'Property'

4. —(1) 'Property' includes money and all other property, real or personal, including things in action and other intangible property.
(2) A person cannot steal land, or things forming part of land and severed from it by him or by his directions, except in the following cases, that is to say—
  (a) when he is a trustee or personal representative, or is authorised by power of attorney, or as liquidator of a company, or otherwise, to sell or dispose of land belonging to another, and he appropriates the land or anything forming part of it by dealing with it in breach of the confidence reposed in him; or
  (b) when he is not in possession of the land and appropriates anything forming part of the land by severing it or causing it to be severed, or after it has been severed; or
  (c) when, being in possession of the land under a tenancy, he appropriates the whole or part of any fixture or structure let to be used with the land.
  For purposes of this subsection 'land' does not include incorporeal hereditaments; 'tenancy' means a tenancy for years or any less period and includes an agreement for such a tenancy, but a person who after the end of a tenancy remains in possession as statutory tenant or otherwise is to be treated as having possession under the tenancy, and 'let' shall be construed accordingly.
(3) A person who picks mushrooms growing wild on any land, or who picks flowers, fruit or foliage from a plant growing wild on any land, does not (although not in possession of the land) steal what he picks, unless he does it for reward or for sale or other commercial purpose.
  For purposes of this subsection 'mushroom' includes any fungus, and 'plant' includes any shrub or tree.
(4) Wild creatures, tamed or untamed, shall be regarded as property; but a person cannot steal a wild creature not tamed nor ordinarily kept in captivity, or the carcase of any such creature, unless either it has been reduced into possession by or on behalf of another person and possession of it has not since been lost or abandoned, or another person is in course of reducing it into possession.

'Belonging to another'

5. —(1) Property shall be regarded as belonging to any person having possession or control of it, or having in it any proprietary right or interest (not being an equitable interest arising only from an agreement to transfer or grant an interest).
(2) Where property is subject to a trust, the persons to whom it belongs shall be regarded as including any person having a right to enforce the trust, and an intention to defeat the trust shall be regarded accordingly as an intention to deprive of the property any person having that right.
(3) Where a person receives property from or on account of another, and is under an obligation to the other to retain and deal with that property or its proceeds in a particular way, the property or proceeds shall be regarded (as against him) as belonging to the other.
(4) Where a person gets property by another's mistake, and is under an obligation to make restoration (in whole or in part) of the property or its proceeds or of the value thereof, then to the extent of that obligation the property or proceeds shall be regarded (as against him) as belonging to the person entitled to restoration, and an intention not to make restoration shall be regarded accordingly as an intention to deprive that person of the property or proceeds.
(5) Property of a corporation sole shall be regarded as belonging to the corporation notwithstanding a vacancy in the corporation.

'With the intention of permanently depriving the other of it'

6. —(1) A person appropriating property belonging to another without meaning the other permanently to lose the thing itself is nevertheless to be regarded as having the intention of permanently depriving the other of it if his intention is to treat the thing as his own to dispose of regardless of the other's rights; and a borrowing or lending of it may amount to so treating it if, but only if, the borrowing or lending is for a period and in circumstances making it equivalent to an outright taking or disposal.

(2) Without prejudice to the generality of subsection (1) above, where a person, having possession or control (lawfully or not) of property belonging to another, parts with the property under a condition as to its return which he may not be able to perform, this (if done for purposes of his own and without the other's authority) amounts to treating the property as his own to dispose of regardless of the other's rights.

THEFT, ROBBERY, BURGLARY, ETC

Theft

7. A person guilty of theft shall on conviction on indictment be liable to imprisonment for a term not exceeding [seven years]²

Robbery

8. —(1) A person is guilty of robbery if he steals, and immediately before or at the time of doing so, and in order to do so, he uses force on any person or puts or seeks to put any person in fear of being then and there subjected to force.

(2) A person guilty of robbery, or of an assault with intent to rob, shall on conviction on indictment be liable to imprisonment for life.

Burglary

9. —(1) A person is guilty of burglary if—
   (a) he enters any building or part of a building as a trespasser and with intent to commit any such offence as is mentioned in subsection (2) below; or
   (b) having entered any building or part of a building as a trespasser he steals or attempts to steal anything in the building or that part of it or inflicts or attempts to inflict on any person therein any grievous bodily harm.

(2) The offences referred to in subsection (1)(a) above are offences of stealing anything in the building or part of a building in question, of inflicting on any person therein any grievous bodily harm [. . .]³ therein, and of doing unlawful damage to the building or anything therein.

[(3) A person guilty of burglary shall on conviction on indictment be liable to imprisonment for a term not exceeding—
   (a) where the offence was committed in respect of a building or part of a building which is a dwelling, fourteen years;
   (b) in any other case, ten years.

(4) References in subsections (1) and (2) above to a building, and the reference in subsection (3) above to a building which is a dwelling, shall apply also to an inhabited vehicle or vessel, and shall apply to any such vehicle or vessel at times when the person having a habitation in it is not there as well as at times when he is.]⁴

Aggravated burglary

10. —(1) A person is guilty of aggravated burglary if he commits any burglary and at the time has with him any firearm or imitation firearm, any weapon of offence, or any explosive; and for this purpose—
   (a) 'firearm' includes an airgun or air pistol, and 'imitation firearm' means anything which has the appearance of being a firearm, whether capable of being discharged or not; and
   (b) 'weapon of offence' means any article made or adapted for use for causing injury to or incapacitating a person, or intended by the person having it with him for such use; and
   (c) 'explosive' means any article manufactured for the purpose of producing a practical effect by explosion, or intended by the person having it with him for that purpose.

---

² Amended by the Criminal Justice Act 1991.
³ Repealed by the Sexual Offences Act 2003.
⁴ Amended by the Criminal Justice Act 1991.

(2) A person guilty of aggravated burglary shall on conviction on indictment be liable to imprisonment for life.

Removal of articles from places open to the public

11. —(1) Subject to subsections (2) and (3) below, where the public have access to a building in order to view the building or part of it, or a collection or part of a collection housed in it, any person who without lawful authority removes from the building or its grounds the whole or part of any article displayed or kept for display to the public in the building or that part of it or in its grounds shall be guilty of an offence.

    For this purpose 'collection' includes a collection got together for a temporary purpose, but references in this section to a collection do not apply to a collection made or exhibited for the purpose of effecting sales or other commercial dealings.

(2) It is immaterial for purposes of subsection (1) above, that the public's access to a building is limited to a particular period or particular occasion; but where anything removed from a building or its grounds is there otherwise than as forming part of, or being on loan for exhibition with, a collection intended for permanent exhibition to the public, the person removing it does not thereby commit an offence under this section unless he removes it on a day when the public have access to the building as mentioned in subsection (1) above.

(3) A person does not commit an offence under this section if he believes that he has lawful authority for the removal of the thing in question or that he would have it if the person entitled to give it knew of the removal and the circumstances of it.

(4) A person guilty of an offence under this section shall, on conviction on indictment, be liable to imprisonment for a term not exceeding five years.

Taking motor vehicle or other conveyance without authority

12. —(1) Subject to subsections (5) and (6) below, a person shall be guilty of an offence if, without having the consent of the owner or other lawful authority, he takes any conveyance for his own or another's use or, knowing that any conveyance has been taken without such authority, drives it or allows himself to be carried in or on it.

(2) A person guilty of an offence under subsection (1) above shall [. . .]⁵ [be liable on summary conviction to a fine not exceeding level 5 on the standard scale, to imprisonment for a term not exceeding six months, or to both.]⁶

    [. . .]⁷

(4) If on the trial of an indictment for theft the jury are not satisfied that the accused committed theft, but it is proved that the accused committed an offence under subsection (1) above, the jury may find him guilty of the offence under subsection (1) [and if he is found guilty of it, he shall be liable as he would have been liable under subsection (2) above on summary conviction.]⁸

[(4A) Proceedings for an offence under subsection (1) above (but not proceedings of a kind falling within subsection (4) above) in relation to a mechanically propelled vehicle—

    (a) shall not be commenced after the end of the period of three years beginning with the day on which the offence was committed; but

    (b) subject to that, may be commenced at any time within the period of six months beginning with the relevant day.

(4B) In subsection (4A)(b) above 'the relevant day' means—

    (a) in the case of a prosecution for an offence under subsection (1) above by a public prosecutor, the day on which sufficient evidence to justify the proceedings came to the knowledge of any person responsible for deciding whether to commence any such prosecution;

---

⁵ Repealed by the Criminal Justice Act 1988.
⁶ Amended by the Criminal Justice Act 1988.
⁷ Repealed by the Police and Criminal Evidence Act 1984.
⁸ Inserted by the Criminal Justice Act 1988.

(b) in the case of a prosecution for an offence under subsection (1) above which is commenced by a person other than a public prosecutor after the discontinuance of a prosecution falling within paragraph (a) above which relates to the same facts, the day on which sufficient evidence to justify the proceedings came to the knowledge of the person who has decided to commence the prosecution or (if later) the discontinuance of the other prosecution;

(c) in the case of any other prosecution for an offence under subsection (1) above, the day on which sufficient evidence to justify the proceedings came to the knowledge of the person who has decided to commence the prosecution.

(4C) For the purposes of subsection (4A)(b) above a certificate of a person responsible for deciding whether to commence a prosecution of a kind mentioned in subsection (4B)(a) above as to the date on which such evidence as is mentioned in the certificate came to the knowledge of any person responsible for deciding whether to commence any such prosecution shall be conclusive evidence of that fact.][9]

(5) Subsection (1) above shall not apply in relation to pedal cycles; but, subject to subsection (6) below, a person who, without having the consent of the owner or other lawful authority, takes a pedal cycle for his own or another's use, or rides a pedal cycle knowing it to have been taken without such authority, shall on summary conviction be liable to a fine [level 3 on the standard scale.][10]

(6) A person does not commit an offence under this section by anything done in the belief that he has lawful authority to do it or that he would have the owner's consent if the owner knew of his doing it and the circumstances of it.

(7) For purposes of this section—

(a) 'conveyance' means any conveyance constructed or adapted for the carriage of a person or persons whether by land, water or air, except that it does not include a conveyance constructed or adapted for use only under the control of a person not carried in or on it, and 'drive' shall be construed accordingly; and

(b) 'owner', in relation to a conveyance which is the subject of a hiring agreement or hire-purchase agreement, means the person in possession of the conveyance under that agreement.

[Aggravated vehicle-taking

12A. —(1) Subject to subsection (3) below, a person is guilty of aggravated taking of a vehicle if—

(a) he commits an offence under section 12(1) above (in this section referred to as a 'basic offence') in relation to a mechanically propelled vehicle; and

(b) it is proved that, at any time after the vehicle was unlawfully taken (whether by him or another) and before it was recovered, the vehicle was driven, or injury or damage was caused, in one or more of the circumstances set out in paragraphs (a) to (d) of subsection (2) below.

(2) The circumstances referred to in subsection (1)(b) above are—

(a) that the vehicle was driven dangerously on a road or other public place;

(b) that, owing to the driving of the vehicle, an accident occurred by which injury was caused to any person;

(c) that, owing to the driving of the vehicle, an accident occurred by which damage was caused to any property, other than the vehicle;

(d) that damage was caused to the vehicle.

(3) A person is not guilty of an offence under this section if he proves that, as regards any such proven driving, injury or damage as is referred to in subsection (1)(b) above, either—

(a) the driving, accident or damage referred to in subsection (2) above occurred before he committed the basic offence; or

(b) he was neither in nor on nor in the immediate vicinity of the vehicle when that driving, accident or damage occurred.

---

[9] Inserted by the Vehicles (Crime) Act 2001.
[10] Inserted by the Criminal Justice Act 1982.

(4) A person guilty of an offence under this section shall be liable on conviction on indictment to imprisonment for a term not exceeding two years or, if it is proved that, in circumstances falling within subsection (2)(b) above, the accident caused the death of the person concerned, [fourteen years.][11]

(5) If a person who is charged with an offence under this section is found not guilty of that offence but it is proved that he committed a basic offence, he may be convicted of the basic offence.

(6) If by virtue of subsection (5) above a person is convicted of a basic offence before the Crown Court, that court shall have the same powers and duties as a magistrates' court would have had on convicting him of such an offence.

(7) For the purposes of this section a vehicle is driven dangerously if—

(a) it is driven in a way which falls far below what would be expected of a competent and careful driver; and

(b) it would be obvious to a competent and careful driver that driving the vehicle in that way would be dangerous.

(8) For the purposes of this section a vehicle is recovered when it is restored to its owner or to other lawful possession or custody; and in this subsection 'owner' has the same meaning as in section 12 above.][12]

Abstracting of electricity

13. A person who dishonestly uses without due authority, or dishonestly causes to be wasted or diverted, any electricity shall on conviction on indictment be liable to imprisonment for a term not exceeding five years.

Extension to thefts from mails outside England and Wales, and robbery etc. on such a theft

14. —(1) Where a person—

(a) steals or attempts to steal any mail bag or postal packet in the course of transmission as such between places in different jurisdictions in the British postal area, or any of the contents of such a mail bag or postal packet; or

(b) in stealing or with intent to steal any such mail bag or postal packet or any of its contents, commits any robbery, attempted robbery or assault with intent to rob; then,

notwithstanding that he does so outside England and Wales, he shall be guilty of committing or attempting to commit the offence against this Act as if he had done so in England or Wales, and he shall accordingly be liable to be prosecuted, tried and punished in England and Wales without proof that the offence was committed there.

(2) In subsection (1) above the reference to different jurisdictions in the British postal area is to be construed as referring to the several jurisdictions of England and Wales, of Scotland, of Northern Ireland, of the Isle of Man and of the Channel Islands.

[. . .][13]

FRAUD AND BLACKMAIL

Obtaining property by deception

15.—[. . .][14]

Obtaining a money transfer by deception

15A.—[. . .][15]

---

[11] Amended by the Criminal Justice Act 2003.
[12] Inserted by the Aggravated Vehicle-Taking Act 1992.
[13] Repealed by the Postal Services Act 2000.
[14] Repealed by the Fraud Act 2006.
[15] Repealed by the Fraud Act 2006.

Section 15A: supplementary

15B.—[...]¹⁶

Obtaining pecuniary advantage by deception

16.—[...]¹⁷

False accounting

17. —(1) Where a person dishonestly, with a view to gain for himself or another or with intent to cause loss to another,—

(a) destroys, defaces, conceals or falsifies any account or any record or document made or required for any accounting purpose; or

(b) in furnishing information for any purpose produces or makes use of any account, or any such record or document as aforesaid, which to his knowledge is or may be misleading, false or deceptive in a material particular;

he shall, on conviction on indictment, be liable to imprisonment for a term not exceeding seven years.

(2) For purposes of this section a person who makes or concurs in making in an account or other document an entry which is or may be misleading, false or deceptive in a material particular, or who omits or concurs in omitting a material particular from an account or other document, is to be treated as falsifying the account or document.

Liability of company officers for certain offences by company

18. —(1) Where an offence committed by a body corporate under section [...]¹⁸ 17 of this Act is proved to have been committed with the consent or connivance of any director, manager, secretary or other similar officer of the body corporate, or any person who was purporting to act in any such capacity, he as well as the body corporate shall be guilty of that offence, and shall be liable to be proceeded against and punished accordingly.

(2) Where the affairs of a body corporate are managed by its members, this section shall apply in relation to the acts and defaults of a member in connection with his functions of management as if he were a director of the body corporate.

False statements by company directors, etc

19. —(1) Where an officer of a body corporate or unincorporated association (or person purporting to act as such), with intent to deceive members or creditors of the body corporate or association about its affairs, publishes or concurs in publishing a written statement or account which to his knowledge is or may be misleading, false or deceptive in a material particular, he shall on conviction on indictment be liable to imprisonment for a term not exceeding seven years.

(2) For purposes of this section a person who has entered into a security for the benefit of a body corporate or association is to be treated as a creditor of it.

(3) Where the affairs of a body corporate or association are managed by its members, this section shall apply to any statement which a member publishes or concurs in publishing in connection with his functions of management as if he were an officer of the body corporate or association.

Suppression, etc. of documents

20. —(1) A person who dishonestly, with a view to gain for himself or another or with intent to cause loss to another, destroys, defaces or conceals any valuable security, any will or other testamentary document or any original document of or belonging to, or filed or deposited in, any court of justice

---

¹⁶ Repealed by the Fraud Act 2006.
¹⁷ Repealed by the Fraud Act 2006.
¹⁸ Repealed by the Fraud Act 2006.

or any government department shall on conviction on indictment be liable to imprisonment for a term not exceeding seven years.

(2) [. . .][19]

(3) For purposes of this section [. . .][20] 'valuable security' means any document creating, transferring, surrendering or releasing any right to, in or over property, or authorising the payment of money or delivery of any property, or evidencing the creation, transfer, surrender or release of any such right, or the payment of money or delivery of any property, or the satisfaction of any obligation.

Blackmail

21. —(1) A person is guilty of blackmail if, with a view to gain for himself or another or with intent to cause loss to another, he makes any unwarranted demand with menaces; and for this purpose a demand with menaces is unwarranted unless the person making it does so in the belief—

(a) that he has reasonable grounds for making the demand; and

(b) that the use of the menaces is a proper means of reinforcing the demand.

(2) The nature of the act or omission demanded is immaterial, and it is also immaterial whether the menaces relate to action to be taken by the person making the demand.

(3) A person guilty of blackmail shall on conviction on indictment be liable to imprisonment for a term not exceeding fourteen years.

OFFENCES RELATING TO GOODS STOLEN ETC

Handling stolen goods

22. —(1) A person handles stolen goods if (otherwise than in the course of the stealing) knowing or believing them to be stolen goods he dishonestly receives the goods, or dishonestly undertakes or assists in their retention, removal, disposal or realisation by or for the benefit of another person, or if he arranges to do so.

(2) A person guilty of handling stolen goods shall on conviction on indictment be liable to imprisonment for a term not exceeding fourteen years.

Advertising rewards for return of goods stolen or lost

23. Where any public advertisement of a reward for the return of any goods which have been stolen or lost uses any words to the effect that no questions will be asked, or that the person producing the goods will be safe from apprehension or inquiry, or that any money paid for the purchase of the goods or advanced by way of loan on them will be repaid, the person advertising the reward and any person who prints or publishes the advertisement shall on summary conviction be liable to a fine not exceeding [level 3 on the standard scale].[21]

Scope of offences relating to stolen goods

24. —(1) The provisions of this Act relating to goods which have been stolen shall apply whether the stealing occurred in England or Wales or elsewhere, and whether it occurred before or after the commencement of this Act, provided that the stealing (if not an offence under this Act) amounted to an offence where and at the time when the goods were stolen; and references to stolen goods shall be construed accordingly.

(2) For purposes of those provisions references to stolen goods shall include, in addition to the goods originally stolen and parts of them (whether in their original state or not),—

(a) any other goods which directly or indirectly represent or have at any time represented the stolen goods in the hands of the thief as being the proceeds of any disposal or realisation of the whole or part of the goods stolen or of goods so representing the stolen goods; and

[19] Repealed by the Fraud Act 2006.
[20] Repealed by the Fraud Act 2006.
[21] Inserted by the Criminal Justice Act 1982.

(b) any other goods which directly or indirectly represent or have at any time represented the stolen goods in the hands of a handler of the stolen goods or any part of them as being the proceeds of any disposal or realisation of the whole or part of the stolen goods handled by him or of goods so representing them.

(3) But no goods shall be regarded as having continued to be stolen goods after they have been restored to the person from whom they were stolen or to other lawful possession or custody, or after that person and any other person claiming through him have otherwise ceased as regards those goods to have any right to restitution in respect of the theft.

(4) For purposes of the provisions of this Act relating to goods which have been stolen (including subsections (1) to (3) above) goods obtained in England or Wales or elsewhere either by blackmail or[, subject to subsection (5) below, by fraud (within meaning of the Fraud Act 2006)][22] shall be regarded as stolen; and 'steal', 'theft' and 'thief' shall be construed accordingly.

[(5) Subsection (1) above applies in relation to goods obtained by fraud as if—

(a) the reference to the commencement of this Act were a reference to the commencement of the Fraud Act 2006, and

(b) the reference to an offence under this Act were a reference to an offence under section 1 of that Act.][23]

[Dishonestly retaining a wrongful credit]

[24A —(1) A person is guilty of an offence if—

(a) a wrongful credit has been made to an account kept by him or in respect of which he has any right or interest;

(b) he knows or believes that the credit is wrongful; and

(c) he dishonestly fails to take such steps as are reasonable in the circumstances to secure that the credit is cancelled.

(2) References to a credit are to a credit of an amount of money.

[(2A) A credit to an account is wrongful to the extent it derives from—

(a) theft;

(b) blackmail;

(c) fraud (contrary to section 1 of the Fraud Act 2006); or

(d) stolen goods.][24]

[. . .][25]

(5) In determining whether a credit to an account is wrongful, it is immaterial (in particular) whether the account is overdrawn before or after the credit is made.

(6) A person guilty of an offence under this section shall be liable on conviction on indictment to imprisonment for a term not exceeding ten years.

(7) Subsection (8) below applies for purposes of provisions of this Act relating to stolen goods (including subsection [2A][26] above).

(8) References to stolen goods include money which is dishonestly withdrawn from an account to which a wrongful credit has been made, but only to the extent that the money derives from the credit.

(9) ['Account' means an account kept with—

(a) a bank;

(b) a person carrying on a business which falls within subsection (10) below; or

(c) an issuer of electronic money (as defined for the purposes of Part 2 of the Financial Services and Markets Act 2000).

---

[22] Inserted by the Fraud Act 2006.
[23] Inserted by the Fraud Act 2006.
[24] Inserted by the Fraud Act 2006.
[25] Repealed by the Fraud Act 2006.
[26] Amended by the Fraud Act 2006.

(10) A business falls within this subsection if—

    (a) in the course of the business money received by way of deposit is lent to others; or

    (b) any other activity of the business is financed, wholly or to any material extent, out of the capital or of the interest on money received by way of deposit.

(11) References in subsection (10) above to a deposit must be read with—

    (a) section 22 of the Financial Services and Markets Act 2000;

    (b) any relevant order made under that section; and

    (c) Schedule 2 to that Act;

but any restriction on the meaning of deposit which arises from the identity of the person making it is to be disregarded.

(12) For the purposes of subsection (10) above—

    (a) all the activities which a person carries on by way of business shall be regarded as a single business carried on by him; and

    (b) 'money' includes money expressed in a currency other than sterling.][27]

POSSESSION OF HOUSEBREAKING IMPLEMENTS, ETC

Going equipped for stealing, etc

25. —(1) A person shall be guilty of an offence if, when not at his place of abode, he has with him any article for use in the course of or in connection with any [burglary or theft][28]

(2) A person guilty of an offence under this section shall on conviction on indictment be liable to imprisonment for a term not exceeding three years.

(3) Where a person is charged with an offence under this section, proof that he had with him any article made or adapted for use in committing a [burglary or theft][29] shall be evidence that he had it with him for such use.

    [...][30]

(5) For purposes of this section an offence under section 12(1) of this Act of taking a conveyance shall be treated as theft [...].[31]

ENFORCEMENT AND PROCEDURE

Search for stolen goods

26. —(1) If it is made to appear by information on oath before a justice of the peace that there is reasonable cause to believe that any person has in his custody or possession or on his premises any stolen goods, the justice may grant a warrant to search for and seize the same; but no warrant to search for stolen goods shall be addressed to a person other than a constable except under the authority of an enactment expressly so providing.

    [...][32]

(3) Where under this section a person is authorised to search premises for stolen goods, he may enter and search the premises accordingly, and may seize any goods he believes to be stolen goods.

    [...][33]

(5) This section is to be construed in accordance with section 24 of this Act; and in subsection (2) above the references to handling stolen goods shall include any corresponding offence committed before the commencement of this Act.

---

[27] Inserted by the Fraud Act 2006.
[28] Amended by the Fraud Act 2006.
[29] Amended by the Fraud Act 2006.
[30] Repealed by the Serious Organised Crime and Police Act 2005.
[31] Repealed by the Fraud Act 2006.
[32] Repealed by the Police and Criminal Evidence Act 1984.
[33] Repealed by the Criminal Justice Act 1972.

Evidence and procedure on charge of theft or handling stolen goods

27. —(1) Any number of persons may be charged in one indictment, with reference to the same theft, with having at different times or at the same time handled all or any of the stolen goods, and the persons so charged may be tried together.

(2) On the trial of two or more persons indicted for jointly handling any stolen goods the jury may find any of the accused guilty if the jury are satisfied that he handled all or any of the stolen goods, whether or not he did so jointly with the other accused or any of them.

(3) Where a person is being proceeded against for handling stolen goods (but not for any offence other than handling stolen goods), then at any stage of the proceedings, if evidence has been given of his having or arranging to have in his possession the goods the subject of the charge, or of his undertaking or assisting in, or arranging to undertake or assist in, their retention, removal, disposal or realisation, the following evidence shall be admissible for the purpose of proving that he knew or believed the goods to be stolen goods:—

    (a) evidence that he has had in his possession, or has undertaken or assisted in the retention, removal, disposal or realisation of, stolen goods from any theft taking place not earlier than twelve months before the offence charged; and

    (b) (provided that seven days' notice in writing has been given to him of the intention to prove the conviction) evidence that he has within the five years preceding the date of the offence charged been convicted of theft or of handling stolen goods.

(4) In any proceedings for the theft of anything in the course of transmission (whether by post or otherwise), or for handling stolen goods from such a theft, a statutory declaration made by any person that he despatched or received or failed to receive any goods or postal packet, or that any goods or postal packet when despatched or received by him were in a particular state or condition, shall be admissible as evidence of the facts stated in the declaration, subject to the following conditions:—

    (a) a statutory declaration shall only be admissible where and to the extent to which oral evidence to the like effect would have been admissible in the proceedings; and

    (b) a statutory declaration shall only be admissible if at least seven days before the hearing or trial a copy of it has been given to the person charged, and he has not, at least three days before the hearing or trial or within such further time as the court may in special circumstances allow, given the prosecutor written notice requiring the attendance at the hearing or trial of the person making the declaration.

[(4A) Where the proceedings mentioned in subsection (4) above are proceedings before a magistrates' court inquiring into an offence as examining justices that subsection shall have effect with the omission of the words from 'subject to the following conditions' to the end of the subsection.][34]

(5) This section is to be construed in accordance with section 24 of this Act; and in subsection (3)(b) above the reference to handling stolen goods shall include any corresponding offence committed before the commencement of this Act.

28.—[. . .][35]

29.—[. . .][36]

GENERAL AND CONSEQUENTIAL PROVISIONS

[Spouses and civil partners][37]

30. —(1) This Act shall apply in relation to the parties to a marriage, and to property belonging to the wife or husband whether or not by reason of an interest derived from the marriage, as it would apply if they were not married and any such interest subsisted independently of the marriage.

---

[34] Inserted by the Criminal Procedure and Investigations Act 1996 and to be repealed by Criminal Justice Act 2003.

[35] Repealed by the Powers of Criminal Courts (Sentencing) Act 2000.

[36] Repealed by the Courts Act 1971.

[37] Amended by the Civil Partnership Act 2004.

(2) Subject to subsection (4) below, a person shall have the same right to bring proceedings against that person's wife or husband for any offence (whether under this Act or otherwise) as if they were not married, and a person bringing any such proceedings shall be competent to give evidence for the prosecution at every stage of the proceedings.

[. . .]³⁸

(4) Proceedings shall not be instituted against a person for any offence of stealing or doing unlawful damage to property which at the time of the offence belongs to that person's wife or husband [or civil partner], or for any attempt, incitement or conspiracy to commit such an offence, unless the proceedings are instituted by or with the consent of the Director of Public Prosecutions:

Provided that—

(a) this subsection shall not apply to proceedings against a person for an offence—

(i) if that person is charged with committing the offence jointly with the wife or husband [or civil partner]; or

(ii) if by virtue of any judicial decree or order (wherever made) that person and the wife or husband are at the time of the offence under no obligation to cohabit; [or

(iii) an order (wherever made) is in force providing for the separation of that person and his or her civil partner.]

[(5) Notwithstanding [section 6 of the Prosecution of Offences Act 1979] subsection (4) of this section shall apply—

(a) to an arrest (if without warrant) made by the wife or husband [or civil partner], and

(b) to a warrant of arrest issued on an information laid by the wife or husband [or civil partner].]³⁹

Effect on civil proceedings and rights

31. —(1) A person shall not be excused, by reason that to do so may incriminate that person or [the spouse or civil partner]⁴⁰ of that person of an offence under this Act—

(a) from answering any question put to that person in proceedings for the recovery or administration of any property, for the execution of any trust or for an account of any property or dealings with property; or

(b) from complying with any order made in any such proceedings; but no statement or admission made by a person in answering a question put or complying with an order made as aforesaid shall, in proceedings for an offence under this Act, be admissible in evidence against that person or (unless they [married or became civil partners after the making of the statement or admission) against the spouse or civil partner]⁴¹ of that person.

(2) Notwithstanding any enactment to the contrary, where property has been stolen or obtained by fraud or other wrongful means, the title to that or any other property shall not be affected by reason only of the conviction of the offender.

Effect on existing law and construction of references to offences

32. —(1) The following offences are hereby abolished for all purposes not relating to offences committed before the commencement of this Act, that is to say—

(a) any offence at common law of larceny, robbery, burglary, receiving stolen property, obtaining property by threats, extortion by colour of office or franchise, false accounting by public officers, concealment of treasure trove and, except as regards offences relating to the public revenue, cheating; and

---

³⁸ Repealed by the Police and Criminal Evidence Act 1984.

³⁹ Section appears as amended or repealed by: Civil Partnership Act 2004; Criminal Jurisdiction Act 1975; and Prosecution of Offences Act 1979.

⁴⁰ Amended by the Civil Partnership Act 2004.

⁴¹ Inserted by the Civil Partnership Act 2004.

(b) any offence under an enactment mentioned in Part I of Schedule 3 to this Act, to the extent to which the offence depends on any section or part of a section included in column 3 of that Schedule;

but so that the provisions in Schedule 1 to this Act (which preserve with modifications certain offences under the Larceny Act 1861 of taking or killing deer and taking or destroying fish) shall have effect as there set out.

(2) Except as regards offences committed before the commencement of this Act, and except in so far as the context otherwise requires,—

(a) references in any enactment passed before this Act to an offence abolished by this Act shall, subject to any express amendment or repeal made by this Act, have effect as references to the corresponding offence under this Act, and in any such enactment the expression 'receive' (when it relates to an offence of receiving) shall mean handle, and 'receiver' shall be construed accordingly; and

(b) without prejudice to paragraph (a) above, references in any enactment, whenever passed, to theft or stealing (including references to stolen goods), and references to robbery, blackmail, burglary, aggravated burglary or handling stolen goods, shall be construed in accordance with the provisions of this Act, including those of section 24.

Miscellaneous and consequential amendments, and repeal

33. —(1) [...][42]

...

(4) No amendment or repeal made by this Act in Schedule 1 to the Extradition Act 1870 or in the Schedule to the Extradition Act 1873 shall affect the operation of that Schedule by reference to the law of a British possession; but the repeal made in Schedule 1 to the Extradition Act 1870 shall extend throughout the United Kingdom.

SUPPLEMENTARY

Interpretation

34. —(1) Sections 4(1) and 5(1) of this Act shall apply generally for purposes of this Act as they apply for purposes of section 1.

(2) For purposes of this Act—

(a) 'gain' and 'loss' are to be construed as extending only to gain or loss in money or other property, but as extending to any such gain or loss whether temporary or permanent; and—

(i) 'gain' includes a gain by keeping what one has, as well as a gain by getting what one has not; and

(ii) 'loss' includes a loss by not getting what one might get, as well as a loss by parting with what one has;

(b) 'goods', except in so far as the context otherwise requires, includes money and every other description of property except land, and includes things severed from the land by stealing[; and

(c) 'mail bag' and 'postal packet' have the meanings given by section 125(1) of the Postal Services Act 2000.][43]

Commencement and transitional provisions

35. —(1) This Act shall come into force on the 1st January 1969 and, save as otherwise provided by this Act, shall have effect only in relation to offences wholly or partly committed on or after that date.

(2) [Section 27 of this Act and section 148 of the Powers of Criminal Courts (Sentencing) Act 2000][44] shall apply in relation to proceedings for an offence committed before the commencement of this

---

[42] Repealed by SI 2001/1149.
[43] Inserted by SI 2003/2908.
[44] Amended by the Powers of Criminal Courts (Sentencing) Act 2000.

Act as they would apply in relation to proceedings for a corresponding offence under this Act, and shall so apply in place of any corresponding enactment repealed by this Act.

(3) Subject to subsection (2) above, no repeal or amendment by this Act of any enactment relating to procedure or evidence, or to the jurisdiction or powers of any court, or to the effect of a conviction, shall affect the operation of the enactment in relation to offences committed before the commencement of this Act or to proceedings for any such offence.

Short title, and general provisions as to Scotland and Northern Ireland

36. —(1) This Act may be cited as the Theft Act 1968.

[. . .]⁴⁵

(3) This Act does not extend to Scotland or [. . .]⁴⁶ to Northern Ireland, except as regards any amendment or repeal which in accordance with section 33 above is to extend to Scotland or Northern Ireland.

SCHEDULES

SECTION 32.

SCHEDULE 1
OFFENCES OF TAKING, ETC. DEER OR FISH

[. . .]⁴⁷

Taking or destroying fish

2. —(1) Subject to subparagraph (2) below, a person who unlawfully takes or destroys, or attempts to take or destroy, any fish in water which is private property or in which there is any private right of fishery shall on summary conviction be liable to a fine not exceeding fifty pounds or, for an offence committed after a previous conviction of an offence under this subparagraph, to imprisonment for a term not exceeding three months or to a fine not exceeding one hundred pounds or to both.

(2) Subparagraph (1) above shall not apply to taking or destroying fish by angling in the daytime (that is to say, in the period beginning one hour before sunrise and ending one hour after sunset); but a person who by angling in the daytime unlawfully takes or destroys, or attempts to take or destroy, any fish in water which is private property or in which there is any private right of fishery shall on summary conviction be liable to a fine not exceeding [level 1 on the standard scale.]

(3) The court by which a person is convicted of an offence under this paragraph may order the forfeiture of anything which, at the time of the offence, he had with him for use for taking or destroying fish.

(4) Any person may arrest without warrant anyone who is, or whom he, with reasonable cause, suspects to be, committing an offence under subparagraph (1) above, and may seize from any person who is, or whom he, with reasonable cause, suspects to be, committing any offence under this paragraph anything which on that person's conviction of the offence would be liable to be forfeited under subparagraph (3) above.

---

⁴⁵ Repealed by the Northern Ireland Constitution Act 1973.
⁴⁶ Repealed by the Northern Ireland Constitution Act 1973.
⁴⁷ Repealed by the Deer Act 1980.

APPENDIX 2

Theft Act 1978

An Act to replace section 16(2)(a) of the Theft Act 1968 with other provision against fraudulent conduct; and for connected purposes. [20th July 1978]

BE IT ENACTED by the Queen's most Excellent Majesty, by and with the advice and consent of the Lords Spiritual and Temporal, and Commons, in this present Parliament assembled, and by the authority of the same, as follows:—

Obtaining services by deception

1.—[. . .]¹

Evasion of liability by deception

2.—[. . .]²

Making off without payment

3.—(1) Subject to subsection (3) below, a person who, knowing that payment on the spot for any goods supplied or service done is required or expected from him, dishonestly makes off without having paid as required or expected and with intent to avoid payment of the amount due shall be guilty of an offence.

(2) For purposes of this section 'payment on the spot' includes payment at the time of collecting goods on which work has been done or in respect of which service has been provided.

(3) Subsection (1) above shall not apply where the supply of the goods or the doing of the service is contrary to law, or where the service done is such that payment is not legally enforceable.

(4) [. . .]³

Punishments

4.—(1) Offences under this Act shall be punishable either on conviction on indictment or on summary conviction.

(2) A person convicted on indictment shall be liable—

[. . .]⁴

(b) for an offence under section 3 of this Act, to imprisonment for a term not exceeding two years.

(3) A person convicted summarily of any offence under this Act shall be liable—

(a) to imprisonment for a term not exceeding six months; or

(b) to a fine not exceeding the prescribed sum for the purposes of [section 32 of the Magistrates' Courts Act 1980]⁵ (punishment on summary conviction of offences triable either way: 1,000 or other sum substituted by order under that Act),

or to both.

---

¹ Repealed by the Fraud Act 2006.
² Repealed by the Fraud Act 2006.
³ Repealed by the Serious Organised Crime and Police Act 2005.
⁴ Repealed by the Fraud Act 2006.
⁵ Amended by the Magistrates' Courts Act 1980.

Supplementary

5.—(1) [. . .]⁶

(2) Sections 30(1) (husband and wife), 31(1) (effect on civil proceedings) and 34 (interpretation) of the Theft Act 1968, so far as they are applicable in relation to this Act, shall apply as they apply in relation to that Act.

(3) [. . .]⁷

(4) In the Visiting Forces Act 1952, in paragraph 3 of the Schedule (which defines for England and Wales 'offence against property' for purposes of the exclusion in certain cases of the jurisdiction of United Kingdom courts) there shall be added at the end—'(j) the Theft Act 1978'.

(5) In the Theft Act 1968 section 16(2)(a) is hereby repealed.

Enactment of same provisions for Northern Ireland

6. An Order in Council under paragraph 1(1)(b) of Schedule 1 to the Northern Ireland Act 1974 (legislation for Northern Ireland in the interim period) which contains a statement that it operates only so as to make for Northern Ireland provision corresponding to this Act—

(a) shall not be subject to paragraph 1(4) and (5) of that Schedule (affirmative resolution of both Houses of Parliament); but

(b) shall be subject to annulment by resolution of either House.

Short title, commencement and extent

7.—(1) This Act may be cited as the Theft Act 1978.

(2) This Act shall come into force at the expiration of three months beginning with the date on which it is passed.

(3) This Act except section 5(3), shall not extend to Scotland; and except for that subsection, and subject also to section 6, it shall not extend to Northern Ireland.

---

⁶ Repealed by the Fraud Act 2006.
⁷ Repealed by the Extradition Act 1989.

APPENDIX 3

Theft (Amendment) Act 1996

1996 c.62

An Act to amend the Theft Act 1968 and the Theft Act 1978; and for connected purposes.

[18th December 1996]

Be it enacted by the Queen's most Excellent Majesty, by and with the advice and consent of the Lords Spiritual and Temporal, and Commons, in this present Parliament assembled, and by the authority of the same, as follows:—

1. [...]¹

Dishonestly retaining a wrongful credit.

2.—(1) After section 24 of the Theft Act 1968 insert—

'**Dishonestly retaining a wrongful credit.**

24A.—(1) A person is guilty of an offence if—

  (a) a wrongful credit has been made to an account kept by him or in respect of which he has any right or interest;

  (b) he knows or believes that the credit is wrongful; and

  (c) he dishonestly fails to take such steps as are reasonable in the circumstances to secure that the credit is cancelled.

(2) References to a credit are to a credit of an amount of money.

(3) A credit to an account is wrongful if it is the credit side of a money transfer obtained contrary to section 15A of this Act.

(4) A credit to an account is also wrongful to the extent that it derives from—

  (a) theft;

  (b) an offence under section 15A of this Act;

  (c) blackmail; or

  (d) stolen goods.

(5) In determining whether a credit to an account is wrongful, it is immaterial (in particular) whether the account is overdrawn before or after the credit is made.

(6) A person guilty of an offence under this section shall be liable on conviction on indictment to imprisonment for a term not exceeding ten years.

(7) Subsection (8) below applies for purposes of provisions of this Act relating to stolen goods (including subsection (4) above).

(8) References to stolen goods include money which is dishonestly withdrawn from an account to which a wrongful credit has been made, but only to the extent that the money derives from the credit.

(9) In this section "account" and "money" shall be construed in accordance with section 15B of this Act.'

(2) This section applies to wrongful credits made on or after the day on which this Act is passed.

---

¹ Repealed by the Fraud Act 2006.

The new offences: jurisdiction.

3.——(1) In section 1(2) of the Criminal Justice Act 1993 (Group A offences for the purposes of the jurisdictional provisions) paragraph (a)(list of offences under the Theft Act 1968) shall be amended as follows.

(2) [. . .]²

(3) After the entry relating to section 22 insert——

'section 24A (retaining credits from dishonest sources, etc.);'.

4. [. . .]³

Short title and extent.

5.——(1) This Act may be cited as the Theft (Amendment) Act 1996.

(2) Subject to subsection (3), this Act extends to England and Wales only.

(3) An Order in Council under paragraph 1(1)(b) of Schedule 1 to the Northern Ireland Act 1974 (legislation for Northern Ireland in the interim period) which contains a statement that it is made only for purposes corresponding to the purposes of this Act——

(a) shall not be subject to paragraph 1(4) and (5) of that Schedule (affirmative resolution of both Houses of Parliament); but

(b) shall be subject to annulment by resolution of either House.

---

² Repealed by the Fraud Act 2006.
³ Repealed by the Fraud Act 2006.

APPENDIX 4

Fraud Act 2006

CONTENTS

Fraud

Obtaining services dishonestly

Supplementary

FRAUD ACT 2006
2006 CHAPTER 35

An Act to make provision for, and in connection with, criminal liability for fraud and obtaining services dishonestly. [8th November 2006]

BE IT ENACTED by the Queen's most Excellent Majesty, by and with the advice and consent of the Lords Spiritual and Temporal, and Commons, in this present Parliament assembled, and by the authority of the same, as follows:—

Fraud

1 Fraud

(1) A person is guilty of fraud if he is in breach of any of the sections listed in subsection (2) (which provide for different ways of committing the offence).

(2) The sections are
    (a) section 2 (fraud by false representation),
    (b) section 3 (fraud by failing to disclose information), and
    (c) section 4 (fraud by abuse of position).
(3) A person who is guilty of fraud is liable—
    (a) on summary conviction, to imprisonment for a term not exceeding 12 months or to a fine not exceeding the statutory maximum (or to both);
    (b) on conviction on indictment, to imprisonment for a term not exceeding 10 years or to a fine (or to both).
(4) Subsection (3)(a) applies in relation to Northern Ireland as if the reference to 12 months were a reference to 6 months.

2 Fraud by false representation

(1) A person is in breach of this section if he—
    (a) dishonestly makes a false representation, and
    (b) intends, by making the representation—
        (i) to make a gain for himself or another, or
        (ii) to cause loss to another or to expose another to a risk of loss.
(2) A representation is false if—
    (a) it is untrue or misleading, and
    (b) the person making it knows that it is, or might be, untrue or misleading.
(3) 'Representation' means any representation as to fact or law, including a representation as to the state of mind of—
    (a) the person making the representation, or
    (b) any other person.
(4) A representation may be express or implied.
(5) For the purposes of this section a representation may be regarded as made if it (or anything implying it) is submitted in any form to any system or device designed to receive, convey or respond to communications (with or without human intervention).

3 Fraud by failing to disclose information

A person is in breach of this section if he—
    (a) dishonestly fails to disclose to another person information which he is under a legal duty to disclose, and
    (b) intends, by failing to disclose the information—
        (i) to make a gain for himself or another, or
        (ii) to cause loss to another or to expose another to a risk of loss.

4 Fraud by abuse of position

(1) A person is in breach of this section if he—
    (a) occupies a position in which he is expected to safeguard, or not to act against, the financial interests of another person,
    (b) dishonestly abuses that position, and
    (c) intends, by means of the abuse of that position—
        (i) to make a gain for himself or another, or
        (ii) to cause loss to another or to expose another to a risk of loss.
(2) A person may be regarded as having abused his position even though his conduct consisted of an omission rather than an act.

5 'Gain' and 'loss'

(1) The references to gain and loss in sections 2 to 4 are to be read in accordance with this section.
(2) 'Gain' and 'loss'—
    (a) extend only to gain or loss in money or other property;

    (b) include any such gain or loss whether temporary or permanent; and 'property' means any property whether real or personal (including things in action and other intangible property).

(3) 'Gain' includes a gain by keeping what one has, as well as a gain by getting what one does not have.

(4) 'Loss' includes a loss by not getting what one might get, as well as a loss by parting with what one has.

6 Possession etc. of articles for use in frauds

(1) A person is guilty of an offence if he has in his possession or under his control any article for use in the course of or in connection with any fraud.

(2) A person guilty of an offence under this section is liable—
    (a) on summary conviction, to imprisonment for a term not exceeding 12 months or to a fine not exceeding the statutory maximum (or to both);
    (b) on conviction on indictment, to imprisonment for a term not exceeding 5 years or to a fine (or to both).

(3) Subsection (2)(a) applies in relation to Northern Ireland as if the reference to 12 months were a reference to 6 months.

7 Making or supplying articles for use in frauds

(1) A person is guilty of an offence if he makes, adapts, supplies or offers to supply any article—
    (a) knowing that it is designed or adapted for use in the course of or in connection with fraud, or
    (b) intending it to be used to commit, or assist in the commission of, fraud.

(2) A person guilty of an offence under this section is liable—
    (a) on summary conviction, to imprisonment for a term not exceeding 12 months or to a fine not exceeding the statutory maximum (or to both);
    (b) on conviction on indictment, to imprisonment for a term not exceeding 10 years or to a fine (or to both).

(3) Subsection (2)(a) applies in relation to Northern Ireland as if the reference to 12 months were a reference to 6 months.

8 'Article'

(1) For the purposes of—
    (a) sections 6 and 7, and
    (b) the provisions listed in subsection (2), so far as they relate to articles for use in the course of or in connection with fraud,
'article' includes any program or data held in electronic form.

(2) The provisions are—
    (a) section 1(7)(b) of the Police and Criminal Evidence Act 1984 (c. 60),
    (b) section 2(8)(b) of the Armed Forces Act 2001 (c. 19), and
    (c) Article 3(7)(b) of the Police and Criminal Evidence (Northern Ireland) Order 1989 (S.I. 1989/1341 (N.I. 12));
(meaning of 'prohibited articles' for the purposes of stop and search powers).

9 Participating in fraudulent business carried on by sole trader etc.

(1) A person is guilty of an offence if he is knowingly a party to the carrying on of a business to which this section applies.

(2) This section applies to a business which is carried on—
    (a) by a person who is outside the reach of section 458 of the Companies Act 1985 (c. 6) or Article 451 of the Companies (Northern Ireland) Order 1986 (S.I. 1986/1032) (N.I. 6)) (offence of fraudulent trading), and
    (b) with intent to defraud creditors of any person or for any other fraudulent purpose.

(3) The following are within the reach of section 458 of the 1985 Act—
    (a) a company (within the meaning of that Act);

(b) a person to whom that section applies (with or without adaptations or modifications) as if the person were a company;

(c) a person exempted from the application of that section.

(4) The following are within the reach of Article 451 of the 1986 Order—

(a) a company (within the meaning of that Order);

(b) a person to whom that Article applies (with or without adaptations or modifications) as if the person were a company;

(c) a person exempted from the application of that Article.

(5) 'Fraudulent purpose' has the same meaning as in section 458 of the 1985 Act or Article 451 of the 1986 Order.

(6) A person guilty of an offence under this section is liable—

(a) on summary conviction, to imprisonment for a term not exceeding 12 months or to a fine not exceeding the statutory maximum (or to both);

(b) on conviction on indictment, to imprisonment for a term not exceeding 10 years or to a fine (or to both).

(7) Subsection (6)(a) applies in relation to Northern Ireland as if the reference to 12 months were a reference to 6 months.

10 Participating in fraudulent business carried on by company etc.: penalty

(1) In Schedule 24 to the Companies Act 1985 (punishment of offences), in column 4 of the entry relating to section 458 of that Act, for '7 years' substitute '10 years'.

(2) In Schedule 23 to the Companies (Northern Ireland) Order 1986 (punishment of offences), in column 4 of the entry relating to Article 451 of that Order, for '7 years' substitute '10 years'.

OBTAINING SERVICES DISHONESTLY

11 Obtaining services dishonestly

(1) A person is guilty of an offence under this section if he obtains services for himself or another—

(a) by a dishonest act, and

(b) in breach of subsection (2).

(2) A person obtains services in breach of this subsection if—

(a) they are made available on the basis that payment has been, is being or will be made for or in respect of them,

(b) he obtains them without any payment having been made for or in respect of them or without payment having been made in full, and

(c) when he obtains them, he knows—

(i) that they are being made available on the basis described in paragraph (a), or

(ii) that they might be,

but intends that payment will not be made, or will not be made in full.

(3) A person guilty of an offence under this section is liable—

(a) on summary conviction, to imprisonment for a term not exceeding 12 months or to a fine not exceeding the statutory maximum (or to both);

(b) on conviction on indictment, to imprisonment for a term not exceeding 5 years or to a fine (or to both).

(4) Subsection (3)(a) applies in relation to Northern Ireland as if the reference to 12 months were a reference to 6 months.

SUPPLEMENTARY

12 Liability of company officers for offences by company

(1) Subsection (2) applies if an offence under this Act is committed by a body corporate.

(2) If the offence is proved to have been committed with the consent or connivance of—
   (a) a director, manager, secretary or other similar officer of the body corporate, or
   (b) a person who was purporting to act in any such capacity, he (as well as the body corporate) is guilty of the offence and liable to be proceeded against and punished accordingly.
(3) If the affairs of a body corporate are managed by its members, subsection (2) applies in relation to the acts and defaults of a member in connection with his functions of management as if he were a director of the body corporate.

13 Evidence

(1) A person is not to be excused from—
   (a) answering any question put to him in proceedings relating to property, or
   (b) complying with any order made in proceedings relating to property, on the ground that doing so may incriminate him or his spouse or civil partner of an offence under this Act or a related offence.
(2) But, in proceedings for an offence under this Act or a related offence, a statement or admission made by the person in—
   (a) answering such a question, or
   (b) complying with such an order,
   is not admissible in evidence against him or (unless they married or became civil partners after the making of the statement or admission) his spouse or civil partner.
(3) 'Proceedings relating to property' means any proceedings for—
   (a) the recovery or administration of any property,
   (b) the execution of a trust, or
   (c) an account of any property or dealings with property,
   and 'property' means money or other property whether real or personal (including things in action and other intangible property).
(4) 'Related offence' means—
   (a) conspiracy to defraud;
   (b) any other offence involving any form of fraudulent conduct or purpose.

14 Minor and consequential amendments etc.

(1) Schedule 1 contains minor and consequential amendments.
(2) Schedule 2 contains transitional provisions and savings.
(3) Schedule 3 contains repeals and revocations.

15 Commencement and extent

(1) This Act (except this section and section 16) comes into force on such day as the Secretary of State may appoint by an order made by statutory instrument; and different days may be appointed for different purposes.
(2) Subject to subsection (3), sections 1 to 9 and 11 to 13 extend to England and Wales and Northern Ireland only.
(3) Section 8, so far as it relates to the Armed Forces Act 2001 (c. 19), extends to any place to which that Act extends.
(4) Any amendment in section 10 or Schedule 1, and any related provision in section 14 or Schedule 2 or 3, extends to any place to which the provision which is the subject of the amendment extends.

16 Short title

This Act may be cited as the Fraud Act 2006.

SCHEDULES

SCHEDULE 1 Section 14(1)
MINOR AND CONSEQUENTIAL AMENDMENTS

Abolition of various deception offences

1   Omit the following provisions—
   (a) in the Theft Act 1968 (c. 60)—
      (i) section 15 (obtaining property by deception);
      (ii) section 15A (obtaining a money transfer by deception);
      (iii) section 16 (obtaining pecuniary advantage by deception);
      (iv) section 20(2) (procuring the execution of a valuable security by deception);
   (b) in the Theft Act 1978 (c. 31)—
      (i) section 1 (obtaining services by deception);
      (ii) section 2 (evasion of liability by deception);
   (c) in the Theft Act (Northern Ireland) 1969 (c. 16 (N.I.))—
      (i) section 15 (obtaining property by deception);
      (ii) section 15A (obtaining a money transfer by deception);
      (iii) section 16 (obtaining pecuniary advantage by deception);
      (iv) section 19(2) (procuring the execution of a valuable security by deception);
   (d) in the Theft (Northern Ireland) Order 1978 (S.I. 1978/1407 (N.I. 23))—
      (i) Article 3 (obtaining services by deception);
      (ii) Article 4 (evasion of liability by deception).

Visiting Forces Act 1952 (c. 67)

2   In the Schedule (offences referred to in section 3 of the 1952 Act), in paragraph 3 (meaning of 'offence against property'), after sub-paragraph (l) insert— '(m) the Fraud Act 2006.'

Theft Act 1968 (c. 60)

3   Omit section 15B (section 15A: supplementary).
4   In section 18(1) (liability of company officers for offences by company under section 15, 16 or 17), omit '15, 16 or'.
5   In section 20(3) (suppression etc. of documents—interpretation), omit '"deception" has the same meaning as in section 15 of this Act, and'.
6   (1) In section 24(4) (meaning of 'stolen goods') for 'in the circumstances described in section 15(1) of this Act' substitute ', subject to subsection (5) below, by fraud (within the meaning of the Fraud Act 2006)'.
   (2) After section 24(4) insert—
      '(5) Subsection (1) above applies in relation to goods obtained by fraud as if—
         (a) the reference to the commencement of this Act were a reference to the commencement of the Fraud Act 2006, and
         (b) the reference to an offence under this Act were a reference to an offence under section 1 of that Act.'
7   (1) In section 24A (dishonestly retaining a wrongful credit), omit subsections (3) and (4) and after subsection (2) insert—
      '(2A) A credit to an account is wrongful to the extent that it derives from—
         (a) theft;
         (b) blackmail;
         (c) fraud (contrary to section 1 of the Fraud Act 2006); or
         (d) stolen goods.'
   (2) In subsection (7), for 'subsection (4)' substitute 'subsection (2A)'.

(3) For subsection (9) substitute—

'(9) "Account" means an account kept with—

    (a) a bank;

    (b) a person carrying on a business which falls within subsection (10) below; or

    (c) an issuer of electronic money (as defined for the purposes of Part 2 of the Financial Services and Markets Act 2000).

(10) A business falls within this subsection if—

    (a) in the course of the business money received by way of deposit is lent to others; or

    (b) any other activity of the business is financed, wholly or to any material extent, out of the capital of or the interest on money received by way of deposit.

(11) References in subsection (10) above to a deposit must be read with—

    (a) section 22 of the Financial Services and Markets Act 2000;

    (b) any relevant order under that section; and

    (c) Schedule 2 to that Act;

but any restriction on the meaning of deposit which arises from the identity of the person making it is to be disregarded.

(12) For the purposes of subsection (10) above—

    (a) all the activities which a person carries on by way of business shall be regarded as a single business carried on by him; and

    (b) "money" includes money expressed in a currency other than sterling.'

8 In section 25 (going equipped for burglary, theft or cheat)—

    (a) in subsections (1) and (3) for 'burglary, theft or cheat' substitute 'burglary or theft', and

    (b) in subsection (5) omit ', and "cheat" means an offence under section 15 of this Act'.

Theft Act (Northern Ireland) 1969 (c. 16 (N.I.))

9 Omit section 15B (section 15A: supplementary).

10 In section 19(3) (suppression etc. of documents—interpretation), omit '"deception" has the same meaning as in section 15, and'.

11 (1) In section 23(5) (meaning of 'stolen goods') for 'in the circumstances described in section 15(1)' substitute ', subject to subsection (6), by fraud (within the meaning of the Fraud Act 2006)'.

(2) After section 23(5) insert—

'(6) Subsection (1) applies in relation to goods obtained by fraud as if—

    (a) the reference to the commencement of this Act were a reference to the commencement of the Fraud Act 2006, and

    (b) the reference to an offence under this Act were a reference to an offence under section 1 of that Act.'

12 (1) In section 23A (dishonestly retaining a wrongful credit), omit subsections (3) and (4) and after subsection (2) insert—

'(2A) A credit to an account is wrongful to the extent that it derives from—

    (a) theft;

    (b) blackmail;

    (c) fraud (contrary to section 1 of the Fraud Act 2006); or

    (d) stolen goods.'

(2) In subsection (7), for 'subsection (4)' substitute 'subsection (2A)'.

(3) For subsection (9) substitute—

'(9) "Account" means an account kept with—

    (a) a bank;

    (b) a person carrying on a business which falls within subsection (10); or

    (c) an issuer of electronic money (as defined for the purposes of Part 2 of the Financial Services and Markets Act 2000).

(10) A business falls within this subsection if—
    (a) in the course of the business money received by way of deposit is lent to others; or
    (b) any other activity of the business is financed, wholly or to any material extent, out of the capital of or the interest on money received by way of deposit.

(11) References in subsection (10) to a deposit must be read with—
    (a) section 22 of the Financial Services and Markets Act 2000;
    (b) any relevant order under that section; and
    (c) Schedule 2 to that Act;
but any restriction on the meaning of deposit which arises from the identity of the person making it is to be disregarded.

(12) For the purposes of subsection (10)—
    (a) all the activities which a person carries on by way of business shall be regarded as a single business carried on by him; and
    (b) "money" includes money expressed in a currency other than sterling.'

13 In section 24 (going equipped for burglary, theft or cheat)—
    (a) in subsections (1) and (3), for 'burglary, theft or cheat' substitute 'burglary or theft', and
    (b) in subsection (5), omit ', and "cheat" means an offence under section 15'.

THEFT ACT 1978 (C. 31)

14 In section 4 (punishments), omit subsection (2)(a).
15 In section 5 (supplementary), omit subsection (1).

THEFT (NORTHERN IRELAND) ORDER 1978 (S.I. 1978/1407 (N.I. 23))

16 In Article 6 (punishments), omit paragraph (2)(a).
17 In Article 7 (supplementary), omit paragraph (1).

LIMITATION ACT 1980 (C. 58)

18 In section 4 (special time limit in case of theft), for subsection (5)(b) substitute—
'(b) obtaining any chattel (in England and Wales or elsewhere) by—
    (i) blackmail (within the meaning of section 21 of the Theft Act 1968), or
    (ii) fraud (within the meaning of the Fraud Act 2006);'.

FINANCE ACT 1982 (C. 39)

19 In section 11(1) (powers of Commissioners with respect to agricultural levies), for 'or the Theft (Northern Ireland) Order 1978,' substitute ', the Theft (Northern Ireland) Order 1978 or the Fraud Act 2006'.

NUCLEAR MATERIAL (OFFENCES) ACT 1983 (C. 18)

20 In section 1 (extended scope of certain offences), in subsection (1)(d), omit '15 or' (in both places).

POLICE AND CRIMINAL EVIDENCE ACT 1984 (C. 60)

21 In section 1 (power of constable to stop and search persons, vehicles etc.), in subsection (8), for paragraph (d) substitute—
'(d) fraud (contrary to section 1 of the Fraud Act 2006).'

LIMITATION (NORTHERN IRELAND) ORDER 1989 (S.I. 1989/1339 (N.I. 11))

22 In Article 18 (special time limit in case of theft), for paragraph (5)(b) substitute—
   '(b) obtaining any chattel (in Northern Ireland or elsewhere) by—blackmail (within the meaning of section 20 of the Theft Act (Northern Ireland) 1969), or
      (ii) fraud (within the meaning of the Fraud Act 2006);'.

POLICE AND CRIMINAL EVIDENCE (NORTHERN IRELAND) ORDER 1989 (S.I. 1989/1341 (N.I. 12))

23 In Article 3 (power of constable to stop and search persons, vehicles etc.), in paragraph (8), for sub-paragraph (d) substitute—
   '(d) fraud (contrary to section 1 of the Fraud Act 2006).'

CRIMINAL JUSTICE ACT 1993 (C. 36)

24 (1) In section 1(2) (Group A offences), omit the entries in paragraph (a) relating to sections 15, 15A, 16 and 20(2) of the Theft Act 1968.
(2) Omit section 1(2)(b).
(3) Before section 1(2)(c) insert—
   '(bb) an offence under any of the following provisions of the Fraud Act 2006—
      (i) section 1 (fraud);
      (ii) section 6 (possession etc. of articles for use in frauds);
      (iii) section 7 (making or supplying articles for use in frauds);
      (iv) section 9 (participating in fraudulent business carried on by sole trader etc.);
      (v) section 11 (obtaining services dishonestly).'
25 (1) Amend section 2 (jurisdiction in respect of Group A offences) as follows.
(2) In subsection (1), after 'means' insert '(subject to subsection (1A))'.
(3) After subsection (1) insert—
   '(1A) In relation to an offence under section 1 of the Fraud Act 2006 (fraud),
   "relevant event" includes—
      (a) if the fraud involved an intention to make a gain and the gain occurred, that occurrence;
      (b) if the fraud involved an intention to cause a loss or to expose another to a risk of loss and the loss occurred, that occurrence.'

CRIMINAL JUSTICE (NORTHERN IRELAND) ORDER 1994 (S.I. 1994/2795 (N.I. 15))

26 In Article 14 (compensation orders), in paragraphs (3) and (4)(a) for 'or Article 172 of the Road Traffic (Northern Ireland) Order 1981' substitute ', Article 172 of the Road Traffic (Northern Ireland) Order 1981 or the Fraud Act 2006'.

CRIMINAL JUSTICE (NORTHERN IRELAND) ORDER 1996 (S.I. 1996/3160 (N.I. 24))

27 (1) In Article 38(2) (Group A offences), omit the entries in sub-paragraph (a) relating to sections 15, 15A, 16 and 19(2) of the Theft Act (Northern Ireland) 1969.
(2) Omit Article 38(2)(b).
(3) Before Article 38(2)(c) insert—
   '(bb) an offence under any of the following provisions of the Fraud Act 2006—
      (i) section 1 (fraud);
      (ii) section 6 (possession etc. of articles for use in frauds);
      (iii) section 7 (making or supplying articles for use in frauds);
      (iv) section 9 (participating in fraudulent business carried on by sole trader etc.);
      (v) section 11 (obtaining services dishonestly).'

28 (1) Amend Article 39 (jurisdiction in respect of Group A offences) as follows.

(2) In paragraph (1), after 'means' insert '(subject to paragraph (1A))'.

(3) After paragraph (1) insert—

'(1A) In relation to an offence under section 1 of the Fraud Act 2006 (fraud), "relevant event" includes—

(a) if the fraud involved an intention to make a gain and the gain occurred, that occurrence;

(b) if the fraud involved an intention to cause a loss or to expose another to a risk of loss and the loss occurred, that occurrence.'

POWERS OF CRIMINAL COURTS (SENTENCING) ACT 2000 (C. 6)

29 In section 130 (compensation orders), in subsections (5) and (6)(a), after 'Theft Act 1968' insert 'or Fraud Act 2006'.

TERRORISM ACT 2000 (C. 11)

30 (1) In Schedule 9 (scheduled offences), in paragraph 10, at the end of subparagraph (d) insert 'and' and omit paragraph (e).

(2) After paragraph 22A of that Schedule insert—

'*Fraud Act 2006*

23 Offences under section 1 of the Fraud Act 2006 (fraud) subject to note 2 below.'

(3) In note 2 to Part 1 of Schedule 9, for 'paragraph 10(a), (c) or (e)' substitute 'paragraph 10(a) or (c) or 23'.

31 (1) In Schedule 12 (compensation), in paragraph 12(1), omit '(within the meaning of section 15(4) of the Theft Act (Northern Ireland) 1969)'.

(2) After paragraph 12(1) of that Schedule insert—

'(1A) "Deception" means any deception (whether deliberate or reckless) by words or conduct as to fact or as to law, including a deception as to the present intentions of the person using the deception or any other person.'

CRIMINAL JUSTICE AND COURT SERVICES ACT 2000 (C. 43)

32 (1) In Schedule 6 (trigger offences), in paragraph 1, omit the entry relating to section 15 of the Theft Act 1968.

(2) After paragraph 2 of Schedule 6 insert—

'3 Offences under the following provisions of the Fraud Act 2006 are trigger offences—

section 1 (fraud)

section 6 (possession etc. of articles for use in frauds)

section 7 (making or supplying articles for use in frauds).'

ARMED FORCES ACT 2001 (C. 19)

33 In section 2(9) (definition of prohibited articles for purposes of powers to stop and search), for paragraph (d) substitute—

'(d) fraud (contrary to section 1 of the Fraud Act 2006).'

LICENSING ACT 2003 (C. 17)

34 In Schedule 4 (personal licence: relevant offences), after paragraph 20 insert—

'21 An offence under the Fraud Act 2006.'

ASYLUM AND IMMIGRATION (TREATMENT OF CLAIMANTS, ETC.) ACT 2004 (C. 19)

35 (1) In section 14(2) (offences giving rise to immigration officer's power of arrest), omit paragraph (g)(ii) and (iii), in paragraph (h), '15, 16' and paragraphs (i) and (j).

(2) After section 14(2)(h) insert—
    '(ha) an offence under either of the following provisions of the Fraud Act 2006—
        (i) section 1 (fraud);
        (ii) section 11 (obtaining services dishonestly),'.

SERIOUS ORGANISED CRIME AND POLICE ACT 2005 (c. 15)

36 In section 76 (financial reporting orders: making), in subsection (3), for paragraphs (a) and (b) substitute—
    '(aa) an offence under either of the following provisions of the Fraud Act 2006—
        (i) section 1 (fraud),
        (ii) section 11 (obtaining services dishonestly),'.

37 In section 78 (financial reporting orders: making in Northern Ireland), in subsection (3), for paragraphs (a) and (b) substitute—
    '(aa) an offence under either of the following provisions of the Fraud Act 2006—
        (i) section 1 (fraud),
        (ii) section 11 (obtaining services dishonestly),'.

GAMBLING ACT 2005 (c. 19)

38 After paragraph 3 of Schedule 7 (relevant offences) insert—
    '3A An offence under the Fraud Act 2006.'

SCHEDULE 2 Section 14(2)
TRANSITIONAL PROVISIONS AND SAVINGS

MAXIMUM TERM OF IMPRISONMENT FOR OFFENCES UNDER THIS ACT

1   In relation to an offence committed before the commencement of section 154(1) of the Criminal Justice Act 2003 (c. 44), the references to 12 months in sections 1(3)(a), 6(2)(a), 7(2)(a), 9(6)(a) and 11(3)(a) are to be read as references to 6 months.

INCREASE IN PENALTY FOR FRAUDULENT TRADING

2   Section 10 does not affect the penalty for any offence committed before that section comes into force.

ABOLITION OF DECEPTION OFFENCES

3   (1) Paragraph 1 of Schedule 1 does not affect any liability, investigation, legal proceeding or penalty for or in respect of any offence partly committed before the commencement of that paragraph.
(2) An offence is partly committed before the commencement of paragraph 1 of Schedule 1 if—
    (a) a relevant event occurs before its commencement, and
    (b) another relevant event occurs on or after its commencement.
(3) 'Relevant event', in relation to an offence, means any act, omission or other event (including any result of one or more acts or omissions) proof of which is required for conviction of the offence.

SCOPE OF OFFENCES RELATING TO STOLEN GOODS
UNDER THE THEFT ACT 1968 (c. 60)

4   Nothing in paragraph 6 of Schedule 1 affects the operation of section 24 of the Theft Act 1968 in relation to goods obtained in the circumstances described in section 15(1) of that Act where the obtaining is the result of a deception made before the commencement of that paragraph.

DISHONESTLY RETAINING A WRONGFUL CREDIT UNDER THE THEFT ACT 1968

5 Nothing in paragraph 7 of Schedule 1 affects the operation of section 24A(7) and (8) of the Theft Act 1968 in relation to credits falling within section 24A(3) or (4) of that Act and made before the commencement of that paragraph.

SCOPE OF OFFENCES RELATING TO STOLEN GOODS UNDER THE THEFT ACT (NORTHERN IRELAND) 1969 (C. 16 (N.I.))

6 Nothing in paragraph 11 of Schedule 1 affects the operation of section 23 of the Theft Act (Northern Ireland) 1969 in relation to goods obtained in the circumstances described in section 15(1) of that Act where the obtaining is the result of a deception made before the commencement of that paragraph.

DISHONESTLY RETAINING A WRONGFUL CREDIT UNDER THE THEFT ACT (NORTHERN IRELAND) 1969

7 Nothing in paragraph 12 of Schedule 1 affects the operation of section 23A(7) and (8) of the Theft Act (Northern Ireland) 1969 in relation to credits falling within section 23A(3) or (4) of that Act and made before the commencement of that paragraph.

LIMITATION PERIODS UNDER THE LIMITATION ACT 1980 (C. 58)

8 Nothing in paragraph 18 of Schedule 1 affects the operation of section 4 of the Limitation Act 1980 in relation to chattels obtained in the circumstances described in section 15(1) of the Theft Act 1968 where the obtaining is a result of a deception made before the commencement of that paragraph.

LIMITATION PERIODS UNDER THE LIMITATION (NORTHERN IRELAND) ORDER 1989 (S.I. 1989/1339 (N.I. 11))

9 Nothing in paragraph 22 of Schedule 1 affects the operation of Article 18 of the Limitation (Northern Ireland) Order 1989 in relation to chattels obtained in the circumstances described in section 15(1) of the Theft Act (Northern Ireland) 1969 where the obtaining is a result of a deception made before the commencement of that paragraph.

SCHEDULED OFFENCES UNDER THE TERRORISM ACT 2000 (C. 11)

10 Nothing in paragraph 30 of Schedule 1 affects the operation of Part 7 of the Terrorism Act 2000 in relation to an offence under section 15(1) of the Theft Act (Northern Ireland) 1969 where the obtaining is a result of a deception made before the commencement of that paragraph.

POWERS OF ARREST UNDER ASYLUM AND IMMIGRATION (TREATMENT OF CLAIMANTS, ETC.) ACT 2004 (C. 19)

11 (1) Nothing in paragraph 35 of Schedule 1 affects the power of arrest conferred by section 14 of the Asylum and Immigration (Treatment of Claimants, etc.) Act 2004 in relation to an offence partly committed before the commencement of that paragraph.

(2) An offence is partly committed before the commencement of paragraph 35 of Schedule 1 if—
  (a) a relevant event occurs before its commencement, and
  (b) another relevant event occurs on or after its commencement.

(3) 'Relevant event', in relation to an offence, means any act, omission or other event (including any result of one or more acts or omissions) proof of which is required for conviction of the offence.

SCHEDULE 3 Section 14(3)
REPEALS AND REVOCATIONS

Title and number	*Extent of repeal or revocation*
Theft Act 1968 (c. 60).	Sections 15, 15A, 15B and 16 In section 18(1), '15, 16 or'. Section 20(2). In section 20(3), '"deception" has the same meaning as in section 15 of this Act, and'. In section 25(5), ', and 'cheat" means an offence under section 15 of this Act'. Section 24A(3) and (4).
Theft Act (Northern Ireland) 1969	Sections 15, 15A, 15B and 16. Section 19(2). In section 19(3), '"deception" has the same meaning as in section 15, and'. Section 23A(3) and (4). In section 24(5), ', and "cheat" means an offence under section 15'.
Theft Act 1978	Sections 1 and 2. Section 4(2)(a). Section 5(1).
Theft (Northern Ireland) Order 1978	Articles 3 and 4 Article 6(2)(a). Article 7(1).
Nuclear Material (Offences) Act 1983	In section 1(1)(d), '15 or' (in both places).
Criminal Justice Act 1993	In section 1(2), the entries in paragraph (a) relating to sections 15, 15A, 16 and 20(2) of the Theft Act 1968. Section 1(2)(b).
Theft (Amendment) Act 1996	Sections 1, 3(2) and 4.
Criminal Justice (Northern Ireland) Order 1996	In Article 38(2), the entries in sub-paragraph (a) relating to sections 15, 15A, 16 and 19(2) of the Theft Act (Northern Ireland) 1969. Article 38(2)(b).
Theft (Amendment) (Northern Ireland) Order 1997	Articles 3, 5(2) and 6.
Terrorism Act 2000	In Schedule 9, paragraph 10(e). In Schedule 12, in paragraph 12(1), '(within the meaning of section 15(4) of the Theft Act(Northern Ireland) 1969)'.
Criminal Justice and Court Services Act 2000	In Schedule 6, in paragraph 1, the entry relating to section 15 of the Theft Act 1968
Asylum and Immigration (Treatment of Claimants, etc.) Act 2004	In section 14(2), paragraph (g)(ii) and (iii), in paragraph (h), '15, 16' and paragraphs (i) and (j).

APPENDIX 5

Criminal Law Act 1977 ss 1 and 5

An Act to amend the law of England and Wales with respect to criminal conspiracy; to make new provision in that law, in place of the provisions of the common law and the Statutes of Forcible Entry, for restricting the use or threat of violence for securing entry into any premises and for penalising unauthorised entry or remaining on premises in certain circumstances; otherwise to amend the criminal law, including the law with respect to the administration of criminal justice; to provide for the alteration of certain pecuniary and other limits; to amend section 9(4) of the Administration of Justice Act 1973, the Legal Aid Act 1974, the Rabies Act 1974 and the Diseases of Animals (Northern Ireland) Order 1975 and the law about juries and coroners' inquests; and for connected purposes.

[29th July 1977]

PART I
CONSPIRACY

The offence of conspiracy

1. —[(1) Subject to the following provisions of this Part of this Act, if a person agrees with any other person or persons that a course of conduct shall be pursued which, if the agreement is carried out in accordance with their intentions, either—
   (a) will necessarily amount to or involve the commission of any offence or offences by one or more of the parties to the agreement, or
   (b) would do so but for the existence of facts which render the commission of the offence or any of the offences impossible,
   he is guilty of conspiracy to commit the offence or offences in question.][1]
   (1A) [. . .][2]
   (1B) [. . .][3]
   (2) Where liability for any offence may be incurred without knowledge on the part of the person committing it of any particular fact or circumstance necessary for the commission of the offence, a person shall nevertheless not be guilty of conspiracy to commit that offence by virtue of subsection (1) above unless he and at least one other party to the agreement intend or know that that fact or circumstance shall or will exist at the time when the conduct constituting the offence is to take place.
   (3) [. . .][4]
   (4) In this Part of this Act 'offence' means an offence triable in England and Wales [. . .][5]

---

[1] Amended by the Criminal Attempt Act 1981.
[2] Inserted by the Computer Misuse Act 1990 and repealed by the Criminal Justice (Terrorism and Conspiracy) Act 1998.
[3] Inserted by the the Computer Misuse Act 1990 and repealed by the Criminal Justice (Terrorism and Conspiracy) Act 1998.
[4] Repealed by the Trade Union and Labour Relations (Consolidation) Act 1992.
[5] Repealed by the Criminal Justice (Terrorism and Conspiracy) Act 1998.

(5) [. . .]^6
(6) [. . .]^7

. . .

Abolitions, savings, transitional provisions, consequential amendment and repeals

5. —(1) Subject to the following provisions of this section, the offence of conspiracy at common law is hereby abolished.

    (2) Subsection (1) above shall not affect the offence of conspiracy at common law so far as relates to conspiracy to defraud, [. . .]^8

    (3) Subsection (1) above shall not affect the offence of conspiracy at common law if and in so far as it may be committed by entering into an agreement to engage in conduct which—

        (a) tends to corrupt public morals or outrages public decency; but

        (b) would not amount to or involve the commission of an offence if carried out by a single person otherwise than in pursuance of an agreement.

    (4) Subsection (1) above shall not affect—

        (a) any proceedings commenced before the time when this Part of this Act comes into force;

        (b) any proceedings commenced after that time against a person charged with the same conspiracy as that charged in any proceedings commenced before that time; or

        (c) any proceedings commenced after that time in respect of a trespass committed before that time;

    but a person convicted of conspiracy to trespass in any proceedings brought by virtue of paragraph (c) above shall not in respect of that conviction be liable to imprisonment for a term exceeding six months.

    (5) Sections 1 and 2 above shall apply to things done before as well as to things done after the time when this Part of this Act comes into force, but in the application of section 3 above to a case where the agreement in question was entered into before that time—

        (a) subsection (2) shall be read without the reference to murder in paragraph (a); and

        (b) any murder intended under the agreement shall be treated as an offence for which a maximum term of imprisonment of ten years is provided.

    (6) The rules laid down by sections 1 and 2 above shall apply for determining whether a person is guilty of an offence of conspiracy under any enactment other than section 1 above, but conduct which is an offence under any such other enactment shall not also be an offence under section 1 above.

    (7) Incitement [. . .]^9 to commit the offence of conspiracy (whether the conspiracy incited [. . .]^10 would be an offence at common law or under section 1 above or any other enactment) shall cease to be offences.

    (8) The fact that the person or persons who, so far as appears from the indictment on which any person has been convicted of conspiracy, were the only other parties to the agreement on which his conviction was based have been acquitted of conspiracy by reference to that agreement (whether after being tried with the person convicted or separately) shall not be a ground for quashing his conviction unless under all the circumstances of the case his conviction is inconsistent with the acquittal of the other person or persons in question.

    (9) Any rule of law or practice inconsistent with the provisions of subsection (8) above is hereby abolished.

---

    ^6 Inserted by the Computer Misuse Act 1990 and repealed by the Criminal Justice (Terrorism and Conspiracy) Act 1998.
    ^7 Inserted by the Computer Misuse Act 1990 and repealed by the Criminal Justice (Terrorism and Conspiracy) Act 1998.
    ^8 Repealed by the Criminal Justice Act 1987.
    ^9 Repealed by the Criminal Attempts Act 1981.
    ^10 Repealed by the Criminal Attempts Act 1981.

(10) In section 4 of the Offences against the Person Act 1861—
  (a) the words preceding 'Whosoever' shall cease to have effect; and
  (b) for the words from 'be kept' to 'years' there shall be substituted the words 'imprisonment for life'.

(11) [. . .]¹¹

---

¹¹ Repealed by the Trade Union and Labour Relations (Consolidations) Act 1992.

Proceeds of Crime Act 2002 ss 327–40

327 Concealing etc

(1) A person commits an offence if he—
  (a) conceals criminal property;
  (b) disguises criminal property;
  (c) converts criminal property;
  (d) transfers criminal property;
  (e) removes criminal property from England and Wales or from Scotland or from Northern Ireland.
(2) But a person does not commit such an offence if—
  (a) he makes an authorised disclosure under section 338 and (if the disclosure is made before he does the act mentioned in subsection (1)) he has the appropriate consent;
  (b) he intended to make such a disclosure but had a reasonable excuse for not doing so;
  (c) the act he does is done in carrying out a function he has relating to the enforcement of any provision of this Act or of any other enactment relating to criminal conduct or benefit from criminal conduct.
[(2A) Nor does a person commit an offence under subsection (1) if—
  (a) he knows, or believes on reasonable grounds, that the relevant criminal conduct occurred in a particular country or territory outside the United Kingdom, and
  (b) the relevant criminal conduct—
    (i) was not, at the time it occurred, unlawful under the criminal law then applying in that country or territory, and
    (ii) is not of a description prescribed by an order made by the Secretary of State.
(2B) In subsection (2A) 'the relevant criminal conduct' is the criminal conduct by reference to which the property concerned is criminal property.
(2C) A deposit-taking body that does an act mentioned in paragraph (c) or (d) of subsection
  (1) does not commit an offence under that subsection if—
    (a) it does the act in operating an account maintained with it, and
    (b) the value of the criminal property concerned is less than the threshold amount determined under section 339A for the act.][1]
(3) Concealing or disguising criminal property includes concealing or disguising its nature, source, location, disposition, movement or ownership or any rights with respect to it.

328 Arrangements

(1) A person commits an offence if he enters into or becomes concerned in an arrangement which he knows or suspects facilitates (by whatever means) the acquisition, retention, use or control of criminal property by or on behalf of another person.
(2) But a person does not commit such an offence if—
  (a) he makes an authorised disclosure under section 338 and (if the disclosure is made before he does the act mentioned in subsection (1)) he has the appropriate consent;
  (b) he intended to make such a disclosure but had a reasonable excuse for not doing so;

---

[1] Inserted by Serious Organised Crime and Police Act 2005.

(c) the act he does is done in carrying out a function he has relating to the enforcement of any provision of this Act or of any other enactment relating to criminal conduct or benefit from criminal conduct.

[(3) Nor does a person commit an offence under subsection (1) if—

    (a) he knows, or believes on reasonable grounds, that the relevant criminal conduct occurred in a particular country or territory outside the United Kingdom, and

    (b) the relevant criminal conduct—

        (i) was not, at the time it occurred, unlawful under the criminal law then applying in that country or territory, and

        (ii) is not of a description prescribed by an order made by the Secretary of State.

(4) In subsection (3) 'the relevant criminal conduct' is the criminal conduct by reference to which the property concerned is criminal property.

(5) A deposit-taking body that does an act mentioned in subsection (1) does not commit an offence under that subsection if—

    (a) it does the act in operating an account maintained with it, and

    (b) the arrangement facilitates the acquisition, retention, use or control of criminal property of a value that is less than the threshold amount determined under section 339A for the act.][2]

329 Acquisition, use and possession

(1) A person commits an offence if he—

    (a) acquires criminal property;

    (b) uses criminal property;

    (c) has possession of criminal property.

(2) But a person does not commit such an offence if—

    (a) he makes an authorised disclosure under section 338 and (if the disclosure is made before he does the act mentioned in subsection (1)) he has the appropriate consent;

    (b) he intended to make such a disclosure but had a reasonable excuse for not doing so;

    (c) he acquired or used or had possession of the property for adequate consideration;

    (d) the act he does is done in carrying out a function he has relating to the enforcement of any provision of this Act or of any other enactment relating to criminal conduct or benefit from criminal conduct.

[(2A) Nor does a person commit an offence under subsection (1) if—

    (a) he knows, or believes on reasonable grounds, that the relevant criminal conduct occurred in a particular country or territory outside the United Kingdom, and

    (b) the relevant criminal conduct—

        (i) was not, at the time it occurred, unlawful under the criminal law then applying in that country or territory, and

        (ii) is not of a description prescribed by an order made by the Secretary of State.

(2B) In subsection (2A) 'the relevant criminal conduct' is the criminal conduct by reference to which the property concerned is criminal property.

(2C) A deposit-taking body that does an act mentioned in subsection (1) does not commit an offence under that subsection if—

    (a) it does the act in operating an account maintained with it, and

    (b) the value of the criminal property concerned is less than the threshold amount determined under section 339A for the act.][3]

(3) For the purposes of this section—

    (a) a person acquires property for inadequate consideration if the value of the consideration is significantly less than the value of the property;

---

[2] Inserted by Serious Organised Crime and Police Act 2005.
[3] Inserted by Serious Organised Crime and Police Act 2005.

(b) a person uses or has possession of property for inadequate consideration if the value of the consideration is significantly less than the value of the use or possession;

(c) the provision by a person of goods or services which he knows or suspects may help another to carry out criminal conduct is not consideration.

330 Failure to disclose: regulated sector

(1) A person commits an offence [if the conditions in subsections (2) to (4) are satisfied].[4]

(2) The first condition is that he—

    (a) knows or suspects, or

    (b) has reasonable grounds for knowing or suspecting, that another person is engaged in money laundering.

(3) The second condition is that the information or other matter—

    (a) on which his knowledge or suspicion is based, or

    (b) which gives reasonable grounds for such knowledge or suspicion, came to him in the course of a business in the regulated sector.

[(3A) The third condition is—

    (a) that he can identify the other person mentioned in subsection (2) or the whereabouts of any of the laundered property, or

    (b) that he believes, or it is reasonable to expect him to believe, that the information or other matter mentioned in subsection (3) will or may assist in identifying that other person or the whereabouts of any of the laundered property.

(4) The fourth condition is that he does not make the required disclosure to—

    (a) a nominated officer, or

    (b) a person authorised for the purposes of this Part by the Director General of the Serious Organised Crime Agency, as soon as is practicable after the information or other matter mentioned in subsection (3) comes to him.

(5) The required disclosure is a disclosure of—

    (a) the identity of the other person mentioned in subsection (2), if he knows it,

    (b) the whereabouts of the laundered property, so far as he knows it, and

    (c) the information or other matter mentioned in subsection (3).

(5A) The laundered property is the property forming the subject-matter of the money laundering that he knows or suspects, or has reasonable grounds for knowing or suspecting, that other person to be engaged in.

(6) But he does not commit an offence under this section if—

    (a) he has a reasonable excuse for not making the required disclosure,

    (b) he is a professional legal adviser [or other relevant professional adviser][5] and—

        (i) if he knows either of the things mentioned in subsection (5)(a)and (b), he knows the thing because of information or other matter that came to him in privileged circumstances, or

        (ii) the information or other matter mentioned in subsection (3) came to him in privileged circumstances, or

    (c) subsection (7) [or (7B)][6] applies to him.][7]

(7) This subsection applies to a person if—

    (a) he does not know or suspect that another person is engaged in money laundering, and

    (b) he has not been provided by his employer with such training as is specified by the Secretary of State by order for the purposes of this section.

---

[4] Amended by Serious Organised Crime and Police Act 2005.
[5] Amended by SI 2006/308.
[6] Amended by SI 2006/308.
[7] Amended by the Serious Organised Crime and Police Act 2005.

[(7A) Nor does a person commit an offence under this section if—
    (a) he knows, or believes on reasonable grounds, that the money laundering is occurring in a particular country or territory outside the United Kingdom, and
    (b) the money laundering—
        (i) is not unlawful under the criminal law applying in that country or territory, and
        (ii) is not of a description prescribed in an order made by the Secretary of State.][8]
[(7B) This subsection applies to a person if—
    (a) he is employed by, or is in partnership with, a professional legal adviser or a relevant professional adviser to provide the adviser with assistance or support,
    (b) the information or other matter mentioned in subsection (3) comes to the person in connection with the provision of such assistance or support, and
    (c) the information or other matter came to the adviser in privileged circumstances.][9]
 (8) In deciding whether a person committed an offence under this section the court must consider whether he followed any relevant guidance which was at the time concerned—
    (a) issued by a supervisory authority or any other appropriate body,
    (b) approved by the Treasury, and
    (c) published in a manner it approved as appropriate in its opinion to bring the guidance to the attention of persons likely to be affected by it.
 (9) A disclosure to a nominated officer is a disclosure which—
    (a) is made to a person nominated by the alleged offender's employer to receive disclosures under this section, and
    (b) is made in the course of the alleged offender's employment [. . .][10]
[(9A) But a disclosure which satisfies paragraphs (a) and (b) of subsection (9) is not to be taken as a disclosure to a nominated officer if the person making the disclosure—
    (a) is a professional legal adviser [or other relevant professional adviser],[11]
    (b) makes it for the purpose of obtaining advice about making a disclosure under this section, and
    (c) does not intend it to be a disclosure under this section.][12]
(10) Information or other matter comes to a professional legal adviser [or other relevant professional adviser][13] in privileged circumstances if it is communicated or given to him—
    (a) by (or by a representative of) a client of his in connection with the giving by the adviser of legal advice to the client,
    (b) by (or by a representative of) a person seeking legal advice from the adviser, or
    (c) by a person in connection with legal proceedings or contemplated legal proceedings.
(11) But subsection (10) does not apply to information or other matter which is communicated or given with the intention of furthering a criminal purpose.
(12) Schedule 9 has effect for the purpose of determining what is—
    (a) a business in the regulated sector;
    (b) a supervisory authority.
(13) An appropriate body is any body which regulates or is representative of any trade, profession, business or employment carried on by the alleged offender.
[(14) A relevant professional adviser is an accountant, auditor or tax adviser who is a member of a professional body which is established for accountants, auditors or tax advisers (as the case may be) and which makes provision for—
    (a) testing the competence of those seeking admission to membership of such a body as a condition for such admission; and

---

[8] Inserted by the Serious Organised Crime and Police Act 2005.
[9] Inserted by SI 2006/308.
[10] Repealed by the Serious Organised Crime and Police Act 2005.
[11] Amended by SI 2006/308.
[12] Inserted by the Serious Organised Crime and Police Act 2005.
[13] Amended by SI 2006/308.

(b) imposing and maintaining professional and ethical standards for its members, as well as imposing sanctions for non-compliance with those standards.][14]

331 Failure to disclose: nominated officers in the regulated sector

(1) A person nominated to receive disclosures under section 330 commits an offence if the conditions in subsections (2) to (4) are satisfied.

(2) The first condition is that he—
  (a) knows or suspects, or
  (b) has reasonable grounds for knowing or suspecting, that another person is engaged in money laundering.

(3) The second condition is that the information or other matter—
  (a) on which his knowledge or suspicion is based, or
  (b) which gives reasonable grounds for such knowledge or suspicion, came to him in consequence of a disclosure made under section 330.

[(3A) The third condition is—
  (a) that he knows the identity of the other person mentioned in subsection (2), or the whereabouts of any of the laundered property, in consequence of a disclosure made under section 330,
  (b) that that other person, or the whereabouts of any of the laundered property, can be identified from the information or other matter mentioned in subsection (3), or
  (c) that he believes, or it is reasonable to expect him to believe, that the information or ther matter will or may assist in identifying that other person or the whereabouts of any of the laundered property.

(4) The fourth condition is that he does not make the required disclosure to a person authorised for the purposes of this Part by the Director General of the Serious Organised Crime Agency as soon as is practicable after the information or other matter mentioned in subsection (3) comes to him.

(5) The required disclosure is a disclosure of—
  (a) the identity of the other person mentioned in subsection (2), if disclosed to him under section 330,
  (b) the whereabouts of the laundered property, so far as disclosed to him under section 330, and
  (c) the information or other matter mentioned in subsection (3).

(5A) The laundered property is the property forming the subject-matter of the money laundering that he knows or suspects, or has reasonable grounds for knowing or suspecting, that other person to be engaged in.

(6) But he does not commit an offence under this section if he has a reasonable excuse for not making the required disclosure.

(6A) Nor does a person commit an offence under this section if—
  (a) he knows, or believes on reasonable grounds, that the money laundering is occurring in a particular country or territory outside the United Kingdom, and
  (b) the money laundering—
      (i) is not unlawful under the criminal law applying in that country or territory, and
      (ii) is not of a description prescribed in an order made by the Secretary of State.][15]

(7) In deciding whether a person committed an offence under this section the court must consider whether he followed any relevant guidance which was at the time concerned—
  (a) issued by a supervisory authority or any other appropriate body,
  (b) approved by the Treasury, and
  (c) published in a manner it approved as appropriate in its opinion to bring the guidance to the attention of persons likely to be affected by it.

(8) Schedule 9 has effect for the purpose of determining what is a supervisory authority.

---

[14] Inserted by SI 2006/308.
[15] Inserted by Serious Organised Crime and Police Act 2005.

(9) An appropriate body is a body which regulates or is representative of a trade, profession, business or employment.

332 Failure to disclose: other nominated officers

(1) A person nominated to receive disclosures under section 337 or 338 commits an offence if the conditions in subsections (2) to (4) are satisfied.

(2) The first condition is that he knows or suspects that another person is engaged in money laundering.

(3) The second condition is that the information or other matter on which his knowledge or suspicion is based came to him in consequence of a disclosure made under [the applicable section.][16]

[(3A) The third condition is—

    (a) that he knows the identity of the other person mentioned in subsection (2), or the whereabouts of any of the laundered property, in consequence of a disclosure made under the applicable section,

    (b) that that other person, or the whereabouts of any of the laundered property, can be identified from the information or other matter mentioned in subsection (3), or

    (c) that he believes, or it is reasonable to expect him to believe, that the information or other matter will or may assist in identifying that other person or the whereabouts of any of the laundered property.

(4) The fourth condition is that he does not make the required disclosure to a person authorised for the purposes of this Part by the Director General of the Serious Organised Crime Agency as soon as is practicable after the information or other matter mentioned in subsection (3) comes to him.

(5) The required disclosure is a disclosure of—

    (a) the identity of the other person mentioned in subsection (2), if disclosed to him under the applicable section,

    (b) the whereabouts of the laundered property, so far as disclosed to him under the applicable section, and

    (c) the information or other matter mentioned in subsection (3).

(5A) The laundered property is the property forming the subject-matter of the money laundering that he knows or suspects that other person to be engaged in.

(5B) The applicable section is section 337 or, as the case may be, section 338.

(6) But he does not commit an offence under this section if he has a reasonable excuse for not making the required disclosure.

(7) Nor does a person commit an offence under this section if—

    (a) he knows, or believes on reasonable grounds, that the money laundering is occurring in a particular country or territory outside the United Kingdom, and

    (b) the money laundering—

        (i) is not unlawful under the criminal law applying in that country or territory, and

        (ii) is not of a description prescribed in an order made by the Secretary of State.][17]

333 Tipping off

(1) A person commits an offence if—

    (a) he knows or suspects that a disclosure falling within section 337 or 338 has been made, and

    (b) he makes a disclosure which is likely to prejudice any investigation which might be conducted following the disclosure referred to in paragraph (a).

(2) But a person does not commit an offence under subsection (1) if—

    (a) he did not know or suspect that the disclosure was likely to be prejudicial as mentioned in subsection (1);

---

[16] Amended by Serious Organised Crime and Police Act 2005.
[17] Amended by the Serious Organised Crime and Police Act 2005.

(b) the disclosure is made in carrying out a function he has relating to the enforcement of any provision of this Act or of any other enactment relating to criminal conduct or benefit from criminal conduct;

(c) he is a professional legal adviser and the disclosure falls within subsection (3).

(3) A disclosure falls within this subsection if it is a disclosure—

(a) to (or to a representative of) a client of the professional legal adviser in connection with the giving by the adviser of legal advice to the client, or

(b) to any person in connection with legal proceedings or contemplated legal proceedings.

(4) But a disclosure does not fall within subsection (3) if it is made with the intention of furthering a criminal purpose.

334 Penalties

(1) A person guilty of an offence under section 327, 328 or 329 is liable—

(a) on summary conviction, to imprisonment for a term not exceeding six months or to a fine not exceeding the statutory maximum or to both, or

(b) on conviction on indictment, to imprisonment for a term not exceeding 14 years or to a fine or to both.

(2) A person guilty of an offence under section 330, 331, 332 or 333 is liable—

(a) on summary conviction, to imprisonment for a term not exceeding six months or to a fine not exceeding the statutory maximum or to both, or

(b) on conviction on indictment, to imprisonment for a term not exceeding five years or to a fine or to both.

[(3) A person guilty of an offence under section 339(1A) is liable on summary conviction to a fine not exceeding level 5 on the standard scale.]¹⁸

335 Appropriate consent

(1) The appropriate consent is—

(a) the consent of a nominated officer to do a prohibited act if an authorised disclosure is made to the nominated officer;

(b) the consent of a constable to do a prohibited act if an authorised disclosure is made to a constable;

(c) the consent of a customs officer to do a prohibited act if an authorised disclosure is made to a customs officer.

(2) A person must be treated as having the appropriate consent if—

(a) he makes an authorised disclosure to a constable or a customs officer, and

(b) the condition in subsection (3) or the condition in subsection (4) is satisfied.

(3) The condition is that before the end of the notice period he does not receive notice from a constable or customs officer that consent to the doing of the act is refused.

(4) The condition is that—

(a) before the end of the notice period he receives notice from a constable or customs officer that consent to the doing of the act is refused, and

(b) the moratorium period has expired.

(5) The notice period is the period of seven working days starting with the first working day after the person makes the disclosure.

(6) The moratorium period is the period of 31 days starting with the day on which the person receives notice that consent to the doing of the act is refused.

(7) A working day is a day other than a Saturday, a Sunday, Christmas Day, Good Friday or a day which is a bank holiday under the Banking and Financial Dealings Act 1971 (c. 80) in the part of the United Kingdom in which the person is when he makes the disclosure.

---

¹⁸ Inserted by the Serious Organised Crime and Police Act 2005.

(8) References to a prohibited act are to an act mentioned in section 327(1), 328(1) or 329(1) (as the case may be).

(9) A nominated officer is a person nominated to receive disclosures under section 338.

(10) Subsections (1) to (4) apply for the purposes of this Part.

336 Nominated officer: consent

(1) A nominated officer must not give the appropriate consent to the doing of a prohibited act unless the condition in subsection (2), the condition in subsection (3) or the condition in subsection (4) is satisfied.

(2) The condition is that—
  (a) he makes a disclosure that property is criminal property to a person authorised for the purposes of this Part by the Director General of the [Serious Organised Crime Agency],[19] and
  (b) such a person gives consent to the doing of the act.

(3) The condition is that—
  (a) he makes a disclosure that property is criminal property to a person authorised for the purposes of this Part by the Director General of the [Serious Organised Crime Agency],[20] and
  (b) before the end of the notice period he does not receive notice from such a person that consent to the doing of the act is refused.

(4) The condition is that—
  (a) he makes a disclosure that property is criminal property to a person authorised for the purposes of this Part by the Director General of the [Serious Organised Crime Agency],[21]
  (b) before the end of the notice period he receives notice from such a person that consent to the doing of the act is refused, and
  (c) the moratorium period has expired.

(5) A person who is a nominated officer commits an offence if—
  (a) he gives consent to a prohibited act in circumstances where none of the conditions in subsections (2), (3) and (4) is satisfied, and
  (b) he knows or suspects that the act is a prohibited act.

(6) A person guilty of such an offence is liable—
  (a) on summary conviction, to imprisonment for a term not exceeding six months or to a fine not exceeding the statutory maximum or to both, or
  (b) on conviction on indictment, to imprisonment for a term not exceeding five years or to a fine or to both.

(7) The notice period is the period of seven working days starting with the first working day after the nominated officer makes the disclosure.

(8) The moratorium period is the period of 31 days starting with the day on which the nominated officer is given notice that consent to the doing of the act is refused.

(9) A working day is a day other than a Saturday, a Sunday, Christmas Day, Good Friday or a day which is a bank holiday under the Banking and Financial Dealings Act 1971 (c. 80) in the part of the United Kingdom in which the nominated officer is when he gives the appropriate consent.

(10) References to a prohibited act are to an act mentioned in section 327(1), 328(1) or 329(1) (as the case may be).

(11) A nominated officer is a person nominated to receive disclosures under section 338.

337 Protected disclosures

(1) A disclosure which satisfies the following three conditions is not to be taken to breach any restriction on the disclosure of information (however imposed).

---

[19] Amended by the Serious Organised Crime and Police Act 2005.
[20] Amended by the Serious Organised Crime and Police Act 2005.
[21] Amended by the Serious Organised Crime and Police Act 2005.

(2) The first condition is that the information or other matter disclosed came to the person making the disclosure (the discloser) in the course of his trade, profession, business or employment.

(3) The second condition is that the information or other matter—

(a) causes the discloser to know or suspect, or

(b) gives him reasonable grounds for knowing or suspecting, that another person is engaged in money laundering.

(4) The third condition is that the disclosure is made to a constable, a customs officer or a nominated officer as soon as is practicable after the information or other matter comes to the discloser.

[(4A) Where a disclosure consists of a disclosure protected under subsection (1) and a disclosure of either or both of—

(a) the identity of the other person mentioned in subsection (3), and

(b) the whereabouts of property forming the subject-matter of the money laundering that the discloser knows or suspects, or has reasonable grounds for knowing or suspecting, that other person to be engaged in, the disclosure of the thing mentioned in paragraph (a) or (b) (as well as the disclosure protected under subsection (1) is not to be taken to breach any restriction on the disclosure of information (however imposed).][22]

(5) A disclosure to a nominated officer is a disclosure which—

(a) is made to a person nominated by the discloser's employer to receive disclosures under [section 330 or][23] this section, and

(b) is made in the course of the discloser's employment [. . .][24]

338 Authorised disclosures

(1) For the purposes of this Part a disclosure is authorised if—

(a) it is a disclosure to a constable, a customs officer or a nominated officer by the alleged offender that property is criminal property,

(b) [. . .][25] and

(c) the first[, second or third][26] condition set out below is satisfied.

(2) The first condition is that the disclosure is made before the alleged offender does the prohibited act.

[(2A) The second condition is that—

(a) the disclosure is made while the alleged offender is doing the prohibited act,

(b) he began to do the act at a time when, because he did not then know or suspect that the property constituted or represented a person's benefit from criminal conduct, the act was not a prohibited act, and

(c) the disclosure is made on his own initiative and as soon as is practicable after he first knows or suspects that the property constitutes or represents a person's benefit from criminal conduct.][27]

(3) The [third][28] condition is that—

(a) the disclosure is made after the alleged offender does the prohibited act,

(b) there is a good reason for his failure to make the disclosure before he did the act, and

(c) the disclosure is made on his own initiative and as soon as it is practicable for him to make it.

(4) An authorised disclosure is not to be taken to breach any restriction on the disclosure of information (however imposed).

[22] Inserted by the Serious Organised Crime and Police Act 2005.
[23] Amended by the Serious Organised Crime and Police Act 2005.
[24] Repealed by the Serious Organised Crime and Police Act 2005.
[25] Repealed by the Serious Organised Crime and Police Act 2005.
[26] Amended by the Serious Organised Crime and Police Act 2005.
[27] Inserted by the Serious Organised Crime and Police Act 2005.
[28] Amended by the Serious Organised Crime and Police Act 2005.

(5) A disclosure to a nominated officer is a disclosure which—

    (a) is made to a person nominated by the alleged offender's employer to receive authorised disclo-sures, and

    (b) is made in the course of the alleged offender's employment [. . .]²⁹

(6) References to the prohibited act are to an act mentioned in section 327(1), 328(1) or 329(1) (as the case may be).

339 Form and manner of disclosures

(1) The Secretary of State may by order prescribe the form and manner in which a disclosure under section 330, 331, 332 or 338 must be made.

[(1A) A person commits an offence if he makes a disclosure under section 330, 331, 332 or 338 otherwise than in the form prescribed under subsection (1) or otherwise than in the manner so prescribed.

(1B) But a person does not commit an offence under subsection (1A) if he has a reasonable excuse for making the disclosure otherwise than in the form prescribed under subsection (1) or (as the case may be) otherwise than in the manner so prescribed.

(2) The power under subsection (1) to prescribe the form in which a disclosure must be made includes power to provide for the form to include a request to a person making a disclosure that the person provide information specified or described in the form if he has not provided it in making the disclosure.

(3) Where under subsection (2) a request is included in a form prescribed under subsection (1), the form must—

    (a) state that there is no obligation to comply with the request, and

    (b) explain the protection conferred by subsection (4) on a person who complies with the request.]³⁰

(4) A disclosure made in pursuance of a request under subsection (2) is not to be taken to breach any restriction on the disclosure of information (however imposed).

(5) [. . .]³¹

(6) [. . .]³²

(7) Subsection (2) does not apply to a disclosure made to a nominated officer.

[339A Threshold amounts

(1) This section applies for the purposes of sections 327(2C), 328(5) and 329(2C).

(2) The threshold amount for acts done by a deposit-taking body in operating an account is £250 unless a higher amount is specified under the following provisions of this section (in which event it is that higher amount).

(3) An officer of Revenue and Customs, or a constable, may specify the threshold amount for acts done by a deposit-taking body in operating an account—

    (a) when he gives consent, or gives notice refusing consent, to the deposit-taking body's doing of an act mentioned in section 327(1), 328(1) or 329(1) in opening, or operating, the account or a related account, or

    (b) on a request from the deposit-taking body.

(4) Where the threshold amount for acts done in operating an account is specified under subsection (3) or this subsection, an officer of Revenue and Customs, or a constable, may vary the amount (whether on a request from the deposit-taking body or otherwise) by specifying a different amount.

---

²⁹ Repealed by the Serious Organised Crime and Police Act 2005.
³⁰ Amended by the Serious Organised Crime and Police Act 2005.
³¹ Repealed by the Serious Organised Crime and Police Act 2005.
³² Repealed by the Serious Organised Crime and Police Act 2005.

(5) Different threshold amounts may be specified under subsections (3) and (4) for different acts done in operating the same account.

(6) The amount specified under subsection (3) or (4) as the threshold amount for acts done in operating an account must, when specified, not be less than the amount specified in subsection (2).

(7) The Secretary of State may by order vary the amount for the time being specified in subsection (2).

(8) For the purposes of this section, an account is related to another if each is maintained with the same deposit-taking body and there is a person who, in relation to each account, is the person or one of the persons entitled to instruct the body as respects the operation of the account.][33]

340 Interpretation

(1) This section applies for the purposes of this Part.

(2) Criminal conduct is conduct which—

    (a) constitutes an offence in any part of the United Kingdom, or

    (b) would constitute an offence in any part of the United Kingdom if it occurred there.

(3) Property is criminal property if—

    (a) it constitutes a person's benefit from criminal conduct or it represents such a benefit (in whole or part and whether directly or indirectly), and

    (b) the alleged offender knows or suspects that it constitutes or represents such a benefit.

(4) It is immaterial—

    (a) who carried out the conduct;

    (b) who benefited from it;

    (c) whether the conduct occurred before or after the passing of this Act.

(5) A person benefits from conduct if he obtains property as a result of or in connection with the conduct.

(6) If a person obtains a pecuniary advantage as a result of or in connection with conduct, he is to be taken to obtain as a result of or in connection with the conduct a sum of money equal to the value of the pecuniary advantage.

(7) References to property or a pecuniary advantage obtained in connection with conduct include references to property or a pecuniary advantage obtained in both that connection and some other.

(8) If a person benefits from conduct his benefit is the property obtained as a result of or in connection with the conduct.

(9) Property is all property wherever situated and includes—

    (a) money;

    (b) all forms of property, real or personal, heritable or moveable;

    (c) things in action and other intangible or incorporeal property.

(10) The following rules apply in relation to property—

    (a) property is obtained by a person if he obtains an interest in it;

    (b) references to an interest, in relation to land in England and Wales or Northern Ireland, are to any legal estate or equitable interest or power;

    (c) references to an interest, in relation to land in Scotland, are to any estate, interest, servitude or other heritable right in or over land, including a heritable security;

    (d) references to an interest, in relation to property other than land, include references to a right (including a right to possession).

(11) Money laundering is an act which—

    (a) constitutes an offence under section 327, 328 or 329,

    (b) constitutes an attempt, conspiracy or incitement to commit an offence specified in paragraph (a),

    (c) constitutes aiding, abetting, counselling or procuring the commission of an offence specified in paragraph (a), or

---

[33] Inserted by the Serious Organised Crime and Police Act 2005.

(d) would constitute an offence specified in paragraph (a), (b) or (c) if done in the United Kingdom.

(12) For the purposes of a disclosure to a nominated officer—

(a) references to a person's employer include any body, association or organisation (including a voluntary organisation) in connection with whose activities the person exercises a function (whether or not for gain or reward), and

(b) references to employment must be construed accordingly.

(13) References to a constable include references to a person authorised for the purposes of this Part by the Director General of the [Serious Organised Crime Agency.][34]

[(14) 'Deposit-taking body' means—

(a) a business which engages in the activity of accepting deposits, or

(b) the National Savings Bank.][35]

---

[34] Amended by the Serious Organised Crime and Police Act 2005.
[35] Inserted by the Serious Organised Crime and Police Act 2005.

APPENDIX 7

Fraud Protocol: Control and Management of Heavy Fraud and Other Complex Criminal Cases

A Protocol issued by the Lord Chief Justice of England and Wales—22 March 2005

INTRODUCTION

There is a broad consensus that the length of fraud and trials of other complex crimes must be controlled within proper bounds in order:

(i) To enable the jury to retain and assess the evidence which they have heard. If the trial is so long that the jury cannot do this, then the trial is not fair either to the prosecution or the defence.

(ii) To make proper use of limited public resources: see *Jisl* [2004] EWCA Crim 696 at [113]–[121].

There is also a consensus that no trial should be permitted to exceed a given period, save in exceptional circumstances; some favour 3 months, others an outer limit of 6 months.

Whatever view is taken, it is essential that the current length of trials is brought back to an acceptable and proper duration.

This Protocol supplements the Criminal Procedure Rules and summarises good practice which experience has shown may assist in bringing about some reduction in the length of trials of fraud and other crimes that result in complex trials. Flexibility of application of this Protocol according to the needs of each case is essential; it is designed to inform but not to prescribe.

This Protocol is primarily directed towards cases which are likely to last eight weeks or longer. It should also be followed, however, in all cases estimated to last more than four weeks. This Protocol applies to trials by jury, but many of the principles will be applicable if trials without a jury are permitted under s. 43 of the Criminal Justice Act 2003.

The best handling technique for a long case is continuous management by an experienced Judge nominated for the purpose.

It is intended that this Protocol be kept up to date; any further practices or techniques found to be successful in the management of complex cases should be notified to the office of the Lord Chief Justice.

A. THE INVESTIGATION

(i) The role of the prosecuting authority and the judge

(a) Unlike other European countries, a judge in England and Wales does not directly control the investigative process; that is the responsibility of the Investigating Authority, and in turn the Prosecuting Authority and the prosecution advocate. Experience has shown that a prosecution lawyer (who must be of sufficient experience and who will be a member of the team at trial) and the prosecution advocate, if different, should be involved in the investigation as soon as it appears that a heavy fraud trial or other complex criminal trial is likely to ensue. The costs that this early preparation will incur will be saved many times over in the long run.

(b) The judge can and should exert a substantial and beneficial influence by making it clear that, generally speaking, trials should be kept within manageable limits. In most cases 3 months should be the target outer limit, but there will be cases where a duration of 6 months, or in exceptional circumstances, even longer may be inevitable.

(ii) Interviews

(a) At present many interviews are too long and too unstructured. This has a knock-on effect on the length of trials. Interviews should provide an opportunity for suspects to respond to the allegations against them. They should not be an occasion to discuss every document in the case. It should become clear from judicial rulings that interviews of this kind are a waste of resources.

(b) The suspect must be given sufficient information before or at the interview to enable them to meet the questions fairly and answer them honestly; the information is not provided to give the suspect the opportunity to manufacture a false story which fits undisputable facts.

(c) It is often helpful if the principal documents are provided either in advance of the interview or shown as the interview progresses; asking detailed questions about events a considerable period in the past without reference to the documents is often not very helpful.

(iii) The prosecution and defence teams

(a) *The Prosecution Team*

While instructed, it is for the lead advocate for the prosecution to take all necessary decisions in the presentation and general conduct of the prosecution case in court. The prosecution lead advocate will be treated by the court as having that responsibility.

However, in relation to policy decisions, the lead advocate for the prosecution must not give an indication or undertaking which binds the prosecution without first discussing the issue with the Director of the Prosecuting authority or other senior officer.

'Policy' decisions should be understood as referring to non-evidential decisions on: the acceptance of pleas of guilty to lesser counts or groups of counts or available alternatives: offering no evidence on particular counts; consideration of a re-trial; whether to lodge an appeal; certification of a point of law; and the withdrawal of the prosecution as a whole.

(for further information see the 'Farquharson Guidelines' on the role and responsibilities of the prosecution advocate).

(b) *The Defence Team*

In each case, the lead advocate for the defence will be treated by the court as having responsibility to the court for the presentation and general conduct of the defence case.

(c) In each case, a case progression officer must be assigned by the court, prosecution and defence from the time of the first hearing when directions are given (as referred to in paragraph 3 (iii)) until the conclusion of the trial.

(d) In each case where there are multiple defendants, the LSC will need to consider carefully the extent and level of representation necessary.

(iv) Initial consideration of the length of a case

If the prosecutor in charge of the case from the Prosecuting Authority or the lead advocate for the prosecution consider that the case as formulated is likely to last more than 8 weeks, the case should be referred in accordance with arrangements made by the Prosecuting Authority to a more senior prosecutor. The senior prosecutor will consider whether it is desirable for the case to be prosecuted in that way or whether some steps might be taken to reduce its likely length, whilst at the same time ensuring that the public interest is served.

Any case likely to last 6 months or more must be referred to the Director of the Prosecuting Authority so that similar considerations can take place.

(v) Notification of cases likely to last more than 8 weeks

Special arrangements will be put in place for the early notification by the CPS and other Prosecuting Authorities, to the LSC and to a single designated officer of the Court in each Region (Circuit) of any case which the CPS or other Prosecuting Authority consider likely to last over 8 weeks.

(vi) Venue

The court will allocate such cases and other complex cases likely to last 4 weeks or more to a specific venue suitable for the trial in question, taking into account the convenience to witnesses, the parties, the availability of time at that location, and all other relevant considerations.

B. Designation of the Trial Judge

(i) The assignment of a judge

(a) In any complex case which is expected to last more than four weeks, the trial judge will be assigned under the direction of the Presiding Judges at the earliest possible moment.

(b) Thereafter the assigned judge should manage that case 'from cradle to grave'; it is essential that the same judge manages the case from the time of his assignment and that arrangements are made for him to be able to do so. It is recognised that in certain court centres with a large turn-over of heavy cases (e.g. Southwark) this objective is more difficult to achieve. But in those court centres there are teams of specialist judges, who are more readily able to handle cases which the assigned judge cannot continue with because of unexpected events; even at such courts, there must be no exception to the principle that one judge must handle all the pre-trial hearings until the case is assigned to another judge.

C. Case Management

(i) Objectives

(a) The number, length and organisation of case management hearings will, of course, depend critically on the circumstances and complexity of the individual case. However, thorough, well-prepared and extended case management hearings will save court time and costs overall.

(b) Effective case management of heavy fraud and other complex criminal cases requires the judge to have a much more detailed grasp of the case than may be necessary for many other Plea and Case Management Hearings (PCMHs). Though it is for the judge in each case to decide how much pre-reading time he needs so that the judge is on top of the case, it is not always a sensible use of judicial time to allocate a series of reading days, during which the judge sits alone in his room, working through numerous boxes of ring binders.

See paragraph 3 (iv) (e) below.

(ii) Fixing the trial date

Although it is important that the trial date should be fixed as early as possible, this may not always be the right course. There are two principal alternatives:

(a) The trial date should be fixed at the first opportunity—i.e. at the first (and usually short) directions hearing referred to in subparagraph (iii). From then on everyone must work to that date. All orders and pre-trial steps should be timetabled to fit in with that date.

All advocates and the judge should take note of this date, in the expectation that the trial will proceed on the date determined.

(b) The trial date should not be fixed until the issues have been explored at a full case management hearing (referred to in subparagraph (iv), after the advocates on both sides have done some serious work on the case. Only then can the length of the trial be estimated.

Which is apposite must depend on the circumstances of each case, but the earlier it is possible to fix a trial date, by reference to a proper estimate and a timetable set by reference to the trial date, the better.

It is generally to be expected that once a trial is fixed on the basis of the estimate provided, that it will be **increased** if, and only if, the party seeking to extend the time justifies why the original estimate is no longer appropriate.

(iii) The first hearing for the giving of initial directions

At the first opportunity the assigned judge should hold a short hearing to give initial directions. The directions on this occasion might well include:

(a) That there should be a full case management hearing on, or commencing on, a specified future date by which time the parties will be properly prepared for a meaningful hearing and the defence will have full instructions.

(b) That the prosecution should provide an outline written statement of the prosecution case at least one week in advance of that case management hearing, outlining in simple terms:

(i) The key facts on which it relies.

(ii) The key evidence by which the prosecution seeks to prove the facts.

The statement must be sufficient to permit the judge to understand the case and for the defence to appreciate the basic elements of its case against each defendant. The prosecution may be invited to highlight the key points of the case orally at the case management hearing by way of a short mini-opening. The outline statement should not be considered binding, but it will serve the essential purpose in telling the judge, and everyone else, what the case is really about and identifying the key issues.

(c) That a core reading list and core bundle for the case management hearing should be delivered at least one week in advance.

(d) Preliminary directions about disclosure: see paragraph 4.

(iv) The first Case Management Hearing

(a) At the first case management hearing:

(i) The prosecution advocate should be given the opportunity to highlight any points from the prosecution outline statement of case (which will have been delivered at least a week in advance).

(ii) Each defence advocate should be asked to outline the defence.

If the defence advocate is not in a position to say what is in issue and what is not in issue, then the case management hearing can be adjourned for a short and limited time and to a fixed date to enable the advocate to take instructions; such an adjournment should only be necessary in exceptional circumstances, as the defence advocate should be properly instructed by the time of the first case management hearing and in any event is under an obligation to take sufficient instructions to fulfil the obligations contained in s 33–39 of Criminal Justice Act 2003.

(b) There should then be a real dialogue between the judge and all advocates for the purpose of identifying:

(i) The focus of the prosecution case.

(ii) The common ground.

(iii) The real issues in the case. (Rule 3.2 of the Criminal Procedure Rules.)

(c) The judge will try to generate a spirit of co-operation between the court and the advocates on all sides. The expeditious conduct of the trial and a focussing on the real issues must be in the interests of **all** parties. It cannot be in the interests of any defendant for his good points to become lost in a welter of uncontroversial or irrelevant evidence.

(d) In many fraud cases the primary facts are not seriously disputed. The real issue is what each defendant knew and whether that defendant was dishonest. Once the judge has identified what is in dispute and what is not in dispute, the judge can then discuss with the advocate how the trial should be structured, what can be dealt with by admissions or agreed facts, what uncontroversial matters should be proved by concise oral evidence, what timetabling can be required under Rule 3.10 Criminal Procedure Rules, and other directions.

(e) In particularly heavy fraud or complex cases the judge may possibly consider it necessary to allocate a whole week for a case management hearing. If that week is used wisely, many further weeks of trial time can be saved. In the gaps which will inevitably arise during that week (for example while the advocates are exploring matters raised by the judge) the judge can do a substantial amount of informed reading. The case has come 'alive' at this stage. Indeed, in a really heavy fraud case, if the judge fixes one or more case management hearings on this scale, there will be need for fewer formal reading days. Moreover a huge amount can be achieved in the pre-trial stage, if all trial advocates are gathered in the same place, focussing on the case **at the same time**, for several days consecutively.

(f) Requiring the defence to serve proper case statements may enable the court to identify:
   (i) what is common ground and
   (ii) the real issues.
   It is therefore important that proper defence case statements be provided as required by the Criminal Procedure Rules; Judges will use the powers contained in ss 28–34 of the Criminal Proceedings and Evidence Act 1996 (and the corresponding provisions of the CJA 1987, ss. 33 and following of the Criminal Justice Act 2003) and the Criminal Procedure Rules to ensure that realistic defence case statements are provided.

(g) Likewise this objective may be achieved by requiring the prosecution to serve draft admissions by a specified date and by requiring the defence to respond within a specified number of weeks.

(v) Further Case Management Hearings

(a) The date of the next case management hearing should be fixed at the conclusion of the hearing so that there is no delay in having to fix the date through listing offices, clerks and others.

(b) If one is looking at a trial which threatens to run for months, pre-trial case management on an intensive scale is essential.

(vi) Consideration of the length of the trial

(a) Case management on the above lines, the procedure set out in paragraph 1 (iv), may still be insufficient to reduce the trial to a manageable length; generally a trial of 3 months should be the target, but there will be cases where a duration of 6 months or, in exceptional circumstances, even longer may be inevitable.

(b) If the trial is not estimated to be within a manageable length, it will be necessary for the judge to consider what steps should be taken to reduce the length of the trial, whilst still ensuring that the prosecution has the opportunity of placing the full criminality before the court.

(c) To assist the judge in this task,
   (i) The lead advocate for the prosecution should be asked to explain why the prosecution have rejected a shorter way of proceeding; they may also be asked to divide the case into sections of evidence and explain the scope of each section and the need for each section.
   (ii) The lead advocates for the prosecution and for the defence should be prepared to put forward in writing, if requested, ways in which a case estimated to last more than three months can be shortened, including possible severance of counts or defendants, exclusions of sections of the case or of evidence or areas of the case where admissions can be made.

(d) One course the judge may consider is pruning the indictment by omitting certain charges and/or by omitting certain defendants. The judge must not usurp the function of the prosecution in this regard, and he must bear in mind that he will, at the outset, know less about the case than the advocates. The aim is to achieve fairness to all parties.

(e) Nevertheless, the judge does have two methods of pruning available for use in appropriate circumstances:
   (i) Persuading the prosecution that it is not worthwhile pursuing certain charges and/or certain defendants.

(ii) Severing the indictment. Severance for reasons of case management alone is perfectly proper, although judges should have regard to any representations made by the prosecution that severance would weaken their case. Indeed the judge's hand will be strengthened in this regard by rule 1.1 (2) (g) of the Criminal Procedure Rules. However, before using what may be seen as a blunt instrument, the judge should insist on seeing full defence statements of all affected defendants. Severance may be unfair to the prosecution if, for example, there is a cut-throat defence in prospect. For example, the defence of the principal defendant may be that the defendant relied on the advice of his accountant or solicitor that what was happening was acceptable. The defence of the professional may be that he gave no such advice. Against that background, it might be unfair to the prosecution to order separate trials of the two defendants.

(vii) The exercise of the powers

(a) The Criminal Procedure Rules require the court to take a more active part in case management. These are salutary provisions which should bring to an end interminable criminal trials of the kind which the Court of Appeal criticised in *Jisl* [2004] EWCA 696 at [113]–[121].

(b) Nevertheless these salutary provisions do not have to be used on every occasion. Where the advocates have done their job properly, by narrowing the issues, pruning the evidence and so forth, it may be quite inappropriate for the judge to "weigh in" and start cutting out more evidence or more charges of his own volition. It behoves the judge to make a careful assessment of the degree of judicial intervention which is warranted in each case.

(c) The note of caution in the previous paragraph is supported by certain experience which has been gained of the Civil Procedure Rules (on which the Criminal Procedure Rules are based). The CPR contain valuable and efficacious provisions for case management by the judge on his own initiative which have led to huge savings of court time and costs.

Surveys by the Law Society have shown that the CPR have been generally welcomed by court users and the profession, but there have been reported to have been isolated instances in which the parties to civil litigation have faithfully complied with both the letter and the spirit of the CPR, and have then been aggrieved by what was perceived to be unnecessary intermeddling by the court.

(viii) Expert Evidence

(a) Early identification of the subject matter of expert evidence to be adduced by the prosecution and the defence should be made as early as possible, preferably at the directions hearing.

(b) Following the exchange of expert evidence, any areas of disagreement should be identified and a direction should generally be made requiring the experts to meet and prepare, after discussion, a joint statement identifying points of agreement and contention and areas where the prosecution is put to proof on matters of which a positive case to the contrary is not advanced by the defence. After the statement has been prepared it should be served on the court, the prosecution and the defence. In some cases, it might be appropriate to provide that to the jury.

(ix) Surveillance Evidence

(a) Where a prosecution is based upon many months' observation or surveillance evidence and it appears that it is capable of effective presentation based on a shorter period, the advocate should be required to justify the evidence of such observations before it is permitted to be adduced, either substantially or in its entirety.

(b) Schedules should be provided to cover as much of the evidence as possible and admissions sought.

D. DISCLOSURE

In fraud cases the volume of documentation obtained by the prosecution is liable to be immense. The problems of disclosure are intractable and have the potential to disrupt the entire trial process.

(i) The prosecution lawyer (and the prosecution advocate if different) brought in at the outset, as set out in paragraph 1 (i)(a), each have a continuing responsibility to discharge the prosecution's duty of disclosure, either personally or by delegation, in accordance with the Attorney General's Guidelines on Disclosure.

(ii) The prosecution should only disclose those documents which are relevant (i.e. likely to assist the defence or undermine the prosecution—see s. 3 (1) of CPIA 1996 and the provisions of the CJA 2003).

(iii) It is almost always undesirable to give the 'warehouse key' to the defence for two reasons:

(a) This amounts to an abrogation of the responsibility of the prosecution;

(b) The defence solicitors may spend a disproportionate amount of time and incur disproportionate costs trawling through a morass of documents.

The Judge should therefore try and ensure that disclosure is limited to what is likely to assist the defence or undermine the prosecution.

(iv) At the outset the judge should set a timetable for dealing with disclosure issues. In particular, the judge should fix a date by which all defence applications for specific disclosure must be made. In this regard, it is relevant that the defendants are likely to be intelligent people, who know their own business affairs and who (for the most part) will know what documents or categories of documents they are looking for.

(v) At the outset (and before the cut-off date for specific disclosure applications) the judge should ask the defence to indicate what documents they are interested in and from what source. A general list is not an acceptable response to this request. The judge should insist upon a list which is specific, manageable and realistic. The judge may also require justification of any request.

(vi) In non-fraud cases, the same considerations apply, but some may be different:

(a) It is not possible to approach many non-fraud cases on the basis that the defendant knows what is there or what they are looking for. But on the other hand this should not be turned into an excuse for a 'fishing expedition'; the judge should insist on knowing the issue to which a request for disclosure applies.

(b) If the bona fides of the investigation is called into question, a judge will be concerned to see that there has been independent and effective appraisal of the documents contained in the disclosure schedule and that its contents are adequate.

In appropriate cases where this issue has arisen and there are grounds which show there is a real issue, consideration should be given to receiving evidence on oath from the senior investigating officer at an early case management hearing.

E. Abuse of Process

(i) Applications to stay or dismiss for abuse of process have become a normal feature of heavy and complex cases. Such applications may be based upon delay and the health of defendants.

(ii) Applications in relation to absent special circumstances tend to be unsuccessful and not to be pursued on appeal. For this reason there is comparatively little Court of Appeal guidance: but see: *Harris and Howells* [2003] EWCA Crim 486. It should be noted that abuse of process is not there to discipline the prosecution or the police.

(iii) The arguments on both sides must be reduced to writing. Oral evidence is seldom relevant.

(iv) The judge should direct full written submissions (rather than 'skeleton arguments') on any abuse application in accordance with a timetable set by him; these should identify any element of prejudice the defendant is alleged to have suffered.

(v) The Judge should normally aim to conclude the hearing within an absolute maximum limit of one day, if necessary in accordance with a timetable. The parties should therefore prepare their papers on this basis and not expect the judge to allow the oral hearing to be anything more than an occasion to highlight concisely their arguments and answer any questions the court may have of them; applications will not be allowed to drag on.

F. The Trial

(i) The particular hazard of heavy fraud trials

A heavy fraud or other complex trial has the potential to lose direction and focus. This is a disaster for three reasons:

(a) The jury will lose track of the evidence, thereby prejudicing both prosecution and defence.

(b) The burden on the defendants, the judge and indeed all involved will become intolerable.

(c) Scarce public resources are wasted. Other prosecutions are delayed or—worse—may never happen. Fraud which is detected but not prosecuted (for resource reasons) undermines confidence.

(ii) Judicial mastery of the case

(a) It is necessary for the judge to exercise firm control over the conduct of the trial at all stages.

(b) In order to do this the judge must read the witness statements and the documents, so that the judge can discuss case management issues with the advocates on—almost—an equal footing.

(c) To this end, the judge should not set aside weeks or even days for pre-reading (see paragraph 3 (i)(b) above). Hopefully the judge will have gained a good grasp of the evidence during the case management hearings. Nevertheless, realistic reading time must be provided for the judge in advance of trial.

(d) The role of the judge in a heavy fraud or other complex criminal trial is different from his/her role in a "conventional" criminal trial. So far as possible, the judge should be freed from other duties and burdens, so that he/she can give the high degree of commitment which a heavy fraud trial requires. This will pay dividends in terms of saving weeks or months of court time.

(iii) The order of the evidence

(a) By the outset of the trial at the latest (and in most cases very much earlier) the judge must be provided with a schedule, showing the sequence of prosecution (and in an appropriate case defence) witnesses and the dates upon which they are expected to be called. This can only be prepared by discussion between prosecution and defence which the judge should expect, and say he/she expects, to take place: See: Criminal Procedure Rule 3.10.

The schedule should, in so far as it relates to Prosecution witnesses, be developed in consultation with the witnesses, via the Witness Care Units, and with consideration given to their personal needs. Copies of the schedule should be provided for the Witness Service.

(b) The schedule should be kept under review by the trial judge and by the parties. If a case is running behind or ahead of schedule, each witness affected must be advised by the party who is calling that witness at the earliest opportunity.

(c) If an excessive amount of time is allowed for any witness, the judge can ask why. The judge may probe with the advocates whether the time envisaged for the evidence-in-chief or cross-examination (as the case may be) of a particular witness is really necessary.

(iv) Case management sessions

(a) The order of the evidence may have legitimately to be departed from. It will, however, be a useful tool for monitoring the progress of the case. There should be periodic case management sessions, during which the judge engages the advocates upon a stocktaking exercise: asking, amongst other questions, 'where are we going?' and 'what is the relevance of the next three witnesses?'. This will be a valuable means of keeping the case on track. Rule 3.10 of the Criminal Procedure Rules will again assist the judge.

(b) The judge may wish to consider issuing the occasional use of 'case management notes' to the advocates, in order to set out the judge's tentative views on where the trial may be going off

475

track, which areas of future evidence are relevant and which may have become irrelevant (e.g. because of concessions, admissions in cross-examination and so forth). Such notes from the judge plus written responses from the advocates can, cautiously used, provide a valuable focus for debate during the periodic case management reviews held during the course of the trial.

(v) Controlling prolix cross-examination

(a) Setting **rigid** time limits in advance for cross-examination is rarely appropriate—as experience has shown in civil cases; but a timetable is essential so that the judge can exercise control and so that there is a clear target to aim at for the completion of the evidence of each witness. Moreover the judge can and should indicate when cross-examination is irrelevant, unnecessary or time wasting. The judge may limit the time for further cross-examination of a particular witness.

(vi) Electronic presentation of evidence

(a) Electronic presentation of evidence (EPE) has the potential to save huge amounts of time in fraud and other complex criminal trials and should be used more widely.
(b) HMCS is providing facilities for the easier use of EPE with a standard audio visual facility. Effectively managed, the savings in court time achieved by EPE more than justify the cost.
(c) There should still be a core bundle of those documents to which frequent reference will be made during the trial. The jury may wish to mark that bundle or to refer back to particular pages as the evidence progresses. EPE can be used for presenting all documents not contained in the core bundle.
(d) Greater use of other modern forms of graphical presentations should be made wherever possible.

(vii) Use of interviews

The Judge should consider extensive editing of self serving interviews, even when the defence want the jury to hear them in their entirety; such interviews are not evidence of the truth of their contents but merely of the defendant's reaction to the allegation.

(viii) Jury Management

(a) The jury should be informed as early as possible in the case as to what the issues are in a manner directed by the Judge.
(b) The jury must be regularly updated as to the trial timetable and the progress of the trial, subject to warnings as to the predictability of the trial process.
(c) Legal argument should be heard at times that causes the least inconvenience to jurors.
(d) It is useful to consider with the advocates whether written directions should be given to the jury and, if so, in what form.

(ix) Maxwell hours

(a) Maxwell hours should only be permitted after careful consideration and consultation with the Presiding Judge.
(b) Considerations in favour include:
   (i) Legal argument can be accommodated without disturbing the jury;
   (ii) There is a better chance of a representative jury;
   (iii) Time is made available to the judge, advocates and experts to do useful work in the afternoons.
(c) Considerations against include:
   (i) The lengthening of trials and the consequent waste of court time;
   (ii) The desirability of making full use of the jury once they have arrived at court;
   (iii) Shorter trials tend to diminish the need for special provisions e.g. there are fewer difficulties in empanelling more representative juries;
   (iv) They are unavailable if any defendant is in custody.

(d) It may often be the case that a maximum of one day of Maxwell hours a week is sufficient; if so, it should be timetabled in advance to enable all submissions by advocates, supported by skeleton arguments served in advance, to be dealt with in the period after 1:30 pm on that day.

(x) Livenote

If Livenote is used, it is important that all users continue to take a note of the evidence, otherwise considerable time is wasted in detailed reading of the entire daily transcript.

G. OTHER ISSUES

(i) Defence representation and defence costs

(a) Applications for change in representation in complex trials need special consideration; the ruling of HH Judge Wakerley QC (as he then was) in *Asghar Ali* has been circulated by the JSB.

(b) Problems have arisen when the Legal Services Commission have declined to allow advocates or solicitors to do certain work; on occasions the matter has been raised with the judge managing or trying the case.

(c) The Legal Services Commission has provided guidance to judges on how they can obtain information from the LSC as to the reasons for their decisions; further information in relation to this can be obtained from *Nigel Field, Head of the Complex Crime Unit, Legal Services Commission, 29–37 Red Lion Street, London, WC1R 4PP*.

(ii) Assistance to the Judge

Experience has shown that in some very heavy cases, the judge's burden can be substantially offset with the provision of a Judicial Assistant or other support and assistance.

APPENDIX 8

Guidance on the Use of the Common Law Offence
of Conspiracy to Defraud

Summary

1. This guidance concerns the issues which the Attorney General asks prosecuting authorities in England and Wales to consider before using the common law offence of conspiracy to defraud, in the light of the implementation of the Fraud Act 2006. It may be supplemented by Departmental-specific guidance issued by individual Directors of the prosecuting authorities.

Background

2. When the Fraud Act 2006 comes into force on 15 January 2007, the prosecution will be able to use modern and flexible statutory offences of fraud. The 2006 Act replaces the deception offences contained in the Theft Acts 1968–1996 with a general offence of fraud that can be committed in three ways:
   - fraud by false representation;
   - fraud by failing to disclose information; and
   - fraud by abuse of position.

   It also introduces other offences which can be used in particular circumstances, notably;
   - new offences to tackle the possession and supply of articles for use in fraud; and
   - a new offence of fraudulent trading applicable to sole traders and other businesses not caught by the existing offence in section 458 of the Companies Act 1985.

3. The new offences are designed to catch behaviour that previously fell through gaps in the Theft Acts and could only be prosecuted as conspiracy to defraud. Indeed the Act is based on a Law Commission report (Cm 5560) which also recommended the abolition of the common law offence of conspiracy to defraud. The argument is that the offence is unfairly uncertain, and wide enough to have the potential to catch behaviour that should not be criminal. Furthermore it can seem anomalous that what is legal if performed by one person should be criminal if performed by many.

4. However, consultations showed a widespread view in favour of retention of common law conspiracy to defraud, and the Government decided to retain it for the meantime, but accepted the case for considering repeal in the longer term. Whether there is a continuing need for retention of the common law offence is one of the issues that will be addressed in the Home Office review of the operation of the Fraud Act 2006, which will take place 3 years after its implementation.

5. In 2003, 14,928 defendants were proceeded against in England and Wales for crimes of fraud; 1,018 of these were charged with the common law crime of conspiracy to defraud of which 44% were found guilty (compared with 71% for the statutory fraud offences).

   The expectation now is that the common law offence will be used to a significantly lesser extent once the Fraud Act 2006 has come into force.

Issues to be considered in using the common law offence

6. In selecting charges in fraud cases, the prosecutor should first consider:
   - whether the behaviour could be prosecuted under statute—whether under the Fraud Act 2006 or another Act or as a statutory conspiracy; and
   - whether the available statutory charges adequately reflect the gravity of the offence.

7. Statutory conspiracy to commit a substantive offence should be charged if the alleged agreement satisfies the definition in section 1 of the Criminal Law Act 1977, provided that there is no wider

dishonest objective that would be important to the presentation of the prosecution case in reflecting the gravity of the case.

8. Section 12 of the Criminal Justice Act 1987 provides that common law conspiracy to defraud may be charged even if the conduct agreed upon will involve the commission of a statutory offence. However, Lord Bingham said in *R v Rimmington* and *R v Goldstein* (2005) UKHL 63]:

   *'I would not go to the length of holding that conduct may never be lawfully prosecuted as a generally-expressed common law crime where it falls within the terms of a specific statutory provision, **but good practice and respect for the primacy of statute do in my judgment require that conduct falling within the terms of a specific statutory provision should be prosecuted under that provision unless there is good reason for doing otherwise.'***

9. In the Attorney General's view the common law charge may still be appropriate in the type of cases set out in paragraphs 12–15, but in order to understand the circumstances under which conspiracy to defraud is used **prosecutors should make a record of the reasons for preferring that charge.**

Records of decisions

10. Where a charge of common law conspiracy to defraud is proposed the case lawyer must consider and set out in writing in the review note:
    - how much such a charge will add to the amount of evidence likely to be called both by the prosecution and the defence; and
    - the justification for using the charge, and why specific statutory offences are inadequate or otherwise inappropriate.

    Thereafter, and before charge, the use of this charge should be specifically approved by a supervising lawyer experienced in fraud cases. Equivalent procedures to ensure proper consideration of the charge and recording of the decision should be applied by all prosecuting authorities in their case review processes.

11. Information from these records will be collected retrospectively for the review to be conducted in 3 years. It will enable the identification of where and why the common law offence has been under. It could then also form the basis for any future work on whether, and if so how, to replace the common law or whether it can simply and safely be repealed. It is expected that in 3 years the Government will be able to review the situation in the light of the practical operation not only of the new fraud offences, but of other relevant changes. These include the Lord Chief Justice's protocol on the control and management of heavy fraud cases, and the sample count provisions in the Domestic Violence, Crime and Victims Act 2004. Any actual or proposed changes to the law on assisting and encouraging crime in the light of the Law Commission's study of that issue *[Cm 6878, published in July 2006]* will also be taken into account.

A. Conduct that can More Effectively be Prosecuted as Conspiracy to Defraud

12. There may be cases where the interests of justice can only be served by presenting to a court an overall picture which cannot be achieved by charging a series of substantive offences or statutory conspiracies. Typically, such cases will involve some, but not necessarily all of the following:
    - evidence of several significant but different kinds of criminality;
    - several jurisdictions;
    - different types of victims, e.g. individuals, banks, web site administrators, credit card companies;
    - organised crime networks.

13. The proper presentation of such cases as statutory conspiracies could lead to:
    - large numbers of separate counts to reflect the different conspiracies;
    - severed trials for single or discrete groups of conspiracies;
    - evidence in one severed trial being deemed inadmissible in another.

14. If so, the consequences might be that no one court would receive a cohesive picture of the whole case which would allow sentencing on a proper basis. In contrast a single count of common law conspiracy to defraud might, in such circumstances, reflect the nature and extent of criminal conduct in a way that prosecuting the underlying statutory offences or conspiracies would fail to achieve.

B. Conduct that can Only be Prosecuted as Conspiracy to Defraud

15. Examples of such conduct might include but are not restricted to agreements to the following courses of action:
    - The dishonest obtaining of land and other property which cannot be stolen such as intellectual property not protected by the Copyright, Designs and Patents Act 1988 and the Trademarks Act 1994, and other confidential information. The Fraud Act will bite where there is intent to make a gain or cause a loss through false representation, failure to disclose information where there is a legal obligation to do so, or the abuse of position;
    - Dishonestly infringing another's right; for example the dishonest exploitation of another's patent in the absence of a legal duty to disclose information about its existence;
    - Where it is intended that the final offence be committed by someone outside the conspiracy; and
    - Cases where the accused cannot be proved to have had the necessary degree of knowledge of the substantive offence to be perpetrated;

HER MAJESTY'S ATTORNEY GENERAL

Dated this 9th day of January 2007

Attorney General's Chambers

9 BuckinghamGate

London SWIE 6JP

APPENDIX 9

Criminal Procedure Rules on Case Management
(Parts 1 and 3)

PART I
THE OVERRIDING OBJECTIVE

Contents of this Part

rule 1.1 The overriding objective

rule 1.2 The duty of the participants in a criminal case

rule 1.3 The application by the court of the overriding objective

1.1 The overriding objective

(1) The overriding objective of this new code is that criminal cases be dealt with justly.

(2) Dealing with a criminal case justly includes—
    (a) acquitting the innocent and convicting the guilty;
    (b) dealing with the prosecution and the defence fairly;
    (c) recognising the rights of a defendant, particularly those under Article 6 of the European Convention on Human Rights;
    (d) respecting the interests of witnesses, victims and jurors and keeping them informed of the progress of the case;
    (e) dealing with the case efficiently and expeditiously;
    (f) ensuring that appropriate information is available to the court when bail and sentence are considered; and
    (g) dealing with the case in ways that take into account—
        (i) the gravity of the offence alleged,
        (ii) the complexity of what is in issue,
        (iii) the severity of the consequences for the defendant and others affected, and
        (iv) the needs of other cases.

1.2 The duty of the participants in a criminal case

(1) Each participant, in the conduct of each case, must—
    (a) prepare and conduct the case in accordance with the overriding objective;
    (b) comply with these Rules, practice directions and directions made by the court; and
    (c) at once inform the court and all parties of any significant failure (whether or not that participant is responsible for that failure) to take any procedural step required by these Rules, any practice direction or any direction of the court. A failure is significant if it might hinder the court in furthering the overriding objective.

(2) Anyone involved in any way with a criminal case is a participant in its conduct for the purposes of this rule.

1.3 The application by the court of the overriding objective

The court must further the overriding objective in particular when—
    (a) exercising any power given to it by legislation (including these Rules);
    (b) applying any practice direction; or
    (c) interpreting any rule or practice direction.

Part 3

Case Management

Contents of this Part

3.1 The scope of this Part

This Part applies to the management of each case in a magistrates' court and in the Crown Court (including an appeal to the Crown Court) until the conclusion of that case.

[Note. Rules that apply to procedure in the Court of Appeal are in Parts 65 to 73 of these Rules.]

3.2 The duty of the court

(1) The court must further the overriding objective by actively managing the case.

(2) Active case management includes—
    (a) the early identification of the real issues;
    (b) the early identification of the needs of witnesses;
    (c) achieving certainty as to what must be done, by whom, and when, in particular by the early setting of a timetable for the progress of the case;
    (d) monitoring the progress of the case and compliance with directions;
    (e) ensuring that evidence, whether disputed or not, is presented in the shortest and clearest way;
    (f) discouraging delay, dealing with as many aspects of the case as possible on the same occasion, and avoiding unnecessary hearings;
    (g) encouraging the participants to co-operate in the progression of the case; and
    (h) making use of technology.

(3) The court must actively manage the case by giving any direction appropriate to the needs of that case as early as possible.

3.3 The duty of the parties

Each party must—
    (a) actively assist the court in fulfilling its duty under rule 3.2, without or if necessary with a direction; and
    (b) apply for a direction if needed to further the overriding objective.

3.4 Case progression officers and their duties

(1) At the beginning of the case each party must, unless the court otherwise directs—
    (a) nominate an individual responsible for progressing that case; and
    (b) tell other parties and the court who he is and how to contact him.

(2) In fulfilling its duty under rule 3.2, the court must where appropriate—
    (a) nominate a court officer responsible for progressing the case; and
    (b) make sure the parties know who he is and how to contact him.

(3) In this Part a person nominated under this rule is called a case progression officer.

(4) A case progression officer must—
    (a) monitor compliance with directions;
    (b) make sure that the court is kept informed of events that may affect the progress of that case;
    (c) make sure that he can be contacted promptly about the case during ordinary business hours;
    (d) act promptly and reasonably in response to communications about the case; and
    (e) if he will be unavailable, appoint a substitute to fulfil his duties and inform the other case progression officers.

3.5 The court's case management powers

(1) In fulfilling its duty under rule 3.2 the court may give any direction and take any step actively to manage a case unless that direction or step would be inconsistent with legislation, including these Rules.

(2) In particular, the court may—
    (a) nominate a judge, magistrate, justices' clerk or assistant to a justices' clerk to manage the case;
    (b) give a direction on its own initiative or on application by a party;
    (c) ask or allow a party to propose a direction;
    (d) for the purpose of giving directions, receive applications and representations by letter, by telephone or by any other means of electronic communication, and conduct a hearing by such means;
    (e) give a direction without a hearing;
    (f) fix, postpone, bring forward, extend or cancel a hearing;
    (g) shorten or extend (even after it has expired) a time limit fixed by a direction;
    (h) require that issues in the case should be determined separately, and decide in what order they will be determined; and
    (i) specify the consequences of failing to comply with a direction.

(3) A magistrates' court may give a direction that will apply in the Crown Court if the case is to continue there.

(4) The Crown Court may give a direction that will apply in a magistrates' court if the case is to continue there.

(5) Any power to give a direction under this Part includes a power to vary or revoke that direction.

[Note. Depending upon the nature of a case and the stage that it has reached, its progress may be affected by other Criminal Procedure Rules and by other legislation. The note at the end of this Part lists other rules and legislation that may apply.]

3.6 Application to vary a direction

(1) A party may apply to vary a direction if—
    (a) the court gave it without a hearing;
    (b) the court gave it at a hearing in his absence; or
    (c) circumstances have changed.

(2) A party who applies to vary a direction must—
    (a) apply as soon as practicable after he becomes aware of the grounds for doing so; and
    (b) give as much notice to the other parties as the nature and urgency of his application permits.

3.7 Agreement to vary a time limit fixed by a direction

(1) The parties may agree to vary a time limit fixed by a direction, but only if—
    (a) the variation will not—
        (i) affect the date of any hearing that has been fixed, or
        (ii) significantly affect the progress of the case in any other way;

(b) the court has not prohibited variation by agreement; and

(c) the court's case progression officer is promptly informed.

(2) The court's case progression officer must refer the agreement to the court if he doubts the condition in paragraph (1)(a) is satisfied.

3.8 Case preparation and progression

(1) At every hearing, if a case cannot be concluded there and then the court must give directions so that it can be concluded at the next hearing or as soon as possible after that.

(2) At every hearing the court must, where relevant—

(a) if the defendant is absent, decide whether to proceed nonetheless;

(b) take the defendant's plea (unless already done) or if no plea can be taken then find out whether the defendant is likely to plead guilty or not guilty;

(c) set, follow or revise a timetable for the progress of the case, which may include a timetable for any hearing including the trial or (in the Crown Court) the appeal;

(d) in giving directions, ensure continuity in relation to the court and to the parties' representatives where that is appropriate and practicable; and

(e) where a direction has not been complied with, find out why, identify who was responsible, and take appropriate action.

3.9 Readiness for trial or appeal

(1) This rule applies to a party's preparation for trial or (in the Crown Court) appeal, and in this rule and rule 3.10 trial includes any hearing at which evidence will be introduced.

(2) In fulfilling his duty under rule 3.3, each party must—

(a) comply with directions given by the court;

(b) take every reasonable step to make sure his witnesses will attend when they are needed;

(c) make appropriate arrangements to present any written or other material; and

(d) promptly inform the court and the other parties of anything that may—

(i) affect the date or duration of the trial or appeal, or

(ii) significantly affect the progress of the case in any other way.

(3) The court may require a party to give a certificate of readiness.

3.10 Conduct of a trial or an appeal

In order to manage the trial or (in the Crown Court) appeal, the court may require a party to identify—

(a) which witnesses he intends to give oral evidence;

(b) the order in which he intends those witnesses to give their evidence;

(c) whether he requires an order compelling the attendance of a witness;

(d) what arrangements, if any, he proposes to facilitate the giving of evidence by a witness;

(e) what arrangements, if any, he proposes to facilitate the participation of any other person, including the defendant;

(f) what written evidence he intends to introduce;

(g) what other material, if any, he intends to make available to the court in the presentation of the case;

(h) whether he intends to raise any point of law that could affect the conduct of the trial or appeal; and

(i) what timetable he proposes and expects to follow.

3.11 Case management forms and records

(1) The case management forms set out in the Practice Direction must be used, and where there is no form then no specific formality is required.

(2) The court must make available to the parties a record of directions given.

[Note. Case management may be affected by the following other rules and legislation:

Criminal Procedure Rules

Parts 10.4 and 27.2: reminders of right to object to written evidence being read at trial

Part 12.2: time for first appearance of accused sent for trial

Part 13: dismissal of charges sent or transferred to the Crown Court

Part 14: the indictment

Part 15: preparatory hearings in serious fraud and other complex or lengthy cases

Parts 21–26: the rules that deal with disclosure

Parts 27–36: the rules that deal with evidence

Part 37: summary trial

Part 38: trial of children and young persons

Part 39: trial on indictment

Regulations

Prosecution of Offences (Custody Time Limits) Regulations 1987

Criminal Justice Act 1987 (Notice of Transfer) Regulations 1988

Criminal Justice Act 1991 (Notice of Transfer) Regulations 1992

Criminal Procedure and Investigations Act 1996 (Defence Disclosure Time Limits) Regulations 1997

Crime and Disorder Act 1998 (Service of Prosecution Evidence) Regulations 2000

Provisions of Acts of Parliament

Sections 5, 10 and 18, Magistrates' Courts Act 1980: powers to adjourn hearings

Sections 128 and 129, Magistrates' Courts Act 1980: remand in custody by magistrates' courts

Part 1, Criminal Procedure and Investigations Act 1996: disclosure

Schedule 2, Criminal Procedure and Investigations Act 1996: use of witness statements at trial

Section 2, Administration of Justice (Miscellaneous Provisions) Act 1933: procedural conditions for trial in the Crown Court

Section 6, Magistrates' Courts Act 1980: committal for trial

Section 4, Criminal Justice Act 1987: section 53, Criminal Justice Act 1991: section 51,

Crime and Disorder Act 1998: other procedures by which a case reaches the Crown Court

Section 7, Criminal Justice Act 1987; Parts III and IV, Criminal Procedure and Investigations

Act 1996: pre-trial and preparatory hearings in the Crown Court

Section 9, Criminal Justice Act 1967: proof by written witness statement]

INDEX

References are to paragraph numbers, e.g. 2.344 refers to Chapter 2, paragraph 344.